P9-DFL-811

STUDENT WRITERS AT WORK

and in the company
of other writers

JUDGES OF THE 1985 BEDFORD PRIZES
IN STUDENT WRITING

Frederick Crews
Janet Emig
Donald McQuade
Donald M. Murray
Nancy Sommers
Lynn Quitman Troyka
William Zinsser

JUDGES OF THE 1983 BEDFORD PRIZES
IN STUDENT WRITING

Wayne Booth
Edward P. J. Corbett
Ellen Goodman
Maxine Hairston
Donald McQuade
Nancy Sommers
Alice Trillin
Calvin Trillin

STUDENT WRITERS AT WORK

and in the company
of other writers

The Bedford Prizes

SECOND SERIES

Edited by

Nancy Sommers & Donald McQuade

Rutgers University   University of California, Berkeley

A Bedford Book
ST. MARTIN'S PRESS · NEW YORK

Library of Congress Catalog Card Number: 85-62181
Copyright © 1986 by St. Martin's Press, Inc.
All rights reserved.
Manufactured in the United States of America

9 8 7 6
f e d c b a

For information, write St. Martin's Press, Inc.,
175 Fifth Avenue, New York, NY 10010
Editorial Offices: Bedford Books of St. Martin's Press,
29 Commonwealth Avenue, Boston, MA 02116

ISBN: 0-312-76942-3

Acknowledgments

Michael Arlen. "Ode to Thanksgiving" from *The Camera Age* by Michael Arlen. Copyright © 1976, 1977, 1978, 1979, 1980, 1981 by Michael J. Arlen. Reprinted by permission of Farrar, Straus and Giroux, Inc.

Caroline Bird. "College Is a Waste of Time and Money" from *The Case Against College* by Caroline Bird. Reprinted by permission of the author.

Emily Dickinson. "I Heard a Fly Buzz–When I Died" by Emily Dickinson from *The Poems of Emily Dickinson*, Thomas H. Johnson, ed., Cambridge, Mass.: Harvard University Press. Copyright 1951, © 1955, 1979, 1983 by the President and Fellows of Harvard College. Reprinted by permission of the publishers.

Patrick Fenton, "Confessions of a Working Stiff" by Patrick Fenton (*New York* Magazine), reprinted by permission of the author.

Samuel G. Freedman. "Live Aid and the Woodstock Nation" by Samuel G. Freedman (*The New York Times*, July 18, 1985). Copyright © 1985 by The New York Times Company. Reprinted by permission.

Bob Green. "How Unwritten Rules Circumscribe Our Lives" by Bob Greene. Reprinted by permission of Tribune Media Services, Orlando, Florida.

Donald Hall. "Four Kinds of Reading" by Donald Hall (*The New York Times*, January 26, 1969). Copyright © 1969 by The New York Times Company. Reprinted by permission.

William Humphrey. "The Salmon Instinct" excerpted from the book *Farther from Heaven* by William Humphrey. Copyright © 1976, 1977 by William Humphrey. Reprinted by permission of Delacorte Press/Seymour Lawrence.

(Continued on page 735)

PUBLISHER'S NOTE

The Bedford Prizes in Student Writing is now an annual nationwide contest for essays written for a freshman composition class. It is sponsored by Bedford Books, an imprint of St. Martin's Press. Contest rules can be found at the back of this book.

The first Bedford Prize contest was open to essays written in 1982. It drew over twelve hundred entries from over five hundred colleges and universities in forty-eight states. A list of the thirty-one winners, who came from twenty-nine schools in twenty states, is printed on the inside back cover.

The second contest, which produced the winning essays reprinted in this book, was open to essays written in 1984. It drew almost two thousand entries from over six hundred colleges and universities in all fifty states. All the entries were read at least twice by a panel of experienced composition instructors, and this preliminary screening produced the essays sent to the seven contest judges for a final reading. In neither the preliminary nor the final judging were the readers aware of the students' names or schools.

The thirty-five winning essayists come from thirty-two two- and four-year schools in twenty-two states across the country. They and their instructors received cash awards as well as formal certificates. (Students who performed additional writing tasks in connection with the preparation of this book received additional compensation.) We congratulate our winners, their instructors, and their writing programs. We also thank everyone who entered or otherwise supported the contest for helping to make it such a success.

We at Bedford Books are grateful to the distinguished panel of writers and educators who served as our judges—Frederick Crews, Janet Emig, Donald McQuade, Donald M. Murray, Nancy Sommers, Lynn Quitman Troyka, and William Zinsser. We thank them for their enthusiastic support and participation in the contest. To Donald McQuade and Nancy Sommers, who have been at the heart of this project from its onset—not only as contest judges but also as contest coordinators and co-editors of this anthology and its bestselling predecessor—we offer special thanks for their good will and good spirits, their high standards and hard work, for their belief in the worth of such a contest and their vision of the potential in a book containing its winners.

PREFACE

The second series of *Student Writers at Work* continues our commitment to making student writing the *primary* text in a composition course. The new edition reflects what we have learned from the Bedford Prize winners, from their instructors, from our own students, and from instructors who have enthusiastically used the first edition. *Student Writers at Work* has been more successful than we dared anticipate: we are told it is the most widely used collection of student writing ever published. We take this as confirmation that a steadily increasing number of freshman composition programs have begun to see students as *writers* and to place student writing at the center of their composition courses.

In its second series, *Student Writers at Work* again celebrates the writing of students and particularly the accomplishments of the thirty-five winners of the Bedford Prizes in Student Writing. But the book is more than merely celebratory. It accords student writing the attention and regard it deserves, not only by publishing it, but also by subjecting it to critical attention like that brought to bear on professional essays in the typical composition anthology. And it explores the composing processes of the prize-winning writers, letting them speak in their own voices about their purposes and strategies, their struggles and satisfactions.

The book is designed to serve either or both of two functions in the classroom. First, it provides a collection of accessible essays comparable to those students will be asked to write, essays that can be used in place of or along with a collection of professional essays. Second, it provides a comprehensive instructional resource for courses in which the primary focus is on student writing.

The collection of Bedford Prize winners in *Student Writers at Work* is in some ways similar to the traditional composition reader and in other ways very different. On the one hand, these essays are as diverse as any group of professional essays. The writers vary widely in age, background, and experience; each of their voices is distinctive. Their subjects include political and social issues, twentieth-century phenomena, and literature as well as personal experience. Their aims and purposes range from expressive to explanatory to argumentative. On the other hand, unlike the writing in professional collections, these essays were written by students for the freshman composition course and thus represent readily accessible and attainable models. Because of the contest's scope, these models reflect a broader demographic range than could be found in any single school or classroom.

Moreover, the material surrounding the student essays is unprecedented in a reader. Because the Bedford Prize contest rules stipulated that all entries be accompanied by preliminary notes and drafts, and because all the winning essayists and their instructors completed detailed questionnaires, the headnotes and discussion questions explore the writers' composing processes as well as their finished products. The headnotes provide not only biographical information about the writers but also quotations from them about their intentions and their writing habits.

The questions after the essays fall into two groups. Those questions on reading address the standard rhetorical concerns of content and form. The questions on revising focus on revision in one of two ways: either by highlighting the writer's strategies and choices or by posing "What if" questions that invite students to consider the effects of further changes in the essay. Together, the two groups of questions are intended to encourage students to read critically and to evaluate carefully the relative success of various writing strategies in particular circumstances. The suggestions for writing that follow each essay include at least one topic related to the essay's rhetorical form, one related to its theme, and one that extends its thematic implications in a different rhetorical form. More particularly, each personal experience essay is followed by an expository or argumentative topic, in keeping with our conviction that the real challenge of the freshman composition course is to show our students how to move from personal experience essays to exposition and argumentation.

We have created a completely new—and unprecedented—part for this second edition entitled "Moving from Personal Experience to Exposition and Argument." The part guides students step by step from writing firsthand accounts of their own experience to broader and more objective approaches to the same material. We asked two Bedford Prize winners, Beverly Dipo and Julie Reardon, to develop new essays from the ones they had originally submitted. The part records their progress: Dipo's from narration to argument, Reardon's from description to exposition. Each writer kept detailed notes on her writing process, from brainstorming to outlining and then to drafting and revising. Reinforcing these examples are specific advice on how to make the transition from personal to expository or argumentative writing and exercises to help students get started.

We have retained and refined four special sections from the first edition of *Student Writers at Work* designed to help students strengthen their own writing:

Students on Writing. This introduction provides an overview of the writing process through the voices of the winning essayists. They discuss their satisfactions and frustrations as writers and their specific strategies for getting started, drafting, and revising. In the second edition we have included more student comments on invention, along with an example of brainstorming.

Three Student Writers at Work. This part focuses on the composing processes of three prize-winning essayists. Guided by editorial comments, students first examine the complete notes and the rough draft of one of the prize-winning essays, along with the writer's own explanations of her intentions. Then, guided by questions, students analyze the choices of two other prize-winning writers as their essays developed from rough drafts to final versions.

Peer Editors at Work. This part prepares students to be effective peer editors and to respond as writers to the editing of their fellow students. We begin with an explanation of the principles and procedures of peer editing. Next, students see the comments of four composition students on one of the winning essays. Through questions, they are then guided to analyze the peer editors' comments and to evaluate the essay on their own. The writer of the essay responds to the peer editors' comments and revises his essay, and students are again invited by questions to examine the results. Further exercises in peer editing with a second example of peer editing are also included.

The Professional Editor at Work. This part demonstrates what happens to writing when it is prepared for publication. We found that many users of the book appreciated this demonstration of close critical editing as an example of the kinds of comments professional editors make to encourage writers to revise. The professional editor's work also illustrates—and emphasizes—how even first-rate essays can be revised. After an introduction explaining the goals and procedures of editing, the professional editor offers specific recommendations for two of the winning essays, focusing on how to improve communication between the writer and the reader. Both writers then revise their essays, commenting on the revision and on the experience of being edited. Through a series of questions, we help students examine the editing of each essay and the writer's response to it.

An additional feature in this edition of *Student Writers at Work* is a glossary of rhetorical terms. We have included a particularly full discussion of each rhetorical pattern to help students recognize these forms in the essays they read and to work with them in those they write.

THE EXPANDED EDITION

We have added a supplement to the second series of *Student Writers at Work* that places the Bedford Prize winners *in the company of other writers*. We reprint in this supplement thirty-five professional texts—twenty-four essays, five short stories, and six poems—connected in theme or rhetorical form or both to the student essays that precede them. As the lowercase title suggests, these additional writings are meant to enhance the student essays, not to overshadow them as is typically the case in nearly all composition textbooks. Our aim is to dissolve the mysterious barrier that separates writing assigned by an instructor from writing commissioned by an editor or inspired by one's own talent and determination. Every professional writer started out as a student, and every student who works with words enters the community of writers.

We designed *in the company of other writers* to satisfy three instructional purposes. First, the essays awarded a Bedford Prize included a large number of narrative, descriptive, and illustrative pieces based on students' personal experiences. Adding a carefully chosen collection of professional essays that connect thematically to the student essays also enables us to adjust for pedagogical purposes the book's rhetorical balance. For example, *in the company of other writers* presents at least two examples of every rhetorical pattern and four examples of argument. Second, many users of the first edition reported that while their main focus in the course is on student writing, they like to have their students work as well with some professional writing. The new supplement provides that opportunity within a single volume.

Finally, we wanted to expand the teaching possibilities of *Student Writers at Work*. By closely examining a student essay, a magazine feature or editorial, a short story, and a poem, all on the same theme, students learn to appreciate the numerous variations writers can develop from one starting point—and the diverse techniques and forms available for creating those variations. Each professional selection links thematically with at least one student essay, approaching the student's theme from a different point of view and usually in a different form. In some cases, several professional selections link with a single student essay. For example, Beverly Dipo's prize-winning narrative about the death of an elderly hospital patient is complemented by the perspectives of a doctor (Richard Selzer), a nurse (Barbara Huttman), a psychiatrist specializing in cultural attitudes toward death (Elisabeth Kübler-Ross), a short-story writer (Katherine Anne Porter), and a poet (Emily Dickinson).

The biographical headnotes preceding the professional pieces, as well as the Questions for Reading and the Suggestions for Writing following them, serve purposes similar to those for the student essays. That is, each of these elements focuses on the process of writing: the numerous choices the writer makes, large and small, at every step from conception to final draft and the circumstances that hinder or facilitate these choices. A special set of Questions on Connections after each professional selection highlights its thematic and rhetorical links to its student counterparts.

Each of the distinctive features of *Student Writers at Work* as well as *in the company of other writers* receives special attention in the complimentary *Instructor's Manual* prepared with the expertise of Miriam Baker of Dowling College. The manual discusses each feature as well as each essay thoroughly and offers teaching suggestions, discussion questions, and writing topics. It also provides a syllabus with ideas for using *Student Writers at Work* as well as *in the company of other writers* throughout a semester and a detailed arrangement of the essays by elements of composition.

We continue to be influenced by the more than two hundred members of the Council of Writing Program Administrators who responded to our survey on the uses of student writing in the classroom. Among many other ideas, the respondents shared their almost unanimous belief that student writing should be the primary text in the composition class; as one administrator put it, no book can replace "the living, breathing student in the class who is there to speak up, to argue, to defend, to explain, to accept, and to reject." *Student Writers at Work* and *Student Writers at Work and in the company of other writers* do not attempt such replacement. Instead, each offers a collection of essays that are both worthy of emulation and possible to emulate. And each supplements the work of students in the class with the work of their peers across the nation, giving them an opportunity to sharpen their critical skills, to study how successful writers make the composing process work for them, and to see themselves as members of a community of writers that extends well beyond the classroom walls.

Acknowledgments

Sherwood Anderson once said that "the whole glory of writing lies in the fact that it forces us out of ourselves and into the lives of others." Behind this second edition of *Student Writers at Work* stands a large—and steadily increasing—number of colleagues and friends who graciously allowed us into their already crowded lives to seek advice and encouragement.

Before we could prepare this new edition of *Student Writers at Work*, we conducted a second national contest to determine the winners of the Bedford Prizes in Student Writing. And before there could be a contest, there were rules to be checked and written. For their counsel during this phase of the project, we would like to thank David Kaye, Paul Slevin, and Hans Smit, Esq. Most importantly, we would like to acknowledge both the instructors across the country who supported the contest by submitting their students's work and the nearly two thousand students who wrote essays worthy of submission.

We are indebted to the kind people who kept track of the essays as they were submitted and who prepared them to be read anonymously by our judges: Chitrita Banerji, Janet Campbell, Judson Evans, Alison Luterman, and especially Carla Johnson. The generosity of Joe McDermott, the Vice President of Local 237 of the Teamsters Union in New York, and Ed Quinn, the former Director of the Center for Worker Education in the City University of New York, provided us with a warm shelter from February snow to read—and re-read—essay after essay.

We are also grateful to the writers, editors, and teachers of writing who served as judges in the first reading: Carla Asher, Deborah Asher, Carol Bamdad, Donald Billiar, Gerald Coleman, Catherine Costa, Jaqueline Costello, Anthony DeLuca, Robert DiYanni, Linda Farhood-Karasavva, Pam Farrell, Beverly Fenig, Bruce Forer, Halima Gutman, Patricia Haag, Barbara Hardy, George Held, Virginia Hlavsa, Siri Hustvedt, Dexter Jeffries, William P. Kelly, Kathleen Kier, Lori Lefkovitz, Mitchell Levenberg, Norman Lewis, Blaise Marino, Phyllis McCord, Catherine McKenna, Stephen Olsen, Barney Pace, John Pufahl, Judi Sandler, Stephen Schmidt, Jonna Semeiks, Susan Stock, Joyce Warren, Robert Webb, Peter Weiss, Gordon Whatley, and Scott Zaluda. Once again special thanks are due Deborah Asher, who helped recruit many of our first-round judges, and especially to Sue Shanker, who also helped recruit judges, then trained them, and choreographed with great skill and delightful humor the multiple readings of each essay. Working with the distinguished panel of judges who chose the winners of the Bedford Prizes in Student Writing remains one of the special pleasures of this project. For their careful readings and thoughtful comments, we would like to thank Frederick Crews, Janet Emig, Donald M. Murray, Lynn Quitman Troyka, and William Zinsser.

We would also like to thank the many instructors who so generously shared with us their experience of working with *Student Writers at Work* in their classes over the past two years: William Arfin, University of North Carolina, Chapel Hill; Eugene Baer, Wisconsin Lutheran College; Dennis Baeyen, Iowa State University; Carol Bamdad, Union County College; Sheila Bender, Seattle Central Community College; Daryl Coats, University of Mississippi; Terri Cook,

Westmont College; Donald Daiker, Miami University, Ohio; Patricia Daire, Pima Community College; Dorothy Fillmore, Virginia Commonwealth University; Paulette Flowers, Vanderbilt University; Beth Franklin, University of Minnesota; J. L. Funston, James Madison University; Margie Garner, Freeman Junior College; Lt. Jill Garzone, United States Naval Academy; E. R. Gelber-Beechler, University of North Carolina, Charlotte; George Greenlee, Missouri Southern State College; Quay Grigg, Hamline University; Susan S. Hankins, University of Mississippi; Susanne E. Hill, Maria Regina College; John K. Hoernig, Niagara County Community College; Diane Horan, Montgomery County Community College; David Jolliffe, University of Illinois; Jim Kolsky, Western Nevada Community College; Mary Beth Lake, Normandale Community College; Sherry Mon Lidaka, Northern Illinois University; Pamela Liebing, Harper College; Darlene Lister, California State University, Dominguez Hills; Nancy G. Little, Motlow State Community College Theresa L. McLain, University of Texas, San Antonio; Barbara C. McMillan, University of Mississippi; Adelio F. Maccentelli, Essex Community College; Harry Marks, Temple University; Vernon G. Miles, University of Arkansas, Fayetteville; Mary Frances Minton, Virginia Commonwealth University; Kathy Morris Murray, University of Mississippi; Edward M. O'Keefe, Niagara County Community College; J. Daniel Patterson, Kent State University; Paul Perry, University of Texas, San Antonio; Douglas Roycraft, Erie Community College; Joseph Sanders, Lakeland Community College; Judi Sandler, Union County College; Paul Sladky, University of Texas, Austin; Mary Ann Smith, Boston College; Cheryl A. Staunton, Mary Washington College; Mary Kathryn Stein, University of Arkansas, Little Rock; Mary Stein, Evergreen Valley College; Judith Straffin, Rock Valley College; Edward F. Sundberg, Cabrillo College; Marilynn Talal, University of Texas, San Antonio; Gilbert Tierney, W. R. Harper College; Erskine S. White, University of North Carolina, Charlotte; Gerald C. Wood, Carson-Newman College.

We are also extremely grateful to the following colleagues for their detailed readings of *Student Writers at Work* and for their many helpful suggestions: Carolyn Beck, Kent State University; Thomas Blues, University of Kentucky; Margaret Butler, Motlow State Community College; Robert Connors, University of New Hampshire; Michele Czosnek, University of Wisconsin, Milwaukee; Anne Hall, University of North Carolina, Chapel Hill; Miriam Baker, Dowling College; Marge McMinn, University of Arkansas, Little Rock; Steven Rayburn, University of Mississippi; Bonnie Rudner, Boston College; John Ruszkiewicz, University of Texas, Austin; and Judith Stanford. For their advice and encouragement, we'd like to thank Deborah Asher, Robert DiYanni, Edward Dornan, Betsy B. Kaufman, William P. Kelly, Elaine Maimon, Robert Roth, and Mimi Schwartz. Laura Novo, Columbia University, helped us locate an elusive text, and David Richter, Queens College, C.U.N.Y., generously made his vast knowledge of fiction available to us. We admire his intelligence and appreciate his help. Gary Goshgarian graciously consented to let us print drafts of one of his many first-rate essays on culture in the chapter on the professional editor. We'd also like to acknowledge Edward P. J. Corbett. His collegiality, accomplishments in print, and intellectual integrity stand as models for our profession.

We continue to be indebted to Jane Aaron, who was once again an eloquent and encouraging voice in "The Professional Editor at Work." Miriam Baker, Dowling College, has lived through two editions of this book with us, and she has been a constant friend and a limitless source of first-rate ideas and teaching strategies. Hers is the strongest of our three voices in the *Instructor's Manual*, and reports of its success in the first edition are a tribute primarily to her accomplishments as an outstanding teacher and writer as well as to her vision of the book's potential.

We would like to acknowledge our colleagues in England and the United States whose work helped shape the section on peer editing: M. L. J. Abercrombie, Lil Brannon, John Clifford, Richard Gebhardt, Thom Hawkins, Edwin Mason, Stephen Tschudi, and especially Ken Bruffee, Rosemary Deen, and Marie Ponsot. For their invaluable help on this section, we would also like to thank the student writers and peer editors at Queens College, C.U.N.Y.: Nicholas Balamaci, Jason Eskenazi, Nelson Farias, and Frances Osborne. Their intelligent, sensitive readings of another, and rather distant, student's writing broadened and enriched the limits of a productive community of writers.

For helping us to recognize the need for the new part on moving from personal experience to exposition and argument, asking us difficult questions, and offering generous advice, we would like to add a special note of thanks to Ron Strahl, Barbara Cambridge, and their colleagues at Indiana University/Purdue University at Indianapolis. Anne Middleton pursued a similarly helpful and rigorous series of questions in conversation at the University of California, Berkeley for which we are grateful. The work of James Moffett as well proved helpful in developing this new part. We would also like to acknowledge the generous cooperation of Nancy Jones of the University of Iowa and Joyce Kinkead of Utah State University.

For the elegant look of their work, we would like to thank Anna Post, who once again designed the book and contest poster, and Richard S. Emery, who deftly repeated his success in designing the book's cover. Linda Howe skillfully copyedited the manuscript, and Anne Richmond was an outstanding proofreader. John Repp, University of Pittsburgh, and Rebecca Saunders, Tufts University, contributed first-rate research to the professional writing supplement. Virginia Creeden Bogucki skillfully managed assembling the permissions for the professional writing included in the supplement, and Sue Dunham graciously did the necessary typing.

One of the most important contributors to this new edition is Carol Verburg. She most generously allowed us to enter her life on the shortest of notice, and she has worked tirelessly on our behalf ever since. This new edition could not have gone to press without her help, we are grateful for her innumerable contributions to *Student Writers at Work and in the company of other writers.*

Our continuing thanks go to the kind people of Bedford Books. Chris Rutigliano coordinated the complex administrative work of the contest and helped see the book through production with a remarkable blend of intelligence, efficiency, and good cheer. Karen Henry coordinated the book's review program and assisted in setting up the contest's first round of judging with great skill and intelligence. Stephen Scipione deserves an MVP as a utility infielder; he played an important role in virtually every phase of this project. The uncommon energy, skill, and irrepressible good humor of Nancy Lyman, Advertising and Promotion Manager, helped keep both the contest and the book on course since their inception. Elizabeth Schaaf, Managing Editor, guided the manuscript through a maze of production problems with an extraordinary amount of intelligence and energy and with an unflappable professionalism. Joan Feinberg, Associate Publisher, not only gave us generous, rigorous comments on every aspect of the manuscript but also repeatedly encouraged us to take the kinds of intellectual risks that made working on this book at once exhausting and yet enormously satisfying. She is the kind of editor every writer hopes to work with and the kind of reader every writer hopes to write for. And Chuck Christensen, Publisher, who enticed us with the idea of the Bedford Prizes, has continued to offer us wise and genial support and the kind of confidence in his authors that makes each sentence easier to write. Both *Student Writers at Work and in the company of other writers* have been truly collaborative enterprises.

Finally, we would like to thank the friends who gave us either time to work or ideas to work with or, in several cases, both: Robert Atwan; Hans Dieter, Sarah, and Amelia Batschelet; Fred, Jill, and Alexander Buell; William Harris; Janine Karoly; William P. Kelly; Helene Kessler; Robert and Bridget Lyons; Judy and Amanda Myers; Kurt Spellmeyer. Gerry McCauley once again helped at both ends of this project. Most importantly, we can only hope that in this sentence Patrick, Rachel, and the recently born Alexandra Hays as well as Susanne, Christine, and Marc McQuade will know how much they have helped us and how much their help has meant to us.

Nancy Sommers
Donald McQuade

CONTENTS

> To "know thyself" is not always to like what you see. Benson's encounter with George Kelly's *Theory of Personality* revolutionizes her concept of herself and everyone around her. CAUSE AND EFFECT

> In this chilling vignette, pressure to succeed turns a military recruit's daytime buddies into his nighttime enemies. NARRATION

STUDENTS
ON WRITING

Part I

O NE OF THE MOST reassuring discoveries any student of writing can make is that there is no single way to write, no fail-proof formula to produce successful essays. Anyone seriously interested in learning to write can benefit from listening to what other writers have to say about the challenges and pleasures of the composing process. The pages that follow will give you a special opportunity to examine the writing process from the point of view of student writers. The thirty-five winners of Bedford Prizes in Student Writing explain their successes and frustrations as writers as well as their particular methods of composition. From their detailed responses to a questionnaire on their specific habits and goals, their strategies and concerns as writers, we have drawn practical information on many aspects of writing—from how these student writers search for an idea and then develop it in a first draft to how they revise and then prepare that idea for presentation in a finished essay.

What do these student writers talk about when they are invited to discuss writing? Like all writers, they invariably speak of the problems and the pleasures of struggling to convey a clear sense of their ideas. They also talk about the purpose and structure of their essays, their use of language, and their relation to an audience. They frequently touch on their respect for and anxiety about mastering the skills required to write good prose. And they describe in detail the distinctive ways in which they compose: how they go about generating ideas for a paper, how they brainstorm and freewrite about that idea, how they organize and develop their first drafts, how they contend with the procrastination and the dead ends that threaten their progress, how they revise, and how they determine when their essays are finished and ready to be read by their peers and submitted to their instructors. Given the academic context within which they work, they also touch on their concern about grades and discuss their perceptions of the place of writing in their career goals.

The perspectives these student writers present on the composing process are as varied as their backgrounds and interests. But the procedures they follow when writing can be grouped into three general phases: getting started, drafting, and revising. Writers usually start by searching for and then deciding on a subject to write about, developing their ideas about the subject, clarifying their purpose in writing, organizing their thoughts, and considering the audience they want to address. In the drafting phase, they usually carry out their detailed plan in a first draft; in the revising phase, they study what they have written and determine how they can improve it. These designations are not a lockstep series of discrete stages that writers work through in exactly the same manner each time. They are simply patterns of activities that describe what happens when writers write. As every writer knows, at least intuitively, writing is not a linear but a recursive process. Writing rarely proceeds neatly from one phase to the next. Rather, the phases frequently overlap, making the process often appear messy. Many writers, for example, revise what they have written as soon as the word or the sentence appears on the page. Each writer participates in the writing process in a different way, at a different pace, and with a different result. In tracing the exact movements of a writer's mind at work on an idea, it is possible to discover and describe patterns, but the specific circumstances and the particular moves are never exactly the same every time.

Yet reading what other students have to say about writing should assure you that all writers—whether they are professionals, prize-winning student essayists, or classmates—grapple with many of the same basic problems. You may be surprised—and pleased—to learn that in many instances the observations and solutions of the prize-winning student writers are similar to those you may have developed in your own writing. In addition, these prize-winning student writers may offer new suggestions that can help you improve your writing. Recognizing both the unique and the shared elements of the writing experience will enable you to place yourself in the company of other writers while distinguishing your own voice from theirs. What follows is not a comprehensive survey of every facet of the writing process but a detailed report on what happens when successful student writers work productively.

1 GETTING STARTED

In the first of the three phases of the writing process, a writer usually chooses a subject to write about if one has not been assigned, discovers a purpose for writing about the subject, generates a thesis or a controlling idea about the subject, considers the audience to be addressed, and then develops that idea in freewriting and brainstorming exercises, in an outline, or in some other form that will be the basis of a first draft of an essay. This is the most difficult phase of writing for most people. Because they usually face so many problems and obstacles here, most writers seem to have more to say about it than any other phase.

Procrastination

Perhaps the single most common obstacle the prize-winning student writers face when they write is their tendency to procrastinate — a trait they share with most other writers, students and professionals alike. For many writers, the easiest part of writing is putting it off. Matthew Holicek identifies the problem quite succinctly: "About the easiest thing for me to do when I write a paper is getting out a sheet of paper and a pen. After that, nothing is really *easy.*" Holicek may well also speak for many when he recognizes his own tendency to delay writing. "I'm a chronic procrastinator," he observes, "I'll say things like 'Oh, the paper isn't due until next week,' but that soon turns into 'It's due on Monday, so I'll start on the weekend.' " He usually starts writing an essay "one or two nights before it is due. I try to put the thought of writing out of my head until the last possible moment. . . . Then, when I've put it off long enough, I just sit down and force myself to do it, constantly reminding myself about when it is due, and that if I don't do it I'll fail. That usually works." As Holicek suggests, some writers apparently can produce only under great pressure, usually the looming presence of a deadline. Johnna Lynn Benson observes: "I like to procrastinate, but I don't know any cute tricks for that bad habit. It usually takes a panicked glance at the calendar to make me decide to start." Frances Taylor elaborates on much the same point: "I try to avoid writing by answering the phone, calling people I suddenly decide I'm worried about, turning on the TV, or playing my guitar. I don't overcome it on my own primarily because most of the things I want to write about are too painful and the rest is boring. So I need classroom deadlines. I need orders."

The stratagems these student writers use to put off writing are often almost as ingenious as the methods they finally discover to write successfully. Ravenel Boykin Curry's account of his preparation for writing includes a catalogue of procrastination techniques, several of which may be familiar to other students: "I do anything to avoid writing. . . . I stand up and pace. I read, reread, and reread. . . . I eat. I daydream. I chew my pencil. I chew the paper. I tell myself that I have to let my ideas 'settle' for a while. . . ." Sandra Casillas would add "drawing pictures" to that list, while Brenda Jacobs explains her reasons for her procrastination this way:

> I avoid writing seriously at all times for two principal rea-
> sons: (1) the process is so very difficult, requiring more
> effort and time that I am normally willing to give; (2) I
> am never fully satisfied with anything that I write, feeling
> that in the end I am pursuing an impossible dream. I avoid

writing in many ways: reading "how to write" books, reading magazines, rereading old assignments. Anything at all
is a good excuse. I have found only two ways to overcome
this — either an obligation to someone or a deadline that
absolutely must be met. Then, and only then, am I able
to sit down and actually complete a particular essay.

The road Ann Field routinely travels on her way to a first draft includes a few
visual and gastronomic detours: "First, I make sure there is nothing on TV
that I have to watch, because once I get started I can't stop. Then I make
sure that my other homework is completed or can wait without putting me
too far behind in my studies. Then I make sure I'm running on a full stomach
and then I begin. I always eat shortly before I begin writing." As Ann Field's
comment suggests, the kitchen is an especially appealing place for student
writers both to prepare for writing and to procrastinate, and eating is the most
common source of pleasurable distraction for writers intent on postponing the
work they need to do.

Eating is hardly the only sure-fire way to avoid writing. Erik Field recounts
a simpler, fail-safe, method: "I avoid writing essays by enrolling in a minimal
number of composition courses. I write well when I have to. I prefer not to
have to."

The student writers whose essays are gathered in this book could identify
any number of equally successful tactics to combat procrastination. Barbara
Carter explains: "My body gets nervous when I don't want to write. With a
will of its own, it needs a walk, or a drink, or a change of pace. When this
happens, I usually take a walk and think about what I'm writing. Often I
return with a different perspective on my work that helps me to get going."
Ravenel Boykin Curry also tries to refresh his mind "and cast away nervous
energy and restlessness with exercise. Fifteen minutes of jumping rope intensely
can make sitting down to a desk far easier." David Christman relies on an
equally determined but less strenuous method for battling his tendency "to put
off writing in lieu of other things. I have partially overcome this by leaving
my typewriter on the table where I can't avoid it," quickly adding, "I don't
live alone, so I can't leave it there all the time." Earnestine Johnson imposes
deadlines on herself and scrupulously, if somewhat "begrudgingly," observes
them.

The Writing Environment

Most writers are as finicky about the circumstances of where and when they
write as they are about whether they will start writing at all. Kelly Mays

describes a rather elaborate ritual for postponing—and then completing—the first draft of an essay:

> I will usually do anything to avoid actually sitting down to do this first writing. . . . I look down at the empty paper, knowing that I have to write this paper tonight. I get up, pour myself a glass of orange juice and sit back down. I tap the pen on the desk several times, then get up and call my mother or a friend. I complain about the paper and then talk about anything else that I can think of. I soon feel guilty or the other person makes me get off the phone. Then I pace around the room, sometimes cleaning it up. Finally, I gather up what little determination I possess along with my materials and drive to the library.
>
> At the library, I always go up into the book stacks and sit in the same carrel. I like it because it is on the floor with the art and literature books and because it is in the very back corner so that there is no human traffic to create distractions. I always eat before I go to the library and smuggle a drink in with me. These two precautions give me no excuse for leaving, except for going to the bathroom (which I usually allow myself). I prescribe for myself an amount of the paper to complete, taking the available time into consideration. Usually I have four hours because I tend to write from 8:00 to 12:00 at night. I always use the same notebook, a plastic folder with a clipboard full of notebook paper and a pocket to hold notes, index cards or assignment instructions. I never bring anything else with me (except the text and a pen) because I will use it to distract myself.

The student writers in this book seem to be divided on the issue of whether writers need a quiet work space to concentrate on practicing the skills required to write successful essays. Judy Jennings represents one extreme when she reports that she needs "total quiet" to write. William Malley's ideal enviroment for writing is "perfectly quiet and absolutely free from distractions." For Brenda Jacobs, writing best takes place near midnight, when the only break in her concentration might come when "the night sounds of crickets ricochet against the open-screened window." The relative stillness of the night envelops her as she works: "Paper covers the round oak table—page after page, coffee-stained and dog-eared, some crumpled into vindictive wads, each white sheet desecrated front and back with inky scribble and crisscrossed with long, bold lines. A still life composed of precariously balanced dictionaries and reference books, coffee cups, overflowing ashtrays, and a pencil sharpener completes the writer's work table. Trancelike, the writer sits in her ladder-back chair, staring at the paper before her, the word puzzle the focus of her attention."

At the other extreme, many students need some form of sound in the background to offset the silence and solitude of writing. Some students prefer to work in front of a television set, and a few even report that they write only during the commercials. Terry Burns's sound is the stereo: "I know most people like it quiet when they write, but I just can't think when it's quiet. Crank up the stereo, and I'm in business." Amber Kennish amplifies this point when she explains: "I usually listen to music when I write because silence only makes distracting thoughts louder." Karen Kramer describes herself in her "ideal" environment for writing: "in my room, alone, with a stereo on, playing some kind of music that I won't feel inclined to sing along with, dance to, or stare out the window and reminisce with. I like it dark, too, with just one desk light on. Makes it cosier somehow." John Mason prefers to "surround myself with pictures of people that have influenced me and that I care about."

Discarded food and packaging, half-filled coffee cups, jugs of Kool-Aid, three-liter bottles of soda, crumpled papers, mangled pencils, disgruntled expressions, furrowed brows, and lingering curtains of cigarette smoke are fairly common features of the productive writing environment many students describe. Linda Lavelle describes a representative sampling of such circumstances for composition: "If someone walked into my room and observed me trying to get started, the first thing they would notice is the mess. Books and papers are scattered on the table; cigarettes, crackers, and a coffee mug fill in the spaces. In the middle of this confusion I sit, tapping my pen on the dictionary, staring into space for long stretches of time. This is followed by bouts of frantic writing. This person would also observe me gulping coffee, chain smoking, crumpling papers, and (so I am told) making faces, twirling my hair, and talking to myself."

Yet student writers do get started on their papers, however perilously close to the deadline they may be, and even if it means, as some report, using "favorite" pens or pencils, wearing "lucky" clothes, or consuming special foods while writing. Julie Reardon, for example, usually wears "a fuzzy blue robe and fuzzy pink slippers" while writing during what she calls "Minnesota's eleven months of winter." She always writes, as she explains, with "treats close at hand. . . . Chocolate is necessary to the writing process, as is diet caffeine-free Coke. A black hard-tip magic marker and lined pad complete my required list of items to write with." Karen Kramer reports that when she writes "sometimes I do like to wear a silly hat and sunglasses." Whatever the quirk, the superstition, the ritual, or the curious concern, many writers feel that certain circumstances must be present before they can even begin to write.

William Malley reports that he relies almost exclusively on determination to complete his writing assignments: "Writing is hard work that requires concentration and effort. For this reason, I never eat, listen to music, or carry on a conversation while writing. I do attempt to write at a time when my head is clear and I am well-rested. I never drink coffee or take any stimulant to keep me awake; that just fools the body and muddles the mind."

Some writers find the time and circumstances of composition unimportant. Nelsy Massoud, a recent émigré from war-ravaged Lebanon, reports, almost casually, that "I write my essays anywhere — a bomb shelter, a car, a bar — and at any time — four in the morning or three in the afternoon — whenever the feeling is there." And she is always prepared: "I always carry on me a very small notebook and pen." Ann Field offers a more tranquil version of the same conviction: "I can write anywhere. If I don't have a place to sit and a surface to rest the paper on, then I just write in my head. I've written brilliant essays while washing dishes, pulling weeds, and scrubbing the bathtub."

Finding a Topic

For many writers, ideas often come when they least expect them — while taking a shower, riding a bicycle, or reading a newspaper. Sandra Casillas reports, for example, that she has little difficulty writing "when I'm ready. But getting ready is something that can go on for days or weeks. It is not a process anyone can observe. It goes on only in my head. It takes time. The 'voice in my head' talks when I'm driving, washing dishes, and doing things completely unconnected with writing." In contrast, Karen Kramer explains that "if getting started means picking a topic, then the best thing for me to do is to sit and wait. It'll come to me. If I try to think actively about it, I usually panic because I feel under the gun as the assignment deadline nears. However, after several of these intense little panic sessions, interspersed by my doing something completely unrelated to the task at hand, I usually end up with a good topic. I know it's a good topic if I get excited about it, or if I just smile in anticipation of writing about it."

Writing invariably involves a great deal of both patience and self-discipline. Barbara Seidel explains the difficulties of each: "If the subject is not of my choosing, I have to wait until an idea hits me like a ton of bricks, and I am not good at waiting. If the subject is of my choosing, I have to restrain myself to get one word at a time out, rather than one paragraph at a time, and I am not good at self-control."

The number of different tactics the student writers use to find their topics and to get started on exploring their ideas about them is virtually endless —

from deliberate reading and research to peer group discussions and random mental association. Ravenel Boykin Curry has found that "the best way to get ideas (and a more interesting way to live your life) is to look for some kind of significance in little things you observe each day":

> A mother slaps her whining kid on the beach. You can pursue the aesthetic — the sun is shining on thousands of people laughing and playing in the water, but all that fills this kid's being right now is the pain and anger. . . . You can be psychological — is the child a brat because the mother responds with violence? Or could negative incentive help the kid to understand that the world doesn't tolerate a whiner? Take a political angle — should the state be able to intervene in minor family violence? What if the husband slapped the wife? What constitutes child abuse, and who should decide? You can expand anything; ideas are endless.

Monika Jerabek has found that the best way to generate ideas to write about is to read in areas of personal interest. Other students prefer to review the material they are studying in either their writing class or in the other courses they are taking. The assigned reading in these courses may well provide a subject to focus on. Magazines and television news and documentary programs also offer ready sources for topics to write about, subjects that will engage your interest — and your reader's. Have confidence in your ability to decide on an interesting subject to write about. As John Mason observes: "The easiest thing for me to come up with is an idea to write about. The world is filled with subjects to write about." But Mason also reminds us that writing involves a good deal of hard work: "Sitting down and explaining that idea in writing is another matter."

A *journal* is one excellent way to keep track of your ideas about a subject. A journal is a daily record in writing of your experiences and thoughts on particular subjects. Journal entries are usually more focused and related than those in a diary, which poses no restrictions on subject or focus. Beverly Dipo uses her journal to discover — and rediscover — her hopes and aspirations, her fears and anxieties: "I keep my journal hidden as if it were top secret. I feel this writing stuff bares my innermost self to the world and that is uncomfortable for me. How does one go about overcoming that? . . . Writing in a journal is a free psychiatric session that would cost upwards of $50.00 an hour. It recalls feelings you thought were buried long ago, returns your mistakes to haunt you, and for me, it gives me an insight into a self that I am surprised to find." Earnestine Johnson connects her journal entries more directly to her essay assignments. Keeping a journal provides her with useful starting points for writing: "What works best for me is sitting down and writing whatever comes to mind on the subject. I may write ten pages, and once I have reviewed them all, I may find that only two or three pages are useful, but they give me a starting point."

Many writers find that they can discover ideas about a subject by writing down everything they know about it. Barbara Seidel relies on a technique known as *freewriting*, also called *nonstop writing*. She begins writing by "pouring out words, thoughts, feelings down on paper, without concern for grammar or punctuation or neatness. I write in a mad rush and want to be undisturbed at this point in the writing process." Seidel's work as a writer comes later, "in organizing those poured-out feelings and thoughts, in getting them to make sense to someone other than me. Words trip over each other, each demanding to be first." As Seidel implies, the key to using freewriting successfully is to put your pen to paper and continue writing without pausing between words or sentences to consider such elements of composition as grammar, sentence structure, word choice, and spelling. Should you find yourself stuck along the way, repeat an important word and expand on it. For Amber Kennish, free-writing "allows my ideas to work and build upon themselves. To write a paper from these ramblings is usually only a matter of lifting a section of the free-writing from my journal and organizing and focusing it into a coherent essay." She finds it especially useful to freewrite "at different times of the day, while I'm in different moods. From these notes it should be easy to form some kind of thesis."

Many writers follow up on their initial thoughts with another round of freewriting, often called *focused freewriting*. In focused freewriting, the writer reviews the first round of freewriting, selects what seems to be a promising lead in it, and then freewrites about that more limited topic. Judy Jennings offers an instructive sample. Having spent some time freewriting about her marriage and children, Jennings decided to loop back over the subject of her stepchildren to focus more deliberately on, as she says, "the injustices of step-parenting" and "to make a few clarifications about a very misunderstood role."

I don't really know what to say or where to start when I try to talk (or write) a logical something about my relationship with my stepchildren! I think all the time "How did I get myself into this?" When Les and I got married, I was an extremely naive 24 and never realized that I was marrying not only a man, but a man with three kids — a package deal so to speak. The first thing I think of when I remember back to our early marriage is the second weekend after we were married. It was Les' weekend to have his children. The older son rode with him to pick up the other two. On the way back they came across an old man on the side of the road selling (or rather giving away) puppies — Mongrel dogs if ever there were such. Some awful mixture that looked like a cross between a bloodhound and a chihuahua. They stopped and took not one but two of the horrible bloodshot-eyed pups.

These notations, still in rough form, served as the basis for Jennings's first draft of her essay "Second-Class Mom." Freewriting and focused freewriting are effective means to deal with what Ravenel Boykin Curry calls the "horrible experience" of having a "piece of paper [that] sits there empty, that white sheet just staring back at you." Frances Taylor aptly summarizes the value of freewriting: "freewriting helps because it liberates ideas at their source while they're still connected up with a great deal of raw power. A lot of writing is generated from which to cull all sorts of marvelous notions."

Other writers prefer to develop ideas through *brainstorming*. Unlike freewriting, which produces ideas by linking or associating one thought with another, brainstorming records thoughts as they come, with no regard for their relation to one another. When writers brainstorm, they often leap from one thought to another without stopping to explore the connections between what may well be two completely unrelated ideas. When Brenda Jacobs set out to write an essay on regional expressions, she decided to brainstorm to come up with a list of words and phrases. Here is what part of it looked like:

Regionalistic expressions

flip flap — fly swatter   pitch a fit — mad
britches — pants   fixin to go
poor — skinny   hand down grace — say

chaps ⎫
chil'l'un ⎬ kids
younguns ⎭
yonder- far, there
sister/ brother
ailing - sick
liter⸗ kindling
sang - community
   singing affair
pot liquor-from greens
⎧ took up with
⎨ took a cold
⎩ took sick

Black dog bit -depressed
2 much sugar for a dime
   tuckered out- tired
I swanee- I declare
   chopping ax
squarehills (squirrels)
   risen - boil
   hollerin - crying
skirttail- hem
            coattails
      ya'll
colorful
rural Southern mystique

Brainstorming, like freewriting, is a writing exercise that can be done virtually anywhere, at any time, and at any pace. When Petrea Galloway is at work developing ideas for an essay, she is concerned that she will get, as she notes, "too much ahead" of herself: "so I hurry and write it anywhere. I've written on the bottom of Kleenex boxes, in book matches, on theater tickets, my shoe. . . ." Her advice about this stage of thinking in writing is simple: "just get it down."

Exercises such as freewriting and brainstorming are excellent confidence builders, especially for relatively inexperienced writers. Such writers can produce a great deal of writing in a very short time. These exercises also enable writers to see rather quickly just what they have to say about a subject while resisting the urge to edit their work prematurely. Whether you write in a leather-bound journal or on the inside of a matchbook, doing your thinking in writing is perhaps the best way to discover a subject. A practiced writer is usually an effective writer.

Purpose

Once they have settled on a subject, most student writers decide on a purpose for writing about that subject; they make decisions about what to say and how to say it. The first of these concerns establishes the general content and the overall goal of the essay. The second focuses on the structure and tone of the essay. Whether an essay is designed to narrate, describe, explain, convince, or persuade, a clearly stated purpose helps ensure its effectiveness and marks most of the essays printed in this book. In most cases, the students' motives for writing include, but are rarely restricted to, the understandable desire to earn an outstanding grade. For some student writers, the pure pleasure of working with words is an added attraction of writing. For others, writing offers the prospect of helping change attitudes and behavior: to defeat a prejudice or upset a stereotype, to underscore the dignity of the oppressed or the terminally ill, to change long-standing opinion on public issues. Steve West wanted to demonstrate "the inadequacy of the Reagan administration's justifications for the Grenada invasion"; Greg Weekes "to show others the horrors of the modern whale hunt and to impress upon my readers that the 'romance' of the nineteenth century whale hunt is gone"; Linda Lavelle "to show that blue-collar workers are not necessarily illiterate or lacking in ambition. I wanted the reader to remember to view people as individuals, not write them off as a group."

A clear purpose need not be as public or as issue-oriented. For many writers, the principal purpose for writing is as simple as wanting to narrate or describe an experience, record a personal anecdote, remember a family story, or recover the pleasure of reading a book, hearing a concert, or seeing a film or play. Just as there is no single, sure-fire way to succeed at writing, there is no single definition of an appropriate subject or purpose in writing. Whatever your purpose, try to make it as clear as possible. As Kelly Mays reminds us, "It is important to gain the reader's interest with a clear and interesting statement of purpose, which then should be heightened and fulfilled by careful and organized evidence within the body of the paper." Deciding on a clear purpose for writing can be, as she notes, "a very creative process."

Audience

Imagining an audience looms large in the mind of every writer. The writer's view of the reader invariably helps determine the extent of an essay's success. The writer usually asks, "Who is my reader? What do I have to do to lead that person to understand what I want to say about the subject?" The first question addresses the knowledge, background, and predispositions of the reader toward the subject. The second points to the kinds of information or appeals that the reader is most likely to respond to. Yet, not all writers begin to concern themselves with the issue of audience from the beginning of their work on an essay.

The primary concern of most writers, however experienced they may be, is to establish authority over their own experience, to express as clearly and as deliberately as possible a sense of control over their own ideas. Johnna Benson puts it this way: "When I start, I'm trying to find my ideas and make them meaningful to myself. I try to get a hold of what I want to say, but my ideas don't always make sense to other people in that form. Then I start trying to present the ideas, but the ideas are set." For William Malley, the initial stage of the composing process is "a very private thing." Like many other student writers, he doesn't consider the issue of audience until he feels that he understands fully what he is trying to say in an essay. Karen Kramer underscores this point when she notes: "The fact that someone is going to read my writing doesn't really influence me as far as I'm aware. . . . I don't think about my audience when I'm getting started. When I begin writing, I set out to produce something that I enjoy writing and reading, and I hope everyone else will enjoy it too." As Terry Burns explains, writing with an audience in mind initially "made me very nervous. But as I gained confidence, the nervousness lessened. Now I encourage people to read my writing. The influence an outsider can have on your work can be invaluable. I usually don't think much about my reader until my last couple of drafts; the first drafts are for me."

Since all student writers prepare papers to satisfy course requirements, they are also mindful of their instructor's presence in their audience. Some student writers deal with what they regard as their instructor's intimidating presence by imagining themselves writing for teachers with whom they can relax. Others, practiced in and encouraged by the principles of collaborative learning, write specifically for their peers. But whether they are writing for a teacher, their peers, or an audience beyond the classroom, the fact that someone is going to read their writing imposes a good deal of discipline on most student writers. Thinking about their readers will help student writers make decisions about appropriate subjects, the kinds of examples to include, the type and level of language to use, and the overall organization of the essay. Every writer wants to be clear and convincing; most consciously try to minimize the risks of being misunderstood.

Outlining

To reduce the possibility that they will be misunderstood and to maximize the likelihood that they will appreciate the implications of their own ideas, all writers find it particularly useful to plan the scope and sequence of their ideas carefully before or during the course of writing a first full draft. For many students, outlining figures prominently in that effort. Yet *when* they turn to outlining varies greatly. Some student writers routinely outline their essays in their minds before they ever set pen to paper. David Christman, for example, notes his habit of composing "the main idea and some supporting ideas in my head." Amber Kennish creates "a basic outline in my head of where the paper will start, progress, and end. The actual writing is a matter of fitting my ideas logically into this outline." Linda Lavelle lets "the idea for an essay rattle around in my head for a few days until a few key phrases or sentences develop. With these few key phrases in mind, I can sit down to plan and write an essay and then come up with something that resembles a first draft."

Beverly Dipo reports "My writing process may be unique. I can write, and have written, an entire outline and the first paragraphs of an essay at night, in bed, in my head." As she explains, "I pretty well have my outline in my head before I actually start writing. I sit down at the typewriter and start typing my thoughts on paper. I'm a pretty organized person, so my first thoughts seem to organize themselves; sentences fall into paragraphs naturally for me. I sometimes use an outline to get an idea going, but I seem to outline in my head better. This was easy with the short essays we were required to do. I imagine it would be difficult for longer works." Carol Oberhaus describes a method of composing that is equally unique: "I make an outline to help me limit the topic. When that is done, I study it for a few moments, then put it aside. My next step is always to do a lot of freewriting and note-taking. I simply empty my mind onto the paper. Later on, I fit the ideas I've made notes on into the framework. I *have* to have a very tight outline because my ideas come from all over the place when I am freewriting and brainstorming. Having the outline gives me the freedom to think because the disciplined part of the essay is done for me."

Other student writers reserve outlining until their writing is well under way. John Siegrist suggests that "brainstorming and freewriting help to select a topic and to determine if it can be adequately covered in a paper. Outlining works well after this because it divides the material into paragraphs." Similarly, Brenda Jacobs's method of composing usually starts with "a list of ideas or words associated with the topic. Depending on the length of the paper, the list is often expanded into an outline—a fairly brief one for short essays, a detailed one for term papers." For Pamela Garrettson, outlining is a handy device to use when a writer gets "stuck": "When I am stuck on a first draft, a rough outline helps me organize my ideas into a coherent order. Also to write down anything, no matter how badly worded or thought out, is preferable to staring at a blank piece of paper. I can always go back and change it later."

Kelly Mays describes an even more intricate system for organizing her essays:

> "Despite the fact that I have always been told of the necessity of an outline, I have never been able to write one. Instead, I tend to brainstorm, thinking about the paper for a long time, even unconsciously, before I actually sit down to write. By the time I do begin, this thinking process has usually helped me to fully formulate my ideas into some cohesive order in my mind and to assemble the evidence which I think supports those ideas. Sometimes for the latter process I also use index cards with quotations and evidence on them which I think are important and pertinent. Physical sorting of these cards can help to organize the evidence when it begins to become too complex to be arranged mentally. When I have gotten to this stage of my thought process, I simply have to make myself sit down and begin to write. The actual process of writing helps further to organize my thoughts and evidence.

In contrast, Johnna Benson finds outlining inhibiting: "Outlining encourages me to discard ideas. I use it later in revising sometimes, but never in the beginning." Matthew Holicek reports that he starts a paper by "just throwing ideas around in my head until I feel I've come up with a satisfactory opening. The rest of the paper works basically the same. I'm one of those people who just hates to waste paper, and I would rather get it right the first time. I hate outlining and brainstorming. However, sometimes I have to if they are required, but in the end I rarely go back to my outline. I don't think I need an outline: I've already got a basic master plan inside my head once I begin writing."

The student writers whose work appears in this book would not be likely to agree on whether it is most helpful to outline an essay before, during, or after writing a first draft. Yet no doubt they would agree that all writers should develop a clear sense of the particular strategies for getting started that work best for them. Practicing these strategies frequently should result in increasing skill and confidence.

DRAFTING

It would not be practical to enumerate all the different ways writers work during the second phase of the writing process — completing a full draft of an essay. Instead, both the introduction to each essay printed in Part II and the Questions for Reading and Revising, along with the Suggestions for Writing that appear after each essay, include detailed information about the specific circumstances in which each essay was written. Here we present just a few general statements from the student writers on their characteristic styles of drafting.

Some writers write to discover what they want to say. In one sense, such writers must see their ideas on paper in order to explore, develop, and revise them. They must write in order to discover and shape their own meaning. William Malley's description of his writing process exemplifies the main features of this style of composing:

> I write the paper in longhand—I never compose at a typewriter, and I do not own a computer. . . . I sometimes sketch a brief outline, but more often I simply begin to write. The first few paragraphs are almost always fairly rough, but within a few minutes I usually fall into a groove. The writing then comes in spurts. I'll write a paragraph or even a page, then go back and look things over. Usually, I write pages and pages in this manner, several of which say the same thing in different ways. The process is time-consuming but worthwhile, because it is in these brief spurts that I churn out the good sentences, the nuts and bolts that can be rearranged and reworked into a good paper.

Writers like Malley usually need to examine their ideas as they are unfolding to clarify, develop, or revise them. Johnna Benson describes herself as "definitely a person who needs to see her ideas on paper before she can evaluate them." To this end, Terry Burns reports that he writes as much as he can in his first draft, without paying "any attention at all to things like punctuation, spelling, and grammar. I just write whatever comes into my head and worry about the mechanics later. I guess this works for me because it frees my mind for writing what I feel, and I don't get bogged down in technicalities." Nelsy Massoud extends Burns's point: "The easiest thing to do is to fill up pages and pages. It's like drawing, the lines must be on the paper." Such writing works incrementally: the writer quickly produces a very rough first draft to sketch out, explore, and develop the controlling idea of the essay and then focuses in subsequent drafts on organizing and polishing that idea. Here is how Beverly Dipo puts it: "Writing for me now is like painting a picture. I have a painting of horses that I did hanging in my living room. It turned out fairly well, but only after much effort. Writing is also something I can accomplish fairly well, with some effort. I am not a 'natural' at anything, including writing."

Some writers proceed at a slower pace. They think carefully about what they are going to say before they commit themselves to writing it out. These writers generally are more comfortable composing in their heads than on paper. They usually regard thinking and writing as separate, and in fact sequential, intellectual activities. David Christman summarizes this method of drafting when he notes: "For the most part I develop the idea in my mind and then sit down at the typewriter and just start in. . . . Most of the time my organization is mental, and I don't put anything down until I start typing." Kelly Mays describes her composing style in slightly different terms:

> I tend to compose in my head a good deal. I often compose whole sentences of the introduction mentally before I sit down to write. By having a very good idea of this portion of the paper prior to actual composition, I order my ideas into the form which they will take in the body of the paper. I think that this process becomes an almost mental outline by which I organize the paper before writing. It is true, however, that the actual writing of the paper greatly aids me in exploring and clarifying my ideas. As they take shape on paper, they often seem to change and take a clearer form in my own mind.

For Terry Burns, careful planning can sometimes produce surprising results: "Most of what I write has been carefully thought out. I can spend weeks turning an idea over and over in my head, until I know exactly what I want to write. Then I sit down and write something totally different."

Many student writers feel most comfortable creating their own distinctive blends of both the write/rewrite and think/write styles of drafting. Matthew Holicek is most comfortable writing when he has worked out beforehand the basic ideas and direction of his essay: "If I know basically what I am going to say and the direction I'm headed, I can usually come up with some lively and somewhat complex sentences right out of my head." Yet, as he explains, he also follows those sentences to wherever they may lead him: "Many times I just get on a roll and everything spills out into place almost perfectly. That's why when I start writing I don't like to stop until I finish the paper or at least that paragraph—for fear of losing my train of thought and the ideas that are floating around in my head." Ann Field makes a similar point when she describes her method of composition:

> I do most, if not all, of my prewriting in my head so it looks as if I'm starting in the middle when I sit down and write. I also try to write my first draft in one sitting. Once I get to the sit-down-and-write stage I know what I want

to say and how I want to try to say it. And once I get
started I just can't stop. It's as if the ideas are running away,
and if I don't get them down on paper in some crude form
they will be lost forever. In the past I have forced myself
to stop in the middle of a first draft, and when I've come
back I have been unable to pick up where I left off.

Karen Kramer prepares her essay carefully enough to be able to rely confidently
on writing two drafts: "Generally speaking, the body of the essay was already
in my head before I sat down and started typing. Once I think up an introduction, the rest just flowed naturally from there. . . . I typed the paper out,
and then I went back and reread it, out loud, and added what I thought was
appropriate, changed a few words here and there, etc. I only write two drafts,
a rough draft and a final draft. . . . I know I'm finished with the essay when
I read it and I wouldn't change, add, or delete anything." And as is the case
with most accomplished writers, Kramer knows better than to violate the
methods that work best for her.

Most of these writers continue to be aware of their audience as they write,
and that awareness helps shape the ways in which they write. But for some,
the anxiety about having their work read continues to haunt their efforts to
compose. Barbara Carter, for example, pictures her readers as "a passionate
group of red-pencil-slashing freshman English students." And Steve West's
consciousness of an audience for his writing exacerbates, as he says, "my tendency to want to work out in a first draft every little imperfection as it comes
up. I have a hard time leaving something that doesn't sound right, even though
I'm aware that I can come back and fix it up later." For many writers, such
issues help expedite the process of writing an essay. For an equally large number
of others, such questions prompt them to revise.

 REVISING

Many writers appreciate the power and permanence that revision can add
to the act of writing. When writers revise, they reexamine what they have
written with an eye on strengthening their control over their ideas. As they
revise, they expand or delete, substitute or reorder. In some cases, they revise
to clarify or emphasize. In others, they revise to tone down or reinforce particular points. And, more generally, they revise either to simplify what they
have written or to make it more complex. Revising gives writers an opportunity
to rethink their essays, to make them accomplish their intentions more clearly
and fully. Revising includes larger concerns such as determining whether the
essay is logically consistent, whether its main idea is supported adequately,
whether it is organized clearly enough, and whether it addresses its intended

audience in engaging and accessible terms to satisfy their specific needs or demands. Revising involves looking at the whole essay as well as at each part, at paragraph as well as sentence structure, at ideas as well as specific word choice. Revising enables writers to make sure that their essays are as clear, precise, and effective as possible.

Although revising is often the most painstaking phase of the writing process, it is crucial to successful writing. The student writers included here value the opportunity revising provides to clarify their ideas, sharpen their purpose in writing, tighten and strengthen the structure of their paragraphs and sentences, and refine their selection of examples and word choices. In describing her own procedures for revising, Brenda Jacobs offers an informative overview of this phase of the composing process. For her, revising involves:

> eliminating superfluous words, and sentences that sound terrific, but either don't fit or are redundant. It also means rearranging sentence patterns for smooth, even flow, improving paragraph transition, finding more precise wording, and rearranging paragraphs in a more logical sequence. . . . Normally, while revising, I find myself adding details that I hope add character to the work—description, examples, etc. — things I tend to leave out in the beginning. . . . Each progressive draft deals with smaller details, until finally (ideally) the little bells that go off in my head when something strikes a wrong note quit sounding.

Pamela Garrettson turns to a different metaphor to explain how she knows she is finished revising her essays: "when I read and start grinning like a fool. I get a big kick reading anything I have written well." As Garrettson reports, there are fundamental differences between drafting and revising an essay: "When I begin writing, I have to think divergently, opening my mind to various possibilities and writing techniques. When I revise, however, I must progress toward a particular goal or point and express my arguments and examples in clear, concrete terms." Barbara Seidel underscores this point by observing that revising provides writers with the occasion to distance themselves from their work: "Revising means taking my emotional likes and dislikes out of the writing process, and looking at my work objectively. This is truly difficult to do, because, like most creative people, I am insecure and therefore uncertain of what should stay and what should go."

Writers like Ravenel Boykin Curry revise as they work on their first drafts: "I usually revise as I write, with about three or four sentences to a page (unless I'm using a word processor). My main structure doesn't usually change too much — if something just doesn't work I'd rather start with something fresh. When a page becomes so messy with arrows and cross-outs that I can't read anything on it any more, I'll recopy it on a new sheet, but otherwise I really only have two drafts—my original and my final one, which is written a few days later." Erik Field also rereads each sentence and paragraph several times before moving on to the next one, adding, "the degree to which I revise is directly proportional to the degree of difficulty of the essay."

Other writers revise after they have written a very quick and usually very rough draft. Once they have something on paper, they revise for as long as they have time and energy. Patrick Kinder Lewis accentuates this point when he describes how he revises: "Length and overall development of structure seem the first factors which I weigh. Then I move slowly through the text actually listening to how it sounds to me. Sometimes I just have to take a breather, or I lapse into verbose stiltedness." Beverly Dipo's method of revision produces numerous drafts, each less messy than the preceding: "I take my typewritten rough draft with its double or triple spacing and wide margins and a red pencil. Then I proceed to thoroughly mess up the rough draft with slashes, marks, underlines, parentheses, arrows, exclamation points, secret codes, doodles, and assorted expletives. I will then retype what is left and repeat the procedure until I produce a whole essay without one single red mark!"

Still other student writers require more distance from their first draft in order to revise effectively. Earnestine Johnson reports that "I try to give myself several days between my first draft and my revision. The several days allow me to return to my writing, after what I call putting my work in 'cold storage.' I can review it later with a more critical eye." Petrea Galloway uses a similar method: "I try to get away from my piece for a few days. If that is not possible, a complete change of scenery for a few hours will help. When I return and read it, I may say, 'Really great!' or I might laugh at it and start over." As Ann Field notes, distance from a first draft enables her to "see the essay as if I were not the one who wrote it. Passages that are unclear or unnecessary are easier to see. And sometimes I have thought of new things to write or new ways to write the old things."

Many of the student writers mention the value of reading their work aloud as an aid to revision. Karen Kramer enumerates the benefits of reading essays aloud:

> I read the paper *out loud.* This is very important. I could read a paper a hundred times to myself and never catch something, but if I read it out loud, I'll catch it. Sometimes you have to actually *hear* what you wrote before you realize that it sounds like something a fourth-grader wrote. So, I read it aloud and change what doesn't sound right. Clumsily constructed sentences, weak words, questionable modifiers, etc. all come to light when I read it aloud to myself.

Other students remind themselves of an audience for their writing by asking family or friends to read their essays aloud to them. Johnna Benson, for example, reports that "I recruit people who live on my floor, members of study-groups, and anyone I can get to read my drafts. I have my victims read for the sense of it, not for grammar, though many can not help but comment on grammar. I also ask them to read aloud. That way I can tell if they get the jokes, understand the phrases, etc., without asking them if they noticed it. This technique really helps me . . . because I knew my readers were mainly unwilling, and that forced me to rework anything boring, technical, or that sounded like dead space."

Barbara Carter thinks about her potential readers in very different terms. "Honing down an essay is always difficult for me. I try to picture a classroom filled with students yelling 'Who cares?' when I revise my work." Jonathan Schilk no doubt speaks for many other students writers on the issue of audience in revision when he observes:

> When I first start a paper, the reader is not really that important. I feel at that stage, subject matter is most important. When the first draft has been completed, then it's time to consider readability. . . . Knowing that it is possible that I may have an audience for my work does influence me and my writing. The audience is just as important as the subject material and must be treated with all due regard given to the subject matter. I feel the reader must be treated as an intelligent person with common sense and at the same time I feel obliged to help him or her along on little-known subjects.

Thinking about an audience for their writing also helps many writers revise and edit their essays. When writers and publishers *edit* a piece of writing, they read it with an eye to preparing it for publication, whether that occurs literally in a newspaper, magazine, or a book, or figuratively in the exchange of essays within the community of a classroom, department, college, or university. When writers *proofread*, they reread their final drafts to detect any errors — misspellings, omitted lines, inaccurate information, and the like. Several student writers recommend what they call a "fail-safe" method for proofreading their essays — "read the essay backwards." Doing so enables writers to see the words more clearly outside the context of the sentence.

In general, more experienced writers concentrate on the larger concerns of writing — their purpose, ideas, evidence, structure — before they give attention to such matters as strengthening syntax and searching for the "right word." The student writers here tend to be interested in both when they revise. And they revise well because they are both practiced writers and readers.

An increasing number of students use word processors when preparing their essays. Yet, for Ravenel Boykin Curry, writing with a word processor comes only after he has written his first page: "I still need a pen and paper to write out the opening paragraph with scratches and cross-outs and arrows and scribbles. I have to face the machine with something *real.*" For many other students, using a word processor makes revising simpler and less time-consuming. As Ann Field notes, word processors eliminate the drudgery of retyping and offer an added attraction: "The hardest part of revising is cutting out unnecessary parts. It feels like I'm throwing away something important. Now that I have a word processor, I can save all the unnecessary parts and use them someday somewhere else."

When asked to offer some final, general advice to first-year college students to help them improve their writing, the thirty-five Bedford Prize winners gave responses as varied as their descriptions of the distinctive ways in which they compose. Common responses were such good-natured imperatives as "Trust your own experience," "Write about what you know or about what you are interested in learning," "Don't be too critical of yourself," "Don't fear failure," "Listen to your teachers," and "Keep it simple!" Steve West amplifies this last recommendation when he notes that "the biggest problem I think young writers have is a tendency to try to sound too polished and artificially intellectual." "It's not hard," he adds, "for readers to tell when authors are trying to adopt a voice they are not comfortable with, and I would advise students to stick to a simple style that seems natural for them." Perhaps not surprisingly, "Write and write and write" and "rewrite, again and again" are the most frequent refrains in the advice these Bedford prize winners offer their peers. Barbara Carter puts the point most simply: "Write! I've heard it said that no one could write 365 bad essays a year; if you write every day, you are bound to come up with something that is good."

These student writers also urge their peers to read as widely, voraciously, and rigorously as possible. "Be curious about everything," Sandra Casillas urges, "and read everything, even cereal boxes." Earnestine Johnson underscores this advice when she says, "Read as much and as often as possible. I would also encourage other student writers to take as many writing courses, labs, and workshops as possible. I believe growth is through knowledge, be it in life experience or in writing experience."

These prize-winning writers take this advice and enjoy reading—for knowledge *and* pleasure. Asking Petrea Galloway what she likes most about reading is, as she explains, "like asking what I like most about food. First, it keeps the body alive. Then there are the different flavors of the various foods. In reading, I like the learning, the discovery, the thoughts provoked, the pleasure of a good tale, the laughing at great humor, and even the sadness of a tragedy." For Linda Lavelle, "Every well-written story is a teacher, and I love to learn."

Yet these student writers often distinguish between reading for pleasure and reading for an assignment. "Reading for pleasure is direct enjoyment," John Siegrist observes, "while reading for an assignment is indirect enjoyment (getting a good grade)." Terry Burns draws the distinction in slightly more wry terms: "The main difference is that reading for pleasure can keep me up late; reading for an assignment can put me to sleep early." Barbara Carter pushes the distinction even further: "When reading for an assignment, you need to keep a grip on reality and study the structure and composition of the work. This does pay off in your writing process."

Nearly all of the student writers recognize the benefits of reading. Patrick Kinder Lewis, for example, describes himself as *not* being a "reader in the traditional sense in which writers seem to be. That is not to say I don't read: I read voraciously — I can almost never be caught anywhere without a book in my possession. But the habit is more a thirst for wisdom than from any learned-pleasure of reading for its own sake. I didn't grow up reading, but thinking and doing instead." Yet, as he explains, he recognizes in reading the opportunity to "look out of a different window onto the same wonderfully complex world. Like learning a new language, reading is truly liberating." Reading also provides, as Brenda Jacobs notes, the possibility to be "transported to other places and times, allowing me to experience vicariously those things apart from my own reality." "Reading," Barbara Seidel explains, "relaxes me, teaches me, reaches my heart, makes me think about people and lifestyles different from me and mine. It expands my limits of tolerance and makes me realize how fortunate I am in life. I could not think of a life without words." The motivations for writing vary widely among these student writers — from the reasonable desire to earn a good grade to the understandable need to discover more about oneself and one's relation to the larger world. Karen Kramer is fully aware that writing can sometimes be a "chore," but she also regards it as "an incredibly enjoyable experience. I know no greater pleasure than when I have written something I really like. Writing is also one of the easiest ways I know of obtaining a sense of accomplishment." "Besides," she quickly adds, "someone has to keep the liquid paper people in business." For Barbara Seidel, writing is "an emotional release, a very selfish pleasure. It is the only time in my life I am totally selfish. I write for my own sanity."

Most important, these writers are all students who write because they have something to say. "I find," Kim Sport says, "that many, many students fear writing courses and do not see the advantage of taking such a course. Learning to write is the most important element in their education. If they can write, they can pass all other courses that require writing with ease. . . . The ability to write is also a measure of a person's qualifications. It is not to be feared or taken lightly. Everyone should always be proud of what and how they write." "Be a person when you write," Johnna Benson urges. "The more you write what you think, the better you think." Finally, as Frances Taylor explains, the act of writing is a truly distinctive way to assert your presence in the world: "Writing belongs to you. There is no voice on earth like your own, and that equals power, so learn to craft it, and read, read, read."

QUESTIONS FOR THINKING AND WRITING

This exercise gives you an opportunity to examine your own attitudes toward writing in general and, more specifically, toward each stage of the composing process outlined in this chapter. Respond in writing to each of the following questions in as much detail as possible.

1. What are your earliest recollections of writing?

2. Have any members of your family, teachers, or anyone else encouraged you to write? Explain the circumstances.

3. What is the easiest thing for you to do when you write an essay?

4. What is the most difficult aspect of writing for you?

5. What method of getting started is most successful for you? Why do you think that method works for you?

6. If someone walked into your room and observed you trying to get started writing, what would this person see? Write your answer in a paragraph or two.

7. Do you try to avoid writing? If so, what do you do to avoid it?

8. What special habits do you have when you write?

9. What is the ideal environment for you as a writer?

10. How does the fact that your writing has an *audience* influence the way you write? How do you take an audience into account when you are writing an essay?

11. Describe in detail the specific procedures you follow when writing the first draft of an essay.

12. What does revising mean to you? Describe your methods of revision. How

many drafts do you usually write? How do you decide when a paper is finished and there is nothing more that you can do with it?

13. How would you describe yourself as a writer? As a reader?

14. What do you like most about reading? What do you like least? What have you learned about writing as a result of your reading? Identify what you do when you read that helps you when you write.

15. What general advice would you offer other first-year students to help them improve their writing?

16. Add any comments on or clarifications of any aspect of your writing that was not addressed adequately in these questions.

THE ESSAYS

Part II

JOHNNA LYNN BENSON

Brigham Young University
Provo, Utah
Brian S. Best, instructor

Johnna Lynn Benson reports that she drafts most of her papers late at night in her dorm room, a place that "has privacy and yet is near people who will listen to drafts and make comments. . . . I wouldn't recommend my method for writing papers. I need more time to write a paper than most of my friends would. I have to start soon after an assignment is given, and I need time between drafts for my ideas to soak down. I like writing this way because I end up with papers no one else would write—papers that sound like me. And even though I agonize over my papers, I enjoy working at them more than throwing together forgettable papers I never thought about. Some people don't like my kind of paper, and some people includes some professors. It's a choice I made."

Benson's choice to express her own distinctive voice marks virtually every aspect of her life. The eldest of six children, she was born in Santa Monica, California. She explains that the "biggest influence on me was my name, Johnna. It's a combination of my Dad's little-used first name and an unrecognizable portion of my Mom's first name. I always felt like I could take the components of my life and put them together in my own new way." A 1984 graduate of El Camino Real High School in Woodland Hills, California, she has earned two academic scholarships—the Mattel Foundation Scholarship and the Presidential Scholarship at Brigham Young University. "I don't have a major, but it won't be English," she notes. "I don't have a career goal, except to have a career and be able to write in it."

Benson explains that the assignment for her paper was "basically to pick any topic we'd studied in the writing colloquium and talk about it. In a class that jumped from evolution to psychology to philosophy, . . . I should have felt like I was at a topic banquet. But I didn't feel like I had anything to say. In connection with the class, I had an advisor who had the title 'writing lab instructor,' whom I was supposed to meet by such-and-such a date, topic in hand, to plan my paper. I mixed up my appointments and showed up without a subject as my advisor, Chris, was leaving for work. She sat on her moped and made suggestions for topics—all ideas I had looked at and discarded in disgust. I tried to explain to her that I needed a topic I could 'soapbox' on, yell and scream about injustice and ignorance. (My previous paper had been on homosexuality.) She asked me why, and I tried to explain that I was different, that I couldn't present an idea someone else might have thought of. In groping for an example of how I am unique I remembered a book we had been reading, George Kelly's A Theory of Personality. Chris said, 'Look at you, you're yelling at me. I think you'd better do your paper on Kelly.' And she buzzed off to work."

"By now," Benson reports, "I had not only made my writing lab instructor late for work but I had also made myself late to math. I found an empty seat in the back of the class, but I have a weakness in not paying attention to a teacher when more than one hundred people separate us. I turned over my homework and started writing about Kelly,

31

*or more accurately, about the things I wanted to say to Chris when she had escaped. I
ended up with a page and a half of sarcasm and jokes, mainly about myself. Later
I . . . ended up showing a friend what I wrote. . . . He said he also felt different than
everyone else. . . . He showed me that he understood what was under the sarcasm.
From then on, I wanted to write the paper using Kelly's* Theory of Personality *only for
what light Kelly threw on the topic of myself. I wanted to make my sometimes abstract
sense of uniqueness understandable."*

For an exercise in peer editing, see Benson's essay in Part V.

Rotten at the Core

George A. Kelly's *Theory of Personality* has scrubbed me on a washboard   1
and put me through the wringer. Discovering what I actually am under the
dirt and debris has been bewildering and has left me wondering if I would be
better off blissfully ignorant. I had thought "to know thyself" an admirable
pursuit, especially since I believed truth was beauty. Now I see I have been
beautifully wrong about who I am and who everybody else is.

When the colloquium introduced me to *Theory of Personality*, I was sure we   2
would get along great. I have always loved dabbling in psychology. My friends
and I would make Freudian jokes or play shrink-games, using those little tests
in women's magazines designed to save on psychoanalysis costs. You could say
I won those games; my free associations were always more bizarre than anyone
else's. I wasn't even trying to be shocking or clever. That is just a bad habit.
My only feud with psychology was that I aspired to be more than a product of
my environment, a multiplication of Mormonism by a materialistic middle-
class suburb. *Theory of Personality* eliminated that limitation for me.

I loved it instantly. Kelly's treatise holds that people create their own per-   3
sonalities. As a person tries to make sense of the circus around him, he picks
up on recurring themes in his life and makes deductions about what is going
on. The individual creates these explanations, called "constructs," for his
convenience in anticipating what the world is going to hit him with next. As
a person construes, he builds an inner road map of himself, of life, and of what
he can expect from it. The psychology I had been exposed to before treated
man like an organism poked and prodded into reactions. I found the concept
of deciding for yourself who you are and what you can expect from life far
more palatable. Claiming total responsibility for my outlook on life filled me
with satisfaction.

Theory of Personality created a little garden paradise in the corner for me,   4
but it also unearthed something upsetting. As part of our colloquium study of

constructs, we were asked to write about our core roles, or how we viewed ourselves. I kept putting the assignment off because every time I started it, my query led me down the same path. If you do not want to go to Rome, finding that all roads go there is rather dismaying. Suddenly it was the day to hand in the assignment, and I discovered, as I frantically wrote the thing in the Harris Fine Arts Center an hour before class, that I had spent enough time trying not to think about it that I knew exactly what I didn't want to know.

With Fresh, Original, and Bizarre as my highest ideals, my core role seems   5
to be that I must be different. And I am different, which makes me exceptional, though not in a way the general population appreciates. This arrogant idea actuates my every thought and emotion, a realization that makes me shudder. Exploring the fact that I'm rotten at the core reduced me to tears.

Yet I can't seem to get around it. I look at how I hate get-acquainted parties.   6
To adhere "Hello, my name is . . ." on my lapel is to assume common ground exists between these strangers and me. But my core role says my lifeline runs geometrically askew to theirs. Kelly defines guilt as an awareness of contradicting one's core role structure, and guilty well describes the uncomfortable feeling I get pretending such parties aren't futile. I forget that I actually do share significant parallels and intersections with family and friends. I like the differences. By the time I was six I introduced myself by saying, to the consternation of my playmates, that I did not like chocolate cake or soda-pop. For years my favorite color was chartreuse, sienna, or puce. My favorite number is 3.02875×10^{14}. I took up origami because I thought no one had heard of it. In short, anything popular was not worth my time, while anything obscure or new was mine by right.

Moreover, I felt unique enough to assume that although rules were necessary   7
to keep the regulars in line, they did not apply to me. Because rules were necessary, I never quite broke them but found interpretations to suit me. For example, when an elementary class punishment to copy five pages from the dictionary was handed down, my paper always included a few words outside the assigned alphabetical range, like "despot," "toupee," or "maltreatment." Lights-out at camp meant it was dark enough to leave the cabin unnoticed and go for a moonlight walk. Going to parties where friends were too drunk to really notice my abstinence was showing my love and understanding for people with problems, not to mention making them aware of the Mormon Church. And of course, as long as my boyfriend and I didn't go all the way, whatever we wanted to do was fine. We were toying with the idea of marriage anyway. Other people needed rules. I did not.

I have been carried away with my own individuality enough to hypothesize   8
that when I was a zygote, some stray cosmic ray zapped my DNA, making me

a daughter of chance and not of Terry and Dianna Benson. On a similar note, I latched onto the idea that I have always existed, that before I was a spirit I was an entity, an intelligence bobbing out somewhere like a chartreuse soap bubble. I did not want to be someone else's creation. I figured God recognized the special and distinctive thing I was and handpicked me to be his child.

Being Mormon has been convenient in other ways. It is a guaranteed way   9 to stick out like a sore thumb. I always felt a swell of pride as I answered astonished cries of "You've never done such and such?" I could spend hours elaborating on LDS precepts with the sole intent of blowing an innocent Protestant mind. I have had so much fun being Mormon that I have to wonder how much of my testimony is based on faith and how much on the attention it garners. I created my outlook on life according to my convenience, says Kelly. My convenient testimony thus becomes as meaningful as my green argyle earrings; I would probably join any group that boasted of being a peculiar people.

Yet my testimony of the gospel encapsulates some of my strongest emotions 10 and most important rational convictions. I founded my belief on study, con-templation, and prayer, not whim. If such a testimony is invalid, there is little I think or feel that is valid. But I must consider I may have forced my person-ality to grow in unnatural and indirect ways because I wanted to be different, cultivating a taste for mustard on my french fries and a taste for LDS doctrine. I have created my personality and maybe I could have done a better job. Yet the thought of supplanting myself with a new and improved model based on different criteria scares me. It would be personality suicide; although someone would be here named Johnna, I would cease to exist.

And what about all these other people? I always pictured my intelligence 11 as a chartreuse bubble in contrast with their monochromatic assembly of lemon yellow bubbles. If Kelly gives me the right to be self-made, he also extends that right to all those dumb slobs. Besides, I doubt Kelly was lemon yellow. If he and I can be different, then probably everyone else is on a slightly different wavelength, can be a slightly different color. This means I probably don't stand out at all. I have always understood why people were worried that God might not know them specifically. There was no reason for him to bother when they were all the same. But if everyone is a unique individual, how does Heavenly Father remember which fingerprint I am? In my place in the sun, I did not notice all those stars out there, each one shining bright for someone. I do not feel important or special while gazing at billions of stars.

For the first time in my life I feel truly lost, an electron carrying practically 12 no weight, fairly indistinguishable from any other electron, whose orbit is an unknown in a probability cloud. I am looking at life in a new and startling way, and this is the ultimate test of my taste for the new and startling. I find myself attempting to straddle the importance of my uniqueness and the existence of 4.5 billion other unique individuals. I do not like wondering who I am. I could always tell before by the stark contrast between me and anyone else. I had three dimensions and the other person only had two. Now I see that I just had no depth perception.

How everyone can be different intimidates and amazes me. Without its   13
former base, my sense of identity has become as fragile as the chartreuse soap bubble I imagine as its beginnings. I fear the existence of all the variegated personalities that might crowd and pop it. Yet in returning to that sense of fragile newness, I see the world freshly. I have bemoaned the fact that no one could appreciate my special outlook. Now I see there are countless other outlooks for me to explore, each a world as strange and wonderful as mine. For the first time there is an impetus for me to get to know people. This potential soothes my battered psyche and fills me with wonder in proportion to my fear.

QUESTIONS FOR READING AND REVISING

1. Johnna Benson's instructor, Brian Best, reports that her interdisciplinary writing colloquium had been reading George Kelly's A *Theory of Personality*, "which discusses the roles, or 'constructs,' people adopt and stresses that all of us have alternative possibilities if we are willing to re-examine our constructs and experiment with other ways of going about creating our self-identity. We had also read Lao Tse, the *Tao Te Ching*, and the *Book of the Hopi*, with the intent of getting some idea of how other cultures view their world. All of this apparently worked for Johnna, and she found herself in something of an identity crisis. Her journal and her rough drafts of this paper became her personal battleground with some long-held personal constructs which she began to question." Outline the major points that Johnna Benson makes in her essay. How is each of these points specifically connected to George Kelly's book, A *Theory of Personality*? How does Benson use Kelly's book to help organize her essay?

2. What assumptions does Benson seem to make about her audience's familiarity with A *Theory of Personality*? Where and how does Benson provide her readers with information about Kelly's theory? Consider, for example, paragraph 6. In writing it, Benson notes that she "spent a great deal of time trying to find concrete examples to back up the connection between Kelly's theories and my own." How successful is she in this paragraph at accomplishing that goal? What overriding point does she make about herself in this essay? What examples does

she offer to support it? How does she connect it to Kelly's theory? What exactly does she mean when she judges herself to be "rotten at the core"? How does she expect her *audience* to react to her use of this phrase?

3. Benson reports that one of the goals of her essay is "to make my sometimes abstract sense of uniqueness understandable." What specific examples does Benson use to make this abstract notion understandable to her audience? Do these examples suggest that her self-awareness increased gradually or occurred suddenly in a moment of revelation while reading Kelly? Point to specific words and phrases to verify your response.

4. One of the strengths of Benson's essay is the lively, honest voice she uses to address her readers. Figurative language helps make this voice memorable. See, for example, paragraph 1, where she notes that "Kelly's *Theory of Personality* has scrubbed me on a washboard and put me through the wringer." What is the nature of this metaphor? Why is it particularly appropriate to Benson's overall *purpose* in writing? Point to other examples of Benson's use of metaphors and assess what each contributes to the points she wants to emphasize.

5. In describing how she writes, Benson notes: "I also cram initial drafts with jokes and cynical parenthetical comments. They keep me entertained and sometimes evolve into relevant subtopics." For example, in paragraph 2, she speaks of how "My friends and I would make Freudian jokes or play shrink-games, using those little tests in women's magazines designed to save on psychoanalysis costs." What is the nature of the cynicism expressed here? Reread Benson's essay and identify other moments when her voice seems to be marked by lingering traces of "jokes and cynical parenthetical comments." What does each contribute to the overall effectiveness of her essay?

6. Benson explains that she drafted this essay "in sections rather than just plodding through the whole paper. I spent a lot of time on the third paragraph, trying to explain Kelly without getting overtechnical or breaking the tone." Reread that paragraph carefully and evaluate how successful she has been. What writing strategies does she use to avoid being "overtechnical"? How successful is she in maintaining the overall *tone* of her essay in this particular paragraph? Point to specific words and phrases to support your response.

7. In discussing the satisfactions and frustrations of writing this essay, Benson observes: "Finding a way to say what I really mean plagued me in the paragraphs on religious attitudes. I would draft and ask myself, 'Is that what I think?' " Reread paragraphs 7 through 10. What role have her religious beliefs and practices played in her increasing self-awareness? What exactly does she mean at the end of paragraph 10 when she talks about "personality suicide"?

8. Benson explains that she worked her way through "one package of notebook paper and half a package of typing paper" as she prepared the multiple drafts of this essay. "I write on every other line in drafts and then cross most every-

thing out. I'm hard on trees." Here is one of Benson's earliest drafts of what became paragraph 6:

> Yet I can't seem to get around it. Kelly defines guilt as "awareness of dislodgement of the self from one's core role structure," a realization that you've contradicted your core role. Guilt can act as a trailmaker pointing to the core role maligned. No wonder I feel guilty at parties where everyone runs around with "Hello, my name is." It's not right for me to act that way, anxious to meet and make friends because people are not my peer group. My lifeline runs geometrically skew, no parallels and no intersections. Of course a logical voice in the back of my head will intone that for me to be so alien to the human race is simply not true. Interactions with family and friends deny the possibility. Logic is thereby, however, ignored. Since I believed I was so set apart, I set myself apart; the conviction was a self-fulfilling prophecy.

Compare and contrast this very early version of paragraph 6 with the final draft of Benson's essay. Which points from this early draft does Benson preserve in the final version and how is each developed? What are the choices she made as a writer in moving from one draft to another? In what specific ways does Benson's revised version more successfully support the overriding point of her essay? How might her final draft of this paragraph be strengthened further?

9. The conclusion of her essay posed special problems for Benson. "Since I don't draft straight through, there is no exact number of drafts. Some parts were only worked about three times, but the ending had at least twenty attempts. . . . Ending the essay was difficult because I felt I had really reached no conclusions; I had a diagnosis but no prescription." Reread Benson's essay carefully, with special emphasis on the relationship between the final paragraph and the rest of the essay. Show how she is—or is not—accurate in her assessment that her essay provides a "diagnosis but no prescription" and point to specific words and phrases to support your response. If Benson had the opportunity to revise her essay, what specific recommendations would you offer her to help strengthen her final paragraph?

SUGGESTIONS FOR WRITING

1. In paragraph 7, Johnna Benson notes: "I felt unique enough to assume that although rules were necessary to keep the regulars in line, they did not apply to me. Because rules were necessary, I never quite broke them but found interpretations to suit me." She then offers as an example to support this point

an anecdote about "an elementary class punishment to copy five pages from the dictionary" and that she included several words "outside the alphabetical range." Consider an incident in your own experience in which you thought that, "although the rules were necessary to keep the regulars in line, they did not apply" to you and write an expository essay in which you recount an incident that illustrates this point. What "lesson" did you learn about yourself— and rules—as a result of this experience?

2. Each of us has had one or more experiences that have fundamentally changed our perceptions of ourselves and of our relationship to those around us. This changed perception might well have also led to substantial changes either in our way of doing something or in our relationships with others. Write an essay in which you re-create that experience. Show how it changed not only your perception of yourself but also your behavior.

3. One of the features that makes Benson's essay effective is her deft use of humor. Psychology and psychiatry have often been the subjects of both cynical and good-spirited humor. Gather as many "professional" jokes about one occupation as you can. What traits do these jokes have in common? Write an *expository* essay using these jokes as *examples* to illustrate what you take to be the general public's prevailing perception of this profession.

TERRY L. BURNS

Canisius College
Buffalo, New York
Robert Durante, instructor

"Being the youngest in a large family made it hard to be taken seriously. I always had things to say, but it was difficult to get anyone to listen. I find writing a better way to say what is on my mind. If I get words just right, I can make people listen." Terry Burns needs no special circumstances or environment to write. "I can write just about anywhere," he notes, "at work, on the bus, in a bar, anywhere but at my desk. . . . All I need is a pen, some paper, and a very large ashtray." Given the size of his family, Burns has no difficulty writing in the midst of commotion: "I know most people like it quiet when they write, but I just can't think when it's quiet. Crank up the stereo and I'm in business." He writes his drafts in longhand, and then types only his final version: "I don't type well, and I can lose a thought before I can put it on paper."

Terry Burns was born in Buffalo, New York, the youngest of nine children. A self-described apathetic student in his "younger" years, Burns has become increasingly interested in writing. He plans to major in English and pursue a career as a free-lance writer. Reading a great deal of fiction occupies a good portion of his time away from classes, and he includes Edgar Allan Poe, Dick Francis, and Kurt Vonnegut among his favorite writers. "The main difference between reading for pleasure and reading for an assignment," he observes, "is that reading for pleasure can keep me up late and reading for an assignment can put me to sleep early."

In the following essay, Burns re-creates the response of "a scared eighteen-year-old, far from home," to a violent initiation into military life and ritual.

The Blanket Party

Crickets chirped in the grass surrounding the compound as four men, dressed   1
only in white government issue underwear, made their way through the dark barracks. Airman Goodrich woke as the rough, military blanket settled over his head and chest. He tried to move, but the four men held the blanket securely, pinning him to his bunk. His feet kicked as a fifth man rose from his neighboring bunk and began to pummel him to unconsciousness. Goodrich's screams shattered the night, yet no one moved a muscle to help. Though the snoring, which was incessant at night, had stopped abruptly and completely, everyone pretended to sleep. When the screaming and pleading had finally died away, Goodrich was motionless. The moonlight poured through the windows, casting unearthly shadows across his body.

After ten minutes of total silence, the taps on Sgt. Siat's shoes could be   2
heard echoing in the long, tile hallway. The fluorescent, overhead lights blinked
on, momentarily blinding the entire flight. Everyone was standing at "Attention," as Sgt. Siat, perfectly creased and polished, walked the length of the
barracks, the taps on his shoes adding an exclamation point to each step. He
stopped at Goodrich's bunk and pulled the blood-soaked blanket from his face.
As he turned and surveyed the entire flight, Sgt. Siat's lips bent to form a
smile that didn't quite reach his eyes. If any concern showed on his face it
was certainly not for Goodrich. Why should he waste his concern on Goodrich? He couldn't march, he couldn't make his bed, he couldn't even shine
his shoes right. The Sergeant threw the blanket on the foot of Goodrich's
bunk, turned on his heel, and headed toward his office to call the base ambulance.

The ambulance arrived, along with two Military Police officers. As the   3
ambulance attendants piled the broken, battered body of Goodrich onto a
stretcher, the MPs finished their cursory investigation and left, thinking nothing of the fact that a man could be mercilessly beaten as one hundred men
slept on in the same room.

The "Blanket Party" was a rarely mentioned, but highly encouraged method   4
of dealing with malingerers and incompetents. It was the favorite method of
some of the "best" instructors. Give extra duty to everyone when one man
consistently made mistakes, and eventually some of his peers would visit him
in the night. The training missed while in the hospital would cause him to be
recycled into a younger flight and then he was someone else's problem. The
"Blanket Party" seemed to work just fine when a man could do the work but
wouldn't. Airman Goodrich, a meek, nervous, unhealthy-looking young man,
just could not do the work. He was easily shaken and seemed on the verge of
tears anytime anyone raised his voice. But the men who are your comrades
and buddies can easily become your enemies when deprived of even a few of
the already meager privileges.

The young men who had joined this organization with the dream of becom-   5
ing "men" had been betrayed by the people they had trusted. They had in
reality become a mob, skulking in the darkness, preying on people as they
slept, always making sure to cover their victim's face, not so much to avoid
being seen as to avoid seeing. The act of felonious assault is much easier when
your victim is faceless. Back at the barracks, life went on as usual, but not for
Goodrich; two flights and two "Blanket Parties" later, Goodrich was discharged
for a defective attitude. The men who had assaulted him, as well as those who
had looked on, went on to graduate. But Goodrich, his face still swollen and
his hair just a shadow on his head, was sent home to face his family.

QUESTIONS FOR READING AND REVISING

1. Terry Burns's advice to other students in first-year writing courses is to "get a good first sentence. A reader can decide if he likes a story very quickly, and you have to hook them as soon as possible." Reread the opening sentence of Burns's essay carefully. In what specific ways does that sentence demonstrate the soundness of his own advice? What features of the sentence encourage—and even impel—his readers to continue reading?

2. Characterize Burns's *point of view* in this essay: Is he detached and objective? Involved and subjective? Some other combination? Where and how is his point of view established? Does it remain consistent throughout the essay? If not, when and how does it change, and with what effect? Support your response with an analysis of specific words and phrases from the essay.

3. What larger significance does Burns find in the ritual of beating Airman Goodrich? When and how does he signal this significance to his readers? What overall point is he trying to make in his essay?

4. Reread Burns's first two paragraphs. How does his choice of phrasing reinforce the ominous story he tells? What, for example, is the effect of his repeating *taps* in paragraph 2? In what other ways is this an effective word choice? Point to additional examples of phrasing in these two paragraphs that heighten the effect Burns tries to create.

5. Consider Burns's final paragraph. What is the effect of using "organization" in sentence 1? What attitude toward the military does this word choice express? Toward Airman Goodrich? Does Burns's attitude toward the military—and toward Goodrich—remain the same throughout this paragraph? What issue is embedded in the final sentence? Why would Goodrich's facing his family be an issue—either for him or for Burns? What does the last sentence tell his readers about Burns's attitude toward Goodrich?

6. Burns wrote several drafts of this essay. The following is his first draft of the opening paragraph:

> Screams shattered the sleep of one hundred men in the dark barracks as Airman Goodrich pleaded for help. Everyone knew what was happening. Three men were holding a blanket over Goodrich's upper torso and head as the fourth pummeled him into unconsciousness, yet no one moved a muscle to help. Everyone pretended to be asleep, though the snoring, which was incessant at night, had stopped abruptly and completely. When the screaming finally stopped the room was deadly silent. The only sounds to be heard were the chirping of the crickets in the grass surrounding the compound and the ominous buzz of the

locust in the trees. Goodrich lay still on his bunk, the moonlight pouring through the windows, casting eerie shadows across his body.

Compare the two drafts of the opening paragraph of this essay. What specific changes do you notice? Comment on the effectiveness of each change. Which version do you prefer? Why?

7. Burns notes that, "while revising is not the easiest part of writing, I find it to be the most satisfying part. Rearranging sentences and searching for just the right word or phrase until I have a clear and concise finished product is very gratifying to me." Here is Burns's last sentence as it stood *before* the final draft: "Airman Goodrich was sent home to face his family, discharged, according to his separation papers, for a 'Defective Attitude.' " Reread the final draft sentence of Burns's essay and consider the revisions he made as he prepared the final draft. Which version do you prefer? Why? How well do the terms *clear* and *concise* apply to his revisions?

SUGGESTIONS FOR WRITING

1. In an earlier draft of his essay, Terry Burns added a series of sentences to his final paragraph that read, in part: "Goodrich, as well as the rest of these young men had been betrayed by a group of people they had trusted to show the way to adulthood, to lead them away from the simple world of childhood to the complex world of men." Write an essay in which you *argue* that the "way to adulthood" should (or should not) include experience with violence. What role should violence play in the move from "the simple world of childhood to the complex world" of adulthood? Support your position with evidence from your own experience and from contemporary world events.

2. The world we live in is filled with various rituals: hazing for fraternities and sororities, joining a team, preparing to jog, studying for exams, and the like. Choose a ritual that is part of your own life and write an essay in which you explain your participation in—and reaction to—this ritual.

3. In the final paragraph of his essay, Burns notes that the soldiers who had beaten Airman Goodrich acted like a mob, "preying on people as they slept, always making sure to cover their victim's face, not so much to avoid being seen as to avoid seeing." Choose a contemporary example of such "faceless" violence and write an essay in which you re-create the nature of the incident and draw some conclusions about the effects of this incident on those involved and on American society in general.

BARBARA J. CARTER

Rogue Community College
Grants Pass, Oregon
Mary Slayter, instructor

"Early evening is the best writing time for me," reports Barbara Carter. "The thoughts of the day are still with me; the commitments of the day are behind. If someone walked in and observed me writing they would see a woman (me) with one hand on a coffee cup and the other gripping a pencil, staring alternatively from the window to the pages spread before her with a mildly mad look in her eye. In spurts of decision, she gulps her coffee and rapidly scribbles words on the paper until her shoulders relax and the madness seems to be replaced with a bemused smile."

Barbara Carter was born in Whittier, California, into a "solid middle-class family that encouraged artistic expression." She is interested in music and theater, and manages a dinner theater in Santa Barbara that encourages the production of plays by new playwrights. Her advice to fellow writers is to "Write! No one could write 365 bad essays a year; if you write every day, you are bound to come up with something good."

Asked to write a "snapshot" description of a person or place, Carter reports: "I wanted my memories to speak to the memories of others. The way that I remember the cupboard is not the same as others do—it may not even be the way it was—but I wanted to promote the idea that our recollections shape our future. My essay is written primarily from a childhood perspective and should be read with that in mind. We all have a cupboard of some kind in our mind."

Momma's Cupboard

In the back of the house, down the long hall between bedrooms and past 1 the laundry chutes, the pantry squatted cramped and dark. It looked like a wart on the house, an architectural afterthought. It was ugly with its weak-tea-stained-plywood veneer and wonderful with its bounty and visions.

Momma called her crowded pantry the guest cupboard and under threats of 2 a sound shaking, we knew better than to sneak a treat. How longingly we children dreamed of the delicacies stacked up in there; how patiently we awaited the guests that never came to relish and sup the goodies that lay within. With every Christmas the gift packs of smoked meats would arrive, make their way into the pantry, and never come out again. Valentine's Day meant one more can of Almond Roca to be set on the second shelf. Every birthday that went by meant one more bottle of vanilla flavoring bought in good faith for the cake to come—but it seemed there was never a child that was good long enough for it to be made.

Sometimes, late in the evening when Momma was at school, we would line   3
our little bodies up at the pantry door like stacking dolls and dream of the
dinner party that was sure to come some day. Stored on the bottom shelf were
my favorite supplies: canned sardines, oysters, salmon packs, and Dinty Moore
Beef Stew. My big sister liked the second shelf with its Almond Roca, candies,
mandarin orange segments, and maraschino cherries. Jim wanted the salty stuff:
pretzels, shoestring potatoes, peanuts, and pecans. Linda settled for whatever
was left over: popcorn kernels, canned clam chowder, apricot nectar, Beeman's
Gum. Robert, the oldest and tallest, lay general claim over it all as befitted
his position. We never ate anything from Momma's pantry, but I remember,
on one occasion, my eldest brother passing around a bottle of vanilla flavoring
that we ceremoniously drained dry.

There weren't a lot of shared plans and dreams in my childhood home, but   4
that pantry was a focal point for everyone. We have all developed opinions
and theories about its effect on our lives—the denials and broken dreams, the
promise that never came. No guest ever did arrive in time for dinner; to my
knowledge no one was ever invited. The day we drank the vanilla flavoring
was the day we stopped believing in birthday cakes or cupboard fantasies.
Although we kept up the illusion for a while, by the time I was in my teens
the pantry was only mentioned when new supplies arrived. We could all be
trusted by then to put the goodies away into that little back room, pausing
only long enough to wipe the shelf dust off our fingertips.

Last year when I moved my parents out of the old childhood home, I   5
followed Momma's explicit instructions, packed up the contents of the pantry
into little cardboard boxes, and donated them all to the church. Someone,
someplace, is having dreams for dinner. Someone is eating my sardines.

QUESTIONS FOR READING AND REVISING

1. Barbara Carter creates a picture of her childhood by focusing on her mother's
   pantry. What did the pantry represent to Carter as a young girl? What does
   the pantry represent to her now as an adult?

2. Carter's essay reflects on an important place in her childhood. It is easy to be
   sentimental and romantic about such places; how does Carter avoid sentimentality?

3. Carter never comes out and makes any direct statements about her mother.
   Rather, we learn everything indirectly through Carter's *description* of the pantry. For instance, in paragraph 4 Carter writes: "No guest ever did arrive in

time for dinner; to my knowledge no one was ever invited." What does this detail tell the reader about her mother? What other passages are similarly indirectly revealing? How is this an effective strategy?

4. One of the most powerful pictures in Carter's essay is that of Carter and her siblings: "Sometimes, late in the evening when Momma was at school, we would line our little bodies up at the pantry door like stacking dolls and dream of the dinner party that was sure to come some day." Why does Carter tell us what each sibling liked in the pantry? How does this information advance her purpose?

5. Carter uses details very effectively. Find specific details and explain what they tell us about the pantry, about Carter's family, and about Carter herself. To what senses do these details appeal?

6. Does Carter maintain a clear, definite *point of view* toward her subject? If so, how?

7. Compare Carter's description of the pantry in paragraph 1 with her reference to it at the end of paragraph 4 as "that little back room." Why is each *description* appropriate for her *purpose*?

8. Carter ends her essay with these simple, but powerful lines: "Last year when I moved my parents out of the old childhood home, I followed Momma's explicit instructions, packed up the contents of the pantry into little cardboard boxes, and donated them all to the church. Someone, someplace, is having dreams for dinner. Someone is eating my sardines." Why is this an effective *conclusion*?

9. In an earlier draft, the last sentence in paragraph 2 read: "Every birthday that went by meant one more bottle of vanilla flavoring bought in good faith for a cake never made." Compare this sentence with her revised version. What is the effect of the change?

10. Carter begins her description of the pantry in her introductory paragraph. Yet in an earlier draft, these two paragraphs introduced the essay:

> There were seven of us tugging, shoving, and scrambling up together in a medium-sized home in a very large suburban track. Our neighborhood—in its vast pretense of privacy—was one where you could walk for miles without getting anywhere and yet always feel a little lost. Inside our cluttered home, filled with elbows, secrets, and twenty years of *National Geographic,* that same feeling prevailed.
>
> I have few vivid memories of my childhood. Most of the years and the times that were my youth are a mist in my mind. I am the youngest child; many of my memories are stories that I heard so often I made up my own recollections for them. Some of my memories might not be true.

But then there are those few that are grounded in their
childlike perception—persistent in their visits—and real.
One of these is the memory of Momma's pantry.

Why do you think Carter dropped these two paragraphs? What effect does
the revised introduction have on the reader? What is the effect of beginning
in such a direct way?

SUGGESTIONS FOR WRITING

1. Select a place that represents the color and texture of your childhood. Write
an essay *describing* this place and showing how it represents some important
aspect of your childhood.

2. Consider an important person or place from your childhood. Interview your
siblings, if possible, to see what this person or place meant to them. Write an
essay *describing* this person or place that incorporates the various perceptions
of each sibling. *Compare and contrast* these various perceptions.

3. Choose an incident in your life that marked the turning point between childhood and adulthood. Write an essay in which you reflect on this turning point
and explain its significance to you.

4. *Compare and contrast* two kitchens or bedrooms or any two rooms in a house.
Explain how the personalities of the inhabitants are reflected in the possessions
and arrangement of the rooms.

SANDRA CASILLAS

University of Texas at El Paso
El Paso, Texas
Alicia Gaspar de Alba, instructor

"Writing was a magic I could hardly wait to learn," Sandra Casillas confesses. *"I used to get my older cousin to write words for me on my drawings, and then I would copy them and go over them when they faded."* Sandra Casillas traces her interest in writing to the encouragement of her mother but decided early on to concentrate on art. *"Writing took second place,"* she notes. Now an art major at the University of Texas at El Paso, Casillas combines her study of art with work in advertising and art instruction at a nearby Episcopal school.

Born in Phoenix, Arizona, Sandra Casillas grew up in an artistic family. Her father was a jeweler, her mother a poet, her brother a sculptor. Art remains a central fact in her life:

> To be an artist, it is necessary to be as serious and as free in
> your thinking as possible. I have always kept a journal since
> high school but I have never done any writing for other people
> until I was forced to take freshman English courses.

Asked by her instructor to write a research paper about a ceremony or ritual from a foreign culture, Sandra Casillas was determined to write about a subject related to her major interest.

She began her research by focusing on the beauty of Raku pottery, which, she later discovered, plays a prominent role in the Japanese tea ceremony. *"My idea developed as I read, and each book and bit of information led me to new ideas and questions, as well as a few answers. It was very exciting to immerse myself in this completely new and unknown subject."* The result is an essay that examines the fascinating process of an ancient Japanese ceremony, a ceremony used for centuries, as Casillas notes, *"to teach the people of Japan tranquility, respect, aesthetics, and restraint."*

Cha-No-Yu,
the Japanese Tea Ceremony

Imagine yourself in a loose flowing robe of pure silk, sitting on a cushion 1
in a small austere room so sparse of decoration that you might compare it with
a cell but for the warmth of the lovely woodwork and the delicate balance of
its simple lines. Imagine that you came to this quiet room in a series of modes
of travel so foreign to this setting that you might have come by sheer magic.

The manner in which we matter-of-factly accept the incredible heights and speeds of transoceanic flight and ride across Japan at over 100 mph in the futuristic "Bullet," electric miracle of public transportation, is an act of faith in modern technology, if not an acceptance of magic.

The transition from chaotic modern life to the tiny tranquil chamber in 2 which you now find yourself has been provided by entering through a rustic gate into a miniature garden of almost other worldly charm. Each paving stone has been set in a carefully thought-out design. You feel that each pebble in the garden has been counted and has a special significance. The sand around the large rocks to one side of the path has been raked into a pattern of ridges that represent ocean waves. Each tree and shrub has been carefully pruned to perfection. Though foreign, you cannot help but admire the controlled beauty of the scene and forget the outside world. You are asked to sit on a small bench with a rustic shelter overhead in case of rain. The spot has been carefully chosen to give you a moment for quiet contemplation of this garden-of-an-other-world. When you continue on your way, you will find you are noticing more of nature than you thought possible in so small a garden. Even the sound of the pines is intriguing in this tight little area. Small is big, you think, as you look at the lovely details of landscape design reflected in a single pool. A rock tied up like a gift with a single rope is found sitting at forks in the path to show where you need not travel (Nishihara 99). Very near the tea house is a stone basin with water running through for the purification ritual of washing your hands and rinsing your mouth.

The entrance to the tea house is an opening three-feet tall. By sitting on 3 the threshold and removing your shoes, you can easily swing your feet inside and enter. The patina of the wooden floor is soft and glowing, mellow and smooth, never touched by anything but stockinged feet. The room is small, a bare ten feet square. You remember what you read about a tea room where the very holy Manjushiri received 84,000 disciples of Buddha and it was fine since space is of no consequence to the truly enlightened (Repplier 140). The empty room, a place "to create your own universe of calm and peace away from the world (Nishihara 96) is reminiscent of the isolation tanks used by many to find tranquility ("Nirvana"). You admire an ancient scroll in the *tokonoma* (sanctuary) that has been especially chosen for this occasion. A slight noise of the host outside at the purification basin is your cue to be seated.

Now, as the ceremony proceeds, you observe each detail of the meticulous 4 ritual, each precise movement of incredible economy and grace. Little tea cakes, subtle of taste, close and firm of texture, are served first. You are impressed with the gentle, quiet courtesy with which each guest is treated, the gracious appreciation of each response. You are impressed with the silence.

You realize that you have slowed down to a time so quiet and peaceful that time does not exist. The only sounds are the boiling of the water on the hearth. You are told later this is called the sound of the soughing of the pines and at times pieces of iron are placed in the iron kettle in order to enhance the sound (Okakura 35). The tea bowl is passed around. It is thin tea.

Imagine that now it is your turn to taste the tea. Your first sip reveals that ⁵ which you had already observed by its strange green color, its frothy texture— Lipton's, this is not! As your tastebuds evaluate the unique, rather bitter flavor, you remind yourself to appreciate its delicate quality as well and assume that this tea is something for which you must acquire a taste.

Contemplating the flavor and aroma of the tea, you become aware of the ⁶ small, simple tea bowl held on the palm of your left hand. Your right hand cradles the cup and enjoys the smooth, slightly pebbly surface of the cup. Its shape is so humble, almost prehistoric in essence. Its balance and weight seem just right; it is pleasant to the hand. You express your admiration of the tea bowl to your host and you are told, as you suspected, that it is a Raku tea bowl of a shape designed by Chojiro, a potter of the sixteenth century. There are seven of these traditional designs by Chojiro that are used by modern potters. They have whimsical, descriptive names such as: fast ship, priest's peach blossom, wet crow, and iris (Chikamatsu 149). The word *raku* means enjoyment, pleasure, ease, and Raku pottery is considered the perfect tea bowl for this ceremony. A continuous line of craftsmen in Kyoto have been producing these bowls since the technique was evolved by Chojiro.

Until now, the conversation has been formalized statements, which began ⁷ with the main guest saying, *Osakini,* meaning, "Excuse me for preceding you" (Ross 55). You are forgiven, being a foreigner, for breaking the pattern, but your questions are really not that out of line. As each guest finishes his tea, he admires the tea bowl, comments on the tea and its very special preparation, and compliments the host. This is an appropriate time for the host to comment on the history of the article mentioned and even to include an account of how it came to belong to his family. Often the tea bowl may be a valuable treasure dating back for several generations. There are times during an informal tea ceremony that you exchange pleasantries with your neighbor between formalized comments, but never are you "to mention work, politics, or topics pertaining to human glory or vanity. You discard rank or station at the door. Each present is free" (Nishihara 99). This is one of the reasons special training in the tea ceremony is sought, even today, by many Japanese as a necessary social grace. Important family occasions, such as contracting a marriage, are negotiated in this way. It helps the families of the young couple begin their relationship in a positive way (Kawashima). Training, besides enhancing your enjoyment of the ritual, teaches you grace and economy of motion. It is no mean trick to sit around on your knees for two or three hours at a time. Even modern day Japanese have a problem with this. You need to be in top physical condition to enjoy the Way of the Tea.

If you were taking part in a more formal situation and the tea ceremony 8 was to include a dinner, this would only be a beginning. The guests would retire to the garden after partaking of the thin whipped tea, *Usuda*, and would relax, smoke, or maybe converse a bit. The sound of the gong, struck gently but firmly, would signal the time to return. The purification ritual at the water basin would be repeated and shoes again removed before entering. Stopping at the *tokonoma*, you would admire and contemplate a special flower arrange-ment of remarkable simplicity in a quaint bamboo vase, replacing the scroll previously displayed (Fukukita 29).

Flower arranging is an art, like the making of the tea bowl, that has forms 9 particular to the tea ceremony. Bamboo vases of this type, a simple hollowed out section of bamboo, have been favored since the time of Rikyu, the Zen teacher who first formalized the tea ceremony as it is practiced today. Rikyu favored the artless and natural such as leaving droplets of water on the flower to enhance the freshness of the bloom—as if just plucked from the garden (Okakura 57). In keeping with his teachings, showy or loud flowers are avoided as are flowers with obvious meanings that would be inappropriate—such as white plum blossoms on a snowy day. These would be considered an excess, too much of a good thing, in the same way as would displaying a scroll at the end of autumn with the inscription, "Leaves fall down like raindrops" (Chick-amatsu 50). This aspect of the tea ceremony, like all its aspects, is studied in Japan as part of understanding culture. The Flower-Masters, the Tea-Masters, potters, and poets are proclaimed National Living Treasures and are supported and protected. Schools are formed under their leadership to insure their art forms for posterity.

After absorbing the significance of this flower, you again take your place at 10 the hearth. Your host serves the dinner himself. The tea this time is *Koicha*, thick tea, about the consistency and appearance of creamed spinach soup. (Both types of tea are made from powdered green tea.) The procedure this time is also a bit different. With the thin tea, the cup was passed back to the host each time and a new cup was prepared for the next guest in line. With *Kiocha*, the same tea bowl is passed around from person to person in a tedious ritual of turning the cup slightly each time and wiping the rim. The folding of the cloth, the *Fukasa*, in a careful ceremonial fashion is so difficult to learn that it is called "taming the *Fukasa*" (Ross 54).

It is curious to note that the sharing of the tea bowl with attendant for- 11
malized ritual is more than reminiscent of the Catholic ceremony of Holy
Communion. However, any modern Japanese person (and indeed all reference
material) will assure you that *Cha-No-Yu* is a completely secular ritual with no
religious overtones inherent or intended. The lessons to be learned from *Cha-
No-Yu* are harmony, respect, purity, and tranquility. This communion service
with a tea-bowl, while definitely not a Christian communion, is indeed a true
communion of these goals for those present. The ideals of life and art as taught
through the disciplines of Tao and Zen are found in the tea ceremony. Tao is
the Way, the essence of all life and divine order. One who knows the Way
goes with the flow, so to speak. Zen is a manner of being in contact with this
Way, as through meditation. It is said that "Taoism furnished the basis for
aesthetic ideals and Zennism made them practical" (Okakura 29). The original
tea ceremony is believed to have begun in southern China by a group of
Buddhist monks who incorporated many Tao doctrines with their Zen beliefs.
For them the tea ceremony was a profound holy sacrament in which they drank
tea from a single bowl (Okakura 15–16). It was this Zen ritual that was finally
developed in Japan by Rikyu, the celebrated Tea-Master of the sixteenth century, as a way to instill in his people an ethic of humility and tranquility and
respect for one another—so needed for survival for a group living so closely
on such a tiny island.

It was a Zen Buddhist teacher who is said to have discovered tea after an 12
act of self-mutilation. Daruma, while wandering through China, attempted to
meditate for nine years. After seven years, he fell asleep. Realizing what had
happened, in anger he ripped off his eyelids, so as not to sleep anymore, and
threw them on the ground. The next day he noticed they had been transformed
into a plant. Chewing the leaves, he found they kept him alert and he slept
no more while meditating. Zen Buddhists used tea often as an infusion to assist
in their meditation, and gradually the use of tea spread around the world
(Seeger 168–70).

Another island nation, Great Britain, also has its tea ceremony, consisting 13
of a litany of "One lump or two?" and "Do you care for cream?" accompanied
by a chorus of banal small talk and scones, rolls, and bread and butter. Tea
became so popular it was a taxable necessity, even in the New World in the
eighteenth century, where Americans invented their own famous tea ceremony, the Boston Tea Party, that rebellious act that heralded the beginning
of the American Revolution.

The refinement of the Japanese tea ceremony has given an ethic of dignity, 14
restraint, and refinement to peasant and wealthy alike. As the world grows

smaller, the population more condensed, and the pollution runs rampant, we all might learn ceremonies of self-restraint, courtesy, and tranquility—to preserve our sanity and to relate more fully to our neighbors. These ceremonies might well be an escape from our environment. The Japanese will do well to continue to treasure their tea ceremony and their master artisans. They will need them more than ever with the future they are creating of computers and transportation like the Maglev (magnetic train) now being perfected to travel at 300 mph. Who can relate to that speed? (Sato 95).

Imagine yourself in the year 2084, in a small cubicle with subdued lighting. 15 Six other people are in sitting position levitated on magnetic mats seven inches above the floor around a microwave oven. Tiny, cordless Walkmen in their ears transmit the sound of boiling water. The scroll in the sanctuary is a Dow Jones printout from a Wang computer. The garden you just passed through, though very tiny, boasted of lovely hydroponic tea gardens under glass belljars. The host passes you a humble Raku tea bowl and you turn to the guest next to you and politely ask, "*Osakini?*"

Works Consulted

Blaser, Werner. *Japanese Temples and Tea-Houses.* New York: F. W. Dodge, 1956.

Bruce, William. *Religions in Japan.* Rutland, VT: Charles E. Tuttle, 1962.

Chikamatsu, Shigenori. *Stories from a Tearoom Window.* Trans. Kozaburo Mori. Rutland, VT: Charles E. Tuttle, 1982.

Fukukita, Yasunosuke. *Tea Cult of Japan.* Tokyo: Board of Tourist Industry, 1934.

"History of Tea," *World Book Encyclopedia.* 1976 ed.

Hutchison, Mike. "Isolation Tanks: The State of the Art." *Esquire* Aug. 1983: 124.

"Japan." *Encyclopedia Americana.* 1979 ed.

"Japanese Tea Ceremony." *Encyclopedia Americana.* 1979 ed.

Kawashima, Dr. Yasuhide. Personal interview. 15 June 1984.

King, Francis. "Japan." *Man, Myth and Magic.* Ed. Richard Cavendish. 24 vols. New York: Marshall Cavendish, 1970. 11:1486–94.

Lilly, John C. *The Center of the Cyclone.* New York: Julian Press, 1972.

Mano, D. Keith. "Sensory Deprivation." *National Review* 10 Dec. 1982: 1564.

McFarland, H. Neill. *The Rush Hour of the Gods.* New York: Macmillan, 1967.

"Nirvana in a Dank, Dark Tank" *Time* 24 Mar. 1980: 105.

Nishihara, Kiyoyuki. *Japanese Houses, Patterns for Living.* Trans. Richard L. Gage. Tokyo: Japan Publications, 1968.

Okakura, Kakuzo. *The Book of Tea.* New York: Dover, 1964.

Repplier, Agnes. *To Think of Tea.* Boston: Houghton Mifflin, 1932.

Rhodes, Daniel. *Clay and Glazes for the Potter.* Rev. ed. Radnor, PA: Chilton, 1975.

Riegger, Hal. *Raku: Art and Technique.* New York: Van Nostrand Reinhold, 1970.

Rosenthal, Ernst. *Pottery and Ceramics.* London: Penguin Books, 1949.

Ross, Nancy. "Chanoyu: The Art of Tea." *Sphere* Feb. 1974: 54–56.

Sadler, A.L. *Cha-No-Yu: The Japanese Tea Ceremony.* Rutland, VT: Charles E. Tuttle, 1963.

Sato, Akihiro. "Beyond the Bullet." *Popular Mechanics* Apr. 1980: 95.

Seeger, Elizabeth. *The Pageant of Chinese History.* New York: Longmans, Green, 1944.
Terry, Charles S. *Contemporary Japanese Houses.* Tokyo: Kodansha, 1968.
Thompson, Bob. *Shiga the Potter.* New York: Van Nostrand Reinhold, 1983.
Woodhouse, Charles Platten. *The World's Master Potters.* London: Pitman Publishing, 1974.

QUESTIONS FOR READING AND REVISING

1. The overall purpose of Sandra Casillas's essay is to *explain* the process of an ancient Japanese ritual. Outline each step in the tea ceremony. Which does Casillas handle most effectively? Why? Reread paragraph 9 on flower arranging as an art. Explain why this paragraph does/does not digress from her purpose. How does it reinforce the overall *purpose* of the essay?

2. Casillas's essay opens with a direct address to the reader. Point to other instances later in the essay where she maintains this form of address. What is its effect? When and how does she vary this direct address? With what effect? What would be the advantages/disadvantages if Casillas had written the essay consistently in either the first or third person? Before responding, rewrite one of Casillas's paragraphs using the first or third person *point of view.*

3. In discussing how she sharpened the focus of her essay, Casillas notes: "Sometimes getting too close to a subject can narrow your vision and cause tunnel vision. The opposite proved true in the case of Cha-No-Yu. I developed 'Grand Central vision.'" Given the context of her essay, what do you suppose Casillas is suggesting here? Point to specific words and phrases that illustrate your reading of her *metaphor.*

4. Casillas explains that one of the aims of her research paper is to describe "an atmosphere of escape into an inner world"—and that "contrast at times was used to help the reader visualize" this idea. Reread Casillas's essay carefully and identify the nature—and the effect—of the *contrasts* she uses. At which points in her essay are these contrasts especially effective? Why?

5. One of the strengths of this essay is the writer's effective use of *description.* Choose one paragraph in the essay that highlights Casillas's successful use of description and list each example of *concrete,* sensory *detail.* In the second paragraph Casillas notes, "you will find you are noticing more of nature than you thought possible in so small a garden." Where—and how—does she use description to help her readers fulfill the promise created in this sentence?

6. Imagine that you are the writer of this essay and that one of the peer editors in your class recommends that you eliminate the section on the history of the tea ceremony as distracting and irrelevant. On what grounds would you defend the inclusion of this particular section of the essay? What does it contribute to the overall *purpose* of the essay?

7. Look carefully again at the opening paragraph. What are its strengths? How, for example, does Casillas capture her reader's attention? What is the function of the second sentence in this paragraph? Of the third sentence? Explain what each contributes to the paragraph and to the essay as a whole.

8. Reread the opening sentence of paragraph 11. In the previous draft it read: "The sharing of the tea bowl and attendant ritual accomplished by formalized strict ceremony is more than reminiscent of the Catholic ceremony of Holy Communion." What specific changes do you notice in these two drafts? Which version do you prefer? Why? Characterize the verb forms in the same paragraph and identify their strengths and weaknesses. Rewrite the paragraph, making the verbs as effective as possible.

9. Review the final paragraph of Casillas's essay. In what specific ways does the paragraph return to—and recapitulate—the *themes* and syntax of earlier parts of the essay? How—in its *tone* and *diction*—does the paragraph head off in a new direction? Explain why the essay would/would not be stronger if the final paragraph were omitted.

SUGGESTIONS FOR WRITING

1. Near the end of her essay, Sandra Casillas observes that "as the world grows smaller, the population more condensed, and the pollution runs rampant, we all might learn ceremonies of self-restraint, courtesy, and tranquility—to preserve our sanity and to relate more fully to our neighbors." Examine carefully some ceremony that emphasizes one or more of these qualities—"self-restraint, courtesy, and tranquility." Write an essay in which you *explain* the process of the ceremony and the specific ways in which it emphasizes these qualities.

2. What ethnic rituals did you and your family participate in on a regular basis during your childhood? Write an expository essay in which you re-create with detail the specific steps in the *process* of that ceremony and the occasion on which it was performed. Explain why the ritual was important to you as a child and how you view it today. What did you learn—either positively or negatively—about your own ethnic heritage and about yourself from having participated in it?

3. Write an *expository* essay in which you explain in detail the precise nature of some social ritual you engage in each year—preparing Thanksgiving dinner, making New Year's Eve resolutions, sending Valentine's Day cards, and the like. How does this social ritual serve as an expression of a particular cultural sensibility? What does it reveal about the culture in which it functions?

DAVID A. CHRISTMAN

New York University
New York, New York
Tony Giffone, instructor

"Don't limit yourself to only the easiest, most obvious topics," David A. Christman urges other students of writing. *"Try to be original in your approach to assignments. Not only will it impress teachers, but, more importantly, it will make writing a much more vital and rewarding experience."* Christman's essay, *"Nietzsche and the Art of Tattooing,"* demonstrates the soundness of his advice. Having read Nietzsche's definitions of *"Dionysian"* and *"Apollonian"* in A World of Ideas, *edited by Lee A. Jacobus, Christman was asked to "choose some form of cultural manifestation" and write an essay analyzing "its Dionysian and Apollonian aspects."* Christman quickly settled on the art of tattooing. *"How exactly I arrived at tattooing for this, I'm not sure. My awareness of tattooing had been somewhat heightened by a trip to the Museum of Tattooing in San Francisco and also by a chance meeting at a party with Spider Webb, one of the better known American tattoo artists."* Christman's interest in tattooing converged with his reading of Nietzsche to produce an essay that compares and contrasts, as Christman notes, *"tattooing as both an ancient and modern art and as a personal and cultural phenomenon."*

In addition to tattooing, Christman cultivates several other, and equally *"visible,"* artistic interests. A movie buff, he is also an accomplished singer and songwriter. Born in New York City and educated at Northfield Mount Herman School in Massachusetts, Christman has played with a rock band, Debroy Rebop, and has cut a record:

> My musical abilities influenced me in a number of ways. For one, the success my band enjoyed gave me a sense of confidence in my own ability to succeed. Secondly, it was really songwriting that led me to writing: first to poetry, then to fiction, and on to nonfiction. My writing is an extension of my total self, including all my experiences and abilities.

Christman is majoring in English at New York University, principally because, as he explains, *"NYU does not offer a degree program in writing."* And while his career goals remain somewhat uncertain at this point, he quickly adds: *"I am sure they will include writing in some capacity."*

Nietzsche and the Art of Tattooing

It is a sorry development of modern civilization that the art of tattooing 1
has come to be associated with only the lowest members of the social strata.
Despite a lengthy tradition as a symbol of nobility and achievement, it is
regarded by many as a sign of either low self-esteem or of low moral character.
Yet to deny this unique form of self-expression the term "art" would be to do
it an injustice. One glance at the powerful imagery of the traditional Japanese
full-body tattoo makes this clear. It is a discipline that requires not only unerring dexterity, but an eye for both the beautiful and the grotesque.

I have long been interested in tattooing, having been tattooed twice, once 2
in 1977 and then again in 1981. But it was only this past summer (1984) that
I began to learn about some of tattooing's history. The catalyst for this, and
the reason for my intensified interest in the field, was a visit to Lyle Tuttle's
Museum of Tattooing in San Francisco. The museum is a fascinating compen-
dium of tattooing history, both in folklore and in fact.

Where the art of tattooing differs from more traditional artistic efforts is 3
that it requires not one, but two willing participants. That is, both the artist
and his "canvas" must agree on the work to be performed. Without question
though, the "tattooee" is the more active participant in the primary decision
of whether to be tattooed at all.

Although by no means an acid test for tattooing's worthiness as art, it is 4
interesting to note that many aspects of it can be related to Nietzsche's concepts of Apollonianism and Dionysianism, both in terms of tattooing's historical development and, more importantly, the individual's decision to be tattooed.

Although Nietzsche states that Dionysos represents the "non-visual art of 5
music," (212) Dionysianism can be extended, as we will see, to encompass
the visual arts as well, especially one that requires an actively collaborative
effort, as tattooing does.

Tattooing is an ancient art. The mummy of the Egyptian princess Hathor, 6
believed to have died around 2000 B.C., was found to be tattooed. In its present
day form, tattooing is usually done with an electric tattooing needle which
cuts through the skin, injecting pigments below the epidermis. However, different cultures have developed other methods for tattooing. The tribal Moko
tattooing practiced by the Maori tribes of New Zealand used chisel-like pieces
of ivory which were hammered into the skin, the cleaved flesh then rubbed
with soot or dyes. In Japan, long bamboo sticks with anywhere from one to
thirty needles protruding from them are slipped effortlessly in and out of the
flesh by hand.

The reasons for tattooing vary widely. In most of its early manifestations, 7 tattooing was primarily for chiefs and warriors of tribal cultures, including the Incan and Mayan Indians. In Borneo, only the upper-class women of the Kenyah and Kayan tribes were allowed to be tattooed. This habit permeated Western civilization as well, when, around the turn of the twentieth century, much of Europe's nobility and aristocracy was tattooed, including King George V and Kaiser Wilhelm II.

Nietzsche states that Apollo is the "apotheosis of the principium indivi- 8 duationis" (223) or as text commentator Lee Jacobus elucidates, "the god in whom the concept of the individual is best expressed" (223). Is not the tattooing of nobility an embodiment of this Appolonian trait—that those people, who either by birthright or bravery are chosen to rule, should wish to reinforce their superior "self" by indelibly marking their bodies as a reminder of "the beguiling image of their own existence" (220)? That these members of nobility would hope for a long and prosperous reign would be no surprise. And a tattoo against which to continually mark the successful passing of time would seem to be representative of what Nietzsche calls "man's . . . desire to remain on earth" (221), another Apollonian trait, as well perhaps as a veiled attempt to defy mortality. Princess Hathor's tattoos outlived her by four thousand years.

Of course the majority of tattooed people are not royalty. So for what 9 reasons might an "average" person get tattooed? This too varies with different cultures. In Japan, the tattooed person (usually a man) enters a type of particularly close-knit club, called a *nakama,* once tattooed. So, as Donald Richie points out in *The Japanese Tattoo,* it is a rite of communal membership. In the Maori culture it was a rite of passage required by all members of the tribe. A man or woman without Moko was held in low esteen by the rest of the community. In the West, many people are tattooed simply because their friends or associates are tattooed. This differs somewhat from Japan in that in the United States, oftentimes the person who is tattooed is not trying to associate himself with tattooed people in general but rather is tattooed to identify himself as a member of some other group, for example: motorcyclist, musician, or sailor. It is interesting to note that these people are often tattooed in a group and that it is not uncommon for them to be drunk. Dionysos is the god of wine and drunkenness.

In all these instances the underlying motive for being tattooed is conformity, 10 either to friends or tradition, or as an initiation to a fraternal setting. This notion of conformity is one of the fundamental concepts of Nietzsche's Dionysianism. "Man now expresses himself . . . as a member of the community," says Nietzsche (216). In Japan, where a strong sense of unity exists between tattooed people, this is especially true. In the annual Buddhist festivals, thousands of fully tattooed men come together, usually wearing nothing more than their fundoshi (loincloths), dancing and swaying to traditional music. And so as Nietzsche states, "the abrogation of the principium individuationis become(s) an esthetic event" (218).

Tattooing is not an aesthetic event only in Japan, though the festivals have 11 an obvious association with the Dionysian celebrations that Nietzsche talks about, but the conformity, the Dionysianism of tattooing, can be seen in other ways too. For instance, it is often noted that most tattoos are based on a rather limited number of motifs. Flowers, animals, and religious imagery are among the most common. This is another tenet of Dionysianism. Nietzsche says that the Dionysiac dithyramb incites "the desire to express the very essence of nature symbolically" (219). What more obvious way to do this than to wear these symbols as adornments of the body? And it is interesting to note that these symbols are rarely the accurate Homeric representations of nature inherent in Apollonianism but rather are caricatures or approximations of nature.

The decision to be tattooed need not always be of a Dionysian nature, 12 though obviously many aspects of the art are. To observe or enjoy the art from afar is a much different thing than to wear it. To consider or conceptualize about being tattooed is an Apollonian exercise, one of fantasy and illusion. But to be tattooed steps over what Nietsche calls the "thin line which the dream image may not cross" (214) and becomes the Dionysian. That is, the conceptualizer, considering the motifs or their placement on his body, by choosing them and being marked with them, is "no longer the artist, he has himself become a work of art" (216).

Although Eastern and tribal tattooing is largely an exercise in conformity, 13 as is a lot of tattooing in the West, many people are tattooed for precisely the opposite reason. These are people who see tattooing as an individualistic and nonconformist exercise. Sometimes they feel they are outcast from society and their tattoos reflect this: "Hell Raiser," "Born To Lose," etc. are common manifestations of these feelings. Other times people see tattooing as an aesthetically pleasing thing to do. They like tattoos and they like they way they themselves look, or would look, with tattoos.

This relates closely to some of Nietzsche's Apollonian concepts. He men- 14 tions an "Apollonian need for beauty" (221), which is really what this aspect of tattooing is all about; the beautification of the body. And an "unabashed delight in colors" (217) is an inherent part of this, for these are people who are being tattooed not simply to carry a mask but to carry a symbol that embodies their ideas of fashion and beauty. They work closely with the tattooist in conceptualizing this custom piece of work, usually ignoring standard tattoo motifs and concentrating instead on brightly colored, highly detailed works of their own design.

Over the past ten years tattooing has been enjoying a renaissance of sorts, 15 especially in the United States. Custom tattooing has generated some beautiful pieces of work which in turn have been accorded a lot of attention and respect by the media. In part this is due to the fact that many of today's top tattooists were trained in "traditional" art schools like Pratt and the Rhode Island School of Design. It is also due to the rising sentiment that tattooing is not just for bikers and sailors but is a respectable and legitimate art form for all types of people.

Though it is unlikely that Nietzsche's work was even remotely connected 16 to tattooing, it is startling that so many passages from his work seem perfectly suited to this discussion. For instance, in his discussion of the Dionysiac celebration, which correlates closely to the Buddhist festivals of Japan, Nietzsche describes nonparticipating onlookers as "cadaverous and ghostly" (215) when compared with "the intense throng of Dionysiac revelers" (215), perhaps in much the same way that nontattooed spectators might seem to appear at a Buddhist festival. And later Nietzsche describes what could be a scene from a Westernized version of the Japanese iconographic tattoo, "the savage beasts of mountain and desert approach . . . the chariot of Dionysos is bedecked with flowers and garlands; panthers and tigers stride beneath his yoke" (215).

More importantly, would Nietzsche have even acknowledged the Apollon- 17 ian and Dionysian elements of tattooing? Or would he have been one of those people who, in his own words, "either from lack of experience or out of sheer stupidity, turn away from such phenomena, and strong in their own sanity, label them either mockingly or pityingly" (215)? For this we have no answer except to presume that a man as attuned to the social and historical implications of art would have a difficult time ignoring those so obviously inherent in the curious art of tattooing.

Works Consulted

King, Michael, and Marti Friedlander. *Moko: Maori Tattooing in the Twentieth Century.* Wellington, NZ: Alister Taylor, 1972.
Nietzsche, Friedrich. "Apollonianism and Dionysianism." *A World of Ideas: Essential Readings for College Writers.* Ed. Lee A. Jacobus. New York: Bedford Books of St. Martin's Press, 1983.
Richie, Donald, and Ian Buruma. *The Japanese Tattoo.* New York: John Weatherhill, 1980.
Scutt, Ronald, and Christopher Gutch. *Art, Sex and Symbol.* Cranbury, NJ: A. S. Barnes, 1974.

QUESTIONS FOR READING AND REVISING

1. David Christman talks about the Dionysian and Apollonian aspects of tattooing. How are *Dionysian* and *Apollonian* defined in this essay? How does a standard college dictionary definition in each instance differ from those pro-

vided in the essay? What points, if any, would you like to add to the definition supplied by Christman?

2. Outline Christman's analysis of the art of tattooing. Which aspects of tattooing does he consider Dionysian? Which does he think are Apollonian? What evidence does he use to verify each of these points? Do you agree or disagree with his conclusions? Why?

3. One of Christman's goals of this essay, as he tells us, was to contrast "tattooing as both an ancient and modern art and as a personal and cultural phenomenon." Where does he introduce the ancient/modern contrast? Outline the comparison as Christman develops it in the essay. Which version of tattooing does Christman prefer? Why?

4. In presenting this writing exercise, Christman's instructor noted, "Remember, your audience for the piece is not necessarily someone who is totally familiar with the work or event you are analyzing. Some information about the work is necessary." What kind of information does Christman work into the essay? How well does Christman satisfy the requirements of the exercise in this respect? What additional information, if any, would you recommend that he include? Rewrite one paragraph including whatever additional information you think necessary.

5. David Christman's writing course included a good deal of peer editing. (For an explanation of peer editing procedures, see Part V.) Here is Christman's explanation of what happened:

> The original rough draft was read to students in my writing class, where, for the most part, it was not very well received. Most people felt that the historical information drew the reader's attention away from the topic. Others simply could not see any viable connection or validity for the essay's central thesis. A second draft, which was handed in for the grade (an A), made some slight changes. I tried to simplify those passages containing historical data so as to make them more palatable to the reader. At this point, I was already satisfied with the essay.

Reread Christman's essay and focus on his use of historical information. Where and with what effect is historical information used in the essay? What additional changes, if any, would you suggest Christman make in the way he handles it?

6. The peer editors who responded to Christman's rough draft "could not see any viable connection or validity for the essay's central thesis." What is the thesis of this essay? Where is it stated? What specific changes, if any, would you recommend that Christman make to clarify and strengthen his thesis statement?

7. Christman's first draft of this essay did not include what is currently the last

sentence in the opening paragraph. In his second draft, Christman added the following sentence: "It is a discipline which by its permanent nature requires unerring dexterity coupled with an eye for beauty and mystery." Christman later changed the sentence to read: "It is a discipline that requires not only unerring dexterity, but an eye for both the beautiful and the grotesque." List the specific changes in these versions of the same sentence and assess the advantages of each.

8. Reread paragraph 8 of Christman's essay, paying special attention to the sentence: "That these members of nobility would hope for a long and prosperous reign would be no surprise." In Christman's first draft, this sentence is preceded by one that he removed from later drafts, which reads: "If we define existence as the ability to chart progress or changes against some standard then what better standard than a permanent mark." Based on your reading of both these paragraphs and the entire essay, how could you defend or challenge Christman's decision to eliminate this sentence?

9 Review the verbs in this essay. What do you notice about them? What consistency do you recognize among them? How might they be improved? What other consistencies can you identify in Christman's *diction* and *tone?* What are the strengths of these two aspects of his essay? What suggestions, if any, would you offer to reinforce their effectiveness?

10. Analyze Christman's use of personal experience to illustrate points in his essay. What reasons would you offer to support—or challenge—Christman's decision not to invoke personal experience at the end of his essay?

SUGGESTIONS FOR WRITING

1. One of the strengths of David Christman's essay is the *contrast* he draws between ancient and modern tattooing. Consider another activity, one that can trace its origins to ancient times (for example, playing a musical instrument or engaging in sports competition) and write an expository essay contrasting the ancient and modern ways of doing it. Include in your essay a clear sense of the procedures involved in each method and show the superiority of one.

2. Choose some activity in contemporary American experience and write an essay in which you analyze its Dionysian and Apollonian elements. You may choose to work with either a standard dictionary definition of these terms or with Nietzsche's, but be sure to support each of your points with detailed references to the activity you have chosen.

3. Christman's essay raises issues about what constitutes art and whether tattooing can claim for itself the respect due to art. Consider the case of advertising. D. H. Lawrence once observed that "some of the cunningest American literature is to be found in advertisements of soap suds." So too, Aldous Huxley regarded

advertisements as "the most exciting, the most arduous literary form of all, the most difficult to master. . . ." But Thomas Wolfe regarded advertisements as nothing more than "fat, juicy, sugar-coated lies for our great Boob public to swallow." Write an *argumentative* essay in which you argue for—or against— the position that the language of advertising should be regarded as art and ought to command respect comparable to that afforded literature.

RAVENEL BOYKIN CURRY

Yale University
New Haven, Connecticut
Fred Strebeigh, instructor

"Having a good idea is a lot easier than establishing it in an essay. The hardest part is pulling your emotions and impressions together well enough to get the first sentence on the page. From there, you may change your direction many times, but at least you have something in front of you to see, at the very least something to cross out and replace. The most horrible experience has got to be sitting at a desk with forty-three ideas swimming and colliding in your mind while the piece of paper sits there empty, that white sheet just staring back at you," notes Ravenel Boykin Curry.

Born in Charlottesville, Virginia, Curry lived in North Carolina for several years before moving to Summit, New Jersey, where he graduated from Summit High School in 1984. The first teenager to appear on the Common Cause National Governing Board ballot, Curry has also been active in the campaigns of many Democratic candidates in national and local elections. He has traveled a great deal with his family (*"to Europe, Asia, and the Soviet Union"*) and has also worked at a newspaper, a gas station, on a peach farm, and at Bloomingdale's department store. He currently operates a vegetable stand with a friend. About his interests at Yale, Curry notes *"I will probably double major in history and economics. . . . I hope to be an investor, but I will maintain a constant involvement in politics. If my writing skills develop, I would love to keep writing."*

Asked to write a nonfiction portrayal of a place, Curry chose to focus on "A Small Town" in rural South Carolina where his parents grew up. And from his earliest draft, as he explains, the audience and purpose he had in mind for his essay were intertwined: *"not the people of Chesterfield (they would probably find it boring) but people who had grown up in some Eastern suburb and had no understanding about the lives of people living just twelve hours (if you hurry) away. I didn't want them to come away with some saccharine picture of a bucolic paradise where Farmer Brown rides around on his tractor while his wife bakes pies and the kids happily milk the cows. On the other hand, some northerners have mistaken the lack of worldly sophistication among southerners in small towns for shallow naiveté. The popular southern myth that results is a condescending view of the happy, ignorant farmer, oblivious to the important problems of the 'real world.' I tried to break the simplistic stereotype by showing people who are complex, who live lives with important cares and tragedies and successes. I wanted the reader to laugh without condescending. To admire without romanticizing. To understand better that no people can be so simply understood."*

A Small Town

Junior Boy is thirty-nine and he has made it. But his is no Horatio Alger 1
story. He was born December 26 in the four-room shack that would be shared
for the next eighteen years with two parents and four sisters. His best friend
was Jay Calvin Rivers until they realized Jay was rich and white and Junior
Boy was poor and black and that all of that meant much more than they had
thought. While Jay went off to Pawley's Island, Junior Boy suffered through
the scorching summers of the South. One especially hot August afternoon
when he was thirteen, Junior Boy made a pledge in the style of Scarlet O'Hara.
"I promised me that no matter what, someday I would have an air-conditioning
box and a telephone to talk to people."

Today, the front of Junior Boy's house, at least the part that isn't a porch 2
with a weight bench, is decked with imitation-brick-pattern linoleum that
suggests a cross between a kitchen floor and a factory wall. Junior Boy is
standing in front of this three bedroom structure next to an old rusty water
pump in the front yard while he discusses his cars. One of them is a dusty
black '79 Buick rested in front of the porch. He is still making payments on
it, but he bought the new, rarely used Thunderbird (bright white) parked just
outside the kitchen because, "If I can't make a payment and they come and
take one of them away, then, tell me, what would I have to ride around in?"

Both cars still have Jimmy Carter bumper stickers on them. "He was such 3
a good man. He was just so *good.*"

Junior Boy's wife Nora comes to the door and calls us inside, interrupting 4
the political discussion. The main room has a black vinyl sofa with white fluff
bursting from a long rip in one arm. A purple shag carpet covers the floor,
and an iron wood stove, taunting us in this hundred-degree heat, stands waiting
for the winter next to the wall on our right.

The door to the bedroom is open and Junior Boy sees me looking inside. 5
There are no windows, so it is very dark, but everything is neat. "Nora keeps
this place clean," he says, and in a time when many sneer at the labors of
"just a housewife," Nora restrains a breaking smile and pokes at Junior Boy
for making it so hard. "By the time I get one room straight, Junior Boy and
the kids've all gone and destroyed another one. If they didn't go to sleep, I'd
never be caught up."

One thing Junior Boy likes is his comfort, so when the telephone man came 6
to install his first phone, Junior Boy had to think about where he wanted it.
He finally walked over to his bed, lay down, reached his right hand up, and
asked for the phone to be installed where his hand was. And there it is.

Junior Boy and his house and his two cars are all in Chesterfield, a tiny,   7
semidusty farm town in the state of South Carolina. The land is sandy, but
the workers who live on the unyielding ground wrench what they can from it.
The buildings on the four blocks that make up downtown Chesterfield are too
new to be quaint and too old to be fresh. Architecture is mid-1950s-Cement
Block, and the flashiest it ever gets is when they put up the plastic Christmas
trees on the street lights in late October.

On one of these blocks, twenty-five years ago, Lee Davis and his wife Dell   8
used to run the Chesterfield Theater where they showed Westerns and serials,
fourteen cents for kids, twenty-five cents for adults. Blacks in the balcony only
please. Dell would take the money as kids filed in and Lee would yell at them
and kick out anyone who talked during the movie.

Now the building is the ultra-up-to-date, air-conditioned Da-Le Discount   9
Drugs and Cosmetics, the biggest store in town. Dell is very pale, pretty fat,
and a little crippled now. She sits behind the register and Mr. Davis shoos out
any kids who are reading the comic books without buying them. There is no
soda fountain in the back yet, but just inside the door is a machine that spits
out cold sandwiches for seventy-five cents and lukewarm hotdogs for a dollar.
Junior Boy is one of their best customers and today he's buying plastic flowers
for Lizzie's funeral.

Lizzie would be seventy-one today if she still lived on the farm in her little   10
home. A fence surrounds the yard to hold all the chickens who scratch around .
outside—and occasionally inside—the house, and a screen porch with too
many holes to discourage any kind of insect dominates the facade. She had
lots of chickens and thirteen children. When my mom was four, Lizzie had
her last child, and a few weeks later my mom came by to see him. Lizzie said
she had run out of names, and asked the girl what name *she* liked. Thinking
of a song she had just learned, my mom said that Billy Boy sounded best to
her. Billy Boy is thirty-eight now and he's in Chesterfield for the funeral with
his son, Billy Boy, Jr.

Lizzie locked herself up in her house and shut her windows for three days   11
and suffocated in the heat.

Chesterfield is not a thriving center of commerce and it rarely makes even   12
the South Carolina papers. The nearest major city is Atlanta, two hours away
in a plane, five by pickup (though most people in Chesterfield have never
gone beyond Cheraw, the nearest town with a movie screen). People driving
through on the way to Myrtle Beach to the east or the Blue Ridge Mountains
in the west probably think it seems like a pretty boring place, if they notice
it at all. But before they glibly conclude that this small town builds small

minds, they should talk to Junior Boy, who wonders what kind of minds come from kids who have to play in crowded city streets instead of ponds and fields and giant silos. What comes from men and women who type the same boring letters and listen to the same boring customers for eight hours every single day. Who build the same houses, read the same magazines, and discuss the same topics over cocktails with the same identical neighbors every single night.

Junior boy's family has tomatoes to pick and one of the mother pigs won't 13 feed her six piglets and a teacher says one of the kids might get a college scholarship if they push him a little harder and one of the little tractors has to be fixed and it's looking like fall might be too wet for the pecans and now Elizabeth is saying she wants to get married before she's finished with high school.

There is a lot of humor and a lot of drama in a tiny town in the sandhills 14 of South Carolina. People say New York has a rhythm, and you can feel the pulsing, blasting, pounding movement as soon as you enter. Well, Chesterfield has a rhythm too, and if you listen, you can hear.

QUESTIONS FOR READING AND REVISING

1. Ravenel Boykin Curry explains that "inspiring me to write this essay was a combination of desires: to solidify some impressions of my mother's farm, to show friends that small towns aren't mindless, and to get a paper finished for my English class before the 5:00 deadline. It started out as a character portrayal—a local color type essay of something I knew well. But as I explained each character and the way they interrelated, I began to discover other themes which in turn helped me to organize the mini-vignettes in a specific way." As you reread Curry's essay, what do you regard to be the central theme? Where is that theme stated? What other themes emerge as you read, and how does each help organize the essay?

2. What do you think Curry means when he talks about "mini-vignettes"? Examine each carefully. What does each contribute to the overall success of the essay? How does Curry manage to unify them into a portrait of "A Small Town?" How does his essay demonstrate that his portrayals of the town and its inhabitants are "interrelated"? What function does Curry's portrait of Junior Boy serve in the essay? What purpose is served by Curry's returning to Junior Boy in paragraphs 13 and 14?

3. Consider the organization of Curry's essay. Does he follow a pattern of moving from the general to the particular? from the particular to the general? some

other pattern of organization? Explain. Several of Curry's paragraphs (see, for example, paragraph three) are one sentence long. Identify these paragraphs and comment on their effectiveness. Why—or why isn't—the length of these paragraphs appropriate to the effect Curry tries to create?

4. When asked how he would like readers of his essay to respond to what he had written, Curry noted:

> I would ask the reader to let his mind wander a little. There are nineteen different scenes (changes in time or place) in a very small space, and each of them can do something different. Do you think Junior Boy's ambitions were inspiring or pathetic? Is Nora a woman oppressed by sexism, or does she have a responsibility to maintain a traditional role to keep the family going? Were Lee and Dell evil when they were racist? Could you say the same thing if you were the one being put in the balcony? Let ideas bubble around and try to make some concrete conclusions.

Sketch out the "nineteen different scenes (changes in time or place)" Curry refers to here. How does each illustrate his overriding point? Answer the questions Curry poses to his readers, supporting your responses with a detailed study of specific sentences.

5. *Compare and contrast* the rhythm of the sentences used to describe this small town and its inhabitants with the cadences of the sentences characterizing urban life. Show how Curry uses the verbal rhythms of his sentence structure to evoke and then reject the city dwellers who might drive through Chesterfield "on the way to Myrtle Beach to the east or the Blue Ridge Mountains in the west." How does the rhythm of his sentences underscore the controlling idea of his essay?

6. One of the most successful aspects of Curry's essay is his ability to use specific details to evoke particular responses in his readers. Consider, for example, the "imitation-brick-pattern linoleum that suggests a cross between a kitchen floor and a factory wall . . ." in paragraph 2. Point to other equally evocative specific details that make his description of Chesterfield and its inhabitants so vivid and memorable. Consider the effectiveness of Curry's verb choices. What makes them effective? Do the same for his adjectives.

7. How does Curry prevent his depiction of Chesterfield and its inhabitants from being "condescending"? Recall Curry's depiction of the lives of urban dwellers and of "kids who have to play in crowded city streets instead of ponds and fields and giant silos." In this section of his essay, how does Curry succeed in avoiding lapsing into the kind of condescending tone that he criticizes city residents for adopting in their view of the rural South? Support your response with a detailed examination of specific sentences.

8. Curry wrote several drafts of this essay. Here is an earlier version of his ending:

> Chesterfield is not the epicenter of any megalopolis, and the nearest major city is Atlanta, two hours away in a plane, five by pick-up (though most people in Chesterfield have never gone beyond Cheraw, the nearest town with a movie screen). But there is a lot of humor in a tiny Southern town that you might think looks like Sinclair Lewis's *Main Street.* You might also think this town builds small minds, but Junior Boy probably wonders what kind of minds come from kids who have to play in some crowded city streets instead of ponds and fields and giant silos. What comes from men and women who type the same boring letters, and listen to the same boring customers for eight hours every single day, who build the same boring houses, read the same boring magazines and discuss the same boring topics over cocktails with the same boring neighbors every single night.
>
> They have tomatoes to pick, and one of the mother pigs won't feed her six piglets and one of the teachers says Alexander might get a college scholarship if they push him a little harder and one of the tractors had to be fixed and the fall might be too wet for pecans. And Elizabeth wants to get married before she's finished with school.
>
> They have things to do in Chesterfield.

What specific differences do you notice between this draft and Curry's final version? Comment on the effectiveness of each change. If Curry had yet another opportunity to revise these paragraphs, what specific changes would you suggest he make? Why?

9. Compare Curry's depiction of the rural South with Ann Louise Field's of the rural West (see "The Sound of Angels") and Julie Reardon's of the rural Midwest (see "The Unmarked Road"). What specific strengths do these essays seem to have in common? What distinguishes each—thematically and stylistically— from the others? How, for example, does each writer handle his or her character's recognition of poverty? Which essay do you find most successful and memorable? Why?

SUGGESTIONS FOR WRITING

1. One of Ravenel Boykin Curry's *purposes* in writing this essay is to use his *description* of Chesterfield and its inhabitants to break simplistic stereotypes.

Write an essay using Curry's essay as a model to "break" some stereotype about the people around you that you find condescending and offensive. As you develop your essay, try to include a detailed description of the nature of the stereotype and the specific ways in which the people you have chosen to write about defeat it with the complex richness of their lives.

2. The success of Curry's essay depends on his sense, which is not made explicit, of what the word *home* means. How would you define this term? What would you regard as the essential and distinguishing feature of a home. Bret Harte, the late-nineteenth century American writer of local color stories, once had this to say about a related subject: "Nobody shoulders a rifle in defense of a boarding house." Write an essay in which you use your own experience to illustrate Harte's point. As you proceed, try to work in your own definition of a *home* and contrast it to your definition of a *boarding house.*

3. Observe a place in your hometown or neighborhood—a street corner, a park, a bar, a convenience store—where people tend to congregate. What is there about this place that encourages people to gather there? Write an essay *describing* it. As you write, try to make each of the specific points of your description support some overriding and more general idea about that place.

BEVERLY P. DIPO

Utah State University
Logan, Utah
Joyce Kinkead, instructor

Beverly Dipo can recall with remarkable detail and winsome irony the first day she worked on cursive writing:

> I was in the third grade. My wooden desk was, even then, ancient and bore the history of previous academic scholars and shirkers. The glossy surface had acquired its glow more from the sweaty palms of test takers and greasy elbows of second-base sliders than from wood polish. The dark embedded pencil scratches attested to the fact that Shirley had once sat here; Patrick was a lousy speller; J. K. did unspeakable things to S. D.; and much to my relief, someone had kindly left me the seven times table.

With her feet wrapped around what she describes as the desk's "de-painted metal legs," Beverly Dipo spent hours practicing large, wire-thin, continuous circles, impelled by her teacher's well-intentioned cautioning: " 'Be sure to use your whole arm to glide evenly over the paper; do not use just your wrist,' she warned, 'or you will have a sloppy slinky'." Born in Hayward, California and a 1984 graduate of Sky View High School in Smithfield, Utah, Beverly Dipo writes these days on an old, water-stained bathroom door that has "no pencil marks or times tables to entertain or inform me." It is cluttered, she reports, "with books, cans of pencils and colored pens, paint brushes, a vase of ugly brown and yellow flowers, a recipe file, a clock, a basket of scissors, tape, paper clips, and other assorted junk, all of which I pay little attention to until they come up missing." Such painstakingly careful observations reflect the strength of her work both as a licensed practical nurse and as a writer at Utah State University, where she is pursuing a degree as a registered nurse.

Asked to write a narrative that focuses on an experience in which she gained some insight, Beverly Dipo responded with what is at once an incisive description and a moving account of the personal and clinical routines that attend the quietly dignified death of an elderly victim of cancer. "Death happens in my profession," Beverly Dipo observes, "it is not uncommon. I think it is difficult for nurses to remember sometimes that these experiences are special and that we need to cherish them more than we do."

For a more detailed discussion of Dipo's essay, see Part IV.

No Rainbows, No Roses

I have never seen Mrs. Trane before, but I know by the report I received 1
from the previous shift that tonight she will die. Making my rounds, I go from
room to room, checking other patients first and saving Mrs. Trane for last,
not to avoid her, but because she will require the most time to care for.
Everyone else seems to be all right for the time being; they have had their
medications, backrubs and are easily settled for the night.

At the door to 309, I pause, adjusting my eyes to the darkness. The only 2
light in the room is coming from an infusion pump, which is flashing its red
beacon as if in warning, and the dim hall light that barely confirms the room's
furnishings and the shapeless form on the bed. As I stand there, the smell hits
my nostrils, and I close my eyes as I remember the stench of rot and decay
from past experience. In my mouth I taste the bitter bile churning in the pit
of my stomach. I swallow uneasily and cross the room in the dark, reaching
for the light switch above the sink, and as it silently illuminates the scene, I
return to the bed to observe the patient with a detached, medical routineness.

Mrs. Trane lies motionless: the head seems unusually large on a skeleton 3
frame, and except for a few fine wisps of grey hair around the ears, is bald
from the chemotherapy that had offered brief hope; the skin is dark yellow
and sags loosely around exaggerated long bones that not even a gown and
bedding can disguise; the right arm lies straight out at the side, taped cruelly
to a board to secure the IV fluid its access; the left arm is across the sunken
chest, which rises and falls in the uneven waves of Cheyne-Stokes respirations;
a catheter hanging on the side of the bed is draining thick brown urine from
the bladder, the source of the deathly smell.

I reach for the long, thin fingers that are lying on the chest. They are ice 4
cold, and I quickly move to the wrist and feel for the weak, thready pulse.
Mrs. Trane's eyes flutter open as her head turns toward me slightly. As she
tries to form a word on her dry, parched lips, I bend close to her and scarcely
hear as she whispers, "water." Taking a glass of water from the bedside table,
I put my finger over the end of the straw and allow a few droplets of the cool
moisture to slide into her mouth. She makes no attempt to swallow; there is
just not enough strength. "More," the raspy voice says, and we repeat the
procedure. This time she does manage to swallow and weakly says, "thank
you." I touch her gently in response. She is too weak for conversation, so
without asking, I go about providing for her needs, explaining to her in hushed
tones each move I make. Picking her up in my arms like a child, I turn her
on her side. She is so very small and light. Carefully, I rub lotion into the
yellow skin, which rolls freely over the bones, feeling perfectly the outline of

each vertebrae in the back and the round smoothness of the ileac crest. Placing a pillow between her legs, I notice that these too are ice cold, and not until I run my hand up over her knees do I feel any of the life-giving warmth of blood coursing through fragile veins. I find myself in awe of the life force which continues despite such a state of decomposition.

When I am finished, I pull a chair up beside the bed to face her and taking   5 her free hand between mine, again notice the long, thin fingers. Graceful. There is no jewelry; it would have fallen off long ago. I wonder briefly if she has any family, and then I see that there are neither bouquets of flowers, nor pretty plants on the shelves, no brightly crayon-colored posters of rainbows, nor boastful self-portraits from grandchildren on the walls. There is no hint in the room anywhere, that this is a person who is loved. As though she has been reading my mind, Mrs. Trane answers my thoughts and quietly tells me, "I sent . . . my family . . . home . . . tonight . . . didn't want . . . . them . . . to see. . . ." She cannot go on, but knowingly, I have understood what it is she has done. I lower my eyes, not knowing what to say, so I say nothing. Again she seems to sense my unease, "you . . . stay. . . ." Time seems to have come to a standstill. In the total silence, I noticeably feel my own heartbeat quicken and hear my breathing as it begins to match hers, stride for uneven stride. Our eyes meet and somehow, together, we become aware that this is a special moment between us, a moment when two human beings are so close we feel as if our souls touch. Her long fingers curl easily around my hand and I nod my head slowly, smiling. Wordlessly, through yellowed eyes, I receive my thank you and her eyes slowly close.

Some unknown amount of time passes before her eyes open again, only this   6 time there is no response in them, just a blank stare. Without warning, her breathing stops, and within a few moments, the faint pulse is also gone. One single tear flows from her left eye, across the cheekbone and down onto the pillow. I begin to cry quietly. There is a tug of emotion within me for this stranger who so quickly came into and went from my life. Her suffering is done, yet so is the life. Slowly, still holding her hand, I become aware that I do not mind this emotional tug of war, that in fact, it was a privilege she has allowed me, and I would do it again, gladly. Mrs. Thane spared her family an episode that perhaps they were not equipped to handle and instead, shared it with me, knowing somehow that I would handle it and indeed, needed it to grow, both privately and professionally. She had not wanted to have her family see her die, yet she did not want to die alone. No one should die alone, and I am glad I was there for her.

Two days later, I read Mrs. Trane's obituary in the paper. She had been a   7 widow for five years, was the mother of seven, grandmother of eighteen, an

active member of her church, a leader of volunteer organizations in her community, college-educated in music, a concert pianist and a piano teacher for
over thirty years.

Yes, they were long and graceful fingers.   8

QUESTIONS FOR READING AND REVISING

1. Beverly Dipo reports that in writing this essay, "I just sat down and typed up
   a rough draft, made some minor wording changes, typed a second draft and
   turned in that." This second draft was "critiqued" by the peer editors in her
   class: "I was worried about its needing some sort of introduction, like 'I'm a
   nurse and I work the night shift,' or something like that. I couldn't come up
   with anything that didn't sound like Jack Webb, so I left it out." Reread the
   opening paragraph of the essay carefully. When—and how—do we know in
   unequivocal terms that the speaker is a nurse? Comment on the alternative she
   chooses to sounding like Jack Webb of *Dragnet* fame ("I'm a nurse and I work
   the night shift"). What choices does Dipo make to increase the effectiveness
   of her opening paragraph?

2. "No Rainbows, No Roses" begins with the first person pronoun. When—and
   how—does that *point of view* shift in the first paragraph? Reread each of the
   subsequent paragraphs. Is the emphasis in each personal? impersonal? some
   blend of the two? Support your response with specific examples. Dipo notes
   that one of her readers suggested she revise paragraph 3 by adding personal
   pronouns. As a writer, however, she exercised her authority over her own work
   and resisted, explaining: "As a nurse I frequently observe *things* before I ever
   speak to a patient or get to know them as human beings. Right or wrong, it's
   the way we are trained." What do you think are the "things" Dipo has in mind
   here? What reasons would you offer to support—or to challenge—her decision
   that her essay ought "to remain impersonal at that point"?

3. Dipo describes outlining in her head as the most effective method of getting
   started: "I sit down at the typewriter and start typing my thoughts on paper.
   I'm a pretty organized person, so my first thoughts seem to organize themselves;
   sentences fall into paragraphs for me." Which paragraphs in this essay strike
   you as well organized? Why? Less well organized? Why? What would you suggest
   that she do to strengthen those you judged less effective?

4. How does Dipo's careful attention to detail in the first two paragraphs reinforce
   the atmosphere she seeks to create in her *narrative*? At the end of the second
   paragraph, she announces that she will "observe the patient with a detached,
   medical routineness." Point to specific examples of her "detached" *point of view*.
   What is the effect in each instance?

5. In the final sentence of paragraph 4, Dipo shifts the focus of her essay from the woman to her own reaction to rubbing lotion on this woman's frail body: "I find myself in awe of the life force which continues despite such a state of decomposition." Comment on the effectiveness of this sentence. How does it either add to or distract from the overall point of this paragraph and of the essay as a whole.

6. One of the appreciable strengths of Dipo's essay is its use of evocative *diction*. Identify at least three instances where the writer chooses an especially effective word or phrase to underscore the effect she aims to create. Explain why each is so effective.

7. Identify the contending forces in the "emotional tug of war" the writer describes in paragraph 6. Why does Dipo note that she "needed" this experience "to grow, both privately and professionally"? Our familiarity with superficially similar movie scenes and soap operas threatens to reduce the painful intensity and emotional integrity of this woman's dignified death. At what moments does the essay come closest to melodrama, and how does Dipo prevent her essay from slipping into it?

8. Dipo explains that she knew her essay was finished "when I remembered [Mrs. Trane's] obituary and recalled thinking then how appropriate that she had played the piano; her hands were the hands of a piano player." When—and how—does she introduce the detail of Mrs. Trane's hands in the essay? with what effect? Explain whether or not you think she should have given more attention to Mrs. Trane's hands throughout her essay. Explain whether you think her title ought to reflect this controlling image.

SUGGESTIONS FOR WRITING

1. Beverly Dipo's account of Mrs. Trane's death exemplifies the medical profession at its best: well-trained people who can display both rigorous objectivity and generous compassion. Consider other careers that require such seemingly paradoxical qualities as objectivity and compassion. Choose one and write an expository essay using concrete examples to explain why such qualities are necessary in that particular line of work, and how one can create a proper balance between them. You may find it useful to explore not only the external but also the psychological aspects of the job.

2. Part of the success of Dipo's essay depends on the element of surprise—both at how Mrs. Trane responds to her own impending death and the reaction this elicits from the professional who cares for her. Write a *narrative* essay recounting in detail how someone you know behaved in ways that defeated the expectations of those around him or her.

3. As a nurse, Dipo notes that she sees "human suffering, weaknesses, triumphs,

and tragedies on a daily basis." Write an essay describing the ways in which someone you know has had to deal with a serious illness, a family member's death, or an awareness of his or her own impending death. What changes has this knowledge brought about in both the person most directly affected and in those around him or her? What insight have you gleaned from this experience? Recalling what Beverly Dipo has accomplished in her essay, include as many evocative details as possible.

ANN LOUISE FIELD

University of Iowa
Iowa City, Iowa
Nancy Jones, instructor

"When I was about three, I packed all of my clothes in a paper sack and informed my parents that I was running away to an alligator farm and could they please tell me where to find one. Ever since then I've been making up all kinds of stories in my head. Many of the stories were based on things that my brother Brett and I had done or wanted to do. Those stories never left my head or ended up on paper until after Brett died in 1977. It was in remembering all that Brett and I had shared that I realized the stories in my head about our youth were interesting even without the parts I made up. I felt as if I had something to say that others might be interested in reading."

Asked to write an essay on some aspect of her hometown or childhood, Field reports that she knew she would write about Brett and herself. "Brett was my childhood. We spent every minute together. He taught me how to climb trees, how to peel an orange in one continuous piece, how to spit, how to throw dirt clods, and how to shoot rubberbands across the room."

Ann Louise Field was born in Ukiah, California, spent the first sixteen years of her life in Redlands, and now calls Bellingham, Washington her hometown. She is studying nursing at the University of Iowa and plans to become a nurse-midwife. Field has worked as a manager for McDonald's, a seamstress in a drapery business, and as a maid in a motel in order to help pay for her college education.

The Sound of Angels

When I was nine I lived in Southern California. Redlands was a small town, as California towns go, and not an exciting place to live. My life in Redlands was as predictable as the fact that we always had tacos for dinner on Saturday, chili on Sunday, and tamale pie on Monday. Every day was a carbon copy of all the previous days. Nothing ever seemed to change. But in spite of this sameness I wasn't unhappy. My brother Brett and the orange groves at the top of our street were both a big part of the sameness and the source of happiness.

Brett had an afternoon paper route in the summer of 1969. The route and the money he earned were something that he and I shared. Every afternoon at two he'd deliver *The Daily Facts* to 107 paying customers and I would ride with him on the last half of the route. I didn't really help deliver any of the papers on the paper route. I was still too new at riding a bike to hold the bike steady with one hand and heave a rolled-up paper onto the porch of a house with the other, but I don't think Brett wanted the help—he wanted the company. Brett never let me go with him to the newspaper office to pick up the papers because some of the other boys would say nasty things to me. He didn't want me to hear the things these boys would say, and he was concerned that the long uphill ride home would be too much for me, so Brett did the first half of the route alone. And I would wait, in the front yard if it wasn't too hot, for Brett to come riding around the corner on his new orange ten-speed.

Brett's bike was the most beautiful bike I had ever seen. It was much too 3
expensive for Mom and Dad to buy so Brett had helped pay for it by selling greeting cards. It was nicer than my bike. My bike was blue and it didn't have any speeds, just stop and go. It was the first bike I had ever owned and I had finally gotten it for Christmas when I was eight after having wished for a bike since I was six. The bike was used and had been painted over and the purple basket on the handlebars was faded, but I didn't care. Brett liked my bike almost as much as I liked his. He never treated my bike as if it were any less valuable than the one he had. He took good care of his own bike, washing and waxing it on the weekends, and he helped me do the same to mine.

Brett bought things for the two of us with the money he made from his 4
paper route. He bought things that we never seemed to get enough of at home; a dozen doughnuts that we didn't have to share with anyone, plastic vampire teeth and fake blood at Halloween, toys from the five- and ten-cent machines just inside the door of the store, and a note pad of pink paper with matching envelopes that he had seen me admiring. When I saw these things in the store I never asked Brett to buy them for me. He just did. Whenever he chose something for himself he chose one for me too. But the doughnuts were the best of all. I can remember getting up early on cool Saturday mornings in the fall or spring and riding with Brett two miles to the Winchell's doughnut house. We would spend thirty minutes just looking in the window at all the different shapes and sizes and kinds of doughnuts. Then, when we had decided which twelve we wanted, Brett would buy them. We would bicycle two blocks over to the high school and eat them there on the lawn in front of one of the buildings. I would eat four and he would eat the rest. They were just for us. If we decided that we didn't like one of the doughnuts that we chose we just left it there for the birds. They were our doughnuts and we could do with them whatever we pleased.

Brett and I also spent a lot of time in the orange groves at the top of our 5
street. Running through these groves were sankies, open drainage ditches that caught the runoff from the groves. When the groves ended the sankies went underground and continued, for miles sometimes, until they reached the next

grove. The sankies were lined on the sides and bottom with rock and cement. Sometimes they had a few inches of water in the bottom and sometimes they were dry. We weren't supposed to play in the orange groves but we did anyway. The orange groves supplied us with rotten oranges that we liked to throw at passing cars. It was into the sankies that we dove for cover when an angry motorist stopped to locate the source of the rotten orange, but not even the most ardent pursuer could catch us once we went underground.

The orange groves were always a pleasant place, winter or summer. In   6
summer we had the shade of the trees and the dust rising from the dry dirt to fill our nostrils and stick to our sweaty skin. We could sit in the sankies with our feet in the water and feel the coolness of the rock wall against our backs as we ate sweet, stolen oranges. In the winter the wind whispered through the leaves bringing with it the pungent odor of oil from the smudge pots burning nearby to keep the trees and their fruit warm. There was a crispness to the cold that could carry the smell of a chimney fire a mile away and bring the stars in the sky within reach.

It was in this cold that Brett and I would steal Christmas lights off of houses.   7
We would go out after dark for a walk to look at the houses decorated for the holiday and we would steal the lights. Never very many though. Only one or two from each house and never more than a handful each trip. It was a challenge for Brett to sneak up to the front of a well-lit house and take the bulbs without getting caught. I was too chicken to leave the safety of the shadows so I was always the lookout. Once we had the bulbs we would return to the orange grove at the top of our street and break them. As they struck the ground there was a hollow POP! followed by the tinkling of colored glass. It was such a pretty sound. Brett said it was the sound of angels. That sound put me at peace and made me happy in a way I had never known. By the smile in his eyes and the way he held my hand as we walked home, I knew it made Brett feel the same way.

We loved our orange groves, our bicycles, the dozens of doughnuts we   8
shared, and the carefree life they gave us. It was the only side of life we knew. I figured that one morning I would wake up and find that I had grown up during the night, but I didn't think that it would change things. Nothing could possibly matter more than paper routes, climbing trees, eating oranges, and crawling around on our bellies in the sankies under the streets.

It was sometime during the latter half of 1969 that I realized we were poor.   9
It was 6:15 one fall evening and the sun would be setting in about an hour. I was standing on a footstool in front of the kitchen sink doing the dinner dishes and I could see Dad and Brett out of the window. Dad was talking and Brett was shaking his head and saying "no" with an intensity I had never seen before.

I thought Brett might be crying. After a few moments they both came in the house and my dad handed Brett two empty grocery sacks.

"Go with your brother, please," was all my dad said. 10

Something in his voice frightened me so I went without asking why. Word- 11 lessly, Brett and I left the house and climbed over the back fence. We crossed the dirt field of the junior high school and passed the buildings until we came to an orange grove on the other side of the school. We climbed this fence too and went back into the trees. I wondered what we were doing there because we never played in this orange grove. Brett opened his sack and began picking oranges and dropping them into it.

"What are you doing?" I screeched. "Dad will kill us if we steal oranges!" 12

Brett looked at me with tears running down his cheeks. "Dad said to take 13 them."

"Why? Dad would never let us steal." 14

"Just shut up and do it!" Brett yelled at me. 15

I stomped my foot. "Not until you tell me why." 16

"Because we're poor!" he shouted. "If we don't steal these oranges we won't 17 have anything for lunch tomorrow." With that he threw the two oranges in his hands at me. They hit me on the head and the arm and I gave a startled cry. Brett wiped his eyes and nose with the sleeve of his shirt and said more quietly, "Just pick the damn oranges."

As our house came into view on the walk home I saw it as if for the first 18 time. The paint was peeling and the yard was overgrown with bushes and ivy. The run-down condition embarrassed me. From inside the house I could hear two people yelling at each other. I saw my whole life in that frame; my hand-me-down clothes that had been Brett's before mine and somebody else's before his, and my used and shabby bike with rust and dents under the cheap blue paint. I remembered a time when I was six and we had "camped out" in front of the fireplace for a week. It had been fun sleeping on the floor, pretending we were pioneers and cooking over the fire. I also remember trying to turn the bathroom light on and my mother's strange look when I asked her why it wouldn't work. I knew now why it wouldn't—the electricity had been shut off. That same year a box of food and some presents appeared on the front porch Christmas morning. My mother cried when I scolded her for not leaving the door unlocked for Santa.

We were poor. I had three oranges as my lunch the next day to remind me. 19

The days went on and so did Brett and I. We continued to play the way 20 we always had, but I think it was easier for me than for him. Sometimes I felt that he was simply going through the motions of play for my sake. At times he would grow tired of our games and want to just sit quietly in one of the trees. I sensed that things weren't the same because the more we did the things we once loved to do, the more withdrawn Brett became. I didn't like seeing him this way so I was glad when we drifted away from the orange grove. I knew that something had taken the fun out of our orange grove, but I wasn't sure what it was or what it meant.

I'm not sure exactly when it happened, but my brother and I drifted apart. 21 We occasionally went for doughnuts on Saturdays and stole Christmas lights each year, but we weren't as close as we had been. And then puberty came along and gave Brett longer legs and me wider hips and I could no longer wear his old clothes and that somehow set us farther apart. The unpleasant memories associated with that day in the orange grove faded and were almost forgotten until I was fourteen and in the ninth grade. I came home one afternoon to find that my mother had tried to kill herself. I was angry at her for doing it. Not so much because she had almost died but because she had brought reality back into my life once and for all. I didn't want to see what reality had to show me. I didn't want to see the shabbiness of the blue bike or the hand-me-down clothes that filled my closet. I didn't want to grow up if it was going to be so complicated that it made some people want to die so bad that they could cut their own wrists. I wanted camping in front of the fireplace to be just camping, not keeping warm because the electricity had been shut off. I wanted to eat an orange without remembering that week when they were all we had to eat. I wanted to share a dozen doughnuts with Brett on a Saturday morning and disappear laughingly into the sankies where reality, like the angry motorist, wouldn't follow. I wanted to close my eyes and hear the hollow POP! and the tinkling of colored glass. I wanted the sound of angels to mask the fact that life wasn't always as easy as orange groves and sankies and a dozen doughnuts.

But the sound of angels couldn't help me anymore. As my mother lay in 22 the hospital and my life went on I said goodbye to the magic, the predictability and the simplicity of a life filled with paper routes, colored Christmas lights, and a dozen doughnuts to share with Brett. These things were gone, and with their going came the knowledge that they could never return.

QUESTIONS FOR READING AND REVISING

1. Ann Louise Field tells us that when she was nine her life was as predictable as the fact that "we always had tacos for dinner on Saturday, chili on Sunday, and tamale pie on Monday. Every day was a carbon copy of all the previous days. Nothing ever seemed to change. But in spite of this sameness I wasn't

unhappy." What are the happy memories that Field remembers about this time in her life? How did she think of these events as a child? How does she think of these events now?

2. What was the major event that caused Field to see her life differently? How did this event change her life?

3. What do we learn about Brett in paragraph 2? How is this impression of him maintained throughout the rest of the essay? How did he react to the stealing of oranges?

4. How many different stories does Field tell us about her childhood? Why does Field choose to tell a number of stories and present a number of memories to her readers instead of just one? How does this strategy serve her *purpose*?

5. Field writes with tremendous care and detail in describing her relationship with Brett: "Brett bought things for the two of us with the money he made from his paper route. He bought things that we never seemed to get enough of at home; a dozen doughnuts that we didn't have to share with anyone, plastic vampire teeth and fake blood at Halloween, toys from the five- and ten-cent machines just inside the door of the store, and a note pad of pink paper with matching envelopes that he had seen me admiring." Identify details that you found vivid and evocative in the essay. How does Field use these details to create the picture we have of her younger self and her relationship with Brett?

6. Field presents a number of recurring *images*—the orange groves, the paper route, eating doughnuts, the sound of angels. What strategies does Field use to keep these images with her readers throughout the essay? How do these images change in meaning for a reader as Field's understanding changes? Why are these images repeated in the last two paragraphs?

7. Field does not indulge in self-pity or sentimentality in writing about her childhood. Describe her *tone*. How does she achieve this tone? What effect does her tone have on your reading of this essay?

8. In Field's first draft, her essay began this way:

> I grew up in southern California. When I tell this to people their next comment is always along the lines of how nice it must have been to live near a beach. Redlands, California, was far enough away from any beach for adults to say "inconvenient" or "too much driving involved" whenever we asked to go. Sun and sand and surfers were not a part of my life. Nor was much of anything else in the summer of 1969.

Why do you think Field deleted this paragraph as her introduction? Why is her revised introduction a more effective one?

9. Field reports: "The biggest problem I had in writing this essay was cutting

unnecessary parts out of the essay. To me everything belonged in the essay and I wanted to find some way to work it all in. Normally I can revise essays with no problems, but revising this paper was like cutting off bits of my arms and legs."

Field wrote and revised her conclusion many times before she was satisfied with it. Here are two earlier versions:

> From draft 1:
> I was growing up, but not overnight. It had been happening little by little for I didn't know how long. The sameness of my life that I hoped to leave behind was partly responsible for my maturity. And as my mother lay in the hospital and my life went on I was comforted in knowing that the sameness would never leave me completely.

> From draft 2:
> Five years before I had tried to leave the orange groves because everything Brett and I did there seemed to remind us that we were poor. The sameness and the peace that I knew there had been everything to me once. That sameness that I had hoped to forget was now what I wanted most. As my mother lay in the hospital and my life went on I was comforted in knowing that the sameness would never leave me completely.

Compare these two conclusions with the conclusion in the final draft. What are the differences between these rough draft conclusions and the final draft conclusion? How does the revised conclusion more successfully tie together the various ideas in the essay?

SUGGESTIONS FOR WRITING

1. Write an essay about some aspect of life in the town where you grew up. You may decide to tell a number of stories as Field has done, or you may decide to write at length about a single memory. Whatever strategy you choose, try to give your readers a sense of your younger self and of the particular town, city, or rural area you called home.

2. Field successfully writes about the vivid edges of experience that children know and the small pleasures that give childhood its meaning. Select an experience— or a series of experiences—from your childhood and reflect on its meaning.

3. Field's essay illustrates the idea that life looks a lot different to a child than to an adult. Do you think that Field's parents should have told her that she was poor and explained to her what that meant? Should children be protected and sheltered from the realities of life? Write an essay to illustrate your point of view on this issue.

ERIK FIELD

Iowa State University
Ames, Iowa
Patricia L. Cagwin, instructor

"There really is nothing easy about writing an essay," Erik Field observes, even when the subject is as familiar as popular music. In describing his own writing process, Field notes: "I usually freewrite the body of the paper first. I let the body dictate what I am going to write in the introduction and the conclusion rather than beginning with the introduction and running into a dead end." Most often he prepares for writing by "lying in bed with all the lights turned off. It would be one o'clock in the morning. I do my best thinking under these conditions. I am more creative when I am on the verge of sleep. . . . Nearly all of the essays that I write are conceived immediately before, or during, sleep, and then written the following morning." Field spends much of the rest of his day avoiding writing, if he can. "I avoid writing letters by making phone calls. I avoid writing essays by enrolling in a minimal number of composition courses. I write well when I have to. I prefer not to have to." With a major in statistics, Erik Field plans to pursue a career as an actuary.

Born in Poughkeepsie, New York, Field graduated from Wheaton Central High School in Wheaton, Illinois. Both his parents are Iowa State graduates and, as Field notes, have "had the greatest influence on me. . . . They have always emphasized hard work, honesty, and the importance of a good education." Field's extracurricular interests and hobbies include intramural sports, the statistics clubs, baseball cards, music, and reading (Joseph Heller, John Irving, Dave Marsh, Ken Follett, and Stephen King).

Given a wide range of subjects and structures to work with, one of which was an essay classifying the people and experiences that comprise much of ordinary life in contemporary America, Field chose "to categorize the phonograph records that I own." Setting out "to make my readers realize that there are such things as good and bad rock music," he creates a strikingly fresh analogy for grading the latest cuts from the world of rock and roll.

Rock Around the World

On my tenth birthday I received a transistor radio as a gift from my parents. 1
Ever since that day I have been truly enamored with rock and roll music. I started out as just a casual listener, but I soon became a rabid rock fanatic. However, as my knowledge and my appreciation of good rock increased, so did my contempt for truly awful rock. If that makes me a snob then so be it, but I honestly believe that there are such things as good rock and bad rock. I

believe that there is such a thing as good taste and that good taste comes with education. Just as surely as a wine connoisseur would refuse to drink muscatel, and as a gourmet chef would refuse to serve Spam, I refuse to listen to low-grade rock.

However, in recent years the radio airwaves have been flooded with Spam.   2
Personally, I am more partial to filet mignon than to Spam so I have been relegated to listening to my own records rather than to the radio. Through the years I have accumulated several hundred records which encompass a vast musical spectrum. Certainly any attempt to classify every one of these albums would prove to be futile, so I have decided to concentrate on what I feel are the six most musically prolific geographical regions, all of which have a definitive rock and roll style. The music from these areas has had a profound influence on me, and I feel that by sharing my musical views with you I am revealing my character as well as my musical tastes, or if you prefer, my B-side as well as my A-side.

The first, and undoubtedly the largest, geographical segment of my record   3
collection falls under the heading "British Invasion" music. The British Invasion era began in early 1964 with the arrival of the Beatles and is considered to have ended by about 1966. During this relatively short period of time, literally dozens of British musical acts found success in the United States. These artists, most notably the Beatles, the Rolling Stones, the Kinks, the Yardbirds, the Who, and the Animals, are well represented in my album library, and deservedly so. The hallmarks of British Invasion rocks are jangly guitars, remarkably tight vocal harmonies, and a general air of adolescent innocence (the Rolling Stones notwithstanding). This was arguably the golden age of rock and roll.

Throughout the 1960s, Detroit was virtually a musical assembly line, pro-   4
ducing one hit record after another. Motown, a Detroit-based record company, continually produced records that were equally irresistible to black and white listeners alike. The Motown recipe consisted of relatively simple lyrics and intense rhythm and blues backing music seasoned with slick pop craftsmanship. The end result was a mile-long list of gold records which included some of the finest dance and party music ever preserved on wax. Detroit musicians employed by Motown include such superstars as Marvin Gaye, Diana Ross and the Supremes, the Four Tops, Smokey Robinson and the Miracles, the Temptations, and Stevie Wonder. Any comprehensive record collection should be well marbled with records by these legends. Mine is.

As segregated as the southern United States were in the late 1950s and   5
early 1960s, it seems only fitting that Memphis, the music capital of the South, should have two entirely different sounds; one white and one black. The white

Memphis sound was a combination of southern rhythm and blues and country made famous in the late 1950s by rock's founding fathers (e.g., Elvis Presley, Roy Orbison, Jerry Lee Lewis). The black Memphis sound, on the other hand, was beautifully soulful. Otis Redding, Sam and Dave, Booker T and the MGs, Aretha Franklin, and Wilson Pickett are but a few of the performers who helped to define the Memphis soul sound of the sixties. No music collection should be lean on Memphis representation. A sizable portion of my collection is devoted to these gems.

Prior to the mid-1960s the city of Los Angeles had no definitive rock and 6 roll sound. However, as the folk rock style became increasingly popular throughout the United States, the city of Los Angeles seemed to adopt this mode. Artists such as the Byrds, the Mamas and the Papas, Buffalo Springfield, and in later years Randy Newman and Jackson Browne combined traditional folk and country with mainstream rock to create a sound that revolutionized folk rock and also contributed heavily to the cultural revolution that was the 1960s. My album collection is peppered with choice cuts by these rock heroes.

As was the case with Los Angeles, San Francisco also became a major rock 7 and roll center in the mid-1960s. However, while the Los Angeles sound was purely folk rock, the San Francisco sound consisted more of psychedelic experimentalism and eclecticism. San Francisco rock heavily influenced (and was influenced by) the hippie subculture of the middle and late 1960s. While this music all seems quite dated today, the raw talent of such San Franciscans as Janis Joplin, the Jefferson Airplane, Steve Miller, the Grateful Dead, the Quicksilver Messenger Service, and Country Joe and the Fish is undeniable. My rock library is thick with psychedelic flavor.

As the 1960s came to a close, a new era in rock music dawned. Psychedelia 8 and hippiedom had become passé. A new generation of rock and rollers had emerged, and they were hungry for a new sound. This new sound was punk, and the pioneers of this style came from New York City. The music that came out of New York in the late 1960s and the early 1970s has proven to be remarkably influential. The sound and stance of artists such as the Velvet Underground, the Ramones, the New York Dolls, and Patti Smith were of seminal importance to modern day and new wave and punk acts. New York rock of this era was dominated by hard-driving guitar work and vocals that were abrasive and often offensive. This music is about as stripped down as rock can get. That may not sound like much of a recommendation; however, what these precursors of punk lacked in talent, they more than made up for in spirit and energy. These rough-edged rockers also displayed a keen sense of social and political awareness that in the "Me Decade" of the 1970s was quite refreshing. These prime New York cuts are some of my most prized possessions.

These are the artists and the sounds that I feel are the filet mignon of rock   9
and roll. They are the living embodiment of all that rock and roll should be.
This is music performed with enthusiasm, sincerity, and intelligence, but without pretension, pomposity, or patronization. So whenever someone asks me,
"How do you like your rock and roll," I reply with a smile, "Well done."

QUESTIONS FOR READING AND REVISING

1. According to what principle does Erik Field classify his record collection? What
   other methods can you think of to classify records? Where and how does Field
   introduce his analogy into the essay? With what effect? How consistently does
   he maintain analogy throughout the essay? In which sections might it be
   strengthened?

2. In commenting on his method of writing this essay, Field explains:

   > First, I made a list of all the geographical areas that have
   > a definitive rock and roll style. Then I wrote a mini-essay
   > about each region, explaining each style and citing ex-
   > amples of musicians who helped to popularize these styles.
   > Next, I decided on the order in which I was going to present
   > these mini-essays. After that, I wrote an introduction and
   > a conclusion. These were the most difficult parts. Then I
   > converted these mini-essays into one long, continuous es-
   > say by adding transitional devices.

   How many geographical mini-essays can you identify in Field's essay? Comment
   on the structure and coherence within each of these mini-essays. How well is
   each organized? What "transitional devices" does Field rely on to link them.

3. How would you characterize Field's *tone* in the opening paragraph? How consistently is this tone maintained throughout the essay? Point to specific words
   and phrases to support your response. Which region of the country—which
   form of rock and roll—does the language of Field's essay suggest he favors?
   Why?

4. Reread carefully the introduction to this essay. Field notes that "writing the
   introduction to an essay is the most difficult aspect of writing for me. I usually
   save that for last." Point to specific words and phrases that suggest Field wrote
   his opening paragraph last.

5. What does Field assume about his audience's knowledge of his subject? Where
   and how does he provide his readers with information that they might not be
   likely to know, but that they need to understand the points he makes? Char-

acterize Field's attitude toward his audience. Does he, for example, regard himself as superior to his readers? inferior? at the same level? Point to specific words and phrases to support your responses.

6. In what ways does the *purpose* of this essay extend beyond *classifying* and *illustrating* the essential features of rock and roll music in this country? When and how do larger points about the general appeal of rock and roll music emerge? about the audience for such music? What are the cultural implications of Field's essay?

7. In the first draft of his essay, Field cast the fourth sentence of paragraph 4 as follows: "The end result was to create records that are among the best dance and party music ever made." What revisions does Field make in the final draft of this sentence? Which version do you prefer? Why?

8. Consider the revisions Field makes at the end of paragraph 8. His first draft reads:

> This music is about as stripped down as rock can get. However, what these prime precursors lacked in talent, they more than made up for in spirit and energy. What makes this music so great is that it is so completely unpretentious and it is never boring. These prime New York cuts are some of my most prized possessions.

Identify the changes in the second version. Which do you think is more effective? Why? Point to specific words and phrases in your response.

9. Now that you have worked through this essay carefully, consider its title. Compare "Rock Around the World" to Field's original title: 'A Geographical Look at the Album Library of Erik Field." What problems—both syntactically and thematically—does Field eliminate in changing his title. Can you think of any ways to improve the title further?

SUGGESTIONS FOR WRITING

1. Despite the success of his essay, Erik Field noted "I never was able to complete the essay to my satisfaction. I would have liked to have included a segment about the Philadelphia soul sounds of the early 1970s and a segment about the Greenwich Village folk sounds of the early and middle 1960s." Choose one of these possibilities—or another "area" of popular music—and write an expository essay in which you follow the method of Field's *analogy* between meat and music.

2. How would you *classify* the books you have read or the films you have seen recently? Are they mostly horror stories? spy thrillers? tales of extraterrestrials?

What essential characteristics does each have, and which of these character-istics does each share? Write an essay in which you *define* the essential ingre-dients of one such genre and explain why the books or films in that genre appeal to a particular segment of the American public.

3. The legendary American songwriter Irving Berlin is reported to have advised the equally popular American songwriter Cole Porter: "Listen, kid, take my advice, never hate a song that has sold a half-million copies." While the statistical standard for success in the music world may have increased since the time when Berlin made his remark, the principle implicit in his advice remains the same: success in the music business can be measured in sales. Consider the pros and cons of Berlin's statement. To what extent do sales determine success? Quality? Does commercial success preclude quality? Prepare an essay in which you argue in support of—or against—this proposition.

PETREA GALLOWAY

Yuba College
Marysville, California
Timothy May, Instructor

"I have been writing something as long as I can remember," Petrea Galloway reports, *"but I kept my writing private until I was in college."* Galloway is a published writer who has had her short stories, poems, and essays printed in her school's literary magazine, the Yuba Review. *About her writing process Galloway reports:* "I begin with ragged notes and ideas and compose in my head. If I get too much ahead of myself, I hurry to write my ideas down anywhere since I don't want to forget my ideas before I sit down at a typewriter. I have written on the bottom of Kleenex boxes, in matchbooks, on theater tickets, even on my shoes."

Besides writing, Galloway is an accomplished artist who has received prizes for her paintings. She has worked at various jobs—driving a delivery truck, operating a drill press, and waitressing. As she tells us: "I was married, had three sons, and divorced all by the time I was twenty-three years old. This provided me with the unique opportunity to experience the working world in a way most young mothers would never know. I re-married after three years, my sons young enough to adjust well to their stepfather, and I inherited two more sons. My husband and I and our five sons enjoy cross-country skiing, motorcycle riding, and walking in the hills of northern California."

Asked to write a process essay, Galloway reports that she immediately knew what to write about: "The subject for my essay was a natural choice because at the time of the events described within the essay, I remember saying 'Some day I'm going to write a book or an essay, and this is going in it.' I often say this to myself when I see, hear, or experience anything out of the ordinary."

How to Fill a Car or
Freezer with Meat

I live with my husband and sons in an old two-story house in the California foothills. The old place is isolated. It is situated like an island in a sea of forest and pasture. The pasture part leads me to my story about filling the freezer. Many hundreds of acres around us are leased to a cattle owner. He lives about fifty miles away so as a neighborly gesture, my family looks out for the cows. Now, this is not a job. We just do simple things. We may chase a cow back through the fence, then call the owner so he can come and repair the barbed wire. Cows are something I have always considered good freezer filler; and we are surrounded by them!

One lazy summer morning, I was enjoying sleeping in. My boys were watch- 2
ing television. A man came to the door. He had just seen a cow out in the
road. He said it had been hit by a pickup truck but he didn't think it was
dead.

He left and I could hear one of the boys saying, "Go tell Mom!"   3

When we reached the cow, whoever had hit it was gone. There it was,   4
making frightful sounds, lying on the side of the road. A man was trying in
vain to put it out of its misery. He had a tiny little twenty-five caliber pistol
and was popping the semiconscious beast between the eyes. It kept trying to
get up—up to its knees, then down—down to the blacktop it would roll. Even
I knew that between the eyes is a thick skull bone. I suggested that he shoot
it in the ear. That location had been most effective for the butcher who once
came and killed our pigs. But the anxious man said. "I . . . I don't have any
more time. I'm late for a meeting in town. I have to go!" And go he did—
leaving me in the road with a half-dead cow and two small boys looking on.

"Well," I thought, "I see I shall have to do something myself." I ran back 5
to the house to get my deer rifle. It was a forty-four magnum. I had shot it a
time or two and knew what I was doing . . . well, almost.

Thankfully, I found a highway worker talking to my watchful boys when I 6
returned with my big gun. The dear man took my gun and skillfully, quickly,
laid the cow to rest. Then he was gone. This time I was left standing in the
road with a dead cow and two small boys looking on.

The next step in this whole mess was obvious: phone Fred, the owner of 7
the cows. I did just that and he was not there. His wife said she would send
him up as soon as he came in.

We decided we'd better wait for Fred out by the poor dead cow. We waited 8
and waited and waited. The sun was rising fast. So was the temperature. As
we were waiting in the increasing heat, our local highway patrol officer stopped
to see what had happenned.

"You're going to butcher it aren't you?" He was serious!   9

"Are you kidding?" I asked, knowing that he wasn't kidding.   10

"Hey, it's getting hot. Don't want all that meat to spoil do you?" Actually, 11
I had not yet thought of the poor unfortunate bovine as "meat."

"The owner will be here soon," I said, "He'll take care of it."   12

"Well, you'd better bleed it at least," said the officer.   13

"Why don't you?" I asked hopefully. "I don't know how to."   14

He got out of his vehicle, removed his pocket knife, and knelt down over 15
the poor old charge. Going at the neck with gusto, but no result, he gave up
and announced, "My blade is too dull. You need a good butcher knife. Better

do it or it'll go bad. I've gotta get on down the road." Climbing back into his car he offered, "Good luck!"

Back to the phone. Back to Fred's wife.   16

"What?" I said with disbelief, "He left two hours ago?" He should have 17 been here easily by now! "Yes, he could have gone about some other business first." (I could not imagine anything more pressing than this dead cow.) "Well," I went on, "I was thinking about bleeding it so your meat won't ruin . . . What? . . . go ahead?" Fred's wife seemed to be under the delusion that I knew what I was doing.

What now? A sharp knife. For some reason I decided to take a towel and 18 a bucket of water back with me. As I was loading this equipment into my pickup, a friend drove up my driveway with her daughter. It just took a hurried explanation and I gained valuable reinforcements.

Now it was my turn to kneel down over the cow. As my friend and now 19 three kids watched, I lowered my sharp butcher knife to the animal's neck. I then discovered just how tough the hide of a cow is. I had to stretch the hide taught, then jab. It took all my force to get the tip of the blade started. Then, using both hands, I had to pull upward in order to cut at all. I was sweating. I was working so hard I forgot all about the poor cow, but my friend hadn't. Although she was turning green, her moral support never wavered. She did ask if we could use the towel to cover the cow's eyes because it was looking at her. Towel in place, I went back to the bloody mess and groped around in the wound I'd made searching for a main vein. My friend closed her own eyes and tried to help by pulling hide out of the way. This was done with two fingers. I continued to probe. I couldn't believe I was doing this. The helpful children pointed out that it was "gross." I had already figured out that part, what with the blood all over my jeans and hands, not to mention the sight of it all.

A low gurgle from deep within the gut of the cow rolled up and became a 20 mighty roar that sent us all back several feet. With all our vast experience, we thought the cow had come vengefully to life! When the panic subsided from our thumping hearts we realized that we had met success. The vein had been cut. Proof poured out of the cow's neck. Somehow, this had caused the loud rumble. We thought there must be more blood inside that would need the aid of gravity to bring it out. We decided to get a rope, tie it to the cow's hind legs, throw it over a tree, tie the other end to my pickup, and haul the cow upside down.

While I was back at the house trying to find a good, strong rope (we did 21 realize the animal would be heavy), Fred showed up.

Fred was pleased that the cow had been bled but said he wouldn't have a 22
chance to get it to a butcher. He turned to me, just returning with the rope,
"Do you want it? Can you get it to a butcher?"

"Sure," I said. No one had ever offered to give me a cow before.   23

Fred filled out a bill of sale for me so I wouldn't be accused of rustling. From 24
that paper I learned that this was not a cow, it was a steer. A cow is female
and raised for milk or breeding calves. A steer is male and raised strictly for
beef. As Fred and his husky partner proceeded to load my steer, with considerable strain, into the back of my pickup, the remaining blood left the animal.

My pick-up had a cracked radiator. It was useless for a trip to town, where 25
a butcher could be found, but I didn't have the heart to tell Fred. Also, I
didn't want to risk not getting the meat, so I kept quiet until the men were
gone. Then I told my friend about the radiator.

"Whatever are you going to do about this animal?"   26

"We'll just have to move it into the back of my Pinto station wagon," I   27
said with confidence. I did not realize what I was asking of the Pinto or of
ourselves.

We parked the pickup in my sloped driveway facing up the hill. Then I   28
opened the back of the Pinto and backed it up until it was just about to touch
the open tailgate of the pickup. We folded the back seats and the front pas-
senger seat of the pinto down and spread an old tarp inside. Now, I thought,
we'll simply roll the steer out of one vehicle into the other. Wrong! Six
hundred pounds of dead weight, cushioned in fat, does not roll. It doesn't
even slide, scoot, or otherwise move. We tied the rope to the steer's leg. We
then passed the rope through the open Pinto and out the driver window where
my friend grasped its frayed end. I was in the back of the pickup with my back
against the cab and my boots planted firmly upon the black, hairy hide. One,
two, three, heave! Again! Our faces were red. We gained two inches. Again,
and again. Finally it slid but the head fell into the slight gap between the
tailgate and Pinto. The neck flopped, like a wedge, blocking all efforts. We
called to the kids.

"Lift up the head so it will slide!" The girl wasn't about to touch the dead 29
cow's head, and it was too heavy for the little boys. I got down from the back
of the pickup and told the kids to slide a shovel under the head as I gingerly
lifted it—by the ear. Now it was looking at me!

With the kids stationed at either end of the shovel holding the head up, I 30
got back to my post. My friend, Janice, was still on the end of the rope. All
together, kids lifted, I pushed, and Janice pulled. We got most of it into the
little station wagon. We did have one problem with a stiff leg. It was pre-

venting the back of the car from shutting. We pulled and tugged and were just considering the chainsaw when it bent enough for the car to close. That was lucky because I don't think any of us knew how to start the chainsaw.

There was only room left in my car for the driver. The boys rode into town 31 with Janice and her daughter. If you have never ridden with a dead steer and about five thousand flies on a hot day, you can't imagine the unpleasantness of the trip. The smell was outrageous. One hind leg hung over my shoulder; a reminder of my grisly deeds, and the flies buzzed incessantly! The thirty-five miles to town seemed a year's journey.

At the butcher shop in town I explained that I had a steer in my car and 32 asked if they could take care of it for me. The man, dressed in a blood-stained white apron, accompanied me to my car.

"If you could back over to the rear door, we have a hoist to unload it with," 33 he explained. He quietly went about his business, throwing strange glances at me from time to time. I'm not very large, about five foot three and one hundred fifteen pounds. Finally, his grin broke through his composure and he blurted out, "Lady, how the hell did you get it in the car?"

After a few days I went back to the butcher shop and picked up over seventy 34 packages of hamburger, steaks, and roasts. The butcher got about fifty dollars for his trouble and I went home and filled my freezer, the hard way.

So you see, there are only four simple steps to filling a freezer. First, obtain 35 a steer. (If this is not possible, you may have to purchase a live one and have it killed. Some butcher shops have them already dead. You will usually get a better price buying them in volume from a butcher than you would at a supermarket.) Second, have a butcher prepare it. Third, pay the butcher, and fourth, take the meat home and fill your freezer. It's as simple as one, two, three—four.

QUESTIONS FOR READING AND REVISING

1. Petrea Galloway succeeds in writing a lively piece about a dead cow. She reports that her *purpose* was "to write something that will inform and entertain."How does she achieve this purpose?

2. Galloway writes: "Cows are something I have always considered good freezer filler; and we are surrounded by them!" What effect does Galloway achieve by

telling us this in her introduction? What is Galloway's attitude toward killing the cow? Does her attitude remain consistent throughout the essay?

3. What does Galloway assume about her reader's knowledge and assumptions about the processes of killing a cow or filling a freezer? Does she give her readers adequate information to understand the *process* she describes?

4. What do we learn about Galloway from reading her essay? What kind of person is she? She entertains her readers with her humor, but what do we learn about her in watching her response to being left "in the road with a half-dead cow and two small boys looking on"?

5. Into what stages has Galloway divided the *process* of filling a freezer?

6. Galloway tells us: "I would love to get to the feelings of the reader, without being overly sentimental, but with real truth, with real life." What details make the essay taste of "real life"? Find the details that are most effective and vivid. Explain how these details work in the essay to establish Galloway's purpose.

7. Galloway uses dialogue in telling her story. What does she achieve by using so much dialogue? Find instances of effective dialogue and explain their function in the essay.

8. In her rough draft, Galloway wrote her introduction this way:

> Everything is expensive today. Meat is something Americans are learning to cut down on for health reasons and because of the cost. But I believe most red-blooded Americans still enjoy good red meat and are willing to pay for it.
>
> In order to fill your freezer with meat, you could just go to your local supermarket and invest a large sum of money for it. It will cost from one dollar and eighty-nine cents to about four dollars a pound. It depends upon the cut. The way I filled my freezer took a good deal more effort but was easier on the budget.

Why do you think Galloway dropped these paragraphs? What does she gain by beginning her essay without them?

SUGGESTIONS FOR WRITING

1. By killing a cow, Galloway filled her freezer in a way she had never done so before. Think of a *process* that you completed in an unusual way. Write an essay detailing this process for your readers that assumes your readers' unfamiliarity with your way of completing this process.

2. Using a humorous *tone*, write an essay in which you offer advice to someone. Some possible topics might include: how to get rich; how to write an "A" paper; how to raise a child; how to lose weight; how to read a poem.

3. Galloway narrates how a disaster (the dead cow) had its good side (a full freezer). Narrate an event that similarly seemed dire at the time but turned out to have valuable consequences. Use dialogue and try to make the story as realistic as Galloway's.

PAMELA GARRETTSON

University of Maryland Baltimore County
Baltimore, Maryland
Wallace Shugg, instructor

Pamela Garrettson was born in Washington, D.C., and has lived in Owings Mills, a semi-rural area of Maryland, all her life. "I have lived a stable, if not sheltered life. I was adopted, which means that I tend to ponder some things, such as my family, that most people take for granted. I am a Christian and my religious beliefs greatly influence my writing."

About her writing process, Garrettson reports: "If someone were to walk in and to observe me writing, she would see a mound of notes sitting on my desk, phrases hastily scribbled on napkins, on the back of a chemistry exam, even in the middle of a math notebook. Amid all the clutter, I sit, trying to make sense of it all. I write a few sentences, frown, scratch out some words, and replace them with others, I shuffle my notes and write a few more sentences. Then I sigh, fling my pencil down, and consult a rough outline. I jump up, pace the floor, grin broadly, and rush back to my desk and write furiously."

Pamela Garrettson reports that she never thought much about writing and considered it a chore until high school. "I was a stereotypical, bespectacled bookworm who was always in the library and who even read the encyclopedia for fun. My reading background eventually made me a writer. I learned to write through reading, much as a small child learns to speak by listening to others." Besides reading and writing, Garrettson enjoys listening to music, running, and being outdoors. She is on the cross-country and track teams, writes for her school's newspaper, and is majoring in biochemistry.

Asked to write a persuasive essay arguing for or against some type of government control, Garrettson reports: "I chose public school prayer as my topic because I felt very strongly about the issue. I wanted my readers to put themselves in the place of school children and to realize how uncomfortable many public school students would feel if spoken prayer were instituted in their classrooms."

Prayer in America's Public Schools: Let's Not Start a Religious War

Separation of church and state has been a hotly contested issue in the [1] United States during the past year (1984). Much of the debate has centered on the role of prayer in public schools. President Reagan is said to favor legislation authorizing organized, spoken prayer in public schools, a proposal which is clearly an example of government meddling.

Proponents of organized, spoken prayer in public schools have argued that   2
its prohibition suppressed students' rights to express their religious faith freely.
However, the laws of the United States are based upon the principle that
freedom should not be exercised to the point that others' rights are violated.
Organized, spoken prayer in public schools would infringe on people's rights.

It is impossible to prove a particular religion "right" or "wrong." A Christian   3
might state that Christ was the Messiah, while a Jew might counter that he
was not. The debate ends right there, with mere assertion. Although a believer
will often attempt to use logic to support his views, one's religious beliefs are
only a matter of faith. The founders of the world's major religions emphasized
that abiding by their teachings was a matter of free choice. Jesus, for example,
did not pressure people into joining him; he invited them to "Follow me."
And even within neighborhood congregations everyone interprets his faith a
bit differently than his brethren.

With religious tolerance in mind, America's founders tried to ensure that   4
its citizens could practice their respective religions without interference. Organized, spoken prayer in our public schools would only serve to undermine
this noble ideal. When one is a member of a minority religion, it is all too
easy to feel uncomfortable in the midst of people who are practicing a religion
in which one does not believe. While attending a Hindu service—so radically
different in both theological content and style from my cozy Lutheran church—
I was quite disconcerted. I felt stupid just standing there and almost compelled
to participate. But I believed not a word of what they were saying. It seemed
to me that if I had joined in, it would have been almost blasphemous. The
same would be true, I suspect, for a member of that church visiting mine.

I was so discomfitted, yet I attended the service by choice, and the wor-   5
shippers there tried to make me feel welcome. And, too, I was a seventeen-
year-old with firmly established beliefs. Imagine the distress and confusion that
a younger student might feel if most of his classmates are saying a prayer he
does not believe in. Should he mouth words he does not believe or understand?
Should he just stand there, or perhaps leave the room? Should he have to
make that choice? To adults, this may seem a small matter, but children and
adolescents are generally more sensitive about being "different," and their peers
can be notoriously cruel in taunting them.

Why is organized, spoken prayer needed in our public schools, anyway?   6
According to *Time* magazine (19 March 1984: 12–15), when Congress was
debating this issue in March of 1984, several proponents of school prayer linked
the lack of it with the increase in sexual promiscuity and drug abuse. Virginia
representative Frank Wolf went further, stating that the rate of teenage suicides
"began to climb at approximately the same time that the schools were with-

drawn from prayer two decades ago" (12). These arguments seem illogical, for drug abuse and sexual promiscuity are nothing new, and most psychologists attribute the rise in teenage suicides to America's increasingly mobile, fast-paced society, which pressures young people to "grow up" before they are ready. Representative Wolf attempted to establish a cause-and-effect relationship without concrete evidence connecting the two events.

The question concerning a student's right to express his religious faith in   7 school remains, however. The First Amendment to the Constitution states that "Congress shall make no law establishing a religion or prohibiting free exercise thereof." Clearly, a balance between these two declarations is intended.

The 1963 Supreme Court decisions on the *Abington School District* v. *Schempp*   8 and *Murray* v. *Currlett* cases did not rule against all prayers, just those organized and led by teachers or school officials. The court saw this as "establishing a religion." Clearly, then, a student should be free to pray any time he wants. America's three major religions (according to membership) all hold that silent prayers are heard as well as spoken ones. In fact, most Protestant and Jewish national organizations are opposed to the proposed school prayer amendment, and the Roman Catholic Church in the United States takes a neutral position. A student wishing to pray can do so silently without risk of disturbing or offending anyone. Therefore, the "minute of silence" compromise also proposed by Congress last spring is redundant.

A few months ago, a federal law was passed that addressed students' rights   9 to exercise religious beliefs freely. The law states that if a school provides students with "non-instructional time" to pursue subjects not directly related to curriculum (clubs, for example), then it may not discriminate against student-initiated groups "on the basis of the religious, political, philosophical or other content of the speech at such meetings," and must provide equal access to school facilities for both secular and religious groups. Because this law is qualified by the phrase "student-initiated," it does not violate the Supreme Court rulings banning school-organized religious activity. It was supported by both backers and opponents of the prayer amendments that were proposed, but not passed in the Senate last March.

Since students are not forbidden to pray or to discuss religious matters among 10 themselves while at school, it is obvious that their right to exercise their religious beliefs remains unviolated. Therefore, the authorization of organized, spoken prayer in public schools is not only potentially offensive to students (and their parents and teachers), but also unnecessary.

Aside from the legal quagmire created by the issue of organized prayer in 11 schools, there are practical considerations as well. For example, how and to whom would the students pray? My mother was a librarian at a Baltimore County public high school during the 1950s. She recalls that the Lord's Prayer was recited as part of morning opening exercises, even though about a third of the school's population was Jewish. Though the Lord's Prayer has fairly universal wording, some Jews might object to its being called the Lord's Prayer when it was authored by a man who was not *their* lord. My mother also said that the prayer exercises "very often turned out being irreverent. You know, kids giggling through it." Wouldn't a devout Christian be offended too, by lack of respect accorded to the recital of "his" prayer?

Jerry Falwell, a leading backer of school prayer, proposes instead that each 12 morning, a different student might lead a prayer from his own faith, with other pupils free to join in or abstain as they wish. This idea avoids none of the problems of the 1950s version of school prayer; it just gives "equal time" to all faiths represented.

Government interference in a matter as personal as prayer only serves to 13 infringe upon the rights of its citizens. In many countries where religion and government are closely meshed, the result is dissension and even bloodshed.

Our public schools should impress upon students their common goals as 14 human beings, not alienate them in a battle over their religious faiths.

QUESTIONS FOR READING AND REVISING

1. Pamela Garrettson tells us: "As a Christian, I realize all too well that devout people of all religions can be intolerant or inadvertently insensitive to others' feelings in their fervor." Where in the essay do we see Garrettson's strong feelings about the issue of school prayer? How do her acknowledged religious views make her arguments more or less convincing? How do her views influence the *tone* of her essay?

2. What is Garrettson's *thesis*? Where in the essay does Garrettson state her thesis?

3. Identify the points Garrettson uses to support her thesis. Which are the most convincing and least convincing arguments? What does her use of evidence contribute in each case?

4. *Classify* the different types of evidence Garrettson uses in her essay. Discuss the effectiveness of each piece of evidence.

5. In paragraph 2, Garrettson makes the point: "Organized, spoken prayer in public schools would infringe on people's rights." What are these rights as she defines them in the essay? How does the argument about people's rights con-

nect to the argument about government interference? Does Garrettson establish the connection in a persuasive way?

6. What opposing *arguments* does Garrettson present? Why, in general, is this an effective strategy for arguing? Does this strategy work in Garrettson's essay?

7. In paragraphs 4, 5, and 11 Garrettson uses personal experience as evidence. How could an opponent argue with this evidence?

8. What is Garrettson's strategy for arguing? Does she move from her weakest argument to her strongest, her strongest to weakest, or does she use some other organization? Can you suggest ways to structure her essay more effectively?

9. Garrettson tells us that her "readers could be anyone." What assumptions does she make about her readers' beliefs? Find specific instances in her essay to support your answer.

10. Reread the last two paragraphs of the essay. Do these paragraphs provide an effective *conclusion?* Suggest ways to revise these paragraphs to make them more effective.

SUGGESTIONS FOR WRITING

1. Garrettson presents a strong *point of view* on the issue of school prayer. What is your point of view on this issue? Write an essay in which you illustrate your point of view using personal experience as evidence.

2. Garrettson uses the issue of school prayer as an example of an area in which she feels there should be no government interference. Consider another issue that influences our public, personal, and political lives (e.g., gun control, abortion, speed limits, food stamps, etc.) Write a *persuasive* essay in which you *argue* why there should or should not be government interference in this area.

3. Find an article in a newspaper or magazine arguing one side of an issue. Write an essay in which you argue for the other side of this issue. Use some of your opponent's arguments as support for your position.

MATTHEW J. HOLICEK

The University of Texas at Austin
Austin, Texas
John Ruszkiewicz, instructor

"When I write I like to have everything I need within arm's reach. The telephone, my bag of Fritos or Oreos, a cold drink, paper, and of course my Walkman. I hate silence when I study and writing isn't any different. I sit at my desk with my typewriter, or sit on my bed with my pillow in my lap, a book to write on, and my blank piece of paper. Sometimes I even have the television going. Sounds like impossible working conditions, but they have been working perfectly fine so far."

Matthew Holicek was born in New Berlin, Wisconsin, and moved to Houston, Texas, when he was twelve years old. He cites this move as one of the biggest influences on his life and reports that "living in two different cultures, Wisconsin and Texas, has given me many different ideas for my writing." Holicek has long been interested in both writing and making films. He was feature editor for his high school newspaper and received a journalism award for his articles. Holicek credits his father, a writer for an advertising agency, with encouraging his writing and for allowing him to use the family's 8-mm movie camera to make his own films. Holicek plans to major in radio-TV-film and make a career out of writing and filmmaking.

Asked to write an extended definition, Holicek reports: "I noticed that one of the choices was to define a particular type of movie, and the idea to write about slasher movies hit me immediately. I have seen so many of these films from working at a movie theater and from renting and watching them on my VCR. Seeing so many of these films has made me, I think, somewhat of an expert on horror movies. These slasher movies are forever imprinted in my mind, which actually might not be such a great thing to have in my memory."

For a more detailed study of Holicek's essay and the drafts that led to it, see Part III.

Look Out Behind You!

Most people get upset if they are told how a suspense or horror movie ends. After all, there's no point in seeing a "who-done-it" film if you already know who did it. But when it comes to a genre of horror films know as "slashers," people seem willing to make an exception. Even though they know that one slasher movie is apt to be just like all the others, audiences enjoy them anyway—perhaps because these stories of people being sliced to death by maniacs are so predictable. John Carpenter's masterful *Halloween*, which premiered in 1978, is widely regarded as the original slasher film. It was soon followed by a rash of inferior imitations which audiences nevertheless flocked to see, unconcerned that these totally predictable cinematic clones focused more on high death tolls and gory violence than on developing interesting characters or coherent plots.

Since teenagers are the target audiences for slasher films, the victims in 2
them are almost always independent, fun-loving, just-out-of-high school partyers. Could it be that the filmmakers believe that the teenage audience somehow identifies with other youths being decapitated, knifed, and electrocuted? But the kids portrayed in the movies die so quickly that viewers don't get much chance to learn about them, much less identify with them. The girls all love to take late-night strolls alone through the woods or skinny-dip at midnight in a murky lake. The boys, eager to impress these girls, prove their manhood by descending alone into musty cellars to restart broken generators or chasing psychotic killers into haylofts and attics. Entering dark and gloomy houses, men and women alike decide suddenly that now's a good time to save a few bucks on the end-of-the-month electric bill—so they leave the lights off. After hearing a noise within the house, they always foolishly decide to investigate, thinking it's one of their many missing friends or pets. Disregarding the "safety in numbers" theory, they branch off in separate directions, never to see each other again. Or the teenagers fall into the common slasher-movie habit of walking backwards, which naturally leads them right into you-know-who. Confronted by the axe-wielding maniac, the senseless youths lose their will to survive, close their eyes, and scream.

In short, whatever the logical thing to do is, the characters don't do it. Or 3
what they try to do fails. Calling the police is almost always out of the question. However, if they do decide to call the cops, the phone is dead. Or the lights don't work. If the victims try to get into another room, the door is jammed. If the characters manage to escape from the house, they always make the mistake of heading for the car. Sometimes the doors are locked and, naturally, the kids are without keys. But if they are lucky enough to have keys, the car won't start. Couldn't even rely on a new BMW in these movies. Then, looking at the fuel gauge, they realize they should have stopped at the village gas station on the way home from the 7–11 the night before. If the fumes are enough to get the car going, the next obstacle will be four deflated tires. The mad killer doesn't miss a trick!

Of course, it's always easy to tell exactly who his next victim will be. If a 4
girl goes off alone, she'll be murdered. If a guy walks backwards . . . instant death. Car won't start? Expect company in the back seat. An unlit room? It's lights out, forever. All hope is lost when characters come face to face with The Slasher.

The mad slasher is a once-ordinary person transformed into an indestruc- 5
tible, unstoppable, superhuman menace. In the opening scene of the movie,
through what appears to be the hazy view of someone afflicted with cataracts,
we see a horrifying incident—a burning, a decapitation, a drowning, a lynching, or a car accident—that causes the death or disfiguration of one or more
innocent outcasts. Then we are transported ten years forward, to the present
time. The plot unfolds. We learn that our happy group of teens—or a similar
bunch of kids—is responsible for the incident that maimed or disfigured the
maniac on that day ten years earlier (it was Halloween, or Valentine's Day,
or Friday the 13th or some other special occasion—a prom, a wedding, a loss
of virginity). Or the slasher has seen the teens cause the death of someone
dear to him. He is hot for revenge, but he has decided to wait exactly one
decade (no more, no less) before exacting his vengeance.

We rarely see where these slashers live, but they obviously don't have the 6
sense to get a comfortable apartment. They seem to prefer dismal, rotting
shacks where they dine on furry animals and Chicken McNuggets. They never
take off their masks or change their wardrobe—which consists of flak jackets,
army boots, and institutional pajamas. They don't talk; they just breathe heavily. Slashers do have the uncanny ability to predict exactly where their victims
will be next: teenagers are sure to back right into their killers or open that
very door behind which the madman patiently lurks. When a slasher ends up
having to chase his victims, he doesn't run. Instead, he just plods on zombielike
after his victims who, despite their youthful vigor, are unable to evade him.
He enjoys waiting for the teenagers, girls especially, to trip. Or he waits to
catch them off guard. That's when he makes his move.

When he murders his victims, he puts his imagination into it. To assure 7
the best and most gruesome results, he selects his tools carefully: knives, machetes, axes, arrows, hot pokers, and sometimes just his bare hands. To save a
little time, he'll occasionally put a single spear or pitchfork through two teens
making love—killing two birds with one stone. Or he'll cunningly lure his
victims to death by slamming doors, snapping branches, or turning off the
power in the fuse box.

After the killing spree, the one surviving teenager, usually a hysterical girl, 8
discovers the dead bodies of all of her friends placed neatly and sequentially
in her path—leading her directly to The Slasher. But, of course, she doesn't
see him until he lunges for her. Fortunately for her, this time his knife (or
poker or pitchfork) somehow misses its mark. She escapes and he chases her
(zombielike) through the house or the woods. Then, after endless screaming,
running, and tripping, the heroine cleverly thinks to defend herself and manages to skewer his eye with a sewing needle, split his skull with an axe, or

hang him. He falls to the ground, dead, or so she thinks. The audience groans as the woman stupidly turns around and walks away. The moment she relaxes to catch her breath, this superhuman monster lunges from the darkness again and tackles her. They struggle, and the slasher's true identity is revealed as she strips away his mask.

As the slasher raises his knife for a life-ending blow, two outcomes are   9 possible. One is that, from nowhere, a male hero appears and kills the slasher, saving the girl. The other and more prevalent outcome has the girl discover a butcher knife or machete lying nearby. Just in time, she avoids the maniac's blow and thrusts the knife into his stomach, killing him for good this time— she thinks. In neither ending do the teens actually check to be certain that the slasher is dead. (None of the kids in these slasher movies are destined for careers as coroners; they're all too eager to pronounce anything that doesn't move *dead.*) But the audience knows better. A simple lack of vital signs won't prevent this killer from rising up again, pulling the knife from his stomach (or the axe from his skull, or the machete from his neck), and killing those surviving teens with even greater enthusiasm and ingenuity in the inevitable, and even more dreadful slasher sequel coming soon to your local theater.

QUESTIONS FOR READING AND REVISING

1. Why, according to Matthew Holicek, do audiences enjoy slasher movies?

2. What is Holicek's attitude toward slasher movies? How does he reveal his attitude?

3. Holicek is writing an extended *definition* of slasher movies. What is his definition? What are the essential features of these movies?

4. What techniques does Holicek use in his introduction to bring his readers into the world of his essay?

5. Why do you think Holicek concludes his essay by promising an "even more dreadful slasher sequel coming soon to your local theater"? Why is this an effective *conclusion?*

6. Holicek advises fellow writers: "Details, details, details. Writers need to use as many details as possible so that readers will know that the writer knows what he is talking about." Does Holicek follow his own advice? Find details that you think are vivid and memorable. How does Holicek use these details to support his purpose?

7. In his third paragraph, Holicek has fun with language as he plays with sentence structure, length, repetition, and rhythm. Which sentences do you find especially effective? Why?

8. For whom is Holicek writing this essay? Can you understand the essay if you have never seen a slasher film? Why? What are Holicek's assumptions about his readers familiarity with the slasher genre?

9. Holicek tells us: "I tried to appeal to my readers through subtle humor in poking fun at slasher movies. I hoped people would laugh a little yet also realize at the same time the truth of the points I made." Did you find Holicek's essay humorous? Cite specific instances in the essay to support your answer. Why is Holicek's humorous tone an effective way to express his point of view?

10. In his first draft, Holicek began his essay this way:

    > The slasher movie is a specific type of horror film which concentrates more on the death toll and body count than on developing characters or plot.

    Why do you think Holicek dropped this simple and direct definition as his introductory sentence?

SUGGESTIONS FOR WRITING

1. Holicek explains to his readers the popularity of slasher movies. Using a humorous *tone*, write an essay in which you illustrate the popularity of romance novels, soap operas, award ceremonies, etc.

2. Write an essay defining the essential ingredients of one genre of books or films—spy thrillers, mysteries, tales of extraterrestrials, etc.

BRENDA JACOBS

Mississippi Gulf Coast Junior College
Perkinson, Mississippi
Nelda J. Lott, instructor

Brenda Jacobs describes herself as the only child of middle-income divorced parents. "Being the only child of two working parents shaped me most," she explains. "As such, I was often alone, both physically and emotionally. Reading and daydreaming were my refuge and my consolation. . . . I had a dog-eared library card of which I was extremely proud, and by the age of eight, a used typewriter. Mother taught me the correct finger placement, and I supplied the words. My love for words goes back as far as my memory of learning to read." The power of words has remained a central interest in her life. Born in Quitman, Mississippi, Jacobs spent her childhood years in Wiggins, Mississippi, before moving to Sonora, California, where she graduated from Sonora High School. An English major at Mississippi Gulf Coast Junior College with as yet undefined career goals, Jacobs participates in numerous extracurricular activities. She serves as a college yearbook photographer, a production assistant for the college theater, and a "reluctant editor of the college newspaper, now defunct." She is also the author of two plays for children produced by the college's "Perk Players" and presented to more than twenty-four thousand elementary school children during a recent tour of southern Mississippi. Jacobs's accomplishments are recognized in Mississippi Gulf Coast Junior College's Outstanding Achievement Awards in English, photography, and philosophy.

Brenda Jacobs's goal in "Handing Down Grace" is, as she explains, "to convey the sense of fun in word play—to illustrate that the nature of the English language is widely adaptable to the inventive imagery of the individual." Writing with an audience of both southerners and "nonnatives" in mind, Jacobs seeks to celebrate "the wonderful speech patterns which are as richly diverse as the people who make up our country."

Handing Down Grace

The unpaved road, a worn ribbon of white sand and red clay, bisects the heart of Five Mile, a narrow stretch of land which bears the name of the small creek running through the surrounding woods. Since my grandparents returned "down home" from California, a portion of the lanky pines and kudzu-entangled underbrush has given way to a plowed field where purple hulls and crowders grow in season. Adjoining the field is the "old place," Grandmother's first home, now a dilapidated, ghost-grey structure veiled in wild flowers and tall grasses. Up the road vestiges of a long-abandoned oil well scar the wooded hill; and a bit farther, ruins of the old frame schoolhouse, where Mother received her education, mark the end of this rural Mississippi road. Though somewhat familiar from early childhood visits and family reminiscences, Five Mile is, none the less, far from my western roots. But here I was, a California transplant having dinner in post-Confederate territory, where standard English is shunned like the carpetbagger of old. As family members gathered around the table and bowed their heads, Grandma singled out one to ask the blessing or, as she phrased it, to "hand down grace." Although my ear had already become accustomed to many regional expressions, this one had a decidedly different ring. Irreverently, I began to ponder the "handing down" aspect of grace while grace was still being "handed down." I searched for some common denominator in order to leap logically from the conventional "saying" or "asking" of grace to Grandma's variation and failed miserably. To my mind came the possibility of quasi-literal translation, a connection between "handing down" and passing—say, from one person to another. Yet, there was an upside-downness to the expression that struck a discordant note. Between mouthfuls of butter beans, I mused upon the paradoxical term; reason dictated that if grace were to be "handed" anywhere, surely it would be sent in an upward direction.

Such linguistic oddities, bound by neither logic nor reason, are inherent in 2 the colorful, inventive vernacular of the rural South, teasing the unseasoned, transplanted mind with homegrown fabrications and abstractions. To the westerner nurtured on bland euphemisms and commonplace nouns, the separate ingredients that compose the rich diet of southern colloquialisms are oftentimes difficult to fathom and to digest. Family reunions with three and four generations present are guaranteed to provide a dialectal feast. "Other-mothers" and "mammaws," better known in other parts of the country as grandmothers, happily go about their business of collecting "sugar" and hugs from assorted "chilluns," "chaps," or "younguns." While swapping hunting tales, the men of the family talk of "squarehills" and "hillbillies"—squirrels and rabbits, to the uninitiated. And, on occasion, at least one of the kinfolk is certain to "holler" for the "flyflap," for use on either insects or "younguns."

In a southern setting standard words, familiar even to the westerner, some- 3 times assume entirely new functions and meanings. A community gathering where music, usually gospel music, is played and sung is to the participants a "sang." "Wet" and "dry," when associated with alcoholic beverages, translate as "to have" or "to have not." Though somewhat clarified by the accompanying actions, expressions such as "pitchin' a fit," "fixin' to go," and "raisin' cane," throw the nonnative off balance, if only for the length of time it takes to sigh for the apparent demise of the "-ing" ending. Equally jarring are the vowel sounds that undergo a metamorphosis when uttered by a native speaker. Taken out of context, "tire" and "tar," as well as, "fire" and "far," are often indistinguishable by sound alone. Similarly, the substitution of "ah" for "i" in "wire" and "hire" forms a sort of verbal mutation. Plainly, southerners just don't put much store in the long "i" sound.

Southernese, in all its conglomerate forms, enhances the cultural shock   4
experienced by the westerner who finds herself "to home" in Dixie. Not long after my arrival in Mississippi, I was introduced to "gardens" and "patches," southern style. Since the few gardens on the West Coast are scarcely larger than graveyard plots, it was a revelation to me to come face to face with the enormous "patches" owned and operated by a single family outfitted with ordinary hoes. My education in the ways and words of the South had barely begun when one evening I accepted an invitation to dig potatoes. Not wanting to appear naive, I did not question the notable absence of a shovel, even though "dig" and "shovel" are hitched together in my vocabulary like "salt" and "pepper," and it is my conviction that such words are not lightly separated. Nor did I give voice to what was uppermost in my mind, that is, what dig had to do with potatoes in the first place. But by then I was growing accustomed to words and phrases not quite fitting my preconceived notions. Perhaps, I reflected, we were off to observe the potatoes doing whatever they do before winding up at the local market—as in "wow, dig those spuds." However, on second thought I was confident that, even though outdated, the expression must have bypassed the South completely. It was simple logic that guided me to assume that our true mission was to harvest potatoes, and logic seemed to indicate that "pick" and "dig" were synonyms of a sort. Needless to say, I was in error on all counts. Mother has always contended that the obvious has a way of eluding me.

It was then and there, among the potatoes, that my name became linked   5
to "poor thing." A "poor thing," I learned, was not to be confused with being poor, as penniless, or with being in a poor state of health. "Poor" of body, or skinny, I was very definitely not; nor was I ailing, as in "doin' poorly." No, "poor thing" in my case denoted an overall state of mind, implying either stupidity or ignorance, depending upon the kindness of the speaker.

The southerner's usage of "sister" and "brother" for those related geneal-   6
ogically, by marriage and otherwise, can perplex even the most astute outsider. In those early days, when my mouth stubbornly refused to form the word, "ya'll," it seemed that everyone in the entire South belonged to one extended family. It was a while before dawn broke over the cloudy linguistic horizon to reveal the true meaning of these fraternal terms. It became evident that, as long as the gender matched, anyone qualified as a "sister" or "brother," even if she or he were an only child. Additionally, I had the suspicion that the

given name of every eldest son, who was invariably called Brother, had been long forgotten. Then too, there was Brother Bill, the Baptist preacher, and Brother Bob, the deacon who married Sister Mattie, adding to the confusion. Although Sister Mattie was also known as Miss Mattie, both before and after her marriage, her husband, Brother Bob, quite sensibly called her "Mama." In time I learned to disregard reason and to stick to hunches while attempting to sort and recatalogue definitions in accordance with the southern tradition.

Now that I have at least one foot firmly rooted in Mississippi soil, large portions of the linguistic puzzle, including those seemingly misrepresentative titles, have fallen into their illogical places. It seems perfectly natural that ladies below the Mason-Dixon line "glow" rather than sweat, and that "pot liquor" is a legal substance in both "wet" and "dry" counties. In fact, I've acquired a fondness for the regional expressions annexed, by bits and pieces, to my word store—enough pieces, I'd like to think, to have at last annulled my "poor thing" image.

7

QUESTIONS FOR READING AND REVISING

1. Brenda Jacobs's essay uses details and *examples* effectively. Reread her opening paragraph and point out the important details and examples she introduces. Explain how each reinforces the overall effect of this paragraph and the essay as a whole. What is the effect of including the phrase "between mouthfuls of butter becans" in the last sentence? Reread the remainder of Jacobs's essay and prepare a list of her most effective details and examples. How well does each reinforce the overall effect she hopes to create in the essay?

2. Jacobs notes that her essay should be "read with a sense of humor." Where— and how—is this humorous attitude toward her subject first revealed? Show how this attitude remains consistent or changes as her essay proceeds. How does the *contrast* between western and southern expressions reinforce her humorous attitude? What is the nature of her comparison between southern and western expressions and how does she introduce—and sustain—it?

3. Jacobs reports on some of the aims of her essay:

> I hoped that the southern reader might "see" the language habits that by virtue of familiarity go unnoticed. (Interestingly, many southerners are not aware of their particular speech habits, only of the "funny" way everyone outside the South talks.) The typical "Yankee" response was expected to be one of instant recognition and empathy. By

> playing up the confusion, difficulty, and downright igno-
> rance of the city-bred Yankee, I hoped to balance the scales
> of fair play, and to counter any notion that any slight was
> intended.

As you reread her essay, weigh carefully—and explain specifically—how Jacobs does or does not "balance the scales of fair play" in her essay with humor. Support your response with references to particular words and phrases.

4. Based on the way Jacobs presents herself in this essay, what do we learn about her as the essay proceeds? What impression does she create of herself in the opening paragraph? In paragraph 4? In the final paragraph? Explain how her image remains consistent throughout the essay or where and how it changes. In what respects does Jacobs poke good-humored fun at herself?

5. How familiar does Jacobs assume her audience is with southern expressions? Examine paragraph 1 for words and phrases that reveal Jacob's assumptions. How much background information does she provide her readers? Where in the essay does she include it?

6. Jacobs reports that she began working on her essay by "making a list of words or phrases that seemed particularly southern, as well as noting possible inter-pretations. The catch phrase 'handing down grace' seemed a good opening which would set the tone or mood and the stage for the linguistic oddities to follow. Because I felt more interested in and better suited to a light-hearted approach, I decided to include several facets of southern colloquialisms rather than dwell on one particular thing—say, pronunciation." What central idea controls Jacobs's arrangement of these southern expressions and the examples she chooses to include? Where is it introduced? How is it developed? Does Jacobs organize her essay, for example, by moving from general statement(s) to particular examples? From particular example to general statement(s)? Some combination of the two? Something else? Explain. What prevents her essay from slipping into a "catalogue" of southern expressions?

7. Reread paragraphs 4 and 5 and consider the purpose of the anecdote about digging potatoes. What is there in the phrase, "wow, dig those spuds," that might prompt her to say that "the expression must have bypassed the South completely"? Jacobs explains her inclusion of the potato-digging section in these terms: "The action of the potato-digging episode was included to offset a drift toward 'listing,' and to dramatize the subject matter." How effective is this "episode?" How does Jacobs connect it to the overall aim of her essay? If Jacobs had the opportunity to revise her essay, what would you suggest she do to strengthen her handling of this "episode"?

8. Jacobs observes that "the most difficult aspect of revising is throwing out that which may sound good, but which actually lends nothing to the paper as a whole." Which parts of Jacobs's essay might at first seem to illustrate her point?

Reread these sections carefully and explain why each does or does not warrant retention in the final draft. Consider the title of her essay. Her previous draft was called "Southernese." Which title do you prefer? Why?

9. Brenda Jacobs wrote numerous drafts of her essay. In her first draft, the final paragraph reads:

> With at least one foot now firmly rooted in Mississippi soil, a large portion of the linguistic puzzle, including misrepresentative titles, has fallen into its illogical place. After sixteen years, it seems perfectly natural that women below the Mason-Dixon line "glow" rather than sweat, and that "pot liquor" is a legal substance in both wet and dry counties. In fact, I've acquired a real fondness for the regional expressions annexed, by bits and pieces, to my vocabulary storehouse—enough pieces, I'd like to think, have at last annulled my "poor thing" image.

What differences do you notice between her first and final drafts? Which version do you prefer? Why? How does the version you prefer tie together the most important points of this essay?

SUGGESTIONS FOR WRITING

1. Brenda Jacobs's essay is based on her discovery of what she calls "linguistic oddities" (curious regional expressions) when she returned to rural Mississippi after living in California for many years. Consider your own travels. Write an essay in which you re-create your first encounter with a way of talking that you had some difficulty understanding. For example, you may have been visiting a foreign country or simply another part of the United States. (If you are uncomfortable writing about differences in language, you might want to focus on differences in items of clothing, a particular mannerism, or a kind of food.) *Compare and contrast* the differences between your own way of talking and the one you encountered. What did you infer about this foreign or regional culture as a result of this encounter? Contrast these inferences with what you know about your own national or regional culture.

2. Select some aspect of daily life in your hometown—a place, an event, a person, a way of talking—that represents the special regional spirit and texture of day-to-day life. Write an *expository* essay in which you use a detailed *description* of this person, place, or event to explain that texture.

3. The popular media (television shows, films, songs) often profit from projecting images of how people from different areas of the United States talk and behave. (What image does a television serial like "Dallas," which is seen in more than

fifty countries worldwide, create of wealthy Texans?) When these images are repeated week after week, do they harden into stereotypes? What are the consequences of projecting such images across the country? Around the world? Write an *expository* essay in which you *analyze* the regional stereotypes of Americans as they are presented in one such television serial, one American film, or a popular song.

JUDY JENNINGS

Richland College
Dallas, Texas
Rica Garcia, instructor

"My life affects my writing more than anything. I am twenty-nine years old, married to Les Jennings, and have one son, Christopher. Les and I have a design firm specializing in large aircraft interiors. I have been attending college on a part-time basis. I tend to write about things that happen in everyday living—my child, husband, the plight of the average housewife. It is important for writers to write about things they know about."

Judy Jennings has always lived in Texas; born in Fort Worth, growing up in Greenville, and now living in Plano. Her major hobby is reading, and her favorite authors include Danielle Steele, Jackie Collins, and Thomas Thompson.

Asked to write an essay in which she explained a situation in her life, Jennings decided to write about her situation as a stepmother. "My husband's two children live with us and I feel very strongly about the injustices of stepparenting. I wanted to clarify a misunderstood role."

Second-Class Mom

On March 22, 1980, I married Leslie Floyd Jennings, Jr. On that same clear 1 spring evening, I also married Daniel Brian Jennings (age seventeen), Lesley Nicole Jennings (age six), and Phillip Timothy Jennings (age two), Les's children by two previous marital failures. I had been warned by everyone I knew about the pitfalls of marrying a man with two failed marriages and three children in tow. But marry him I did, and in that dubious deed, settled upon my youthfully naive shoulders the burdens of the label of "stepmother" that history, mythology, ignorance, and misunderstanding allows our society to dictate.

During the first months of our marriage, I wrestled with having to rearrange 2 our schedules to accommodate weekend visits as well as with my resentment of the amount of child support my husband was paying and the hardships it imposed on our already stretched-to-the-limit budget. These factors (and others) made me often wonder if we would ever be able to have a child of our own because of these financial and emotional commitments to my husband's children. Yes, I had considered all these things before making a permanent commitment to this man, but day-to-day reality is quite different, I found, from the dreams we spin when we are blinded by love's passions.

After only five short months of marriage, Les's two younger children came   3 to live with us, and within thirty days, I was expecting a child of my own. Learning about the trials of motherhood from both Les's children and my own child virtually at the same time, has certainly proven to be a unique and unpredictable experience. I feel that in the last four years, I have learned more about patience, compromise, sacrifice, and endurance than I ever thought possible.

I have never wanted to give anyone the impression that I dislike my step-   4 children, or even that I have no feelings for them at all, but they are not mine. There are times when I want to grab Les by the knot of his tie, pulling him down to my level until the tips of our noses touch and we're looking each other straight in the eye, and then snarl at him through clenched teeth, "THEY'RE NOT MINE." Everyone understands the theories of how difficult it would be to live with someone else's children, but they really never do understand the realities of it. Les's mother is always spouting endless streams of well-meant advice on "raising and disciplining Les's children just like they were my own." Yet, even though she will sit nodding her head in approval while I criticize and correct my own child, she will purse her lips and sometimes burst into tears if I get into a shouting match with one of her grandchildren who is not mine. Even after almost five years, I have never ceased to be amazed and appalled at the injustice of it all. I am expected to perform with perfect precision, but without a single trace of prejudice or partiality, all the mothering rituals, but I am also expected to stop just short of throwing any stones at their characters or past disciplinary guidelines. I'm not supposed to show the slightest bit of distaste or nausea or even say "Yuk" when cleaning up the bathroom after a "didn't-quite-make-it-to-the-toilet" bout of diarrhea or vomiting, but heaven forbid that I should criticize their clothes or hairstyles or friends, a privilege, I presume, reserved for "real" mothers.

One of the things that makes stepmothering somewhat less a joy than   5 mothering your "children by choice" is that it is such a thankless job. Even after I've spent an endless day in unfruitful toilet training sessions or sore throat crankiness, my own child will make it up to me by climbing onto my lap and snuggling his baby head up underneath my chin, making goose bumps run up and down my arms. I've endured countless times, after days of driving car pools, organizing school bake sales and carnivals, soccer practices, ballet lessons, and dental appointments, having one of my stepchildren run out to get in the car holding up some crudely fashioned trinket made in school and saying, "Look! Look what I made for Mommy." "Mommy" being their "real" mother.

The mother they see maybe four or five times a year, and who rarely so much as buys them a pair of shoes.

The role of a stepmother is unlike that of any other kind of mother, whether 6 it be foster mother, adoptive mother, or birth mother. Stepmothering is the only type of mothering we do without choice. All children, certainly, are not "planned" children, but even with an unwanted pregnancy, the mother *chooses* not to abort the baby, or give it up for adoption, or something. And certainly, adoptive mothers and foster mothers have a definite choice in the decision to mother or not. The stepmother does not choose the children, she chooses the father. He just comes as a package deal.

Stepchildren also come with an uncanny radar or sixth sense that enables 7 them to zero in with pinpoint accuracy on our vulnerabilities and fire torpedos with deadly insensitivity. Every year, when our whole family assembles to decorate the family Christmas tree, one of my stepchildren will take this one certain ornament out of the box and hold it up for all the rest to see. This particular ornament came with them when they came to live with us. I have always presumed that it was a gift from their natural mother, so I suppose that's why I've never found it in me to throw it away. This ornament is a small pair of very ugly gorillas with toboggans and neck scarves with their arms around each other looking at a book of Christmas carols. They hold it up to everyone in the room (including me) and then announce triumphantly, "This is Mommy and Daddy." Every year I tell myself that they're only children and that they don't know what they're saying, but my face still gets hot and my stomach still flipflops. I don't like being reminded of the "Mommy and Daddy" that used to be. These children are reminder enough. Their very presence seems to almost be a rubber stamp that says, "Your husband used to be in love with someone else," and some things are better left unthought.

I have a very deep sense of responsibility toward these children and a great 8 deal of affection. I will probably never love them the way I love my own son—sometimes I don't love them at all, but they are as much a part of my life as their father or my own child. Just as I am sure about the way I feel about them, I am quite certain that they feel pretty much the same way about me. We have been thrown together by virtue of the mistakes of other people. I can't help the fact that their mother and father couldn't make a go of their marriage, and neither can they, but here we are. We have grown to accept our lives together, and even to depend upon each other somewhat. I am really the only mother they know, and neither I nor they can change that fact.

I would lay down my own life for *any* of my children. For Christopher, I 9 would do it without a backward glance and probably even with a smile on my face. For Nikki and Philip, I would gripe all the way.

QUESTIONS FOR READING AND REVISING

1. Jennings writes with honesty about a subject many people are unwilling to discuss openly. She tells us that she and her stepchildren "have been thrown together by virtue of the mistakes of other people." What does Jennings see as the injustices of being a stepmother?

2. What is Jennings's *thesis?* Does she state her thesis directly? How does she make her ideas clear and convincing?

3. As readers, we have a strong sense of a writer who cares deeply about her subject and who has taken great care to make her essay lively. What strategies does Jennings use to make her ideas interesting to her readers?

4. Jennings writes: "I am expected to perform with perfect precision, but without a single trace of prejudice or partiality, all the mothering rituals, but I am also expected to stop just short of throwing any stones at their characters or past disciplinary guidelines." What details of the mothering ritual does Jennings present to illustrate her thesis? Select details you found effective and explain how these details are used in the essay.

5. Jennings begins her essay in a very direct way: "On March 22, 1980, I married Leslie Floyd Jennings, Jr. On that same clear spring evening, I also married Daniel Brian Jennings (age seventeen), Lesley Nicole Jennings (age six), and Phillip Timothy Jennings (age two), Les's children by two previous marital failures." Do you find this an effective hook for pulling you, the reader, into the world of her essay? Why?

6. In her *conclusion,* Jennings tells us of her willingness to sacrifice herself for any of her children, but that she would be "griping all the way" for her stepchildren. How does her conclusion effectively tie together all the various ideas in her essay?

7. Jennings reports that she envisions her readers as "stepmothers/persons about to become stepmothers." What evidence is there that she is writing for this *audience?* What evidence is there that she is writing for a more general audience? How would paragraphs 4 and 5, for instance, differ if they were written for a different group of readers?

8. We like Jennings even though she confesses to resenting her stepchildren. How do the examples in paragraphs 5 and 7 influence our attitude toward her?

9. Jennings *generalizes* about the role of the stepmother from her own experience. In paragraph 6, for instance, she tells us, "Stepmothering is the only type of mothering we do without choice." Why does Jennings choose to generalize about the role of the stepmother? How does this strategy help to strengthen her essay?

10. In an early draft, Jennings's title was "Number Two Mom." How does her revised title better introduce the essay?

SUGGESTIONS FOR WRITING

1. Jennings illustrates the burdens of the label *stepmother*. Consider a role you have chosen for yourself or have been thrust into and write an essay in which you illustrate what it is like to be cast in the role.

2. Write an essay in which you explain your attitude toward an event or situation in your life that might surprise your readers.

3. Write an essay responding to Jennings's complaints from the stepchild's *point of view.*

MONIKA JERABEK

Harvard University
Cambridge, Massachusetts
Sven Birkerts, instructor

Monika Jerabek regards her immigration to the United States at the age of three as one of the central facts in her life. Born in Prague, Czechoslovakia, Jerabek grew up in California's Silicon Valley and graduated from Henry H. Gunn High School in Palo Alto. "Since immigrating to the United States, I have realized the importance of independence and self-sufficiency while watching my parents create a new life for us and adapt and change to their new-found circumstances." Jerabek has developed her intellectual independence and self-sufficiency in her studies both in high school, where she received an Arthritis Foundation Summer Science Fellowship to work in a DNA lab at Stanford University, and in college, where she serves on the Harvard Advocate Poetry Board and plans to major in philosophy.

Jerabek describes herself as a writer who likes to finish a paper "at one sitting, with a few short breaks," so "that I do not lose the direction and tone of my thoughts." Along with many other student and professional writers, Jerabek finds it most difficult "to strike a balance between a clear, concise approach and a creative flavor." Planning carefully, she feels, makes it easier to balance clarity and originality and increases the likelihood that her essays will succeed. Not surprisingly, her characteristic method of writing involves a good deal of preliminary note-taking and outlining:

> When I start writing I usually write down several general ideas on the topic and try to think of relevant subcategories that would expand on the subject. I further expand these ideas (in my notes and outline) with concrete evidence and examples. That process then leads me to a more obvious focus or thesis for the paper, the explanation of which I include in the opening or closing remarks. After I have completed these preliminaries, I think of the way I want to present the content of the paper—formally, informally, from what perspective, what kind of language—and begin writing, following the guidelines of my notes.

In preparing her essay on Sylvia Plath's poetry, Jerabek set out not only to analyze the father image in Plath's verse but also "to incorporate elements of Plath's life and creative style. I wanted to communicate some of the passion and turmoil in Plath's life as expressed through her poetry."

Sylvia Plath: Electra Inspired

The poet, Sylvia Plath, wrote from a reservoir of experience, motivation, 1
and ambition. One of her main themes, the portrayal of the father figure,
permeates her work and incorporates the autobiographical with other themes—
nature, childhood, death, and suicide. The untimely death of Plath's own
father when she was nine years old left a wound that festered for the poet's
entire life. From the early stages of her writing to the last months before her
death, Plath refers to the father figure, trying to assimilate her reaction to her
father's death.

During her childhood, Sylvia Plath worshipped her father, Otto Plath, a 2
professor of biology and an authority on bees. He took pride in teaching her
science and language, nurturing a close relationship (Salop 10). When he died
after a long illness, Plath's world ripped in two: As she later said, "those nine
first years of my life sealed themselves off like a ship in a bottle—beautiful,
inaccessible, obsolete, a fine white, flying myth" (Aird 4–5). The tragic experience formed a conflict in Plath's mind between feelings of love and feelings
of abandonment, rejection, and guilt, as if her love were somehow responsible
for her father's death. Plath's suicide attempt at twenty—by taking fifty sleeping
pills after visiting her father's grave—illustrates just how intensely she felt the
pain of loss (Salop 13). In her poetry, Plath uses paternal imagery to try to
resolve her inner turmoil.

Her early work not only shows Plath's attempt to define her perceptions of 3
the external world and the relationship of the individual to the outside world
(Aird 5), but includes several poems involving the father-image theme. The
title poem of *The Colossus*, the only collection of poetry published during
Plath's lifetime, creates an encompassing metaphor for Plath's image of her
father after his death: the ruins of an immense statue, representing her shattered image of God-like father, that she can never "put together entirely, /
Pieced, glued, and properly jointed." Searching for the guiding words of a dead
father, she "[labors] / To dredge the silt from your throat" and symbolically
tries to reconstruct the overwhelming figure of her father by uncovering and
rebuilding the statue in "The Colossus." At the end of the poem, however,
Plath concludes that the task is fruitless, that her "hours are married to shadow,"
not only the shadow of defeat, but the shadow of her father. She pictures
herself married to her father—a sign of Freud's Electra complex. Similarly, in
"The Beekeeper's Daughter," the daughter worships her father the beekeeper:
"You move among the many-breasted hives, / My heart under your foot, sister
of a stone." She compares herself to the queen bee, a figure overpowering to
a mere mother, saying, "Here is a queenship no mother can contest." The

autobiographical implications are evident in this case, as Otto Plath was an expert in beekeeping, and Sylvia identified with her mother while loving her father—the pattern of Freud's Electra complex (Salop 11).

Plath further develops the idea of her Electra complex in "Electra on Azalea   4
Path." She describes the aftermath of her father's death: "I went into the dirt, / Into the lightless hibernaculum / Where bees . . . sleep out the blizzard." For twenty years she endures "that wintering," still considering her father God. The scene in which she awakens to reality, on Azalea Path in the graveyard, "a cramped necropolis," parallels her own visit to the graveyard before her first suicide attempt, a result of depression catalyzed by her warring feelings for her father. Depicting her birth as "ill-starred," Plath then tries to blame her mother for "[dreaming] you down in the sea," but at the end of the poem, she blames herself: "your hound-bitch, daughter, friend. / It was my love that did us both to death." Feeling responsible and guilty, just as she felt responsible and guilty as a child, Plath blames his death and her trauma on her love.

Examining the paternal theme in Plath's poetry uncovers other prevalent   5
subjects—nature, for example. In "The Colossus," Plath refers to the "weedy acres" of the statue's brow and the "hill of black cypress," images that not only suggest vivid pictures in the mind but that enhance the metaphor of the statue as her father. The "black cypress" reflects the images of shadows and darkness, while "acres" suggests the vastness of the reconstruction Plath wishes to achieve. The images of nature in "The Beekeeper's Daughter," on the other hand, relate to the sexuality implicit in the Electra complex. With phrases such as "garden of mouthings," "many-breasted hives," and "dark flesh, dark parings," Sylvia Plath subtly illustrates a latent sexual attraction to her father. Similarly, in "Electra on Azalea Path," she speaks of bees like "hieratic stones"— a phrase hinting of the God-like perception of her father. The petals near his grave "drip red" and connect the reader with the blood and death so vividly evident to Plath.

Other related themes emerge in Crossing the Water, the collection of poems   6
judged as the starting point of Sylvia Plath's final development (Aird 39). She continues writing about nature but relates it to more internal experiences. This transitional period finds her fascinated with the trappings of disease and illness and personal isolation, perhaps recalling her hospitalization for psychotherapy and shock treatment after her first suicide attempt the summer of her junior year at Smith College. In "The Surgeon at 2 A.M." Plath compares the intricacies of the inner human body to the multicolored nature. The surgeon finds "the lung tree," the "red-bell bloom" of the heart, and the "sunset" and "hot spring" of the blood, and she senses her power over the "sleepers in gauze sarcophagi," mere "gray faces." She remains completely stoic, almost mes-

merized by the clinical specimen of the body in which she can "worm and hack in a purple wilderness." The patient floats alone in a blue haze to which the "angels of morphia have born him up." One feels as though Plath strongly identifies with the sensations she describes. Her images in *Crossing the Water* are "a powerful expression of the constant feeling of a lack of reality, a substancelessness which pervades [her] later work (Aird 43).

While Plath's early work concentrates on visual descriptions and outer per- 7 ception, her later works *Winter Trees* and *Ariel* plunge into "the inner world of pain and alienation" (Aird 69); a journey into self-examination and perusal—of childhood, men, marriage, death, suicide, and, of course, the father. Here we see a blossoming of Sylvia Plath's craft and creativity. Her husband, Ted Hughes, has written that "Tulips" was "the first sign of what was on the way. She wrote this poem without her usual studies over the Thesaurus, and at top speed, as one might write an urgent letter" (Ames 291). In "Tulips" Plath presents herself in the inanimate, "flat, ridiculous" substancelessness of a "cut-paper shadow" that the intensely red tulips disturb with their reminder of vigorous life. As she lies in a hospital bed, she learns quiet, pleasant peacefulness. Everything around her is white, "snowed-in." Nurses tend her as "water / Tends to the pebbles it must run over," and in this passivity she finds an emptiness and a purity similar to "what the dead close on." In contrast to her inanimation, the "excitable" tulips she has received are so starkly red that they hurt her. The same color as blood, they "talk to my wound" and "eat my oxygen." The air "snags and eddies" around them, forcing her to concentrate her attention upon them instead of remaining uncommitted. The tulips make her realize the infirmity of her body—and mind—as far from health as she is from a happy, vigorous childhood by the sea.

Some poems in *Ariel* return to the personal distress related to Plath's dead 8 father, but they also include a more public, political side regarding Nazis and concentration camps. These last poems, written not long before her death, represent a kind of catharsis for Sylvia Plath as she vents her anger and ambivalence. "Daddy" depicts an attempt to work through the distress connected with a dead father by comparing him to a Nazi. In a reading for BBC radio, Sylvia Plath said of this poem:

> Here is a poem spoken by a girl with an Electra complex.
> Her father died while she thought he was God. Her case
> is complicated by the fact that her father was also a Nazi
> and her mother very possibly Jewish. In the daughter the
> two strains marry and paralyse each other—she has to act
> out the awful little allegory once over before she is free of
> it. (*Collected Poems* 293).

Although the plot is not strictly autobiographical, for Otto Plath could not have been a Nazi soldier since he came from Prussia as an adolescent (Aird 78), the poem effectively incorporates the poet's emotions by using the comparison.

At the beginning of "Daddy" the girl describes the life she has led for thirty 9 years, existing "like a foot" in a "black shoe." Addressing the father as "Daddy" throughout the poem, Plath hearkens back to her childhood by the sea, where she had, instead of a bag of marbles, a "bag full of God" in her father, a giant statue that she associates with the beautiful, "freakish Atlantic." The untimely death of her father while the girl adored and depended on him prompts the girl to try to "recover" the essence of her father and the identity she has lost as a result.

Plath relates this search using descriptions of war, Nazis, and concentration 10 camps to parallel personal feelings of pain, loss, and entrapment. The girl searches "in the German tongue, in the Polish town" for traces of her father; Plath's own father came from the German sector of Poland. The "name of the town is common," however, and like her soul racked by "wars, wars, wars." She feels severed from her background, denied communication with her father, and ultimately trapped in her private hell:

> So I never could tell where you
> Put your foot, your root,
> I never could talk to you.
> The tongue stuck in my jaw.

By using German words and phrases, such as *Ach, du,* or "Oh you," and the repeated *ich,* Plath enhances her parallel of the Nazi and the father. The "barb wire snare" preventing her from speaking becomes the barb wire of the concentration camp. Thinking every German her father and eventually finding "the language obscene," she gets pulled further into the allegory. "An engine, an engine / Chuffing me off like a Jew" brings to mind her role as the victim of persecution just as the Jews were the victims of the Nazis' persecution.

Returning to the idea of the Electra complex, Plath hints that the girl's 11 impurity may be due to a partially Jewish mother or a gypsy ancestress, and that her "weird luck" and her "Taroc pack," intimations of chance and fate, really place the blame for her troubles on herself. She lapses again into ambivalence, saying, "I have always been scared of you," while describing the "neat mustache / And your Aryan eye, bright blue," and pining, "Oh You." Her father at once represents perfection and abomination. Now compared to the symbol of cruelty, a swastika "so black no sky could squeak through," his image tortures the child, who cannot reconcile her love with his cruelty or her hate with his perfection. In a sexual context, Plath intertwines adoration with violence: the "boot in the face" from the "brute heart." Plath flashes again to childhood when "the black man" "at the blackboard," referring to him as a teacher, "Bit [her] pretty red heart in two."

In a final attempt to join her father, the girl remembers how she tried to 12 commit suicide at twenty, another familiar theme for the poet. Unsuccessful, and with the broken pieces of her mind "stuck . . . together with glue," the daughter tries to escape by marrying a model of her father, a husband "who has been chosen for his similarity to the father in the hope that his presence will exorcise the daughter's obsession" (Aird 81). The marriage does not work: she says she has killed "the vampire who said he was you / And drank my blood for a year, / Seven years." Plath's inclusion of the failed marriage could reflect her own separation from her husband around October of 1962, when she wrote "Daddy." Nevertheless, the girl in the poem, having worked through her anguish, concludes that she is "finally through." With passionate persistence, she insists that "There's a stake in your fat black heart." She figuratively dances and stamps on his image with her mind and calls him a bastard, almost as if she doubts that she is free of his memory—as if she is trying to convince herself of it.

The imagery and word usage emphasize the sensual aspects of the poem and 13 bring it to life for the reader. Plath's use of assonance, for example, not only adds cohesiveness to "Daddy," but also highlights recurrent images, such as "boot," "root," "you" (Daddy). In line 1 Plath has "You do not do," followed by "shoe" and "Achoo." Later she continually repeats "you," rhyming it with "gobbledygoo," "blue," "through," "who," "two," "do," and "glue" (stanzas 9–13). By repeating key words, such as "wars, wars, wars" (line 18), "ich, ich, ich, ich" (line 27), "brute" in lines 49 and 50, and "back" in line 59, Plath directs the reader's attention toward the meaning of the poem. Thus, we can notice the double meaning of boot: "an effective image for the obsessional nature of the daughter's neurosis" and "carrying suggestions of the brutality associated with the father as a Nazi officer" (Aird 80). Moreover, Plath chooses words that convey distinct visual or auditory association. For instance, "barb wire snare" (line 26) connotes the entrapment and pain of the mind and in the camps with its harsh r sounds. Similarly, "Chuffing me off" (line 32) sounds like trains chugging away to the concentration camps, and "gobbledygoo" sounds like confusion and garbled language. The "rack and the screw" (line 66) immediately draw up visions of torture, while "drank my blood" (line 73) implies the sapping of strength and life force—both adding to the inner turmoil of the daughter. The frequent use of black in "Daddy" to describe the father and his effects conjures a powerful feeling of evil, darkness, and cruelty; we encounter a black shoe, a black swastika, a black man (the devil), a black telephone, and a fat black heart. Furthermore, images of the grave, the devil, the vampire, and worms all relate to the theme of death and the otherworld. In essence, the extended metaphor of the poem incorporates many of Sylvia Plath's dominant themes enhanced by potent imagery.

Sylvia Plath molded the content of "Daddy" into sixteen, five-line stanzas. 14 Plath herself called it a piece of "light verse," a term which "becomes clearer if we consider the theory of light verse held by W. H. Auden (Aird 81). Auden sees light verse as an attribute of form, not subject matter. In this way, the choppy, conversational swing of the poem, with its direct address to "Daddy" and its simple, sometimes colloquial vocabulary, earns the poem the label "light verse" (Aird 83). The tone changes with the ebb and flow of the daughter's passion. In the beginning she is sentimental about childhood and distraught at her abandoned state. In the middle she wavers between love and hate of her father. At the end she assumes an almost amused, angry sarcasm as she repudiates the father's image. However, throughout the piece, Plath maintains a certain impersonality, since the girl in the poem is struggling to rid herself of these paralyzing emotions. Thus "Daddy" contains the detached attitude of self-examination found in many of Sylvia Plath's other poems.

"Lady Lazarus," another *Ariel* poem written shortly after "Daddy," has that 15 same impersonality of tone set against dramatic content. Plath paints a picture of a woman who is reborn after death and to whom "dying / Is an art like everything else." In the words of Eileen Aird, "the poet again equates her suffering with the experiences of the tortured Jews." Her fascination with death includes images of Nazis, doctors, and power—a curious power over the watching spectators and over men: "I rise with my red hair / And I eat men like air."

Several of the last poems dwell on the subject of death, but in the last week 16 of her life, Sylvia Plath "moved away from an anguished contemplation of the suffering of living to a concentration on the peace of death" (Aird 86). In "Edge," for instance, the woman attains peace with nature and herself by stepping over the edge into death: "The woman is perfected. / Her dead / Body wears the smile of accomplishment." She gathers her dead children "into her body as petals / Of a rose close" when night falls onto the garden like death falls onto the woman. Perhaps in her own life, Plath used similar reasoning to resolve her problems with depression, paternal obsession, and daily pressures. She resolved her situation in favor of death by placing her head in a gas oven in February of 1963.

Although Sylvia Plath's life ended in an expression of desperation, her 17 creative expression during life showed a wealth of experience, emotion, and energy directed at discovering the mysteries of the outer world and the inner self. Through her craft, she created something fresh and original to add to the world—something many wish to accomplish. Even though her problems overcame her, she endures in her poetry, in its riveting subject matter and intricate imagery. Sylvia Plath would be glad to know that she did not live in vain.

Works Cited

Aird, Eileen M. *Sylvia Plath*. New York: Harper, 1973.
Ames, Lois. Biographical Note. *The Bell Jar*. By Sylvia Plath. New York: Harper, 1971.
Plath, Sylvia. *The Collected Poems*. Ed. Ted Hughes. New York: Harper, 1981.
Plath, Sylvia. *The Journals of Sylvia Plath*. New York: Dial Press, 1982.
Salop, Lynne. *Suisong*. New York: Vantage Press, 1978.

QUESTIONS FOR READING AND REVISING

1. What is the *thesis*—the controlling idea—of Monika Jerabek's essay? Where does she state it most explicitly?

2. What assumptions does Jerabek make about her readers' familiarity with Sylvia Plath's poetry? In this respect, approximately what percentage of Jerabek's essay is devoted to paraphrase? To direct quotation?

3. Outline the major points of Jerabek's analysis. Show how each paragraph supports and extends her thesis. What principal themes in Plath's poetry does Jerabek analyze? Where—and how—is each principal theme introduced into the essay? Consider, for example, the theme of nature in paragraph 5. How does Jerabek connect her discussion of this theme to the controlling idea of her father's image? Could the section on nature be eliminated from the essay? Why? Why not? Consider paragraph 8 on her father's "more public, political side." Explain how this paragraph is related to the controlling idea in the essay and why it should/should not be retained in any new draft Jerabek might write.

4. How does Jerabek organize ideas about Plath's poetry: From simple to complex? From Plath's first book of poems to her last? According to some other principle of organization? Explain with specific examples.

5. Jerabek notes that in preparing this essay, "I had to work out transitional problems—between specific points and their relevance to the central topic. . . . Throughout the writing of my paper, I tried to aim for cohesiveness and a flow of ideas." Examine carefully the *transitions* Jerabek develops from one major point to the next and from one paragraph to the next. What specific compositional devices does she use to create effective transitions?

6. Identify the strengths of Jerabek's literary analysis. Where does she draw on evidence from Plath's poems most effectively to support the points she makes? What other strategies does she use? Where—and how—for example, does Jerabek effectively work into her paragraphs the response of other readers of Plath's poetry?

7. Monika Jerabek effectively blends informative biographical details into her essay. Consider paragraph 2 where she notes that Plath's father was "a professor of biology and an authority on bees," that "he died after a long illness," and that Plath tried to commit suicide at twenty "by taking fifty sleeping pills after visiting her father's grave." Point to other examples of Jerabek's inclusion of useful biographical information to support her reading of Plath's poems.

8. In what specific ways does Jerabek reveal her own attitude toward Plath's poetry? Where does she state it, either directly or indirectly? Which part of speech—verbs, adjectives, or adverbs—does she rely on to express her attitude and to voice her own response to Plath's poems?

9. Monika Jerabek reports that she prepared two drafts of her essay. Here are the opening sentences of the first draft:

> In the quest for self-expression, few people have had the intensity of motivation and ambition of Sylvia Plath. As a poet, she examines life through the windows of nature, personal experience, and dramatic situations, seeking to satisfy the senses and vent her emotions. Most would find her poetry rather graphic, blunt or morbid, but in the interweaving of words and images, comparison and metaphor, her central themes of death, nature, childhood, and suicide, for example, come alive to the reader in new perspectives. One of Sylvia Plath's main themes, the portrayal of the father figure, extends throughout her work and incorporates the autobiographical with the other themes.

What specific differences in Jerabek's opening do you notice between the first and second drafts? What specific qualities make one version more effective than the other? Explain.

SUGGESTIONS FOR WRITING

1. A teenager's perception of his or her father can often be quite complex, fluctuating greatly from one year to the next and from one situation to the next. Consider, for example, Mark Twain's comic remark about his relationship with his father: "When I was a boy of fourteen, my father was so ignorant I could hardly stand to have the old man around. But when I got to be twenty-one, I

was astonished at how much he had learned in seven years." Consider your relationship with your father. Write an essay in which you contrast your understanding of your father when you were a child to your current perception of him. Specifically, how has your perception changed? With what effects? Support your thesis with specific examples.

2. In her essay, Monika Jerabek analyzes the image of the father in Sylvia Plath's poetry. In his essay "Of the Affection of Fathers for Their Children," Michel de Montaigne (1533–1592) offers another view of the relationship between fathers and children. Read carefully the following passage from Montaigne's essay:

> A true and well-regulated affection should be born and increase with the knowledge children give us of themselves; and then, if they are worthy of it, the natural propensity going along with reason, we should cherish them with a truly paternal love; and we should likewise pass judgment on them if they are otherwise, always submitting to reason, notwithstanding the force of nature. It is very often the reverse, and most commonly we feel more excited over the stamping, the games, and the infantile tricks of our children than we do later over their grown-up actions, as if we loved them for our pastime, like monkeys, not like men.

After you have read the passage and feel that you understand its meaning, prepare an essay in which you draw on your own experience with your father to support—or challenge—the wisdom and the accuracy of Montaigne's observation.

EARNESTINE JOHNSON

George Mason University
Fairfax, Virginia
Lois Cucullu, instructor

Earnestine Johnson's advice to first-year students interested in improving their writing is to "read as much and as often as possible." Her earliest recollections of her own childhood reading include "my mother's telling me stories at bedtime about Brer Rabbit and Brer Fox. Even though my mother never went beyond the second grade, I never tired of listening to her versions of those stories. I remember to this day the way she made those stories real for me. As a result of that enjoyment I read as much as possible." Johnson was born in Williamsburg, South Carolina, and raised in Philadelphia, where she worked as a volunteer in a local hospital (including reading to patients) while studying at John Bartram High School. After graduating, she settled in Woodbridge, Virginia, and enrolled at George Mason University. Her academic interests include the humanities and the social sciences. She plans to pursue a career in social work, her college major.

Asked to write a three- to five-page paper responding to Alice Walker's The Color Purple, *Johnson discovered in that book "an example of the influence my mother had on my writing." Johnson recognized similarities to the circumstances of her own childhood in the characters and life styles depicted in* The Color Purple. *"The guidance and interpretations of my mother taught me to rise above the circumstances of our life then and now, in my personal life. I wrote the paper because I knew those characters, and it awoke my own lessons of survival."*

Thank You Miss Alice Walker: The Color Purple

I was required to read the book, *The Color Purple*, by my English course 1 professor. I enjoy reading and therefore I did not mind the assignment. I read the first page and closed the book. I was ashamed of the ignorant definitions given to the parts of the body. I was embarrassed by the explicitness of the sex act. I opened and closed the book many times before I could go beyond the first page. But I did read beyond the first page. I understood the lack of communication between Celie and her mother. Celie was fourteen years old and did not understand or appear to know the functions of her body.

A few days after starting to read this book, I was listening to a news report 2 and heard, ". . . ten-year-old mother and baby both doing fine. The young girl and her family did not know she was pregnant until she was ready to give birth, after complaining of severe stomach pains." The newscaster went on to say the authorities were questioning two male acquaintances of the family. Celie's circumstance, like that of the child-mother's, is ageless. Miss Walker, you brought the situation out into the open, awakening my senses. I did not want to see it, read it, feel it, or be a part of it. This was no longer "just a reading assignment." I was enthralled. I had to read on. How else would you shock me, embarrass me, and shame me?

My class is comprised of a mixture of nationalities, but only four of us are   3
black and female. I, embarrassingly, thought of all of them reading the lines of shame and ignorance of my people. I listened as one male classmate disassociated himself from the males in the story. I wondered if it was because the characters were black, or was he so naive that he believed such things did not happen? As a contemporary black female, I have buried the Celies of my past. Then why, Miss Walker, do you awaken those emotions? What do you expect to accomplish by telling me how it was, or is? Why, of all the subjects to write about, do you choose one which hurts me so deeply? I am furious with you.

I knew a lot of Celies in my teenage years. I met a few Sofias. I heard about   4
one or two Shug Averys too. I left them behind along with the old neighborhood. Those encounters were during an impoverished and ignorant period of growth. I chose to forget them. I have grown and expanded from the narrowness of my childhood and developed through the heritage passed on to me. I have also risen through the classes of the ruling society. I speak like them, dress like them, yet I know that I am but a shadow of them.

Miss Walker, I was compelled to go on with the reading of *The Color Purple*.   5
It was the language usage you gave your characters that held my interest this time. My mind's voice spoke the words by Celie so clearly that I could hear Mrs. Brown, from my youth, "Baby, run across to the store. . . ." Sofia became Mama Liz, big boned, dark complected, mammoth breasted, and as stubborn as the day was long, but oh what a heart. She was full of compassion and empathy for all who encountered her. It's the wonderful memories like those that made the reading of your book painful. Celie and Sofia's language was so familiar to me that in spite of the pain, I settled into the good memories the dialogues conjured up. I was also interested in what Nettie had to say, but Nettie's dialogue had connotations of my own language, educated and refined. I heard it every day. It catalyzed no images. But the other characters' dialect brought memories of faces and voices that had long ceased to exist. Those faces had diminished to just a flicker until your book revived them. Those good memories came with the people you portrayed, along with their examples of survival. Some of the people I knew were very much like Shug Avery and many were like Sofia.

Your message was subtle, Miss Walker. Now after the shame, anger, and 6
memories, I continued to read to the end of the story. Your characters came
full circle. They survived. They matured and became wiser from their experiences. You showed me how they accomplished that. Sofia's way was that of
self-reliance and stubbornness. She was not just physically strong, but she had
a strong nature as well. She was also patient and long suffering. I cannot say
that Sofia's way was successful because she lost so much. She lost her husband
and children to another woman. She lost her freedom to the ruling society,
first jail and then to the mayor's family. Shug Avery was independent and
worldly. She learned to stroke the egos of the people she could not easily
maneuver. Shug was a free spirit, her own person. Celie developed and escaped
to a future of her own making by learning another method of survival than
the one she lived. Celie took a portion of Sofia's stubborness and self-reliance
and mixed that with a little of Shug's independence and literally walked with
a survival plan of her own.

I have read your message Miss Walker, and anguished through the learning 7
of it. This teaching of survival will not soon be forgotten because it was too
painful an experience to relearn. It is for the lesson learned that I thank you.

QUESTIONS FOR READING AND REVISING

1. One of the distinguishing features of Earnestine Johnson's essay is her honest
   and intense response to Alice Walker's *The Color Purple*. Reread Johnson's
   essay carefully *aloud*. How would you characterize the sound of her *voice*? Does
   she sound, for example, tough-minded or sentimental, strident or intimidated?
   Young and impetuous, or experienced and worldly? Some combination of these?
   None of them? Do you notice any changes in Johnson's voice as the essay
   proceeds? Support your response with specific words and phrases.

2. At the beginning of paragraphs 6 and 7 Johnson talks about coming to understand Alice Walker's "message" in *The Color Purple*. Based on your reading of
   Johnson's essay only, summarize that "message." With which character in *The
   Color Purple* does she identify? How can you be sure? How did reading Alice
   Walker's novel help Johnson come to terms with—to understand better—her
   own past? What "message" does Johnson's essay offer about the truth of human
   relationships?

3. What recognition prompts Johnson to regard *The Color Purple* as much more
   than "a reading assignment"? What impels her to continue reading the novel
   after her initial reaction to Walker's explicit depiction of sexual experience?

Johnson notes that she "had to read on" and proceeds to address Alice Walker directly: "How else would you shock me, embarrass me, and shame me?" How does the evidence of her essay suggest that Johnson answered her own question? What is "the lesson learned" for which she thanks Alice Walker?

4. Consider Johnson's explanation of the stages in her personal transformation as a result of reading *The Color Purple:* "Upon completing the book, I was able to see the message Ms. Walker conveyed. I found I had a beginning, my anger, a middle, life experiences, and an ending, my expressed gratitude, for my paper." Reread Johnson's essay and identify where each of these three sections begins and ends. List the points Johnson makes in each section.

5. How would you characterize Johnson's relationship with her audience? To what extent does her audience seem to be a presence in her essay? What specific words and phrases can you point to that indicate who Johnson thinks her readers are (their probable level of intelligence, color, age, social and economic class, etc.)? To what extent must Johnson's readers be acquainted with Walker's novel to appreciate each of her points about the book?

6. One of the unusual features of Johnson's essay is her apparent resistance to being specific. She notes that, "being specific . . . was exactly what I was trying to avoid." What do you suspect she hopes to gain by this strategy? What are the advantages and disadvantages of this decision?

7. Johnson explains one of the problems she had writing her essay: "trying to describe the ruling society without actually saying 'white race.' I became so frustrated with the revision of that particular section, I almost gave into being specific. . . . I continued to rework that section until it finally became acceptable to me and with its connotations, understood by others." Reread paragraph 4 and explain with as much detail as possible exactly how Johnson accomplishes her aim. What other moments in the essay can you identify that seem to reflect Johnson's decision to make her points indirectly rather than explicitly? What is the *purpose*—the desired effect—of her resistance to being specific in each instance?

8. Johnson describes the goal of her essay as trying to "induce a sense of empathy with my feelings by the examples I gave." What stylistic strategies does Johnson use to induce empathy in her readers? What exactly are the "examples" she uses? Roughly what percentage of them are drawn from *The Color Purple?* From her own experience?

9. Johnson offers the following advice to her readers: "I would have failed in the writing of my essay if I had to advise the reader how to understand or read what I had written. I will state what I use as a 'rule of thumb': begin reading with an open mind, void of any preconceived ideas. This should allow for the possibility of involvement, and then see what, if anything, has been gained

from the experience." Apply this "rule of thumb" to Johnson's reading of Alice Walker. How well does Johnson's essay satisfy each of the criteria she establishes? Apply this "rule of thumb" to your reading of Johnson's essay. Identify what you have "gained from the experience."

SUGGESTIONS FOR WRITING

1. Discovering books has allowed innumerable readers to explore the life of the mind and discover the self by identifying with the circumstances of literary characters. Richard Wright's autobiography, *Black Boy*, includes the following passage on the transformative power of reading:

> I read Dreiser's *Jennie Gerhardt* and *Sister Carrie* and they revived in me a vivid sense of my mother's suffering; I was overwhelmed. I grew silent, wondering about the life around me. It would have been impossible for me to have told anyone what I derived from these novels, for it was nothing less than life itself. . . . In buoying me up, reading also cast me down, made me see what was possible, what I had missed. My tension returned, new, terrible, bitter, surging, almost too great to be contained. I no longer *felt* that the world about me was hostile, killing; I *knew* it. . . .

   Consider your own experience as a reader. What books have you read that have had a profound effect on your sense of self-identity? Write an expository essay in which you explain how a particular book helped to transform your own sense of who you are.

2. In *Black Boy*, Richard Wright talks about reading as an addiction: "Reading was like a drug, a dope." Consider the nature of this *comparison*. Track out as fully as possible the analogy between reading and taking a drug and write an expository essay in which you develop this analogy between reading and drug addiction.

3. Consider the differences between reading books and watching television as addictions. In what specific ways are these possible "addictions" similar? Different? Write an expository essay in which you *compare and contrast* reading books and watching television as addictive activities.

AMBER KENNISH

New York University
New York, New York
Claire Gleitman, instructor

"*I'll do anything to avoid writing. One of my favorite techniques, especially when avoiding a really difficult assignment, is to tell myself that I shouldn't worry about it because as soon as I really sit down to do some serious writing it will come easily. Sometimes this works; sometimes it doesn't.*" *Asked to write a response to Caroline Bird's frequently reprinted essay, "College Is a Waste of Time and Money," Kennish worked through three drafts, trying "to appeal to my audience through a metaphorical 'boxing match' between my father and me that I thought would be a familiar scene of doubt and anxiety to other people my age."*

Born in Lawrence, Kansas, Amber Kennish grew up in Essex, Connecticut, and graduated from Valley Regional High School in Deep River, where she participated in numerous student organizations and clubs, including the school yearbook, the theater group, and the Connecticut High School Bowl team. A contributor to the school newspaper and literary magazine, Kennish also won awards for excellence in English, history, science, language, and math.

Writing well has figured prominently in Kennish's academic success, and she is quite conscious of the environment in which she feels most comfortable working: "I usually listen to music when I write, because silence only makes distracting thoughts louder. I usually don't work at a desk—I feel too much pressure to write well when I'm sitting at a desk or in a library cubicle, and sometimes my best writing comes from my worst drafts. I usually write in pen because the grating graphite pencils make on the paper annoys and distracts me." At this point in her studies at New York University, she is uncertain about her major, although her plans do include study abroad in her junior year.

Three Rounds with Dad

Armed with Caroline Bird's argument against college education presented in her essay, "College Is a Waste of Time and Money," I challenged my father to three rounds on the issue. He graciously accepted my challenge, and with Bird providing support from my corner, at the sound of the bell I danced into the center of the ring, hoping my father was prepared for a quick defeat.

I did a little footwork around the idea of dropping out of New York University at the semester break in January, stating that I shouldn't be here because I hate school. I followed by explaining that the only reason I had always done so well in high school was because it seemed to me that the only way to "get back" at school and the nuisance it was to me would be to do really well with whatever they tried to challenge me with. I had hoped this would annoy him into taking a swing at me. Unfortunately, it seemed to have little effect, so I stopped, put my hands on my hips, looked him straight in the eye, and defiantly declared that I wanted to support myself. This stunned him a bit, so I seized this opportunity to hit him hard with the idea that I planned to move to North Carolina, become a waitress in the sleaziest diner I could find, and live happily ever after in a leaky mobile home. Seeing him waver, I followed with Bird's best punch—I was only in college because it was expected of me, having graduated second in my high school class. My father gave the appearance of weakening, but I didn't let up. Next was a blow to the wallet, with which I informed him that I was only wasting his money because I didn't know what I wanted to get out of school.

The bell ending Round 1 sounded, and I, having brought forth every valid 3 point in Bird's essay, retired to my corner and to pats on the back from Bird. I confidently awaited Round 2 and the possibility (slim though it was) of a rebuttal from my father.

Rrrring! My father came out fighting with the premise that while Bird refers 4 to a college degree as an "empty credential," due to the fact that much of a college education may never be utilized, it is still a worthy credential to have. I countered with a quick jab, "Why?" Not fazed by my speed and agility, Dad countered by boxing my ears with the fact that Americans today place an enormous amount of emphasis on a college education, and a degree even in something as "impractical" as a liberal arts subject would grant me the diploma that could make all the difference in the tough competition of today's job market. The realization that an employer, faced with a choice, will hire a person with a college degree over the nondegreed applicant left the taste of blood bubbling in my nose and mouth.

My ears still ringing from this blow to my reason, I felt a sharp pain in my 5 chest. I realized that this pain came from my heart, following my father's paraphrase punch borrowed from essayist Newman, "Knowledge for the sake of knowledge." A series of quick punches to the chest brought home the fact that I needn't necessarily attend college for a practical purpose. Another blow told me that to rush through college in pursuit of the "good job" a diploma is supposed to guarantee is wrong—"Learning is the key"—and I knew he was right, as the red acceptance of his argument trickled from the corner of my mouth.

Suddenly, a blow to the gut knocked the wind out of me. My legs weakened 6 under me as my father hit me with the fact that I may never get another chance to go to college. Bird yelled from outside the ropes, "But college is really just a holding pen for eighteen- to twenty-two-year-olds because society does not know what to do with them!!" I lamely hurled this retort at my father, who said that, while most college freshmen are in this age group, it is often because that it is the only time in their lives in which they are not tied down to a family or job—they are responsible only for themselves—and this gives them the freedom to put the time into college that it needs to pay off. College requires time to do an enormous amount of work, time that might not be so easily found at any other point in life.

Luckily, the bell ending the second round rang, and I retreated to my corner 7 bleeding badly. Bird appeared with a rag to wipe away the sweat and blood from my face, but I pushed her away, preferring to let the blood run out of my mouth and nose and onto the mat, for all to see. Through the sweat streaming into my eyes, I stared intently at my father, who appeared not to be hurting at all. As the bell beginning the third round clanged, I wiped some blood off my face and onto the back of my hand. I went to the center of the ring, bruised and near-beaten, to receive my father's final point.

And a pithy point it was for me. I felt my head throbbing to the rhythm 8 of my father's speech. "College will teach you to inquire, to become a questioning, alert member of society." His words pummeled me as I struggled for support from the ropes. "College offers the serious student the chance to move not only in a linear fashion through life, but to expand himself laterally at the same time by learning about different cultures, art forms, and history." I felt lightheaded, I stumbled. My world began to darken as he spoke of sight. "College offers exposure to many aspects of society that might be otherwise overlooked by less educated people. If nothing else, it is this exposure and sight into human nature and society as a whole that makes higher education worthwhile." I slumped to the mat in defeat. I looked up at my father through eyes filled with sweat and admiration. Out of the corner of my eye I saw Bird sulkily slink into the shadows, out of my sight. My father didn't seem to have a scratch on his body, and when he bent down his words washed over me. The smile on his lips was the last thing I saw as he said, "That hurt me more than it did you." I chuckled, content with my injuries, and closed my swollen eyes.

QUESTIONS FOR READING AND REVISING

1. Amber Kennish creates an *analogy* between boxing and arguing with her father. Identify the major points of her analogy. How well does she introduce—and develop—each of these points? How appropriate do you think this *comparison* is to her subject? Explain.

2. Analyze how Kennish is able to make her essay sound reasonable and believable while developing her analogy. What does Kennish assume is her audience's *point of view* on the issue she argues about?

3. Kennish's essay is based on Caroline Bird's "College Is a Waste of Time and Money." Where in her essay does Kennish rely on Bird's essay to support her own *argument*? How effectively does Kennish draw on Bird's ideas? What specific suggestions would you offer Kennish to strengthen her essay in this respect?

4. Summarize the points Kennish's father makes in rebuttal. What tactic does he use to counter his daughter's argument? Which of his points seems to have the most effect on Kennish? Why? Before the end of the "fight," when does Kennish consider "throwing in the towel?" Why doesn't she?

5. One of the strengths of Kennish's essay is her use of colloquial expressions from the world of boxing to reinforce the points she makes. See, for example, the beginning of paragraph 2, where she reports that she "did a little footwork around the idea of dropping out of New York University." Make a list of other similar words and phrases and comment on how effectively she uses each. What general colloquial expressions does she use in the essay? With what effect?

6. Reread paragraph 7. What is the major point Kennish makes in this paragraph? What is the significance of her refusal to let Caroline Bird help her at the end of the second round? How does this decision reinforce that major point?

7. Reconsider Kennish's final paragraph. What is the liberal significance of her father's final comment: "That hurt me more than it did you?" What is its metaphorical significance? Why does Kennish end her essay by "chuckling?" Why do you think she is "content" with her injuries?

8. In discussing her essay, Kennish noted: "I hope that my audience, after reading my essay, would feel that a college education is a worthwhile investment of both time and money." How would you respond to her statement? What additional points would you make to reinforce—or to challenge—her argument?

SUGGESTIONS FOR WRITING

1. Amber Kennish creates an *analogy* between boxing and debating with her father on the merits of a college education. Write an essay in which you develop a similar analogy to argue about a subject that interests you. This debate could focus, for example, on such issues as banning fraternities and sororities from campus or eliminating scholarships from intercollegiate athletics.

2. Kennish's essay is a response to Caroline Bird's essay, "College Is a Waste of Time and Money." Think of an essay you have read recently whose ideas you would like to refute. Write an argumentative essay in which you present the

essay's ideas and then argue against them. Integrate references from the essay you've read into your essay.

3. Kennish's essay argues for the value of an education. Write an expository essay in which you explain what it means to be educated. Your emphasis in this essay should be on explaining what it means to be educated, not on arguing on behalf of the value of an education.

KAREN L. KRAMER

University of Nebraska—Lincoln
Lincoln, Nebraska
Joan Griffin, instructor

"If someone walked into my room while I was trying to get started, I would probably shut off my typewriter and talk to that person for an hour or so about anything and everything except my paper. But let's suppose the person is invisible, or observing me through a one-way mirror or some such thing. They would see me sit down at the typewriter, turn it on, stare at it for a minute, and then turn it off again, get up, pace around the room, return to the typewriter, turn it back on again, line up the paper, turn the typewriter off, pace around the room, sit back down again, turn it on again, type maybe a paragraph, read it, out loud of course, decide that it stinks, yank the paper out and throw it away, put in a new sheet and then just start typing away."

Karen Kramer's description of her own writing habits seems very much in keeping with her general level of energy and accomplishment. A graduate of Daniel J. Gross High School in Omaha, Nebraska, Kramer's extracurricular activities there included playing in the "concert band, pep band, stage band, musical, and dixieland band," as well as writing copy for the yearbook. In her junior and senior years, she was selected for the All-State Band, ranked fourth in her class academically, was elected salutatorian by her classmates, and was chosen to be a member of the All-State Academic Team. A Regents and National Merit Scholarship winner at the University of Nebraska at Lincoln, Kramer continues to develop her interest in music by playing in various bands both within the university and outside it. She plays the trombone and piano, sings, enjoys drawing, and occasionally works with sculpture and computers. While at school, she has also worked part-time at, among other jobs, her dormitory food service, Ponderosa steakhouses, and a local Burger King. She plans to major in English but is uncertain about her career goals.

Asked by her instructor to write a comparison and contrast essay, Karen Kramer decided to write about her high school band experiences. "My years in band in high school inspired me to write my essay. . . . Music was my life then. I had ample opportunity to observe my fellow musicians. Hence, I wrote about them." As to her purpose in writing "The Little Drummer Boys," Kramer quickly adds: "The goal of my essay was to have fun, pure and simple. No earth-shattering messages here."

The Little Drummer Boys

Quick—what do you call a person who plays the trumpet? A trumpeter, of 1 course. A person who plays the flute is referred to as a flutist, or flautist, if you prefer. Someone who plays a piano is usually known as a pianist, unless of course he plays the player piano, in which case he is known as a player piano player rather than a player piano pianist. Got the hang of this yet? Okay, then what do you call someone who plays that set of instruments belonging to the percussion family? Why, you call him a percussionist, don't you? Wrong! It's not quite as easy as all that. There are two types of musicians who play percussion instruments, "drummers" and "percussionists," and they are as different as Quiet Riot and the New York Philharmonic.

You can find an initial difference even in the very names of the percussion-   2
playing musicians. If you called a percussionist a drummer, he would be highly insulted. If you called a drummer a percussionist, he wouldn't know what you were talking about. The two don't really think much of each other. Percussionists generally consider drummers to be what can only be described as "the scum of the earth," two million years behind the rest of mankind in the evolutionary process. Drummers, on the other hand, consider percussionists to be weak, boring, effeminate individuals with questionable sexual preferences. The differences don't end there.

Take the drummers, for example. It is their belief that all drums have to   3
come welded together in a set, not unlike Siamese twins. As for other pieces of drum equipment, cymbals are all to come perched atop a stand and are to be smashed with a stick and never hand-held and clashed together. Cymbals do not ever come in pairs, except for the high hat. Triangles, sleigh bells, woodblocks, etc., are for second-grade rhythm bands, not drummers. As for kettle drums, as far as the drummer is concerned, they're used for boiling water. The xylophone is merely a word in an A-B-C book. Nobody actually plays any of those things professionally.

At least, no self-respecting drummer would because after all, drummers are   4
cool. Some drummers are so cool, they act as though they're on drugs. Some drummers are on drugs. Regardless of the latter fact, most drummers are very cool, hep, and laid-back kind of guys, you dig? Except, of course, for when they play. It is then that the drummer lets the rabid, primordial Neanderthal that lurks just beneath the surface take complete control of his very being. When performing, the drummer throws his head around as though he were trying to toss it from his shoulders. Sweating profusely, his face twisted into a veritable mask of anguished, tormentuous pain, he looks not unlike a mother-to-be who has been in labor for over nine hours. By the time a drummer finishes a solo, he looks as though he had just come in last in the Boston Marathon. Yet it is this very selfsame animalistic behavior that gives the drummer his appeal to the masses. Almost everybody loves the drummer. Women love him because sweaty, hirsute, muscular guys in torn T-shirts are macho. Men respect drummers, too. Not-so-scientific research has found that deep down within every male of the human species there is a burning desire

to beat the hell out of a trap set, and thus men respect those members of their sex who can do that and get paid besides.

Drummers aren't popular with everyone, however. There are those directors 5 and conductors who expect drummers to play slowly or quietly or even— heaven forbid—with a little class. Needless to say, drummers and conductors do not get along, but this is inevitable. The art of drumming requires a total lack of self-control, whereas the conductor is actually trying to impose behavioral controls on the drummer, which naturally leads to confrontation. One simply should not try to rein in a wild, crazy, drugged-out individual who behaves as though he were raised by gorillas.

Percussionist are on the completely opposite end of the spectrum. Percus- 6 sionists always get along with their directors, as they respect them and bend over backward to follow them and cooperate. Percussionists are *not* cool. Rather, they are very clean-cut, square, straightforward individuals. Their hair is always short and neat. Instead of the sweaty muscle T-shirt of the drummer, the percussionist wears a dress shirt, sweater, and sometimes even a tie. Percussionists don't even know what drugs are. On the contrary, percussionists don't drink or smoke, and they make a habit of attending church services regularly. They're the basic Oral Roberts type.

Thus, percussionists don't enjoy the wide popularity of drummers. It's not 7 that people particularly dislike them. It's just that they don't particularly like them, either. Percussionists are somewhat lacking in personality. They're rather bland, not unlike oatmeal or unflavored soda water. They only become somewhat animated when performing.

Whereas the drummer is merely interested in creating as much noise as 8 possible, music in the true sense of the word is of importance to the percussionist. Whether it be a well-placed cymbal crash or a tiny "ting" on the triangle, the percussionist, with utmost precision, makes the most of it without overpowering the ensemble with which he happens to be playing. His face a mask of concentration, the percussionist's eyes bug out as he stares steadily at his lord and master, the conductor. With moves as sharp, quick, and accurate as a frog nabbing flies, the percussionist tings a triangle, whirls to whap a wood block, and with one deft, lightning-swift move, silently drops everything and seizes a pair of mallets with which he gives the tympani a resounding thump to precisely fill the gap in the music. Percussionists, who are able to create the sound illusion of a trotting horse or a babbling brook, are as subtle as a morning breeze blowing across the dew-covered grass, whereas drummers, who do their best to create the illusion of an artillery barrage, are about as subtle as a panzer division smashing through the concert hall. No one notices a percussion section. They complement the band. Drummers *are* the band as far as they are concerned. Such an attitude would appear egotistical and uncouth to a percussionist but would seem perfectly natural to a drummer.

Drummers and percussionists do have one thing in common. They both are 9 in love with their equipment. Tenderly they fondle the drumheads, cymbals, and all of their sticks, brushes, and mallets; a pair for each day of the week. They let nothing come between themselves and their equipment and woe unto the ambitious unassuming amateur who dares to sacrilegiously set sticks to the "skins" or sets of the devoted drummer or perniciously protective percussionist. Such an act is sure to ruffle the feathers of even the least temperamental drummer or percussionist.

Another sure way to ruffle them is to call a drummer a "percussionist" or a 10 percussionist a "drummer." After all, there should be no excuse for this since it is apparent that the two are as different as a piccolo and a tuba. So when addressing a player of a percussion instrument, be sure to get his name right, or at least apologize profusely for getting it wrong. Then, he'll smile at you—parum-pa-pum-pum. He and his drum.

QUESTIONS FOR READING AND REVISING

1. Karen Kramer was asked to write a *comparison and contrast* essay. List all the points Kramer makes about percussionists. How do percussionists differ from drummers? Show how Kramer organizes these points. Does she proceed point by point? Subject by subject? Some combination of the two? Support your response with detailed references to her essay.

2. Characterize Kramer's *point of view* in this essay. Is she detached and objective? Involved and subjective? Some other combination? Support your response with an analysis of specific words and phrases from the essay. What is her attitude toward percussionists? Toward drummers? When is each attitude first expressed? Which group does Kramer seem to favor by the end of her essay? Why? Having read her essay, explain why you agree or disagree with her conclusions.

3. Karen Kramer explains her *purpose* in writing this essay in the following terms: "What I really want is for the readers to enjoy themselves and have a good laugh or at least a slight chuckle. I'd even settle for a warm smile, or a raise of the eyebrow." How would you describe "the readers" Kramer seems to have in mind here? How familiar does she assume her *audience* is with her subject? How familiar need they be? Describe—specifically—the features of Kramer's humorous essay that make it successful.

4. Make a list of as many of the *similes* and *metaphors* Kramer uses in this essay as you can. Which seem especially effective? Why? When asked to clarify how

she intended to appeal to her readers, Kramer replied: "I appeal to the reader by using incongruous comparisons, such as that of a drummer with a Neanderthal, etc. I exaggerate like crazy, because I feel that one aspect of humor is exaggeration." Identify the moments in her essay that are marked by exaggeration and comment on the effectiveness of each.

5. Kramer has an eye for useful detail. Identify as many details as possible. What does each contribute to the sentence in which it appears? To the essay as a whole? How does Kramer's use of detail support her humorous intentions as well as some purpose beyond being humorous? What, in your judgment, might this larger purpose be? Is this essay finally about naming people? Naming things? Some combination of the two? Explain.

6. How would you describe Kramer's *tone* in this essay? What specific strategies does she use to maintain that tone, or does it change as she proceeds in the essay? Comment on Kramer's *diction*. Is it primarily informal or colloquial? Point to specific examples where Kramer has fun playing with the conventional meaning of words and phrases.

7. When describing her methods as a writer, Kramer noted: "The most difficult thing about writing a first draft is thinking of a beginning and a conclusion. I cannot begin writing from anywhere except the beginning. Some people can write the body and then tack on an intro when they're finished. I cannot. I may have the whole body written word for word in my head, but I haven't thought of a snappy intro yet, I can't type one word of it." Consider Kramer's first draft of her opening paragraph:

> Quick—what do you call someone who plays the trumpet? A trumpeter, of course. A person who plays the flute is referred to as a flutist, or flautist, if you prefer. Someone who plays a piano is usually known as a pianist, unless of course he plays the player piano, in which case he is known as a player piano player rather than a player piano pianist. Got the hang of this yet? Okay, then what do you call someone who plays that set of instruments belonging to the percussion family. Why, you call him a percussionist, don't you? Wrong! It's not quite as easy as all that. There are two types of musicians who play percussion instruments, "drummers" and "percussionists," and they are as different as Quiet Riot and the New York Philharmonic.

What changes did Karen Kramer make as she moved from her first to her final draft? Explain the appropriateness—and the effectiveness—of each.

8. When reviewing the procedures she follows in revising an essay, Kramer observed: "I read the paper *out loud*. This is very important. I could read a paper a hundred times to myself and never catch something, but if I read it out loud,

I'll catch it. Sometimes you have to actually *hear* what you wrote before you realize that it sounds like something a fourth-grader wrote. So, I read it out loud, and I change what doesn't sound right. Clumsily constructed sentences, weak words, questionable modifiers, etc. all come to light when I read it and then I correct them." Keeping in mind the criteria Kramer establishes in the last sentence of this quotation, reread this draft *aloud.* If she had an opportunity to revise her essay, what recommendations for revision would you offer her? Why?

SUGGESTIONS FOR WRITING

1. What kind of music do you most enjoy listening to? Who are some of the most respected artists who compose and/or play that music? Write an essay in which you *compare and contrast* the respective styles of these two musicians in performance. If you most enjoy listening to rock and roll, for example, you might want to compare and contrast the musical styles of Elvis Presley and Bruce Springsteen. If classical music interests you more, you might prefer to look at the styles of violinists such as Itzhak Perlman and Isaac Stern.

2. One of the reasons Kramer's essay is successful is that she takes a relatively familiar experience (listening to a drummer and a percussionist) and exaggerates it, both to make a point and to make a lively, amusing essay. Yet Kramer does not exaggerate the differences beyond recognition. In fact, we appreciate her essay all the more because of her effective control of exaggeration. Consider a familiar experience that might be exaggerated in a similar fashion to make a point: preparing for your first date with someone; studying for final exams as opposed to quizzes; taking the road test for your driver's license. Write an account of what happened, playfully exaggerating to make a point.

3. Musicians are often asked to create *similes* to describe their compositional methods. Here are two rather celebrated, if somewhat indecorous, responses: "I produce music as an apple-tree produces apples"—Camille Saint-Saëns (1835–1921); "I write [music] as a sow piddles"—Wolfgang Amadeus Mozart (1756–1791). Here is another, somewhat more dignified comparison: "[Claude] Debussy is like a painter who looks at his canvas to see what more he can take out; [Richard] Strauss is like a painter who has covered every inch and then takes the point he has left and throws it at the canvas"—Ernest Bloch. Analyze your method of writing and write an essay in which you explain your methods in terms of an analogy.

LINDA LAVELLE

Harrisburg Area Community College
Harrisburg, Pennsylvania
Edward McCarthy, instructor

Linda Lavelle appreciates the patience and effort needed to write well. She also trusts herself as a writer. Assigned a topic, she is confident that "an idea will come to mind immediately. What works best for me is to let that idea rattle around in my head for a few days until a few key phrases or sentences develop. With those few key phrases in mind, I can sit down to write and come up with something that resembles a first draft." Yet, as she explains, moving beyond that first draft proves to be the most frustrating aspect of writing for her: "My first draft usually ends up a chaotic stream of ideas. Organizing this mess into a second draft is the most difficult phase." Given this tendency, Linda Lavelle tries to leave little to chance and prepares for long sessions when she works on her essays. She equips herself with, as she notes, "cigarettes, coffee, crackers, and a favorite pen. I also have my dictionaries, a reference manual, and my notes, which consist mostly of those few key phrases."

Amid what she describes as a "mess" of "books and papers scattered on the table," Linda Lavelle sits "gulping coffee, chain smoking, crumpling papers, and (so I am told) making faces, twirling my hair, and talking to myself." This scene often yields to another, one in which Lavelle can be seen "tapping my pen on the dictionary, staring into space for long stretches of time. This is followed by bouts of frantic writing."

Linda Lavelle works hard at her writing, a skill she has been practicing since childhood. "I started making up stories and poems when I was about three years old. By the time I was nine or ten I had started putting them down on paper and dreaming of being a writer." Lavelle describes herself as having led a rather "unconventional" childhood and adolescence: "As a child I traveled frequently, living in many different places, with many different families, and was therefore exposed to a wide variety of lifestyles and philosophies. As a writer this gives me a great deal of experience to draw on. . . . Yet I believe my writing has been most influenced by the people and places of Philadelphia." Born there, Lavelle graduated from that city's Frankford High School. She has worked as a "gofer" in a playhouse, a waitress, and in electronics. She currently divides her time among her family, her work, and her studies. She plans to major in English or journalism and hopes to write professionally.

Asked to write an essay using personal experience as the basis for a commentary on a contemporary social issue or national problem, Lavelle turned to her "own postponed goals as an example." She set out to "show that blue-collar workers are not necessarily illiterate or lacking in ambition. I wanted the reader to remember to view people as individuals, not write them off as a group. . . . My goal was to show that people who work in factories are not mindless machines, just trapped by them."

Confessions of a Blue-Collar Worker

The large brick building was a factory that made circuit breakers. There 1
were assembly lines, spot welding machines, riveting machines, and hundreds
of people handling the same small parts over and over. There were several of
us naive eighteen-year-olds who, courtesy of thoughtful relatives, entered the
world of concrete and noise that day. This was a place where youth had an
advantage. It was bonus work, and we couldn't believe it was possible to earn
so much money for performing such simple tasks.

As the weeks passed, and the overwhelming boredom set in, we began to 2
realize what we were really being paid for. Forty hours a week, while our hands
moved with lightning speed, our minds were free—to wander, to dwell on
problems, to rot. We were being subjected to a form of mental torture—for a
paycheck. Still, we were not discouraged because most of us planned to make
it a temporary stay. I, for one, had my future mapped out: work for a year,
buy a new car, fatten my bank account, then join VISTA (the application
was safely tucked away in my desk drawer), and later start college. My plans
had not allowed for getting caught in the quicksand of money and machinery.

A year passed, and another, and another. We were all still there, still 3
planning to leave. Only now we looked differently at the young women, always
on the verge of divorce, popping their valium, while the life was slowly sucked
out of them with each movement of the assembly line. We looked differently
too at the old ladies with knotted hands and varicose veins who were struggling
to keep pace. It became frightening to realize these stoop-shouldered old ladies
with the bitter smiles had once been young and full of dreams. We looked
into their empty eyes and saw the ghost of things to come.

I lost my VISTA application, but I did acquire my new car, and another, 4
and a houseful of furniture—not to mention the house and husband. I applied
and was hired for more dignified positions, but I always changed my mind. I
just couldn't walk away from the high pay and good benefits. So I continued
to fill circuit breakers with little parts as the assembly line moved on.

Like many of the others, I tried to continue my formal education. And like 5
those others, in the face of frustration and fatigue, I finally gave up. At the
same time my *informal* education flourished beneath the fluorescent lighting,
although the knowledge I was acquiring wasn't taught in any classroom or
found in any text. I studied business up close. I learned the intricacies of the
numbers operations and the going price of stolen goods. I learned how management and unions function on the intimidation of workers, and how to fight
for rights against both of them.

I met people who taught me volumes about human behavior. I saw people 6
take amphetamines to keep up with ever-rising production rates. I saw good
friends, and even relatives, physically attack each other over job assignments
that would mean a few cents' difference. I observed women cheating on their
husbands and men cheating on their wives. I watched women hand over their
entire paycheck to a bookie. I saw pregnant women, their feet too swollen for
shoes, come to work in slippers. I saw women with colds stuff pieces of tissue
up their nostrils so they wouldn't have to keep stopping to blow their nose.

I even studied a new language—"Shop Talk"—which consists of insults and 7
profanities shouted by supervisors and workers at each other. Fluency in this
language is essential to blue-collar work, as the need for it occurs frequently.
I had lessons in vocabulary as well. I learned the definitions of obscenities I
had never even heard before. And while the words "self respect" were being
driven from my vocabulary, the definition of dehumanization was being driven
home each day. I learned the meaning of many words, like humiliation, when
I heard two foremen referring to their workers as "the stupid whores."

In time all the vulgarities became part of the scenery, like the peeling paint 8
on the machines or the faded partitions that covered the windows. And when,
six years after that first day, I climbed out of the quagmire to ring out my time
card for the last time, I had learned the value of a good sense of humor. We
had laughed a great deal. We joked about our "prison uniforms" and being
replaced by chimpanzees. We joked that some people pay large sums of money
to have their fingerprints removed while we were having it done for free. We
laughed about our "fringe benefits," like being able to buy "hot items" on our
breaks. We laughed at so many things that weren't funny. We laughed at the
office workers, with their small paychecks, who looked down their prissy noses
at us. We laughed, but we always glanced at our calloused fingers and knew
that we were becoming something less than human beings.

QUESTIONS FOR READING AND REVISING

1. Linda Lavelle's announced *purpose* in writing this essay is "to show that people
   who work in factories are not mindless machines, just trapped by them." Reread
   her essay carefully. What specific points does she make to *illustrate* and underscore this idea?

2. From what *point of view* does Lavelle recount the events in this essay? Where
   is that point of view first established? Show how this point of view remains

consistent—or changes—as the essay proceeds. Lavelle's essay occasionally shifts between "I" and "we." Who are the people Lavelle associates with this "we"? Whom does she exclude?

3. Lavelle observes that "this was a difficult essay for me to write because I was so personally involved with the subject. I knew what I wanted to say, but I just didn't work it out until I used my own experience as the focus—something I really hadn't wanted to do." Consider the way in which Lavelle presents herself and her own experience in this essay. What do we learn about her as the essay develops? What reaction does her self-portrayal elicit in paragraph 4? Does her self-image in this paragraph remain consistent in the paragraphs that follow? If so, what specific writing strategies does she use to sustain it? If not, where and how does the image change?

4. What motivates Lavelle to climb, as she reports in paragraph 8, "out of the quagmire to ring out my time card for the last time"? What is the "mental torture" Lavelle mentions in paragraph 2? What is the significance of the comment in paragraph 8: "I had learned the value of a good sense of humor"?

5. In describing the difficulties she faced in writing this essay, Lavelle notes: "The next problem was to avoid sounding bitter or sarcastic." What specific strategies does Lavelle use to resist lapsing into bitterness and sarcasm? In paragraph 3, she observes: "It became frightening to realize these stoop-shouldered old ladies with the bitter smiles had once been young and full of dreams." How would you characterize the nature of Lavelle's own smiles in this essay?

6. Lavelle takes a fairly familiar topic—the drudgery of working on an assembly line—and offers a reflective view of the limits of that world and her rejection of it. What specific writing strategies does Lavelle use to make her essay fresh? Which paragraph(s) do you find most successful thematically? Stylistically? Why? Point to specific words and phrases to support your response.

7. Reread Lavelle's essay paying special attention to her use of repetition. Consider the verb choices in paragraph 1. What do you notice about them? Show how they strengthen—or undermine—the effect Lavelle aims at creating in this paragraph. Which paragraphs feature repetition of sentence structure? Why? What is the effect of this repetition in each of the paragraphs where it occurs?

8. Lavelle wrote six drafts of her essay. Here is the opening paragraph of her first draft:

> At eighteen, college held no appeal for me, but my marketable skills consisted of youth and a desire to help my fellow man. VISTA was my answer, but before I had completed my application I was told of a job opportunity too good to ignore. My mother, with the best of intentions, pointed out how it would be to my advantage to have a bank account to draw on while I was completing my VISTA

service. Her ideas made sense, so I decided to work for a
year before I went off to live with the Indians.

Here is the opening paragraph from her fifth draft:

> I was not alone when I first set foot in that large brick
> building. There were several of us naive eighteen-year-olds
> who, courtesy of thoughtful relatives, entered a world of
> concrete, dust, and noise that day. This was a place where
> youth had an advantage. It was bonus work, and we couldn't
> believe it was possible to earn so much money for perform-
> ing such simple tasks.

Compare and contrast each of these opening paragraphs. Identify the strengths
of each. What changes in direction and focus does Lavelle make as she moves
from one draft to another? Which version do you prefer? Why? If Lavelle were
revising her essay, what recommendations would you offer? Why?

9. In Lavelle's first draft of her final paragraph, she wrote:

> In time all the vulgarities were just part of the scenery,
> and when, six years after that first day, I rang out my time
> card for good I had learned the value of a sense of humor.
> We had laughed a great deal. We joked about our "prison
> uniforms," and being replaced by chimps. We joked that
> some people pay a great deal of money to have their fin-
> gerprints removed while we were having it done for free.
> We laughed about our "fringe benefits," like being able to
> discount shop on our breaks. We laughed at the office
> workers, with their clean hands and small paychecks, who
> looked down their prissy noses at us. We laughed, but we
> would always look down at our calloused fingers and know
> that we were becoming something less than human beings.

Compare and contrast this ending to Lavelle's final version. What changes has
she made in the final draft? Evaluate the effectiveness of each. What additional
changes, if any, would you recommend? Why?

SUGGESTIONS FOR WRITING

1. In the fourth and fifth paragraphs of her essay, Linda Lavelle recounts the
    conflict she faced as a young adult working in a factory between "high pay and
    good benefits" and the "frustration and fatigue" of the work she faced each day.
    Write an essay in which you *describe* a serious conflict you faced in your own
    experience on the job or in school and explain how you did—or did not—
    succeed in resolving this conflict.

2. Lavelle talks about being humiliated and dehumanized by her experience as a "blue-collar worker" on an assembly line. At the end of her essay, she and her co-workers laugh in ironic awareness of their own calloused fingers. They knew, as Lavelle reports, "that we were becoming something less than human beings." Examine some line of "blue-" or "white-collar" work today that encourages the people who perform it, whether deliberately or not, to regard themselves as "something less than human beings." Write an essay in which you use a detailed *description* of that work to illustrate this idea.

3. The twentieth-century philosopher José Ortega y Gasset once observed that "an unemployed existence is a worse negation of life than death itself. Because to live means to have something definite to do—a mission to fulfill—and in the measure in which we avoid setting our life to something, we make it empty. . . . Human life, by its very nature, has to be dedicated to something." Consider the circumstances of your own life or those of someone whom you know fairly well. Write an essay in which you use that experience to support— or undermine—the validity of Ortega y Gasset's proposition. You might prefer writing an *argumentative* essay in which you endorse—or refute—the accuracy of Ortega y Gasset's proposition. Either way, try to make your personal experience, or that of someone you know, the basic evidence for verifying your contention.

PATRICK KINDER LEWIS

Wheaton College
Wheaton, Illinois
Sharon Ewert, instructor

Patrick Kinder Lewis describes himself as "not a 'reader' in the traditional sense in which writers seem to be. That is not to say I don't read. I read voraciously—I can almost never be caught anywhere without a book in my possession. But the habit is more from a thirst for wisdom than from any learned-pleasure of reading for its own sake. I didn't grow up reading, but thinking and doing instead. . . ." Lewis has spent nearly all of his life on the move. Born in Moses Lake, Washington, Lewis and his twin brother Mike, along with an older and a younger sister, have lived as U.S. Air Force dependents in various parts of the world. A graduate of Kubasaki High School in Okinawa, Japan, Lewis grew up during years of being what he calls a "perennial traveler. I have lived in over a dozen places since I was fifteen and spent two years traveling through the United States."

Lewis's experience on the road prompt him to characterize himself as "a people-oriented philosopher," a phrase he explains in these terms: "My folks have lent me their own brand of stoical toleration mixed with lots of love. From rather obscure sources, both I and my twin have grown into quixotic convention flouters . . . which has led us to the 'existential edge' of our lives more than once." "Five Minutes North of Redding" recounts one such experience.

In writing this essay on hobos and the saving grace of friendship while riding the rails, Lewis hoped "to create the snapshot which I never took of that epiphanic moment" on board a freight train. The lesson of that experience, Lewis suggests, is that "nothing in this life comes cheaply—nothing of value anyway—but none of us pays anywhere near the face-value for what we get either: what we have, we have been given on loan."

For a revised version of Patrick Kinder Lewis's essay, see Part V.

Five Minutes North of Redding

I rolled out of the weeds into the crisp daylight of that late September morning to catch the north train out of Roseville. The herder had said it would leave about 3:00 A.M. so I had huddled in my coat for at least three hours, wishing in the predawn chill for a cup of hot anything. But the noise and lights of the train yard had filtered through the tall grass and disturbed even those harmless dreams.

Finally she came. Forty cars were in sight before the engines passed me. Moving down to the rail bed, I noticed for the first time that I had not slept alone on this stretch of tracks. Three figures were coming down to claim a rail car 150 yards up the line, and even as I cautiously watched them, two other groups of riders were claiming cars behind me. I bounded onto a flatcar, concerned that the line of empties would soon pass me by—then thought again. A solitary presence on that flat deck, instinct shouted within me warnings about such a vulnerable position. I crossed the ten-foot width and dropped down onto the ground on the other side of the car. This time I watched until everyone was on board before I picked out one of the last empty boxcars. And still there were some fifty closed cars behind mine. This train was surely big enough, I imagined, for all of us.

The line of cars came to its first stop on a siding three hours up the Sacramento Valley as we allowed another train to pass. Groves of plum trees lined the track on either side. Even so late in the season, the trees to the train's right were still full of hard purple fruit. I laid down in a splash of sun on the deck of my car. For the first time that morning warm and relaxed, the startling sound of shouts out the east door caused me to retreat into the shadows again. I peered out to find six men playing among the trees like kids as they picked plums only to pelt each other with them. I watched intently, as if it were some elaborate social experiment, until the sound of boots on gravel brought me back around. Looking to the shadow behind me, I suddenly realized that it was too late to conceal myself. The man whose crunching boots had just announced his approach was somehow already at my back door looking me over.

"There you are. I've been lookin' for you. You're travelin' alone ain't you?" All the wrong questions to ask someone who is already scared of you. Luckily the voice betrayed nothing but a desire for friendship.

"That's right, I am. What . . . are you alone, too?" I sized him up coolly as I moved toward my knapsack in the far corner. In its open front pocket I had a knife if I needed it. He had an eight-inch Bowie knife strapped frontier-style to his right shin.

"No. Couple of beaners and me pick up together in Stockton; but they ain't speakin' nothin' but Spanish, man. You want sumpum to eat? They're gettin' some plums. We got cukes and tomatoes still that they picked in the Valley yesterday. And I got a box of saltines in Roseville."

He had a ruddy face that was roughly pocked, probably from adolescence, and a scraggly mustache that only became noticeable when he looked right at you. I had reached my pack, but simply turned toward him in a crouch to look for my next move.

If I planned to turn down his offer, standing four feet up in a boxcar was the time to do it. His bony frame and large hands gave away his height: I would be at a three- to four-inch disadvantage once down on level ground. And he just looked tough. Shoulder-length, muddy blond hair he had tied back with a lace of dark buckskin; it laced the seams of his chamois pants too. (He was fond of buckskin and wore it well.) Very tough but somehow gentle. He seemed all in all an atavism, a confusing mixture of General Custer with a sixties flower child. I decided to trust my second inclination.

"Sounds good," I said closing my pack. "What's your name?" I grabbed my 9 jacket and hopped down onto the loose shale bed. The train was just pulling away with a halting rumble as we neared his car. On quickening our pace, I noticed he was limping from his hip down. I was in the car before him and offered him a hand. But he ignored it and managed an agile roll into the car by catching hold of a break in the floor.

Alex and the Beaners were the first hobos I was to travel with. For the 10 space of a couple days we ate, drank, slept, and fought like brothers. I learned their pasts and their plans in that short time together and laid awake to think what it would be like to live their lives. At one point, left behind by our train somewhere south of Red Bluff, we hiked together most of the way to the next railhead, ducking many a curious sheriff en route. Finally Alex found us a ride out of a truck stop with an ex-Harley biker. Ambling over the gunwales of his pickup, we rode it all the way to Redding.

That night, we caught the last train out still on its dinner break. Ducking 11 into a store nearby, I quickly bought enough sardines, crackers, and canned sausages for ten men. While the train sat idle we found a boxcar that was open only on its east side. (For the cold trip into the mountains ahead, warmth was a more important concern than a view of the scenery to the west.) We had just finished off the sardines as the train at last began to lumber out of the yard. Our bodies exhausted, our hunger at last abated, we sat on the dirty floor of our boxcar enjoying the last warm breath of the evening. We were now at the northernmost end of California's fertile basin. From here on the land would climb more steeply. Only the Sacramento River lay between us and the Cascade mountains. As we approached the trestle, the track took only one slow curve to the northwest. On ahead, I was sure it would begin a series of slow switchbacks to climb Mt. Shasta's side. But for now, because dead ahead, Shasta was out of sight.

I leaned tiredly against the back door and watched as the scene in front of 12 me began to change. Low on the horizon, a nearly full moon was rising slowly to take its place in the center of our stage. Mt. Lassen's distant volcanic head joined it as we rounded the last turn before the river, showing mutely through a carpet of velvet green peaks. Inside the car, Alex stood up to blow the smoke of his cigarette out into the crystal air. He propped himself like a caryatid supporting the right border of our window on the world. My Mexican compadres sat nearly motionless at the door's left side. Mesmerized, I dug blindly into my pack to find the harmonica which I had saved for just such an inspiring moment. I sucked in a chord or two of "This Train Is Bound for Glory," laughing inside. Suddenly, another actor entered from stage left and I came up to a squatting position to get a better vantage. The wild Sacramento below us had begun to snake its way into view, illumined only by the bright moonlight.

It was all I could do to keep from walking out our door onto that stage. 13 Like something from a dream, it seemed too fantastically beautiful to be real. And finally, unexpectedly, the train itself emerged as a player. The trestlework not only poised the line of cars two hundred feet above the river's surface but managed as well to bend it into a slow arc midway in the crossing. The sweep of that northward arc turned our view to the south. And just for that instant both the front and rear of the train were visible at once. The engines at our head disappeared slowly into the shadow of Mt. Shasta while the cars that trailed our coach paraded behind us across the massive trestle. And on it all was poured the stark quiet of the moonlight reflected in the river below.

The trestle, from south to north, could not have been over a mile long. 14 The entire panorama played before us for less than two minutes. Yet, in a very real way, it has run in my mind's eye ever since.

As that team of Southern Pacific diesels pulled us out of Redding, eternity 15 sat captive for a moment. Like a stolen glimpse of childbirth, I shared in that peaceful feeling of something both beginning and ending at once. And like a mother smiling at her child born at last, I found myself smiling with a similar relief. It was joy without euphoria. I hunted again for the insights of the moment before but found them fading with the darkness of the mountains ahead. What race had I run to earn such rest? What was born in that moment? I looked to my companions for an answer but found it instead full-formed in the darkness between us. There was the sudden realization of the only bond that we all shared: our passion for life. We were living life moment by moment. That was our race well run. As our moonlight halos began to fade I picked up my harmonica and found myself playing "Bound for Glory" in a different key.

QUESTIONS FOR READING AND REVISING

1. Patrick Kinder Lewis's essay recounts a youthful adventure "on the rails." How does he organize the story he tells? Is it organized, for example, strictly according to chronology? incident? some other principle? explain. What are its major parts? What is the relation of each part to the whole essay?

2. One of the strengths of Lewis's essay is the presence of an engaging *narrative voice*. How would you characterize the narrator? What information are you using to create this characterization? What does the narrator tell us about himself? In discussing his essay, Lewis notes: "I wanted to explain not only what was going on around me but also what was going on inside the narrator as well." How does the narrator change as the essay develops? What is your attitude toward the narrator? At the end of the essay, how has your attitude changed, if at all? Support your answer with examples from the text.

3. Characterize Lewis's *point of view* in telling this story. Is he involved and sub-jective or detached and objective at the beginning of his essay? Where—and how—does his point of view change as the essay proceeds? Where does Lewis restrict himself to reporting his observations of incidents and where does he allow himself to draw inferences based on those observations? With what effect? Point to specific words and phrases to support your response.

4. In explaining his *purpose* in writing this essay, Patrick Lewis notes: "The ex-perience about which I wrote was a brief but meaningful excerpt from a much longer story I hope to write about learning from life-lived-on-the-edge. 'Five Minutes North of Redding' was in a way the fulfillment of a youthful dream and the beginning of a more mature vision." Locate the moments in this essay that illustrate this point. In the final paragraph when Lewis states: "I hunted again for the insights of the moment before," what, exactly, are the insights he refers to? How does the final paragraph amplify each of them?

5. This essay is rich in detail. Readers can sense the presence of a writer working hard—and consciously so—at *description*. One distinguishing feature of effective description is the use of *concrete*, sensory details. List the instances where Lewis appeals to each of his reader's senses. Another characteristic of effective de-scription is its specificity. Consider paragraph 9, and more particularly, the last three sentences in it. How does the final sentence in the paragraph extend and develop the point made about Alex's "limping from the hip down"? How is Lewis's use of detail in action in this paragraph reinforced at other moments in the essay?

6. In paragraph 12 Lewis develops a compelling image of a "stage." Identify each of the "actors" who play on this "stage." In addition to the individuals and groups you have listed, what additional "actors" does Lewis's drama depend on? Show how the *metaphor* of the stage controls the last several paragraphs of Lewis's essay. What other metaphors can you point to in the essay that further his *purpose*? Support your response with specific words and phrases.

7. Reread the final paragraph of this essay. What does Lewis mean, when he talks about "the sudden realization . . . that we all shared: our passion for life." How does the final paragraph serve to clarify this "passion"? How has it been dra-matized in each of the preceding paragraphs? If you had an opportunity to suggest revisions for improving Lewis's essay, what specific changes, if any,

would you encourage Lewis to make in his final paragraph? Would you, for example, recommend that he delete it? Why? Why not?

8. When discussing how he wrote his essay, Lewis noted: "I seem to like writing introductions . . . which lead to several different beginnings. . . . I must have written six or more openings before settling on picking up in the middle of one version. Then I reworked that much shorter approach at least another six times." Here is Lewis's first draft of his opening paragraph:

> There are some memories which you need to recall on cold stormy nights. When a chilling blast begins to whisper the worst sort of misgivings about life, their inner glows can throw dark doubts in the cellar where they belong. And if ever you are sure human beings are simply perpetual self-centered trouble, it may take a real warm memory to shake free from the acid experiences with the more ignoble among us. Someone has said, "Everyone needs certain works of the literary arts to guide them through troubled times." I have expanded the rule. We can create our own art within us to carry us through storms.

Here is a much later draft of the opening paragraph:

> There are memories that chew at your insides and shorten your life. They wake you up on chilly nights and rip the blankets off. Like the time your favorite jacket was stolen from the closet at the high school dance: you shivered all the way home, convinced that the only answer to injustice was to be just as nasty and brutish as everyone else. You shivered, shook, and wanted to cry out, and none of it did any good—the doubts had been planted deep. At such times we need to recall the "angels unawares" and warm puppies in our lives. Like waking up from a bad dream, our only answer may be to hope for a good dream to warm us again from such cold memories—from the inside out. That is when I remember Alex.

Consider Lewis's final draft of his opening. What specific differences do you notice among these three drafts? What does each emphasize? What are the connections among the three? Which version do you prefer? Why?

9. In an earlier draft of his essay, Lewis included several paragraphs recounting the "story" of Alex's life. Here, for example, is one such paragraph:

> Somewhere south of Red Bluff I confessed how new I was at running the rails. Alex wasn't running anymore. He was "tired of all that" and he was simply headed home to

help out his mother. He joked that he might even settle
down with a waitress who had been chasing him for some
time. In any case he had begun to feel at thirty-eight that
the years were wearing him away little by little. Like the
Snake River near his home, he could feel time cutting its
own sort of canyon. And if he was going to lay down roots,
it might as well be near where he began. His father was
long since dead and his mother was getting to a point where
she really needed him, he said. Still, I remember thinking
there was something missing from his story. It just made
too much sense.

Consider the gains—and the losses—of Lewis's decision to delete this paragraph. How would Lewis's essay be strengthened and weakened by adding more
information about Alex?

SUGGESTIONS FOR WRITING

1. Patrick Lewis's first draft of his opening paragraph ends on this point: "Someone
   has said, 'Everyone needs certain works of the literary arts to guide them through
   troubled times.' I have expanded the rule. We can create our own art within
   us to carry us through storms." Examine your own experience carefully, and
   write an essay in which you recount an experience to *illustrate* either of Lewis's
   "rules."

2. At the end of his essay, Lewis notes: "As that team of Southern Pacific diesels
   pulled us out of Redding, eternity sat captive for a moment. Like a stolen
   glimpse of childbirth, I shared in that peaceful feeling of something both beginning and ending at once." We have all had experiences that have changed
   our perceptions so that we develop a new way of understanding something.
   Write an essay in which you recount such an experience to show how your
   perception changed and what this change in perception meant to you.

3. Lewis's essay raises questions about the nature of friendship. Montesquieu, one
   of the most accomplished essayists in literature, once gave the following definition: "Friendship is an arrangement by which we undertake to exchange small
   favors for big ones." Write an expository essay in which you relate an *anecdote*
   that serves to verify or challenge Montesquieu's definition.

WILLIAM G. MALLEY

Harvard University
Cambridge, Massachusetts
Holly Weeks, instructor

"I rely on self-discipline when I write," reports William Malley. "Writing is hard work that requires concentration and effort. For this reason, I never eat, listen to music, or carry on a conversation while writing. The first draft is never easy. I must say that I have not found any short cuts to a good paper."

William Malley was born in Buffalo, New York, and graduated from Canisius High School. His father writes for the Buffalo News and has always encouraged Malley's writing efforts. Malley believes that his own extensive reading has given him a subconscious understanding of how words should look on the printed page and an instinctive feel for language. At Harvard, Malley writes for the Crimson, the school's daily newspaper, and plans to major in history or government.

Asked to write an argumentative essay on a topic of his choice, Malley explains his choice this way: "I had just read The Making of the President 1960 *and was interested in the religious issue in the 1960 campaign. I started by going to the library and reading a wide range of periodicals from 1959 and 1960: popular mass-circulation magazines, Catholic magazines, Protestant magazines, and political journals. I wanted to read articles from a broad spectrum of viewpoints. After weeding out a few of the less useful pieces, I began taking notes from the ones that were left. At first, I took notes on just about everything, because I didn't really know what I was looking for. Later, after reviewing my notes, I began to get a better understanding of the whole debate; at that point, I began to read with a more critical eye."*

An American Catharsis: The Debate Surrounding the Issue of Religion During the 1960 Presidential Campaign

We tend to remember a presidential campaign in terms of a particular issue 1
that dominated it, and indeed we should, for it is often this dominant issue
that determines the character—or even the outcome—of the campaign. More
often than not, this issue is political in nature; the issues of recovering from
Watergate in 1976, of the impending war in 1940, and of the Great Depression
in 1932 are typical. Each of these issues derives its importance not so much
from the attitudes of the particular candidates as from the state of the country

as a whole at the time. Certainly, the positions of the candidates affect the development of the issues, but each of these issues would have been important even if other men had run. The campaign of 1960, however, did not fit this pattern. In that campaign, the issue of whether a Catholic should be president played a dominant role; if John Kennedy had not run, this issue would not have come up. But he did run, and in doing so he forced the nation to face a unique issue, one that differed greatly from the political issues of other elections.

Veterans of presidential campaigns had seen these issues come and go. Every 2 four years, a few new ones arose, and a few old ones died out. These issues were by no means unimportant or insignificant; in fact, they had played pivotal roles in every campaign. But they were manageable. For the most part, they were debated in the context of the campaign and lost much of their importance after the election; those few that lingered on were generally confined to the political arena. The religious issue, however, had a life of its own. It had existed for hundreds of years and had been debated at one time or another or nearly every level of society. It transcended politics. By running for president, John Kennedy brought this old issue out into the open and made it a topic of popular debate. He didn't create the issue—he simply made it relevant. And once he had done that, he was powerless to make it irrelevant. He couldn't push the issue off the stage or out of the spotlight. The situation was further complicated by the fact that this was, after all, an issue of religion. Religious beliefs are not rooted in reason but in faith. The unreason that is a necessary part of religion instills in religious believers an unreasonable bias, prejudice, and fear that often runs nearly as deep as the faith itself. These unfortunate byproducts of religion color the perceptions of any believer and render reasonable argument ineffective as a method of debate.

In terms of politics, then, this debate was nothing but trouble. It hurt both 3 candidates, it divided the American people, and it raised difficult questions that simple political slogans could not put to rest. In another sense, however, the debate was more than a troublesome campaign issue. Religious bias, prejudice, and fear had existed in America for centuries, rarely out in the open but never forgotten entirely; they were chronic, malignant, festering sores on the American subconscious. The debate brought these sores out into the open, compelling Americans to recognize that they existed and to deal with them. The process was one of national catharsis which, though painful, was both necessary and good.

The religious prejudice that Americans confronted in 1960 grew out of a 4 religious division that began centuries before. Protestants, not Catholics, had founded America. Protestants had led the war for independence, drawn up the

Constitution, and passed the first Laws; Protestants had chosen the principles upon which the nation was built. Among the most important of these principles was the one that guaranteed separation of church and state and gave each man the right to worship—or not to worship—as he chose. For the early Protestants, the very antithesis of this idea was the church of Rome, which sought secular as well as religious power (White 284–85). For Protestants in 1960 the situation had changed little. The tradition of suspicion of the Catholic church had become ingrained in the Protestant consciousness; whether the suspicion was still justified had little bearing on the matter. For many Protestants, Roman Catholicism remained synonymous with intolerance and bigotry.

These Protestant feelings were far from unfounded. Even Protestants who   5 supported the right of a Catholic to be president found certain papal statements extremely difficult to digest. These statements could not have been less ambiguous: in 1832, Pope Gregory XVI condemned "the mad belief that every individual must be allowed and guaranteed freedom of conscience"; in 1864, Pius IX supported the view that "the Catholic religion should be considered the only religion of the state to the exclusion of all other forms of worship"; and in 1888, Leo XIII declared that "the state cannot adopt the same attitude toward all religions and grant them the same rights without discrimination" (Andrews 1241). From these statements it was hard to draw any conclusion except that the Catholic church had repeatedly rejected the idea of separation of church and state. Furthermore, as if to erase any hope that teachings had changed since the nineteenth century, the Vatican newspaper *L'Osservatore Romano* published an editorial on May 17, 1960 that budged not an inch from the established church position:

> The church . . . has full powers of true jurisdiction over
> all the faithful and therefore has the duty and the right to
> guide, direct, and correct them on the level of ideas and
> the level of action . . . The Catholic can never overlook
> the teaching and instruction of the church; in every field
> of his life he must base his private and public behavior on
> the guidance and instruction of the hierarchy. ("Vatican
> Paper" 73)

The position of the Catholic church on the religious freedom of its members   6 seemed just as threatening as its position on the religious freedom of those of different faiths. This willingness on the part of the church to intrude so boldly into the secular world was made unmistakeably clear by the bishops of Puerto Rico just a few weeks before the election. These bishops issued a pastoral letter forbidding their parishioners to vote for a certain party, the Popular Democrats, in the uncoming Puerto Rican elections. For speaking out against the letter, the mayor of San Juan was threatened with excommunication, as was any Catholic who chose to disobey the injunction ("Biggest Issue" 36–37).

Even at the beginning of the campaign, before the *L'Osservatore* editorial 7 or the pronouncements of the Puerto Rican bishops, the odds—and the experts—were against John Kennedy. It was a standard political rule of thumb that Catholicism and presidential politics did not mix; the 1928 candidacy of Al Smith was proof of that. Even the Democratic party, whose constituency and leadership were both substantially Catholic, would not hear of a Catholic candidate (White 228). Still, Kennedy had the minimum of support necessary to get a campaign under way. When, on January 2, 1960, he officially declared his candidacy, the first phase of this American catharsis had begun.

Kennedy's route to the presidency led through the Democratic primaries, 8 so it was in the individual states that the issue was first tentatively raised. As the primaries got under way, the issue grew in importance, but it was not until the West Virginia vote in early May that it became a dominant factor. The predominantly Protestant West Virginians had favored John Kennedy by a 70–30 margin over his opponent, Hubert Humphrey, in polls taken in December of 1959; just three weeks before the primary, however, they had reversed their position of 60–40 in favor of Humphrey. When Kennedy asked his advisers for an explanation, they said simply, "No one knew you were a Catholic in December. Now they know" (White 121).

For the Kennedy campaign, this reversal of opinion was certainly disap- 9 pointing but not altogether unexpected. They realized that the campaign had just gotten under way and that neither the candidates nor the issues were very well known; the fact that John Kennedy was a Catholic was one of the few hard bits of information available to the West Virginian voters. Thus, when pollsters asked them to choose between two candidates, the voters chose not between Kennedy and Humphrey but between a Catholic and a Protestant. In a country in which a Catholic had never been president, this could hardly even be called a choice, so it could not have been a surprise when the people picked the Protestant. In rejecting the Catholic, the voters were merely following a centuries-old tradition. And up until this point, Kennedy had given them no reason not to.

The anti-Catholic opposition in West Virginia was not an organized polit- 10 ical effort but rather a gut-level reaction on the part of individual voters. Clearly, this reaction was powerful, but Kennedy realized that it could be manipulated. The reaction was based on the justifiable assumption that a vote for a Catholic was a vote against separation of church and state. To win, Kennedy had to turn this assumption on its head; he had to show that a vote for a Catholic was a vote against intolerance and against those who sought to deny public office to forty million Americans simply because of their religion. Once the decision became a matter of tolerance or intolerance, the voter could only prove his tolerance by voting for Kennedy (White 127).

To effect a massive reversal of public opinion is never easy; to do so in a 11 matter of weeks is almost never possible. Poor odds, however, meant little to the well-oiled Kennedy machine, which now moved briskly into battle. Thousands of Kennedy volunteers flooded the state to provide a broad base of support. Each of the eight area commanders paid his first call to the district leader in the local county courthouse. And Kennedy himself was everywhere. In speeches, in parades, and on television, he relentlessly drove his message home. There was Kennedy the war hero, Kennedy the young father, Kennedy the strong leader—and, above all, Kennedy the believer in separation of church and state (White 127–29). Against this awesome tide of men and money, Humphrey was helpless. On May 10, Kennedy won easily, forcing Humphrey to withdraw. John Kennedy was now the front-runner in the race for the nomination.

Politically, Kennedy's campaign in West Virginia had been a success. His 12 strategists had been able to manipulate the religious issue for political advantages, and it almost seemed possible that this could be done throughout the campaign. This, however, was not to be. In West Virginia the debate was in its first, formative stages. For the most part, it was confined to the level of the individual, and it could be controlled by political game playing. Ultimately, however, all the attention in West Virginia served to fuel the debate rather than to control it. Within weeks, the debate had spread beyond the limits of the political arena, and it soon reached every sector of society.

Both Kennedy and his opponent in the general election, Richard Nixon, 13 quickly realized the difficulties inherent in the religious issue and attempted to avoid it as much as possible. But while the two candidates did their best to ignore it, the debate among the American people grew faster than ever. Up to this point, the debate had taken place mostly in private conversations. The majority of public figures had refrained from taking a stand on the issue; they feared that even an honest attempt to criticize Roman Catholic doctrine would be condemned as bigotry. But now the debate took a new turn. In the last week of May, the annual meeting of the Southern Baptists was held in Miami. Not once in the course of the proceedings was John Kennedy mentioned by name, but the references to him were unmistakable. Dr. Ramsey Pollard of Memphis, reelected president of the group, opened with a harsh attack on the Catholic church. "Roman Catholicism," he declared, "must come to us with clean hands and admit her own sin in the field of religious persecution and bigotry before she can raise a finger at us" ("Dogma" 43). The convention then approved a sharply worded resolution that dealt specifically with the election. "When a public official is inescapably bound by the dogma and demands of his church, he cannot consistently separate himself from these. This is especially true when that church maintains a position in open conflict with our established and constituted American pattern of life" ("Dogma" 43).

With the increasingly vocal support of groups like the Southern Baptists, 14 Protestant leaders began to speak out. The press covered each new development with increasing boldness, and Catholic leaders for the first time began to respond publicly. The issue had broken out into the open and was now recognized as a legitimate topic for debate. Once this had happened, the traditional bias, prejudice, and fear were quickly dragged up from the American subconscious to confuse the debate and to be examined by it.

Back and forth, point and counterpoint, the people puzzled and probed. 15 What they found was interesting. The Catholic church that had traditionally been seen as so monolithic, rigid, and unambiguous was proving to be something quite different. It turned out that the papal pronouncements that had seemed so clear were in fact open to interpretation; the authority of the church hierarchy that had seemed so far-reaching and absolute was in fact limited. American theologians and clergy entered the debate to defend and explain their faith with great vigor. In a lengthy interview with U.S. News and World Report, Monsignor Francis Lally of Boston articulated the opinions of many modern Catholics. Contrary to the beliefs of some Protestants, he explained, papal encyclicals are meant to be "guides" to help Catholics apply their faith, not "blueprints for action." A Catholic president, he went on, would not be obliged to follow these guides, but only to consider them as he would any document that came from a prestigious source. Citing the leaders of France, Italy, and West Germany as examples, Monsignour Lally said that a Catholic leader of a democratic nation could function independently of the Vatican ("If a Catholic" 66–67). From throughout the Catholic church in America there came a new message: Roman Catholicism was more open, more liberal, and far, far less rigid than was popularly supposed; as far as America's Catholic leaders were concerned, there existed absolutely no religious barriers that would restrict a Catholic president's ability to function.

For many Protestants, this was a welcome revelation, and it confirmed what 16 they had hoped all along. For others, however, including many Protestant theologians, this was not the case. One of those who still remained unconvinced was Dr. John Mackey, a former president of the Princeton Theological Seminary. He outlined the principal questions of many of his fellow Protestant theologians in an essay in U.S. News that appeared five weeks after the Monsignor Lally interview. In carefully chosen, unemotional words, he questioned the extent to which a Catholic president would be free to follow his own will and the degree of authority which the church claimed in relation to the state. His feeling, clearly, was that the Catholic president's freedom of conscience was too small and the degree of authority claimed by the church was too great (Mackay 50). He went on to attack what he called "clericalism" and defined as "the pursuit of power, especially political power, by a religious hierarchy carried on by secular methods and for the purposes of social domination" (Mackay 48). This clericalism, Dr. Mackay suggested, was a threat to American institutions, and could only be furthered by the election of a Catholic president.

Throughout the summer, Catholics like Monsignor Lally and Protestants 17 like Dr. Mackay continued the debate. As the weeks passed and the number of participants increased, it became clear that this debate could not be satisfactorily resolved by the time of the election. For this there were several reasons. First, and most obvious, was the fact that a centuries-old conviction cannot be completely reversed in a matter of months even under ideal conditions—and conditions were far from ideal. Protestants who believed that the ultimate aim of the church was control of the state simply would not be persuaded that this was not the case; even when church leaders in America flatly denied all accusations of clericalism, the suspicion persisted. Catholic leaders abroad made the situation even more difficult when they issued orders that seemed to confirm the Protestants' suspicions. Second, and less obvious, is the fact that the question was being debated in the context of politics. Religious beliefs were intimately connected with cultural attitudes and political allegiances. Many people who would have found them difficult to separate in any case found it even more difficult now, as politicians and clergymen alike sought to play upon these connections to influence the outcome of the election. Finally, there is the point which many people probably understood but which few actually brought up. This point is that the only way to know how a Catholic president would act would be through experience. They were debating a question that was, for the time, unanswerable.

So the debate ran on, endlessly, with a momentum of its own, swinging 18 first to one side, then to another. In early September, the Reverend Norman Vincent Peale graced the growing Protestant movement with his prestige, and the anti-Catholic sentiment threatened to crystallize. Kennedy realized that he could not end the debate, but he knew that he had to prevent it from swinging too heavily against him. For Kennedy, the course of action was clear: he had to address the issue directly, and he had to address it soon (White 311).

With this in mind, then, Kennedy accepted an invitation from the Greater 19
Houston Ministerial Association to discuss his religion on September 12 in
Houston. In addressing his Protestant, somewhat hostile audience, Kennedy
spoke powerfully and effectively:

> I believe in an America where the separation of church
> and state is absolute—where no Catholic prelate would tell
> the president, should he be a Catholic, how to act, and
> no Protestant minister would tell his parishioners for whom
> to vote—where no church or church school is granted any
> public funds or political preference—and where no man is
> denied public office merely because his religion differs from
> the president who might appoint him or the people who
> might elect him. ("Both Sides" 74)

In the question-and-answer session that followed, Kennedy addressed all the
areas of Protestant concern over Catholic policy. By the time he had finished,
he had clearly defined the personal doctrine of a modern Catholic in a democratic society and won the respect and friendship of his audience as well
(White 313).

The Houston speech had its intended effect on the debate. It reversed the 20
growing tide of support for the anti-Catholic Protestants and threw the debate
back into a state of relative equilibrium. By the end of September, most American figures, both lay and clergy, had spoken on the issue; the media had made
sure that the basic questions were clear to the American people. During the
last month of the campaign, then, the debate returned to the level of the
individual. Across the country, outside the view of the television camera,
individual Americans made up their minds. Over the course of the campaign,
most of these people had, at one time or another, been forced to face the
difficult issue of religion. They had seen, with varying degrees of clarity, their
own prejudice, bias, and fear, as well as that of others. As election day approached, they were forced to make a decision: would John Kennedy's religion
be a factor or wouldn't it? As each individual voter made that decision, he
helped bring the process of national catharsis to an end.

On November 15, the American people chose John Kennedy, for reasons 21
neither the pollsters, nor the politicians, nor even the people themselves knew
for sure. It could have been a vote for a Catholic, or a vote against bigotry,
but it just as easily could have been a vote that in the end had very little to
do with religion. In spite of all the talk and speculation, in spite of all the
intense feeling and deep emotion, the decision could have rested on what John
Kennedy called the real issues: the issues of the Communist threat in Cuba,

of hunger and poverty in America, of education, and of outer space. Or maybe it rested not on the issues but on the images of the two candidates, who had met for five debates on that new and powerful medium, television.

In one sense, however, the reasons and even the decisions themselves were 22 insignificant. Regardless of how they eventually voted, the American people had accomplished something. As a society and as individuals, they had confronted issues that generations of Americans had tried to ignore. They had engaged in a divisive, painful, but ultimately necessary debate. Their success, in any concrete sense, was difficult to measure, but that, too, was somehow insignificant. In the end, it was the process itself that mattered.

Works Cited

Andrews, Charles R. "A Catholic President: Pro." *Christian Century* 26 Oct. 1960: 1241–43.
"The Biggest Issue." *Newsweek* 7 Nov. 1960: 36–37.
"Both Sides of the Catholic Issue." *U.S. News and World Report.* 26 Sept. 1960: 74–81.
"Dogma and Politics." *Time* 30 May 1960: 43.
"If a Catholic is President." *U.S. News and World Report.* 30 May 1960: 64–69.
Mackay, John A. "The Other Side of the Catholic Issue." *U.S. News and World Report* 4 July 1960: 48–51.
"A Vatican Paper Tells When Church Has Role in Politics." *U.S. News and World Report.* 30 May 1960: 73–74.
White, Theodore H. *The Making of the President 1960.* New York: Pocket Books, 1964.

QUESTIONS FOR READING AND REVISING

1. William Malley explains that "the first few paragraphs were extremely important in setting up the rest of the paper. I had to communicate to my reader my own sense of the wonderful uniqueness and complexity of the religious issue in the 1960 campaign." How does Malley "set up the rest of the paper"? How does he invite his reader into the world of his essay? How did he succeed in communicating to you his own sense of the "wonderful uniqueness and complexity" of his topic?

2. Why does Malley provide the historical background to the religious conflict in paragraphs 4 to 7? Why does a reader need this information? How does this information advance his *argument* and help establish his *purpose?*

3. Malley chose to unfold the story of the religious debate through the democratic primary and general election. His strategy was to provide his interpretation of this debate within the context of the events he *narrates.* Why do you think Malley chose this strategy? What does this strategy offer him as a writer?

4. What is Malley's *thesis?* Classify the various types of *evidence* Malley advances to support his thesis. For instance, in paragraphs 15 and 16, he quotes a monsignor and a Protestant theologian. Did you find these questions effective pieces of evidence?

5. Malley relies heavily on three magazines—*Time, Newsweek,* and *U.S. News and World Report.* Does he rely too heavily on these sources? What other kinds of sources could he have used to document his essay? What would these additional sources have contributed to the essay?

6. Malley reports: "My essay can be read by a fairly wide audience. Any reader with even the slightest knowledge of the campaign should be perfectly able to grasp the ideas presented in the essay." What assumptions does Malley make about his *audience?* How does he provide his readers with information they are unlikely to know, but which they need to understand his essay?

7. Describe Malley's *tone.* What does his tone contribute to the impact of his essay?

8. What is the significance of the first part of Malley's title, *An American Catharsis?*

9. Malley writes: "Regardless of how they eventually voted, the American people had accomplished something. As a society and as individuals, they had confronted issues that generations of Americans had tried to ignore. They had engaged in a divisive, painful, but ultimately necessary debate. . . . In the end, it was the process itself that mattered." How does Malley prepare a reader for this *conclusion?* Do you agree with his conclusion?

SUGGESTIONS FOR WRITING

1. Malley demonstrates that the religious issue in 1960 had "a life of its own . . . it transcended politics." What issues interested you in the 1984 Reagan-Mondale campaign? Was there any issue (for instance, women, taxes, the nuclear freeze) that had a life of its own? Select one issue, research it, and write an *argumentative* essay in which you use your research to present your *point of view* on the issue.

2. Malley writes about the changes in attitude that took place during the 1960 presidential campaign. Select and research a political issue such as Watergate or the Teapot Dome Scandal. What was the background to this issue? What were the dominant attitudes about it? How have attitudes changed?

JOHN E. MASON, JR.

Central Connecticut State University
New Britain, Connecticut
Patricia Lynch, instructor

Like many students, John E. Mason, Jr. has had to work while attending college. Managing the schedules of both can sometimes prove difficult, as Mason's own memorable experience attests: "I was trying to juggle college with work, and I had to work [installing linoleum] before I went to school on that particular day. I thought I could make it home after the job in order to shower and get a change of clothes, but because the job ran over, I was placed in a rather awkward position. The customer, who had gone shopping, wouldn't be home for an hour. I figured since I couldn't make it home to get cleaned up, maybe I could take a shower at the lady's house before she came back. In any case, I got caught in the act when she arrived home early for some reason. There I was, drying myself off."

Charming anecdotes about family, school, and work punctuate John E. Mason's account of his childhood and adolescence. Born in Hartford, Connecticut, Mason attended elementary school in South Windsor, Connecticut, where, in Mrs. Sullivan's second-grade class, he was considered "the king of the 'once upon a time' stories. . . . I don't think anyone knew that I had an interest in writing when I was younger, except for Mrs. Sullivan, who loved my fairy tales." He graduated from South Windsor High School and enrolled in his first writing course in college.

John Mason's goal as a writer is "to write something good enough to be possibly published in the Northeast Magazine [local city paper] so all my friends could go around saying, 'That can't be the same guy'. . . . I usually write so friends and relatives can get a thrill out of seeing their name in print. One measure of my writing success would be to have my best buddy, Groove, call me yelling about why I didn't use his first name!"

Asked to write an essay describing a person in his or her setting, Mason chose to focus on Mrs. Sullivan, his second-grade teacher. In the course of his essay, Mason recalls his trip to Mrs. Sullivan's funeral and the wealth of memories she inspired.

Shared Birthdays

As usual he had waited until the last minute. Route 5 wasn't a very direct route, but it was free of stop lights and he was already late for the funeral. On the other hand, Ellington Road was more direct, but it was a back road littered with stop lights. He knew he couldn't make as good time on Route 5 and from a distance he saw the miniature golf range, which signaled the fork in the road. At the last possible moment he swerved right, just narrowly missing the curb, but managing to cause his wheels to squeal nicely. In spite of the fact

that it was the middle of June, the golf course was closed as usual. He momentarily wondered how people could possibly support themselves on such a
seasonal business. He quickly remembered from his own experience that, when
night rolled around, the place would be packed with teenagers competing for
each other's attention. He chuckled as he read the sign on Lucian's Restaurant,
which used to be called Lou's Drive-In. He could just imagine the steady
customers, mostly truckers, calling Lou by his new name. He wondered if
building a new addition, acquiring a liquor license, and widening the parking
lot had changed his personality the way it did his name.

He checked his watch and realized that no matter how fast he drove, he   2
would be late as usual. After all, it was his trademark. He was blessed at being
able to wait until the last possible moment to do anything. This habit, practiced throughout his life and constantly corrected by his mother, had caused
her to patent the saying, "Someday you're going to give yourself an ulcer."
But now he couldn't really decide whether he wanted to go to the funeral at
all. Mrs. Sullivan, his second-grade teacher, his favorite teacher, had died,
and he was going to pay his respects. But he couldn't for the life of him
remember what she looked like. It had only been twenty-five years.

He whipped around a truck that was traveling thirty-five in the thirty-five   3
mile an hour zone. He looked across the field and even from the road he
noticed that the drive-in movie screen was in desperate need of a paint job.
He shot back to the days as a thirteen-year-old when he and his gang spent
many a summer night sneaking in through the back for the pleasure of watching
the movie standing outside the concession stand. But the main reason wasn't
to watch the movie; the passionate lovers in the back row were their feature
attraction. Pounding on the steamy back windows of young neckers' cars, only
to be chased through the potato field, was at that time a thrill and a half. The
perilous excitement of being chased through a wet and sticky potato field was
comparable to the times when Groove and he would bomb cars with snowballs.
It was a systematic process of a snowball crushing against the side of a car,
brakes squealing, and swear words filling the winter dark, only to be drowned
out by the laughter of kids.

He thought ahead to who would be at the funeral today. Would any of his   4
fellow second graders show? He'd have to run into someone he knew. It was
inevitable. "I remember you . . . what are you doing with yourself?" He didn't
rehearse what he would say, as he usually did. Instead, he again tried to imagine
Mrs. Sullivan, a woman he remembered as nice and kind and sweet . . .
everything a girl scout would envy. But he knew there was something more—
why else would he take a day off from work and drive thirty miles? Reading
the obituary the night before, he racked his brain trying to remember if her

first name was Mary. There are so many Sullivans. She seemed so old, even then. Could this be the same Mrs. Sullivan who was his second grade teacher? The same Mrs. Sullivan who shared the same birthday as he?

He slowed down for the newly installed light in front of Elmore's. Although it was not actually Elmore's since a glass company bought it out, he still insisted on calling it Elmore's. In the same way he called Jerry Z's Restaurant, Dell's, after its original owners. He always felt a twinge of guilt on driving past Elmore's. As a fifteen-year-old it became customary for him, after playing basketball, to walk down from the school and steal ice cream sandwiches. It was a cold and calculated ordeal which sometimes caused him to nearly freeze his private parts. This was mainly because Mr. Elmore, who loved kids, loved to talk. Years later when he found Elmore's had gone out of business, he envisioned poor old Mr. Elmore broke with no place to go, mainly because of the loss of his ice cream sales.

"Today is a very special day and we have some special birthdays to celebrate." Everyone knew it was Mrs. Sullivan's, and he'd tried to tell as many people as possible that it was his. But Al Jankowski's? There Al sat, like a fat cat, purring in the lap of Mrs. Sullivan. He knew that he, and *not* Al, should have been nestled in that warm and secure lap. Thank God for Al's neighbor who finked that Al's birthday was in September and not in March. In the dignified manner in which she seemed to do everything, she kindly asked Al to return to his seat and not to fib in the future. Seeing fat little Al get caught in the act, he quickly promoted himself to the best seat in the house. From the lap of Mrs. Sullivan, he was able to look down on all the little eyes jealously looking at him. He was also able to shoot Al a "better luck next time" smirk. He crossed his arms, resting his head on her breast, and listened as Mrs. Sullivan explained that even though we're all very different, on our birthdays we're that much more unique, because that's the day that God made us specially. The bell rang telling them that lunch was ready, but he would have gladly missed it for a few more moments of playing king.

He tried to imagine what she would have looked like today. He combined what he remembered of the faces of all his old teachers to construct some sort of imaginary face. Even the sight of Pleasant Valley School, the school where she taught, didn't jog his memory; Pleasant Valley School . . . Pigsville . . . as it was so affectionately called by its devoted students. He slowed down just enough to notice that they had built an addition to the back of the school covering the basketball court. The old blacktop . . . it was on that blacktop that he perfected the dying art of chasing a girl to pull her braids. And of course, there was . . . Kathy . . . his first love. He had had his eyes on her, along with half the boys in school, since they went to kindergarten together at the Little Red School House. The blacktop served as his stage to entertain and amuse Kathy. His antics, long forgotten by most, were filed away in his memory bank, always to be relived when passing "Pigsville." The climactic moment of belting a home run, aided by six errors, crossing the plate to have Kathy tell him she liked him more than Graham . . . Even though it only lasted the length of the recess period, it didn't matter. She liked him! Deliberately tripping and falling, getting his new pants dirty was well worth it to see Kathy laughing. Despite the scoldings by his mother, he loved every minute of it. Probably the deciding factor for his crush on Kathy was the head maintenance man in charge of the whole school. He was her grandfather. Everybody wanted to be on a first name basis with the janitor. Two dreams he had had during those early years were to marry Kathy and to be on the safety patrol . . . "Single file under the lights. . . ."

He stopped abruptly for another damn light. The car before him could have 8 made it. He knew he'd definitely be late and decided to drive straight to the church. It's funny, but it was at this specific light that he set the record for the longest kiss in town. It was mostly caused by peer pressure from his eighth-grade friends who seemed to think there was something wrong if you didn't kiss a girl after going with her for eight months. But he loved Anita, he respected her, and what if she slapped his face? On that day, standing at the light waiting for it to change, he again struggled to find a way to say good-bye. "I'll see you in school . . . Call you tonight . . . Going to church tomorrow?" But for some reason unknown to him, he just turned and kissed her. It was a hot and sticky summer day and the sun seemed to melt their lips together. Despite the honking of the passing cars, they managed to stay glued together for three changings of the light. He couldn't even look her in the face as he went to leave, too embarrassed that someone he knew might have seen him. But as he bounced away, had never felt so good about being embarrassed.

What would he talk about if he did run into anybody he knew? He always 9 felt uncomfortable about returning to his home town. If only they didn't ask the same basic and boring questions. "What are you doing now? Are you still working for your father?" He'd always dreaded that twofold question. He couldn't exactly figure out why. Maybe it was because he didn't enjoy the work he inherited from his father; maybe because he didn't enjoy only being his father's son; or maybe because he just didn't enjoy himself. In any case, he was there to pay tribute to a special teacher; so special he couldn't remember what she looked like. If anyone inquired about how he knew the deceased, he could always say they shared the same birthday. He pulled into the church parking lot, scanning the faces of the few people to see if he knew anyone. He was surprised, even relieved, to see the familiar face of his good friend, Nurse Files, the high school nurse. Through the years after high school they had kept in touch. It was only today he was to learn that she was Mrs. Sullivan's sister-in-law.

He took a seat in the last pew, separated from the rest of the mourners. 10 This assured that if he did have to cry, he wouldn't be heard by the others. The preacher in the middle of his eulogy expounded on the fact that through the years, Mrs. Sullivan dedicated her life to not only teaching youngsters, but more importantly, showing love and compassion to people in all walks of life, including the needy and the less fortunate. As the pastor rattled off the list of her finer attributes, he wondered to himself what the difference between teaching youngsters and helping the needy was. For some reason, the way the reverend worded the differences between youngsters and the needy and less fortunate struck him as funny. What would he classify himself as? The only substantial memories he had of her were ones of love that she showed not only for him, but for all her children (including Al). With each story of accomplishments being recited by the proud preacher, he felt tears burning a path down his face. He didn't make an effort to wipe his face, even though people slowly began filing out past him. Farewell tears, because he would miss her, grateful tears for her being a part of his life, tears because he no longer had the need to remember what she looked like.

As the weary family members lined up to receive their condolences, Nurse 11 Files made it a point to introduce him to the family—"This boy was a favorite of your mother's." She was cut short by the pressing line of friends who wanted their say in the matter. He shook hands with the daughter, dying to say her mother's birthday was the same as his, but judging by the look in her eyes, she too wanted to keep the line moving. He kissed Nurse Files goodbye, promising to keep in touch, knowing he wouldn't. The cold air chilled his face where the tears had covered. He felt a strange sense of accomplishment, the way he felt whenever he pushed himself to do something he didn't want to do. He was happy, not only for having attended the funeral, but for having taken the back road, even if as usual he had waited until the last minute.

QUESTIONS FOR READING AND REVISING

1. John E. Mason, Jr. explains one of his purposes in writing this essay: "I wanted people to know that Mrs. Sullivan was a special woman, not just to me, but to everyone who was a part of her life." How does he describe Mrs. Sullivan?

What does he tell us about her life and her teaching? What memories does thinking about her evoke? Based on what he says in this essay, why do you think Mason regards Mrs. Sullivan as "a special woman"?

2. Reflecting on why he wrote this essay, Mason notes: "As we get older, each of us has a tendency to forget special people who helped us along the way. I originally had questioned my motives for attending the funeral of a teacher I'd known so long ago. But the more I wrote, the clearer I saw our relationship." What explanation does Mason offer for attending Mrs. Sullivan's funeral? What does he describe as the nature of their relationship?

3. Mason explains that in writing his essay, "I wanted people to be able to relate, to be able to remember doing the same thing, to say, 'I felt the same way about that,' to just share feelings about growing up in a small town. I wanted people to feel good about themselves." What specific strategies as a writer does Mason use to elicit this response from his readers? Support your response with detailed references to particular paragraphs and sentences. What do you think he means when he reports: "I think I was saying that the things I seem to find the hardest to do in life are usually the most gratifying"?

4. Characterize Mason's *point of view* in this essay. Is he, for example, detached and objective? Involved and subjective? Some other combination? Support your response with an analysis of specific words and phrases. Consider the way Mason presents the "he" in this essay. Why is—or isn't—using the third person point of view here appropriate to his overall purpose? How is this person introduced? Show how his character remains consistent—or changes—as the essay unfolds.

5. What is the primary function of the series of *anecdotes* about the past? What do these anecdotes have in common? What is the effect of each on the overall success of the essay?

6. Mason's essay seems to be divided into two parts: the driver's reflections as he travels to Mrs. Sullivan's funeral and his thoughts while attending the funeral service in church. Outline the major points Mason makes in each section. How does each contribute to the overall effect of the essay? How does Mason unify these two parts of the essay? What frame or overall structure does Mason create for his essay?

7. Mason's essay makes skillful use of *irony*. See, for example, paragraph 1, where he ponders the effects of the change in the name of "Lou's Drive-In" to "Lucian's Restaurant." Find other instances of irony in Mason's essay and comment on their effectiveness. How does irony add to—or detract from—the success of Mason's essay?

8. Mason wrote several drafts of his essay. In discussing the first draft, he observes: "The difficult part about writing the first draft is getting tangled up in how to phrase the lead sentence. Should I have a delayed lead?" What do you think

he means here by a "delayed lead"? What advice would you offer Mason on this question? Consider the first sentence of Mason's first draft: "Like everything in his life, he was waiting until the last minute." Evaluate the effectiveness of this opening sentence. What specific changes does he make in the final draft? Which version is more effective? Why?

9. Here is the complete opening paragraph of Mason's first draft:

> Like everything in his life, he was waiting until the last minute. Route 5 wasn't a very direct route, but it was free of stop lights and he was already late for the funeral. On the other hand Ellington Road was more direct, but was a back road that was littered with stop lights. He knew he couldn't make as good time and from a distance he saw the miniature golf range, which signaled the fork in the road. At the last possible moment he swerved right, just narrowly missing the curb, but managed to cause his wheels to squeal. Despite being the middle of June the miniature golf range was closed as usual. He momentarily wondered how anyone could support themselves on such a seasonal business. But he knew from personal experience that when night rolled around that place would be packed with teenagers competing for each other's attention. He chuckled as he read the sign of Lucian's Restaurant which used to be called Lou's Drive-In. He could just imagine the faithful customers of truckers calling Lou by his new name. He wondered if adding a new addition, acquiring a liquor license and widening the parking lot would change his personality the way it did his name.

Contrast this version to Mason's final draft. What specific differences do you recognize? Which version established a more effective *tone* and direction for the essay?

SUGGESTIONS FOR WRITING

1. In writing his essay, Mason wanted people "to know that Mrs. Sullivan was a special woman, not just to me, but to everyone who was a part of her life." Recall your own elementary, secondary school, and college teachers. Whom among them could you describe as special? Write an essay in which you explain and *illustrate* this teacher's "specialness." You might want to include a detailed *description* of the teacher and recount one or more *anecdotes* to illustrate the points you make.

2. Mason observes near the end of the first paragraph that "Lou's Drive-In" has been changed to "Lucian's Restaurant." Describe a similar change in some business establishment you know about. Write an expository essay in which you *compare and contrast* the old place of business with the new, reborn version. How have the physical appearance, the products or services, the staff, and the management changed since the place assumed a new look and identity?

3. You have accumulated more than enough classroom experience by now to warrant speaking and writing publicly about the qualities that distinguish outstanding teachers. Read the following quotations on teachers and teaching:

> A teacher affects eternity; no one can tell where [a teacher's] influence stops. (Henry Adams)
>
> The mediocre teacher tells. The good teacher explains. The superior teacher demonstrates. The great teacher inspires. (William Arthur Ward)
>
> The art of teaching is the art of assisting discoveries. (Mark Van Doren)
>
> In teaching it is the method and not the content that is the message . . . the drawing out, not the pumping in. (Ashley Montagu)

Choose one of these statements and make it the focus of an essay in which you use your own experience and that of others to verify or refute it.

NELSY MASSOUD

Hunter College
New York, New York
Rebecca Mlynarczyk, instructor

"I used to think about my readers when getting started. It became so confusing that I would give up writing, convinced that I wouldn't be understood, or that my writing was not formal or clear. Then, three months ago, a ninety-five-year-old friend said to me: 'Say it the way you want it, the way it pleases you, the way you see and hear it. It must reflect you. The rest is not your problem, but up to your readers.' Isn't she wonderful."

Born in Damascus, Syria, Nelsy Massoud grew up in Beirut, Lebanon. She reports that she writes "anywhere—a bomb shelter, a car, a bar—and at any time—four in the morning or three in the afternoon, whenever the feeling is there." She always carries a small notebook and pen with her. First drafts are most difficult for her because "my ideas seem so disorganized at this point, they seem to say to me: 'If you don't catch me, you'll lose me.' And they all seem so important at this point. But then I know which ideas are really important. I revise and revise, but I never feel that an essay is finished. The end of one essay is a beginning to another essay."

Asked to describe a personal experience, Massoud reports: "About a month before I wrote my essay, I spent a whole day talking to a friend who had been pushing me to write about the war in Lebanon. It started as a political discussion but then became personal. It was the first time I had shared this experience with someone. I knew I had to write about Lebanon and to appeal to my readers by revealing what the war had done to my parents, friends, and compatriots."

War in Paradise

The story goes that God created the universe and found it beautiful. He admired it and was proud of it. Then God wanted to create a paradise and . . . there was Lebanon. Lebanon was to become the link between Eastern and Western cultures. In time, the Lebanese society was torn apart, some looking toward the East, others toward the West. With growing stakes on both sides and a very complex situation in the Middle East, civil war became unavoidable.

The phases of this war have been so numerous: the Lebanese against the Palestinians; the Christians and the Moslems against each other; the Maronites (a Christian sect) against the government, then against one another; the Left against the Right; the Poor against the Rich; Israel against the Palestinians;

the Syrians first with the Christians, then against them; the Druzes, the Sunnis, and the Shias (three Moslem sects) against the government, then against each other, the Iranians against Imperialism, and the list keeps growing. . . . The Lebanese, civilians, fighters and politicians alike, when asked to sum up nine years of war, explain: "It's an American plot. It's a big game and we are its victims. It's beyond us. The two superpowers, the USA and the USSR, are fighting on our soil. This war should end, but still, do you hear now? What are they bombing? Who are they killing? Us, the civilians. So we say that this war is beyond our comprehension, ala Allah, leave it to God."

I left Lebanon nine months ago, after living through a year and a half of continuous battles. Now I live in New York. Every time I lie down to think about how I can pass along the essence of war to those who are ignorant of it, I can hear the sound of heavy bombs and explosions closing in on me. It's not that I want to share this because it's so awful, but because I hope to do something to stop it. It's been one of my most unrealistic dreams, but the only one that has kept me going.   3

Several weeks ago, I was riding my bike around Washington Square, enjoying the good weather, when right in front of me a motorcyclist fell underneath a bus. I didn't blink. It was as if I had no heart. I just kept going. Suddenly I stopped, shocked by my attitude: no feelings? No, just a flashback: a nineteen-year-old girl, back there, tied up between two cars and split in two when her torturers finally decided to end her suffering by driving off in opposite directions. Then, I had been powerless. I had had to suppress my human instincts, knowing from previous experiences that any effort would be in vain and might be fatal to myself and my family. I had asked a man, watching next to me, "Why?" He said in a tone of total conviction: "She is," (was, I thought) "Moslem, and by doing this publicly, we teach those bastards a lesson and pay them back for their atrocities." That was back in 1976.   4

A very dear friend of mine once came to visit me in 1977, bringing a present created by his own hands—a key ring made from a human ear.   5

"Whose ear is this?" I stammered.   6

"A Palestinian's," he said.   7

I lost all sense of time. What century was this? Were we both of the same generation? Had we grown up together? Had we held the same beliefs in years past?   8

My parents, who had not hesitated to beat me in my childhood to teach me honesty, have accepted stolen goods during the war: televisions, tables, lamps, paintings, and other miscellaneous property from houses deserted by non-Christians in their neighborhood. "If we don't accept them, somebody   9 else will and, besides, everybody is doing it." At one time, there were thirteen TV sets in our living room.

War is not only shooting, fighting, and killing. It's much more personal 10 than that. There is no more normalcy in one's life. There is nothing to hold onto anymore. It kills all valuable principles in one's heart and mind. War is the caricature of life because it means death. One might lose everything over-night, and the only refuge is one's friends, family, co-victims—people, in a word. We are killing each other, although every one of us knows that only a human being can understand and help another.

Let me return to the motorcyclist for a second. Normal people would have 11 stopped and tried to help him. I didn't. I have seen worse. I had been im-munized against suffering by living through a war. In Lebanon, children grow up amidst violence. By the time they are nine, their favorite game is war, leadership their dream.

Most of us believe the problem of war is so big and complicated that we 12 choose not to get involved, feeling impotent before it: "It's beyond us," we say. This is the very attitude that has cost Lebanon nine years of unbearable war. I thought for a while that the solution would be to disband all armies by convincing young people everywhere not to serve. But once in the USA, I realized the complexity of the problem. It is much bigger than the war in Lebanon. We all live with the fear and loathing of a nuclear war. We must all change our way of thinking and admit that we are personally contributing to such disasters with our knowledge, fatalism, and money, and in the case of small, bloody wars such as the Lebanese one, with our silence. Nothing that we create should go beyond us, but it will as long as we don't start acting responsibly and feeling concerned. Every one of us is needed, because it is we who will be the victims.

QUESTIONS FOR READING AND REVISING

1. Massoud's assignment was to describe a personal experience and to indicate what she learned from this experience. What do you see as Massoud's true *purpose* in writing her essay? What message is she trying to leave with her readers?

2. How does Massoud portray herself in her essay? What techniques does she use to create this impression of herself?

3. Massoud includes a lot of information about the war in Lebanon. She invites her readers to imagine that they too not only see, but also feel what she is feeling. How does Massoud draw you into the world of her essay? What gives her writing power and authority?

4. What assumptions does Massoud make about her readers? What information does she feel her readers need? For instance, why does she provide a long list of the phases of the war in paragraph 2? Do we need more information to understand the implications of her essay?

5. Why does Massoud give us the *anecdote* about the motorcyclist? How does this anecdote help establish her purpose? Why does she return to this anecdote in paragraph 11?

6. What is Massoud trying to persuade us to believe or to do? What strategies as a writer could she use to make her ideas more persuasive?

7. Massoud presents her *thesis* toward the end of her essay. What is the effect of delaying the thesis? Is this an effective strategy?

8. Massoud uses her personal experience to make a larger statement about the political situation in Lebanon and war in general. How does she move in her essay between personal writing and *exposition*? Is she successful in both?

9. In an earlier draft, Massoud's *conclusion* was written this way:

> However, we are life; we are family, community, society. Something can be done if only everyone is willing to bear a share of the responsibility. The first step would be to disband all armies by convincing our own brothers, friends, and neighbors not to serve. If we really need to fight, let's do it with our bare hands. Let Lebanon be something God and all those who knew it in the past can be proud of again.

Compare this version with Massoud's final conclusion. What are the differences between these two conclusions? How does the revised conclusion more successfully tie together the various ideas in the essay?

SUGGESTIONS FOR WRITING

1. Most of us have not had personal experiences of living in a war-torn country like Nelsy Massoud. However, we have all had powerful experiences that have changed our lives. *Describe* an experience in which you have seen or heard something but did nothing about it, and later regretted your inaction. Why

did you ignore the experience? Why did you later regret it? What have you learned about yourself from this experience?

2. Do you agree or disagree with Massoud's claim: "We must all change our way of thinking and admit that we are personally contributing to such disasters with our knowledge, fatalism, and money, and in the case of small, bloody wars such as the Lebanese one, with our silence." Write a response to Massoud's claim, illustrating your point of view with convincing ideas.

KELLY J. MAYS

Emory University
Atlanta, Georgia
Jerome Beaty, instructor

Kelly J. Mays traces her interest in writing to the encouragement of her fifth-grade teacher: "She pulled me aside after a creative writing assignment and asked me if I wrote a lot, encouraging me to do so because she felt that my paper was interesting. It mattered to me a great deal, and even now I remember the exact assignment. She asked me to write on the blackboard all the words which we thought of in connection with school, and after we had done so, she asked us to write a story about a day at school without using any of these terms. I don't remember what I wrote, but I think that it was a really interesting assignment, and her encouragement made it even more important to me. Since that time I have gotten a lot of encouragement from teachers, professors, and my family."

The third of four children, Mays was born in Decatur, Georgia, which her family still calls home. Writing and reading have always figured prominantly in her life, both in and out of school. She attended Decatur's Shamrock High School, where she coedited the school newspaper, served as the sports editor of the yearbook, and graduated with the English Department Award and a National Merit Scholarship. Now a member of Sigma Tau Delta (the English Honor Society) at Emory University, Mays plans to pursue a Ph.D. in English literature and to teach in college. In addition to her interest in literature, she enjoys modern dance, acts in campus productions, and lives "in the S.P.I.C.E. dorm on campus (the Saunders Program for International Cultural Exchange)."

Asked to write a five-page paper analyzing the images and structure of Andrew Marvell's "On a Drop of Dew," Mays reports that "the main thing which I wanted the reader to gain from my paper was the awareness of the depth and complex richness of the poem. Poetry is such a compact form that the true poet must be a concise artist whose word and phrase contributes to the poem's effect. I think that this poem is a good example of the multi-layered quality of the poetic form at its best. I hope that reading my paper might reveal this craftsmanship to the reader, as writing it did for me."

An Analysis of Images and Structure Within Andrew Marvell's "On a Drop of Dew"

Within "On a Drop of Dew," Andrew Marvell uses a single comparison to 1 examine the nature of the soul and the possibility of its salvation. Marvell uses a drop of dew and the natural cycle of which it is a part to illustrate the nature of the soul and its relation both to the heaven which creates it as well as to the earthly body in which it lives. His vision of the soul is one of a pure and complete entity which embodies, at birth, the Heaven which created it. Yet, as a drop of dew is threatened with contamination from its contact with the earth, so, he implies, is the soul threatened by the potentially corruptible elements of an earthly form. He ends by suggesting that salvation comes not only from the natural state of the soul, which tends toward the goodness of its creator, but also from the active grace of God and, perhaps from the actions of man himself. Marvell expresses this idea through this overriding comparison with the dew in addition to other underlying images and finally through the structure of the poem itself.

The poem is based on the metaphysical comparison of a drop of dew to the soul. Marvell begins this image by describing the inherent innocence, youth, and purity of the newly created drop through such references as "orient dew," which suggests its connection to the rising sun, "from the bosom of the morn," which implies a childlike connection with the parent-Heaven, "careless," which suggests its innocence of thought, and "little globe," which, as a diminutive phrase, again emphasizes the dew's childlike state. These descriptions not only vividly portray the natural state of the soul, which is inherently connected to God's goodness, but also set up the contrast between this state and the earthly. This contrast is furthered by the darker, more active descriptions of the earth implied by "blowing roses," "purple flow'rs," and the soul's subsequent, "trembling," and "restless" and "unsecure" "roll[ing]." By achieving such a great contrast Marvell points up the fear of the the dew or soul for its own contamination. The image of the drop continues within the second verse paragraph as it is "exhal[ed]" back to its birthplace and so provides the transition within the poem to a more direct comparison between it and the soul. This transition is aided also by the connection between the images of the human flower to the images of the actual flowers in the beginning. The dew image again returns within the last section in active references to manna, and within the first three phrases which connect the characteristics of the soul to those of the dew. That is, "loose" and "easy" refer back to "restless" and "unsecure," "girt" to "round in itself incloses," and finally "moving but on a point below" to "scarce touching where it lies," so that with this last paragraph Marvell rounds off the comparison between the soul and the dew, strengthening both images with the support of the other. This support relies not only on the actively described characteristics but also on the natural cycle of which the dew is known to be a part. By using the cyclical falling-evaporating of the moisture, he emphasizes the transitory and similarly cyclical nature of the soul's states.

In addition, this idea of a perpetuated cycle connects with a second prevalent image of the poem, which is the circular or round ideal. Marvell presents images of the circular throughout his poem. From the beginning he uses such terms as "round," "incloses," "globe," "sphere," "circling," "wound," and "girt," which emphasize this image of roundness. He ties this image, both through implication and active association within the poem, to the heavenly, especially its virtues of purity, eternity, wholeness, and harmony. This idea connects not only with the underlying cycles within the poem but also with the images of the drop, the world and the soul. As a circle or globe, all of these are connected, able to face every way and yet to turn away and so connect both the purity to heaven with the earth, goodness with sin, and disdain with love. Further, this image of the sphere refers not only to the general heavenly sphere but ties in more specifically with the sun at its center.

The sun becomes almost an embodiment or symbol for God's power within   4 the poem. Marvell achieves this powerful image through both the implied power of the sun within the water cycle but also through its active presentation within the action of the poem itself. The first time it is mentioned explicitly it is presented as the powerful body which "pit[ies]" the "pain" of the drop/ soul and "exhal[es]" it back to the sky. Thus it is presented in a Godlike way through its mercy and its ability to bring the drop/soul back to its original state of grace. This idea seems to connect the sun to the "sphere" (line 14) of the dew's actual origin. Further, the sun becomes an active participant again within the last paragraph in Marvell's reference to Manna as well as in his ending, which emphasizes the power of the "almighty sun" to dissolve the body and reclaim the soul. This image is also supported within the poem by the references of "shed" (radiate), "shines with a mournful light," "that ray," and "eternal day."

Many other images also lend richness to the poem. The drop of dew is in   5 some ways compared to a tear since it is "shed" and "shines . . . like its own tear." But it also seems to be compared to a drop of blood in the same references to "shed" and the later phrase "congealed." In these two comparisons, then, Marvell ties the poem to the biblical not only through reference to manna but in this allusion to the blood and tears of Christ. Through these images of active grace and Christ's suffering, in conjunction with the strong and active portrayal of the "almighty sun," Marvell seems to suggest the action of grace within the idea of salvation. To this idea however, he seems to add the suggestion that there is some action necessary on man's part. This idea seems to come through his reference to the drop's "pain," its action of "shun[ning]" and "moving," as well as the idea of "climbing" inherent in the word "ascend." In addition, there may be some connection within the idea of "piety" in the root of "pity."

Connecting images of warmth and light, cold and darkness also play a major   6 role within the poem. Largely, they serve to emphasize the contrast between heaven and earth, good and evil, and yet their ultimate connection. To this and the author uses such phrases as "orient" (shining), "clear region," "shines," "its own light," "warm sun," "bright above," and "white" to refer to the heavenly nature of the soul/drop. These images of light and warmth emphasize the purity of heaven, its goodness and its compassion, and by implication the holy light, the good. Contrasting these images are the dark, colder ones of the earth. These images are found not only in the flower descriptions but also in the phrases "dark beneath" and "congealed and chilled." These images again emphasize the contrast between the qualities of heaven/earth, soul/body through their active portrayal within the poem and through traditional connections between light and dark with goodness and evil. These images also, however, point to the ultimate connection of these forces. Marvell achieves this connection through yet another cycle, that of night-day (where the sun is again the chief power), and through the circular image of the world, which may both reflect and accept light just as the soul connects both good and evil.

Through these images, Marvell has moved the reader from a basic description of a dewdrop, to an active comparison between it and the soul, and finally, to his conclusion of both the comparison and of his vision of the soul. The structure clearly follows and aids the movement of Marvell's ideas by its three verse-paragraph form. Within these paragraphs too, Marvell's structuring mirrors and supports his ideas. As the drop of dew exists in a "restless," "unsecure," and "trembling" state, so the poem begins with an erratic meter and rhyme scheme. As the drop becomes "inclosed" and assumes its "coy figure," so does the poem tighten in form. Within lines 27–32, Marvell increases the regularity of the length and meter of his lines as well as the rhyme scheme so that they, too, move toward harmony and balance with the soul's movement. This regularly also emphasizes the culmination of his active comparison, which occurs within this section. In the third verse paragraph, the same rhyme scheme is retained so that regularity is still apparent, but Marvell uses, too, the somewhat looser, flowing and yet highly regulated iambic lines to emphasize the contrasting description of the soul as being "loose" yet "girt." At the last, the poem again seems to largely lose its regularity perhaps reflecting the dissolution of the soul; yet, there are also many heavy stresses, caesuras, and strong couplet rhyme, which emphasize the summation of his poem, the power of the almighty and the salvation of the soul itself.   7

Through the strong, basic image of the dew, underlying images of the sun,   8
the cycles of water and light, the suffering of Christ, and the eternal circle, in addition to the structure of the poem, Andrew Marvell creates a complex vision of the soul. Through the opposing and yet connecting nature of his images and structures, he creates the portrait of a soul which is similarly divided and whole. He stresses, especially with contrasting imagery, the inherent goodness of the soul and suggests this inherent connection with the good, Heaven,

as the essential element in its salvation. He also, however, hints at the importance of God's active grace and the soul's own attempts (at reconnecting with its good) in the process of salvation. Thus Marvell ends by creating a hopeful vision of life, which is by nature transient and yet eventually connected to the pure and whole of God by its fall from, and eventual return to, grace.

Andrew Marvell
"On a Drop of Dew"

See how the orient dew,
Shed from the bosom of the morn
   Into the blowing roses,
Yet careless of its mansion new,
For the clear region where 'twas born
   Round in itself incloses,
   And in its little globe's extent
Frames as it can its native element;
   How it the purple flow'r does slight,
   Scarce touching where it lies,   10
But gazing back upon the skies,
   Shines with a mournful light
      Like its own tear,
Because so long divided from the sphere.
   Restless it rolls and unsecure,
      Trembling lest it grow impure,
   Till the warm sun pity its pain,
And to the skies exhale it back again.
      So the soul, that drop, that ray
Of the clear fountain of eternal day,   20
Could it within the human flower be seen,
   Rememb'ring still its former height,
   Shuns the sweet leaves and blossoms green;
   And recollecting its own light,
Does, in its pure and circling thoughts, express
The greater heaven in an heaven less.
   In how coy a figure wound,
   Every way it turns away;
   So the world excluding round,
   Yet receiving in the day;   30
   Dark beneath but bright above,
   Her disdaining, there in love;
   How loose and easy hence to go,
   How girt and ready to ascend;

Moving but on a point below,
It all about does upwards bend.
Such did the manna's sacred dew distill,
White and entire, though congealed and chill;
Congealed on earth, but does, dissolving, run
Into the glories of th' almighty sun.   40

QUESTIONS FOR READING AND REVISING

1. In describing how she intended to appeal to her readers, Kelly Mays notes: "I think that the best appeal to any reader is a sense of clarity, control, and purpose within the paper. It is important to gain the reader's interest with a clear and interesting statement of purpose, which then should be heightened and fulfilled by careful and organized evidence within the body of the paper." As you reread Mays's essay, identify this "clear and interesting statement of purpose." Explain how it is "heightened and fulfilled" by her "careful and organized evidence."

2. Outline the major points of Mays's literary analysis. On behalf of what *thesis*— what governing or controlling idea—does she make points? Make a list of each of the images Mays analyzes. Which does she deal with most convincingly? What points does she make about the structure of "On a Drop of Dew"?

3. Mays's announced goal in this essay is "to analyze the metaphysical conceit on which the poem is based, the underlying imagery, and the structure (especially rhyme and meter) to see how the poet utilized these three elements to express his ideas." Consult a dictionary or a handbook of literary terms for the meaning of "metaphysical conceit." With this *definition* in mind, reconstruct Mays's analysis of the extended *comparison* in Marvell's poem between a drop of dew and the soul. Evaluate the effectiveness of her analysis. How thorough has Mays been in covering each point of comparison?

4. What are the specific strengths of Mays's literary analysis? Where in her essay does she examine *diction*—words and phrases from Marvell's poem—most effectively? What other aspects of the poem does she attend to with unusual skill? Given her announced *purpose*, which aspects of the poem, if any, might Mays have devoted more attention to?

5. In organizing her essay, what pattern of sequence does Mays use to control the presentation of her ideas? Does she move from the simple to the complex? From the general to the specific? From the specific to the general? From the beginning to the end of the poem? According to some other pattern of principle? Verify your response with examples.

6. What specific strategies as a writer does Mays use to present her analysis? What

assumptions does she make about her readers' familiarity with Marvell's poem? How does she introduce the poem to her readers in the first paragraph, and what does she have to say about it? What percentage of her essay does she devote to paraphrasing the poem's ideas? To literary analysis?

7. One of the difficulties the writer of a such a detailed literary analysis faces is creating effective *transitions* between one major point and another, between one paragraph and another. What particular devices does Mays use to create graceful transitions? Which transitions, if any, do you think could be strengthened further?

8. Mays wrote three drafts of this essay. Here is the first draft of her opening paragraph:

> Within "On a Drop of Dew," Andrew Marvell uses a single metaphor to illustrate the nature of the soul and its possible salvation. Marvell uses a drop of dew, and the natural cycle of which it is a part, to illustrate the nature of the soul and its relation to heaven which creates it as well as the earthly body wherein it resides. His vision of the soul is of a pure and whole entity which embodies at birth the heaven which creates it. Yet, as a drop of dew is threatened by adulteration from the earth it contacts so he implies is the soul in danger of this impurification. Marvell suggests in his second verse paragraph that it is not only the soul's innate form but also the grace of God symbolized within the tree which helps the soul return to its heavenly state. Marvell uses not only this overriding metaphor but also underlying and implicit images, as well as structure to express this idea.

Compare and contrast this rough draft to the opening paragraph of Mays's final draft. What specific changes has she made? With what effect? Which version do you prefer? Why? If Mays were revising her essay, what additional changes would you recommend? Why?

SUGGESTIONS FOR WRITING

1. Mays obviously admires Andrew Marvell's ability to create a compelling *analogy* for the concept of the soul. Choose some *abstract* word or phrase and write an expository essay in which you create an analogy to define the term and how it functions in our lives.

2. When asked to offer first-year college students some general advice to help

them improve their writing, Mays responded most generously, although not in essay form:

> First, I do think it is really important to approach your reading as if you were going to have to write on the work. This approach might mean slower and more careful reading as well as underlining or jotting down notes to yourself. Listen in class to what the professor has to say about the work and try to expand on these ideas in your own mind. Pay careful attention to the assignment and be sure that you really do understand what the teacher expects from your paper. If you don't understand or don't really know where to begin, ask for help. I used to be really afraid to do this, but professors would probably rather help now than wade through a horrible paper. Everyone will tell you not to procrastinate and that is probably the best as well as the least followed advice in the world. I rarely can follow it myself, so if you do procrastinate on a paper, try not to panic. Instead, spend as much time as you can thinking about the text, the professor's comments, and your own ideas rather than in trying to write blindly. When you do start, it is much easier if you have a clear idea of where you want to begin, where you want to end, and how you're going to get there. It is important to remember that you have to prove what you are contending; you can't expect your reader to read your mind or to understand what you're trying to say if that is not what your writing is saying. It also helps if you pick a topic that you want to write on rather than whatever is the easiest; but don't try to answer the questions of the universe either. For me, a sense of routine is also helpful when I write as is the realization— although I want to write well—that I am not Shakespeare.

Consider Mays's advice on writing. How consistent is what she says with the advice you would offer other first-year students of writing? Write an *expository* essay in which you present, in as much detail as possible, your own composing process. Based on your own writing process, what advice would you offer to other first-year students of writing?

THU HONG NGUYEN

Palomar College
San Marcos, California
Donald S. Pratt, instructor

Thu Hong Nguyen was born in Vietnam, the youngest child in a large family and now lives in Escondido, California. She reports that having lived in two countries is an advantage to her writing; she has learned from the two different cultures and expresses her observations through her writing. Nguyen began writing for herself at the age of nine but reports that her family, most of whom are accomplished writers, did not think much of her writing then. Her teachers, on the other hand, had faith in her writing, encouraged her, and used her short stories as examples. Besides writing, Nguyen enjoys reading and drawing. She plans to study engineering.

About the conditions necessary for writing, Nguyen reports: "I first put on my favorite record of Handel's 'Water Music.' Once the music begins, I walk stealthily to my desk, afraid to awake the peaceful world in my small room."

Asked to write an essay in which she defined a subject, Nguyen decided she wanted to offer a picture of the life that a woman in Vietnam is likely to lead. The model for such a Vietnamese woman is Nguyen's mother—a widow who devoted her life to serving her family.

For an extended discussion of Nguyen's work, see Part VI.

A Good Woman

A good woman means an industrious daughter, a devoted wife, and a loving   1
mother. Thus is the saying that has been a collective belief for many centuries in Viet Nam. As soon as a female infant is born, it is given the middle name Thi—meaning female—to emphasize its role as a woman in later years. Then, in growing up, this child receives lessons about a woman's duties and must practice what she learns. Parents wholeheartedly train their daughters to achieve the qualities expected of a woman. Should they forget, their neighbors promptly remind them. In a Vietnamese village, the entire community helps, by words of praise and by punishment, to bring up a female child to be a good woman, whose service, obedience, and generosity bring much comfort to those around her. With the fear of retribution, the child grows into a woman who follows loyally the instructions of virtue which determines her fate. From the moment her mind is mature enough to understand commands, to the day she is married off, to the time when she bears her own children, a Vietnamese woman con-

tinuously tries to establish a good name as a diligent daughter, a submissive wife, and an altruistic mother.

In order to be approved by everyone, a Vietnamese woman must first be industrious. This begins with her services at the house of her parents who keep her from idling with endless housework. Already at the age of nine, she is the babysitter of her younger siblings. Carrying a baby on her back, she spends the day sweeping the house, carrying messages, and doing errands. As she grows older, she shares more of the housework with her mother. Upon the first crow of the rooster, she rises to brew tea and prepare breakfast. Afterward, she does the laundry by the river bank. At noon she cooks lunch and has just enough time to tidy up the house before she prepares dinner. In the evening she goes to bed, but only after having fixed the shirts or pants that were torn or missing a button. In keeping busy, she has no time to wonder and to dream, which often result from idleness.

Besides working diligently, a good Vietnamese woman must also submit to her husband. She is expected to revere the man whom her parents have chosen for her after they have accepted his valuable gifts. Once married, she must show that she is unequal to her husband. When husband and wife are seen together in the street, she usually keeps a respectful distance behind him. She also has to acknowledge her inferior position in her speech. When addressed by her husband, she always answers in a well-modulated tone. In talking to him, she uses formal address. Even in the most intimate moments, she still cannot use the familiar form of address. If she has permission from her husband, she may speak aloud her opinions but should not try to make the decision. Whatever her husband says, she will listen and not contradict. Remaining silent is usually the most encouraged means for her to be respectful.

Finally, to be recognized favorably, a Vietnamese woman must try to sacrifice herself for the benefit of the children which are her duty to bear. At mealtimes, she eats little, repressing her hunger with the gratifying consolation that her children are growing taller and stronger. She must not dream of any kind of luxuries. Plain clothing gives her an air of modesty and thriftiness. Wearing perfume or lipstick may lead other people to condemn her as wanton and irresponsible. Instead of beautifying herself, she should give her children more food to eat and better clothes to wear. She must also refrain from any kind of pleasure. She spends her evening hours at home looking after the children rather than at a nightclub or theater. A pack of cigarettes, a bottle of beer, or a few piasters lost at the casino can deprive her children of their right to be fed more. A Vietnamese mother does everything for the sake of her children.

In trying to be what one expects of her, a Vietnamese woman continues to   5
serve if not her parents and siblings, then the husband and children of her
own. Year after year, she humbles herself to make her husband happy as a
proud superior, from his youthful days of good health to his time of age and
sickness. Day after day, she dedicates herself to the welfare of her children
even after they grow up. In this lifetime of striving to be a good woman, she
sets herself as an illustrious example to other women who are also trying to
achieve the same desired qualities. Realizing her goal, she is the pride of her
parents, husband, and children. People around her are satisfied with her. They
feel proud and sure of their lasting tradition in bringing up a good woman. In
any generation, they will always have a good Vietnamese woman to admire.
In any century, they will always have a slave to praise.

QUESTIONS FOR READING AND REVISING

1. Thu Hong Nguyen sets boundaries in her essay and tells her readers how Vietnamese culture *defines* a good woman. According to Nguyen, what are the
   essential traits of a good woman? What is she and what is she not?

2. What did you learn about a woman's life in Vietnam? What did you learn
   about life in general in Vietnam? In what way does Nguyen's purpose extend
   beyond defining and illustrating the life of a Vietnamese woman? What are the
   cultural implications of this essay? What is Nguyen's unstated *purpose?*

3. What does Nguyen assume about her readers' attitudes toward women's roles
   in society? What reaction, as a reader, did she intend for you to have toward
   her essay?

4. Analyze the *introduction* to Nguyen's essay. What function does paragraph 1
   serve? Besides telling us the traits of a good woman, Nguyen also tells us about
   her training. Does she provide too much information in her introduction.

5. What is Nguyen's *thesis?* Where does she state her thesis? How does she use it
   to organize her essay?

6. How would you characterize Nguyen's *tone?* Find instances in her essay to
   support your answer. How does her tone serve her *purpose?*

7. Nguyen concludes her essay with these lines: "In any generation, they will
   always have a good Vietnamese woman to admire. In any century, they will
   always have a slave to praise." Did you suspect such a *conclusion?* How did
   Nguyen marshall her information toward this conclusion? Is it satisfying?

SUGGESTIONS FOR WRITING

1. Nguyen writes about the role of the good woman. Consider a role you now fill—daughter, son, wife, student, friend, worker, etc.—and write an essay defining this role as you see it.

2. Nguyen writes about the "good woman" as defined by Vietnamese culture. Write an essay in which you *define* and illustrate the "good woman" or the "good man" as defined by American culture.

3. Here are three statements from Nguyen's essay:

    > A good woman means an industrious daughter, a devoted wife, and a loving mother.

    > [A woman] must try to sacrifice herself for the benefit of the children which are her duty to bear.

    > [A woman] must show that she is unequal to her husband.

    Choose one of these statements and consider how American culture views a woman's role. Does the culture, in general, agree or disagree with these statements? Use examples from television shows and commercials, advertising, and your own experiences and observations to support your thesis.

CAROL A. OBERHAUS

Auburn University at Montgomery
Montgomery, Alabama
Gerald W. Morton, instructor

"Writing is an emotional and intellectual catharsis for me," reports Carol Oberhaus. *"I become very excited when I write, squirming and shifting in my chair, crossing then uncrossing my legs, scratching my arms, and chewing on my lower lip. I sit at my kitchen table consuming large quantities of popcorn and wearing loose-fitting clothes. I need to be physically comfortable and to have complete silence when I write."*

Oberhaus says that for her, the easiest part of writing is getting all the ideas down on paper. She first brainstorms, *"emptying her mind onto the paper,"* and then outlines. An outline gives her a framework yet allows her the *"freedom to think in a disciplined way."* Then she writes a draft and *"revises and revises until it is just right. For me, revising means removing myself from the role of the writer and stepping into the role of the reader. I read what I have written and decide if I have actually communicated what I intended to say."*

Oberhaus reports that until she reached college she was primarily influenced by her conservative rural education, which cast the machines of writing *"in concrete."* Born and raised in Muscatine, Iowa, Oberhaus moved to Montgomery, Alabama, to live with relatives and go to college. She has worked as a nurse for nine years and is now studying to become a veterinarian.

Asked to write a definition essay, Oberhaus reports: *"We were told to have fun with our writing. I had recently had a conversation with my cousin's husband in which we were discussing southern men, and he had used the word Yahoo to describe a certain type. I knew I had my subject; that was all I needed to get started."*

For Ladies Only

I have always been envied by other women for my ability to find unique [1] boyfriends. I know this is true because every time I introduce a boyfriend to my friends, they say, "Boy, she really knows how to pick 'em." Well, I may be skilled, but I'm not selfish. Therefore, I will give you ladies my no-fail method of finding the most unique and desirable type of male, the Yah-Hoo. There are many men who try unsuccessfully to imitate Yah-Hoos. Consequently, you must be able to quickly decide if he is a real Yah-Hoo, or a cheap imitation. Your success will depend on your ability to remember that above all, a Yah-Hoo is characterized by his special dialect, style of clothing, vehicle, restaurant etiquette, and choice of music.

A Yah-Hoo's dialect will distinguish him from other men. His speech is an 2
exciting blend of a southern accent plus the sounds of a mating call of a pair
of corduroy jeans. Certain words will be substituted for others, such as "barn"
for born, "balkx" for box, "far" for fire, and "bode" for board. If you're lucky,
he may "ax" you for a date, but do not be so "far-ward" as to ask *him* for a
date, because he will tell you to mind your own "bidness." Yah-Hoos do not
like women who, "caw-wull" them on the phone or have their own "chorge"
cards. And ladies, do NOT show your ignorance by blushing when a Yah-Hoo
talks about a "wang"; he simply means a wing. Understanding a Yah-Hoo's
speech is definitely a science, which explains "wah" they date only the most
intelligent of women.

A Yah-Hoo can also be identified by his clothing. He will usually be wearing 3
a baseball cap bearing the monogram of either Jack Daniels whiskey or Skoal
Bandits. Incidentally, don't forget to look for the sweat stains around the
headband of the cap. They are a unique characteristic of the Yah-Hoos. Long-
sleeved plaid shirts seem to be popular with Yah-Hoos, even during hot summer
months. Yah-Hoos *never* wear pink shirts. When a Yah-Hoo is out looking for
a date, he will unbutton his shirt just far enough to give you a peek at his
undershirt. Most women find the exposed undershirt a real "turn on." Pressing
on, you must skillfully judge a man's pants. This category requires the most
skill of all because you must be completely inconspicuous. If the man sees you
performing your evaluation, he could misinterpret your intentions, or think
that you are from New York. In either case you would surely offend him if he
were a real Yah-Hoo. Look for jeans that are baggy in the seat with a white
ring on the back pocket where the snuff can has worn through. The white
ring on a real Yah-Hoo's pants is permanent and cannot be ironed out. Yah-
Hoos successfully obtain an element of mystery by obscuring the shape of their
thighs and buttocks with baggy jeans. However, the lower legs of the jeans
must be very tight and too long in order to get their famous punched up look
at the calves. Last, but not least, a Yah-Hoo will always wear boots with worn-
down heels. The worn heels cause a very characteristic rocking, bowlegged
walk that only Yah-Hoos do well.

If your potential Yah-Hoo is still in the running after you've assessed his 4
clothing and dialect, then you must note the characteristics of his vehicle. A
man that does not drive a pickup truck is a counterfeit Yah-Hoo. A Yah-Hoo's
truck will always have all-terrain tires and be jacked up more than any others.
A Yah-Hoo never has to worry about remembering where he parked his truck
in a K-Mart lot because the truck is conspicuously taller than any other vehicle
in the lot and very easy to locate. If you are fortunate enough to be asked to
ride in a Yah-Hoo's truck, *don't panic* because you have to climb four feet.

Resist the temptation to ask for a stepladder, a "leg-up," or any other assistance. Yah-Hoos really detest "whiners," but they love athletic women, so be
thinking in advance of a method that allows you to bound effortlessly into the
cab. (Hints: Boosting yourself by holding onto a street sign works, but may
ruin your panty hose and get rust on your hands. A curb will give you a six-
inch advantage that, with a running start, enables you to vault your way into
the cab.) Yah-Hoos like to drive fast; therefore you must maintain good balance
on your seat to avoid catching your hair on the gun rack behind your head.
No matter how muddy the exterior of the Yah-Hoo's truck may be, the front
license plate will always be wiped clean. The plate will usually say "American
by birth, Southern by the grace of God," or look like a Confederate flag. Yah-
Hoos never have FM radios in their trucks, but they do have CBs with whip
antennas.

Another way to tell if a man is a real Yah-Hoo is by his etiquette in a   5
restaurant. The first hurdle, of course, is locating the kind of restaurant in
which you might find a Yah-Hoo. Yah-Hoos can usually be found in restaurants
that specialize in home-cooked meals twenty-four hours a day. Even more,
Yah-Hoos are attached to establishments that possess a particular ambience,
such as waitresses with beehive hairdos and a missing front tooth, red squirt
bottles for ketchup, small and very thin paper napkins in metal dispensers,
and booths upholstered in solid orange or turquoise vinyl. The musical amen-
ities will be provided by an AM radio on the counter top that is tuned into
the local country-western station. Once you are inside the *truck stop,* you may
begin your assessment for potential Yah-Hoos. Try to sit in a booth where the
upholstery tears have been patched with silver duct tape because trying to sit
on a upholstery tear may cause you to giggle or squeal, and that would attract
too much attention to yourself. In your assessment, you will notice that others
in the restaurant very clumsily refer to the waitress as "Miss" or "Ma'am."
Meanwhile, a real Yah-Hoo has his situation completely under control by
calling the waitress "Darlin'." A Yah-Hoo always knows exactly how to order
food, too. He will always order his prime rib well done. After all, it doesn't
make much sense to put ketchup on your prime rib if all those meat juices are
going to mix with it and dilute it! A real Yah-Hoo's etiquette is more creative
than most peoples'. He isn't satisfied when the waitress asks "How is your
coffee?" to simply answer her, "Fine" or "Good." Instead, he will demonstrate
real flair by saying, "Boy! This stuff will make you want to slap your granny!"

You can always tell an authentic Yah-Hoo by his choice of music. Music is   6
a category that will serve many purposes for you in your search for a Yah-Hoo.
You will be able to readily identify a Yah-Hoo, and if you're smart, you can
use this information to endear yourself to the Yah-Hoo. Let me give you an

example. A man who looks and acts just like a Yah-Hoo, but who is listening to Mantovani, is not only a bogus Yah-Hoo, he is the kind of man that Yah-Hoos hate most—a sissy. One of the quickest ways to score points with a Yah-Hoo is to tell him when you see a sissy in Yah-Hoo clothing. This lets him know that you are his kind of woman. Hippie freaks with new haircuts like to dress like Yah-Hoos too, but you can easily spot one if he's listening to rock music. Yah-Hoos often refer to soft mood music as "elevator" music because that's where they were the first time they heard it. Elevator music is favored by doctors and lawyers but not Yah-Hoos. And God forbid that a real Yah-Hoo, while tuning in his radio, should accidently tune in soul music! I don't know exactly what soul music does to Yah-Hoos except that it seems to be like Mexican food—"bad for yer system." The kind of music that Yah-Hoos claim as theirs is music that is sung by other Yah-Hoos. The more sophisticated Yah-Hoos listen to Charlie Daniels or Hank Williams, Jr. However, the majority of Yah-Hoos aren't particular about *who* is doing the singing as long as the song is country-western style and concerns itself with "drinkin' and cheatin'." Examples of their favorites are songs with lyrics such as, "Your Cheatin' Heart," "Who's Been Makin' Love to Your Old Lady, While You Were Out Makin' Love?," "Colorado Kool-Aid," and "Take This Job and Shove It!" Ladies, you may want to go out and purchase a few of these songs just in case you get the chance to entertain a Yah-Hoo in your home. I must warn you, though "drinkin' and cheatin' " music has been known to have an aphrodisiac effect on Yah-Hoos, so *be prepared!*

Any man who is characterized by my descriptions of dialect, clothing, vehicle, restaurant etiquette, and choice of music is a genuine Yah-Hoo. You must move quickly before another woman catches him. And practice makes perfect, so don't be afraid to try several Yah-Hoo boyfriends. You will know that you've really perfected your selection process when people say, "Boy, you really know how to pick 'em." 7

QUESTIONS FOR READING AND REVISING

1. According to Carol Oberhaus, what are the essential traits of a Yah-Hoo? Which details do you find particularly vivid or memorable? Does Oberhaus make you want to know a Yah-Hoo?

2. Oberhaus uses a good deal of sarcasm, a form of *irony*, in her essay. What is her attitude toward Yah-Hoos? Find instances of sarcasm in her essay and

evaluate their ineffectiveness. How does sarcasm add to or detract from the success of Oberhaus's essay?

3. For whom is Oberhaus writing this essay? Is she writing for Southerners? How much does she assume her readers already know about this type of man? What are her assumptions about her *audience?*

4. How did you react to Oberhaus's *description* of Yah-Hoos? Did you find her essay humorous, persuasive, offensive, etc.? Describe your reaction.

5. Oberhaus is writing an extended *definition* of Yah-Hoos. How has she organized her definition? How does each part of her essay contribute to her definition?

6. Oberhaus has a good ear for dialect, capturing the language of Yah-Hoos and using dialogue to help define the man. Why do you think she chose to present so much of the Yah-Hoos' dialect? Point out instances you found effective.

7. Oberhaus reports: "Even though I really could have written an entire book about Yah-Hoos, I felt the essay was complete when that type of man became recognizable to any woman." Did Oberhaus succeed? Is the Yah-Hoo recognizable? What else might she have added to make the character more recognizable?

SUGGESTIONS FOR WRITING

1. Oberhaus *defines* one kind of stereotyped character—the Yah-Hoo. Write an essay in which you define another kind of stereotyped character. Give your readers those characteristics which represent this character's appearance, manners, speech, etc.

2. Select several popular magazines and study the advertisements directed to male and female readers. How are these ads similar? How are they different? How do these ads stereotype males and females? Write an essay in which you analyze the nature of these ads by *comparing and contrasting* the stereotypes advertisers have created.

MAX RAMSEY

University of Richmond
Richmond, Virginia
Joy M. Barnes, instructor

Max Ramsey reports that he comes from a very average lower-middle-class family. "My father is a minister, which meant we moved around a great deal. I never really achieved anything in high school. I guess one could say I was an undermotivated over-achiever."

Born in St. Louis, Missouri, Ramsey graduated from St. Stephen's School in Alexandria, Virginia, and now lives in Richmond. He credits his family with encouraging him to write even though his first memory of writing is when, at the age of three, he wrote his name on the living room wall and got spanked for it (he figures he received the spanking because he must have spelled his name wrong). About his writing process, Ramsey tells us: "When I write I try to remember everything exactly as it happened by forming a mental picture. I close my eyes and picture events, re-create feelings, and then jot them down in jumbled words and half-sentences. The paper is done in the rewrite."

Asked to write a personal narrative, Ramsey reports: "After high school I joined the army and trained with the Special Forces. In September 1983 we were sent to Lebanon. I have had a very difficult readjustment to civilian life and an especially hard time dealing with my experience in Lebanon. I wrote the essay, as the title suggests, for myself. It started out as a journal entry. I just scratched down what was in my mind. Later, after rereading it, I decided to flesh it out. I rewrote it four times before I was finished. I knew it was finished because it felt right."

For Myself

Every night I see her face etched upon my dreams. An endless nightmare that wracks my brain and jolts me awake like a slap in the face, her image returns to haunt me. I sometimes wonder if she will ever fade away.

She was like gold on a charcoal background, a flower in a desert of death and deprivation. Her eyes were big and chocolate brown and peered right into your soul. And when she smiled, it was as if the sky opened up and a ray of light poked through and illuminated everything around her.

For me, the war in Lebanon really began three months before I met her. I was a member of a Special Forces advisory team assigned to the beleaguered Lebanese Army in their seemingly endless war for stability. My war began one Sunday morning in late October with the sound of an enormous explosion, crumbling cement, and twisting steel. It was my first taste of death, so close you had to peel its fingers from around your throat. Since that day, I saw life in nothing but black and white. Nothing was in color. My senses had been numbed by the smell of death, an unmistakable stench that consumes and overwhelms your senses and hangs heavily in the air like humidity. It clings to you, and it won't wash off. Somewhere along the line, I had lost that esthetic part of me that gave me the gift of feeling. Death had not come for me yet, but it had left its mark on my heart. A sheet of thick, cold ice coated my emotions.

Then, one hazy day in late December, my unit was engaged in a firefight 4 across Rue Damur, a rubbled street in Moslem-held West Beirut. Out of the corner of my eye, I saw a ball roll out into our cross fire. Right behind it was a little girl in a dirty white linen dress.

"Shit, she's gonna get blown away," I thought, and I gave the order to 5 cease fire. Apparently, so did the Shi'ite militia leader. We just sat and stared through the thick, sulfurous smoke as this dirty-faced little wisp of a girl picked up her ball, held it to her stomach loosely with both hands, cocked her head to the side, and looked at us, her piercing eyes clearly visible through the silver haze. She turned and looked at the Moslems across the street and then ran off out of sight.

I called my men off, as did the militia leader, and we all went home. I 6 don't know why, but her intervention caused a calm to fall over our private little war, and suddenly nobody wanted to fight any more.

I found her playing in the street the next day while I was on a security 7 patrol through the Shatila refugee camp, about three blocks from where we had been fighting the day before.

Shatila. The land of lost souls. Empty shells of human beings who have 8 nowhere left to go scurry through the muddy, rubbled streets, afraid someone will come to send them away again. The crumbling, blown-out buildings are their homes, the garbage heaps their clothing stores, and the gutters their toilets.

But this little girl glowed in all of Shatila's gloom, playing, oblivious to her 9 surroundings. I walked up and sat down next to where she was bouncing her precious ball. I took out a chocolate bar and handed it to her. She smiled that toothy smile of hers and a warmth fell over me like a blanket. It must have melted part of that ice, because I felt something, admiration I guess you'd call it, for this little twelve-year-old girl with the big brown eyes. How those frail shoulders could hold up under all the shells, disease, fighting, and dying that engulfs that stinkhole of a country was beyond me.

I made patrols through Shatila at least three times a week just to see her, 10 in the hope that some of her warmth would rub off on me. I felt alive inside myself when she and I would talk. I loved to hear her tell stories in her broken English of how she was going to come to America and be a beautiful movie star like Linda Evans. God, she made me feel good again about what I was doing in Lebanon. She was what it was all about.

In mid-February—it was the second Wednesday night of the month is all I 11 remember—the Druze shelled Shatila in an attempt to hit the government positions there. They shelled it for seven straight nerve-racking hours. There was an empty feeling inside me that told me she was dead before I even left the bunker the next morning to help dig out the camp.

I remember the exact feeling I had when I found her body among the dead 12 that were laid out in the street for identification and burial. Her tiny legs were off at the knees and her abdominal cavity was exposed. But what cut right through me were her big brown eyes staring blindly at me and a look frozen on her blood-caked face that asked accusingly, "Why?"

My knees felt weak. My bowels felt loose. I felt as if my heart weighed ten 13 pounds and was pushing down on my stomach. I wanted to throw up and I wanted to cry. I fought back the tears: "A soldier never cries and he never asks questions."

I staggered off to a sandbagged barricade across the street. There I puked 14 up six months of hate, of disillusionment, of betrayal, of fear, and with them the last remnants of my youth.

By the time I'd finished retching, I was raging. It was a white-hot, out-of- 15 control anger that builds and builds and can't be turned off or toned down.

"Fuck this place. Where the hell are all the goddamned liberals who think 16 we shouldn't be here? Why aren't they here now, huh? Fuck this place and the government that sent me here. Why doesn't the rest of the wise and mighty United States have to see this shit? And why the hell is it that the innocent have to pay for these people's fucking ignorance? Tell me that, you bastards. You answer the girl. It's your fucking country. It's your fucking war. You tell her why."

I was screaming at everybody and everything. As I felt the last bit of strength 17 drain out of me, I slumped down against the sandbags.

And then I felt something unfamiliar rolling down my cheek. Tears. I cried 18 like a baby that day. Sitting against the sandbags on the mud-covered street, I cried like a damn baby. I cried for the soul of that blindly innocent little girl that was going to be a movie star. And I cried for a dying Lebanon and its hopeless questions without answers. But most of all, I cried for myself. I cried for the death of a part of me. I cried for the shattering of ideals. And I cried because her death meant to me that life really was in black and white, and emotions and colors were just illusions for somebody else to experience.

They say that time heals all wounds, but some wounds are deeper than 19
others. In time, I'm sure her face will fade from my dreams. But there will
always be that unanswerable and yet inevitable question engraved in my
memory—Why?

QUESTIONS FOR READING AND REVISING

1. Max Ramsey tells a powerful story and succeeds in holding our attention
   throughout his *narrative*. What *purpose* other than offering a personal narrative
   do you find in Ramsey's essay? What messages is Ramsey trying to leave with
   his readers?

2. What gives Ramsey's writing authority and credibility? Find specific details to
   support your answer.

3. As readers, we feel the strong presence of the writer in this essay; we hear
   him and feel we know him through his writing. What strategies does Ramsey
   use in his essay to give us this sense of himself?

4. What *details* does Ramsey use to make the little girl memorable to his readers?
   What do these details reveal about the little girl? About Ramsey himself? Why
   does the little girl remain nameless?

5. Look closely at the selection of events and the dramatic sequence Ramsey
   gives us. How does this organization serve his *purpose?* Determine the purpose
   of each scene. What has he deliberately left out?

6. The title of the essay is "For Myself." For whom does Ramsey seem to be
   writing? To what extent does his sense of *audience* influence his writing? Why
   do you think he gave this title to his essay?

7. Ramsey's narrative is about the little girl, but although she dies in paragraph
   12, the essay continues for another seven paragraphs. Why?

8. Do you find the *introduction* effective? Does it succeed in bringing you into
   the world of this essay? Could you suggest to Ramsey any way in which he
   might revise his introduction to make it more effective?

9. Ramsey sometimes uses phrases such as "Death had not come for me yet" and
   "I felt alive inside myself," which might be classified as *clichés*. Does the
   overfamiliarity of these phrases make them ineffective? Identify these *clichés*
   and explain what feeling Ramsey is trying to create. How else might he have
   expressed these feelings?

10. Ramsey reports: "The only problem I had in rereading and revising my paper
    was the harsh language I used. I didn't know if it was acceptable in college.
    I had no intention of taking it out. I finally said the hell with it and turned

it in. I guess it worked out okay." Do you agree with Ramsey's conclusion that his language "worked out okay"? In what way does his "harsh" *diction* help him achieve his purpose? How would it have changed his essay if he had tried to soften his language?

11. Ramsey tells us that the hardest part of revising is "deciding what needs changing and omitting. It is hard to throw out a memory even if it doesn't fit the paper. What is meaningful to me is not necessarily meaningful to someone else." Was Ramsey successful in revising? Has he included any details of memories that are extraneous? Is there anything in his essay that doesn't fit or advance his purpose?

SUGGESTIONS FOR WRITING

1. About his Lebanese experience Ramsey writes: "There will always be that unanswerable and yet inevitable question engraved in my memory—Why?" Write a personal *narrative* about a powerful experience in your life which you asked, "Why?"

2. Ramsey writes about his disillusionment and the loss of his youth. Select an incident in your life that led to disillusionment and shattered your ideals. Write a *narrative* essay in which you show your readers how this experience affected you.

3. Both Max Ramsey and Nelsy Massoud wrote about the Lebanese War. How do their differing positions—Ramsey as an American soldier and Massoud as a Lebanese civilian—influence their *point of view?* Write a summary-response essay in which you first summarize Ramsey and Massoud's points of view on war and then respond by showing how you agree or disagree with them.

JULIE REARDON

Normandale Community College
Bloomington, Minnesota
Mary Beth Lake, instructor

"Chocolate is necessary to the writing process," reports Julie Reardon, "as is caffeine-free diet Coke. A black-tip magic marker and lined pad complete my required list of items to work with. I have a special writing spot—the couch. I wear a fuzzy blue robe, pink slippers, and keep my cat close at hand during Minnesota's eleven months of winter. If my writing is going well, other people are allowed in the room to watch TV or listen to the stereo. If I am having difficulty, though, my husband and son retreat to their alternate areas—basement or bedroom. Only the cat is brave enough to stay during all phases of the writing process."

Born and raised in Mason City, Iowa, Julie Reardon now lives in Shakopee, Minnesota. She credits her uncle with stimulating her interest in writing. At the age of ten, she began writing letters to him and they maintained a twenty-year correspondence. In addition, Reardon has a close friend, an aspiring writer, to whom she sends examples of her writing for criticism and encouragement.

About her prize-winning essay, Reardon tells us: "My assignment was to illustrate my first encounter with a foreign culture. The life I encountered in a small town in Iowa was like another culture. I had strong memories from that experience and had wanted for years to tell other people the story of the lives of my neighbors. I thought of nothing else but this essay for a week after receiving the assignment. I sat down and wrote nonstop for about three hours. As the story emerged, I finally felt able to deal with all the old emotions that resurfaced as I thought and wrote about this experience."

For a more detailed discussion of Reardon's work, see Part IV.

The Unmarked Road

When I was sixteen, I married and moved to a small town to live. My new [1] husband nervously showed me the house he had rented. It was after dark when we arrived there, and I remember wondering why he seemed so apprehensive about my reaction to the house. I thought the place seemed shabby but potentially cozy and quite livable inside. The morning sun revealed the reason for his anxiety by exposing the squalor outdoors. Up to that point, my contact with any reality but that of my own middle-class childhood had come from books. I had read extensively on a variety of topics and considered myself grown-up and fairly aware of the world. The next four years in a small Iowa town taught me that I was far from adult, and that reading about poverty is a lot different from living with poverty.

Our own house was an appalling sight from the outside. The siding, origi- 2 nally white, sprouted leprous gray patches where the paint was peeling away. Bark hung down from the huge dead elm in the front yard like long, limp scabs. The tree and a doorless garage leaned ominously toward our house. To the north, weeds grew up around a lonely, abandoned shack. To the south, a run-down house covered with rotting, gray asbestos shingles crouched, a weathered outhouse several steps from the back door. Farther south along the frozen, muddy road huddled a tiny one-room dwelling isolated in a swampy hollow. Barely glimpsed through a sea of stiffly dried weeds, the roofs of two ramshackle chicken coops rounded out the view from our yard. Our forgotten lane lacked street lamps and house numbers and was denied even the dignity of a street sign at the corner.

Madonna was the first neighbor I met. She and her two illegitimate children 3 occupied the miserable shack in the hollow. Madonna's occupation belied her saintly name. The number of cars risking axle damage by bumping along the rutted path to her house after dark confirmed she was supplementing her welfare money with prostitution. Her older son was disfigured with a bulging navel hernia that protruded visibly through his dirty clothing. I tried tactfully on several occasions to persuade Madonna to take Shawn to the doctor and have this repaired. Her dull, moon face stayed expressionless throughout my pleas. Shawn's hernia remained.

My closest neighbor to the south, Fanny, knocked on our door soon after 4 we moved in. She bore a steaming jar of homemade bean soup and a small, dense loaf of homemade bread. After several weeks of my newlywed culinary disasters, the kindness and the delicious aroma brought tears to my eyes. In my gratitude, Fanny's lined, weather-beaten face, sparse gray hair, and missing teeth were quite beautiful. I was already feeling the isolation and loneliness of that unfamiliar town and nearly deserted lane, and I attempted to coax her to come in for a visit. She told me she had to go right home because her husband was there alone. Gradually, I learned the circumstances of her life. Her husband, Buck, was blind, incontinent, and as afraid of being left alone in his permanent darkness as a child. Too proud to ask for help and too poor to pay for it, Fanny took total care of him without even the assistance of a washing machine or indoor plumbing. They eked out a bare existence on Buck's tiny disability pension by cutting out all but the most basic necessities. There was no money to style Fanny's limp gray hair or to have her much-needed dental work done. The often laundered and mended sheets she hung out to dry on the line were so thin as to be nearly transparent. Fanny was able to hurry the two blocks to the grocery store for food, but often as not, Buck's plaintive cries of "Fanny, Fanny, where are you?" greeted her return. He was unable to remember for fifteen minutes where she had gone.

One morning I was startled by a grotesque sight. An enormously fat man 5 with a vivid orange tangle of artificially colored and curled hair was slowly pedaling between the ruts down our road. He was so heavy he overflowed the bicycle seat and squashed down the old-fashioned balloon tires. The tires were barely turning as he wobbled past. I walked over to Fanny's house and asked who he was. Fanny pointed at the larger of the two "chicken coops." "That's Louie. He lives in that house." House! I could barely imagine him able to squeeze his immense bulk inside that tiny shack, let alone live there. Fanny continued. "He works part time cleaning up at the meat locker." That was his sole source of income—barely enough to pay taxes on his piece of land and keep himself in cheap, starchy foods. Fanny hesitated a moment, then decided to tell me the rest of his story. "Louie's father caught him when he was a boy, fooling with his sister. His father castrated him with the pig knife." I was stunned. Louie's unhealthy size hinted at a glandular problem, but this was incredible. I made Louie's acquaintance later on, and found him to be a quiet, painfully shy man. I don't know whether incest had actually been involved in his past or whether his father had interrupted an innocent game of "doctor."

I thought by now I had discovered all the inhabitants of the neighborhood, 6 but one surprise remained. I had lived in ———— for over a year, and trudging back from the post office one afternoon, I found myself face to face on the path through the tall weeds with a stranger. He was an elderly, stick-thin old man with face and hair so pale he seemed almost albino. I offered him a friendly hello; and was startled to see him start with alarm, nearly fall, and disappear into the weeds. My question to Fanny revealed that he lived in the smaller of the two "chicken coops." This structure was no larger than six feet by six feet. The old man, Sylvan, lived in that metal box winter and summer. Sylvan had been a frail child, and his mother "protected" him by keeping him always at home with her, never letting him go to school or play with other children. The tragic result of this pampering was that Sylvan grew up so frightened of the outside world that he was never able to associate with other human beings. His sister, never subjected to this maternal smothering, grew up able to function. She married and moved to California, leaving Sylvan entirely alone after his mother's death many years earlier. He did trust Fanny, and he signed over his miserable subsistence check he received from the government each month. Out of this check, less than fifty dollars, Fanny paid his fuel oil bill and bought his groceries. Neither Sylvan nor Louie had running water or electricity, and Fanny provided them both with buckets of water from her cold water tap. Sylvan's sister flew in once a year to check on him and take his clothes to the laundromat.

So we lived, each of us isolated from each other and the rest of the world.   7
Fanny was the single thread that sewed together the crazy-quilt patterns of our lives. Ten years ago, I pulled loose the stitches that held me to a failed marriage and that unmarked road. Late at night, I still wonder about the fates of those other unfortunate people. My several letters to Fanny remain unanswered, and my memories are too painful to allow me to ever return there, even for a visit. I never entered those people's lives to any meaningful extent, but they entered mine. I grew up a lot during those four unhappy years, and from the lesson of those wasted lives, I forged a determination not to waste my own.

QUESTIONS FOR READING AND REVISING

1. What overall impression of "the unmarked road" does Julie Reardon create? What is the significance of the fact that "the forgotten land lacked street lamps, house numbers, and was denied even the dignity of a street sign at the corner"?

2. Why does Reardon *describe* the houses on "the unmarked road" before introducing the people? How does paragraph 2 influence the reading of the rest of the essay?

3. What is Reardon's *purpose* in writing this essay? Where in the essay does Reardon state that purpose?

4. What important points does Reardon make about her life on the unmarked road in the small Iowa town? From her essay, what do we learn about the writer herself?

5. Reardon uses *concrete details* very effectively. She tells us, for instance, that her house, "originally white, sprouted leprous gray patches where the paint was peeling away. Bark hung down from the huge dead elm in the front yard like long, limp scabs." Find other instances in the essay where Reardon appeals to each of her readers' five senses. How do these details help Reardon establish her purpose?

6. Reardon reports: "I would advise my readers to read my essay with an open mind; not to let stereotypes of 'welfare mothers' or 'disabled persons' get in the way of seeing these people as individuals." Was Reardon successful? How does she help you to see and understand the lives of Madonna, Fanny, Louie, and Sylvan? What specific *images* and details illustrate how Reardon feels about these individuals?

7. "Fanny was the single thread that sewed together the crazy-quilt patterns of our lives." How does Reardon use the *example* of Fanny to *unify* her essay? Why is this an effective strategy?

8. Why did Reardon save the *example* of Sylvan until last? On what basis did she organize her examples?

9. Reardon reports that she added the *anecdote* in her *introduction* in a final draft. Evaluate the effectiveness of the introductory paragraph. How effective would the last sentence of the introduction be without this anecdote?

SUGGESTIONS FOR WRITING

1. Reardon chose to write about the most foreign culture she has known—the life in a small town in Iowa, a culture which forged her determination not to waste her life. Write an essay in which you illustrate your first encounter with a foreign culture. Explain the assumptions you had about this culture—and, in contrast, about your own—as a result of this encounter. What did you learn about yourself from this encounter?

2. Reardon writes: "The next four years in a small Iowa town taught me that I was far from adult, and that reading about poverty is a lot different from living with poverty." Consider a similar experience you have had in which reading about something has been quite different from the "real" experience. What were your expectations from reading? What was the reality? Develop a *thesis* to explain these differences and write an essay illustrating your thesis through a series of *examples*.

3. Have you known a series of people, like those Reardon knew, who entered your life and taught you something? Write an essay in which you introduce these people and show your readers their importance to you.

4. *Compare and contrast* two towns or two neighborhoods in which you have lived. Is there one person at the center of the town or neighborhood like Reardon's Fanny?

JONATHAN SCHILK

Highline Community College
Midway, Washington
Luke M. Reinsma, instructor

"My ideal writing environment is a well-lit but not too bright room. I like to have a radio playing classical music. And I don't like people tramping through constantly asking what it is I am doing. First drafts are difficult. There are so many questions and ideas that are passing through my head that I can't write them down fast enough. Sometimes I get confused and lost in my own ideas. No matter how confused I am, I keep on going. I often write for ten hours straight without stopping."

Jonathan Schilk joined the Coast Guard in 1980, served aboard a 180-foot buoy-tender out of Grand Haven, Michigan, and also served in Key West, Florida as a small boat crew member during the Cuban-Sealift Operation of 1980. Schilk received a citation for humanitarian duty and advanced to the rank of Quartermaster First Class. He now works in the Coast Guard Rescue Coordination Center in Seattle. Schilk hopes to work for the U.S. Department of Forestry or the Parks Department after graduating from college.

Asked to write a narrative essay about an important event, Schilk chose to use one of his Coast Guard experiences as his subject. He explains: "The main inspiration of this essay was that my writing had been mostly run-of-the-mill mediocre; technically passable, but uninteresting. I thought that a well-told sea story would entertain my readers and hold their attention."

For a more detailed study of Schilk's essay and the drafts that led to it, see Part III.

57 Degrees

At the Coast Guard Training Center in Alameda, California, our instructors stressed that we still had much to learn about the sea's moods and temperaments. Our training, they said, was only inadequate preparation for what could happen to us in open water. "The ocean humbles even the most experienced skipper!" warned one teacher ominously. He often spoke of the *Edmund Fitzgerald,* an ore carrier which had foundered in a winter storm on Lake Superior. Even though the ship was over seven hundred feet from stem to stern and equipped with the latest technology, she went down in less than a sweep of the radar's antenna. But it made no difference to me. After all, those men on the *Fitzgerald* were only civilians; I was a Coast Guardsman. After fifteen weeks at the Center, after long hours delving into the art of navigation and piloting, I could deal with any emergency. Steering—"wheeling" as we called it—was my forte. Several times, in fact, in less-than-perfect conditions, I had brought ships through narrow entrances in the breakwall. I could handle any ship of any tonnage. There was nothing that I couldn't do.

After graduating, I was assigned as a navigator to the *Acacia,* an 180-foot 2 buoy-tender on the eastern shores of Lake Michigan. I've been ordered to an oversized mudpuddle in the Midwest, I thought. It was like giving a man with a Ph.D. in math a grammar-school job. My fears were confirmed when I first saw the lake: it was flat, featureless, unromantic. Then there were the arguments with my shipmates about the storms. It would never get that rough on the lake. If they wanted "rough," if they wanted big storms, I told them, they ought to sail the Gulf of Alaska in autumn or go on a spring patrol on the Caribbean Sea. Besides, the *Acacia* could handle whatever nature could throw at her. She had been fitted with the latest technology—variable ballast tanks, hydroplane stabilizers, and all—to prevent dangerous rolls. The Boatswain never said much; he just nodded and smiled.

One day headquarters ordered us to sail for a point twenty miles northeast 3 of Chicago, where a 23-foot Chris Craft, adrift in bad seas, had radioed an SOS. We loosened the mooring lines at sunset and glided between the piers into open water. Fifty miles to the southwest storm clouds hovered over the horizon like a gigantic bruise. But here, where the ship only rippled the flawless surface of the lake, I fell asleep in my rack, secure in the knowledge that the *Acacia* and I could handle anything—anything short of a tsunami that is.

I awoke to the sound of water crashing and gurgling on the weather deck 4 above me. Lurching to the port, the ship dumped me onto the deck. I sat there, my blankets and mattress draped over me, wondering what had happened. I picked myself up and numbly eyed my shipmates, who had burrowed among their woolly blankets and lashed themselves in—giant cocoons in the dim red light. Clothes on hooks swung like pendulums with each roll, and a figure in the passageway made his way toward me like the proverbial drunken sailor. "What's going on? Where are we?" I asked.

"We're on the edge of a storm front and it's gonna get worse!" he gasped. 5

Before I could reply the ship pitched forward, and he zigzagged down the 6 passageway to the head. A bucket on wheels, loose from its trices, spun across the deck and smashed against the bulkhead, splashing its contents. I glanced to the berths to see if anyone had awakened. The cocoons hadn't budged. The bucket careened into another bulkhead with a crash. The walls closed in and air became putrid. I hoped this was as bad as it would get.

The sailor who had run into the head emerged, swallowed back another 7 retch, and told me I had the next watch in twenty minutes. Even in the passageway's red light, his features had a greenish hue. The ship plunged forward again, and he struggled back to the head.

After dressing, I climbed the ladder to the wheelhouse, leaving the bucket, 8 the messenger from the bridge, the muffled sloshing, coughing, and gagging behind. I fought my way up, sometimes weightlessly as the ship dropped from beneath me, sometimes ponderously as waves forced me to defy gravity. The bulkhead oscillated up and down, back and forth, up and down until I grew dizzy. I opened the wheelhouse door, stepped inside, and saw the helmsman clinging to the large brass wheel and spinning it in an almost futile effort to keep the ship on course. The Boatswain gazed out the porthole nonchalantly puffing on a Dutch Masters. The Skipper had been sitting in his chair forward of the helmsman's wheel. He too was looking out the portholes. Everyone else, including the lookout, the Officer of the Deck, and the Exec, was hanging on to whatever wasn't flying across the deck.

The acrid stench of the Boatswain's cheroot made me queasier than ever. 9 I would have loved to punch him in his smug, self-satisfied face, but I was too ill to bother. All about me, strewn across the deck, were coffee-stained charts, pieces of broken glass, and crockery. Outside, the Quartermaster of the Watch, draped over the bridgewing's edge like a rag doll, finally staggered toward the door and stepped inside. His face was haggard and drawn. Behind him the sea careened toward the gunwales and then receded.

I turned to see what the anemometer read: the needle had pegged out at 10 106 knots. The lake was as I had never seen it before. Even in an ocean storm, the period from the crest of one wave to the next would run at least three hundred feet. But here in the lake the period was seventy-five feet, and the ship was subjected to an endless thrashing, so that it was impossible for her to recover from one wave before confronting the next. Out there waves holding millions of gallons of water broke upon themselves, and the slicing wind sheared off the wave caps. Waves looming above the ship quickly swept on, leaving vast troughs for the ship to fall into—and she did. Many times I felt as if I had left my stomach thirty feet in the air above. Waves of nausea washed over me, and I wished I were dead. I meant it. I would have done anything to stop the misery.

No sooner had I thought this than a rogue wave plowed into our port beam 11 and sent the ship broadside, cork-screwing into a trough. "Brace yourselves!" the Skipper cried. Losing his grip on the wheel, the helmsman catapulted against the radar and landed in a heap. The wheel spun past hard left to a point where it would jam the rudder and leave the ship without steerage control. I jumped for the wheel and brought the rudder to midships and then hard right to bring the port bow into the seas. But before she responded, the ship gave way to the blow of yet another wave that towered above the signal bridge and mast. The *Acacia* heeled wickedly to the starboard—20, 30, then 40, then 50 degrees. At 57 degrees—seven degrees past the point of capsizing— she slowed to a stop. The fo'c'sle disappeared under thousands of tons of water, and the starboard rail dipped into the black waters.

Inside the pilothouse, maps, pencils, and coffee mugs cascaded off the chart   12 table onto the deck. The table lamp swung into the Fathometer, and sparks flew from its shorted circuits and shattered light bulb. And there, through the porthole, past my wild-eyed reflection, the lake boiled at the bridgewing's gunwales. The ship hovered on the edge of eternity. Deep in the ship's heart, rivets and welds strained and groaned, and deck plates jumped from the con- cussion. This is it! I thought. We're going down!

Slowly at first, almost hesitantly, the *Acacia* recovered, and the clinometer   13 climbed up its scale. Water washed from the fo'c'sle's deck in sheets as the *Acacia* swung past even keel, whipped through an arc of 100 degrees, and settled into a sedate 40-degree roll for the remainder of the trip.

In the corner, wedged between the Skipper's chair and the radar, the Boat-   14 swain still stood, puffing on the stub of a Dutch Masters and grinning quietly at me.

QUESTIONS FOR READING AND REVISING

1. Jonathan Schilk tells us proudly in the first paragraph of his essay: "I was a Coast Guardsman." What was Schilk's attitude about his own abilities during his Coast Guard training? How did his attitude influence him when he was assigned to be the navigator of the *Acacia*? How did his experience with the *Acacia* humble "even the most experienced skipper"?

2. Schilk tells a powerful story and succeeds in holding our attention throughout his *narrative*. Does Schilk's essay have any *purpose* other than personal narra- tive? Is Schilk trying to give his readers any message about himself? How do the first two paragraphs set up his purpose?

3. We meet the boatswain in paragraph 2: "The Boatswain never said much; he just nodded and smiled." We meet him again at the end of the essay: "The Boatswain still stood, puffing on the stub of a Dutch Masters and grinning quietly at me." What does the Boatswain represent to Schilk? What is his function in the essay? Why did Schilk end the essay with this image?

4. A reader feels the writer's presence in this essay; we know we are reading an

essay by a writer who cares about what he is saying. What strategies does Schilk use to give his readers this sense of commitment to his subject?

5. Schilk uses details effectively: he writes about a coffee cup flying across the room, the bucket careening down the corridor, etc. Find other instances of specific details you found effective and evocative. How does Schilk use his details to show rather than tell his story?

6. Look closely at the selection of events and sequences Schilk gives us. How does he organize his narrative? How does this organization serve his purpose? Evaluate the function of each scene.

7. Schilk's *tone* is almost conversational, like an old salt sitting in front of us recounting his adventures. What strategies does Schilk use to convey this effect? How does his tone establish his *purpose?*

8. Schilk reports: "I tried to get my readers involved with my tale by appealing to the romantic notions of the sea which most people have." In what way does Schilk appeal to these romantic notions? What else does he appeal to?

9. Schilk uses a lot of nautical terminology in his essay. Were you confused by these terms or did they add a sense of realism to the essay?

SUGGESTIONS FOR WRITING

1. Write a *narrative* essay about something that happened to you that made a difference and that has the potential of making a difference to your readers. Look back with your readers. Recapture some significant event or person or place or turning-point in your life. Help your reader to understand its impact on you.

2. Think of a time in your life when you thought you were invincible. What changed this image of yourself? Was there a particular person, experience, turning point? What humbled you? In a *narrative* essay, explain what changed your understanding of yourself and your world.

3. What does maturity mean to you? Write an essay in which you *define* the word maturity. You might want to use a personal *anecdote* as one *example* to support your definition.

BARBARA SEIDEL

Ocean County College
Toms River, New Jersey
Mary Ellen Byrne, instructor

"My upbringing was traditional," reports Barbara Seidel. "We were a close, volatile family and our home was always filled with relatives. I was the oddball from an early age—hot-tempered, rebellious, imaginative. I always loved to listen to the stories of my relatives; who did what, where, and why. I always wanted to understand peoples' motives, to explain their actions. Even today, I want to lift the lids off peoples' heads, peek inside, and explain the undercurrents of emotion and thought I often sense but cannot see. Writing is the best way to understand the world around me."

Born in Newark, New Jersey, Seidel grew up in Hillside and now lives in Toms River. She has always received praise and encouragement for her writing from her family and teachers. She served as the features editor of her high school newspaper and has written a cooking column and a column on humor in daily life for a county newspaper. About the conditions necessary for writing, Seidel tells us: "I want the house to be silent except for the sporadic squawking of my birds. I need to be left alone, without the phone ringing, or without anyone asking me questions or needing me at the moment."

Asked to write an essay of tribute to someone, Seidel immediately knew she would write about her father. "I knew this paper would be a very personal essay. I made a promise to myself that I would be open and vulnerable in my writing, that I would speak plainly about Dad. If I did otherwise, this paper would not work. I decided not to worry about the reaction my dad or other family members would have because otherwise I would have been paralyzed with the attempt to please everybody. I wrote what I felt and thought, and I hope anyone who reads this essay will understand that it was written with love."

For a more detailed study of Seidel's essay and the drafts that led to it, see Part III.

A Tribute to My Father

Thirty years ago, when his father was dying, he would leave his wife and two small children asleep in the square Cape Cod style house, then drive in the predawn light through the quiet city streets to take his father for outpatient medical care. Much later in his own life, his daughter puzzled over his devotion to a man who had divorced his mother, then ignored him and his brother. A faint look of surprise flickered in his eyes; then he answered concisely, "He was my father." He has always said that actions speak louder than words.

A soft-spoken man with a frequent low chuckle, he is so slow to anger that ₂ some people have been fooled into believing him an easy mark for trickery, a dangerous mistake. He is just as slow and long in remembering anyone who violates his strict set of values. He has no textbook education, yet he possesses an abundance of common sense. He is not religious, yet he is a moral man, consistent in his values on a daily basis, not only on a Sabbath. The inherent boundaries of his life, given and expected, have been loyalty, respect, tradition. Perhaps it is from the wild young hellion who quit school, whose idea of fun was joyriding in his older brother's car while that brother chased after him, that this man of caution and habit emerged.

Yet it was not caution, but sharp, clear instincts that twirled him fast and ₃ dizzy after the woman he would marry. He was already engaged; his fiancée made the fatal mistake of introducing her fair-haired, blue-eyed, slender man to the dark-haired woman whose first sight caused some inner voice to shout at him, firmly, "yes!" This woman would need him, would nurture him; he knew it. He broke his engagement, then immediately proposed, waiting a year before marrying only because of his future mother-in-law's insistence that he do so. He may have been impulsive, but he was, after all, respectful of his elders. And he had clearly chosen not only a wife but a family style. Tradition and warmth, tangled relationships, and rash tempers all spoke of people connecting to one another. His life became one of stability and constancy, of the same meat loaf served on the same day of each week, of the same conservative clothes worn year in and year out, of a man and a woman whose lives revolved around each other, so unlike his own past.

He spoke little about his past. No bitterness over the second-hand shoes ₄ stuffed with newspapers, or the hand-me-down clothing several sizes too large, pushed him to pursue great wealth to power. His dream, he later said, was to be able to work hard and just provide. He found the greatest pleasure in the small things—the ability to buy himself new shoes. Nor did he wield his own meager childhood as a club to inspire guilt or appreciation in his own more fortunate, more spoiled children. Instead, they learned of him through passing comments—or from his mother.

Her divorce came in an era when such an act was brazen. She worked long ₅ days caring for her two boys, who ate one meal daily at the corner candy store. The counterman would wait until they entered, then place a sandwich and a drink in front of them. "Never more or less, and all ordered and paid for in advance," he once said, a respectful, wondering tone in his voice at the sheer order of it all. She passed her stern work ethic on to him. He became very good at being responsible, dependable, at providing.

And the errant, alcoholic, polo-playing father—the womanizer who once 6
told his ladies that this then-nineteen-year-old younger son was his younger
brother—had a few admirable traits of his own left up his sleeve. To his son,
he passed on a love of animals and a fascination with cars, with their sight
and smell and the gas-powered freedom they gave to a man. His son, as a boy,
would drag home one protesting stray after another to a firmly opposed mother.
Years later, a father himself, he would laugh when his own daughter did the
same. After spending forty years selling the mechanical monsters, his love
affair with cars has only dimmed. It is telling of the man that in a profession
where truth is not always a recognizable commodity, he has a staunch reputation for honesty and a loyal following of customers.

If his honesty attracts them, so must his humor, gentle and chiding. And 7
of course, there are the quirks. There are the Hershey chocolate bars hidden
in the night table drawer, the towels folded and placed exactly so in the linen
closet, the sink faucet wiped shiny dry after dishes are washed. If his past did
not create anger to unbridled ambition, it did give him a legacy of sorts:
hoarded candy bars contrast with the giving parent; an obsession with details
fills him with anxiety. He worries over each decision like a dog gnawing on a
bone. He is still the small boy seeking security, the ultimate peacemaker avoiding confrontations, reconciling and rationalizing the good in people and in
issues to the frustration of his children. They, grown, have at last learned to
laugh gently at the habits that once exasperated them. There is the family
favorite—the phone joke. His son speaks to him, hangs up the phone, then
counts, "5-4-3-2—hello, Dad!" He knows his father will hesitate, then call
again. Is everyone happy? Should we talk more?

It is this son who is one of the brief detours on his well-laid road map of 8
life. With his daughter, loving was an easy goal. They shared a silent similarity
of vision, of loving and letting go. With his son, such love was reached only
after struggle; they spoke a different language. His son needed questions answered, challenges met, baseball and other games which had found no place
in his own childhood; he was a man concerned with providing. By the boy's
adolescence, they were like two bucks, antlers locked in a battle of dominance.
Now they are two men, two fathers, who reach gingerly, but often, across the
once-volatile differences of self to touch the love that always existed.

And now, at age fifty-eight, his hair is streaked with gray; his oval face is 9
heavily lined; he is tired. The habits of his lifetime have been altered, a difficult
task for a man who dislikes change, by the death of the woman who needed
and nurtured him. For years, he had watched her slowly die, her illness chipping away small pieces of his own courage, creating small anxieties, worrisome
habits that still linger with him. But he is not a man to live alone; he has

remarried. With his new wife, he can sometimes be found at the cemetery where their respective first spouses are buried. Flat bronze plaques and high white headstones stretch across the green fields. He bends down to clear her grave of grass and dirt. She was, after all, his wife. Actions do, indeed, speak.

QUESTIONS FOR READING AND REVISING

1. What is the dominant impression we get of Barbara Seidel's father in her essay? How does she create this impression? What kind of man is Seidel's father? How does he *define* the role of a father?

2. It is very easy to be sentimental about our parents, but Seidel writes about her father with controlled emotion and restraint. How does she avoid sentimentality? What is the effect of her control?

3. Why do you think Seidel chose to write her tribute in the third person? What advantage does she gain? What effect does this choice have on your reading of her essay? What would have been the difference if she had written her essay in the first person?

4. Seidel uses details very effectively to catch the nuances of her father's behavior. She tells us about his "second-hand shoes stuffed with newspapers" and "the Hershey chocolate bars hidden in the night table drawer." Select details and images you find effective and explain how they support the dominant impression of him that she conveys in her essay.

5. Seidel reports: "The hardest part of writing this paper was establishing order, organizing it so it made sense and did not jump from subject to subject." How does Seidel organize her tribute? Describe what holds the essay together so that it does not "jump from subject to subject."

6. Seidel urges her readers to "read the essay twice. The first time just let yourself be carried along by the rhythm of the words. The second time read the essay just to understand the man." Seidel plays with sentence structure, length, repetition, and rhythm. Which sentences and word choices do you find especially effective? Why?

7. About her *introduction*, Seidel tells us: "The lead paragraph in my first rough draft was simply part of the process of pouring words onto paper. I knew it would have to catch my attention if it would be able to catch the attention of a reader. I knew it did not work." Here is Seidel's rough-draft introduction:

> Actions speak louder than words, he often said. If so,
> then his actions say much about the man. There was that
> moment, thirty years ago, when his father was dying slowly.

> He would arise at dawn, leaving his wife and small children asleep in the tiny house, and drive the distance on quiet city streets. Years later, his own daughter, puzzled, would ask why he showed such devotion to the man who divorced his mother and abandoned him and his brother. He answered, with a faint look of surprise at the question, "He was my father."

What are the differences between the rough-draft introduction and the final-draft introduction? How does the revised introduction more successfully introduce and tie together the various ideas in the essay?

SUGGESTIONS FOR WRITING

1. Select someone about whom you would like to write a tribute. It should of course be someone with whom you are close. Try to *describe* this person's faults as well as merits to give your reader's complete impression of what he or she is like.

2. Americans ritually celebrate the relationship between children and parents on Mother's Day and Father's Day. Analyze your family's particular way of responding to and celebrating these holidays. What rituals have you created? What do they express about your family?

3. Write an essay in which you *explain* what you believe are the biggest mistakes parents make in raising their children. Illustrate your *point of view* with convincing examples.

JOHN S. SIEGRIST

Florence-Darlington Technical College
Florence, South Carolina
Holly Westcott, instructor

"I come from a military family which meant frequent changes in my life. I grew up in a very liberated and educationally free environment. My mother had a great deal to do with my education and desire to gain knowledge because of her open-mindedness and career as a teacher. I did average work in school until college, where I have maintained grade level for the Dean's List."

Born in Greenville, South Carolina, John Siegerist graduated from high school in Lyndon, Kansas, and now lives in Florence, South Carolina. Siegrist remembers his first piece of writing as a hundred-word theme given to the class as punishment. Since then, he has been writing for himself, with the encouragement of his high school and college teachers. About his writing process, Siegrist reports: "When I write, I sit at a desk or table in a quiet place and appear to be staring at an object. I tap my pencil or rub my forehead a lot if ideas are not coming to my mind quickly enough. Once a good idea comes to mind, I begin brainstorming and then outlining until I have enough ideas for my essay. I suppose it looks like I am in a trance until an idea strikes and then I am a flurry of continuous writing until my basic ideas are all on paper."

Asked to write about a process with which he was familiar, Siegrist decided to write about a subject he enjoyed: eating rattlesnake.

For an extended discussion of John Siegrist's work, see Part VI.

Rattlesnake: A Palatable Experience

People usually alienate themselves from things and experiences which are 1 not customary to their lifestyles. They close their minds to ideas which might prove enjoyable if they would only give themselves the opportunity to try something different. This is the kind of resistance met when one mentions the idea of eating rattlesnake.

There are people throughout the world who eat snake and find it not only 2 palatable, but delicious. People eat snake in sandwiches and soups, fried or barbecued. I was fortunate during my Air Force Service to be stationed only thirty miles from the site of the most famous rattlesnake roundup, held annually in Texas. I was able not only to find out how snake meat tastes, but to learn how to catch, skin, and prepare the snake myself.

The first step in tasting fried rattlesnake is to collect the ingredients. While 3 most of these can be found at any grocery store, the main item, the snake, must be sought out in its own habitat. One thing must be said before anyone goes out to catch a rattlesnake: Be careful. A snake is like any other wild animal. It is timid until concerned, but then it will fight to survive with every ounce of energy.

The best areas to look for rattlesnakes are among rock piles, rock fences, 4 heavy brush piles, and abandoned animal burrows. Since one would not want to reach into these places, a flashlight or mirror to reflect the sun into the darkened areas is a necessity. I have heard of people using hoses to pour gasoline into these places, but I feel that method is unsporting and creates an unnecessary fire hazard.

One should take into account the amount of meat needed when looking 5 for a snake. A snake two feet long would be all right for two people. If a family is larger or guests are invited over, a snake four or five feet in length is required. This will save the hostess the embarrassment of not having enough to go around.

Once the proper snake is found, it must be caught. This is usually accom- 6 plished through the use of special poles or hooks. The idea is to pull the snake from its place of refuge, use the pole to hold its head against the ground, then reach down and grab the snake behind his head. This gives the person control of the snake and allows it to be dropped into a burlap sack or other suitable container for transporting back to the house.

I am either too smart or too big a coward to attempt this practice. Since I 7 don't like the idea of coming within inches of an animal that has the potential to kill me, I prefer to shoot the snake from a reasonable distance. Any type of firearm will ensure that the snake is dead before it is picked up; however, I use a small caliber handgun because it destroys less meat. I shoot the snake in the head, as the body is the part to be cooked.

The very first thing to do upon killing the rattlesnake is to remove its head 8 using a knife, machete, axe, or even shovel. The fangs still contain poison and even an accidental scratch from them could result in serious medical problems. Once removed, the head should be buried to keep stray animals from eating it and becoming sick.

The snake is now ready to be skinned and gutted. I remove the tail first 9 and then attempt to cut a straight line from one end of its belly to the other end. This is fairly simple unless the snake's muscles are still contracting; then it can be a moving experience! If you find the snake trying to curl around your arm, either wait a little longer to do the skinning or have a friend hold the body still. This may show you who your friends are. A pair of scissors is much easier to use than a knife, but either is fine. It is important to keep the cut shallow and try not to go into the snake's organs, as that would contaminate the meat.

Once the cut is finished, the skin can easily be peeled back on each side of 10 the snake's body. I accomplish this by placing two fingers between the snake's skin and the meat on the body and running my fingers the entire length on both sides of the body. The skin will peel away just like a banana's. The snake skin is worth saving and can be used to make belts, hatbands, belt buckles, and other attractive items.

The gutting procedure is very similar to that of skinning the snake. Place 11 two fingers between the internal cavity and the meat of the snake's inner body. Running your fingers the entire length will remove the guts in one clean and effortless motion.

We now come to the actual preparation of the meat for cooking. There are 12 numerous ways to prepare any meat, and snake is no different. The seasoning is left up to one's personal taste, as is the style of cooking. Snake can be steamed, fried, baked, broiled, or even eaten raw. I prefer mine fried, although I would like to try it barbecued.

Frying rattlesnake is probably quickest and easiest of all the methods to 13 prepare it. The snake must be cut into portions which are easy to work with. I find two- or three-inch lengths adequate. I use a deep fat fryer, and while the oil is getting warm, I prepare the snake pieces. I combine several ingredients, the amounts of which depend upon the number of pieces to be cooked. I mix beaten eggs, pepper, and a little onion salt in a small bowl. I dip the snake pieces into the mixture and then roll them in flour. This gives them a light covering which becomes crunchy when fried.

The oil should be kept at a medium temperature. Too low a setting can 14 cause the snake to fall apart, and too high a setting can cause the flour crust to harden too much. The meat should be placed in the oil and left there for not more than a few minutes. The snake sections are similar to fillets of fish and fry very quickly. Once done, they should be removed to drain any excess oil. They are now ready to serve, and I guarantee everyone will be waiting in anticipation of their first bite of rattlesnake.

Eating rattlesnake is a rather unique experience. It can be served as the 15 main dish or as an appetizer. It is especially suited when one desires a light meal or a refreshing change from beef, pork, chicken, or fish. Using a fork to eat fried snake is almost useless, and one must rely upon the most basic of eating utensils, the fingers.

The taste of rattlesnake meat has a flavor all its own, close to that of 16 armadillo. Since most people have not tried armadillo, I would describe it as somewhat like turtle meat. I won't lie and say it tastes like chicken because it doesn't. It is a meat with a very mild flavor, possibly just a little sweet. I can only verify that it does taste exceptionally delicious.

I know most people will not have the opportunity or inclination to eat 17 rattlesnake, but if the chance should arise, try it. The taste is surprisingly good, and the experience may open your mind to other culinary delights which you have previously rejected. Forget about those ideas you have of snakes, and think of fried rattlesnake as one more way to experience life's variety of food.

QUESTIONS FOR READING AND REVISING

1. How does John Siegrist make the subject of eating rattlesnake interesting? What specific sentences in his essay help you to understand why this process fascinates him?

2. What does Siegrist assume about his readers knowledge? How does he anticipate and control his readers' expectations? Why, for instance, does he say: "I won't lie and say it tastes like chicken because it doesn't"?

3. Into how many steps does Siegrist break down the *process* he analyzes? What are these steps? Why are they presented in chronological order? How does Siegrist indicate to his readers when one stage of the process stops and the next begins.

4. Could you follow Siegrist's process? Or is this his *purpose* in writing the essay?

5. Describe Siegrist's *tone*. Do you think he is having fun writing about eating rattlesnake? Point out specific words and phrases to support your views.

6. Do you find Siegrist's *introduction* effective? What would be the effect on the essay if this introductory paragraph were deleted?

7. Siegrist shifts from using *one*, to *I*, to *you*. As a reader, does this shift in person bother you? Why? Would complete consistency be desirable? Which person— one, I, or you—seems the most natural?

8. Look at paragraph 13. Rewrite this paragraph to combine sentences, simplify and add greater variety.

SUGGESTIONS FOR WRITING

1. In his essay, Siegrist analyzes the *process* of cooking and eating rattlesnake, an experience most of us are unfamiliar with. Write an essay analyzing a process with which you are familiar but which may not be familiar to most people; for

example, something from your life as a student, a daughter, a parent, etc. or from your work. Detail the process step by step.

2. Using a humorous *tone*, write an essay in which you offer advice to someone. Some possible topics might include how to belly dance, how to write an A paper, how to get rich, how to raise a child, how to lose weight, etc.

3. Write an essay in which you describe in detail the process of preparing and eating a meal (or any ritual) in which every member of the family participates. Describe not only the nature of the process, but also all the sensual and emotional experiences involved.

KIM SPORT

Our Lady of Holy Cross College
New Orleans, Louisiana
Sister Rose Elizabeth Brown, instructor

Kim sport's ideal writing environment is one without distractions. When she writes, she sees no visitors and accepts no phone calls. About her writing, Sport reports: "I used to try to avoid writing, but now I consider it a challenge. Today I have so much to say about so many things that I look forward to sharing my opinions with others. Writing is a fantastic way for me to gather my thoughts together and resolve problems. Learning to write is the most important element of our education. The ability to write is a measure of a person's qualifications. One should always be proud of what and how she writes."

Sport, a nationally registered X-ray and nuclear medicine technologist, plans to graduate with a degree in health sciences and begin law school at Tulane University. Born in New Orleans, Sport grew up in Gretna, Louisiana. Her hobbies include skiing, sailing, and reading.

Asked to write a persuasive essay, Sport says that her personal feelings about capital punishment promoted her to select this subject for her essay.

Capital Punishment

The average American runs a higher risk of being a victim of violent crime 1
than of being hurt in an auto accident. This is the finding of a study done by the Justice Department's Bureau of Justice Statistics (*U.S. News and World Report*, 12 Dec. 1983: 72) It seems as though crime, rape, and murder are becoming ways of life for many people. To deal with crime, America has become a country on the defense. Airports are equipped with weapon scanners; banks are equipped with electronic security devices; individuals carry Mace or guns and equip their homes with security systems and multiple locks. We have started fingerprinting our children because we are afraid someone will kidnap them, and we have started neighborhood watch programs to prevent crime around our homes. The rise in crime can be blamed on many factors, but the main factor is that the punishment for criminal activity has become very lenient. People are not afraid to commit violent crimes. Criminals are comforted by a legal process that is more concerned with their rights than the rights of their victims, life sentences with parole, plea bargaining, and the availability of appellate courts. Criminals deserve punishment for their crimes, and the worst crimes deserve the worst punishment—capital punishment. The act of capital punishment is a point of great controversy in the United States,

and there are those who are pushing for its abolishment. Capital punishment should not be abolished because: it deters crime, unburdens tax payers, prevents overcrowded jails, and provides absolute justice to society in certain cases.

Not everyone feels that capital punishment is necessary. The opponents of capital punishment have raised three major arguments against it. First, opponents consider capital punishment to be cruel and unusual punishment, and therefore, a violation of the Eighth Amendment. Proponents of capital punishment realize that the Constitution forbids cruel and unusual punishment but do not believe that capital punishment falls into this category. The Eighth Amendment was ratified in the eighteenth century to prevent the punishments practiced at that time. These included public hangings, burnings, decapitations, mutilations, torture, and dragging criminals by horses through towns. Nowhere does the Eighth Amendment prohibit the death penalty, which proponents feel is a civilized punishment when compared to the atrocities committed by those sentenced to death. The second argument against capital punishment is that Christianity forbids it in the words "Thou shalt not kill." Proponents of the death penalty feel that the biblical "eye for an eye" is an argument for capital punishment on the grounds that it is fitting and just, and Jesus' dictum, "All who take the sword will perish by the sword," makes clear that the death penalty for murder still stands. Opponents of capital punishment feel, third, that capital punishment is as much a crime as any other reason for taking a human life. The logical argument presented by proponents of the death penalty is that murder is illegal and capital punishment is not. If capital punishment isn't illegal, then it cannot be murder. Clearly, capital punishment is an emotional and moral issue, but to abolish capital punishment will not solve the problems of crime, overcrowded jails, increasing taxes, and those who demand justice for the offenses committed against them.

Capital punishment addresses the crime problem because capital punishment deters crime. Ernest van den Haag of Fordham University believes that "nobody fears prison as much as death." Economist Isaac Ehrlich built a "supply and demand" theory of murder and argued that capital punishment prevents more murders than prison sentences. Because of the 3,411 executions carried out from 1933 to 1967, Ehrlich speculates that enough potential murderers were discouraged that some 27,000 victims lives were saved (*Time*, 24 Jan. 1983: 35). Repeat offenders prove that prison does not deter crime. For example, Charles Manson, who was arrested many times and was convicted of murder, is eligible for parole next year. His cult is waiting for him. Are we to believe that Manson will find a job and settle down with a wife and children? If Manson gets out, is there any reason that he should fear our judicial and criminal systems? I think not. If the death penalty were properly carried out, crime would be deterred even more, but criminals can see that the 1,289 people presently on death row may be alive for a long time (*Time*, 6 Feb. 1984: 56). Criminals must be made to fear the consequences of their actions, and capital punishment, properly carried out, can accomplish this.

While criminals sit on death row or serve life sentences for their offenses 4 to society, society supports them with its tax dollars. A person whose wife and children were murdered pays for the murderer's food, clothing, and shelter. Isn't something wrong here? These criminals are obligated to give nothing back to society. This situation is not only unfair, but it is a waste of precious funds that could be allocated to those in dire need of food, clothing, and shelter. Ted Guest of *U.S. News and World Report* (2 May 1983: 42) says that "the current cost of $20,000 yr. to keep the nearly 500,000 U.S. prisoners locked up is twice as much as the cost to send a child to Stanford University." Also, our judicial system allows for numerous appeals by death row inmates, and last year, the New York State Defenders Association estimated the typical trial costs for death penalty cases to be 1.5 million dollars each (*Time*, 24 Jan. 1983: 39). This money is being wasted on society's worst offenders. Capital punishment would put an end to this travesty of justice.

Capital punishment, while deterring crime, would also prevent jail over- 5 crowding, which has in itself become a serious problem. Opponents of capital punishment favor life sentences at $20,000 a year for criminals over the death penalty, but where are we going to put them? A Justice Department Bureau of Statistics' study concluded that "in actual numbers, prisons held nearly one-half million inmates in mid 1983—more than double [that] of a decade earlier" (*U.S. News and World Report*, 12 Dec. 1983: 72). There is no more room for prisoners; cities have resorted to tents in some cases, and in a terrible situation in New York, a judge ordered the release of 610 prisoners at Attica Institute to relieve prison overcrowding (*Time*, 5 Dec. 1983: 65). To build new prisons is outrageously expensive, with costs approximated at $70 billion for every 100,000 beds. These costs do not even include the costs to operate and staff the prisons. Why should capital offenders be allowed to take up badly needed prison space?

Realistically, capital offenders deserve to die. Their crimes are so horrendous 6 that the only comparable punishment is death. For example, on the night of June 3, 1973, Henry Brisbon, along with three other men, forced a woman off the road. Brisbon ordered her to strip at gun point, then as she begged for mercy, he thrust his gun into her vagina and fired. The woman died after another shot to the throat. As if this were not enough, Brisbon and his friends stopped another car carrying a young engaged couple. He made them lay down on the shoulder of the road and told them to "Kiss your last kiss," then he shot them both in the back. This case, as reported in *Time*'s "An Eye for an Eye" (24 Jan. 1983: 30) was accompanied by another case which should convince even the staunchest opponent of capital punishment to reconsider his position. Lawrence Bittaker is on death row at San Quentin. He and a friend kidnapped, raped, and sodomized five teenage girls for days at a time in front of a camera. Bittacker tortured the girls by using pliers on their nipples and icepicks in their ears; he recorded their screams. He killed all of them, but did something special to the last victim—he strangled her with a coat hanger, mutilated her genitals, then placed her body on a lawn so he could watch the reactions of its discoverers. Repulsively, both Brisbon and Bittaker complain of their prison conditions and think that they do not deserve to die. Regrettably, because of legal red tape, they never will. These men are not insane. They are as sane as the 1,287 others on death row who are guilty of such disgusting acts that the only retribution is their death.

Society should never have to worry that capital offenders such as Manson, 7 Bittaker, and Brisbon are allowed back on the streets, but this is the greatest consequence of the abolishment of capital punishment. Only ten of our fifty states have adopted statutes which abolish parole. This means that in forty states the Bittakers, Mansons, and Brisbons could be freed on parole. If not paroled, capital offenders will continue to be supported by a society at the cost of $20,000 a year each or 257.8 million dollars a year for capital offenders alone. Simply, the abolishment of capital punishment means fear and increased taxes. It is time for innocent Americans to live without fear. Capital punishment is the only way to put fear where it belongs—with those who intend to harm others.

QUESTIONS FOR READING AND REVISING

1. What is Kim Sport's *thesis?* How does she use her thesis to organize her essay? How does she build her *argument?*

2. Do you find Sport's *argument* convincing? Explain by pointing to specific strengths or weaknesses you see in the evidence Sport provides. What issues does she not address?

3. As a reader, how do you know that Sport has a strong opinion on the topic? Describe Sport's *tone.* Does she seem reasonable and believable to you?

4. How does Sport pull you into the world of her essay? Why do you think she refers in her *introduction* to fingerprinting children, burglar alarm systems, and

neighborhood watch programs? What assumptions does she make about her readers' position on capital punishment?

5. In paragraph 3, Sport provides the opinions of two experts who agree with her position. Has she proved her point? How could an opponent refute her? What further evidence does she need?

6. One of Sport's strategies is to present the position of opponents of capital punishment. If she is a proponent of capital punishment, why does she give the opponent's point of view? What does she gain by using this strategy? Is it effective?

7. Why does Sport choose the dramatic examples of Manson, Brisborn, and Bittacker to make her point? What effect did these examples have on you? Why are these effective examples? Why not?

8. Sport reports; "To read my essay, one must separate thoughts on religion from those on law. Even if my readers believe in the 'Thou shalt not kill' commandment, I want them to consider the victims and not the capital offenders themselves." Was Sport successful in achieving her goal?

SUGGESTIONS FOR WRITING

1. Think of an unjust situation that directly affects you in school, in your family or community, or at work. Write a *persuasive* essay in which you present your reasons for believing this situation unjust. Recommend changes to eliminate the injustice.

2. What is your opinion on capital punishment? Do you agree with Sport's ideas? Write a response to Sport's essay in which you either refute her arguments to support them with additional evidence.

3. Write a persuasive essay on a change you would like to see or an opinion you want to defend. Imagine that your readers disagree with your *point of view*.

FRANCES E. TAYLOR

Hunter College
New York, New York
Louise A. DeSalvo, instructor

"My earliest recollections are of writing squiggly lines, and asking my sister if my squiggly lines said anything. She would say, 'What are you trying to say?' And I would say, 'I love you and I'd like to go outside, and can we play with my toys.' She would say, 'You said it!' and then give me a big hug and say 'That's very good Frances.' "

Frances Taylor, born in Brooklyn, New York, describes her background as a working-class Afro-American family. Her interests include composing for guitar, reading, leather work, carpentry, and minority histories. She plans to write, teach, advocate issues relating to disenfranchised people, and pursue a degree in law.

Taylor reports that there were always books in her home from as early as she can remember. From these books she learned to love the written word. Taylor describes writing as "crafting power" and she advises fellow writers: "There is no voice on earth like your own, and that equals power, learn to craft it, and read, read, read."

Taylor's assignment was to write about her first encounter with someone who had made an impact on her life. About her essay, Taylor tells us: "In writing this essay I got in touch with a very important part of my life that I had been trying to write about for years and had not been able to. I wanted my audience to be moved and to think about my experience, even though it was unique and perhaps, to some, bizarre. I ask that my readers bring their humanity to the reading of my essay."

Carol

1   She had a moustache, shiny and black against her brown skin. Her front teeth were outlined with gold fillings—I later learned she hated that—but it didn't keep her from smiling. She wanted you to know she saw you, felt you, was listening to you.

2   She made a hissing sound when she laughed—as if in preparation for an explosion; but she always stopped just before the lid flew off or the sound got too loud. Her body was chestnut brown and sensual, yet tense somehow—as if unhappiness, anger, some long-ago buildup of feeling was locked inside. She wore a red tank top tucked in close to her body. I was immediately afraid of her. She seemed so hot skillet sizzly and those eyes sparkled and caught you like a light out for moths.

3   I was a recluse rescued by a bookmobile librarian who had a head full of Gerard Manley Hopkins and Sara Teasdale and a heart for the odd. I noticed

Carol because I'd just come to my first lesbian dance at a Daughters of Bilitis
meeting room cum dance hall in a musty Prince Street warehouse with a
peeling facade. A gypsy lady with spangles and rouge kept telling me to be
attentive for bells and cymbals and some great shocking quality in the air in
case the woman I dreamed of came through the door. But Carol met someone
else that night; another firstcomer just as new and intimidated as I.

The loft was dark, filled with cigarette smoke and cheap soda cans bent and   4
used for ashtrays. Soda stains and beer puddles dotted the splintered, gray-dirt
planking of the warped wooden floor. Some lone wailing love song for her and
her new love to remember each other and the night by—maybe Roberta Flack—
poured from the juke. I hid behind the sticky counter selling orange and grape
drinks and colas that were tucked down in the melting ice filling the huge
green plastic garbage pail. A skinny Caucasian, dressed all in black—hot pants
over leotards—with dyed black hair and insect wings growing out of her eyelids,
kept offering me bright red kisses in payment for the drinks and flapping the
lids and leaning forward on one elbow, tapping on my cheek with thin red
talons.

Carol invited me to stay in New York that night, driven to West 46th   5
Street by her new love with the riding habit in the boot of her Volvo station
wagon. Her social worker love was a granddaughter of Philadelphia's black
elite "who taught me to respect my elders and how to sit at table." A Roller
Derby aspirant when in her teens, she'd somehow cooled her heft and swagger
by her student travels up the Mediterranean and down some Elysées. "What
have we here?" said Carol admiring all this self-sufficiency. "What a prize!"
The "prize" moved her tennis racket and riding boots, the black velvet domed
hat, crop, training manuals, feminist books, Woman Sports magazines—and
made room in the back for me—escapee from under a bed in Queens.

In flight from that spirit-corset in Queens, I moved into Carol's tiny two   6
rooms and slept on the floor with a finicky Doberman in the tight space used
for storage. Carol always walked around in black lace panties, smoking her
cigarettes, sipping strong drink and mud-black coffee and fighting with her
memories. Her breasts and the rest of her body were firm and full and her
underarms smelled like flowers.

She used to turn her pointing index fingers around each other as though   7
she were outlining a cylinder when she talked intensely—and as she did it
that first morning a light came on like the corona over El Greco's Toledo and
then snapped off. I loved her fully from then on. I can remember the exact
moment. "I feel as if life has chipped away at me—that's why I left my job
. . . I couldn't work anymore—but there's still some part of who I really am
left in the center of my being. I try to keep it safe" (she hunched her shoulders
and spoke in a whisper, pointing at her heart) "guarding it here—in the center

of my being." I got a flash of the lay of the land of her soul and never saw anything that mattered but that part of her ever again.

Somehow I became a communications link between her and the "prize," 8 like Elmer's glue, I thought. My pride in being needed encouraged them to manipulate each other through me. I convinced myself I was the lover she'd love if she didn't love the lover she had. But as she drifted with the "prize" she tried any port in her storm, any port but me.

Her vacations home from Mary MacCloud Bethune's campus in Georgia 9 she spent ironing, washing, and cooking for the college boys in the family. "And don't you know they laughed and watched the ball games and thought it was their due!" She'd spend hours shifting canvases she's stretched and filled, rearranging her small apartment, putting blue hospital sheets on the two mattresses stacked on the floor. She told me about the husband whom she'd left, who was just like her brothers, and then about the woman in her life and how strong she felt in her Florida beach house with the twin brandy-hued Dobermans and the narrowed-down and hollowed-out blonde and the blonde's two kids, and the shake-up-the-world sex. That lover left her for an importunating older woman, a bigot with a laundromat in a nearby town.

Examining her painting of a nude black woman one day, she said, "She has 10 no life, has she? Look! She's static, dead!" and ripped into it with her palette knife so the head hung down, brown and floppy.

Many months later. She called me from Florida after her breakup with the 11 "prize" and told me she'd been "hexed" out of New York but wanted to come back. She was missing *my* ex this time. I said, "And what about me, Carol? You're like a sorry old voice from the past—with bad news. . . ." She hung-up on me—four o'clock in the morning—all the way from Delray.

Three months later. The "prize" called to tell me Carol had shot herself in 12 a women's commune on the South Side of Chicago. And that's what I can't forget. She's all dead and blown apart someplace with the last words from me bitter ones.

Back in Florida, her father, the landscape gardener, and her mother, the 13 nursing instructor, have become Seventh Day Adventists and made her bedroom into a little shrine. Her paintings, some of her photographs, and maybe fresh-cut flowers are kept there. And maybe it smells just a little bit like Carol.

QUESTIONS FOR READING AND REVISING

1. In writing this essay, Frances Taylor tells us: "I felt that I had cracked a code, and that the code was my own voice. I was connecting my voice with my work in a way that I didn't think was possible." Taylor's voice is authentic and we

feel and hear the presence of the writer in her essay. What effect does her clear, authentic voice have on your reading of her essay? How do you know that she is writing about a subject that is very close to her?

2. What overall impression does Taylor create of Carol? What *unifies* Taylor's description?

3. This essay is rich in detail. As readers, we feel the presence of the writer working hard to describe what Carol meant to her. Select details and images that you find especially effective and show how these details support the writer's *purpose.*

4. Taylor uses dialogue very effectively. What does the dialogue reveal about Carol? About the writer herself?

5. Taylor begins her description immediately without any introductory comments. What is the effect of beginning this way? What is the effect of referring to Carol as "she" and "her" before we know her name? How does Taylor succeed in bringing you into the world of her essay?

6. For what *audience* is Taylor writing her essay? She tells us that she wrote her first draft without thinking about a reader and that is why she was able to write about such personal things withoug being blocked. Does Taylor seem to be aware of her audience in her final draft? Find evidence in the essay to support your answer.

SUGGESTIONS FOR WRITING

1. Write about a person in your own life who has made an impact on you and about whom you feel strongly. Describe your initial encounter with this person.

2. What is friendship? Henry Adams tells us: "One friend in a lifetime is much; two are many; three are hardly possible." And Montesquieu: "Friendship is an arrangement by which we undertake to exchange small favors for big ones." Write an essay in which you *explain* the concept of friendship. You might want to use a dramatic personal experience as one of your *examples* to illustrate your *thesis.*

GREG WEEKES

University of Central Florida
Orlando, Florida
Gerald Schiffhorst, instructor

Life and work at sea have figured prominently in Greg Weekes's life. The son of a Navy captain, Weekes was born in Corpus Christi, Texas, and has lived with his family in Europe and the Middle East: "Being in a Navy family and living almost all over the world has greatly influenced my life." A graduate of Rogers High School in Newport, Rhode Island, where he earned nine varsity letters in track and cross-country, Weekes worked as a deckhand and as chief mate on east coast charter boats before enrolling at the University of Central Florida, where he majors in science education and plans to teach high school biology.

"When I get a good idea my mind just keeps going, and I find I can't write fast enough. I have a hard time writing when the idea isn't there. But when I get a brainstorm on a story, it flows out like water." Weekes wrote only one draft of the following essay, in which he contrasts the tranquility of a whale in calm Alaskan waters to an account of the violent death of a whale "Off the Grand Banks." His essay seeks "to show others the horror of the modern whale hunt and to impress upon my readers that the ' romance ' of the eighteenth-century whale hunt is gone."

Off the Grand Banks . . .

Picture, if you can, a dark blue fjord in Alaska. The snowcapped mountains 1 rise high into the sky around the water, and their reflection is clear on the still surface. Patches of evergreen trees top the shoreline, and all you can hear is the cold silence of a still spring day. One lone whale suddenly breaks the glassy surface of the day, coming up for some air. Just the tip of its head shows, and soon the air is alive with spray. As it dives again you catch a glimpse of its tail, strong and powerful, speckled with barnacles. The huge fin slips silently beneath the water, and you think the whale is gone. But it soon comes up again, this time in an almost perpendicular position with the surface. Its face has long white scars all under what would be its chin, probably from raking the muddy bottom searching for food. Or maybe they're reminders of a fierce battle, long forgotten by both combatants. Its large brown eye reminds you of a lonely hound dog, and its mouth is curved into what looks like an eternal grin—a seductive sort of smile. It slides gracefully back into the water the same way it came, leaving barely a ripple on the mirrorlike surface.

The same whale, the one you had admired so much, the one so free and   2
happy, could be the same whale in this story—a story not of whales, but of
men.

I had been crew on the selling ship *Valhalla*, and we were about three-   3
hundred miles offshore in an area called the Grand Banks. The wind was calm
and the sea placid as we made our way east. It was getting late in the day, so
the captain ordered us to take down the jib and reef the main.

In the process I heard what sounded like gunfire in the distance. I wasn't   4
the only one who had heard it, as a few of the other deckhands cocked their
heads curiously, taking note of the strange booming.

Looking in the direction of the sound, we saw a dark voluminous cloud of   5
smoke billowing out of a ship, with many smaller waves breaking around its
bow.

"Whaleship—probably Russian," the first mate told me. Very few of us had   6
ever seen one, and it was nothing like I had expected as it neared our boat.

It was an enormous vessel, painted red with large rust spots dotting the   7
hull. I grabbed some binoculars from below and saw the gunman; he was aiming
a lethal-looking barbed weapon at the water in front of him. The whales were
running in a panic toward us and as the ship got closer a female humpback,
surfacing to get air, gave its position away by expelling its blowhole. The
harpoon sunk in deep, and the whale suddenly dived. The line connecting
the animal to the ship tightened, and a plume of blood-red water filled the air
above the whale as the grenade-tipped harpoon detonated. The whale surfaced
again, and blew out its blowhole a tall geyser of blood. When she rolled over,
we saw where the explosive had left its mark. Exposed flesh cut a gaping hole
at least ten feet wide above its fin, leaving a huge depression in the side of
the whale. Blood started to rush into the hole and changed it from stark white
to a pool of red. She took one last dive, and when she came up again all the
blood had been washed away. As the sea around the whale was reddening, we
heard a small cry. Then she rolled on her side, never to dive again.

As the ship moved in to process the whale, men with small rifles opened   8
fire into the water all around it. Sharks from miles away had sensed the blood
and were tearing huge chunks out of the dead whale. The sea around the whale
was soon churning with sharks, all hoping for an easy meal.

Slowly the whale was hauled onto the ship, its carcass limp on the slanted   9
floor of the processing deck. We could almost smell the stench as the sun
baked the slaughtered animal. The sharks, still crazed with the smell of blood,
had started to attack themselves and were moving away from the area. Some
sharks had remained attached to the whale even onto the deck and were beaten

to bloody pulps by husky crew members, no doubt to end up on that night's dinner table.

The whale doesn't grin as it lies on the deck; the seductive smile is gone. 10 Its sad brown eyes have been plucked out by scavenging seagulls, and its barnacled tail, useless to man, has been thrown back into the water.

Some say that its usefulness to man is just beginning. And some, thinking 11 of a clear blue inlet on a certain spring day, say it has just ended. But the man who killed it will never know for sure. It probably never bothered him before. Because, you see, he knows only one side of the story.

QUESTIONS FOR READING AND REVISING

1. How would you define Greg Weekes's *purpose* in this essay? Is it to highlight the contrast between describing the tranquility of a whale's surfacing in a "fjord in Alaska" and narrating the violence of a whale hunt? Something else? How does Weekes's essay move beyond either *description* or *narration* to express some larger governing idea? What is the idea that governs this essay?

2. In paragraph 2, Weekes notes that this is *not* an account "of whales, but of men." What function does the paragraph serve in the essay? How, specifically, does Weekes's essay fulfill the expectation created in this paragraph? How do the paragraphs that follow demonstrate that this is indeed an account "not of whales, but of men"?

3. Analyze the structure of the essay. Identify its distinct parts. How does Weekes *unify* them? What order does he establish? Specific to general, general to specific, concrete to abstract, abstract to concrete, increasing importance, increasing complexity, step-by-step, something else?

4. What is the effect of Weekes's extended description in paragraph 1? How does the opening paragraph contribute to the overall purpose of his essay? In your judgment, could—or should—the first paragraph be eliminated? Why? Why not?

5. Effective description uses *concrete*, sensory details. List the instances when Weekes appeals to each of his readers's five senses in his *description* of a whale in "a fjord in Alaska" and in his account of the whale hunt off the Grand Banks? Point to specific words and phrases to support your responses.

6. Effective description also uses clear *point of view*, the perspective from which a story is told or a scene is described. Show how Weekes's point of view either

changes or remains consistent as the essay proceeds. Rewrite paragraph 7 (on killing the whale) from the point of view of the "gunman" on board the whaling ship.

7. What assumptions does Weekes make about his audience's familiarity with his setting? With whale hunting? What does Weekes assume about his audience's attitude toward each subject? How much background information is necessary to appreciate the overall point of his essay? How much background information does he provide? What, for example, is the purpose—and the effect—of Weekes's use of the phrase "if you can" in the opening line of the essay?

8. At several points in the essay, Weekes introduces technical details from life at sea ("jib," "reef the main," "wale," etc.). In what specific ways do you think technical *diction* adds to or detracts from the essay? How does Weekes use these terms to increase or diminish his intended effect? How does he make sure that his audience will not be distracted from or put off by unfamiliar language?

9. Show how Weekes's *narrative* of killing the whale does or does not prepare readers for the points he makes in the final two paragraphs of his essay. Suggest how Weekes might revise this narrative to strengthen the overall purpose of his essay.

SUGGESTIONS FOR WRITING

1. One of the reasons for the success of Greg Weekes's essay is the *contrast* he creates between the tranquility of watching the performance of a whale and the violent spectacle of the whale hunt. Choose some aspect of contemporary American life—traveling by train, ship, or plane; attending a Sunday afternoon doubleheader at the ballpark, etc.—and write an essay in which you combine *description* and *narration* to highlight the *contrast* between the pleasure, and at times the serenity, associated with an activity and the possibility that the activity might well be engulfed in violence at any moment.

2. Weekes talks about the "gaping hole" left in the whale's side by the explosion of a "grenade-tipped harpoon"—surely a far different procedure for killing whales than that practiced by, say, Captain Ahab and his crew in Herman Melville's *Moby-Dick*. Consider the process of doing some kind of work that has been transformed in recent years by technology. Write an expository essay *comparing and contrasting* the past and the present processes. Exactly what changes in procedure have occurred, and what are the short-term and long-term consequences.

3. In the opening paragraph of his essay, Weekes depicts a place where the natural

world and people seem to be completely at peace. Do you know such a place, some location in the contemporary world that you feel still reflects such a peaceful relationship? Describe its distinctive characteristics in detail. Then write an essay in which you use your detailed *description* as the basis for making some larger point about preserving such a relationship between people and the natural environment.

STEVE WEST

Columbia University
New York, New York
Laura Novo, instructor

"After I receive an assignment, I often mull it over while doing other things (like jogging) and most of my ideas for my essays come up during this period. Once I get started, I jot down an outline, often in the margin of some other piece of paper, and try to write the introduction. A person who walked in on me during this stage would probably see me with my feet up on the desk, chewing on a pencil or tugging on my hair, and trying to get the paper started. If he looked over my shoulder, he would probably see two or three sentence fragments of introductions that I had abandoned quickly, and probably a doodle or two in the margin. Somewhere near the bottom of the page would begin an introduction that seemed good enough for the moment."

Steve West reports that he enjoys writing analytical pieces and feels that his ability at analytical thought has shaped both his writing and his interest in debate. West was named one of eighteen John Jay Scholars in the Columbia College Class of 1988. He is a reporter for the student newspaper, the Spectator, and spends from fifteen to thirty hours a week writing for the newspaper. West plans to major in history and is thinking about a career in law.

Asked to write an essay in which he analyzed one of the sources he planned to use for his research paper, West chose to analyze Jeane Kirpatrick's speech to the United Nations since "it was the most thorough and well thought out of the Reagan administration's statements on the Grenada invasion." West explains: "Before writing my essay I had already done a considerable amount of research on the Grenada invasion, and I had some idea of what were the disputable facts in Kirkpatrick's speech. A close reading of her speech and an examination of it in light of the other information I had gathered were the bases of my attacks on her reasoning."

Evaluating U.S. Motives
for the Grenada Invasion

Following the U.S. invasion of Grenada in October, 1983, the United   1
Nations General Assembly adopted a resolution condemning the invasion and
calling for the immediate withdrawal of United States troops. The measure
passed, however, before the United States was allowed to present its case, and
in "The U.N. and Grenada: A Speech Never Delivered," U.S. Ambassador
Jeane Kirkpatrick outlines the arguments she had hoped to present in defense
of the invasion. Although her article is probably the most comprehensive

defense of the invasion advanced by any administration official, her arguments suffer from factual distortions and omissions and from their inconsistency with much of United States policy in Central and South America (11–18).

Kirkpatrick provides four different justifications for the invasion. The first 2 (and the one most stressed by administration officials at the time of the invasion) is the possibility that Americans on the island might have been harmed or taken hostage in the upheaval that followed the assassination of Maurice Bishop. She cites the twenty-four-hour shoot-on-sight curfew imposed by the new regime as an example of the threat facing U.S. citizens. She also maintains that the government failed to fulfill its promise to open the airport to foreigners wishing to leave and concludes that the threat facing Americans on the island was "real and imminent."

Kirkpatrick's analysis seems valid on the basis of the evidence she presents, 3 but she ignores a number of facts that suggest that the Americans were in little danger and could have been evacuated without an invasion. The shoot-on-sight curfew, for example, was lifted the day before the invasion, and Americans at the St. George's University Medical School resumed classes the same day (Kenworthy 637). Charles Modica, head of the medical school, was in contact with U.S. officials several times before the invasion and informed them that only 10 percent of his students wished to be evacuated (Kenworthy 637). Furthermore, the airport was not closed, as Kirkpatrick charges; the single commercial airline servicing the island refused to send its aircraft to Grenada, but chartered planes did remove over thirty foreigners (Americans among them) on October 24, and State Department officials were arranging with the government for the evacuation of other Americans (Kenworthy 638). These facts suggest that whatever instability did exist after the October 19 coup had largely abated before the American invasion six days later.

Kirkpatrick's second justification for the invasion is the threat that Grenada 4 posed to other nations in the region and to American security interests. She quotes Jamaican Prime Minister Edward Seaga, who pointed to the presence of Cuban advisors and to the soon-to-be-completed Pt. Salines airstrip as proof of Grenada's threatening military buildup. After the invasion, Kirkpatrick charges, huge stockpiles of weapons and contracts for future arms shipments were discovered, further justifying fears of Grenadian aggression.

One of this justification's major flaws is the fact that much of the evidence 5 on which it is based—evidence about the stockpiles of weapons and the arms transfer agreements—was not discovered until after the invasion and therefore could not have played any role in the initial decision to intervene. In addition, much of the evidence on which the administration did act is not very compelling. Before the invasion, for example, the administration acknowledged in a telegram to Fidel Castro that the Cubans on the island were a mix of poorly armed military advisors and construction workers, hardly a force that posed a significant threat to either U.S. or regional security ("Truth" 678).

And what about the Pt. Salines airstrip? Kirkpatrick insists that it was to have been a military institution but ignores the plausibility of the Grenadian explanation that tourist airliners and not military jets were intended users of the facility. In fact, the latter explanation seems more consistent with the history and design of the facility. The airstrip was not, for example, a primarily Cuban project; funding was provided by the International Monetary fund and by the British, whose contractors also did much of the work (Kenworthy 642). After the invasion, Plessey, one of the British contractors, published a list of eleven features (including military radar and fuel storage tanks) necessary for a military airstrip but lacked by the Pt. Salines facility (Massing 82). Finally, the length of the new airstrip (9,000 feet versus the 4,300-foot runway of the old airport) was a result of the government's desire to accommodate the largest commercial airliners; the shorter length of the old facility required tourists to transfer to smaller planes for the last leg of their trip to Grenada, and the government hoped that direct flights would boost tourism (Massing 82).

Kirkpatrick also justifies the invasion as a legitimate response to requests made by six Caribbean nations and by Grenada's Governor General, Paul Scoon. Arguing that Grenada's military buildup represented a threat to regional security, she concludes that the request of the four members of the Organization of Eastern Caribbean States (Barbados and Jamaica participated in the invasion but are not OECS members) was legal under the OECS charter. In addition, she notes that Scoon's request carried "exceptional moral and legal weight" because he was the only figure of legitimate political authority on the island.

Closer scrutiny of the facts and of international law, however, finds these justifications seriously lacking in credibility. Under the OECS charter, all seven members of the organization must approve any military action undertaken in its name, but only four members sanctioned or participated in the invasion (Joyner 137). Furthermore, the charter allows a military response only in the event of external aggression against a member nation, but the upheaval in Grenada was an internal affair and posed little genuine threat to regional security (Joyner 136). Kirkpatrick also overstates the impact of Scoon's request; the Governor General was stripped of all but ceremonial duties when the country's constitution was rewritten in 1979, and in any event, his request did not reach U.S. officials until thirty-six hours after they had already begun drawing up plans for the invasion (Joyner 139).

Kirkpatrick's final justification for the invasion is the need to restore democracy to the island after the October 19 coup. The ambassador charges that the Grenadians were subjected to a "brutal reign of terror" before the October 25 invasion and that the nation was in danger of becoming a Soviet/Cuban satellite. The invasion, Kirkpatrick says, restored democracy to the island and won the overwhelming support of the Grenadians.

The major flaw in this argument is its inconsistency with much of U.S. 10 policy in Central and South America; the administration seems to have done a rather abrupt about-face from its former insensitivity to regional coups. In the spring of 1982, for example, the administration responded to a right-wing military coup in Guatemala with an offer of a $4 million arms sale ("Generals" 29), and in a situation remarkably similar to that in Grenada, the United States stood silently by in November, 1982, when a group of Marxist military officials overthrew the legitimate government of Surinam and instituted their own bloody reign of terror (Dew 6). Kirkpatrick's fear that Grenada would have lost its national identity to the Cubans or Soviets seems exaggerrated given the limited extent of their involvement on the island and is somewhat ironic given the administration's much greater involvement in Honduras and El Salvador. Apparently, the administration's concern is not so much with sovereignty per se as with the possibility that a nation might lose its sovereignty to the wrong superpower.

Interestingly, recent Administration statements about Grenada have largely 11 ignored Kirkpatrick's arguments. President Reagan, for example, declared last spring that the invasion marked the end of the "doom and defeatism" of the Vietnam era, and George Bush sounded the same note last fall in his debate with Geraldine Ferraro, describing the invasion as a "proud, proud moment for America and democracy." Such statements, coupled with the inadequacy of Kirkpatrick's justifications, suggest that the real motives of the invasion may have been to boost American morale and to reestablish America's role as a police officer to its southern neighbors. In a sense, the administration's presentation of its motives for the invasion resembles its handling of factual information about the affair; just as the truth about the invasion and the situation on the island emerged slowly, after much of the fighting had ended and public interest had dwindled, so the invasion was initially justified with talk about rights and the threat of violence and aggression, leaving the less honorable but more important motives to be acknowledged only when the act was over and almost forgotten.

Works Cited

Dew, Edward. "Surinam Tar Baby: The Signature of Terror." *Caribbean Review* 12 (Spring 1983):
    p. 6.
"The Generals Take Over." *Time* 5 April 1982: p. 29.

Joyner, Christopher. "The United States Action in Grenada—Reflections on the Lawfulness of the Invasion." *American Journal of International Law* 78 (January 1984): 136–139.

Kenworthy, Eldon. "Grenada as Theater." *World Policy Journal* 1 (Spring 1984): 637.

Kirkpatrick. Jeane. "The U.N. and Grenada: A Speech Never Delivered." *Strategic Review* 12 (Winter 1984): 11–18.

Massing, Michael. "Grenada Before and After." *Atlantic Monthly* Feb. 1984: 76–87.

"The Truth About Cuba's Role in Grenada." *Intercontinental Press* 28 Nov. 1983: 678.

QUESTIONS FOR READING AND REVISING

1. Steve West's essay is an example of an *argumentative* essay that starts from the writer's strong response to an issue. What evidence in the essay shows West's strong reaction to Kirkpatrick's speech? What evidence shows West's commitment to his subject?

2. West's strategy is to attack Kirkpatrick's evidence and the assumptions on which she bases her speech. Why is this an effective strategy for *arguing*? Cite specific instances from West's essay to support your answer.

3. Do you find West's *arguments* convincing? How do you think Kirkpatrick would respond to West's points?

4. West turned an assignment that might easily have been just a reaction to Kirkpatrick's speech into a real argument. How does West use Kirkpatrick's speech to provide the structure of his essay?

5. Analyze how West uses and *introduces* his evidence to support his argument.

6. What assumptions does West make about his readers' familiarity with the Grenada invasion? Does he provide enough background information? Do you feel that you need to read Kirkpatrick's speech to understand West's essay?

7. West advises his fellow writers: "The biggest problem young writers have is a tendency to try to sound too polished and too artificially intellectual. It's not hard for a reader to tell when a writer is trying to adopt a voice he's not comfortable with. Writers need to stick to a simple style that is natural for them and not try to adopt an artificially pompous style that the reader will spot and dislike right away." How does West follow his own advice? Describe his *voice* in the essay. How does West's voice serve his *purpose*? How does his voice help to make his ideas more convincing?

8. West reports: "I had a difficult time writing my conclusion. I went through five or six versions of the conclusion and never felt satisfied with any of them. In the end, I simply used the one that dissatisfied me the least."

   One of the versions of West's conclusion was written this way:

   > Recent Reagan administration statements about Grenada
   > have largely ignored Kirkpatrick's arguments and have em-
   > phasized the resurgence of pride in the American military

that took place after the invasion. These statements suggest that the administration's "real motives" for the invasion were to boost American morale and to flex the country's military muscles. Perhaps, then, it should come as no surprise that Kirkpatrick's arguments are less than convincing; she may have intended them simply as a diplomatic smokescreen to conceal the less honorable objectives of the invasion.

What are the differences between this version and the final draft conclusion? In what ways is the final draft conclusion more successful?

SUGGESTIONS FOR WRITING

1. Choose a newspaper or magazine article dealing with a topic with which you are familiar. Write an essay evaluating this article as a source. Does the writer present evidence accurately and fairly? Does the writer have a bias? How is the writer's *argument* structured?

2. Think of someone whose ideas you have read and would like to *argue* against. Write an essay presenting that writer's assumptions and then argue against them. Use your outside reading as the basis for the essay and integrate the readings into the essay.

3. *Define* an ethical problem related to being a student, such as the ethics of term paper writing services or plagiarism. Define your position on the problem, and then write an essay explaining the reasons for your *point of view*.

THREE STUDENT
WRITERS
AT WORK

Part III

MOST PEOPLE WRITE without consciously thinking about what they are doing. There are as many writing habits as there are writers. Some people can write anywhere — riding on buses, waiting in line, sitting in restaurants — while others need special conditions. Barbara Seidel, for instance, reports: "I want the house to be silent except for the sporadic squawking of my birds. I need to be left alone, without the phone ringing, or without anyone asking me questions or needing me at the moment. I sit at my desk, running my fingers through my hair, reaching for pieces of chocolate, or grabbing for a drink of ice water. I move around a lot in my chair, sigh deeply, and stare at the wall. Finally, I put pen to paper and write."

This chapter observes Barbara Seidel at work — getting started, drafting, and revising — and considers writing from her point of view. Seidel talks about her concerns as she worked through her pile of notes and six drafts to a final, prize-winning essay. Even though all writers need to find the conditions and circumstances that work best for them, we can still learn a great deal about the stages of the writing process by studying how one writer made important decisions and revisions as she progressed through these stages.

Too often when a piece of writing is successful, readers do not have the opportunity to see how it was written; the writing carries them along so that they are not concerned with the writer's process. The writing reads smoothly and logically and readers assume, if anything, that it must have flowed equally smoothly from the writer's pen. What readers don't see are the scratch-outs and the drafts, the decisions and conversations that went on in the writer's mind to produce such writing.

Seidel's notes and drafts show that her carefully conceived and balanced essay required a great deal of work. She began with fragments — notes to herself. Her ideas did not spring full-blown from her mind in clear, coherent prose. Rather, they tumbled out in unformed, fragmented ways that she developed in draft after draft as she made decisions, evaluated those decisions, and adjusted her writing so that the new decisions were consistent with what she had already written. What guided Seidel throughout the process were the concerns of subject, audience, and purpose.

This chapter begins with a detailed look at how Seidel wrote her essay, "A Tribute to My Father." It concludes with Jonathan Schilk's drafts for his essay,

"57 Degrees," and Matthew Holicek's drafts for his essay, "Look Out Behind You!" which are given as exercises. The drafts of these three writers reveal how writing evolves, from tentative beginnings, to become good writing. What comes through is the power and possibility of writing.

GETTING STARTED

In her freshman writing class, Barbara Seidel was given the broad assignment of writing a tribute to someone. She reports that she decided immediately to write about her father: "My first reaction to this assignment, though, was a feeling of slight panic. I knew I wanted to write about my Dad and I thought the assignment would give me a chance to further understand him and our relationship. But I kept thinking this is going to be tough; I will have to be open and vulnerable if I am going to write plainly about Dad. I knew if I did otherwise, the essay would not work."

For a writer, having a subject to write about is only the beginning. Seidel knew her subject — she knew she had a strong interest in writing about her father — but she didn't know specifically what she wanted to say about him. She needed to get her thoughts down on paper to see what she wanted to write. Seidel's method of getting started was brainstorming, a strategy that helps a writer to think as quickly and broadly as possible about a subject by writing down everything about the subject that springs to mind. Brainstorming usually takes the form of an unstructured list with words and phrases written as quickly and as uncritically as possible. Brainstorming helps Seidel to get involved with her subject quickly. "I jot down words, ideas, and images to give me a way of remembering what I know; the more I brainstorm, the more I have to work with."

The following notes are copies of Seidel's brainstorming sheets for her essay, "A Tribute To My Father."

SEIDEL'S BRAINSTORMING NOTES

```
--58 years old

--parents divorced when he was young

--1 older brother, Arthur, mom's favorite

--young--white hair, pale skin, blue eyes
```

--young--brother had darker skin, brown eyes,
  black hair

--grew up--wore hand-me-down clothes and shoes--
  used to fold newspapers into shoes

--Mother worked early morn til after dinner

--went to corner store for meal--Mother paid $ in
  advance to store

--hell-raiser as teen; didn't like school, dropped
  out (car and Uncle Art)

--Navy man during WWII; never overseas

--loved animals; always bringing home strays

--saw little of his father who was alcoholic,
  til age of 19 (father dating)

--great common sense, wise man, folk sayings

--not an intellectual; doesn't read; not "learned"

--patient; calm in crisis; resigned

--very hard worker; in car business since hung
  around father's car lot in late teens

--family man; loyal, devoted, dependable

--instinctive, yet never called it that (marrying Mom)

--extremely honest

--non-confronter: peace within family at all costs,
  sometimes to detriment of people

--not religious

--worrier; drives people crazy (5 countdown humorous
  quirk)

--obsessive about details; perfectionist: towels
  just so, etc.

--5'7"

--sandy blond hair, reddish gold, curly, short

--blue eyes, glasses

--long oval face with slightly square jaw

--conservative dresser

--man of habits; does not like change

--homebody; needs family warmth and love;

  gravitated to Mom's family

--dependable (Uncle Art; Mom--illnesses)

--loves candy (would hide his choc. in night table

  drawer and diet sundae--humorous quirks)

--strong sense of traditional values (his father

  ill, etc.; his mom driving him crazy yet he's

  there; grave)

--slow to anger but doesn't forget; stubborn

--drives around corner in car to cool down

--horseback riding when younger with daughter

--closer to daughter than son thru childhood years;

  able to talk with son when grown

--likes to talk things out

--Mother said he and his daughter very alike

  Seidel spent a half-hour brainstorming, letting her mind roam, and generating details and information. Her brainstorming sheets are rich with possibilities; it is clear that she knows her subject well. To an outside observer,
these notes might look rather disorganized and idiosyncratic. We might ask:
What does "5 countdown humorous quirk" mean or what about "perfectionist:
towels just so, etc."? Yet this is how notes at this stage should look. Seidel is
writing these notes for herself, an audience of one, and it is important only
that she can read and interpret them. What outside observers can see in these
notes, however, is that Seidel asked herself important questions as she brain-
stormed in order to collect her thoughts and to see what she wanted to write.

She asked, for instance, What does Dad look like? What can I say about his family — his background — his growing up poor? What are his values? One thought suggested another.

These brainstorming sheets offered Seidel enough information for writing a first draft. She had collected a stock of materials to work with, and this helped her feel confident that she knew where she was headed. As she reports: "My brainstorming served as a road map, pointing me where I should focus my attention, and helping me to see how I wanted to view my subject."

Getting started is often the most difficult stage for writers. They stare at the blank page, waiting for inspiration, expecting to write a perfect opening sentence. Or they write something down, strike it out, crumple up the paper, mumble to themselves, "This isn't what I wanted to say," and begin again — and again. Having no sense of direction to guide them, they are forced to improvise, attempting to find ideas at the same time they are developing and organizing them. The time spent in getting started is time well spent. Writers write with more confidence and ease if they have developed a focus for their first drafts. Such a focus shows writers where they are headed and leads them to a more developed and organized draft.

Seidel's brainstorming notes offered her numerous details, but these details were unsorted and unfocused. She spent some time thinking about her notes and asking herself: Which details seem most interesting? Which details can be developed? How can these details be grouped to provide a focus? As she reports, "Before I wrote my first draft, I read and reread my notes. They clearly pointed me in the direction of *contrasts, honor,* and *principles.* These were factors about my father I intuitively knew were important to me, but I had never before identified or singled out. I realized these factors could be used as a focus to write about my father with both objectivity and compassion."

DRAFTING

Having reread and thought about her notes, Seidel wrote her first draft. She reports: "As I wrote my first draft, I was excited about my essay. I knew I had something important to say about my father. I just let loose in writing this draft so that I could connect all my notes and the ideas that were still rushing through my head. If I try to be too orderly in the first draft, then I am stymied. A first draft is always an experiment; I am still testing and exploring what I want to write. I was still trying to describe my father, make me see and understand him, so that my readers could. My lead sentence, 'Actions speak louder than words, he often said,' kept jumping into my head. I found it to be a very telling phrase and I knew it gave me a good sentence with which to start writing."

The following is Seidel's first draft.

SEIDEL'S FIRST DRAFT

A Tribute to My Father

Actions speak louder than words, he often said. 1
If so, there are actions that say much about the man.
There was that moment, thirty years ago, when his
father was dying slowly of cancer. In order to take
his father to and from the hospital for medical care,
he would arise at dawn, leaving his wife and small
children asleep in the tiny house, and drive the
distance on deserted city streets. Years later, his
own daughter, puzzled, would ask why he showed such
devotion to the man who had divorced his mother and
almost abandoned him and his brother. He answered,
with a faint look of surprise at the question, "He
was my father."

As though such an answer explains it all . . . he 2
is still not a man to say more when less will do. Soft-
spoken, slow to anger but long in remembering, he has
his own set of values. The towels in the linen closet
were always folded just so. The lights in an unused
room turned off, to the exasperation of children
lectured to do likewise. One's word is one's bond, he
said. Loyalty, respect, tradition, honesty . . . these
were the basic tenets of his life, unspoken but inherent.
Perhaps it is because of the young hellion who quit
school, tired of being caught napping, who trailed after
his older brother while his mother worked, that the
older man of rigid values emerged. Nonreligious,

unschooled by textbooks, he is a man of enormous common
sense, ready folk wisdom, and stubborn, instinctive
notions. He has always been a man of instincts,
though never introspective enough to notice their
presence.

Such instincts propelled him, fast and dizzy,   3
toward his future wife. He was engaged to her friend,
who introduced him to the dark-haired, pale-skinned
woman, about whom his inner voice said, firmly, yes.
He broke the engagement, proposed to Marilyn, then
reluctantly waited a year before marrying at the
insistence of his future mother-in-law. He chose a
family of traditions and closeness, of gnarled inter-
dependencies and rash tempers, so unlike his own past.
He knew this woman would need him, nurture him.

But then, he never shared much about his own   4
past. No bitterness over the shoes stuffed with newspapers, or the hand-me-down clothes several sizes too
large. No club of guilt-inspiring comparisons was
wielded over his more fortunate, and often unappre-
ciative, children. Instead they learned of him in
casual answers to direct queries, or from his mother,
a woman divorced in an era when such action was hardly
respectable. She worked long, tiresome days, leaving
him and his older brother Arthur to fetch a meal at
the corner candy store. The counterman, waiting, would
place a sandwich and a drink before them. "Never more
or less, and all paid for in advance," he once said, a
tone of wonder in his voice just at the sheer order of

it all. She passed her stern work ethic on to him;
he became a good provider, obsessed with being
responsible.

And the errant, alcoholic, polo-playing father--   5
the womanizer who told girlfriends his then-nineteen-
year-old younger son was a younger brother--passed on
some traits of his own. A love for animals and a love
for cars that would last a lifetime. The former
caused the young boy to drag home a succession of
dirty pets to an emphatically opposed mother, and the
young man to smile when his own daughter did the same
thing to his wife. The latter prompted an affair
with cars that forty years of selling automobiles has
only dimmed, not ended. It is telling of the man
that in a profession where truth is not a known
commodity, he has a reputation of such staunch
honesty that customers return, year after year.

Perhaps it is his subtle humor, his ability to   6
enjoy people that attracts them as well. Such humor
takes the form of quirks and annoyances in his home.
There is the "diet" dessert of ice milk over bananas
and Hershey chocolate bars, eaten nightly with an
innocent smile. Or the chocolate bars hidden in his
night table drawer. There is the obsession over
details, prompting him to worry over each decision.
And the peacemaker, the small boy within him still
seeking approval and love, who avoids confrontation,
attempting to reconcile people and issues, provoking
frustration in his daughter. And laughter in his son,

who at the end of a phone conversation over any issue,
hangs up the phone, then counts "5-4-3-2-hello, dad,"
knowing his father will immediately re-call to be
certain everyone is pleased.

If there is a failure in his values, it has been,   7
until recently, with this son. It has taken them until
now, when the boy is a father himself, to see the love
that exists beneath their opposite personalities. With
his daughter, being needed and revered was easy; she
idolized him. With his son, there were questions,
wants, swirling energy and demands. And he, working
to provide for his children, had not time for the
baseball or other games that were no part of his own
childhood. Now, two men, two fathers, they reach
across the distance with love.

And now, at age fifty-eight, his blond hair has   8
become a gray-brushed reddish gold. His long, oval,
square-jawed face is heavily lined. The habits of
his lifetime have been altered, a difficult task for
a man who dislikes change, by the death of the woman
who needed and nurtured him, and bore his children.
Years of chronic illness and possible loss of her
created little anxieties, worrisome habits that, he
admits, remain with him still. But he has remarried,
and with his new wife, can often be found walking at
the cemetery where their respective spouses are buried.
He bends down to clear the grave of grass and dirt. She
was, after all, his wife. And his actions continue
to speak.

There is quite a jump between Seidel's rough, disorganized notes and this rough, but organized first draft. The details are beginning to make sense, and the essay is beginning to take shape. Seidel's strategy in writing her first draft was to refer to her notes and establish her purpose by grouping details from these notes. For instance, she took her brief sketchy notes:

— grew up — wore hand-me-down clothes and shoes — used to fold newspapers into shoes

— Mother worked early morn til after dinner

— went to corner store for meal — Mother paid $ in advance to store

and developed these details about her father's boyhood into paragraph 4 of her first draft. Seidel also combined and grouped details from different places in her notes. Details such as "hell raiser," "slow to anger," "not religious," and "perfectionist," scattered throughout her notes, all are grouped together in paragraph 2 about her father's values.

As she wrote her first draft, Seidel found that she needed to go beyond her notes in order to define her purpose. New ideas came out in writing as one idea stimulated another and new possibilities emerged. She added the details about her Mother in paragraph three, for example, when she realized that she needed this information to illustrate her father's complex set of principles. Seidel was open and receptive, as writers need to be while drafting, discovering new ideas and following her writing where it took her. Because she spent so much time brainstorming and developing her ideas, and because her notes were so well developed, Seidel was able to write a detailed, focused first draft. Her first draft was indeed a very good beginning.

REVISING

Seidel put her draft aside for one day before beginning to revise. With time, she reports, she gains the necessary distance to rethink what she has written and to see her writing more objectively. "Most of my time 'writing' is really revising. I first revise by reading my draft from start to finish. Next, I begin scribbling changes on the draft — additions, deletions, arrows, circles, notes to myself, and ideas for moving paragraphs around. The draft really looks chewed over at this point. Then, I type a new draft, make more changes on the draft, and continue and continue. I have often felt alone and very strange because I write so many drafts, but I can rarely complete even a very short piece of writing without multiple drafts. It is only through revising that I can keep refining my writing and hope to reach my readers."

Seidel's major concern as she read her first draft was that she had not captured her father and achieved her purpose in writing about him. She describes her thinking at this point: "I was very uneasy about my tribute to my father. I saw too many of my opinions of his actions and realized that I had not distanced myself emotionally from my subject. I had to take my emotional likes and dislikes out of my essay and try to see my work more objectively. In the third paragraph of my first draft, for instance, I described my mother's physical appearance, not my father's. I was getting carried away with my memories. I began to ask myself, 'Well, what is it I want to say? What is my purpose in writing this essay?' I knew I was trying to achieve a sense of flowing movement from one idea to another, so the man I was writing about would just seem to 'appear' to be 'real' the way he was in my mind's eye. I wanted my father to tell his own story; I wanted to show that his actions do speak louder than his words. One of my goals in revising was to remove myself from the essay. I shortened my sentences to let simple statements and my father's actions speak for themselves. I recognized that the more I interjected ME into describing HIM, the less of HIM could be seen."

To revise means, literally, "to see again," and that is what Seidel was able to do. While getting started, she could see her writing only as parts and pieces, but having written an entire draft, she could see from the perspective of the whole if her draft was consistent with her purpose. As she moved from draft to draft, Seidel revised by adding, deleting, and reordering. She refined her writing, searching for a precise word or a more descriptive phrase, rearranging sentences, and tightening her writing. As Seidel tells us: "My sentences were just too wordy. The essay, in fact, was so bloated with words that my father's actions could not speak for themselves. Wordiness is always a first draft problem because it is part of the process of pouring out ideas and discovering a purpose. In revising, I work for a rhythm and mood in my writing that is only possible by removing every excess word and phrase.

Seidel maintained the basic structure of her essay throughout her drafts, but the focus on her father's personality, his contrasts, his honor, and his principles, became more vivid. It was the accumulation of small changes from draft to draft, so that each sentence, phrase, and word fit her purpose, that made the difference in Seidel's prize-winning essay. Seidel reports: "I knew my essay was finished when I saw a clear pattern. I had created a logical transition from paragraph to paragraph. It no longer mattered if I wanted to add anything else; I could 'hear' the essay was complete."

It was through revising that Seidel was able to "reach the hearts of her readers" and achieve the essay she wanted — a vivid and memorable tribute to her father. As we learn from her, the best reason for putting anything down on paper is to allow a writer to see it, understand it, and know how to change it. In revising, Seidel patiently brought her ideas and her imagination together.

On the following pages Seidel's final draft appears alongside her first draft so that you can study the major decisions and changes she made. New sentences or phrases in the final draft have been underlined.

SEIDEL'S FIRST DRAFT

A Tribute to My Father

Actions speak louder than words, he often said.   1
If so, there are actions that say much about the man.
There was that moment, thirty years ago, when his
father was dying slowly of cancer. In order to take
his father to and from the hospital for medical care,
he would arise at dawn, leaving his wife and small
children asleep in the tiny house, and drive the
distance on deserted city streets. Years later, his
own daughter, puzzled, would ask why he showed such
devotion to the man who had divorced his mother and
almost abandoned him and his brother. He answered,
with a faint look of surprise at the question, "He
was my father."

As though such an answer explains it all . . . he   2
is still not a man to say more when less will do. Soft-
spoken, slow to anger but long in remembering, he has
his own set of values. The towels in the linen closet
were always folded just so. The lights in an unused
room turned off, to the exasperation of children
lectured to do likewise. One's word is one's bond, he
said. Loyalty, respect, tradition, honesty . . . these
were the basic tenets of his life, unspoken but inherent.

SEIDEL'S FINAL DRAFT

```
                A Tribute to My Father
        Thirty years ago, when his father was dying, he        1
    would leave his wife and two small children asleep in
    the square Cape Cod style house, then drive in the
    predawn light through the quiet city streets to take
    his father for outpatient medical care.  Much later
    in his own life, his daughter puzzled over his devotion
    to a man who had divorced his mother, then ignored him
    and his brother.  A faint look of surprise flickered in
    his eyes; then he answered concisely, "He was my father."
    He has always said that actions speak louder than words.
```

1. The phrase, "actions speak louder than words," functioned as a touchstone for Siedel's ideas, a way of getting at what she wanted to say about her father and finding the words to express her central idea about his values. In revising, Seidel moved this phrase from her lead sentence to the last sentence. She wanted to make her lead sentence more specific, to draw her readers into her essay by showing one of her father's most telling actions. The last sentence of the final draft, "He has always said that actions speak louder than words," unifies the paragraph and summarizes Seidel's dominant impression of her father. In revising, Seidel has also condensed six sentences into four in order to create a more forceful impression of her father.

```
            A soft-spoken man with a frequent low chuckle, he        2
    is so slow to anger that some people have been fooled
    into believing him an easy mark for trickery, a dan-
    gerous mistake.  He is just as slow and long in
    remembering anyone who violates his strict set of
    values.  He has no textbook education, yet he possesses
    an abundance of common sense.  He is not religious, yet
    he is a moral man, consistent in his values on a daily
    basis, not only on the Sabbath.  The inherent boundaries
```

Perhaps it is because of the young hellion who quit
school, tired of being caught napping, who trailed after
his older brother while his mother worked, that the
older man of rigid values emerged. Nonreligious,
unschooled by textbooks, he is a man of enormous common
sense, ready folk wisdom, and stubborn, instinctive
notions. He has always been a man of instincts,
though never introspective enough to notice their
presence.

        Such instincts propelled him, fast and dizzy,   3
toward his future wife. He was engaged to her friend,
who introduced him to the dark-haired, pale-skinned
woman, about whom his inner voice said, firmly, yes.
He broke the engagement, proposed to Marilyn, then
reluctantly waited a year before marrying at the
insistence of his future mother-in-law. He chose a
family of traditions and closeness, of gnarled inter-
dependencies and rash tempers, so unlike his own past.
He knew this woman would need him, nurture him.

of his life, given and expected, have been loyalty, respect, tradition. Perhaps it is from the wild young
hellion who quit school, whose idea of fun was joyriding
in his older brother's car while that brother chased
after him, that this man of caution and habit emerged.

2. In revising, Seidel took what was essentially a list of details from her brainstorming notes that she had strung together into sentences in her first draft, and focused them by reorganizing and deleting. She decided to develop this paragraph around her father's values as a man of caution and habit. Thus, she moved the detail about the towels in the linen closet to paragraph 7 and cut the last sentence of the first draft about instincts and introspection. She deleted the phrase "to the exasperation of his children" to shift the focus of the sentence to her father. She added the important detail that "he is so slow to anger that some people have been fooled into believing him an easy mark for trickery" in order to establish her father's values.

Yet it was not caution, but sharp, clear instinct   3
that twirled him fast and dizzy after the woman he would
marry. He was already engaged; his fiancée made the
fatal mistake of introducing her fair-haired, blue-
eyed, slender man to the dark-haired woman whose first
sight caused some inner voice to shout at him firmly,
"yes!" This woman would need him, would nurture him;
he knew it. He broke his engagement, then immediately
proposed, waiting a year before marrying only because
of his future mother-in-law's insistence that he do
so. He may have been impulsive, but he was, after
all, respectful of his elders. And he had clearly
chosen not only a wife but a family style. Tradition
and warmth, tangled relationships and rash tempers
all spoke of people connecting to one another. His
life became one of stability and constancy, of the

But then, he never shared much about his own   4
past. No bitterness over the shoes stuffed with newspapers, or the hand-me-down clothes several sizes too
large. No club of guilt-inspiring comparisons was
wielded over his more fortunate, and often unappre-
ciative, children. Instead they learned of him in
casual answers to direct queries, or from his mother,
a woman divorced in an era when such action was hardly
respectable. She worked long, tiresome days, leaving
him and his older brother Arthur to fetch a meal at
the corner candy store. The counterman, waiting, would
place a sandwich and a drink before them. "Never more
or less, and all paid for in advance," he once said, a
tone of wonder in his voice just at the sheer order of
it all. She passed her stern work ethic on to him;
he became a good provider, obsessed with being
responsible.

same meat loaf served on the same day of each week,

of the same conservative clothes worn year in and year

out, of a man and a woman whose lives revolved around

each other, so unlike his own past.

3. Seidel realized in revising that she could use the story in this paragraph about her mother to show us more about her father's principles. She shortened her sentences, allowing her father's actions to speak for themselves, and added an effective detail: "his life became one of stability and constancy, of the same meat loaf served on the same day of each week."

He spoke little about his past. No bitterness   4

over the secondhand shoes stuffed with newspapers, or

the hand-me-down clothing several sizes too large,

pushed him to pursue great wealth or power. His

dream, he later said, was to be able to work hard and

just provide. He found the greatest pleasure in the

small things--the ability to buy himself new shoes.

Nor did he wield his own meager childhood as a club to

inspire guilt or appreciation in his own more fortunate,

more spoiled children. Instead, they learned of him

through passing comments--or from his mother.

Her divorce came in an era when such an act was   5

brazen. She worked long days caring for her two boys,

who ate one meal daily at the corner candy store. The

counterman would wait until they entered, then place a

sandwich and a drink in front of them. "Never more or

less, and all ordered and paid for in advance," he once

said, a respectful, wondering tone in his voice at the

sheer order of it all. She passed her stern work ethic

on to him. He became very good at being responsible,

dependable, at providing.

And the errant, alcoholic, polo-playing father--   5
the womanizer who told girlfriends his then-nineteen-
year-old younger son was a younger brother--passed on
some traits of his own. A love for animals and a love
for cars that would last a lifetime. The former
caused the young boy to drag home a succession of
dirty pets to an emphatically opposed mother, and the
young man to smile when his own daughter did the same
thing to his wife. The latter prompted an affair
with cars that forty years of selling automobiles has
only dimmed, not ended. It is telling of the man
that in a profession where truth is not a known
commodity, he has a reputation of such staunch
honesty that customers return, year after year.

4–5. Seidel divided paragraph 4 of her first draft into two paragraphs, giving her father's mother a separate paragraph, which emphasizes her influential role. In paragraph 4 of the final draft, Seidel added the two sentences on her father's adult ambition and his pleasure in buying himself new shoes. These sentences resonate for us, as readers, because we remember the earlier detail about his secondhand shoes stuffed with newspaper. Seidel cut out unnecessary words in her lead sentence in paragraph 4, again allowing her father's actions to speak for themselves. In the new paragraph 5, we see how small changes make the difference, reinforcing Seidel's purpose.

> And the errant, alcoholic, polo-playing father-- 6
> the womanizer who once told his ladies that this then-
> nineteen-year-old younger son was his younger brother--
> had a few admirable traits of his own left up his
> sleeve. To his son, he passed on a love of animals
> and a fascination with cars, with their sight and smell
> and the gas-powered freedom they gave to a man. His
> son, as a boy, would drag home one protesting stray
> after another to a firmly opposed mother. Years later,
> a father himself, he would laugh when his own daughter
> did the same. After spending forty years selling the
> mechanical monsters, his love affair with cars has only
> dimmed. It is telling of the man that in a profession
> where truth is not always a recognizable commodity, he
> has a staunch reputation for honesty and a loyal fol-
> lowing of customers.

6. Here it is the small changes—details added, excess words deleted—that make this paragraph more effective. Seidel added the phrase, "with their sight and smell and the gas-powered freedom they gave to a man," to emphasize her father's fascination with cars.

Perhaps it is his subtle humor, his ability to   6
enjoy people that attracts them as well. Such humor
takes the form of quirks and annoyances in his home.
There is the "diet" dessert of ice milk over bananas
and Hershey chocolate bars, eaten nightly with an
innocent smile. Or the chocolate bars hidden in his
night table drawer. There is the obsession over
details, prompting him to worry over each decision.
And the peacemaker, the small boy within him still
seeking approval and love, who avoids confrontation,
attempting to reconcile people and issues, provoking
frustration in his daughter. And laughter in his son,
who at the end of a phone conversation over any issue,
hangs up the phone, then counts "5-4-3-2-hello, dad,"
knowing his father will immediately re-call to be
certain everyone is pleased.

```
     If his honesty attracts them, so must his humor,        7

gentle and chiding.  And of course, there are the quirks.

There are the Hershey chocolate bars hidden in the

night table drawer, the towels folded and placed

exactly so in the linen closet, the sink faucet

wiped shiny dry after dishes are washed.  If his

past did not create anger or unbridled ambition, it

did give him a legacy of sorts:  hoarded candy bars

contrast with the giving parent; an obsession with

details fills him with anxiety.  He worries over

each decision like a dog gnawing on a bone.  He is

still the small boy seeking security, the ultimate

peacemaker avoiding confrontations, reconciling and

rationalizing the good in people and in issues to the

frustration of his children.  They, grown, have at

last learned to laugh gently at the habits that once

exasperated them.  There is the family favorite--the

phone joke.  His son speaks to him, hangs up the phone,

then counts, "5-4-3-2--hello, Dad!"  He knows his

father will hesitate, then call again.  Is everyone

happy?  Should we talk more?
```

7. Seidel's skill as a writer is evident in her revisions of this paragraph. She has revised every sentence, cut out every excess word, and removed every unnecessary detail so that her father's idiosyncrasies become real to us. Paragraph 7 of her first draft was baggy and lacked a clear focus. In revising, Seidel shows how her father's quirks have been shaped by the legacy of his childhood: "hoarded candy bars contrast with the giving parent; an obsession with details fills him with anxiety. He worries over each decision like a dog gnawing on a bone." Seidel dropped the detail about the diet dessert because it didn't fit in, inserted the example from paragraph 2 about the folded towels, and added the

If there is a failure in his values, it has been,   7
until recently, with this son. It has taken them until
now, when the boy is a father himself, to see the love
that exists beneath their opposite personalities. With
his daughter, being needed and revered was easy; she
idolized him. With his son, there were questions,
wants, swirling energy and demands. And he, working
to provide for his children, had not time for the
baseball or other games that were no part of his own
childhood. Now, two men, two fathers, they reach
across the distance with love.

new detail about "the sink faucet wiped shiny dry." Her sentences become much more direct: Instead of writing, "Such humor takes the form of quirks and annoyances in his home." Seidel's revision says, "And, of course, there are the quirks." The phone joke also becomes more concrete as we hear the father's voice saying, "Is everyone happy? Should we talk more?"

> It is this son who is one of the brief detours on 8
> his well-laid road map of life. With his daughter,
> loving was an easy goal. They shared a silent simi-
> larity of vision, of loving and letting go. With his
> son, such love was reached only after struggle; they
> spoke a different language. His son needed questions
> answered, challenges met, baseball and other games
> which had found no place in his own childhood; he was a
> man concerned with providing. By the boy's adolescence,
> they were like two bucks, antlers locked in a battle
> of dominance. Now they are two men, two fathers, who
> reach gingerly, but often, across the once-volatile
> differences of self to touch the love that always
> existed.

8. Seidel developed this paragraph to make the conflict between father and son more real to us. She straightened out the chronology of the paragraph so that she first describes the conflict and then explains its resolution, by moving the second sentence to the end. Her revision of the lead sentence is important. In the first draft, she wrote of the conflict as a "failure in the father's values," but "failure" was inexact, Seidel realized, because the conflict has since been resolved. In her first draft, she described this conflict between father and son in vague language: "With his son, there were questions, wants, swirling energy and demands." In revising, Seidel wrote: "With his son, such love was reached only after struggle; they spoke a different language. . . . By the boy's adolescence, they were like two bucks, antlers locked in a battle of dominance."

And now, at age fifty-eight, his blond hair has   8
become a gray-brushed reddish gold. His long, oval,
square-jawed face is heavily lined. The habits of
his lifetime have been altered, a difficult task for
a man who dislikes change, by the death of the woman
who needed and nurtured him, and bore his children.
Years of chronic illness and possible loss of her
created little anxieties, worrisome habits that, he
admits, remain with him still. But he has remarried,
and with his new wife, can often be found walking at
the cemetery where their respective spouses are buried.
He bends down to clear the grave of grass and dirt. She
was, after all, his wife. And his actions continue
to speak.

```
         And now, at age fifty-eight, his hair is streaked        9

    with gray; his oval face is heavily lined; he is tired.

    The habits of his lifetime have been altered, a dif-

    ficult task for a man who dislikes change, by the

    death of the woman who needed and nurtured him.  For

    years, he had watched her slowly die, her illness

    chipping away small pieces of his own courage, creat-

    ing small anxieties, worrisome habits that still

    linger with him.  But he is not a man to live alone;

    he has remarried.  With his new wife, he can sometimes

    be found at the cemetery where their respective first

    spouses are buried.  Flat bronze plaques and high white

    headstones stretch across the green fields.  He bends

    down to clear her grave of grass and dirt.  She was,

    after all, his wife.  Actions do, indeed, speak.
```

9. Seidel has removed all excess words from this paragraph so that her father stands before us in his final actions. In the first draft, she wrote about his first wife by saying: "Years of chronic illness and possible loss of her created little anxieties." In the final draft, her father becomes the actor in the sentence: "For years, he had watched her slowly die, her illness chipping away small pieces of his own courage." Finally, we see Seidel's father in the cemetery, bending down to clear the grass and dirt from his first wife's grave, and honoring her memory. In revising, Seidel brings her essay full circle by connecting the beginning and ending.

EXERCISE:
TWO DRAFTS BY JONATHAN SCHILK

This exercise looks at Jonathan Schilk's second and final drafts to understand the decisions and changes Schilk made as he developed his prize-winning essay.

Schilk was given the broad assignment of writing a narrative essay about an important event. He decided to use one of his Coast Guard experiences because, as he reports, "I thought that a well-told sea story would entertain my audience." Schilk's initial idea was to write about his first experience with seasickness, and the focus of his first draft was the psychological effects of seasickness. Schilk tells us: "I realized after reading what I had written that the focus was all wrong. I didn't really want to read a paper about seasickness and I didn't think that my readers would either. I began to ask myself, 'What is the purpose of this essay?' As I reread my first draft, I began to think that the most interesting idea in this draft was the picture of me being seasick, sitting in the corner, holding my gut, surrounded by water, and feeling very small. In fact, it was my first bout with seasickness that humbled me and made me recognize how small and insignificant I was in comparison to the vastness of the sea. I decided to move on to a second draft, entitling this draft, "The Sea and Me," and to tell the tale of my first experience with seasickness and what it taught me about the sea."

The following is Schilk's second draft.

SCHILK'S SECOND DRAFT

The Sea and Me

To those who sail or steam, the sea is something   1
to be feared and respected. Mariners hold it in the
highest esteem because he knows that his life is
pitifully small and insignificant in relation to its
vastness. The inexperienced person, however, cannot
fathom this basic maritime tenet. The unguided novice
usually goes to sea overestimating his abilities and
underestimating the sea. More times than not, these
jaunts end in disaster. Books are filled with chilling sea-stories about unlucky sailors caught in
whirling maelstroms. They often lost their lives in
the desperate battle against the elements.

Until I went to sea, the idea of my life being   2
threatened by wind and wave had never occurred to me.
I had never been to sea before and I naively believed
that I had no reason to fear it. Little did I know
that I was about to learn one of the most terrifying
lessons of my life. The following is an account of
that experience that changed my relationship with the
sea for the rest of my life.

Before I graduated from the Coast Guard Training   3
Center, the instructors told us that we had much more
to learn about the sea and its ways. They said that
we should remember that the ocean humbles even the
most experienced of skippers. Still, I was cocky
and felt I had the world by the tail. I felt very

confident in my abilities to do any task or to deal
with anything that came my way. No problem seemed
too large.

The first time I put to sea, we had been ordered   4
to search for a boat that was flooding twenty miles
northeast of Chicago. We loosened the mooring lines
at sunset and steamed for the distressed craft. As
the ship slowly glided between the pier heads into
open water, her newly painted sides were gently buf-
feted by tiny ripples. Distant storm-clouds splashed
with a hundred brilliant colors filled the horizon.
Later, I lay awake in my bunk and wondered what my
first watch would be like. The seas were calm and
unimportant; they were the last thing on my mind.
Soon, the gentle rolling of the ship rocked me to
sleep. I later awoke to the sound of water crashing
and gurgling on the deck above me. This was the beginning of the end of my delusion of the sea. The
ship violently lunged to the port and I was suddenly
emptied on to the deck. As I gathered myself up, I
saw a seaman making his way down a dimly lit passageway like a drunken sailor. With each wave, the ship
sickeningly heeled to the port and then to the starboard, and in like manner, so did he. I shouted to
him and I asked what was going on. He said that the
ship was on the edge of a gale and things were going
to become worse. A feeling of claustrophobia was
creeping over my slowly crumbling constitution. In

my mind, the creaking walls were sickeningly swaying
back and forth. With every nauseating tilt, I could
hear something in the next compartment as it spun
across the deck and smashed against some bulkhead.
I began to wonder what I had gotten myself into. Not
only was I beginning to experience my first of many
bouts of seasickness, a cold feeling of dread was
also churning in my stomach. On the way to the wheelhouse, I stopped at a porthole to see how bad it
really was. There, I saw mountainous waves pound
into the bow and explode into billowing spray that
engulfed the ship. I continued upwards and pondered
the tremendous energy of that wall of water. When I
stepped into the wheel-house, I noticed someone bent
over the bridgewing, their arching back showed inter-
mittant convulsive wretches. I felt my own stomach
give increasingly wrenching twists as a succession of
waves sent the ship into a dizzying, oscillating roll.
Everyone, including the captain, was clutching and
grabbing at whatever wasn't flying across the compartment. All about me, strewn on the deck, were
coffee-stained charts, pieces of broken glass and
other things I could not make out in the gloom. As
I made my zig-zag way to the man I was relieving, the
ship gave way to what appeared to be the largest wave
yet. But, before she could recover, another hit us.
The skipper shouted, "Brace yourselves!" The helmsman lost his grip on the wheel. Half-stumbling and

half-airborne, he piled into the radar. Deep in the
ship's heart, we could hear a shudder as metal
strained to hold in one piece. The world seemed to
be turning upside down as we came precariously close
to the point of capsizing. The ship's movement
slowed and she hung there, groaning, for what seemed
hours. I really thought that this was it, the ship
was going down and me with it. Hesitatingly and
almost reluctantly, she came back to an even keel.
Although we had no other experiences with waves of
that proportion again, we still took a beating for
the next sixteen hours.

This shaking experience taught me something.   5
The sea was no longer an unimportant detail as I had,
up to then, believed. No longer could I view the
sea with the same attitude. I saw her change from a
placid, restful friend to a distorted furious malev-
olent whirlpool. With all of the intricate machinery,
high technology, that made the ship so advanced in
our sight, we were still belittled by the elements.
I came to the conclusion that no matter how much
knowledge puny man accumulates, he can never come to
the point of mastering the overwhelming vastness and
limitlessness of the sea.

Questions on Schilk's Second Draft

1. Schilk's second draft provided him with a good place to begin developing his ideas. Describe the strengths and weaknesses of this draft.

2. What point is Schilk trying to make about the "Sea and Me"? What lessons did he learn? As a reader, do you feel that Schilk told you what he learned or showed you?

3. Schilk describes the storm in paragraph 4. From this description are you able to see, hear, smell the storm? What additional information would you like Schilk to provide?

4. Paragraph 4 is a rather lengthy paragraph. In fact, it is the heart of the essay. Is there anything confusing or unclear about this paragraph? What changes would you suggest?

5. Schilk's final paragraph begins: "This shaking experience taught me something." He reports that he wrote his conclusion this way because he was always taught to "tell my readers what I want them to know in my conclusion." Do you think this final paragraph is effective? Could you suggest ways to revise it?

Schilk wrote three more drafts, before he wrote his final prize-winning essay. Here is his final draft.

SCHILK'S FINAL DRAFT

57 Degrees

At the Coast Guard Training Center in Alameda,   1
California, our instructors stressed that we still
had much to learn about the sea's moods and temperaments. Our training, they said, was only inadequate
preparation for what could happen to us in open water.
"The ocean humbles even the most experienced skipper!"
warned one teacher ominously. He often spoke of the
Edmund Fitzgerald, an ore carrier which had foundered
in a winter storm on Lake Superior. Even though the
ship was over seven hundred feet from stem to stern
and equipped with the latest technology, she went
down in less than a sweep of the radar's antenna.
But it made no difference to me. After all, those
men on the Fitzgerald were only civilians; I was a
Coast Guardsman. After fifteen weeks at the Center,
after long hours delving into the art of navigation
and piloting, I could deal with any emergency.
Steering--"wheeling" as we called it--was my forte.
Several times, in fact, in less-than-perfect conditions, I had brought ships through narrow entrances
in the breakwall. I could handle any ship of any
tonnage. There was nothing that I couldn't do.

After graduating, I was assigned as a navigator   2
to the Acacia, an 180-foot buoy-tender on the eastern
shores of Lake Michigan. I've been ordered to an
oversized mudpuddle in the Midwest, I thought. It

was like giving a man with a Ph.D. in math a grammar-
school job. My fears were confirmed when I first saw
the lake: it was flat, featureless, unromantic.
Then there were the arguments with my shipmates about
the storms. It would never get that rough on the
lake. If they wanted "rough," if they wanted big
storms, I told them, they ought to sail the Gulf of
Alaska in autumn or go on a spring patrol on the
Caribbean Sea. Besides, the Acacia could handle
whatever nature could throw at her. She had been
fitted with the latest technology--variable ballast
tanks, hydroplane stabilizers, and all--to prevent
dangerous rolls. The Boatswain never said much; he
just nodded and smiled.

One day headquarters ordered us to sail for a   3
point twenty miles northeast of Chicago, where a
23-foot Chris Craft, adrift in bad seas, had radioed
an SOS. We loosened the mooring lines at sunset and
glided between the piers into open water. Fifty
miles to the southwest storm clouds hovered over the
horizon like a gigantic bruise. But here, where the
ship only rippled the flawless surface of the lake,
I fell asleep in my rack, secure in the knowledge
that the Acacia and I could handle anything--anything
short of a tsunami that is.

I awoke to the sound of water crashing and gur-   4
gling on the weather deck above me. Lurching to the
port, the ship dumped me onto the deck. I sat there,

my blankets and mattress draped over me, wondering what
had happened. I picked myself up and numbly eyed my
shipmates, who had burrowed among their woolly blankets and lashed themselves in—giant cocoons in the
dim red light. Clothes on hooks swung like pendulums
with each roll, and a figure in the passageway made
his way towards me like the proverbial drunken sailor.
"What's going on? Where are we?" I asked.

  "We're on the edge of a storm front and it's   5
gonna get worse!" he gasped.

  Before I could reply the ship pitched forward,   6
and he zigzagged down the passageway to the head.
A bucket on wheels, loose from its trices, spun
across the deck and smashed against the bulkhead,
splashing its contents. I glanced to the berths to
see if anyone had awakened. The cocoons hadn't
budged. The bucket careened into another bulkhead
with a crash. The walls closed in and air became
putrid. I hoped this was as bad as it would get.

  The sailor who had run into the head emerged,   7
swallowed back another retch, and told me I had the
next watch in twenty minutes. Even in the passageway's red light, his features had a greenish hue.
The ship plunged forward again, and he struggled
back to the head.

  After dressing, I climbed the ladder to the   8
wheelhouse, leaving the bucket, the messenger from
the bridge, the muffled sloshing, coughing, and

gagging behind. I fought my way up, sometimes
weightlessly as the ship dropped from beneath me,
sometimes ponderously as waves forced me to defy
gravity. The bulkhead oscillated up and down, back
and forth, up and down until I grew dizzy. I opened
the wheelhouse door, stepped inside, and saw the
helmsman clinging to the large brass wheel and
spinning it in an almost futile effort to keep the
ship on course. The Boatswain gazed out the porthole nonchalantly puffing on a Dutch Masters. The
Skipper had been sitting in his chair forward of the
helmsman's wheel. He too was looking out the portholes. Everyone else, including the lookout, the
Officer of the Deck, and the Exec, was hanging on
to whatever wasn't flying across the deck.

 The acrid stench of the Boatswain's cheroot   9
made me queasier than ever. I would have loved to
punch him in his smug, self-satisfied face, but I
was too ill to bother. All about me, strewn across
the deck, were coffee-stained charts, pieces of
broken glass, and crockery. Outside, the Quartermaster of the Watch, draped over the bridgewing's
edge like a rag doll, finally staggered toward the
door and stepped inside. His face was haggard and
drawn. Behind him the sea careened toward the gunwales and then receded.

 I turned to see what the anemometer read: the   10
needle had pegged out at 106 knots. The lake was

as I had never seen it before. Even in an ocean
storm, the period from the crest of one wave to the
next would run at least three hundred feet, But
here in the lake the period was seventy-five feet,
and the ship was subjected to an endless thrashing,
so that it was impossible for her to recover from
one wave before confronting the next. Out there
waves holding millions of gallons of water broke
upon themselves, and the slicing wind sheared off
the wave caps. Waves looming above the ship quickly
swept on, leaving vast troughs for the ship to fall
into--and she did. Many times I felt as if I had
left my stomach thirty feet in the air above. Waves
of nausea washed over me, and I wished I were dead.
I meant it. I would have done anything to stop the
misery.

No sooner had I thought this than a rogue wave   11
plowed into our port beam and sent the ship broadside, cork-screwing into a trough. "Brace yourselves!" the Skipper cried. Losing his grip on the
wheel, the helmsman catapulted against the radar and
landed in a heap. The wheel spun past hard left to
a point where it would jam the rudder and leave the
ship without steerage control. I jumped for the
wheel and brought the rudder to midships and then
hard right to bring the port bow into the seas. But
before she responded, the ship gave way to the blow
of yet another wave that towered above the signal

bridge and mast. The <u>Acacia</u> heeled wickedly to the
starboard--20, 30, then 40, then 50 degrees. At 57
degrees--seven degrees past the point of capsizing--
she slowed to a stop. The fo'c'sle disappeared under
thousands of tons of water, and the starboard rail
dipped into the black waters.

Inside the pilothouse, maps, pencils, and coffee   12
mugs cascaded off the chart table onto the deck. The
lamp swung into the Fathometer, and sparks flew from
its shorted circuits and shattered light bulb. And
there, through the porthole, past my wild-eyed reflection, the lake boiled at the bridgewing's gunwales. The ship hovered on the edge of eternity.
Deep in the ship's heart, rivets and welds strained
and groaned, and deck plates jumped from the con-
cussion. This is it! I thought. We're going down!

Slowly at first, almost hesitantly, the <u>Acacia</u>   13
recovered, and the clinometer climbed up its scale.
Water washed from the fo'c'sle's deck in sheets as
the <u>Acacia</u> swung past even keel, whipped through an
arc of 100 degrees, and settled into a sedate 40-
degree roll for the remainder of the trip.

In the corner, wedged between the Skipper's   14
chair and the radar, the Boatswain still stood,
puffing on the stub of a Dutch Masters and grinning
quietly at me.

Questions on Schilk's Final Draft

1. Schilk's final draft is polished, interesting, and highly readable. What has Schilk accomplished in his final draft? What has Schilk achieved in revising?

2. In his final draft, Schilk dropped the first two paragraphs from his second draft. As he reports: "I had been taught to tell my readers what I was going to tell them and I was following this formula in these paragraphs." Describe the tone of these two paragraphs? What were their weaknesses?

3. In his final draft, Schilk plunges right in and starts his essay with a picture of himself. Why is this an effective *introduction*? How does this introduction more effectively draw his readers into the world of his essay?

4. In the third paragraph of his second draft, Schilk gives his readers the cliché that he felt he had the world by the tail. He drops this cliché from the final draft and instead *shows* his readers how cocky and confident he was. What information about himself does he add to his essay? How does this information help to set himself up for a fall?

5. In revising, Schilk built up the details of the storm. Why do Schilk's readers need to see the storm? Find specific details that Schilk added that help you to visualize the storm.

6. In revising, Schilk also developed the character of the boatswain. What did he represent to Schilk? What is his function in the essay? How does the boatswain help Schilk to show his readers what he learned?

7. In his final draft, Schilk ends with the image of the boatswain "puffing on the stub of a Dutch Masters and grinning quietly at me." Compare this ending to the final paragraph of the second draft. Why do you think he dropped that paragraph? Why is the image of the boatswain a more effective conclusion?

8. Schilk's original idea to write about seasickness became a minor point in his final draft. What does this suggest to you about the process of revising?

9. Schilk reports: "When I first start writing an essay, the reader is not really that important. I feel that at this stage my subject and *purpose* are most important. When I revise, though, I begin to consider my readers and the readability of my essay. I try to keep in mind as I revise that my natural way of writing is rather stiff, and I pay attention to that problem. In my early drafts of this essay, I wrote as if I had a collar on that was too tight and that itched." In what specific ways has Schilk considered the needs of his readers in his final draft?

10. Summarize what you have learned about revising from studying Schilk's two drafts.

EXERCISE:
TWO DRAFTS BY MATTHEW HOLICEK

This exercise looks at Matthew Holicek's first and final drafts to understand the decisions and changes Holicek made as he developed his prize-winning essay.

Holicek was given the broad assignment of writing an extended definition. As he reports: "My reaction to this assignment was very different from that of other assignments. Most of the time when an assignment is given, I scan it over for a while, and when no ideas come to my mind, I just put it aside so I don't have to think about it until later. This assignment, though, was a little different. An extended definition paper didn't sound too interesting, but one of the topics my professor suggested, a type of movie, interested me. 'Horror Movies,' I thought: 'Perfect.' I have seen so many horror movies, especially slasher movies, that I am somewhat of an expert on them. I went into the writing of my essay with a fairly good idea of what I was going to say and how I was going to say it. I started out with a simple and direct definition of a slasher movie. Then I thought about all of the different categories within horror movies that are common, such as plot, victims, and locale. I used these categories as a focus for writing my first draft. I tried to rethink a couple of memorable slasher movies so I could poke fun at the many actions that are common to almost all these movies. Because these actions themselves are so funny, I decided to appeal to my readers through humor. By poking fun at these movies, I hoped my readers would laugh and see the truth of what I had written."

The following is Holicek's first draft.

HOLICEK'S FIRST DRAFT

Look Out Behind You!

A slasher movie is a specific type of horror film   1
which concentrates more on the death toll and body
count than on developing characters or any form of a
coherent plot.

The victims in these slasher horror movies are   2
almost always teenagers. But they are murdered so
quickly that the audience doesn't even get a chance to
learn about them. The characters are almost all the
same and all act as stupidly as each other. Girls
love to go through late-night strolls alone through
the woods or take a midnight skinnydip in the lake.
All the men want to be heroes and go by themselves to
find out where the strange noise is coming from. Upon
entering dark and gloomy houses, men and women decide
that now is a good time to conserve energy and save a
few extra bucks at the end-of-the-month electric bill;
so they leave the lights off. After hearing a noise
coming from within the house, they always foolishly
decide to investigate, thinking it's one of their
missing friends. Disregarding the "safety in numbers"
theory, they branch off in separate directions, never
to see each other again. Then teenagers fall into the
common habit of walking backwards, which almost always
means certain death. When confronted with the axe-
wielding maniac, the characters lose their will to live,
and just close their eyes and scream, not once making an
effort to get away. Whatever the logical thing to do is,

the characters don't do it. It's hard to believe that
any real person would act the way they do in the
situation they're in. Calling the police is always
out of the question, as is just leaving the place
altogether. It's so easy to tell exactly who will be
the next victim. If the person goes off alone, they'll
be murdered; if they walk backwards . . . death; an
unlit room . . . it's all over. All the characters
just lose any common sense they might have to be a
prime target of the killer.

The mad slasher was once an ordinary person who   3
has somehow been transformed into a superhuman, indestructible and unstoppable menace to whoever crosses
his path. Masks are worn to cover their hideously
deformed faces. Although we usually don't see his
house, we are led to believe that he lives alone in a
secluded shack. (He obviously can't get a job to pay
for a nice apartment, and has to get food on his own.)
Slashers never talk, but rather only breathe heavily.
But these maniacs do have an uncanny gift to predict
exactly what his victim's next moves will be. The
victim walks right in his direction so that he doesn't
have to waste time chasing them around. When he does
chase them, however, he doesn't run after them. He just
walks zombielike after his victims who never seem to be
able to evade him. The slasher seems to have no purpose
in life other than to murder people. But when he murders
them, he puts his imagination into it. Knives, machete,

axes, arrows, hot poker sticks, and sometimes just
his bare hands are used to kill defenseless victims.
Sometimes, when two teenagers are having sex he can
kill two birds with one stone and put a spear or
pitchfork through both of them at the same time.
Otherwise he'll use his cunning and lure his victims
to death, such as by making faint noises or by turning
off the power in the fuse box. By whatever method it
may be, the mad slasher never fails to stop until the
last victim is finally dead, which usually ends up
being himself.

The story most often centers around a certain   4
group of ignorant teenagers being the target of one
mad maniac. Apparently, ten years earlier (commonly
a holiday or other specific day) an unfortunate
incident caused by our teenagers (or a similar bunch
of teenagers) has left an innocent man disfigured
and out for revenge. But he decides to wait until
exactly one decade later to don a mask and purchase an
assortment of sharp instruments through which he intends to exact his vengeance. Luckily for the slasher,
all of his intended victims just happen to still be
together and easy to find. Summer camps and other
isolated wilderness areas are always a good place to
hang out; they also happen to be a favorite spot for
our slasher as well. Night comes around and the fun-
loving teenagers decide to do a little wandering around.
That's when the mad man begins to intentionally make

noises to draw the curiosity of our hapless victims.
As the characters split up, the killer sets each one
up to be butchered. One by one while everyone is
looking for each other, they only find the cold, steel
blade of the slasher's knife. Finally, there's only
one teenager left, aimlessly running around. Suddenly,
the hero (usually a girl) discovers all of her friends'
dead bodies, neatly and sequentially placed leading her
right to the slasher. Somehow, though, the killer
misses in his attempt to kill her. Then, through endless chaoos, the heroine finally decides to defend herself and stabs the killer. He falls to the ground, dead,
or so she thinks. The audience groans as the woman
stupidly turns around and walks away. The moment she
begins to relax and catch her breath, this superhuman
monster lunges out of the darkness and tackles her. In
the struggle, the slasher's true identity is revealed
as the mask is stripped away. At the moment the
slasher is at his peak for the final kill, there are
two possible outcomes. One possibility is that, from
out of nowhere, a male hero appears and kills the
slasher, saving the girl. The more prevalent outcome
has the girl discover a fairly large knife or machete
just in time to avoid the killer's blow and thrust the
knife into his stomach, killing him for good this time
. . . supposedly. Many times the last shot of the movie
is of the killer's arm or leg moving, or else he is gone
altogether, signifying that another similar dreadful
sequel will soon be out.

Questions on Holicek's First Draft

1. Holicek's first draft provided him with a good place to begin. Describe the strengths of this draft. What are its weaknesses?

2. Holicek's introductory paragraph is a direct *definition*. "A slasher movie is a specific type of horror film which concentrates more on the death toll and body count than on developing characters or any form of a coherent plot." Is this an effective introduction? Does it succeed in pulling you into the world of the essay?

3. Paragraph 2 is lengthy. Is there anything confusing or unclear about this paragraph? How would you advise Holicek to revise it? What needs to be added, deleted, or rearranged?

4. Paragraph 4 is also long. Is there anything confusing or unclear about this paragraph? How would you advise Holicek to revise it?

5. There are no direct references in this first draft to any specific slasher movies. How could such references strengthen this draft?

6. Do you find Holicek's conclusion effective? Could you suggest ways to revise it?

Holicek wrote two more drafts before he wrote his final prize-winning essay. As he tells us: "I always tend to write more than I have to and so when I revise I have to decide what sentences to cut out, trim, or combine so my writing will flow smoothly and coherently. The easiest part of revising for me is reworking individual sentences. When I wrote the introduction, I just thought it should be short, quick, simple, and to the point. But when I reread it I saw the introduction didn't work. I knew that I needed a longer introduction so that the essay didn't just appear from nowhere. I needed to give my readers some background information and slowly prepare them for what they were about to read."

Here is Holicek's final draft.

HOLICEK'S FINAL DRAFT

Look Out Behind You!

Most people get upset if they are told how a   1
suspense or horror movie ends. After all, there's no
point in seeing a "who-done-it" film if you already
know who did it. But when it comes to a genre of
horror films known as "slashers," people seem willing
to make an exception. Even though they know that one
slasher movie is apt to be just like all the others,
audiences enjoy them anyway--perhaps because these
stories of people being sliced to death by maniacs
are so predictable. John Carpenter's masterful
<u>Halloween</u>, which premiered in 1978, is widely regarded
as the original slasher film. It was soon followed by
a rash of inferior imitations which audiences nevertheless flocked to see, unconcerned that these totally
predictable cinematic clones focused more on high death
tolls and gory violence than on developing interesting
characters or coherent plots.

Since teenagers are the target audience for   2
slasher films, the victims in them are almost always
independent, fun-loving, just-out-of-high school
partyers. Could it be that the filmmakers believe
that the teenage audience somehow identifies with
other youths being decapitated, knifed, and electrocuted? But the kids portrayed in the movies die so
quickly that viewers don't get much chance to learn
about them, much less identify with them. The girls

all love to take late-night strolls alone through the
woods or skinny-dip at midnight in a murky lake. The
boys, eager to impress these girls, prove their
manhood by descending alone into musty cellars to restart broken generators or chasing psychotic killers
into haylofts and attics. Entering dark and gloomy
houses, men and women alike decide suddenly that now's
a good time to save a few bucks on the end-of-the-month
electric bill--so they leave the lights off. After
hearing a noise within the house, they always foolishly
decide to investigate, thinking it's one of their many
missing friends or pets. Disregarding the "safety in
numbers" theory, they branch off in separate directions,
never to see each other again. Or the teenagers fall
into the common slasher-movie habit of walking backwards, which naturally leads them right into you-know-
who. Confronted by the axe-wielding maniac, the
senseless youths lose their will to survive, close
their eyes, and scream.

        In short, whatever the logical thing to do is, the   3
characters don't do it. Or what they try to do fails.
Calling the police is almost always out of the question.
However, if they do decide to call the cops, the phone
is dead. Or the lights don't work. If the victims try
to get into another room, the door is jammed. If the
characters manage to escape from the house, they always
make the mistake of heading for the car. Sometimes the
doors are locked and, naturally, the kids are without

keys. But if they are lucky enough to have keys, the
car won't start. Couldn't even rely on a new BMW in
these movies. Then, looking at the fuel gauge, they
realize they should have stopped at the village gas
station on the way home from the 7-11 the night before.
If the fumes are enough to get the car going, the next
obstacle will be four deflated tires. The mad killer
doesn't miss a trick!

    Of course, it's always easy to tell exactly who   4
his next victim will be. If a girl goes off alone,
she'll be murdered. If a guy walks backwards . . .
instant death. Car won't start? Expect company in
the back seat. An unlit room? It's lights out, forever. All hope is lost when characters come face to
face with The Slasher.

    The mad slasher is a once-ordinary person trans-   5
formed into an indestructible, unstoppable, superhuman
menace. In the opening scene of the movie, through
what appears to be the hazy view of someone afflicted
with cataracts, we see a horrifying incident--a burning,
a decapitation, a drowning, a lynching, or a car acci-
dent--that causes the death or disfiguration of one or
more innocent outcasts. Then we are transported ten
years forward, to the present time. The plot unfolds.
We learn that our happy group of teens--or a similar
bunch of kids--is responsible for the incident that
maimed or disfigured the maniac on that day ten years
earlier (it was Halloween, or Valentine's Day, or

Friday the 13th or some other special occasion--a prom,
a wedding, a loss of virginity). Or the slasher has
seen the teens cause the death of someone dear to him.
He is hot for revenge, but he has decided to wait
exactly one decade (no more, no less) before exacting
his vengeance.

We rarely see where these slashers live, but they   6
obviously don't have the sense to get a comfortable
apartment. They seem to prefer dismal, rotting shacks
where they dine on furry animals and Chicken McNuggets.
They never take off their masks or change their ward-
robe--which consists of flak jackets, army boots, and
institutional pajamas. They don't talk; they just
breathe heavily. Slashers do have the uncanny ability
to predict exactly where their victims will be next:
teenagers are sure to back right into their killers or
open that very door behind which the madman patiently
lurks. When a slasher ends up having to chase his
victims, he doesn't run. Instead, he just plods on
zombielike after his victims who, despite their youthful vigor, are unable to evade him. He enjoys waiting
for the teenagers, girls especially, to trip. Or he
waits to catch them off guard. That's when he makes
his move.

When he murders his victims, he puts his imagi-   7
nation into it. To assure the best and most gruesome
results, he selects his tools carefully: knives,
machetes, axes, arrows, hot pokers, and sometimes just

his bare hands. To save a little time, he'll
occasionally put a single spear or pitchfork through
two teens making love--killing two birds with one
stone. Or he'll cunningly lure his victims to death
by slamming doors, snapping branches, or turning off
the power in the fuse box.

    After the killing spree, the one surviving teen-   8
ager, usually a hysterical girl, discovers the dead
bodies of all her friends placed neatly and sequentially
in her path--leading her directly to The Slasher. But,
of course, she doesn't see him until he lunges for her.
Fortunately for her, this time his knife (or poker or
pitchfork) somehow misses its mark. She escapes and he
chases her (zombielike) through the house or the woods.
Then, after endless screaming, running, and tripping,
the heroine cleverly thinks to defend herself and
manages to skewer his eye with a sewing needle, split
his skull with an axe, or hang him. He falls to the
ground, dead, or so she thinks. The audience groans as
the woman stupidly turns around and walks away. The
moment she relaxes to catch her breath, this superhuman
monster lunges from the darkness again and tackles her.
They struggle, and the slasher's true identity is
revealed as she strips away his mask.

    As the slasher raises his knife for a life-ending   9
blow, two outcomes are possible. One is that, from
nowhere, a male hero appears and kills the slasher,
saving the girl. The other and more prevalent outcome

has the girl discover a butcher knife or machete lying
nearby. Just in time, she avoids the maniac's blow
and thrusts the knife into his stomach, killing him for
good this time--she thinks. In neither ending do the
teens actually check to be certain that the slasher is
dead. (None of the kids in these slasher movies are
destined for careers as coroners; they're all too
eager to pronounce anything that doesn't move <u>dead</u>.)
But the audience knows better. A simple lack of vital
signs won't prevent this killer from rising up again,
pulling the knife from his stomach (or the axe from
his skull, or the machete from his neck), and killing
those surviving teens with even greater enthusiasm and
ingenuity in the inevitable, and even more dreadful
slasher sequel coming soon to your local theater.

Questions on Holicek's Final Draft

1. Holicek's final draft is lively, interesting, and polished. What has Holicek's revision accomplished?

2. Compare the introductory paragraphs from the first and final drafts. Describe the differences between these two paragraphs. How does the revised introduction more effectively draw readers into the world of the essay?

3. Compare the way in which Holicek began his second paragraph in both the first and final drafts and describe the differences. What has Holicek added to make the sentences in the final draft more interesting? Why are these sentences more effective?

4. In paragraph 3 of the final draft, Holicek added these sentences: "However, if they do decide to call the cops, the phone is dead. Or the lights don't work. If the victims try to get into another room, the door is jammed. If the characters manage to escape from the house, they always make the mistake of heading for the car." Why was this information added to the essay? Why does the information make the essay more interesting and effective?

5. Holicek reports: "My paragraphs in my first draft were dreadfully long and an eyesore on the page. They needed to be separated to contain their own ideas while still maintaining the flow of the essay. I took some of the subtopics and created new paragraphs giving these subtopics more emphasis and attention." What has Holicek done with paragraphs 2 and 4 from his first draft? Has he succeeded in giving the subtopics in his essay more emphasis and attention?

6. Holicek tells us: "I had difficulty with the conclusion. The ending in my first draft sounded very awkward. I kept thinking about this paragraph when the coroner idea came to me and everything just seemed to fit together." Compare the conclusions from the first and final drafts. What has Holicek achieved in revising his *conclusion*? How does the revised conclusion more effectively tie together the various threads in the essay?

7. One of Holicek's goals was to entertain his readers. Do you find the final draft more entertaining than the first draft? What specifically is more interesting and humorous in the final draft? Do you feel that Holicek's strategy to poke fun at the slasher movies was effective?

8. Summarize what you have learned about revising from studying Holicek's two drafts.

MOVING FROM PERSONAL EXPERIENCE TO EXPOSITION AND ARGUMENT

Part IV

T HE POET ROBERT FROST once observed, "All thought is a feat of association: having what's in front of you bring up something in your mind that you almost didn't know you knew. Putting this and that together. That click." Frost's description of "That click" may well remind you that one of the most appreciable pleasures of writing is recognizing the connections between one of your ideas and another. This recognition usually comes at the most unexpected moments, often after you have struggled for hours trying to express your thoughts clearly in writing. Yet part of the *enduring* satisfaction of writing is precisely that element of surprise, that life-long pleasure of discovering your own resourcefulness with language, of finding new ways to explore your own intelligence and to contribute in some original and visible way to improving the world of ideas. And as Frost's remark implies, one useful way to approach mastering the art of thinking in writing is to learn how to multiply connections—between the ideas you have, and between the essays you write.

How is one essay connected with another? No paper you write is ever a unique, self-contained task; each is a step in the learning process. Any subject you write about involves two important types of connection: building on what you already know and linking your ideas into a coherent presentation. Suppose you are asked to write an essay for your history class on the post-Civil War South. You may have personal memories of the South or a sense of the post-Civil War era from high school reading that will help you to approach the topic with greater confidence and authority. Once you have written your essay, you may be able to adapt the research and thinking you have already done when you are asked to write, say, an essay on William Faulkner for your English class. Professional writers very often follow this strategy, choosing a single subject — congressional lobbyists, microcomputers, public education budgets — that they can write about from several different angles for different publications. The crucial point, as Robert Frost suggested, is to be attuned to the connections between ideas. The work you do in a freshman composition course can sharpen your awareness of such connections and give you valuable practice at building related ideas into a lucid essay. So too, the effort to recognize and develop productive connections between one essay and another is very much akin to the process of *revising* your ideas within the boundaries of a single essay. In both instances, you *re-see* (re-vise) your thinking from a fresh perspective. More generally, frequent practice in recognizing—and developing—the productive connections between the ideas you generate and the essays you write will also better prepare you to discover the intellectual connections between the courses you take.

We have designed *Student Writers at Work* to encourage you to recognize and develop the abundant resources of your own intelligence by practicing your skills as a writer—one who is able to connect and extend ideas both within an essay and from one essay to another. The discussion questions following each of the thirty-five student essays in this book focus on analyzing how each writer has developed an essay governed by a powerful idea. The ability of these writers to create clear and convincing relationships, both between and among the ideas in the sentences they write in an essay, has earned them the special recognition of a Bedford Prize in Student Writing. Their explanations of the strategies they used to come up with ideas, draft, and revise offer accessible models for *every* student writer, whether practiced or inexperienced. In the previous chapter, three student writers—Barbara Seidel, Jonathan Schilk, and Matthew Holicek—explained in even greater detail the specific strategies they used to plan, draft, and rewrite their essays. Part IV extends those same principles and strategies to a larger issue: how can student writers most successfully connect the ideas in one essay form to the intellectual demands of working in another essay form?

COMPARING THE PERSONAL ESSAY
WITH EXPOSITION AND ARGUMENT

Our correspondence and conversations with teachers and students across the country underscore what we have noticed in our own composition classes: many student writers find it difficult to move from writing personal experience essays to writing expository and argumentative ones. For most first-year students, personal essays seem easier to write because they focus on what we think we know best. Expository and argumentative essays, however, can also focus on what we know. The difference lies less in the subject matter than in the way the writer approaches and organizes it.

All writing fundamentally expresses an idea about a subject, but the purpose, the language and forms used, the evidence summoned, the point of view adopted, and the audience imagined may vary greatly. Personal experience essays most often *narrate* an event (report what occurred) or *describe* a person, place, object (record appearance in sensory terms). For example, you could write an essay in which you describe in detail a favorite hometown hangout that is now gone. Or you could write a narrative essay in which you recount a memorable incident of your adolescence that occurred at that hangout. In both descriptive and narrative essays, the perspective or point of view from which you write is usually first person. The evidence you present to convey a clear sense of that place (description) or a vivid rendition of what happened there (narration) is normally bounded by the limits of your own experience. The audience writers envision for personal experience essays can be either themselves or others as well. And because the emphasis in personal experience essays is usually on narration and description, such writing may not explicitly assert an idea about the subject rendered.

What distinguishes expository and argumentative writing from personal experience essays is the nature of — and the critical prominence given to — asserting an idea about a subject. "Exposition" is a form of nonfiction prose that puts forth facts and ideas about a subject. But more importantly and specifically, expository writing *asserts and explains an idea about a subject.* That subject can be a person, place, object, or an event, or an abstraction such as *justice* or *liberty.* Because it asserts or explains an idea about a subject, exposition often involves generalizing; that is, it requires a greater distance between the speaker and the subject than would occur in a personal essay. And since its purpose is to explain, exposition assumes an audience beyond the speaker.

Consider again the example of the favorite hometown hangout. A descriptive essay about the hangout would emphasize what the place looked like several years ago. A narrative essay might recount a memorable incident that occurred there. In contrast, an expository essay about the hangout might assert the following idea about it: the hangout has changed a great deal in the years since you last spent some time there. Given the fact that the purpose of the exposition is to explain an idea about a subject, you might well want to explain how (comparison and contrast) or why (cause and effect) the hangout has changed. (For a complete list of the forms of exposition, see the Glossary.) The audience imagined by writers of expository essays always includes other readers.

"Argumentation" is another form of nonfiction prose in which the speaker attempts *to convince an audience that a specific claim or proposition is true.* What makes the claim or proposition true is that it is supported by a body of logically connected statements that are true. Argumentation is, in effect, a form of theorizing; proposing that a specific claim or proposition would be true if certain statements proved to be true. When writers move from personal experience essays to exposition and argumentation, they broaden considerably their point of view, their range of evidence, and their conception of the real or imagined audience to whom they are writing.

Return to the example of the hangout once again. An argumentative essay on this subject might address the issue of whether urban redevelopment displaces more people than it helps. Or the writer of an argumentative essay might formulate the following proposition or claim: urban renewal programs destroy the architectural character indigenous to a neighborhood in favor of governmentally sanctioned standards. The purpose of such an essay would be to convince an audience of the validity of the proposition or claim by citing evidence, which might range from personal anecdote to research reports. The writer of an argumentative essay wants to do more than explain an idea; he or she wants to convince an audience of the truth of a proposition or claim.

The purpose of this chapter is to help you apply the range of options available to you as a writer to your own essays and practice your skills in moving from personal experience essays to expository and argumentative ones. As a starting point, let's observe how two student writers—Julie Reardon and Beverly Dipo—discovered ample resources in their original prize-winning essays for writing other papers. Because Reardon's "The Unmarked Road" (p. 202) and Dipo's "No Rainbows, No Roses" (p. 70) are both strongly felt personal accounts of topics with broad implications, each writer was invited to write a second essay, using her original paper as a springboard into a different rhetorical pattern. The following sections trace Reardon's and Dipo's progress—from carefully rereading their personal essays to generating ideas to formulating and ultimately writing a new composition.

JULIE REARDON: FROM DESCRIPTION TO EXPOSITION

In her essay "The Unmarked Road," Julie Reardon responded to an assignment in which she was asked "to relate my reaction to a foreign culture." Her life in the small town she chose to write about was "like being thrust into another country. I had strong memories from that experience, and writing the essay gave me a chance to form my feelings about that period in my life . . . . The goal of my essay was to show the other students in my class how differently and how miserably other people can live in our country, not so far from home. I tried to appeal to these readers by relating the confines of my neighbors' lives. I tried to appeal to the reader's sense of compassion for those less fortunate than themselves. I wanted them to really see the borders of my characters' lives."

As you reread "The Unmarked Road" (p. 202), notice the techniques Reardon uses to accomplish these goals. Watch particularly closely how she organizes her description: the type of language she uses, the evidence she summons, the point of view she adopts, and the ways in which all these elements suit her purposes and her intended audience. These are the tools you will see Reardon using in new ways when she reaches the writing stage of her second essay.

When she first approached the challenge of moving from description to exposition, Reardon's main concern, of course, was to find an appropriate topic. What aspect of "The Unmarked Road" might become the core of a new essay? Here is Reardon's explanation of how she proceeded to generate ideas:

> Step 1: I reread my essay.
>
> Step 2: To generate new topics for an essay, I thought about my original paper and then freewrote about as many new thoughts as I could. Some of the ideas I came up with were:
>
> —How life experiences shape a person's outlook on life.
> —Compassion for others.
> —How much money is enough? Interview several people. Thesis: "amount of money not as important as person's attitude toward money."
> —The importance of friends.
> —Neighborliness — once restricted to neighbors but not found at the office.
> —Determination to succeed.
> —Poverty — compare life of the poor in earlier times with now.
> —Isolation — literature is full of people isolated in a strange culture.
> —Fanny's influence on me.
> —Stereotypes of the poor in literature.
> —Teen marriages — why they fail.
>
> Most of these ideas were quickly discarded. I thought I had covered developing compassion in my original essay, so I also abandoned that idea. Ditto with life experienced affecting a person's life. The idea to interview several people about their attitudes toward money was stymied by a lack of people at the higher end of the income levels for me to interview. Determination to succeed and teen marriages have been done to death already in the media. The idea of neighbors now being found at the office rather than next

door was my favorite idea, but I had read a similar article in *Newsweek* some time earlier, and I was afraid of plagiarism, even unconscious plagiarism. I finally narrowed down my choices to poverty—compare and contrast today with many years ago or examine stereotypes of the poor in literature. Poverty as a subject finally sparked my interest when the thought occurred to me to compare grandmother's hard life with what her life would be like today.

Here is the final draft of Julie Reardon's new essay. Notice how, in addition to moving from description to exposition, she has also moved from autobiography to biography. Her point of view is no longer that of the central character in her essay, but of a narrator writing in the third person. Though her language is not dramatically different, her descriptive passages are focused toward a different purpose. Both her language and the organization of her material are adapted as well to the new kinds of evidence she incorporates. Her intended audience remains the same, but her change in purpose and point of view means a change in the tone with which she addresses her readers. Reardon did not decide these aspects of her essay in advance; they fell into place as she began work.

REARDON'S EXPOSITORY ESSAY

A Woman of the Times

Poverty has always been synonymous with a hard life   1
and deprivation. Just two generations ago, being poor
meant an endless struggle to find work and to obtain
food, clothing, and shelter. My grandmother raised her
family in those days on very little money and coped with
difficulties impossible to imagine today. If she were
raising her family in modern America, her life
would be much easier. Yet she would face new problems
that she never had to deal with in earlier times.

My grandmother, Molly Halvorson, was born on a   2
small farm in Iowa in 1891 (Westcott). Always dis-
pleased with her name, Molly maintained that she was
named after the family cow. Her firm sense of right
and wrong revealed itself in her small, determined
chin and serious blue eyes. She loved growing flowers
and could happily root about in her garden for hours,
amazingly not getting her hands dirty. She protected
her exquisite Nordic coloring from the sun with a wide-
brimmed straw hat, and was somewhat vain about her small,
dainty feet. She began school speaking only Norwegian
but quickly learned English and became an enthusiastic
student. She loved to read, wrote an elegant hand, and
won many school spelling bees. In an era when many farm
children attended only a few semesters of school, Molly
resolved to learn all that she could. She insisted on
staying in school and proudly graduated from the eighth
grade.

Molly's job opportunities were exceedingly limited.   3
As a woman, she was forbidden to even consider a "man's
job." The options available to her were teaching,
nursing, or domestic service. Teaching and nursing required training her family couldn't afford; domestic
labor was her only realistic choice. Throughout her
life, Molly supplemented the family's income by cooking,
cleaning, and ironing for others. At times, she was the
sole support of the family. Her domestic skill was
highly prized by her employers, yet she was paid no more
than the prevailing wage for "hired girls," twenty-five
cents per hour.

She married Leroy Abbott in 1910. They had their   4
first son, Arthur, the following year. My mother, Viola,
was born five years later, Don the next, and Betty in
1924. Leroy supported them with a variety of short-term,
low-paying jobs: horse trader, meat packer, dairy
delivery. Occasionally he could barter a horse meant
for the rendering works to someone for a pound of butter
or perhaps a dollar cash. Depressions in 1907, 1919,
1921, and the Great Depression in the thirties period-
ically terminated Leroy's employment. There was no
unemployment insurance; he was let go without notice,
and until he could find a new job, no money came in.

The family moved often in search of work. Molly   5
sometimes had to sell her few sticks of furniture to
pay for the move and would arrive at the next rented
house without even a bed to set up. Molly loathed dirt

and would immediately dig into scrubbing down the place,
which was invariably filthy and sometimes rat infested.
Molly brightened the rooms with hand-sewn curtains and
rag rugs crocheted from scraps.

At each house, Molly had to carry water indoors   6
from a spring for cooking, cleaning, and washing. This
icy water had to be heated in a copper boiler, then
carried outside after use to be dumped. Molly kept
their home and the family's clothes spotless with the
only cleaning and laundry aids available to her:
boiling water, harsh lye soap, and sunshine.

Molly kept her big, black stove handsome with stove   7
blacking. Molly had to build the fire in the morning,
feed it throughout the day, and bank it at night to heat
the house. During World War I, coal and wood for the
stove were scarce and very expensive. Molly's house,
drafty and cold at best, was even chillier during
those years. The same stove was used for cooking and
heating water, making the house unbearably hot in
summer. Molly grew much of the family's food and spent
many long, airless August days over the stove canning
shining jars of fruits and vegetables for winter use.

Molly's children never had to feel like "trash,"   8
the common term for poor families with numerous, dirty
children. Their house and clothes, though shabby, were
clean. It was important that their clothes were patched
with tiny, invisible stitches, a skill Molly had perfected early in her life. The family always managed to

scrape by on their meager income without the humiliating experience of "going on the county" for money.
Viola and her friend Eloise entertained themselves
with homemade paper dolls cut from the Sears-Roebuck
catalog. Though only a year older than her brother
Don, often Viola was responsible for his care while
Molly was occupied with household duties or out working.

Molly's days and evenings were filled with never-   9
ending tasks and backbreaking chores. It took her hard
work and sacrifice to see her family decently taken
care of. Yet this bleak life was softened by pleasure
in her children, her love of gardening, and her pride
in the family's ability to be self-supporting.

If Molly was raising her four children today,
chances are that she would be doing it alone. Today's   10
welfare system could support the family far more
adequately than Leroy could. The market for his unskilled labor is not much better in today's recessions
and uncertain economy than it was back in earlier
depressions. The antifamily bias in the modern welfare code would actually encourage him to abandon his
family. "Even today, there are twenty-nine states in
which a two parent family, no matter how poor, cannot
receive welfare payments or Medicaid. . . . And even in
the more enlightened jurisdictions, the de facto policy
is to aid only the broken family" (Harrington 17). If
Leroy compared what his minimum wage earnings could buy
for his family with the wide range of services available

to them should he desert them, he would conclude it
would be foolish to stay.

In addition, the terrible stigma of "going on the   11
county," which led Molly and Leroy to struggle on their
own, is today largely gone. "Simply put, poverty is
coming to be seen not as the fault of the poor but as
a condition imposed on them by society and the economy"
(Harrington 198-99). Consider the changes in Molly and
her four children's lives if they applied for welfare
today in Hennepin County, Minnesota (McNitt).

The family of five would qualify for a three-   12
bedroom, subsidized apartment. Rent would be approximately fifty dollars per month. The housing itself
would be required to meet strict safety codes. The
plumbing, heating system, electricity, and water must
be in working order. This housing is often located in
desirable suburban locations. This apartment would be
a tremendous improvement over Molly's succession of
cramped, ill-heated, rented houses in run-down neighborhoods. Molly's passion for cleanliness would be much
easier to satisfy with the aid of modern inexpensive and
effective cleaning supplies. Water would run at the turn
of a faucet, light and heat turn on at the flip of a
switch. Though heating fuel is as expensive today as it
was in earlier times, a Federal Energy Assistance program
would help Molly with the bills. Her family could stay
warm despite the high cost of fuel.

Molly's respect for education would lead her to   13

continue her schooling. Free tutoring is available to
help her prepare for the GED tests. Passing the test
would reward Molly with her high school equivalency
diploma. Federal grants are then available to pay
tuition at a trade school or college. She would no
longer be limited to a "woman's job." Her love of
reading, beautiful penmanship, and flawless spelling
might cause her to choose the traditional field of
teaching, or her concern for plants and flowers might
encourage her to enter the "man's jobs" of conservation
or horticulture. The Minnesota Job Service would then
provide her with free assistance in locating employment
in her chosen field.

$150 in food stamps, careful shopping, and a monthly   14
grant of $691 would enable Molly to feed and clothe her-
self and the children. They would no longer be dependent
on what Molly could grow in her garden. Her thrifty
nature would doubtless lead her to continue to sew many
of their clothes, but a sewing machine would eliminate
laborous hand sewing and make the task much easier.

Careful saving over several months would enable   15
Molly to purchase a television and join the 97 percent
of American homes that own a set (Rosenberg and Rosenberg
269). Since television is such an inexpensive form of
entertainment, it seems logical that the family would
follow the average viewing pattern of nearly seven hours
daily (Information Please 269). During that time, they
would be bombarded with programs featuring families much

more affluent than their own, and commercial messages
urging them to buy, Buy, BUY! Toys such as "action
figures," for example, "are backed by heavy market
research and cross-promoted by cartoon shows aimed at
young children" (Barol 54). A survey of one five-hour
period of Saturday morning cartoons revealed the following parade of cartoons blatantly pushing related
toys: Snorks, Muppet Babies, Smurfs, Dungeons &
Dragons, Rubik the Amazing Cube, The Littles, Mr. T.,
and Spiderman. With the dazzling array of toys
advertised on their favorite programs, it seems
unlikely that Viola and Eloise would be content with
their homemade paper dolls. More likely, Molly would
be subjected to whiney demands for the items seen on
television and would feel guilty at not being able to
afford them for her children.

Molly's days would still be busy. School during   16
the day, homework, and being both a father and mother
to her children would occupy much of her time. She
would have to substitute pride in continuing her
education for her former pride in being self-supporting.
Freed from grinding daily chores and endless worry about
employment, today's Molly could lead a more enjoyable
life.

A lifetime of hard work and frugality enabled the   17
real Molly to eventually own her own small home with
flowers blooming indoors and out. With the opportunities
for education and the career choices available to her

today, it is likely that her same hard work and thriftiness would lead her to a similar happy ending. Along
the way, modern inventions would greatly ease her daily
routine. She would be able to improve her lot in life,
but the assistance isn't free. The cost she would pay
would be the loss of her husband and of the family's
self-sufficiency. It might be too high a price to pay.

Works Cited

Barol, Bill. "War Toys on the March." Newsweek
        1 July 1985: 54.

Harrington, Michael. The New American Poverty.
        New York: Holt, Rinehart and Winston, 1984.

Information Please Almanac 1985.

McNitt, Michael. Personal interview with caseworker.
        25 July 1985.

Rosenberg, Norman, and Emily Rosenberg. In Our Times.
        2nd ed. Englewood Cliffs, New Jersey: Prentice-
        Hall, 1982.

Westcott, Viola Abbott. Personal interview. 24 July
        1985.

Julie Reardon wrote three drafts of her new essay, her first being "merely an attempt to get started. I just keep on writing until I'm finished, even though I am well aware of the aromatic quality of what I am turning out." In her second draft, she attempted "to smooth the writing a bit . . . and to begin developing a feel for the information I want to use in the final version, along with the wording I want to retain, the length that will feel comfortable, and the sources I wish to use." Then she turned to the final draft:

> Before starting the final draft, I reread carefully my second draft, I list the facts I wish to include, and I decide the order in which I want to present them. This version received an enormous amount of rewriting and editing. I decide to let the opening and closing paragraphs, which I feel are very weak, simmer in my head overnight.
>
> My original thesis was how much easier it is to be poor today than it was in Grandma's day. The first research I did bore out this assertion. And indeed, physically my grandmother did endless, backbreaking labor no longer necessary today. But the cost of public welfare is high in terms of breaking up a family, and television today is a very big influence on everyone, but possibly more so on poor people. The contrast between what they see on the tube and what they have in their life must be numbing. So my final thesis points out that there were both advantages and disadvantages to each era.
>
> I considered my readers when I decided to use a member of my family as an example. I hoped that decision would appeal to a typical college student more than a dry analysis of "Poverty—Then and Now."
>
> I chose the block form of comparison and contrast rather than the point-by-point method because of the awkwardness of switching decades while keeping the same person as the subject in each paragraph. In the final draft, I attempted to give equal weight to both 1910 and 1985 and to compare each point I wanted to make in similar order.
>
> I edited the final version even as I typed. Rereading it aloud before the final typing suggested more changes. I finally know I'm done because I am REALLY sick of the whole thing. I avoid reading it now that the "final" copy is typed because I am always very dissatisfied with it right after I finish. Later I can appreciate it more.

Questions on Reardon's Two Essays

1. Identify the general subject of Julie Reardon's new essay. What specific idea does she assert about that subject? What specific *evidence* does she offer to support her assertion about that subject? What additional evidence might you suggest to help her strengthen her assertion? Where should that additional evidence be placed? Why?

2. What specific differences can you point to between Reardon's strategies—and accomplishments—as the writer of both "The Unmarked Road" and "A Woman of the Times"? In what specific ways do you think she might be able to strengthen the expository qualities of "A Woman of the Times"?

3. What specific thematic connections can you identify between "The Unmarked Road" and "A Woman of the Times"? What stylistic consistencies link these two essays? Analyze the word choice, phrasing, and sentence structure of Reardon's two essays. Point to specific *evidence* that would verify the fact that these two essays were written by the same person.

4. Review Reardon's explanation of her *purpose* in writing this new essay. Explain in detail how she achieved that purpose. What aspects of her new essay do you think would benefit from additional work? Explain why.

5. Reardon reports that she had a great deal of difficulty "narrowing the points to be covered in the essay. There was so much material I wanted to use that this piece could easily have been ten times longer. I tried to pick what was the strongest contrast between then and now, and to include information that the average student wouldn't be aware of. It was very difficult finding information about a woman's life around 1910; the topic isn't covered in most history texts. I was glad that my mother could furnish me with so many recollections." Identify "the strongest contrast between then and now" in Reardon's essay and comment on how effectively she handles it. Discuss her use of the information her mother provided. How successfully does she work this information into her essay? What sources, in addition to "most history texts," might she have consulted for "information about a woman's life around 1910"?

6. In discussing her essay, Reardon observes that "the easiest part was, as usual, the rewriting. I really enjoy revising my essays. It gives me pleasure to sift through words to find the exact one that I want to use, a phrase that reflects what I want to say." With this in mind, observe the changes Reardon makes in the opening paragraphs of each of her three drafts. Here is the opening paragraph in her first draft:

> The life of the poor is never easy, but survival today for a low income family is much easier than it was in my grandma's day.

Here is the opening paragraph in her second draft:

> Survival today is easier for a low-income family than it
> was in my grandmother's day. There is help available to
> her, but at a cost to her family life.

Compare and contrast these opening paragraphs with the final version. What changes do you notice in each draft? Which version do you prefer? Why?

7. Reardon lists a number of possible subjects that emerged from rereading her original essay. What other possibilities for writing a new essay can you identify in "The Unmarked Road"?

BEVERLY DIPO:
FROM NARRATION TO ARGUMENT

Beverly Dipo is a licensed practical nurse who enrolled at Utah State University to "try to get my RN." In her work as a nurse, she sees "human suffering, weaknesses, triumphs, and tragedies on a daily basis. It provides a unique perspective that many do not have." Asked to write a narrative essay focusing on a personal experience in which she gained some insight, Dipo responded with a compelling account of the death of one of her patients, Mrs. Trane. "I was asked to write about a moving experience, and Mrs. Trane's death was just that. I felt I could give an accurate account of the situation. . . . As a nurse, I frequently observe *things* before I ever speak to patients or get to know them as human beings. Right or wrong, it's the way we are trained. . . . All I did in this paper was to describe in detail a situation that really happened and my reactions to it."

When asked to describe herself as a writer, Beverly Dipo observed that "I am not a 'natural' at anything, including writing. . . . In fact my writing process may be unique. I can, and have, written an entire outline and the first paragraphs of a work at night, in bed, in my head. The next time I sit down at the typewriter, I put my rough draft on paper. I will make a second rough draft to redo spelling, punctuation, basic structure, and make revisions as needed. . . . Then I will proceed to thoroughly mess up the rough draft with slashes, exclamation points, secret codes, doodles, medical shorthand, and assorted expletives. . . . I will then retype what is left and repeat the procedure until I produce a whole essay without one single red mark!" In writing her essay, "No Rainbows, No Roses," Dipo notes that "the final draft practically ended up word for word the same as my first rough draft"—a testament to the emotional intensity of her narrative as well as to her own dictum that writers ought to "keep it simple."

Beverly Dipo's claim that she is not a natural at writing seems overly modest in view of her impressive work in "No Rainbows, No Roses" (p. 70). As you reread that essay, watch how Dipo uses the skills of observation she has developed as a nurse. "All I did in this paper was to describe in detail a situation that really happened and my reactions to it," she says. In writing down her observations, however, Dipo shows a strong sense of what details to include, how to translate sensory images into verbal ones, and how to balance setting, characters, action, and emotion. To do this requires skills that almost every beginning writer finds elusive, but that improve markedly with practice. As Dipo notes, the innate simplicity and intensity of the incident she chose to write about counted heavily in her favor.

Picking a subject for her second essay proved more difficult than Dipo had hoped. She kept track of her efforts to identify and explore ideas for a new essay based on "No Rainbows, No Roses" in the form of journal entries. After rereading her original essay several times, Dipo was able to note little progress: "Somewhere in my mind I have the general idea of what is expected of me. An 'expository or argumentative essay.' They make it sound so easy. Do I make it a more difficult task than it should be? Yes, I do. I want it to be a good paper." After several more readings, Dipo reports: "I'm still stuck for a subject. I've put it aside — thinking it will 'come to me' in a brilliant flash of light. Well I was hoping. Now I must sit down and do some brainstorming." Here is Dipo's record of the results of that effort:

> Possible subjects:
>
> 1. Avoid death; it's too morbid.
> 2. Nursing the terminally ill — good possibility — a subject dear to me, but still too morbid.
> 3. Why do I want to avoid it? Doesn't everybody?
> 4. How about rainbows? That's as far as I can get from death and still be considered part of my original essay. But what on earth could I contribute to the subject?
> 5. Obituaries? Back to the death thing again.
> 6. Am I going to be able to avoid it?
> 7. Families of patients as a subject comes to mind. A possibility. Families of the terminally ill?
> 8. Nursing in general? Too broad!
> 9. Nursing the elderly — a good possibility — something I really love. They can be so special: the gray, thinning hair, a twinkle in the eye, some with such a sense of humor. It's a joy but it can be painful. I find old folks more afraid of living than dying, especially if they're ill. This may be the choice. I will have to think about it.

Several days of preparing for summer school examinations intervened before Dipo could find adequate time to return to thinking about an appropriate subject for a new essay. When she did, her ideas developed quickly:

> I have been studying for exams; had little time to think about writing an essay. At work this morning, I found a patient's chart on which the Dr. had written: 'patient to be allowed to die with dignity, only supportive care to be given at the pt.'s request.' I wondered: how many times have I seen this actually written on a chart? Once, maybe twice before. And, from this same physician. Why are doctors so reluctant to do this? "The God Syndrome" we nurses call it. Doctors do not actually believe that they are God; they just try to act like Him. What is it that is taught in medical school that tells these people that they can *save everybody*?? It is so foolish, because *everybody* dies, sooner or later!! I admire the few who know when they have done enough, the few who are honest enough to give their patients realistic expectations. I remember Judy, whom you will meet in my essay, and I remember Mrs. Trane. They both died of the same disease. And my essay is pouring out into my brain. I sat down and scribbled out the first two pages before being summoned elsewhere and having to put it aside. My subject: Does a patient have the right to die the way *he* chooses? Is he informed enough to be able to choose? If not, why not? Is it the physician's responsibility to give his patient *informed* choices? These are questions my paper should include. So, I have my subject. The paper is started. Some research is needed.

Several days later, Dipo made the following entry in her journal: "I wish writing were easy! I wonder if I'm making myself understood. The essay is developing — my thoughts ramble though. This will take some organization. An outline may have been of some help, but the first five or six paragraphs came so easily; but now I seem stuck. Will plunge onward!"

Later that same day, Dipo made the following notations in her journal:

> —Euthanasia: "A painless *putting* to death of persons having an incurable disease; an easy death. Also mercy killing."
> —Suicide: "One who intentionally *takes* one's own life. The intentional taking of one's own life; to kill oneself."
> —Murder: "The act of unlawfully killing a human being by another human with premeditated malice; to commit murder." (Not applicable.)

—Ethical: "Pertaining to morals or morality; right and wrong
  in conduct."

The final entry in Dipo's journal, made a few days later, reads: "Received articles from library. Wow! So *many* different arguments—some good, some bad. I will be very limited in how much of the subject I can present. My first draft is done. Think—as time is limited—I will have to stick with what I've already done."

Beverly Dipo eventually wrote three drafts of her new essay. The final version follows. Notice as you read it that although Dipo opens with a specific case, as she did in "No Rainbows, No Roses," her thesis this time is a general one. She uses the concrete examples of Judy and Mr. Syms to illustrate the abstract principle of "dying with dignity." To do this, she gives up (as Julie Reardon did) the central character's point of view for that of a narrator writing mainly in the third person. Dipo thus draws on her nursing experience for illustrations and information rather than for characterization. Her language and organization show that she is less concerned now with setting a mood— appealing to her readers' emotions—and more concerned with building a case based on claims, evidence, and logic. Although the issue itself is highly emotional, and so is some of Dipo's supporting evidence, her tactics are not. She is still writing for a general audience, but her purpose has changed significantly.

DIPO'S ARGUMENTATIVE ESSAY

A Time to Die

Judy had been looking awfully tired recently. 1
Her husband, Clair, had been in and out of the
hospital over the last six months following his
heart attack, and Judy had been naturally concerned
about his failing health. She had managed to continue working at her full-time job as a registered
nurse, but the effort was beginning to show. There
were now creases in her once smooth brow, dark
circles under dull eyes, and an ashen hue seemed to
dim not only her complexion, but her personality as
well. The vigor which she had once applied to all
her tasks was gone. A number of her friends began
encouraging her to get a checkup, but she claimed
she just did not have the time.

Three months passed, and Judy began to lose 2
weight, have bouts of nausea, and back pain. She
finally decided to find the time for a physical
examination. After numerous tests, X-rays, scans,
and an admission to the hospital for a biopsy, Judy's
doctor told her she had pancreatic cancer. He informed her that with chemotherapy and radiation,
the probability of her living another year, maybe
two, was pretty good. As a nurse, Judy was well
informed about her disease, its treatments, and her
prognosis. She knew her doctor was being optimistic
and kind. She talked to Clair at length about what

her future would be, and then weighing her options carefully, she chose to refuse treatment. Both Clair and her doctor pleaded with her to accept the treatments, but she remained adamant. She knew she might have extra time with the help of the drugs and radiation, but she also knew that the extra time would be a time in and out of the hospital, nausea, vomiting weakness, emaciation, and to Judy, the worst side effect of all, the loss of control of her life. Finally, as a person whose life was spent in concern for others, typically, her concern was now for Clair. Since his heart attack, their income and savings had dwindled, and she seriously doubted Clair's ability, either physically or emotionally, to handle her prolonged illness. It was not the way she wanted to die. To Judy, her death was the natural and inevitable consequence of living, and she accepted it with grace and dignity.

Judy went home from the hospital, arranged her affairs, painted her last landscapes, and died within five months.   3

Was Judy's decision a right one? Did she have the right to determine how she was going to die?   4

Her husband never agreed with her but finally came to accept it as her decision. Her doctor, on the other hand, maintained that she did not have the right to refuse treatment. As a matter of fact, he refused to support her choice. Judy, as a nurse,   5

knew a doctor who would, and it was easy for her to
seek him out. Other patients are not that lucky.
Most patients do whatever is recommended to them by
their doctors, without question and without the knowledge that they do have a right to refuse treatment because the doctor never gives them that option. A
doctor will explain a terminal illness to his patient
by telling him of the medicines and procedures that
are available to combat the disease. Doctors believe,
and it is sometimes true, that this is what the patient
wants to hear and that this is the treatment the
patient expects to receive. Some doctors will explain to the patient that while there are side effects
to the treatments, they can be controlled by changing
the chemotherapy or by giving more medications to
counteract the effects of the chemotherapy. An
occasional physician will tell his patient he has "a
50/50 chance of living another two years or so with
treatment." Rarely is a patient told that, even after
the chemotherapy, radiation, surgery, and the "two
years or so" of extended life, he is going to die
anyway. A doctor is trained to treat illness and
cure the patient. To him, by not acting to prevent
death, he is allowing his patient to die. To a doctor,
death is an enemy and failure. Every measure is taken
to ensure that the patient does not become a "failure."
When his patient dies, the doctor feels personal
failure.

With today's technology, a patient's appointment   6
with death, while still inevitable, can be rescheduled
according to the arbitrary wishes of the physician.
If a patient's lungs fail, put him on a ventilator to
do his breathing for him; if his kidneys fail, start
dialysis; even if his heart fails, he can be maintained mechanically. Here again, patients are rarely
given information about the effects, the costs, or the
benefits of these treatments, let alone informed of
the potential harm they may cause. Often the institution of these treatments by the physician are afterwards explained to the patient or family as "necessary
to prevent death." Should not the patient be allowed
to decide if and when and which treatments he wants
to have, prior to their use? Some physicians will
argue that their patients do not have sufficient
knowledge to be able to determine whether or not they
need to be put on a respirator or started on dialysis
or receive any other medical treatment that might be
necessary. I will counter that such a physician has
a responsibility to educate his patients in such
matters. The patient does not need a medical degree
to make decisions about his own care. He needs only
the information pertaining to his specific condition,
and all the options that are open to him, including
his right to refuse any or all of those options.

What about the patient who is unable to make in-   7
formed decisions? Is it possible that medical treatment could become medical abuse?

Mr. Syms was a 73-year-old gentleman who, while   8
walking home from visiting his wife at a local nursing
home, was struck by a car. Besides a shattered left
femur, a fractured pelvis and a ruptured bladder, and
fractured ribs and abdominal bleeding, he suffered
head injuries, the extent of which could not be determined on admission. An emergency operation removed
his lacerated spleen and repaired his abdominal injuries and the ruptured bladder. His left leg was
set as best as it could be, but useful function of
the leg would be doubtful. He lay in the intensive
care unit, his leg in a cast from hip to toe; a
catheter drained his still bloody urine from his
bladder out through his abdomen; he had a nasogas-
tric tube draining his stomach contents out through
his nose; two IV lines were running, one in each arm,
to provide him with fluids. He remained comatose and
an electroencephalogram showed only minimal brain
activity. His wife had Alzheimer's disease and was
not even aware that he was missing from her life. He
had no other family.

Mr. Syms remained in critical condition for two   9
days. On the third day after the accident he had a
heart attack, but with resuscitation was revived.
Within twenty-four hours, he had two more heart attacks
and was again revived each time. In the following
three days, he had two more heart attacks and was
twice again revived and placed on a respirator to keep

him alive. Finally, on the tenth day after the accident and after developing pneumonia, he died even while attempts to resuscitate him continued.

Here was a body trying desperately to die. Who 10 among the medical profession would step up and say "enough is enough"? None did. Was Mr. Syms's medical treatment medical abuse?

In my opinion it was. Had efforts to keep Mr. 11 Syms alive succeeded, he would have been eventually transferred to a nursing home to be "maintained" in a vegetative state until he died, a silent reminder of miraculous medicine.

Besides the obvious ethical issues in Mr. Syms's 12 treatment, there are two questions I feel need to be asked. First, what about the cost of Mr. Syms's care, not only his hospital care, but what about the care he would have needed should he have survived? His hospital bill was over $46,000, which was paid for by Medicare (you and me). Should cost be a factor in anyone's care? Mr. Syms's early treatment, right after the accident, was certainly justified, but when it was known that he would not ever recover, continued efforts to keep him alive were highly questionable.

What about his age? If Mr. Syms had been a six- 13 year-old hit by a car while playing in the street would his treatment be justified, even when there was no hope of recovery? While most children have parents or guardians to make decisions for them, it is still the physician who has the responsibility to inform those decision makers about reasonable expectations of re- covery and the options they have concerning treatment, including the right to stop or refuse treatment.

Physicians are devoted to a moral duty to heal   14
their patients. They are also faced with an ethical dilemma which invariably involves taking some risks in making judgments. In making life-or-death decisions, they must employ wisdom and judgment. They cannot act on whims or prejudices, and decisions must be support- able with the desires and well-being of the patient in the forefront, even when those desires counter the physician's own beliefs, and even when they may consti- tute death to his patient. Conflict arises when the doctor's moral duty to heal impedes the patient's right to die.

Euthanasia is a term defined by the dictionary as   15
"a painless putting to death of persons having an in- curable disease; an easy death." The medical profession has conveniently broken that definition down into two: "active euthanasia" or the hastening of death by de- liberate action, and "passive euthanasia" or the alle- viating of symptoms, even though life may be shortened and nature be allowed to take its course. This was the course Judy chose. Was Judy's decision a right one? It was for her. She made her choice based on a knowledgeable foundation.

There are not any hard and fast rules within the   16

medical community concerning euthanasia. It is a word
never spoken in hospitals even though passive euthanasia
is practiced by some physicians like the one Judy found.
The right to die is basically a decision now made by
doctors based on their own morals and beliefs, even
though it is a decision that should be based on the
patient's morals and beliefs. Some doctors are thoughtful and reasonable about their expectations of a
patient's course of disease. They are considerate of
the desires of the patient and discuss openly all
options open to the patient, including what will
happen should the patient elect to refuse treatment.
That is as it should be. Other physicians, however,
never give in to that old enemy death. These doctors
will frequently confuse patients and families by offering hope through medications and treatments that are
only temporary measures to prolong life. To them, the
quality of life is not even a matter that needs consideration or discussion. They fully believe they are
doing their best for the patient by saving him from
death, even for a short while, even in misery.

The right to die has been slow in being brought   17
forth for open discussion. Gradually, medical schools
are beginning to recognize that the life of a dying
patient becomes steadily less rich and less worth
living, and that as the pain and suffering involved
in maintaining what is left of life are mounting,
there comes a point when decisions must be made.

These decisions must be made by a knowledgeable patient
and family, clergy and physician, all together.

There are no absolute rules that will resolve all   18
the questions with the same answer. Each case and
each patient are different and need to be considered
on an individual basis. I cannot advocate active
euthanasia or mercy killing. That involves one person
ending the life of another. I do not advocate patients
refusing all treatments, when there are certainly
patients who can benefit. I am saying that all of us
are going to die sooner or later. I am saying that
the medical profession has a duty to accept that fact,
that it be given to the patient as an alternative to
all other treatments he may be asked to consider, and
that his wishes in the choices he makes be accepted
gracefully. I do hope that in the near future the
medical profession allows that to each individual
there is a time to die and that that time is the
patient's rightful choice.

As it is written in Ecclesiastes: "To everything   19
there is a season, and a time to every purpose under
heaven: a time to be born, and a time to die; a time
to plant, and a time to pluck up that which is
planted."

Amen!   20

When Beverly Dipo completed the final draft of "A Time to Die," she wrote the following commentary on the process of writing the essay:

It's done! It is always a great relief to get something that is difficult finished. I did find writing an argumentative essay difficult. A personal experience essay requires only that you describe something and report your responses to it. An argumentative essay requires some thought and research. Also, I suppose I had some difficulty because I am basically a passive and introverted person. While I may have some strong feelings and opinions, I do not usually publicize them.

Medical abuse is one subject I do have strong feelings about. I work with it daily, and it is so very frustrating. Nurses are somehow caught in the middle of a great dilemma between the medical hierarchy on one side and just wanting to help people on the other. As for my paper, I am not sure I stated that position as well as it could have been. I hope I gave some good examples and expounded on some of the problems that confront the dying patient. But — being my own worst critic — I feel it probably could have been said better by someone else.

The most difficult aspect of the assignment was to restrain and contain the subject. I did do some research on it and found it to be much more involved than I could possibly cover in one paper. My theme could have covered "codes" or the lack of them, "slow codes," living wills, malpractice, families, or hospice care, among other things. I did feel at times a certain limitation and at other times that I had picked a subject which was more than I could handle.

During the process of writing this essay, my mind frequently wandered back to Mrs. Trane and to so many other dying patients I have taken care of over the years. I wonder, had they really known what their remaining time would be like after a terminal diagnosis was made, how many of them would have agreed to treatment? Would they have refused treatment if they had been given all the facts? I remember one man being so angry about not being told what would happen to him that, much against his family's wishes, he ordered that his remains be cremated, without funeral services. He had shunned every friend and all but his closest family. He did not want to have them see him, during his illness or after his death. He not only blamed his doctors, but the nurses as well. He died an angry and hostile man. One of his last remarks to me was, "This disease didn't kill me, my fellow man did." Well, his disease may have killed his body, but it probably was his fellow man who killed his spirit.

It is people like this that I thought about when writing this essay. It is my argument for them and to them. They are the ones who need to be educated about their rights. They are the ones who need to realize that doctors are only humans, not gods, and that medicine cannot keep everyone alive forever. This argumentative essay let me make that point, whereas the one on Mrs. Trane did not.

Thinking about it now, after the essay is done, I find I like the idea of being able to say right out loud how I feel about the issue. It is not such a bad thing to be able to do. That is probably the thing I enjoyed most about this paper.

In my personal experience essay, I suffered Mrs. Trane's death silently and alone. In this argumentative essay, I gave the burden of sharing death over to those who are experiencing it. Maybe someone will learn something from it, or think about death differently than they had before, or discover that they do indeed have control over their own lives — and deaths.

Questions on Dipo's Two Essays

1. Beverly Dipo's journal entries include "some brainstorming." What relation does this brainstorming exercise have to "A Time to Die"? Which notations, if any, provide an early indication of the eventual focus and direction of "A Time to Die"?

2. At what point in her journal entries does Dipo seem to settle on a subject for her new essay? What specific thoughts trigger her decision to write about a patient's "right to die in the way he chooses"?

3. Once Dipo has begun to write her essay, what concerns does she express about finishing it? Based on your reading of her final draft, how did she resolve those "problems"? Support your response by pointing to specific words and phrases.

4. Dipo's journal entries include several *definitions*. In what specific ways does Dipo incorporate these *definitions* — either explicitly or implicitly — in "A Time to Die"? Where and how does she include information from the library research she has done?

5. Reread Dipo's explanation of her goal in writing this essay. Assess as specifically as possible the extent to which she achieves that goal. Outline Dipo's *argument* in "A Time to Die." What are the specific strengths of her argument? In what ways do you think she might strengthen it?

6. What specific thematic connections can you identify between "No Rainbows, No Roses" and "A Time to Die"? What stylistic features link both essays? What evidence can you point to in the word choice, phrasing, sentence structure, and overall organization that would verify Dipo's authorship of both?

7. Review the brainstorming notes and journal entries exploring possible subjects that resulted when Dipo reread her original essay. What other possibilities for writing a new essay can you identify in "No Rainbows, No Roses"?

TURNING A PERSONAL EXPERIENCE ESSAY
INTO EXPOSITION OR ARGUMENT

Now that you have observed how two student writers developed new essays —one expository, the other argumentative—from personal experience essays, you can apply the procedures they followed in your own writing. The whole process, from start to finish, consists of five basic steps:

1. Reread your personal experience essay carefully several times and generate as many new subjects as possible.

2. Generate as many ideas about each of these subjects as possible.

3. Decide on a new subject to write about.

4. Assert a specific idea about that subject.

5. Write a new essay in which you explain (exposition) or verify a claim or proposition about that new subject (argumentation).

You have probably noticed that both Julie Reardon and Beverly Dipo devoted a large proportion of their efforts to steps 1 and 2. For these writers, as for many others, steps 3 and 4 happened together as step 2 progressed. That is, once you have come up with a list of subjects and are thinking about how you might approach each of them, you may well find that a thesis—an interesting idea to assert about a workable subject—occurs to you almost spontaneously. Very often steps 1 and 2, generating possible subjects and ideas, are the most daunting and time-consuming steps in the process. Let's look at them closely.

As Beverly Dipo's and Julie Reardon's examples indicate, the personal experience essays you have already written contain rich and ready resources for writing other types of essays. Although Reardon moved from description to exposition, while Dipo moved from narration to argument, it is clear from their freewriting and brainstorming that Reardon's original paper might just as well have led her to an argumentative essay and Dipo's to an expository one. The choice of which kind of essay to write may depend on your assignment, or on the combination of subject and idea that strikes you as the most promising thesis. Keeping an open mind is wise. Recall Beverly Dipo's initial reluctance to write an argumentative essay; once she did it, however, she commented: "I find I like the idea of being able to say right out loud how I feel about the issue. . . . This is probably the thing I enjoyed most about this paper."

Step 1 involves rereading your original personal experience essay carefully, several times, and listing every subject that comes to mind as you think about what you are reading. When you return to your earlier work after a lapse of time, you are better able to see it from a fresh perspective. Ask yourself questions: What made me feel strongly enough about my original topic to write about it? What controversies does it suggest? What broader subjects does it relate to that would allow me to generalize (exposition) or theorize (argumentation) about my experience? Your goal at this point is simply to list as many new subjects to write about as possible.

After completing step 1, you may conclude that only one of your possible subjects is worth pursuing or that one subject is significantly stronger than the others. If so, go on to step 2 and ask yourself: What idea can I assert about this topic? Focus your thinking about the subject — or issue — until you are reasonably confident you can assert a specific idea about it. Now consider what information, what data you can provide to support and clarify your idea about this subject or issue. Explaining that idea will become your new expository essay. Or, when you have narrowed your list of possible topics to one, ask yourself: what claim or proposition can I assert about this topic? Presenting logically related statements in support of your claim or proposition will lead to a new, argumentative essay.

In most cases, more than one subject on your list will have good potential as an essay topic. Step 2, then, is to generate as many ideas as you can about each of your "finalists." Some possible theses or approaches to a thesis probably will have occurred to you while you were considering topics. Even if these do not look promising, write them down; they may suggest other possibilities later. As you did when you thought of subjects, you can try brainstorming, as Beverly Dipo did — let ideas swirl around in your head and write down everything that might lead to a thesis. Or you can freewrite, as Julie Reardon did — go through your original essay again and list all the thoughts it inspires.

Another Bedford Prize winner, Ravenel Boykin Curry, has described the kind of chain of associations from which he gleans ideas. Curry's essay, "A Small Town" (p. 63), is the result of looking at ordinary personal experience from as many angles as possible. Cultivating this kind of "writer's eye" not only generates a continual supply of ideas but suggests ways of asserting those ideas in an essay. As Curry notes:

> I have found that the best way to get ideas (and a more
> interesting way to live your life) is to look for some kind
> of significance in little things you observe each day. A
> mother slaps her whining kid on the beach. You can pur-
> sue the aesthetic — the sun is shining on thousands of
> people laughing and playing in the water, but all that fills
> this kid's being right now are the pain and anger. You
> can be psychological — is the child a brat because the
> mother responds with violence? Or could negative incen-
> tive help the kid to understand that the world doesn't
> tolerate a whiner? Take a political angle — should the state
> be able to intervene in minor family violence? What if
> the husband slapped the wife? What constitutes child abuse
> and who should decide? You can expand anything; ideas
> are endless.

It sometimes happens, however, that even after rereading your original essay
and listing possible subjects and ideas, you still have no workable thesis for an
expository or an argumentative essay. If so, you may find the following additional questions helpful. Consider all four sets of questions and then choose
one set to guide you as you develop your new essay.

1. *Move from the specific to the general.* A narrative or descriptive essay focuses
on a specific event, person, place, or object. Beverly Dipo's "No Rainbows,
No Roses" related the death of Mrs. Trane; Julie Reardon's "The Unmarked
Road" re-created the rural neighborhood where the author spent four years.
Every specific case can be viewed as an example of a generality: people
dying in hospitals; people living in poverty. To move from the specific
subject of your personal experience essay to a more general topic, think
about how your experience can be considered representative of many people's experience. The goal here is to broaden your point of view, to extend
your thinking to take in that of others besides yourself. Once you have
done this, you may want to choose one segment within that general topic,
as Beverly Dipo chose "people dying in hospitals *with dignity.*" Or your first
generalization may lead you to others: people dying at home; the value of
funerals; the importance of making a will.

   Questions: What general topic is implied in your specific personal experience? What general subject does your personal experience exemplify?
What general issue or issues does your experience raise? What other general
subjects or issues emerge from rereading your original essay and thinking
about its larger implications?

2. *Move from autobiography to biography.* Another way to move from personal experience to exposition and argumentation is to shift the focus of your original essay from autobiography to biography, from a first- to third-person point of view. The shift from a subjective to an objective perspective carries you beyond the limitations of your own experience. It also enables you to understand—and participate in—a multiplicity of cultures and life-experiences that, in turn, may well help to illuminate your own life.

   Questions: As you reread your personal experience essay, pay special attention to whether you talk about anyone else during the course of your essay. Consider each such person carefully. What aspects of this person's life do you think are worth writing about—consider beliefs, attitudes, accomplishments, or perhaps an incident or an anecdote in which he or she figures prominently? What ideas can you assert about this person? What general concept is this person's life a specific example of? What proposition or claim can you make on the basis of this person's views or behavior?

3. *Move from the concrete to the abstract.* Narrative and descriptive essays are based in large part on concrete information: sensory details about how something looked, felt, or sounded; actions that occurred; the writer's response to those details and actions. In Patrick Kinder Lewis's essay, "Five Minutes North of Redding" (p. 150), we feel the predawn chill of a railway roadbed, and we share the author's tension as he bounds onto a flatcar. But Lewis's essay also alludes to such abstract concepts as freedom, risk-taking, and friendship. As you reread your own personal experience essay, look for the abstractions it suggests.

   Questions: What abstract nouns come to mind as you reread your essay? You may very well think of several abstractions that are associated with your specific, concrete experience. Choose one of these and work at developing its potential as the subject of another essay. Why did this particular abstract noun surface in your mind as you reread your essay? What aspects of your essay suggested it? How does it summarize the point of your essay or indicate what your essay is about? What idea, claim, or proposition might you assert that conveys your thoughts regarding this abstract concept?

4. *Move from observation to inference.* Yet another way to find a suitable subject to develop into a new essay is to move from observation to inference. (For our purposes, an "observation" may be defined as a statement about the visible facts in a specific situation, a statement about which there can be no disagreement. An "inference" is a conclusion based on a premise drawn

from observations, a statement about what is still uncertain made on the basis of what is certain. For additional information about observations and inferences, see Part V. In one sense, your original essay might well be considered a series of observations about your experience.

Questions: What inferences about experience in general can you draw from your essay? What theory or pattern of behavior seems to govern the experience you wrote about? Consider that theory or pattern carefully and list as many observations as you can about it. Based on your observations, what inferences can you draw about this theory or pattern? To what conclusion about experience, however tentative, do these observations and inferences lead you? Turn this tentative conclusion into the thesis — the controlling idea — for either an expository or an argumentative essay. How can you use the evidence of your own experience, or your inferences about experience in general, to support this thesis?

Having considered these four broad sets of questions aimed at helping you move from writing personal experience essays to expository and argumentative ones, you need next to decide which cluster seems most appropriate to the purpose of your new essay. Once you have made that determination, you might well want to work with the following summary of useful procedures. As you reread your personal experience essay, what new "angles," what new approaches to this subject can you think of? What broader subjects does this essay suggest? Keep track of these subjects in note form and develop each by following your usual methods of developing an idea about a subject: brainstorm, freewrite, and so on. Narrow your list of possible subjects to one and examine it further. Then ask yourself: what idea can I assert about this subject? Explaining that idea will become your new, expository essay. Or, when you've narrowed your list of possible subjects to one, ask yourself: What claim or proposition can I assert about this subject? Presenting logically related statements in support of your claim or proposition will lead to a new argumentative essay.

Discovering and learning how to develop the connections between the ideas in one successful essay and another are important skills to master, especially for writers who are not only respectful of the richness of their own intelligence but also committed to exploring that richness fully. Learning to explore the connections between one idea and another, between one essay and another, and between one course and another also helps every writer to recognize — and strengthen — both the interrelations of writing and reading and the common threads that weave together the seemingly disparate verbal elements of our lives into a practiced, confident, and unique intellectual identity.

Three Exercises for Moving from Personal Experience
to Exposition and Argument

1. Reread Ann Louise Field's essay, "The Sound of Angels" (p. 76). Here are some possible subjects — and ideas asserted about those subjects — that Field prepared after rereading her essay:

—Paper routes
   1. Early jobs build responsibility.
   2. Forcing children to work at too early an age robs them of their youth.

—Sibling relationships
   1. A little bit of rivalry can be a good thing.
   2. Traditions of childhood; experiences common to all kids.
   3. Love-hate feelings between siblings.

—Orange groves
   1. The rise and fall of the Southern California citrus industry.
   2. The pros and cons of growing oranges for Minute Maid.
   3. The art of tree-climbing.
   4. Linus Pauling and the vitamin C/cancer controversy.

—Childhood pranks
   1. Lead to delinquency.
   2. Encourage imagination and creativeness in youth.

—Christmas
   1. Holiday traditions.
   2. The evolution of commercialism at Christmas.

—Loss of innocence
   1. The effects of economic stress on the contemporary American family.
   2. The need for everyone to recognize reality.
   3. The nature of adolescent rebellion.
   4. The increase in teenage suicide — the inability to function in an adult world?

Based on your reading of Field's essay, which of these possible subjects — and assertions — for expository and argumentative essays do you think Field would handle best in a new essay? Why? Point to specific passages in "The Sound of Angels" to verify your response. Which seems to offer the least potential as the subject — and the assertion — for a new essay? Why?

2. Write an expository or argumentative essay based on a personal experience essay you have written. Follow the questions and procedures outlined above.

3. Write as detailed a commentary as possible on how you wrote your new essay. For instance, how did the idea — or claim — you chose to assert about your new subject develop and change as you actually wrote the essay? What particular problems did you have to work out from one draft to the next? What was the goal of your new essay? Whom did you see as the readers of your new essay? How did you try to appeal to these readers? What did you want them to think or feel after they read your essay? What advice would you offer your readers on how to respond to and understand your new essay?

PEER EDITORS
AT WORK

Part V

THE TWO PREVIOUS CHAPTERS examined the composing process from the writer's point of view. In Part III, "Three Student Writers at Work," Barbara Seidel, Jonathan Schilk, and Matthew Holicek reconstructed the different approaches they used to get started, write, and then revise their essays. In Part IV, "Moving from Personal Experience to Exposition and Argument," Beverly Dipo and Julie Reardon explored the personal experience essays they had already written to generate new topics for additional expository and argumentative essays. This chapter studies the composing process from the points of view of both the writer and the reader by focusing on how writers can work with their peers to improve each other's essays. Like their professional counterparts (see Part VI, "The Professional Editor at Work"), peer editors serve as supportive readers, ready to understand a writer's purpose and to assist the writer in achieving that purpose. In such circumstances, a writer can sense the immediacy of an audience — other students who are willing to read his or her work thoughtfully and offer detailed comments on how effectively a particular draft expresses that writer's intentions. As a peer editor you can provide both specific praise and practical advice about how to strengthen the already successful features of an essay and how to revise its weaknesses. And by responding to and evaluating your peers' writing, you will be better able to write, read, revise, and edit your own essays.

Peer editors and writers can work one on one, in small groups, or within the class as a whole to help each other get started, draft, revise, and edit essays that will satisfy themselves and their course requirements. Although the principles and procedures of peer editing can be applied to any stage of the composing process, peer editing usually works best after writers have produced a first draft of an essay, when they can benefit most from detailed and supportive responses to what they have written. By working collaboratively with peer editors, writers are not limited to their own perspective on the composing process; they can see how other writers — the peer editors — would deal with exactly the same circumstances and challenges.

This chapter examines the most effective techniques peer editors can use when responding to the writing of other students. The chapter first presents an example of peer editing: several students offer detailed responses to and

341

recommendations for Patrick Kinder Lewis on how he might improve his essay, "Five Minutes North of Redding." The chapter then considers in general terms how a writer might work most productively with the peer editors' responses to plan more effective revisions based on their comments and recommendations. More specifically, the chapter presents Lewis's explanations of how and why he incorporated, modified, and occasionally rejected the peer editors' suggestions in working on his revision. A newly revised draft of Lewis's essay follows, along with several peer editing exercises in which you can apply the principles and procedures of peer editing, first to Johnna Lynn Benson's "Rotten at the Core" and then to your own writing.

THE PEER EDITOR'S RESPONSE TO WRITING

The most effective peer editor is an interested and sensitive reader. To be a sympathetic and helpful critic of another student's writing, you should be willing to work diligently to understand the writer's purpose and to offer thoughtful and specific advice about how the writer might best achieve that purpose. You need to be interested in helping other students write better—not by suggesting ways to avoid errors but by assisting them in articulating their ideas fully.

When approaching another student's writing, you should think, talk, and write about it seriously and respectfully; any writer will respond more appreciatively and energetically to criticism—be it positive or negative—that has been tactfully worded. Judicious comments also signal that you are genuinely interested in helping another writer improve; the most helpful comments are specific, direct, and encouraging. A peer editor who says simply that he or she "liked" or 'disliked" an essay doesn't help the writer understand either the essay's strengths or weaknesses. But noting, for example, that the writer has emphasized a particular point by developing a striking metaphor in the third sentence of the second paragraph makes that achievement more appreciable —and the skill more repeatable—for both the writer and the peer editor. And it is, after all, the ability to repeat success that can make writing so satisfying and enduring an intellectual enterprise.

As a peer editor, you can respond in innumerable ways to another student's writing. The most typical and widely used strategies for peer editing fall into two categories: specific comments in the margin of the essay and a general statement, usually at the end of the essay. These specific and general comments most often serve two functions: to describe what the writer has actually said in the essay and to evaluate its strengths and weaknesses.

Perhaps the most valuable service that you, as a peer editor, can perform for a writer is to return a clear and, at least initially, nonjudgmental description of what the writer has written. One of the best ways to do that is to write as many specific observations as possible about the essay, either directly on the manuscript or on a separate sheet of paper to be given to the writer. In peer editing, an *observation* is a statement about which there can be no disagreement. In this sense, an observation is concrete, limited, verifiable, and often fairly obvious. It is also nonjudgmental. The purpose of your observations is to help the writer understand and appreciate a reader's perceptions of what he or she has actually written. Your observation might address, for example, fundamental problems in logic and organization: "You mention the same point about the effects of nuclear weapons in paragraphs 4 and 7." A seemingly obvious observation such as, "I notice that you begin the first five sentences in your essay with 'It is' and 'There are,' " may lead the writer to reread the essay with an eye to varying its verbs and sentence structure. But the decision, and in fact the authority, to do so remains where it belongs—solely with the writer.

Evaluative comments shift the emphasis from describing what the essay says to assessing its specific strengths and weaknesses and suggesting particular revisions. In making evaluative comments, the peer editor writes detailed marginal notations about such elements of composition as word choice, tone, use of examples, logic, and organization. You identify both what the writer does well in the essay and what the writer needs to spend more time on. The more honest your assessments are, the more helpful they will be.

A particularly useful kind of evaluation is for the peer editor to summarize as succinctly as possible the thesis of the essay and to note specifically how the writer develops that controlling idea in each paragraph. The aim of this evaluation is to assist the writer in expressing, clarifying, and developing completely the main point of the essay as well as the assertions in each paragraph that support it.

The peer editor usually writes a general evaluation at the end of the essay based on the specific marginal notations made throughout the paper. Your goal in this general evaluation is to give a balanced overview of the essay's strengths and weaknesses, not simply a summary of its flaws. You should also include suggestions to help the writer develop a detailed and achievable plan for revision. These suggestions should be selective rather than exhaustive and should help the writer set clear priorities for revising. These general comments are also the most appropriate place to review the essay with an eye to helping the writer make it as concise, engaging, and elegant as possible. These are also quite likely the last suggestions the writer can draw on before revising the essay and submitting it to the instructor for an additional reading and eventually a grade.

Student writers who serve as peer editors will be both practiced writers and practiced readers, since the skills of writing and reading are truly integrated. What peer editors learn about the interaction between reading and writing will help them a great deal when they turn to their own writing.

PEER EDITING PATRICK KINDER LEWIS'S ESSAY

To demonstrate how a writer can improve an already successful essay with the help of peer editors, this section presents several peer editors' responses to Patrick Kinder Lewis's essay, "Five Minutes North of Redding." We have chosen this essay because of its complexity and ambition. Lewis writes knowledgeably and dramatically about a youthful adventure "riding the rails" in northern California. Aboard a freight train traveling north from Sacramento, Lewis discovers a great deal about himself and his relation to the world around him.

Lewis spent roughly a year on the road, trying "to figure out what made life tick — and whether there was really anything that made one's life worth all the pain. What I came back with was the beginnings of something more than simple self-worth. That was there too. But that year, more than any other, assured me that life is really only as absurd as we choose to make it. . . . I also came back with a new realization of the value God has placed on every human life. The hobos and mixed-up kids I met were no less worthy of the meagre amount of grace that I was able to show them than any others I might meet under other circumstances. Nothing in this life comes cheaply — nothing of value anyway — but none of us pays anywhere near the face value for what we get either: what we have, we have been given on loan. I began to live in the midst of that antinomy, to be liberated by it. The world of others around me continues to be bathed in that strange light for me."

With this recognition in mind, Lewis set out to write an essay about the chain of events that led to his realization about the profound dignity of each human life, "to create the snapshot which I never took of that epiphanic moment. And I wanted to create the peace of that moment. . . . The experience about which I wrote was a brief but meaningful excerpt from a much longer story I hope to write about learning from life-lived-on-the-edge. 'Five Minutes North of Redding' was in a way the fulfillment of a youthful dream and the beginning of a more mature vision."

At the end of the spring 1985 semester, we invited four writing students at Queens College in the City University of New York to respond as peer editors to Patrick Lewis's essay. At that time, the students—Nicholas Balamaci, Jason Eskenazi, Nelson Farias, and Fran Osborne — had accumulated virtually a semester's worth of peer-editing experience. These students read and responded to Lewis's essay as though he were a classmate. Then Lewis responded in writing to their comments and suggestions and planned and wrote a revision based on their recommendations.

Here are both the specific marginal notations the peer editors made on Lewis's essay and their general comments at the end of the essay. Read the essay as it appears on pages 150 – 153 without any comments on it. Then reread it as it appears below, this time considering the peer editors' responses.

LEWIS'S EDITED ESSAY

This title puts the incident in both time and place.

Five Minutes North of Redding

You tell us where we are immediately. (NF)

I rolled out of the weeds into the crisp daylight of that late September morning to catch the

I notice you use a technical term. Is this the language of hobos? of railroad people? both? (JE)

north train out of Roseville. The herder had said

Powerful description of your state of mind (FO).

it would leave about 3:00 am; so I had huddled in

Is this necessary? (NF)

my coat for at least three hours, wishing in the

predawn chill for a cup of hot anything. But the

You transform wishes to dreams here. (FO)

You create a strong sense of anticipation at the end of the first paragraph. (NB)

noise and lights of the train yard had filtered
through the tall grass and disturbed even those
harmless dreams.

I notice that you equate wishing and dreaming here. Your equation is very indirect, however. Make it clearer? (JE)

Finally she came. Forty cars were in sight

Who is this "she"? (NB)

before the engines passed me. Moving down to the

How about: "As I moved down"? I think it reads better that way. (NB)

I notice that you use many participial phrases. (JE)

rail bed, I noticed for the first time that I had
not slept alone on this stretch of tracks. Three
figures were coming down to claim a rail car 150
yards up the line, and even as I cautiously watched

them, two other groups of riders were claiming cars

What is this other thought? Is it the next sentence? (JE)

behind me. I bounded onto a flatcar, concerned that
the line of empties would soon pass me by--then
thought again. A solitary presence on that flat

This is a dangling modifier. (NB)(JE)(FO)

How about: "I was a solitary presence on that flat deck, and within me instinct..."? (NB)

You make me feel how sensitive you are to your own vulnerability here. (NB)

deck, instinct shouted within me warnings about such
a vulnerable position. I crossed the ten-foot width
and dropped down onto the ground on the other side
of the car. This time I watched until everyone was

1

2

on board before I picked out one of the last empty

boxcars. And still there were some fifty closed

cars behind mine. This train was surely big enough, *All references to the journey between Rockville and Sacramento are left out. Can we assume that you got on board, the train started, and you travelled? (FO)*

I imagined, for all of us.

The line of cars came to its first stop on a 3

siding three hours up the Sacramento Valley as we *I notice that you refer to yourself and the train collectively. (JE)*

allowed another train to pass. Groves of plum trees

There are lots of details here. They work well. (NP)

lined the track on either side. Even so late in the

season, the trees to the train's right were still

full of hard purple fruit. I laid down in a splash

Who was warm and relaxed? (FO)(NB)

of sun on the deck of my car. For the first time

I was

that morning warm and relaxed, *but* the startling sound

Another dangling modifier? Add: "I was" and "but"? (NB)

of shouts out the east door caused me to retreat *If they are playing, then this should be fun. "Experiments" are for rats. (NF)*

into the shadows again. I peered out to find six

There is an innocence here that fights against the alienation you say you feel. (NB)

men playing among the trees like kids as they picked

plums only to pelt each other with them. I watched

intently, as if it were some elaborate social experi-

By whom? You seem to want to generalize here. Why? (JE)

ment, until the sound of boots on gravel brought me

back around. Looking to the (shadow) behind me, I

suddenly realized that it was too late to conceal *Whose shadow? Your participial phrase keeps me guessing. (JE)*

Excellent aural and visual description. (NB)

myself. The man whose crunching boots had just

announced his approach was somehow already at my

back door looking me over. *Is this word necessary? What does it add to your sentence? (NB)*

"There you are. I've been lookin' for you. 4

You make this sound ominous. It works! (NB)

You're travelin' alone ain't you?" All the wrong questions to ask someone who is already scared of you. [Luckily the voice betrayed nothing but a desire for friendship.] "That's right, I am. What . . . are you alone, too?" I sized him up coolly as I moved toward my knapsack in the far corner. In its open front pocket I had a knife if I needed it. He had an eight-inch Bowie knife strapped frontier-style to his right shin.

"No. Couple of beaners and me pick up together in Stockton; but they ain't speakin' nothin' but Spanish, man. You want sumpum to eat? They're gettin' some plums. We got cukes and tomatoes that they picked in the Valley yesterday. And I got a box of saltines in Roseville."

He had a ruddy face that was roughly pocked, probably from adolescence, and a scraggly mustache that only became noticeable when he looked right at you. I had reached my pack, but simply turned toward him in a crouch to look for my next move. If I planned to turn down his offer, standing four feet up in a boxcar was the time to do it. His bony frame and large hands gave away his height: I

Handwritten annotations:

- But only one is asked. (JE)
- It would be interesting for a reader to know why you would need to carry a knife. It would create tension if the danger was dramatically present. (NF)
- Is this necessary? It seems to me that this phrase reduces the relief caused by the discovery. (NF)
- I like how you showed friendship with his voice instead of simply telling us about it. (JE)
- You give your audience lots of details here. You make it easier for us to see the knife. (NF)
- There's a real sense of voice, of personality here. These lines back up your point that the stranger is friendly. (Fo)(JE)
- You separate the dialogue with lines of description. That gives the effect of coolness, of distance, between the speakers. (Fo)
- Is this necessary? It doesn't seem like essential information to me. What does it add? (NF)
- There is excellent control in here. The tension begins to grow, but its reduced by the following sentence. ("If I planned...")
- Do we "look out" for our next move? Don't we get "ready" for it? (NF) This is an unusual way of saying this, and the phrase works well. (NB)
- Can "standing" be a time? (NB)
- This is a concise description. (Fo)

would be at a three- to four-inch disadvantage once *You repeat this word later. (NF)*

down on level ground. And he just looked (tough.) *Move to beginning of sentence? (NF)*

Shoulder-length, muddy blond hair (he had) tied back *Do you need this? Isn't this understood? (NF)*

This is a sentence fragment. (NF)

with a lace of dark buckskin; it laced the seams of

his chamois pants too. (He was (fond) of buckskin and *How do you know this unless he told you? And if he did, then*

wore it well.) [Very (tough) but somehow gentle.] He *why not let him speak here? (JE)*

How?

The contrast needs to be developed. (NF)

seemed all in all an atavism, a confusing mixture of

General Custer with a sixties flower child. I de- *I think it's a good idea to let us figure out what that was. It's more fun for your readers. (NB)*

cided to trust my second inclination.

"Sounds good," I said closing my pack. "What's   8

your name?" I grabbed my jacket and hopped down onto

Where else would he limp from? Sounds like he kicked the door! (JE)

the loose shale bed. The train was just pulling away *I notice that you use the word "him" here twice in one sentence. (JE)*

with a halting rumble as we neared his car. On

quickening our pace, I noticed he was limping from

his hip down. I was in the car before him and

offered him a hand. But he ignored it and managed *This is an excellent sentence. You show his experience in action. This is filled with great details! (JE)*

an agile roll into the car by catching hold of a

break in the floor.

Use "in" here instead? (JE)

Alex and the Beaners were the first hobos I (was)   9

You need to give some examples here. (NB) (Fo)

to travel with. (For) the space of a couple days we *Was seems out of place here. It's like looking back on something you're looking back on? (JE)*

ate, drank, slept, and (fought) like brothers. I

I'm not sure that this is the right word. If you meant "fought" literally, then that seems like a cliché. You need to work harder here on your language. (NB)

learned (their) pasts and (their) plans in that short

time together and laid awake to think what it would *I notice that you use the word "their" three times in one sentence. (JE)*

be like to live (their) lives. At one point, left

behind by our train somewhere south of Red Bluff, *Same train? New train? (JE)*

This paragraph confuses me. I've lost a clear sense of time and place. (FO)

we hiked together most of the way to the next rail-

head, ducking many a curious sheriff en route.

Finally Alex found us a ride out of a truck stop

with an ex-Harley biker. Ambling over the gunwales

of his pickup, we rode it all the way to Redding.

Which night? (FO) (NB)

That night, we caught the last train out still

on its dinner break. Ducking into a store nearby, I

nearby what? (NB)

Why ducking if you are a legitimate customer? (JE)

This is ambiguous. Can a train be on a dinner break? (JE)

quickly bought enough sardines, crackers, and canned

sausages for ten men. While the train sat idle we

found a boxcar that was open only on its east side.

(For the cold trip into the mountains ahead, warmth

was a more important concern than a view of the

scenery to the west.) We had just finished off the

This implies that you're impatient for it to move. If so, why? (NF)

sardines as the train at last began to lumber out of

Why? (FO) Show us. Don't tell us. (JE)

the yard. Our bodies exhausted, our hunger at last

abated, we sat on the dirty floor of our boxcar en-

joying the last warm breath of the evening. We were

You make me feel this sentence! Well done. (JE)

now at the northernmost end of California's fertile

basin. From here on the land would climb more steeply.

Only the Sacramento River lay between us and the Cas-

cade mountains. As we approached the trestle, the

You move back to being more specific here. That's very effective. (FO)

I notice that you use another technical term. (JE)

track took only one slow curve to the northwest. On

ahead, I was sure it would begin a series of slow

switchbacks to climb Mt. Shasta's side. But for now,

Read this aloud. Doesn't it sound awkward? (NF)

Something missing? (NF)

because dead ahead, Shasta was out of sight.

The naming of places does not fully produce a feeling of movement. This is especially true for readers unfamiliar with the geography of California! (NF)

10

Why? (FO)

Is there such a word? (NB)

I leaned tiredly against the back door and *Your use of this metaphor from drama is very effective.* watched as the scene in front of me began to change.

Low on the horizon, a nearly full moon was rising *It's almost poetic!) (FO)*

You shift here from the concrete to a metaphor → (NF) slowly to take its place in the center of our stage.

Mt. Lassen's distant volcanic head joined it as we *I'm not sure what "it" refers to. (JE)* rounded the last turn before the river, showing mutely

through a carpet of velvet green peaks. Inside the

I think it would have been more effective to mention their origin earlier. (NF) car, Alex stood up to blow the smoke of his cigarette *This sentence sounds awkward. (JE)* out into the crystal air. He propped himself like a *This simile seems out of place. → (FO)* caryatid supporting the right border of our window on *Excellent word choice, suggesting oneness with each other and emphasizing the feeling of the paragraph. (FO)*

Your words grow more affectionate here, and that seems appropriate. (JE) the world. My Mexican compadres sat nearly motion- less at the door's left side. Mesmerized, I dug blindly into my pack to find the harmonica which I

had saved for just such an inspiring moment. I sucked

Why? (JE)(NF) Are you using this phrase ironically & talking about pure pleasure? (FO) in a chord or two of "This Train Is Bound for Glory," *But you don't develop the metaphor of the stage until six sentences after it introduced. (NF)*

The Sacramento? → (FO) laughing inside. Suddenly, another actor entered *The river? If not, who? → (JE)*

You make us figure this out for ourselves. I like that. (NB) from stage left and I came up to a squatting position to get a better vantage. The wild Sacramento below *Your essay picks up momentum in these past few sentences, and the momentum increases with each new sentence. (JE)* us had begun to snake its way into view, illumined only by the bright moonlight.

What is "it"? (JE) It was all I could do to keep from walking out 12

What is "it"? (JE) our door onto that stage. Like something from a *This is an overused word, but here you use it effectively. (FO)* dream, it seemed too fantastically beautiful to be

real. And finally, unexpectedly, the train itself

Excellent! You reinforce your metaphor of the stage nicely. (JE)
This is wonderful! The train has been a silent player all along, and here you finally see it too, and consciously. (FO) emerged as a player. The trestlework not only poised

the line of cars two hundred feet above the river's

surface but managed as well to bend it into a slow

arc midway in the crossing. The sweep of that north–

You return here to talking about yourself and the train in collective terms. (JE) ward arc turned our view to the south. And just for

that instant both the front and rear of the train

were visible at once. The engines at our head dis– *This seems like a peacocky word to use here. (FO)*

appeared slowly into the shadow of Mt. Shasta while

the cars that trailed our coach paraded behind us

This verb makes it sound a little melodramatic. (NB)
across the massive trestle. And on it all was poured

the stark quiet of the moonlight reflected in the
I love the idea of quiet being "stark." It's
river below. *really a good example of how you control your*
language in the last two paragraphs so that it sounds greeting-card like. (FO)
The trestle, from south to north, could not have   13

This sounds philosophical and therefore a little risky for some readers.
been over a mile long. The entire panorama played

before us for less than two minutes. Yet, in a very

Would something like "Time stood still" work here? (NB)
real way, it has run in my mind's eye ever since.

As that team of Southern Pacific diesels pulled   14

us out of Redding, eternity sat captive for a moment.

(NB) These are very powerful images. You handle them well! (JE)
Like a stolen glimpse of childbirth, I shared in that

The metaphor of birth doesn't work as well as your others. It seems inappropriate. (FO)(NF)
peaceful feeling of something both beginning and

ending at once. And like a mother smiling at her

child born at last, I found myself smiling with a

similar relief. It was joy without euphoria. I

hunted again for the insights of the moment before

but found them fading with the darkness of the

mountains ahead. What race had I run to earn such

These sentences seem to contrast, if not contradict each other. (JE)

But what were they? (NB) I'm not sure that you explained them clearly. (NF)

rest? What was born in that moment? I looked to my

I don't understand companions for an answer but found it instead full-

this. How does an appreciation for beauty formed in the darkness between us. There was the

sudden realization of the only bond that we all

show a passion for life? shared: our passion for life. We were living life

(FO) moment by moment. That was our race well run. As

our halos began to fade I picked up my harmonica

and found myself playing "Bound for Glory" in a

different key.

The problem of this last paragraph is — unlike the rest of your essay — you tell me this. I want you to show me. I want to experience what you're talking about here so that I can also feel it. (JE)

General Comments at the End of the Essay

The four peer editors added these general comments, in addition to their marginal notes, to the end of Lewis's essay.

NICHOLAS BALAMACI —This is even-keeled, controlled writing. It is also vivid; I "saw" the story. Your essay is also philosophical, and because of that, risks being sentimental. Yet I feel that you avoid this problem very well, although there are just a few lapses (for example "tough but gentle," and "ate, drank, slept, and fought like brothers"). You narrate an important experience in your life, and you emphasize the particular with lots of concrete details. You also use those details to make more general and abstract statements. That's why the essay is so well-crafted.

The only part of your essay that seems a little shaky is the ending. Your words there seem mostly abstract, and you run the risk of letting your essay slide off into impor-tant-*sounding* talk. You should think about saying this more simply or less abstractly. Also, there's one repeated me-chanical problem: you allow loose connections at times between your modifiers and their referents and between your subjects and the participial phrases that modify them. But I want to say also that I could have written beside every paragraph: This essay comes ALIVE! It really makes the experience come to life for the reader. I feel as if I had been there. It's vivid and yet matter-of-fact writing. I look forward to reading it again and owning my own copy of it!

JASON ESKENAZI —When writing for others, we sometimes write more elabo-rately than we need to, changing sentences for complexity, for example. I think you need to watch out for this. Some-times you exchange complexity for clarity. I think you should be clear first.

This essay approaches being a short story. You have the main character come to a moment of insight, and that moment seems to change him at the conclusion. Why did you decide to write an essay? What makes this an essay and not a short story?

If you're going to revise this essay, I'd suggest thinking more about the opening paragraphs. You seem to be much more indirect in the opening paragraphs than you are in the final ones. I think you should be more consistent about this.

The momentum of your essay builds up nicely to the conclusion. Your realization about how the train became a "player" is terrific! Your realization became mine! In moments like that you use a good deal of poetic language. I hear you! The chances you've taken are worth it! You've created many intriguing images and ideas, and you make me want to think more about your story and what it means.

NELSON FARIAS   —Your story has lots of fine word choices and effective metaphors. And these choices give your essay its tone. In this respect, your word choices are appropriate to the mood you want to create. But your sentences are sometimes incomplete and your metaphors aren't developed fully. The way to improve these weaknesses is to place metaphors and ideas that are connected closer together.

You also seem to use lots of proper nouns in your story. That's both effective and ineffective. It's effective because you really draw the reader into your experience, but it's ineffective when the nouns are obscure or confusing. For example, what is a "herder"? Also much of the terminology of the trains is hard to understand. What and where is the "east door"? Is a "closed' car the opposite of an "empty" car? What are "switchbacks"? How can you be sure that your reader will understand what these terms mean? I think your essay could be improved if you'd concentrate on who your audience is. If these railroad terms aren't essential to the overall point you're making in your essay, then maybe you should eliminate them. They distracted me. I guess they'll distract other readers. How important are these terms to what you really want to say in your paper? Maybe you should write another paper on the technical parts of railroading! I'm just not sure that these terms contribute anything to your essay. Besides, I'm more interested in reading about what happens to you than I am about what happens to the train! I'd suggest eliminating some of what you say about the train and adding more about yourself and your experiences with Alex and the beaners.

FRAN OSBORNE   —Up to this point [paragraph 9], there's a real caution in your word choices. (See all the words marked by +.) But when you come to the end of this paragraph, that caution seems to disappear. Did you intend to do that?

This essay has real power to move your audience, power which stems from your ability to communicate "the magic of a moment." It seems to me that paragraphs 12 and 13 capture that moment very effectively. But these paragraphs also contribute much more to your essay. The metaphor of the "stage" that you introduce in paragraph

11 brings all the elements ("the players") of the essay together into a powerful moment of recognition for you. And
you have prepared your audience well for that moment —
even from the very beginning of your essay. You express
the basic idea of your essay in a beautifully understated
way in the title.

If the moment of recognition in your essay is presented
in paragraphs 12 and 13, then I think you should consider
eliminating most, if not all, of your final paragraph in your
revision. The metaphor of the childbirth, for example, seems
inappropriate to the context you have created. Also, your
tone changes in the last paragraph. You seem to want to
summarize, but you do that in a very different voice. Perhaps you should leave out most of the final paragraph and
end by returning to "playing 'Bound for Glory' in a different
key."

The essay needs some "fixing" in a purely technical sense.
I need to understand better the architecture of the train
more clearly (What does it look like?). I also need to understand better the passing of time more clearly (How much
time elapses while you're on the train?). Finally, I also need
to understand better the relationships between you, Alex,
and the beaners more clearly (How much more can you
tell us about them that will strengthen your story?).

All in all, though, I think your essay borders on the
poetic, and it is all the more effective for it. I enjoyed
reading it and thinking about what you accomplished.

Questions on Lewis's Edited Essay

1. Reread the peer editor's statements about Patrick Lewis's essay. On which
aspects of the essay does Nicholas Balamaci focus his attention? Jason Eskenazi?
Nelson Farias? Fran Osborne? What overall advice does each offer? What specific changes in focus, tone, and word choice do you notice between the peer
editors' general concluding statements and their marginal comments? Which
parts of the essay does each regard as most successful? Least successful? Why?

2. Review the peer editors' detailed marginal notations. Which of the comments
are observations (statements about which there can be no disagreement)? Which
are evaluations that try to summarize the main idea of the essay and then show
the relation between specific paragraphs and this idea?

3. Examine Fran Osborne's comments at the end of the essay. What is her response
to the overall structure of Lewis's essay? to his use of *diction* and figurative

language? to the speaker's voice? Which of these aspects of composition does Osborne think Lewis handles best? Why? Point to specific words and phrases to support your response.

4. List the points the peer editors agree on; disagree on. On what points do you agree with them? On what points do you disagree?

5. Reread Nicholas Balamaci's final comments. Sketch out what Lewis would need to do in a revision to respond adequately to what Balamaci says. Then reread Jason Eskenazi's concluding statement. In what specific ways might Lewis's plan for revision be altered by what Eskenazi says?

THE WRITER'S RESPONSE TO PEER EDITING

As a writer, you will benefit most from peer editing when you listen attentively to what your peer editors have to say about your essay and then examine with them the implications of their observations and recommendations. But peer editing — like writing — is a skill that takes time and frequent practice to develop. So you and your peer editor need to remind each other, at least occasionally, that even the most well-intentioned efforts at peer editing — and especially the first few tries at it — may not bring immediate improvement. There are few quick fixes in the world of ideas.

As a writer about to work with peer editors, you can anticipate receiving a good deal of generous and supportive criticism from readers who are familiar with — and sympathetic to — your purpose. And the presence of a real audience, who will read and respond to what you have written, may well be all you need to reassure yourself that writing is worth the effort involved, especially when you face moments, as nearly every writer does, when ideas seem hard to discover and energy and interest falter.

To make the best possible use of the peer editor's responses and advice, you need to listen thoughtfully to their observations and recommendations and take advantage of them when you write a final draft of your essay. By listening purposefully, you are less likely to be distracted from examining the strengths and weaknesses of your essay by what may occasionally be a peer editor's poorly phrased comment or ill-advised judgment.

When done rigorously, peer editing is as much a writing exercise as a reading exercise. When your peer editors are searching quickly for the best way to convey their responses to your essay, they, too, may occasionally slip into awkward or even inappropriate phrasing. But such moments, however uninstructive they may appear at first glance, can be opportunities for you to reciprocate by helping your peer editors express themselves more effectively. Sometimes their comments may not be entirely clear, and in such cases you should not hesitate to press for clarification. This process often results in a dialogue in which you have a chance to explain more fully your purpose or sense of audience, and the peer editors have an opportunity to clarify and develop some of their comments and suggestions. But whatever the particulars of such dialogue, writing is clearly the source—and the result—of productive conversation.

Writing should be at the center of peer editing. You should leave a peer-editing session with more than the impression of your peer editors' response. You should carry away, and later evaluate and act on, their detailed written responses to your essay, responses that have been amplified in your discussion with them. Having all the peer editors' comments in writing not only makes particular points of the discussion recoverable later, it also enables you to evaluate their comments and enumerate your priorities for revision.

With the benefit of peer editors' responses, you should improve—and per-haps dramatically so—your ability to evaluate the reactions of many different readers, each of whom may read your essay in a slightly different way. You ought to pay special attention to any comments about strengths and weaknesses pointed out by more than one peer editor. In each instance, *you* as the writer must decide what to change and what to retain in your new draft. Although the peer editors can help, the authority and the responsibility for those deci-sions remain yours, and yours alone as the writer.

Discussing and then evaluating peer editor comments should help you de-velop a clear sense of how to improve your essay. Your detailed plan for revision should include the peer editor recommendations you have decided to accept and act on and your own ideas about how to reinforce your essay's strengths and eliminate its weaknesses. The peer-editing process encourages you to treat your essay as a work-in-progress, to understand your specific strengths and shortcomings as a writer, and eventually, to produce stronger writing at every phase of the composing process.

ONE WRITER'S RESPONSE TO PEER EDITING

In this section we present Patrick Lewis's response to the peer editing of Nicholas Balamaci, Jason Eskenazi, Nelson Farias, and Fran Osborne. Patrick Lewis's comments explain his decisions to include, adapt, and sometimes reject their recommendations in the revised version of his essay. Lewis's reactions to the peer editors' final general comments and then to their specific marginal notations are followed by his overall response to peer editing itself—its prin-ciples and practices and its value in the composing process.

The final comments gave me a general idea of the temperament of my audience. Did they like me and the paper, or did they think I was from another planet? I wanted to know about any big gaps that I needed to bridge. I have taken four general guidelines for revision from the peer editors' end notes:

1. Nicholas comments about my tendency to philosophize to the point of sentimentality. I knew exactly the passages in which I made the offenses. The question I had to ask was, "Is that so bad?" After talking things over with my writing teacher, I came away feeling that, whatever I did — as in so many things — it was always going to be better to use silver polish than a sandblaster. A little philosophy never hurt anyone, so long as it isn't overblown — "important-*sounding* talk" as Nicholas calls it. Since some kind of expository essay seems to be my natural mode, I guess I had better learn to do it well if I can.

2. The same question in my mind comes up in Jason's query about whether I hadn't really wanted to write a short story. The truth is that I would have liked to write one, but that was not the assignment. I decided that, if I hope to really "assay" my thoughts on the story I want to tell, then I should do it engagingly, and without resorting to any abrupt mood shifts.

3. Nelson asked for more development of the "I" character. That in fact prompted the most obvious change in the paper, that is, its opening. Nelson made me realize that the central character was the only thing that made the story coherent. So I worked myself into every line in a more conscious way. Enough said! This begins to sound self-aggrandizing, which is not my intent at all.

4. Fran made me see more clearly that it was the "magic of the moment" which needed to be the teleos of the work. I am glad that she liked it, because I was beginning to lose sight of why I felt I *had* to write this paper in the first place. She also agreed with the haunting feeling I had that the last paragraph was somehow overkill.

Fran also raises a very interesting question for me. She wanted to understand better the relationship between me and the other characters. In fact, she went through and marked words [with a + sign] that seemed to indicate my isolation from them up to the point where I met Alex.

In the revision I have tried to make that theme more

consistent and the transition more obvious. I *was* afraid and then resolved not to live in that unfounded fear. So, as to the basics of human friendship, I wanted to show that change as one that was/is evident to even me. But there is another distance that separated us, which is not as central.

It was interesting to find Fran in a marginal note assuming that we (that is, the travelers) were all in the same boat. There is a barely legible note on my "General Directions" outline where I ask myself (to explain) where the ignorant and illiterate fit into my scheme of the world. I see quite a distance separating me from the fellows that I am writing about. But it is not the same sort of distance I mentioned above (fear), nor the sort I mentioned in the paragraph about hobo life (ignorance and uncaring). I am not isolated from them by my choice as much as by "our choice." I feel for and with them, but there is no less a real distance of understanding. But I resolve that it not be a distance of appreciation. My empathy, born in our exposures (and the sometimes palpable misunderstanding that exposure brought), affords them a very special place in my world—perhaps akin to the place which Jesus intimates in the beatitudes (and in fact throughout his teaching ministry). The poor in spirit *are* blessed. Not simply because of their ignorance nor in spite of it. It is for both of these reasons and more. And somehow, it makes them my *superiors*, in a realm that I don't understand well, but respect very much. The uncomfortable distance which I feel between the "ignorant" and the "enlightened" is the result of *our* misunderstanding—both sides are guilty. It is bridged, then by admission of our own ignorance. The bridge seems intensely spiritual.

ON THE PEER
EDITORS' MARGINAL
NOTATIONS

I am not a detail person, so I guess it shouldn't surprise me that the big things worked in my essay, while, often as not, the sentences struggled to make themselves even coherent. I took Jason's comments about "exchanging complexity for clarity" and "writing too elaborately" to heart. I hope that most of the sentences in the new version are at least readable . . . . Let me quickly mention no more than a dozen marginal comments that got me thinking.

What is so mystifying about the relationship between wishing and dreaming? I added the phrase "half-awake" to a sentence from the old paragraph 1 to clarify the point. I hope it works. I think that more than likely, the heavy opposition was due to first paragraph overzealousness. Anyway, it does read better.

I am truly indebted to Nicholas (my tongue is *not* in my cheek this time!) for two very specific suggestions which I think improve paragraph 2 immensely: just the kind of cleaning up that Jason drew to my attention in his general comments—a misplaced participial phrase and a predicate with a (mis)understood subject.

At the end of the same paragraph, I dropped the last two sentences because they were a weak attempt at developing the "fear" theme. The more direct reference two paragraphs above made them superfluous.

Everyone got their wish in paragraph 3 when I interrupted a very difficult sentence (again with a misunderstood subject) to make a detour for Fran and Nelson's benefit. Actually, I had wanted to put more of the hobo's eye view description in my original, but couldn't seem to make it fit. I hope the addition gives new insights, though I suspect it has a few difficulties of its own.

I was disappointed that everyone seemed to concur with Nelson's remark that "experiments are for rats," a little later in the same paragraph (old number 3). The sense of observer-observed isolation is exactly what I had felt up to that time. And it is what I tried to convey by that word choice.

Again in the same paragraph, Fran made a practical, seemingly obvious, suggestion that vastly improved the feel of the prose. I substituted the simple Anglo-Saxon verb "hide" for a difficult Latin reflexive phrase "conceal myself."

Both Nelson and Jason helped me clean up the next paragraph (that is, number 4 in the original).

I was trying all along to keep Alex down to a "manageable size." Several of the peer editors, in the paragraph describing Alex's appearance, wanted me to somehow expand on "tough but gentle." Though Alex was a real person, I really wanted him, for the purposes of this essay, to stand for a character type: the good guy, gentleman-of-the-rails. Having to develop *two* characters to everyone's satisfaction threatened to diffuse the overall direction of the essay and add an unnecessary dimension.

The old paragraph 10 has a whole new look for the same sort of reason: too much detail with not enough direction.

Both to introduce a paragraph that contains what I consider to be some "important talk" and to satisfy the urgings of Nicholas and Fran (that is, to expand the somewhat sappy line about "fighting like brothers"), I cut out much of that paragraph and some of the next. Most of the next paragraph in the revision (as well as parts of the new introduction and conclusion) came from the material that I cut out from the original for lack of space.

I thought the question about technical terms perplexing. Anyone who has grown up around mountains should have encountered "switchbacks" as the only practical way for a road or a trail (or a railroad track) to climb a steep grade. Words like "herder" and "beaners" I assumed would be obvious by their contexts (who else in California speaks "nothing but Spanish, man"?).

For the rest of the story, I had spent great pains in getting a very difficult picture in my mind's eye on paper. So I felt comfortable about the generally favorable comments and with leaving it much the same. I made one very specific change suggested by Nelson, shifting the first sentence of paragraph 13 with the last one of 12.

ON PEER EDITING
AND WRITING

I certainly hope that the peer editors like the new look and feel of the essay. It took a while to get started after the preliminary notes I made on everyone's ideas. I didn't really hit a groove until a few hours of working on the revision. Then, and only then, did I start to enjoy what I was doing again. The final product seems more focused than before, moving with a kind of concerted effort it didn't have before. And I also came to feel a lot more comfortable with the distinct voice that an essay should have. It just sounds more controlled than before, less rambling and storylike.

When I began the process of this revision, after reading through both the peer editors' final comments and their marginal notes, I was ready to make a broad statement about the greater relative value of the end-type comments. I thought I would reject 90 percent of the marginal stuff. Now that I have finished, I can no longer make that statement. I ended up weighing every comment carefully, and I would guess that 90 percent of them have affected the new essay in some way or other. I hope the peer editors can see the extent of each of their contributions to the new version. And I very much appreciated the strongly personal approach each took. It made their recommendations "stand apart" with much less overlapping than I anticipated. What's more, they wrote very lucidly about rather difficult subjects. All that said, I am glad there were no more than four peer editors — even five would have been overwhleming.

As a new writer, I suppose it is natural that I am a rather unselfconscious writer. I enjoy writing. I suppose that there is a similar feeling in the neophyte painter. If nothing else, writing always seems to sharpen my perception of what I have seen. The peer-editing process has rushed me into the world of the conscious. There is an almost unimaginable benefit in simply the suggestion that someone is taking something I have written seriously enough to respond to it personally. That feeling of "someone watching," if not allowed to dominate our mind, can probably be the greatest single factor in encouraging seminal talent. But you must, I think, enjoy writing first.

I am also, I think, an unassuming preacher/teacher without a pulpit/classroom. Though I have to guard myself against "manufactured solutions," there is probably nothing wrong with sermons which might not sound like sermons, but still contain real value. To a great extent, that is what I had hoped for in "Five Minutes North of Redding." That is also why the last paragraph is so much different. There is nothing I said in the original which I would in any way call false or contrived. I believed every word. But to believe so strongly can be synonymous with robbing the mystery from truth to leave only bare bones. That kind of truth dies a sudden death of exposure. And dead "truth" becomes confused with the worst sort of lie. The message which I have tried to convey by this essay, because it is existential, is bound to be a little obscure. But then so is life! At its best, it is full of mystery — at its worst, it is full of doubt, especially self-doubt and distrust of others.

Now that you have had the opportunity to read Patrick Lewis's responses to the peer editor's observations and recommendations, examine the revised version of his essay, which he prepared after considering their reactions and advice.

LEWIS'S REVISED ESSAY

Five Minutes North of Redding

My twentieth-fifth year was a mixed-up time   1
for me, full up with broken relationships and lost
hope, all-day school and all-night jobs. I was
"living in the shade of a freeway" (as Jackson
Browne so aptly put it) in a worn-out mobile home
with a Siamese cat on loan from a friend, and a
primer gray Datsun 110 with a bad transmission:
the whole thing was rather comical for a while, but
I was slowly becoming more desperate for whatever
was next. And so it was that I began to notice the
routine of a work train that daily came out of a
cement yard over on the other side of the through-
way fence.

"Riding the rails" had wooed me for several   2
years, from the time I had first seen three modern
hobos jump off their "coach" on the outskirts of
Las Vegas. From that moment on, the romance of life
seen from the door of a boxcar had captured my
imagination. I even resurrected an old harmonica
that I had used in high school and began playing
woeful tunes late at night, while the open road sang
along in a familiar voice. The words of the ballad
promised to tell a tale yet untold, but then they
drifted off into the soft stillness outside my door.

I left the L.A. basin with only one change of   3

clothes, a bedroll, and a little bit of money hidden
so well that it took me ten minutes to get to it. I
waited until I heard the train pulling into the cement
plant and locked the door of my trailer behind me as
I ran to meet it. Twenty minutes later I was riding
my first freight. Alone. And that was just fine.
I had heard too many stories about shifty bums who
would kill for a pair of shoes. I stayed wide of
their campfires and always traveled by myself.

Two weeks later found me near Sacramento, wait-   4
ing for another train on the outskirts of the biggest
rail yard in northern California. This time I was
bound for Seattle. I rolled out of the weeds into
the crisp daylight of that late September morning
to catch the north train out of Roseville. The
herder had said it would be leaving about 3:00 a.m.
So I had huddled half-awake in my coat for at least
three hours, wishing in the predawn chill for a cup
of hot anything. But the noise and lights of the
train yard had filtered through the tall grass and
disturbed even that harmless dream.

Finally she came. Forty cars were in sight   5
before the engines passed me. As I moved down to
the rail bed, I noticed for the first time that I
had not waited alone on this stretch of tracks.
Three figures were coming down to claim a rail car
150 yards up the line, and even as I cautiously
watched them, two other groups of riders were

claiming cars behind me. With what looked like
seasoned confidence, I bounded onto a flat car,
concerned that the line of empties would soon pass
me by--then thought again. I was a solitary presence
on that flat deck, and, within me, instinct shouted
warnings about such a vulnerable position. I crossed
the ten-foot width of the car and dropped down onto
the ground on the other side. This time I watched
until everyone was on board before I picked out one
of the last empty boxcars.

The line of cars came to its first stop on a   6
siding three hours up the Sacramento Valley as we
allowed another train to pass. Groves of plum
trees lined the track on either side. Even so
late in the season, the trees to the train's right
were still full of hard purple fruit. I lay down
in a splash of sun on the deck of my car. For the
first time that morning, I was warm and relaxed.
The world of the hobo seemed at the moment to be
everything I had hoped for. Maybe more. For one
thing, I hadn't figured on the dust, but there was
plenty of it to go around. My first hour reclining
against the wall of a boxcar left me smudged with
enough soot to convince anyone that I had been
hoboing all my life. Nor had I counted on the
noise. The crashing clatter, especially of start-
ups, made me wish often enough for the luxury of
earplugs. Even the click of the rails inside this

car (with both doors pushed open wide) was less than
soothing after an hour or so. Still, all that seemed
to make stops like this one the more enjoyable. The
view and the solitude of such regular pauses lured
me into the kind of romantic reverie that had inspired this adventure. Later, after a nap, I would
get out to step away from the train far enough to
see what was up ahead. But for now, what I could
see through my door was all the world I had wished
for.

Suddenly, the startling sound of shouts out the 7
east door caused me to retreat into the shadows
again. I peered out to see six men playing among
the fruit trees like kids as they picked plums only
to pelt each other with them. I watched intently, as
if it were some elaborate social experiment, until
the sound of boots on gravel out the other door
brought me back around. Looking back to the
shadows of the car's interior, I suddenly realized
that it was too late to hide. The man whose
crunching boots had just announced his approach
was already at the west door looking me over.

"There you are. I've been lookin' for you. 8
You're travelin' alone ain't you?" The wrong
question to ask someone who is already scared of
you. Luckily the tone of his voice betrayed only
a desire for friendship.

"That's right, I am. What . . . are you alone, 9

too?" I sized him up coolly as I moved toward my
knapsack in the far corner. In its open front
pocket I had a knife if I needed it. He had an
eight-inch Bowie knife strapped frontier-style to
his right shin.

"No. Couple of beaners and me pick up together   10
in Stockton; but they ain't speakin' nothin' but
Spanish, man. You want sumpum to eat? They're
gettin' some plums. We got cukes and tomatoes still
that they picked in the Valley yesterday. And I
got a box of saltines in Roseville."

He had a ruddy face that was roughly pocked,   11
probably from adolescence, and a scraggly mustache
that only became noticeable when he looked right at
you. I had reached my pack, but simply turned
toward him in a crouch to look for my next move.

If I planned to turn down his hospitality,   12
standing there four feet up in a boxcar was the
moment to do it. His bony frame and large hands
gave away his height. He would be three to four
solid inches taller than me on level ground. He
had tied his shoulder-length, muddy blond hair back
with a lace of dark buckskin; it laced the seams of
his chamois pants too. (He was fond of buckskin
and wore it well.) But, tough as he looked, there
was an obvious gentleness to him as well. He
seemed all in all an atavism, a confusing mixture
of General Custer with a sixties flower child. I

decided to trust my second inclination.

"Sounds good," I said closing my pack. "What's   13
your name?" I grabbed my jacket and hopped down
onto the loose shale bed. The train was just pulling away with a halting rumble as we neared his car.
As we quickened our pace, I noticed he was limping
from his hip down. I was in the car before him and
offered him a hand. But he ignored it and managed
an agile roll into the car by catching hold of a
break in the floor.

Alex and the Beaners were the first hobos I   14
was to travel with. Their friendship wore away the
edge of the fear I had felt since hearing my first
hobo story. Over the space of a few days we ate,
drank, slept, and fought like brothers. I shared
my rations, and at one point, even my bedroll, with
my Mexican companions who had come less prepared,
while Alex laughingly looked on and told story after
story. I learned something of their pasts and their
plans in that short time together, and lay awake to
think what it would be like to live their lives.

Life in a downtown rail yard is much farther   15
away from most of us than simple distance suggests.
The bums, drying out from damp nights by fires
built under the bridges, rarely venture into our
world from their environs plaited out of steel and
wood. Sometimes they make the trip to downtown

skid rows for the social interaction offered at
missions and overnight shelters. But hobos are
really in a class by themselves. Not quite as
permanently debilitated as the downtown drunks,
they generally live their private lives without pan-
handling, building a world of their own in the hobo
jungles that spring up among the weeds and warehouses surrounding train yards. Few of them have
anything resembling a year-round home. Transience
and seasonal migrations are the more general rule.
Some do venture in and out of institutional life:
missions, dry-out centers, acute psychiatric wards.
Paranoid schizophrenia is surely their most common
syndrome; alcohol is their drug of choice. But
there are also, of course, many exceptions. Alex
and the beaners were three of them.

While the train sat idle in Redding, we found   16
a boxcar that was open only on its east side. (For
the cold trip into the mountains ahead, warmth was
a more important concern than a view of the scenery
to the west.) We had just finished off several tins
of sardines as the train at last began to lumber out
of the yard. Our bodies exhausted, our hunger at
last abated, we sat on the dirty floor of our boxcar, enjoying the last warm breath of the evening.
We were now at the northernmost end of California's
fertile basin. From here on the land would climb

more steeply. Only the Sacramento River lay between
us and the Cascade mountains. As we approached the
river's trestle, the track took only one slow curve
to the northwest. On ahead, it was sure to begin a
series of slow switchbacks to climb Mt. Shasta's
side. But for now, because dead ahead, Shasta was
out of sight.

I leaned tiredly against the back door and   17
watched as the scene in front of me began to change.
Low on the horizon, a nearly full moon was rising
slowly to take its place in the center of our stage.
Mt. Lassen's distant volcanic head joined it as we
rounded the last turn before the river, showing
mutely through a carpet of velvet green peaks. Inside the car, Alex stood up to blow the smoke of his
cigarette out into the crystal air. He propped himself like a caryatid supporting the right border of
our window on the world. My Mexican compadres sat
nearly motionless at the door's left side. Mesmerized, I dug blindly into my pack to find the
harmonica which I had saved for just such an inspiring moment. I sucked in a chord or two of
"This Train Is Bound for Glory," laughing inside.
Suddenly, another actor entered from stage left and
I came up to a squatting position to get a better
vantage, as the river below came into view. It
was all I could do to keep from walking out our
door onto that stage.

The wild Sacramento below us had begun to snake   18
its way into view, illumined only by the bright
moonlight. Like something from a dream, it seemed
too fantastically beautiful to be real. And
finally, unexpectedly, the train itself emerged as
a player. The trestlework not only poised the
line of cars two hundred feet above the river's
surface, but managed as well to bend it into a slow
arc midway in the crossing. The sweep of that
northward arc turned our view to the south. And
just for that instant, both the front and rear of
the train were visible at once. The engines at
our head disappeared slowly into the shadow of
Mt. Shasta while the cars that trailed our coach
paraded behind us across the massive trestle. And
on it all was poured the stark quiet of the moonlight reflected in the river below.

The trestle, from south to north, could not   19
have been over a mile long. The entire panorama
played before us for less than two minutes. Yet,
in a very real way, it has run in my mind's eye
ever since. As that team of Southern-Pacific
diesels pulled us out of Redding, eternity sat
captive for a moment.

Later that night, I found out that Alex wasn't   20
running away as I had supposed. He was "tired of
all that" and thought it was time to head home
and help out his mother. Maybe he would even

settle down with a waitress who had been chasing
him for years. At thirty-eight, the traveling
seemed to be wearing him away little by little. I
wondered what crisis had brought him to his decision,
but decided not to ask. For it seemed that a similar moment had just passed in my life--one which no
words could explain. The open road had told me its
tale, and now I too was ready to walk into whatever
was next. I closed my eyes for the night, humming
"Bound for Glory" in a different key.

Questions on Lewis's Revision

1. In his responses to the peer editing (pages 358–363), Lewis discusses some of his plans for revising his essay. What did he decide to focus on in his revision? Which points does he accomplish most successfully? Point to specific words and phrases in both his responses and his revision to support your answer.

2. Which of Lewis's responses to the peer editors' comments do you agree with? Which do you disagree with? Why? Which points in his plan for revision would you like to see expanded? dropped? altered slightly? Why?

3. Which aspects of Lewis's essay would benefit from additional attention and revision? Why? Point to specific places where he could make further changes and indicate what those changes might be.

4. Lewis reports that he made substantial revisions in the opening and closing of his essay. How, specifically, has he done this, and with what effect?

5. Write as many observations as you can about the specific differences between Lewis's original essay (pages 150–153) and his revised essay. In what ways is his *purpose* clearer? How does each paragraph relate more clearly to the main point of the essay? How is his handling of Alex and the beaners stronger? How does he consider his audience's knowledge of hobos, trains, and life "on the rails"? How does his choice of words reflect a different consideration for his *audience*? Point to specific words and phrases in the essay to support your responses.

PRACTICING PEER EDITING

In this section you have an opportunity to practice applying the principles and procedures of peer editing, first to Johanna Lynn Benson's "Rotten at the Core" and then to your own writing.

The following checklist points out many of the concerns peer editors keep in mind as they work on an essay. Your instructor may add others.

1. *Purpose.* What is the writer trying to do in the essay? What is the main idea, the essay's thesis or overriding point? What intention or promise does the essay state or imply? Where and how well does the writer act on that intention or promise? What specific examples, ideas, or information would help clarify or reinforce the writer's purpose?

2. *Organization.* How is the essay organized? What is its basic structure? Comment on the logic and effectiveness of the sequence of paragraphs. How well does each paragraph support and develop the essay's main idea? In which paragraphs is the main idea most effectively supported by details and examples?

3. *Choice of Words.* Is the language of the essay primarily abstract or concrete? If it is abstract, do you understand what each abstraction means? Does the writer use special terminology or colloquial terms? How effective is such language? How well does it support the writer's purpose?

4. *Point of View.* Point of view means the point or perspective from which the essay is written or the story is told. From what perspective does the writer approach the subject of the essay? Where is this point of view stated or implied? Does the writer maintain the point of view consistently throughout the essay? Point to those places where the writer's point of view is most clearly stated, where it seems uncertain, and where it is consistent or inconsistent.

5. *Audience.* Characterize the audience the writer seems to have in mind. What does the writer expect the audience to know about the subject? Point to specific words and phrases that reveal the writer's assumptions about the audience's familiarity with the subject.

From your own experience and your study of peer editors at work, what other aspects of composition should peer editors attend to as they read another student's writing? Prepare sets of questions for each aspect.

Exercises in Peer Editing

1. Apply the principles of peer editing to "Rotten at the Core" by Johnna Lynn Benson (pages 31–35), following the peer-editing procedures outlined in this chapter. Read the essay several times and write your observations, evaluations, and recommendations in the margin.

   —Write as many observations as you can about the essay (remember, an observation is a statement about which there can be no disagreement).

   —Summarize the essay's main idea and note how the writer supports and develops that idea in each paragraph.

   —Identify both the strengths and the weaknesses of the essay. In this respect, pay particular attention to Benson's sentence structure and variety, her verb tenses and voice, her paragraph transitions, and her concluding paragraph.

   —Prepare a general final statement noting the essay's overall strengths and weaknesses and offering some specific recommendations for revision.

   After you have completed your work as a peer editor on "Rotten at the Core," write Johnna Benson a letter in which you analyze the strengths and weaknesses of her essay and offer her as much reasonable, practical, and detailed advice as you can about what she might do in another draft to improve her essay.

2. Now that you have completed your peer editing of Benson's essay, you might find it instructive to compare and contrast your marginal notations and final comments with those prepared by Nicholas Balamaci, Jason Eskenazi, Nelson Farias, and Fran Osborne. Here are both the specific marginal notations that these peer editors made on Johnna Benson's essay, along with their general reactions and recommendations for revision at the end of her essay. Reread Benson's essay, which begins on the next page, this time paying special attention to the other peer editors' responses.

BENSON'S EDITED ESSAY

You use a cleaning metaphor to begin with: Rotten at the Core *Your title seems inconsistent with the outcome of your essay. (JE)*

neat because you're going to clean your self off and start over. (FO)

George A. Kelly's <u>Theory of Personality</u> has   1

scrubbed me on a washboard and put me through the

wringer. Discovering what I actually am under the *Cleansing metaphor*

This word repeats "better off," and it can be considered a cliché. (JE) Remove? (NB)

dirt and debris has been bewildering and has left me *works well here. (JE)*

wondering if I would be better off blissfully igno-   *Shakespeare! (JE)*

Reference to Keats's Ode to a Grecian Urn." But are you searching for "Beauty"? (JE)

rant. I had thought "<u>to know thyself</u>" an admirable

pursuit, especially since I believed <u>truth was beauty.</u>

Now I see I have been <u>beautifully</u> wrong about who I *(Your use of "blissfully" and "beautifully" worries me because you do not explain how your ignorance was either. (FO)*

You personify the colloquium. (FO)

am and who everybody else is.

When <u>the colloquium</u> introduced me to <u>Theory of</u>   2

<u>Personality</u>, I was sure we would get along great. I *colloquial language (FO)*

have always loved dabbling in psychology. My friends

But you do try to be "shocking" and "clever." Why not say so? (And they are not necessarily bad habits.) (NF)

and I would make Freudian jokes or play shrink-games,

using those little tests in women's magazines de-

signed to save on psychoanalysis costs. You could *Combine this sentence with the one before it for the sake of clarity. (FO)*

say I won those games; my free associations were

always more bizarre than anyone else's. I wasn't

even trying to be <u>shocking or clever.</u> That is just *You change tenses here. (NB)*

I don't understand your point here. (JE)

a bad habit. My only feud with psychology was that

I aspired to be more than a product of my environ-

ment, <u>a multiplication of Mormonism by a material-</u>

<u>istic middle-class suburb.</u> <u>Theory of Personality</u>

eliminated that limitation for me.

Your point of view is now clear. (JE)

I loved it instantly. Kelly's treatise holds 3

that people create their own personalities. As a

I notice that you go to the source for a dab of objectivity. I like how you work Kelly in here. (JE)

person tries to make sense of the circus around him,

Do you mean inferences here? (FO)

he picks up on recurring themes in his life and makes

deductions about what is going on. The individual

creates these explanations, called "constructs,"

for his convenience in anticipating what the world

is going to hit him with next. As a person con-

strues, he builds an inner road map of himself, of

life, and of what he can expect from it. The psy-

chology I had been exposed to before treated man like

an organism poked and prodded into reactions. I

found the concept of deciding for yourself who you

are and what you can expect from life far more pal-

atable. Claiming total responsibility for my out-

look on life filled me with satisfaction.

Theory of Personality created a little (garden 4

paradise) in the corner for me, but it also (unearthed)

This is an effective metaphor. (JE)

something upsetting. As part of our colloquium study

of constructs, we were asked to write about our core

Your tone changes here. Is that what you intend? Do you both love and fear the book and what it reveals? (JE)

roles, or how we viewed ourselves. I kept putting

The essay really seems to get under way here. (FO)

the assignment off because every time I started it,

Doing anyway should determination and strength of character. (NF)

my query led me down the same path. [If you do not

want to go to Rome, finding that all roads go there

is rather dismaying.] Suddenly it was the day to

This is an innovative and pleasant way to turn around the old cliché, and to make a point besides. (NB) hand in the assignment, and I discovered, as I fran-

tically wrote the thing in the Harris Fine Arts

What a concise way to put this! Excellent! (NB)

Center an hour before class, that I had spent enough

time trying not to think about it that I knew exactly

This could be a sentence by itself. (NF)

what I didn't want to know.

You return us here to the idea of shocking and clever in paragraph one. (FB)

With Fresh, Original, and Bizarre as my highest　　5

ideals, my core role seems to be that I must be dif-

"Different" is not a quality word.

ferent. And I am different, which makes me excep-

"Exceptional" implies better than average. (FO)

I don't see why being different makes you exceptional. (FO)

tional, though not in a way the general population

appreciates. This arrogant idea actuates my every

This way of talking about yourself seems unwarranted. (FO)

thought and emotion, a realization that makes me

shudder. Exploring the fact that I'm rotten at the

But you haven't explained how you are "rotten at the core," only slightly arrogant. (NB)

core reduced me to tears.

Yet I can't seem to get around it. I look at　　6

how I hate get-acquainted parties. To adhere

You sound a little snobbish and ego-tistical in here. (JE)

"Hello, my name is . . ." on my lapel is to assume

common ground exists between these strangers and me.

But my core role says my lifeline runs geometrically

This is an innovative, clear, and artful way of putting this. (NB)

askew to theirs. Kelly defines guilt as an aware-

ness of contradicting one's core role structure, and

guilty well describes the uncomfortable feeling I

get pretending such parties aren't futile. I forget

that I actually do share significant parallels and

Can parallels be "shared"?

intersections with family and friends. I like the

Can "inter-sections"? (JE)

differences. By the time I was six I introduced

myself by saying, to the consternation of my play- *This is unclear. Did the three colors alternate as your favorite over the years? Aren't you certain which was your favorite? (NB)*

mates, that I did not like chocolate cake or soda-

pop. For years my favorite color (was) chartreuse,

sienna, or puce. My favorite number is 3.02875x10^{14}.

I took up origami because I thought no one had heard

of it. In short, anything popular was not worth my

time, while anything obscure or new was mine by right.

These paragraphs enumerate differences but they also enumerate similarities too. You, like most people, do have a favorite color, number, etc. And you do "obey" rules. The "differences" appear to be semantic rather than substantial. (FO)

Moreover, I felt unique enough to assume that   7

although rules were necessary to keep the regulars *This para-graph gives examples of how you "break" rules without breaking them! (FO)*

in line, they did not apply to me. Because rules

were necessary, I never quite broke them but found

interpretations to suit me. For example, when an

elementary class punishment to copy five pages from

the dictionary was handed down, my paper always in-

cluded a few words outside the assigned alphabetical

range, like "despot," "toupee," or "maltreatment."

Lights-out at camp meant it was dark enough to *Do you see the contradiction here? If friends are "too drunk to really notice" how can you be "showing"? (FO)*

leave the cabin unnoticed and go for a moonlight

walk. Going to parties where friends were too drunk

to really notice my abstinence was showing my love

The idea about the Mormon Church seems unrelated to the rest of the sentence. It would help if you gave an example of what the Mormons have to offer such troubled people. Of what exactly did you make them aware? (NF)

and understanding for people with problems, not to

mention making them aware of the Mormon Church. And

of course, as long as my boyfriend and I didn't go

all the way, whatever we wanted to do was fine. We

were toying with the idea of marriage anyway.

Other people needed rules. I did not.

I have been carried away with my own indi-   8

viduality enough to hypothesize that when I was a

zygote, some stray cosmic ray zapped my DNA, making

me a daughter of chance and not of Terry and Dianna

Benson. On a similar note, I latched onto the idea

This seems to say "before I was spiritual, I was physical." (FO) that I have always existed, that <u>before I was a</u>

<u>spirit I was an entity, an intelligence bobbing out</u>

somewhere like a chartreuse soap bubble. I did not *colloquial (FO)*

want to be someone else's creation. I <u>figured</u> God

recognized the special and distinctive thing I was

and handpicked me to be his child.

Without the religious aspect, your essay still makes sense. Is the sole purpose of your talking about religion to account for your differences? I think not. (JE) Being Mormon has been convenient in other ways.   9

This is a cliché, and judging from your use of language else-where, you can do a lot better than this. (NB) It is a guaranteed way <u>to stick out like a sore</u>

thumb. I always felt a swell of pride as I

answered astonished cries of "You've never done

It would be a lot easier on the reader if you simply spelled it out. (NB) such and such?" I could spend hours elaborating

on LDS precepts with the sole intent of blowing an

innocent Protestant mind. I have had so much fun

There is something arrogant in this: 1) in the impli-cation that you are sophisticated (and so can "blow an innocent mind") and 2) in your focus on Protestant rather than other religious sects. (FO) being Mormon that I have to wonder how much of my

testimony is based on faith and how much on the

attention it garners. I created my outlook on life *You sound like you're condemning yourself in here.) (FO)*

according to my convenience, says Kelly. My con-

venient testimony thus becomes as meaningful as my

green argyle earrings; I would probably join any

group that boasted of being a peculiar people.

The problem you elucidate concerning your faith is never resolved. Is it convenient or is it based on something more? (FO)

Yet my testimony of the gospel encapsulates   10
some of my strongest emotions and most important
rational convictions. I founded my belief on study,
contemplation, and prayer, not whim. If such a
testimony is invalid, there is little I think or
feel that is valid. But I must consider (I may have)
forced my personality to grow in unnatural and indirect ways because I wanted to be different, cultivating a taste for mustard on my french fries and

How do you make the leap here from Kelly's theory being merely possible to its being true? (NB)

This is the heart of your essay. It is clear, thoughtful, and very meaningful. (NF)

a taste for LDS doctrine. (I have created) my personality and maybe I could have done a better job.
Yet the thought of supplanting myself with a new and

The problem of looking at yourself in a new way begins here. (FO)

improved model based on different criteria scares me.
It would be personality suicide; although someone
would be here named Johnna, I would cease to exist.

Is there another way to convey that you looked down on them without resorting to such coarse words?

And what about all these other people? I always   11
pictured my intelligence as a chartreuse bubble in
contrast with their monochromatic assembly of lemon
yellow bubbles. If Kelly gives me the right to be

Don't be insecure here. Take a stand! (NF)

They seem inappropriate because the

self-made, he also extends that right to all those

Is Kelly dead? (FO)

(dumb slobs.) Besides, I doubt Kelly (was) lemon yellow.

rest of your essay is artful and innovative. (FO)(NB)(WE)(NF)

If he and I can be different, then (probably) everyone

Is this necessary? I don't see what it adds. Remove? (NB)

else [is on a slightly different wavelength,] can be a
slightly different color. This means I (probably)

You have used the word "probably" several times. (NF)

I like your realization here. Maybe those previous comments made the necessary contrast. (JE)

don't stand out at all. I have always understood

why people were worried that God might not know them

specifically. There was no reason for him to bother

~~Capitalize?~~
(NB)

when they were all the same. But if everyone is a

This is a very sensitive question to ask! (NF)

unique individual, how does Heavenly Father remember

which fingerprint I am? In my place in the sun, I

did not notice all those stars out there, each one

You cannot stand under the sun and see the stars! (NF)

shining bright for someone. I do not feel important

or special while gazing at billions of stars.

For the first time in my life I feel truly   12

lost, an electron carrying practically no weight,

fairly indistinguishable from any other electron,

whose orbit is an unknown in a probability cloud.

What does this phrase mean? (NB)

I am looking at life in a new and startling way,

and this is the ultimate test of my taste for the

This is an excellent verb here. (NB)

new and startling. I find myself attempting to

You have taken the road to Rome! (NF)

straddle the importance of my uniqueness and the

existence of 4.5 billion other unique individuals.

Yes, and we are not "dumb slobs." It's an inconsistent metaphor, but it's also a strong way to show what you feel. (NF)

I do not like wondering who I am. I could always

tell before by the stark contrast between me and

Before you were talking about people in general.

anyone else. I had three dimensions and the other

person only had two. Now I see that I just had no

depth perception.

Now you're talking about one other person. (FO)

This is very honest. Now you are not afraid to draw definite conclusions. (NF)

How everyone can be different intimidates and   13

amazes me. Without its former base, my sense of

You use the image of the soap bubble in a new way by reference to ~~identity~~ has become as fragile as the chartreuse *substance rather than color. (FO)*

You use this image soap bubble I imagine as its beginnings. I fear the

well. It helps to unify your essay. (NF) existence of all the variegated personalities that

might crowd and pop it. Yet in returning to that

sense of fragile newness, I see the world freshly.

I have bemoaned the fact that no one could appre-

ciate my special outlook. Now I see there are

I feel like I've gone through hell with you and come up a winner! (JE) countless other outlooks for me to explore, each a

world as strange and wonderful as mine. For the

first time there is an impetus for me to get to

know people. This potential soothes my battered

psyche and fills me with wonder in proportion to

my fear. *The fear is minimized by wonder: You have the equipment now with which to move forward. (FO)*

General Comments at the End of the Essay

NICHOLAS BALAMACI

—I thought that the overall structure of your essay was excellent. There is a clear beginning, middle, and end. Your paragraphs and transitions flow well. You seem to be in control of what you want to say and how you want to say it.

—Your essay seems tightly reasoned, yet it also seems spontaneous—straight from your mind and heart.

—The title of your essay is clever, (and therefore tempting to use), but it struck me as inappropriate. "Rotten" is too strong a word and is never really shown or proven.

—Your writing is lean and easy to read. Your use of language is innovative and artful.

—This is an honest and mature essay, and it works in a way that most of us, I think, would have a hard time *ever* achieving. I admire it!

JASON ESKENAZI

—This is an effective essay, but I feel it needs to go through the same wringer you described in order to get at its core.

—Your essay is filled with understatement, which makes my view of your essay sway. But there is a vitality to it that keeps me on the edge of my seat. I'd almost lost my faith that words (books) could transform people, and then you introduce me to Kelly.

—The core of your essay is great, but I needed to read what you wrote two or three times to get it. I think that was because of its complexity. You fill up your sentences with many complex and tenuous ideas. You need to develop them and make the relationship between the sentences and ideas clearer.

—Please invent a word that's ten times better than "fantastic," and I'll use it. The ideas flow and are inspiring. Your emergence into the human community is glorious! Welcome to your life!

—I think I'll read it again—this time purely for fun.

NELSON FARIAS

—You really do take a meaningful conflict in your life and discuss its implications without fear, which is a very difficult thing to do. This essay is at its strongest when you look into yourself.

—Your writing is loaded with colorful metaphors, which are the result of a creative play on words and ideas. However, they are overshadowed by the reality at which the essay arrives.

—Finding that all individuals are unique should not prevent you from experiencing your own individuality. You have accomplished this extremely well in the essay.

FRAN OSBORNE

—The essential idea in this essay seems to me to be about the uniqueness/commonness of each human being. It is an enormous topic, and you deal with it lucidly and intelligently.

—The idea that you are rotten at the core seems incompatible with the honesty that pervades the essay. How can such frankness/honesty be rotten? The title bothers me as a result.

—The religious issues you introduce are so big that they could be looked at again in a separate essay. Is your religion a convenience?

—As for the structure of the essay, I found it to be well organized, with a good, strong beginning, and a strong, optimistic conclusion.

—The introduction seems slightly overdone: you take five paragraphs before getting into the meat of your essay. From there on, the reading is fast, entertaining, and informative. I particularly like the fact that you use specific examples to show how you tried to be different, but I am slightly bothered by the fact that these differences seem superficial.

—I thought the last four paragraphs were particularly strong: you have a core identity (being different), but you are frightened of giving it up (in spite of its arrogance) because such relinquishing might result in a kind of personality suicide. You find a way around this by looking at yourself in a "new and startling way" that straddles individuality and common humanity. Finally, you find in the wonder of looking at—and exploring—yourself a way of overcoming fear.

Exercises in Peer Editing

1. Reread the general statements at the end of Benson's essay. How is each similar to — and different from — the final general comment you have written about her essay? What does each focus on, and how consistent is their overall advice with yours? Review the four peer editors' marginal notations on Benson's essay. Which are observations? Which are evaluations? Which aspects of composition does each focus on? List the points you and the other peer editors agree on; disagree on. Finally, sketch out what Benson would need to do in a revision to respond adequately to what you and the other peer editors have recommended.

2. Your own writing is the focus for this exercise. Prepare a draft of an essay according to your instructor's directions. Then review the various peer-editing activities described on pages 342–344. Bring your own essay to class and present it to your peer editors. After you have received their written observations and recommendations on the essay, their assessment of its specific strengths and weaknesses, and their recommendations for improving it, prepare a detailed plan for revising your essay. Consult with your peer editors about your plans, and then draft a new version of the essay.

3. Review the peer editing process. Write an essay in which you offer a clear sense of what you think you have learned about writing and reading as a result of your experiences with it. How has peer editing helped you improve your writing? In what specific ways has it strengthened your reading? What new insights have you developed about the processes of writing and reading? How will peer editing affect the ways in which you prepare your next essay? What do you see as the limitations of peer editing? How would you suggest improving or extending the peer editing process? Be as specific as possible. The emphasis in your essay should reflect either your reservations about peer editing or your enthusiasm for it.

THE PROFESSIONAL
EDITOR
AT WORK

Part VI

IN PREVIOUS CHAPTERS we have seen how students revise their work, first on their own and then with the help of peer editors. In this chapter we have the opportunity to see a professional editor, Jane Aaron, make suggestions for revisions as she shapes the essays by Thu Hong Nguyen and John Siegrist as if for professional publication.

Observing a professional editor at work teaches several lessons about the place of revision in the composing process. First, all writing, even good writing, can be improved. Good writing takes time, effort, and patience, and often requires further revision, or editing, even after a "final" draft. At this point in the process, the professional editor's goal is to preserve the writer's intentions while suggesting changes to improve the accuracy, emphasis, specificity, and consistency of the text. The process, though, is not predictable, as Jane Aaron tells us, because "each writer's process is unique, and the barriers to clear, effective expression are many."

Second, professional editing provides a model of close and careful reading that we can translate to our reading of our own and other writer's work. The job of the professional editor, like that of a peer editor or an instructor, is to provide an objective view; by standing in for the audience, the editor becomes a collaborator who shows the writer whether he or she has communicated effectively with the intended audience. Aaron's editing of Nguyen's and Siegrist's essays shows how a revised sentence or paragraph, a change in emphasis or tone can allow the writers' intentions to become even clearer to their readers. We see the power and possibility of revising as Nguyen's and Siegrist's essays move from being strong essays to polished pieces.

Third, observing the professional editing process also shows what happens when a piece of writing goes public. For those who publish their work, whether in a commercial magazine or a school paper, editing is the final step in the composing process. As readers, we are not aware of this stage—of the extensive editing that goes on — because the printed page does not reveal how each piece of writing was created. We see only the polished words and are not privy to the suggestions and changes, the additions and deletions that constitute the important work of editing.

Gary Goshgarian, a professor of English at Northeastern University and a novelist, textbook author, and free-lance writer, is one of the many writers with whom Jane Aaron has worked. In the following passage, the fourth paragraph from Goshgarian's essay, "Zeroing in on Science Fiction," we see the suggestions and changes Aaron offered him.

> Science ~~F~~fiction is th~~at~~e branch of literature that imaginatively speculates on the consequences of living in a scientific or technological world.
>
> A closer look at ~~our~~ the definition will help ~~us to understand~~ outline some SF prerequisites. The word "specu-lates" implies the future. Therefore, a writer who "imaginatively speculates" is one who creates experiences and conditions that ~~may or may not~~ have not yet ~~have~~ occurred in the real world. Certainly ~~the~~ humans have experienced ~~of~~ love, hate, and fear; ~~are real,~~ however, the writer may create unreal conditions out of which those experiences evolve, as H. G. Wells did in his War of the Worlds. The point is that SF speculates about some tomorrow conditions. ~~and circumstances. Such~~ The same may be said of any non-historical fiction that presumes some general future time. But—and this is where ~~the rest of our definition separates~~ SF differs from non-SF—the future ~~Those con-ditions and circumstances~~ experiences and conditions are categorically scientific or technological. ~~by nature.~~ In other words, SF is about ~~what it is like to~~ being human in ~~a future of~~ some imagined technological ~~advances.~~ future. ~~Our~~ The definition does not specify locale, so SF stories can be set on earth, in space, or on worlds galaxies away. ~~Likewise, our~~ Nor does the definition ~~does not~~ specify whose technology. In War of the Worlds, ~~it is Martian~~ the

OK to include Conditions here? It's used twice below.

Have not yet seems more accurate, given what you go on to say. See also opposite margin.

You might consider cutting the Wells example here: it may not be familiar enough to readers to make it useful. The intervening points (besides Wells) are really covered in the earlier sentence Therefore . . . real world. And Wells is introduced in more detail at the end of the paragraph.

Here, and later, OK to delete circumstances, redundant with conditions?

Dashes OK to help emphasize shift in focus?

Note that if you cut the earlier Wells example you need to add Wells's name to this sentence.

Changes OK to simplify/ strengthen phrasing? know̲how ~~that permits the~~ bug-eyed ~~invaders to~~ Martians
— of *transports them*
~~journey the~~ millions of miles ~~of space~~ to earth
and then
~~which it~~ nearly devastates ∧ with deadly gases and *the planet*
heat rays.

Aaron's specific suggestions show Goshgarian how to strengthen his paragraph so that his message and purpose are clearer. Her editing suggestions help to simplify his sentences, clarify parts of the paragraph that might be confusing to readers, and improve the accuracy and emphasis of his word choice. Because the interaction between a professional editor and writer demonstrates vividly the very process a writer must follow in preparing a final draft, we invited Jane Aaron to edit the essays of Thu Hong Nguyen and John Siegrist in the same way she worked with Gary Goshgarian. In eighteen years as a professional editor, Jane Aaron has worked with authors of magazine articles, of books for general audiences, and of college textbooks in almost every discipline, including freshman composition. She is the editor of *The Compact Reader*, an anthology of essays for composition courses, and a contributing editor to *The Little Brown Handbook*, a best-selling composition textbook.

Our editing procedure was similar to the standard editing process used by most professional publications. Aaron edited Nguyen's and Siegrist's essays by making some changes, suggesting others, and questioning the writers in places about their meaning and intended effect. With the edited versions of their essays, she sent them a covering letter in which she explained her general response to their essays and offered an analysis to support her comments on their manuscripts. The students were asked not only to revise their essays using Aaron's suggestions but also to describe how they felt to have their work professionally edited. As Jane Aaron wrote to Nguyen and Siegrist, she hoped that they would find her suggestions helpful, but they, as writers, had the final word; all decisions on revision were theirs to make. Before reading the edited versions of these essays, read the unedited essays as they appear on pages 188–190 for Nguyen and 217–220 for Siegrist.

We begin this chapter with Jane Aaron's description of an editor at work.

A PROFESSIONAL EDITOR DESCRIBES HER WORK

In their comments on being edited (pages 401 and 414), Thu Hong Nguyen and John Siegrist describe initial feelings of insecurity and indignation that would sound familiar to any editor. Like most writers who have poured themselves into their work, Nguyen and Siegrist had good reason to believe that their essays were successful. And indeed they were. But, like most manuscripts received by publishers, the essays also had the potential to be better—clearer, more convincing, more enjoyable for readers.

An editor is a kind of messenger between writer and reader, representing each to the other. On the one hand, the editor helps the writer state his or her message as effectively as possible. On the other hand, the editor represents the typical reader for whom the piece of writing is intended, anticipating his or her needs for information, clarity, and readability. At the practical level this dual representation works itself out in one process, as the editor helps shape the writer's work for the reader's maximum understanding and enjoyment.

The goal of the editing process is thus to preserve all the strengths of the manuscript while removing whatever impedes communication between writer and reader. Such a broad goal can encompass any feature of the work, including development, organization, emphasis, pace, specificity, conciseness, consistency, and accuracy. The process is not predictable, however, for each writer's purpose is unique, and the barriers to clear, effective expression are many. From one writer's work to another's, or even from one paragraph to the next in the same work, fresh problems arise to demand fresh solutions. And always the solutions must be conceived in the context of the writer's intentions and the reader's needs.

In order to understand the writer's intentions, diagnose the weaknesses of the manuscript, and conceive appropriate solutions, the editor may read the work as closely and as often as the writer has. Usually the first reading is a quick one to get the gist of the author's ideas and the sound of the author's voice. Then slower readings follow, during which the editor notes any problems in organization, gaps in the development of ideas, shifts in tone, or unnecessary repetitions. These readings require a kind of peripheral vision of the mind, an ability to recall the entire work while concentrating on a bit of it in order to see the connection—or lack of connection—between the part and the whole.

The actual editing is the most time-consuming part of the process, as the editor tries to resolve the larger problems and also weighs every sentence against the author's intentions and the reader's likely response. It is during this stage that the dialogue between editor and writer occurs. The writer's part in the dialogue consists of the words on the page. The editor's consists of changes, questions, comments, and suggestions, either on the manuscript, in the margins, or on separate sheets of paper. Sometimes the editor changes the manuscript without explanation if the need for change seems obvious enough; most corrections of grammatical, spelling, and typographical errors fall into this category. Sometimes the editor explains changes that reflect interpretations of the author's meaning. And sometimes the editor relies solely on suggestions or questions if the meaning cannot be safely assumed or if passages seem to require rewriting that the author is best equipped to handle. (All three approaches appear on Ms. Nguyen's and Mr. Siegrist's essays.) The explanations and suggestions may be lengthy, seemingly out of proportion to the problem being addressed, so that the author will understand why the manuscript is not clear or what impairs its readability. An editor quickly learns that a simple comment like "Not clear" usually prompts the natural response "It's clear to me" — and no revision.

When the editing is completed, the editor returns to the author with a covering letter that includes a general response to the piece — both strengths and any overall weaknesses that will provide some context for the specific comments on the manuscript. (See the letters on pages 396 and 407.) Usually the author's revision is the final round in the process, as it was with Ms. Nguyen's and Mr. Siegrist's essays. But occasionally the editor may negotiate last-minute changes with the author before the manuscript is set in type.

Editing requires a certain amount of mind-reading, to discern the writer's intentions, as well as a sense of the possible solutions, an ear for language, and a firm grounding in the conventions of grammar, punctuation, mechanics, and spelling. It also requires an ability to work "silently," suspending one's own ideas instead of pushing them on the author. Of course, editors sometimes overstep their bounds. Beyond grammer and spelling, few matters in writing are clear-cut: almost everything is a question of choice, of judgment, and judgment calls are endlessly debatable. Although authors have the final word, the good ones, from an editor's standpoint, will always suspend their initial feelings of insecurity and indignation to engage in the debate. By that criterion alone, Ms. Nguyen and Mr. Siegrist are excellent authors.

THU HONG NGUYEN, "A GOOD WOMAN"

What follows is Jane Aaron's editing of Thu Hong Nguyen's essay. We begin with Aaron's letter to Nguyen and her editing of the essay. We then see Nguyen's comments on Aaron's editing and the essay as she revised it in response to Aaron's comments.

EDITOR TO AUTHOR:
JANE AARON'S LETTER TO THU HONG NGUYEN

Dear Ms. Nguyen:

Your essay is affecting and well controlled. You create a clear picture of the life of a Vietnamese woman, eliciting both the respect and sympathy of the reader. Your three-part organization (reinforced by the echoing introductory and concluding sentences of each body paragraph) provides a neat but unforced structure for presenting the complexities of the life you describe.

My suggestions for revision focus mainly on occasional wordiness, some unclear passages, and the introduction. The introduction is too long and detailed, I think: it immerses the reader in explanation before the point of the essay is clear. As you will see, I have suggested that you move some introductory sentences to the next paragraph, where they seem to fit well, and that you cut or condense some of the remaining sentences.

Although most of my suggestions appear in the margins, I have also made some changes in the expectation that editing would clarify my ideas. I hope you find the suggestions helpful and agree that they will strengthen your essay. Of course, the decisions on whether and how to implement them rest with you.

Sincerely,
Jane E. Aaron

NGUYEN'S EDITED ESSAY

A Good Woman

1

Use quotation marks for this saying?

A good woman means an industrious daughter, a devoted wife, and a loving mother. Thus ~~is the~~ saying ~~that~~ has ~~been~~ *expressed* a collective belief for many centuries in Viet Nam. ~~As soon as a female infant~~ *Move this to 2nd sentence of paragraph 2?*

~~is born, it~~ *she* is given the middle name Thi--meaning "female"--to emphasize ~~its~~ *her* role (as a woman in later years.) ~~Then, in~~ growing up, th~~is~~*e* child receives lessons about a woman's duties and must practice what she learns. Parents wholeheartedly train their daughters to achieve the qualities expected of a woman. Should they forget *(OK to add?) their duty,* their neighbors promptly remind them. In a Vietnamese village, *a girl's family and* ~~the~~ entire community ~~helps, by words of~~ *contribute* praise and ~~by~~ punishment *raise her into* to ~~bring up a female child to be~~ a good woman, whose ~~service, obedience, and generosity~~ bring*s* much comfort to those around her. With the fear of retribution, the child grows into a woman who follows loyally the instructions of virtue which determines her fate. From the moment ~~her mind is mature enough~~ *she can* ~~to~~ understand commands, ~~(to) the day she is married~~ *through her own marriage and childbearing, a* ~~off, (to) the time when she bears her own children, a~~ Vietnamese ~~woman~~ *(female?)* continuously tries to establish a good name as a diligent daughter, a submissive wife, and an altruistic mother.

Cut? Doesn't the name emphasize the role in childhood, too?

Should this sentence stress parents' responsibility rather than training (focus of the previous sentence)? Rephrase: Her parents are primarily responsible for her training.

See my letter: Reduce detail and length of introduction by moving these sentences and condensing this part?

repeated in 1st and last sentences of ¶

Since her virtue continues beyond marriage and childbearing, "to the day" and "to the time" are misleading

What does this clause refer to? Could the sentence be cut?

The idea of punishment is in the previous sentence, and loyalty and virtue could be introduced there as well, as modifiers for woman: *a loyal virtuous woman.*

Use female *instead of* woman *when referring to the child as well as the adult?*

Again —
female
instead of
woman?

In order to be approved by everyone, a Viet-   2

female?

namese woman must first be industrious. ~~This~~ begins *Her training* *add section*
                  at birth, when *from first*

~~with her services at the house of her parents who~~ *paragraph as*
The child is kept   *suggested?*

~~keep her~~ from idling with endless housework. ~~Already~~ *Then the*
deleted
   By   *for* *part of this*

always at 9, ~~at~~ the age of (nine,) she is the babysitter ~~of~~ her *sentence seems*
or does the   *unnecessary.*
age vary? younger siblings. Carrying a baby on her back, she
Perhaps: Before
the age of
eight or nine spends the day sweeping the house, carrying messages,
or nine or ten and doing errands. As she grows older, she shares
to make it
more general. more of the housework with her mother. Upon the

first crow of the rooster, she rises to brew tea
Moved because
the first line and prepare breakfast. Afterward, she does the
doesn't apply
to the whole laundry by the river bank. ~~At noon~~ she cooks lunch
sentence. *at noon*
    and has just enough time to tidy up the house before *This phrase*
   ^   *implies that*
she prepares dinner. In the evening she goes to bed, *she keeps*
                      herself busy
but only after having fixed the shirts or pants that *to avoid*
                   reverie. Perhaps
were torn or missing a button. (In keeping busy,) she *delete it and*
                    rephrase to
has no time to wonder and to dream, which often *sharpen the irony*
            I think you
            intend: She has no time for wondering
result from idleness. *and dreaming, ~~the pursuits of the idle~~.*

I think you
need a better Besides working diligently, a good Vietnamese 3
transition
from childhood woman must also submit to her husband. She is ex-
to adulthood.
Perhaps: When pected to revere the man whom her parents have chosen
the girl becomes for her after they have accepted his valuable gifts.
a woman, she
must not Once married, she must show that she is unequal to
only work   *appear*
diligently her husband. When husband and wife ~~are seen~~ to-
but also
submit to gether in the street, she usually keeps a respectful
her husband.

distance behind him. She also ~~has to~~ acknowledges

her inferior position in her speech. When addressed

by her husband, she always answers in a well—modulated

tone. In talking to him, she uses formal address; *The semicolon shows the close relation between clauses.*

Even in the most intimate moments, she still ~~cannot~~ *may not*

use the familiar form of address. If she has per-

mission from her husband, she may speak aloud her

opinions) but *she* should not try to make ~~the~~ decisions.

must

Whatever her husband says, she ~~will~~ listen and not

contradict. ~~Remaining~~ silence is usually the most

encouraged means for her to be respectful.

viewed

     Finally, to be ~~recognized~~ favorably, a Viet-

namese woman must try to sacrifice herself for ~~the~~

it is ~~benefit of~~ the children ~~which are~~ her duty to bear.

~~At mealtimes,~~ she eats little, *at meals,* repressing her hunger

with the gratifying consolation that her children are

growing taller and stronger. She must not dream of

any kind of luxuries. Plain clothing gives her an

air of modesty and thriftiness. ~~Wearing~~ perfume or

lipstick ~~may~~ *might* lead other people to condemn her as

wanton and irresponsible. Instead of beautifying

herself, she ~~should~~ *must* give her children more food to

eat and better clothes to wear. She must also re-

frain from any kind of pleasure. She spends her

evening hours at home looking after the children

Could this be rephrased more simply: silence is the way she demonstrates respect? If the implication about cultural encouragement is important, it should perhaps be stated more directly: she has learned [or has been taught] to show respect through silence.

4

rather than at a nightclub or theater. A pack of

cigarettes, a bottle of beer, or a few piasters lost

at the casino ~~can~~ deprive her children of their right

to be fed more. A Vietnamese mother does everything

for the sake of her children.

In trying to be what *every* one expects of her, a Viet-   5

namese ~~woman~~ *female?* ~~continues to~~ *begins by* serv*ing* ~~if not~~ her parents

and siblings, ~~then the husband and children of her~~

~~own.~~ *Then,* Year after year, she humbles herself to make

her husband happy as a proud superior, from his

youthful days of good health to his time of age and

sickness. Day after day, she dedicates herself to

the welfare of her children even after they grow up.

In this lifetime of striving to be a good woman,

she sets ~~herself as~~ an illustrious example to other

women who are also trying to achieve the same de-

sired qualities. *When she* ~~R~~ealiz*es* ~~ing~~ her goal, she is the

pride of her parents, husband, and children. *The* ~~P~~eople

around her are satisfied with her. They feel

(proud) and (sure of their lasting tradition) *of?* (in) bringing

up *a?* good (wom*e?*an.) In any generation, they will always

have a good Vietnamese woman to admire. In any cen-

tury, they will always have a slave to praise.

Marginal annotations:

add nothing for herself and to stress the sacrifice?

Could this be stated more simply? Perhaps: would mean less food for her children.

The changes here are a suggestion for recalling your 3-part structure, giving equal emphasis to childhood as to other parts.

Note that pride appears two sentences before.

Do you mean that tradition is validated (or perhaps justified) by her success? If so, perhaps make that clearer: Her success validates [or justifies] their lasting tradition of bringing up a good woman.

Effective ending.

THE AUTHOR RESPONDS:
COMMENTARY FROM THU HONG NGUYEN

When I was told that Jane Aaron would edit my essay, I was both surprised and curious. I must say that although it was a pleasant feeling that a professional editor, who must have edited the works of many popular and important writers, would now edit my essay, I could not help feeling nervous. I was also curious about what changes she would make on my essay. After all, the essay had been screened by my peers and instructor before it was sent into the contest. After I read over Ms. Aaron's comments, I was much impressed and felt that her editing was definitely necessary. From a piece of casual writing, she has turned my essay into professional work. I was both amazed and pleased how she suggested changes for some of my sentences and expressions that I was not satisfied with but did not know how to improve. My uneasiness soon left me and I was enthusiastically rewriting my essay using her suggestions. This is still my essay, but it is a stronger essay thanks to the editor's thoughtful comments.

NGUYEN'S REVISED ESSAY

A Good Woman

"A good woman means an industrious daughter, a   1
devoted wife, and a loving mother." This saying has
expressed a collective belief for many centuries in
Viet Nam. In a Vietnamese village, a girl's family
and entire community contribute praise and punishment
to raise her into a good woman who brings much comfort to those around her. With the fear of retribution, the child grows into a loyal, virtuous woman.
From the moment she can understand commands through
her own marriage and child bearing, a Vietnamese
female continuously tries to establish a good name
as a diligent daughter, a submissive wife, and an
altruistic mother.

In order to be approved by everyone, a Viet-   2
namese female must first be industrious. Her
training begins at birth, when she is given the
middle name Thi--meaning "female"--to emphasize her
role. Growing up, the child receives lessons about
a woman's duties and must practice what she learns.
The child is kept from idling with endless housework.
Before the age of nine or ten, she is the babysitter
for her younger siblings. Carrying a baby on her
back, she spends the day sweeping the house, carrying
messages, and doing errands. As she grows older,
she shares more of the housework with her mother.
Upon the first crow of the rooster, she rises to

brew tea and prepare breakfast. Afterward, she does the laundry by the river bank. She cooks lunch at noon and has just enough time to tidy up the house before she prepares dinner. In the evening she goes to bed, but only after fixing shirts or pants that are torn or missing a button. She has no time for wondering and dreaming, the pursuits of the idle.

When the girl becomes a woman, she must not only work diligently but also submit to her husband. She is expected to revere the man whom her parents have chosen for her after they have accepted his valuable gifts. Once married, she must show that she is unequal to her husband. When husband and wife appear together in the street, she usually keeps a respectful distance behind him. She also acknowledges her inferior position in her speech. When addressed by her husband, she always answers in a well-modulated tone. In talking to him, she uses formal address; even in the most intimate moments, she still may not use the familiar form of address. If she has permission from her husband, she may speak her opinions aloud, but she should not try to make decisions. Whatever her husband says, she must listen and not contradict. She has been taught to show respect through silence.

Finally, to be viewed favorably a Vietnamese woman must try to sacrifice herself for the children which are her duty to bear. She eats little at

meals, repressing her hunger with the gratifying
consolation that her children are growing taller
and stronger. She must not dream of any kind of
luxury. Plain clothing gives her an air of modesty
and thrift. Perfume or lipstick might lead other
people to condemn her as wanton and irresponsible.
Instead of beautifying herself, she must give her
children more food to eat and better clothes to
wear. She must also refrain from any kind of
pleasure. She spends her evening hours at home
looking after the children rather than at a nightclub or theater. A pack of cigarettes, a bottle of
beer, or a few piasters lost at the casino would
mean less food for her children. A Vietnamese
mother does nothing for herself and everything for
the sake of her children.

In trying to be what everyone expects of her, a   5
Vietnamese female begins by serving her parents and
siblings. Then, year after year, she humbles herself
to make her husband happy as a proud superior, from
his youthful days of good health to his time of age
and sickness. Day after day, she dedicates herself
to the welfare of her children, even after they
grow up. In this lifetime of striving to be a good
woman, she sets an illustrious example to other
women who are also trying to achieve the same desired
qualities. When she realizes her goal, she is the
pride of her parents, husband, and children. The

people around her are satisfied with her. Her
success validates their lasting tradition of
bringing up good women. In any generation, they
will always have a good Vietnamese woman to admire.
In any century, they will always have a slave to
praise.

Questions on Nguyen's Essay

1. What is Nguyen's *purpose* in writing her essay? How do Jane Aaron's suggested changes help to strengthen Nguyen's purpose?

2. Aaron offers many comments on Nguyen's *introduction*. In general, her comments suggest that the introduction is too long and detailed and that the reader is immersed in explanation before the point of the essay is clear. Do you agree with Aaron's comments? What specific changes has she suggested? Study Nguyen's revised introduction. How do the changes strengthen not only the introductory paragraph, but the entire essay as well?

3. Aaron points out a number of unclear passages in paragraph 2. Study these passages and explain how and why they are unclear. How has Nguyen strengthened this paragraph in her revised essay?

4. Aaron also indicates a number of other unclear passages in other paragraphs. Examine these passages and discuss Aaron's suggested changes. Has Nguyen accepted these changes?

5. Aaron offers Nguyen many suggestions to avoid wordiness. Why, in general, is wordiness a problem for a reader? Study Aaron's suggestions and explain how the edited sentences make the essay more readable.

6. Does Aaron suggest any changes that you disagree with? Explain.

7. Nguyen tells us: "This is still my essay, but it is a stronger essay thanks to the editor's thoughful comments." Summarize the differences between the two drafts. Why is the revised draft stronger?

8. What have you learned about writing, reading, and the editing process from studying Aaron's comments on Nguyen's essay?

JOHN SIEGRIST, "RATTLESNAKE: A PALATABLE EXPERIENCE"

This section continues with Aaron's editing of John Siegrist's essay. Again we see Aaron's letter to Siegrist and her editing of the essay, followed by Siegrist's comments and his revised essay.

EDITOR TO AUTHOR:
JANE AARON'S LETTER TO JOHN SIEGRIST

Dear Mr. Siegrist:

Your essay is intriguing and usually quite clear: like all good process essays, it not only lays the steps out neatly but also makes an interesting point (about experimenting with the unfamiliar).

My suggestions for revision center on problems a reader might see in your essay. The explanations could be clearer in a few places, and sentences could sometimes be combined or condensed for greater conciseness and a smoother flow. In addition, paragraph 12, on various methods of preparing snake, could be revised to integrate information in paragraphs 2 and 15 about ways of preparing and serving snake and to provide a more inclusive and less awkward first sentence. Finally, the actor (the person performing the process) could be more consistent: you now shift among *one*, *I*, and *you* (sometimes stated and sometimes implied in imperative sentences such as "Place two fingers . . . "), or you use the passive voice ("This is usually accomplished . . . "). Shifting subjects are a common difficulty in process essays, and complete consistency is probably neither possible nor desirable. But I have suggested (in my editing) that you stick with *I* whenever possible because the passages in which you now use it seem the liveliest and most natural. *You* seems inappropriate because it would cast the reader as the actor when your message is to persuade the reader to try rattlesnake. *One* can work in isolated sentences, but it's hard to maintain without creating a stuffiness that would conflict with your essay's overall tone. Passives, though sometimes useful or necessary, tend to deaden prose and create confusion about who the actor is.

I have written suggestions and questions in the margins of your essay. When showing seemed easier than telling, I have made changes and usually explained them in the margins. I hope you agree that the suggested changes would make your essay even clearer and more readable then it already is. Of course, the decisions on revision are yours to make.

Sincerely,
Jane E. Aaron

SIEGRIST'S EDITED ESSAY

Often may be less off-putting to readers, who can more easily say, "But not me."

Rattlesnake: A Palatable Experience

People ~~usually~~ *often* alienate themselves from ~~things~~ *the* *unfamiliar.* ~~and experiences which are not customary to their~~ ~~lifestyles.~~ They close their minds to ~~ideas~~ ~~which~~ *new experiences that* might prove enjoyable if ~~they would only~~ give ~~them~~ *n a try* ~~selves the opportunity to try something different.~~ This is the kind of resistance ~~met when one~~ *I usually meet when I* mention~~s~~ ~~the idea of~~ eating rattlesnake.

Several changes in 1st paragraph eliminate unneeded words and help sharpen meaning. The use of experiences in the 2nd sentence rather than 1st focuses attention on a key idea.

Restrictive clauses like this one usually begin with that *instead of* which.

See my letter on the use of I.

~~There are~~ people throughout the world ~~who~~ eat snake and find it not only palatable, but delicious. *(People eat snake in sandwiches, ~~and~~ soups, fried, or barbecued.)* I was fortunate during my Air Force service to be stationed only thirty miles from the site of the most famous rattlesnake roundup, held annually in Texas. I ~~was able~~ not only ~~to find~~ out *found* how snake meat tastes, but ~~to~~ learn*ed* *also* how to catch, skin, and prepare the snake myself.

I suggest putting this information at the end of paragraph 1½ (The editing here shows there are 4 variations.)

Editing avoids repeated I was *in 2 sentences.*

The first step in tasting fried rattlesnake is to collect the ingredients. ~~While~~ *m*ost of these can be found at any grocery store, *but* the main item, the snake, must be sought out in its own habitat. One thing must be said ~~before~~ *to* anyone *who* goes out to catch a rattlesnake: Be careful. A snake is like any other wild animal. It is timid until cornered, but then

1

2

3

In paragraph 6 it sounds as if the light shows where the snake is. If so, change to is necessary to illuminate the darkened areas? Or is the gasoline used to flush the snake out? And if the light is used merely to show where the snake is, how do you flush it out? Or do you shoot it in its hiding place?

it will fight to survive with (every ounce of energy.)

The best ~~areas~~ *places* to look for rattlesnakes are

among rock piles, rock fences, heavy brush piles,

No

and abandoned animal burrows. ~~Since~~ one ~~would not~~

blindly   *so*

want to reach into these places, a flashlight or

mirror to reflect the sun (into the darkened areas

is a necessity.) I have heard of people ~~using hoses~~

snake's hiding

ing
~~to~~ pour gasoline into the~~se~~ places, but ~~I feel~~ that

method is unsporting and creates an unnecessary fire

hazard.

I
(~~One should~~) take into account the amount of meat

family ... guests = How many people? Also I suggest active voice, for example, "a larger group of five or six requires ..."

I
needed (when looking for a snake.) A snake two feet

provides enough meat
long ~~would be all right~~ for two people. If a (family)

is larger or (guests) are invited over, a snake four

long
or five feet ~~in length~~ is required. (This) ~~will~~ save

~~the hostess~~ the embarrassment of not having enough

Why hostess? Cut OK?

to go around.

Change to killed or caught and killed since (caught.) *the next para. on your method doesn't describe catching? Also, at the end of this para., add a brief explanation of how the hook-and-pole hunters kill the snake?*

Once the proper snake is found, it must be

Many snake hunters
(caught.) ~~This is usually accomplished through the~~

use ~~of~~ special poles or hooks. ~~The idea is~~ to pull

and
the snake from its place of refuge, ~~use the pole to~~

The hunter
hold its head against the ground, then reach down

its   *gaining the*
and grab the snake behind ~~his~~ head. (~~This gives the~~)

control necessary to
~~person control of the snake and allows it to be~~

the snake
dropped into a burlap sack or other ~~suitable~~

Right margin notes:

4

Cliché? Instead say briefly what happens when a snake is cornered: ie, a poisonous bite, illness, maybe death?

5

Antecedent unclear: Adequate meat?

6

Change made to set up possibility that this is not the only method, so readers will be prepared for yours.

Changes OK? This was unclear but I assume it refers to grabbing the snake.

container for transporting ~~back to the house.~~ home.

I am either too smart or too ~~big a~~ coward~~ly~~ to   7

Grabbing OK?
You describe
actual contact
in previous
paragraph.
attempt this practice. Since I don't like the idea
of ~~coming within inches of~~ grabbing an animal that has the
potential to kill me, I prefer to shoot the snake

Perhaps just
kill the
snake
instead of
ensure
that ...

from a (reasonable distance.) Any ~~type of~~ firearm will

See query at
paragraph 4
about where
the snake is
when you
shoot it:
still in its
hiding place?
ensure that the snake is dead before it is picked up;
picked up?
however, I use a small-caliber handgun because it
destroys less meat. I shoot the snake in the head,
leaving intact
~~as~~ the body ~~is the part~~ to be cooked.

The ~~very~~ first thing to do ~~upon~~ after killing the   8

rattlesnake is to remove its head using a knife,
a   an   a
machete, axe, or even shovel. The fangs still contain poison, and ~~even~~ an accidental scratch from them
the head is
could result in (serious medical problems.) Once re-

Illness or
death instead
of the less
precise
serious
medical
problems?
I   it   other
moved, ~~the head should be~~ buried to keep ~~stray~~ ani-
(OK? Stray implies "lost"
mals from eating it and becoming sick. *or "out of place."*

The snake is now ready to be skinned and gutted.   9

I remove the tail first and then attempt to cut a

straight line from one end of its belly to the other.

~~end.~~ This is fairly simple unless the snake's

muscles are still contracting; then it can be a
I
moving experience! If ~~you~~ find the snake trying to
my   I
curl around ~~your~~ arm, either wait a little longer to

do the skinning or have a friend hold the body still.

(This ~~may show you~~ way I learn who ~~your~~ my friends are.) A pair of

scissors is much easier to use than a knife, but

either is fine. It is important to keep the cut

shallow ~~and try not to go into~~ because penetrating the snake's organs

~~as that~~ would contaminate the meat.

{handwritten right margin: Do you prefer scissors because it is easier to make a shallow cut with them? If so, I suggest moving this sentence to the end of the ¶ and saying something like: I find it easier to make a shallow cut with scissors than with a knife.}

Once the cut is finished, the skin can easily   10

be peeled back on each side of the snake's body. I

~~accomplish this by~~ placing two fingers between the

snake's skin and the meat on the body and run~~ning~~ my

fingers the entire length on both sides ~~of the body.~~

The skin ~~will~~ pools away just like a banana's. The

snake skin is worth saving ~~and can be~~ used for to make

belts, (hatbands, belt buckles,) and other ~~attractive~~

items.

{handwritten left margin: Does a snake skin have to be tanned? If so, say something like: The snake skin is worth saving; once tanned it can be used in...}

~~The~~ gutting ~~procedure~~ the snake is very similar to ~~that~~   11

~~of~~ skinning ~~the snake.~~ it. I place two fingers between

the internal ~~cavity~~ organs and the meat of the snake's

inner body. ~~Running your~~ Then I my fingers the entire length

~~will~~ to remove the guts in one clean ~~and effortless~~

motion.   *{handwritten: (Seems redundant.}*

{handwritten left margin: Organs OK? Clearer than cavity, I think.}

Skinned and gutted, the meat is ready to be

~~We now come to the actual preparation of the~~ prepared and served in any of

~~meat for cooking. There are~~ numerous ways ~~to pre-~~   12

~~pare any meat, and snake is no different.~~ The

seasoning is ~~left up to one's~~ a matter of personal taste, as is

the style of cooking. Snake can be steamed, fried, meat

{handwritten left margin: See my letter where I suggest these changes to provide a less awkward transition and a more inclusive introduction. (Even if you accept the value of these changes, you may prefer to make them differently. My changes are meant merely as suggestions.)}

It can be served in sandwiches or soups or alone as an appetizer or a main dish. It is especially good for a light meal or a refreshing change from beef, pork, chicken, or fish

baked, broiled, ᵥor even eaten raw. ¶I prefer mine

Sentence moved from previous paragraph → ⎡   *barbecued,*   fried, although I would like to try it barbecued.

Is barbecued the only method you haven't tried?

Frying ~~rattlesnake~~ is probably the quickest and   13

Why do you prefer frying? (Just because it's quick and easy?)

easiest ~~of all the~~ methods *for* ~~to~~ prepare ~~it.~~ *ing the meat I cut* The snake

Sentences here could be combined and simplified as noted to give greater variety to the paragraph.

~~must be cut~~ *meat* into portions which are easy to work

Combine?

with. ①find two- or three-inch lengths adequate.

Simplify? →

(Note: almost all the sentences begin with I.)

⎡ ①use a deep-fat fryer, and while the oil is getting
⎣ warm, I prepare the snake pieces. ①combine several

ingredients, the amounts of which depend upon the

Combine?

number of pieces to be cooked. ①mix beaten eggs,

Meaning the batter and the flour? If so, say: The batter and the flour give the pieces a light, crunchy coating when fried.

pepper, and a little onion salt in a small bowl. ①

dip the snake pieces into the mixture and then roll

them in flour. This gives them a light covering

that ~~which~~ becomes crunchy when fried.

frying

The oil should be kept at a medium temperature: 14

Too low a setting can cause the snake to fall apart,

The colon shows the close relation between these sentences. (The capital letter after the colon is optional but consistent with the style you set in paragraph 3.)

The passives in this paragraph seem preferable to more sentences starting with I.

and too high a setting can cause the flour crust to

harden too much. The meat should be ~~placed in the~~

in the oil

~~oil and~~ left ~~there~~ for no*t* more than a few minutes

because

the snake sections are similar to fillets of fish and

sections

fry very quickly. Once done, they should be removed

and *ed of*

~~to~~ drain any excess oil. They are now ready to serve,

a

and I guarantee everyone will be waiting ~~in anticipa-~~

~~tion of~~ their first bite of rattlesnake.

Agreement problem (everyone...their). OK to say the?

Eating rattlesnake is a ~~rather~~ unique experience.   15

Something either is or isn't unique.

See comment at para. 12 in which I suggest you insert this information at the end of that para. If you do so, then you needn't start a new para. here

It can be served as the main dish or as an appetizer. It is especially suited when one ~~desires~~ a light meal or a refreshing change from beef, pork, chicken, or ~~fish.~~ Using a fork to eat fried snake is almost use-less, and one must rely upon the most basic of eating utensils, the fingers.

Say pointless instead to avoid repetition from using a fork?

Also, why is it useless or pointless?

Taste... flavor is redundant.

~~The taste of~~ rattlesnake meat has a flavor all 16
its own, close to that of armadillo. Since most
people have not tried armadillo, I would describe ~~it~~ rattlesnake as somewhat like turtle meat, ‸ with a mild, slightly sweet flavor◦ I won't lie and say it tastes like chicken because it doesn't. ~~It is a meat with a very mild flavor, possibly just a little sweet.~~ I can only verify that it does taste excep-tionally delicious.

OK to put this info. here instead of two sentences later for the benefit of readers who haven't tried turtle?

I think the shift to you in this paragraph is effective. You could go further and change most people to most of you.

If this sentence immediately follows the one about chicken, a more explicit contrast seems needed. Perhaps: It is, however, exceptionally delicious!

I know most people will not have the opportunity 17
or inclination to eat rattlesnake, but ~~if~~ the chance◦ try it if you have ~~should arise, try it.~~ The taste is surprisingly good, and the experience may open your mind to other
culinary delights ~~which~~ that you have previously rejected.

Avoid the cliché?

Forget about those ideas you have of snakes, and
think of fried rattlesnake as one more way to experi-ence life's variety◦ ~~of food.~~

Of food seems unnecessary. Omitting it ties the last sentence back to your introduction (about shutting off from experiences in general, not just eating experiences).

THE AUTHOR RESPONDS:
COMMENTARY FROM JOHN SIEGRIST

I must admit to being a little surprised at the amount of editing Ms. Aaron did to my essay. This shock was lessened upon my reading the comments and finding that while numerous, the suggestions did not call for major revisions. I feel her comments give my essay that fine polish that only an experienced writer has the ability to give. I appreciated the chance to have my work edited and agree with most of her comments.

I incorporated Ms. Aaron's comments into my essay to give it a better flow from one idea to the next. This is the one element of writing I know I need to improve, and her ideas were clear and simple to use. The comments I did not use were the ones that I felt did not express my ideas in the context I had intended.

I have learned a great deal from the editing of my essay and am able to see where a little change can improve an essay considerably. My essay is now more polished and satisfying. I knew it had rough edges; I just need Ms. Aaron's comments to show me where they were.

SIEGRIST'S REVISED ESSAY

Rattlesnake: A Palatable Experience

People often alienate themselves from the un-familiar. They close their minds to new experiences that might prove enjoyable if given a try. This is the kind of resistance I usually meet when I mention eating rattlesnake.

People throughout the world eat snake and find it not only palatable but delicious. I was fortunate during my Air Force service to be stationed only thirty miles from the site of the most famous rattle-snake roundup, held annually in Texas. I not only found out how snake meat tastes but also learned how to catch, skin, and prepare the snake myself.

The first step in tasting fried rattlesnake is to collect the ingredients. Most of these can be found at any grocery store, but the main item, the snake, must be sought out in its own habitat. One thing must be said to anyone who goes out to catch a rattlesnake: Be careful. A snake is like any other wild animal. It is timid until cornered; then it becomes aggressive, fighting for survival. Rattlesnake hunters must always keep in mind that they are seeking a potentially dangerous animal. Rattlesnake bites can cause serious illness and sometimes, death.

The best places to look for rattlesnakes are among rock piles, rock fences, heavy brush piles,

and abandoned animal burrows. No one wants to reach
blindly into these places, so a flashlight or a
mirror to reflect the sun is necessary to illuminate
the darkened areas. I have heard of people pouring
gasoline into snake's hiding places, but that method
is unsporting and creates an unnecessary fire hazard.

I take into account the amount of meat I need   5
prior to looking for a snake. A snake two feet long
provides enough meat for two people. A larger number
of people will require a larger snake. A good rule
of thumb is to allow one-half to one foot of snake
for each person. Keep in mind that as the snake's
length increases, so does its diameter, and this increases the amount of meat a large snake will yield.
Good judgment in selecting the proper size rattlesnake will save the embarrassment of not having
enough to go around.

Once the proper snake is found, it must be caught   6
or killed. Many snake hunters use special poles or
hooks to pull the snake from its place of refuge and
to hold its head against the ground. The hunter then
reaches down and grabs the snake behind its head,
gaining the control necessary to drop the snake into
a burlap sack or other container for transporting
home. This method keeps the snake alive until time
to cook the meat and ensures the availability of
fresh rattlesnake meat.

I am either too smart or too cowardly to attempt   7

this practice. I prefer to find a snake lying in a relatively open area and shoot it from a safe distance. Any firearm will kill the snake; however, I use a small-caliber handgun because it destroys less meat. I shoot the snake in the head, leaving the body intact to be cooked.

The very first thing to do after killing the rattlesnake is to remove its head, using a knife, a machete, an axe, or even a shovel. The fangs still contain poison, and an accidental scratch from them could result in illness or death. Once the head is removed, I bury it to keep other animals from eating it and becoming sick.

8

The snake is now ready to be skinned and gutted. I remove the tail first and then attempt to cut a straight line from one end of its belly to the other. This is fairly simple unless the snake's muscles are still contracting; then it can be a moving experience! If I find the snake trying to curl around my arm, I either wait a little longer to do the skinning or have a friend hold the body still. (This way I learn who my friends are.) It is important to keep the cut shallow because penetrating the snake's organs would contaminate the meat. I find it is easier to make a shallow cut using scissors rather than a knife.

9

Once the cut is finished, the skin can easily be peeled back on each side of the snake's body. I place two fingers between the snake's skin and the

10

meat on the body and run my fingers the entire length on both sides. The skin peels away just like a banana's. The snake skin is worth saving and, once preserved, it can be used in making belts, belt buckles, hatbands, and other items.

Gutting the snake is very similar to skinning it. I place two fingers between the internal organs and the meat of the snake's inner body. Then I run my fingers the entire length to remove the guts in one clean motion.   11

Skinned and gutted, the meat is ready to be prepared and served in any one of numerous ways. The seasoning is a matter of personal taste, as is the style of cooking. Snake meat can be steamed, fried, baked, broiled, barbecued, or even eaten raw. It can be served in sandwiches or soups or alone as an appetizer or a main dish. It is especially good for a light meal and a refreshing change from beef, pork, chicken, or fish.   12

I prefer snake meat fried because of the crisp texture of the cooked meat, although I would like to try it barbecued. Frying rattlesnake is probably the quickest and easiest method for preparing the meat. I cut the snake meat into portions, two or three inches in length, which are adequate for serving and easy to work with. I use a deep-fat fryer, and while the oil is getting warm, I prepare a coating for the snake pieces which combines beaten   13

eggs, pepper, and a little onion salt. The amounts
used will depend upon the number of pieces of snake
to be cooked and personal taste. The snake pieces
are dipped into the mixture, then rolled in flour.
The batter and the flour give the pieces a light
and crunchy coating when fried.

The frying oil should be kept at a medium tem-   14
perature: Too low a setting can cause the snake to
fall apart, and too high a setting can cause the
flour crust to harden too much. The meat should be
left in the oil for no more than a few minutes because the snake sections are similar to fillets of
fish and fry very quickly. Once done, the sections
should be removed and drained of any excess oil.
They are now ready to serve, and I guarantee everyone will be awaiting the first bite of rattlesnake.

Eating rattlesnake is a unique experience.   15
Using a fork to eat fried snake is almost pointless,
due to the fine texture of the meat, and one must
rely on the most basic of eating utensils, the
fingers. Rattlesnake meat has a flavor all its own,
close to that of armadillo. Since most people have
not tried armadillo, I would describe rattlesnake as
somewhat like turtle meat, with a mild, slightly
sweet flavor. I won't lie and say it tastes like
chicken, because it doesn't. It is, however,
exceptionally delicious.

I know most of you will not have the opportunity   16

or the inclination to eat rattlesnake, but try it
if you have the chance. The taste is surprisingly
good, and the experience may open your mind to other
foods that you have previously rejected. Forget
about those ideas you have of snakes, and think of
fried rattlesnake as one more way to experience
life's variety.

Questions on Siegrist's Essay

1. John Siegrist remarked in his commentary: "I must admit to being a little surprised at the amount of editing Ms. Aaron did to my essay." Were you surprised? What is it about the process of editing that makes a writer surprised, sometimes indignant, when he sees his work edited?

2. Jane Aaron tells us: "An editor is a kind of messenger between writer and reader, representing each to the other. On the one hand, the editor helps the writer state his or her message as effectively as possible. On the other hand, the editor represents the typical reader for whom the piece of writing is intended, anticipating his or her needs for information, clarity and readability." How has Jane Aaron helped Siegrist to state his message more effectively? How has she also helped you, the reader, to understand the essay better? What specifically do you find clearer and more readable in the revised draft?

3. Ms. Aaron identifies Siegrist's shift in person among "one", "I," and "you" as a major problem in his essay. Why does she suggest that he use "I" whenever possible? Why is "I" preferable to "you" or "one"? Do you agree with her suggestion? Locate specific passages in which Aaron suggested to Siegrist to revise his essay using "I" Why do these changes make Siegrist's essay more readable? How do they also help Siegrist achieve his *purpose?*

4. Ms. Aaron also comments: "Shifting subjects are a common difficulty in *process* essays, and complete consistency is probably neither possible nor desirable." Locate instances in which Aaron has suggested to Siegrist to use "you" or "one." Do you agree with her suggestions?

5. Study Aaron's editing of Siegrist's introductory paragraph. She writes to him: "Several changes . . . eliminate unneeded words and help sharpen meaning." Explain how Aaron's editing helps to sharpen Siegrist's meaning in this paragraph.

6. Siegrist writes in his commentary: "I have learned a great deal from the editing of my essay and am able to see where a little change can improve an essay considerably." What are some of the "little" changes Aaron suggested that improved Siegrist's essay? How do these changes improve the essay as a whole?

7. Ms. Aaron suggested to Siegrist that he should combine information for greater conciseness. In paragraph 13 for instance, she edited sentences to combine and simplify. Study the editing of this paragraph. Explain the effect of the changes Ms. Aaron suggested? Has Siegrist combined information to make the essay more readable?

8. Ms. Aaron wrote to Siegrist: "I hope you agree that the suggested changes would make your essay even clearer and more readable then it already is. Of course, the decisions on revision are yours to make." And Siegrist comments: "The comments I did not use were the ones that I felt did not express my

ideas in the context I had intended." Which editing suggestions did Siegrist choose not to use? Find specific examples. Do you agree with his decisions?

9. Which of Aaron's comments did you find most helpful? What did you learn about reading, writing, and revising from studying Aaron's comments on Siegrist's essay?

10. Imagine that you are a professional editor preparing Siegrist's essay for publication. Are there any more changes that you would make? Annotate Siegrist's revised essay, as Aaron did with the original essay, explaining the changes you think are necessary and offering possible solutions. Also write a letter to Siegrist telling him what the strengths of his revision are and what still needs to be done.

IN THE COMPANY
OF OTHER WRITERS

Part VII

MICHAEL J. ARLEN

Michael J. Arlen approaches Thanksgiving with the unique qualifications of having been born in London, the son of a well-known Anglo-Armenian writer, and educated at St. Paul's School in Concord, New Hampshire. After receiving his B.A. degree from Harvard in 1952, Arlen spent four years as a reporter for Life *magazine. In 1957 he became a contributor to and television critic for* The New Yorker, *a job he has continued to hold for nearly thirty years.*

Arlen has twice served as a juror for the Columbia University-Dupont awards for broadcast journalism, and as a faculty member at the Breadloaf Writers' Conference. He received an award for television criticism from the Screen Directors Guild in 1968. He is the author of eight books, from Living-Room War *in 1969 to* Say Goodbye to Sam *in 1984.* Passage to Ararat *(1975), Arlen's story of his pilgrimage to Soviet Armenia in search of his roots, won the 1976 National Book Award for contemporary affairs. "Ode to Thanksgiving" was first printed in* The New Yorker *in 1978 and was reprinted in Arlen's* The Camera Age: Essays on Television *(1981).*

Ode to Thanksgiving

It is time, at last, to speak the truth about Thanksgiving, and the truth is   1
this. Thanksgiving is really not such a terrific holiday. Consider the traditional symbols of the event: Dried cornhusks hanging on the door! Terrible wine! Cranberry jelly in little bowls of extremely doubtful provenance which everyone is required to handle with the greatest of care! Consider the participants, the merrymakers: men and women (also children) who have survived passably well throughout the years, mainly as a result of living at considerable distances from their dear parents and beloved siblings, who on this feast of feasts must apparently forgather (as if beckoned by an aberrant Fairy Godmother), usually by circuitous routes, through heavy traffic, at a common meeting place, where the very moods, distempers, and obtrusive personal habits that have kept them all happily apart since adulthood are then and there encouraged to slowly ferment beneath the cornhusks, and gradually rise with the aid of the terrible wine, and finally burst forth out of control under the stimulus of the cranberry jelly! No, it is a mockery of a holiday. For instance: *Thank you, O Lord, for what we are about to receive.* This is surely not a gala concept. There are no presents, unless one counts Aunt Bertha's sweet rolls a present, which no one does. There is precious little in the way of costumery: miniature plastic turkeys and those witless Pilgrim hats. There is no sex. Indeed, Thanksgiving is the

one day of the year (a fact known to everybody) when all thoughts of sex completely vanish, evaporating from apartments, houses, condominiums, and mobile homes like steam from a bathroom mirror.

Consider also the nowhereness of the time of year: the last week or so in November. It is obviously not yet winter: winter, with its death-dealing blizzards and its girls in tiny skirts pirouetting on the ice. On the other hand, it is certainly not much use to anyone as fall: no golden leaves or Oktoberfests, and so forth. Instead, it is a no-man's-land between the seasons. In the cold and sobersides northern half of the country, it is a vaguely unsettling interregnum of long, mournful walks beneath leafless trees: the long, mournful walks following the midday repast with the dread inevitability of pie following turkey, and the leafless trees looming or standing about like eyesores, and the ground either as hard as iron or slightly mushy, and the light snow always beginning to fall when one is halfway to the old green gate — flecks of cold, watery stuff plopping between neck and collar, for the reason that, it being not yet winter, one has forgotten or not chosen to bring along a muffler. It is a corollary to the long, mournful Thanksgiving walk that the absence of this muffler is quickly noticed and that four weeks or so later, at Christmastime, instead of the Sony Betamax one had secretly hoped the children might have chipped in to purchase, one receives another muffler: by then the thirty-third. Thirty-three mufflers! Some walk! Of course, things are more fun in the warm and loony southern part of the country. No snow there of any kind. No need of mufflers. Also, no long, mournful walks, because in the warm and loony southern part of the country everybody drives. So everybody drives over to Uncle Jasper's house to watch the Cougars play the Gators, a not entirely unimportant conflict which will determine whether the Gators get a Bowl bid or must take another postseason exhibition tour of North Korea. But no sooner do the Cougars kick off (an astonishing end-over-end squiggly thing that floats lazily above the arena before plummeting down toward K. C. McCoy and catching him on the helmet) than Auntie Em starts hustling turkey. Soon Cousin May is slamming around the bowls and platters, and Cousin Bernice is oohing and ahing about "all the fixin's," and Uncle Bob is making low, insincere sounds of appreciation: "Yummy, yummy, Auntie Em, I'll have me some more of these delicious yams!" Delicious yams? Uncle Bob's eyes roll wildly in his head. Billy Joe Quaglino throws his long bomb in the middle of Grandpa Morris saying grace, Grandpa Morris speaking so low nobody can hear him, which is just as well, since he is reciting what he can remember of his last union contract. And then, just as J. B. (Speedy) Snood begins his ninety-two-yard punt return, Auntie Em starts dealing everyone second helpings of her famous stuffing, as if she were pushing a controlled substance, which it well might be, since there are no easily recognizable ingredients visible to the naked eye.

Consider for a moment the Thanksgiving meal itself. It has become a sort 3 of refuge for endangered species of starch: cauliflower, turnips, pumpkin, mince (whatever "mince" is), those blessed yams. Bowls of luridly colored yams, with no taste at all, lying torpid under a lava flow of marshmallow! And then the sacred turkey. One might as well try to construct a holiday repast around a fish — say, a nice piece of boiled haddock. After all, turkey tastes very similar to haddock: same consistency, same quite remarkable absence of flavor. But then, if the Thanksgiving *pièce de résistance* were a nice piece of boiled haddock instead of turkey, there wouldn't be all that fun for Dad when Mom hands him the sterling-silver, bone-handled carving set (a wedding present from her parents and not sharpened since) and then everyone sits around pretending not to watch while he saws and tears away at the bird as if he were trying to burrow his way into or out of some grotesque, fowl-like prison.

What of the good side to Thanksgiving, you ask. There is always a good 4 side to everything. Not to Thanksgiving. There is only a bad side and then a worse side. For instance, Grandmother's best linen tablecloth is a bad side: the fact that it is produced each year, in the manner of a red flag being produced before a bull, and then is always spilled upon by whichever child is doing poorest at school that term and so is in need of greatest reassurance. Thus: "Oh, my God, *Veronica*, you just spilled grape juice [or plum wine or tar] on Grandmother's best linen tablecloth!" But now comes worse. For at this point Cousin Bill, the one who lost all Cousin Edwina's money on the car dealership three years ago and has apparently been drinking steadily since Halloween, bizarrely chooses to say: "Seems to me those old glasses are always falling over." To which Auntie Meg is heard to add: "Somehow I don't remember receivin' any of those old glasses." To which Uncle Fred replies: "That's because you and George decided to go on vacation to Hawaii the summer Grandpa Sam was dying." Now Grandmother is sobbing, though not so uncontrollably that she can refrain from murmuring: "I think that volcano painting I threw away by mistake got sent me from Hawaii, heaven knows why." But the gods are merciful, even the Pilgrim-hatted god of cornhusks and soggy stuffing, and there is an end to everything, even to Thanksgiving. Indeed, there is a grandeur to the feelings of finality and doom which usually settle on a house after the Thanksgiving celebration is over, for with the completion of Thanksgiving Day the year itself has been properly terminated: shot through the cranium with a high-velocity candied yam. At this calendrical nadir, all energy on the planet has gone, all fun has fled, all the terrible wine has been drunk.

But then, overnight, life once again begins to stir, emerging, even by the 5
next morning, in the form of Japanese window displays and Taiwanese Christmas lighting, from the primeval ooze of the nation's department stores. Thus,
a new year dawns, bringing with it immediate and cheering possibilities of
extended consumer debt, office-party flirtations, good—or, at least, mediocre
—wine, and visions of Supersaver excursion fares to Montego Bay. It is worth
noting, perhaps, that this true new year always starts with the same mute,
powerful mythic ceremony: the surreptitious tossing out, in the early morning,
of all those horrid aluminum-foil packages of yams and cauliflower and stuffing
and red, gummy cranberry substance which have been squeezed into the refrigerator as if a reenactment of the siege of Paris were shortly expected. Soon
afterward, the phoenix of Christmas can be observed as it slowly rises, beating
its drumsticks, once again goggle-eyed with hope and unrealistic expectations.

QUESTIONS FOR READING AND REVISING

1. Thanksgiving is a uniquely American holiday and the most widely observed
   holiday in the United States. Like most holidays, it commemorates a past event
   that represents values still held today. Imagine that you are a foreigner with
   no information about Thanksgiving except Arlen's essay. What particular symbols and rituals mentioned here might help you deduce the values this holiday
   represents? What important clues has Arlen left out?

2. Arlen's title, "Ode To Thanksgiving," is an ironic contradiction of the thesis
   expressed in his second sentence: "Thanksgiving is really not such a terrific
   holiday." Later he goes further: "No, it is a mockery of a holiday." On the
   basis of the criticism that follows, how would Arlen define a "real" or "good"
   holiday? Is his definition ironic or serious? What is Arlen really criticizing in
   this essay?

3. Arlen makes his case against Thanksgiving by describing specific objects and
   events that are recognizable, although not necessarily personally familiar, to
   all of us. His strategy is similar to that of a playwright or short-story writer who
   uses a specific setting, props, characters, and plot to convey ideas with wider
   relevance. Which of these elements in Arlen's essay could only apply to
   Thanksgiving? Which ones could appear in an essay on some other holiday?
   What aspects of Thanksgiving make it a better target for this type of attack
   than, say, Halloween or Christmas?

4. As a dramatist Arlen draws his audience into his story, but as an essayist he
   keeps a distance between himself and his audience, continually reminding them
   that their role is to evaluate data presented in support of an argument. How

does Arlen address the reader directly without using the personal *I, we,* or *you?* What other tactics does he use to encourage readers to play the role of observer rather than participant?

5. Arlen's majestic opening sentence alerts his audience that exaggeration is likely to be an important part of his humor throughout this essay. What other exaggerations, both large and small, help Arlen to make his points? What words besides *all* and *none* does he use to create a false impression of universality?

6. Another of Arlen's humorous tactics is contrast. What observations contribute to his overall contrast between the outward richness of a Thanksgiving celebration and its inward sparseness? What incongruous images sharpen the reader's sense of contrast? What kind of contrast is set up by Arlen's alternation at certain points in his essay between active and passive verbs?

QUESTIONS ON CONNECTIONS

1. Sandra Casillas's essay "Cha-No-Yu, the Japanese Tea Ceremony" (p. 47), like Michael Arlen's "Ode to Thanksgiving," describes a traditional event that is unique to a particular culture. What values represented by the Japanese tea ceremony are similar to those of the ideal American Thanksgiving? What aspects of the Japanese ritual are likely to prevent it from ever becoming the kind of "mockery of a holiday" depicted by Arlen? In what ways does Casillas's tea ceremony resemble Arlen's Thanksgiving? How do these resemblances reflect a similarity or contrast in the essays' themes?

2. Casillas's essay, like Arlen's, gives us a vivid sensory picture of an event with the help of a specific setting, props, characters, and plot. How is Casillas's purpose different from Arlen's? How do these two authors use similar stylistic techniques in different ways to achieve different results?

SUGGESTIONS FOR WRITING

1. Michael Arlen's comments about Thanksgiving point up the frequent disparity between the values we as Americans believe in and the values we live by. Thanksgiving is by no means the only occasion when people gather out of regard for tradition, family feeling, religious commitment, or patriotism, only to find the actual festivities centering on food, football, presents, the luxury of a long weekend, a chance to catch up on work, or some other unrelated motive. Choosing an example from your own experience — such as a birthday, anniversary, wedding, holiday, or vacation — write an essay showing how the theoretical focus of a celebration can differ from the actual focus.

2. In "Ode to Thanksgiving," Arlen uses specific symbols (cornhusks, cranberry jelly, plastic turkeys and Pilgrim hats, the carving ceremony, the after-dinner walk) to talk about a complex ritual. Because his audience is already familiar with his topic, Arlen can be highly selective in his choice of symbols, singling out those that will stimulate his readers' negative memories of their own Thanksgivings. In contrast, in "Cha-No-Yu, the Japanese Tea Ceremony," Sandra Casillas chooses her symbols for representative accuracy. Though her purpose is also to create a mood, that mood is inherent in the tea ceremony; Casillas must give us as full a picture as possible. Think of a popular social ritual that interests you—a school dance, a religious ceremony, a rock concert, or a TV awards ceremony, for example. Directing your essay at an audience that either is or is not familiar with it, describe this social ritual in a way that conveys your attitude toward it.

3. Michael Arlen's essay on Thanksgiving takes a humorous approach to a subject usually viewed seriously. Using techniques such as irony, exaggeration, and contrast, write about a phenomenon in modern American life that could benefit from being considered humorously.

CAROLINE BIRD

Caroline Bird wrote "College Is a Waste of Time and Money" out of her experience on both sides of the desk, having attended Vassar College, the University of Toledo, and the University of Wisconsin before serving some forty years later as Froman Distinguished Professor at Russell Sage College and Mather Professor at Case Western Reserve University. The author of nine books and numerous articles, Bird is known as a patient, painstaking researcher with what one critic has called "a far-out feminist vision of the future." In 1968 Gloria Steinem remarked in the New York Times Book Review *that the last chapter of Bird's* Born Female, *entitled "The Case for Equality," "should be sent to all the Presidential candidates just to shake up their thinking."*

Born in New York City in 1915, Bird received her master's degree at the age of twenty-four, after which she spent several years as an editor and researcher for the New York Journal of Commerce, Newsweek, *and* Fortune. *From journalism she jumped to a twenty-year stint in public relations. In 1968, with two books to her credit, she turned to writing full-time, with periodic pauses for teaching and lecturing. Bird and her husband, also a writer, have conquered some of the problems of combining home and work, which are chronicled in her 1979 book,* The Two-Paycheck Marriage. *"Jobs can fit people," she assured an audience of managerial and professional women, with the confidence of one whose own life is the proof. "We can do it if we really try."*

"College Is a Waste of Time and Money" comes from Bird's 1975 book, The Case Against College.

College Is a Waste
of Time and Money

A great majority of our nine million college students are not in school 1 because they want to be or because they want to learn. They are there because it has become the thing to do or because college is a pleasant place to be; because it's the only way they can get parents or taxpayers to support them without working at a job they don't like; because Mother wanted them to go, or some other reason entirely irrelevant to the course of studies for which college is supposedly organized.

As I crisscross the United States lecturing on college campuses, I am dis- 2 mayed to find that professors and administrators, when pressed for a candid opinion, estimate that no more than 25 percent of their students are turned on by classwork. For the rest, college is at best a social center or aging vat, and at worst a young folks' home or even a prison that keeps them out of the mainstream of economic life for a few more years.

The premise — which I no longer accept — that college is the best place for   3
all high-school graduates grew out of a noble American ideal. Just as the United
States was the first nation to aspire to teach every small child to read and
write, so, during the 1950s, we became the first and only great nation to aspire
to higher education for all. During the '60s, we damned the expense and built
great state university systems as fast as we could. And adults — parents, employers, high-school counselors — began to push, shove, and cajole youngsters
to "get an education."

It became a mammoth industry, with taxpayers footing more than half the   4
bill. By 1970, colleges and universities were spending more than 30 billion
dollars annually. But still only half our high-school graduates were going on.
According to estimates made by the economist Fritz Machlup, if we had been
educating every young person until age 22 in that year of 1970, the bill for
higher education would have reached 47.5 billion dollars, 12.5 billion more
than the total corporate profits for the year.

Figures such as these have begun to make higher education for all look   5
financially prohibitive, particularly now when colleges are squeezed by the
pressures of inflation and a drop-off in the growth of their traditional market.

Predictable demography has caught up with the university empire builders.   6
Now that the record crop of postwar babies has graduated from college, the
rate of growth of the student population has begun to decline. To keep their
mammoth plants financially solvent, many institutions have begun to use hard-
sell, Madison-Avenue techniques to attract students. They sell college like
soap, promoting features they think students want: innovative programs, an
environment conducive to meaningful personal relationships, and a curriculum
so free that it doesn't sound like college at all.

Pleasing the customers is something new for college administrators. Colleges   7
have always known that most students don't like to study, and that at least
part of the time they are ambivalent about college, but before the student riots
of the 1960s educators never thought it either right or necessary to pay any
attention to student feelings. But when students rebelling against the Vietnam
war and the draft discovered they could disrupt a campus completely, administrators had to act on some student complaints. Few understood that the
protests had tapped the basic discontent with college itself, a discontent that
did not go away when the riots subsided.

Today students protest individually rather than in concert. They turn in-   8
ward and withdraw from active participation. They drop out to travel to India
or to feed themselves on subsistence farms. Some refuse to go to college at all.
Most, of course, have neither the funds nor the self-confidence for constructive

articulation of their discontent. They simply hang around college unhappily and reluctantly.

All across the country, I have been overwhelmed by the prevailing sadness 9 on American campuses. Too many young people speak little, and then only in drowned voices. Sometimes the mood surfaces as diffidence, wariness, or coolness, but whatever its form, it looks like a defense mechanism, and that rings a bell. This is the way it used to be with women, and just as society had systematically damaged women by insisting that their proper place was in the home, so we may be systematically damaging 18 year-olds by insisting that their proper place is in college.

Campus watchers everywhere know what I mean when I say students are 10 sad, but they don't agree on the reason for it. During the Vietnam war some ascribed the sadness to the draft; now others blame affluence or say it has something to do with permissive upbringing.

Not satisfied with any of these explanations, I looked for some answers with 11 the journalistic tools of my trade — scholarly studies, economic analyses, the historical record, the opinions of the especially knowledgeable, conversations with parents, professors, college administrators, and employers, all of whom spoke as alumni too. Mostly I learned from my interviews with hundreds of young people on and off campuses all over the country.

My unnerving conclusion is that students are sad because they are not 12 needed. Somewhere between the nursery and the employment office, they become unwanted adults. No one has anything in particular against them. But no one knows what to do with them either. We already have too many people in the world of the 1970s, and there is no room for so many newly minted 18-year-olds. So we temporarily get them out of the way by sending them to college where in fact only a few belong.

To make it more palatable, we fool ourselves into believing that we are 13 sending them there for their own best interests, and that it's good for them, like spinach. Some, of course, learn to like it, but most wind up preferring green peas.

Educators admit as much. Nevitt Sanford, distinguished student of higher 14 education, says students feel they are "capitulating to a kind of voluntary servitude." Some of them talk about their time in college as if it were a sentence to be served. I listened to a 1970 Mount Holyoke graduate: "For two years I was really interested in science, but in my junior and senior years I just kept saying, 'I've done two years; I'm going to finish.' When I got out I made up my mind that I wasn't going to school anymore because so many of my courses had been bullshit."

But bad as it is, college is often preferable to a far worse fate. It is better 15 than the drudgery of an uninspiring nine-to-five job, and better than doing nothing when no jobs are available. For some young people, it is a graceful way to get away from home and become independent without losing the financial support of their parents. And sometimes it is the only alternative to an intolerable home situation.

It is difficult to assess how many students are in college reluctantly. The 16 conservative Carnegie Commission estimates from 5 to 30 percent. Sol Linowitz, who was once chairman of a special committee on campus tension of the American Council on Education, found that "a significant number were not happy with their college experience because they felt they were there only in order to get the 'ticket to the big show' rather than to spend the years as productively as they otherwise could."

Older alumni will identify with Richard Baloga, a policeman's son, who 17 stayed in school even though he "hated it" because he thought it would do him some good. But fewer students each year feel this way. Daniel Yankelovich has surveyed undergraduate attitudes for a number of years, and reported in 1971 that 74 percent thought education was "very important." But just two years earlier, 80 percent thought so.

The doubters don't mind speaking up. Leon Lefkowitz, chairman of the 18 department of social studies at Central High School in Valley Stream, New York, interviewed 300 college students at random, and reports that 200 of them didn't think that the education they were getting was worth the effort. "In two years I'll pick up a diploma," said one student, "and I can honestly say it was a waste of my father's bread."

Nowadays, says one sociologist, you don't have to have a reason for going 19 to college; it's an institution. His definition of an institution is an arrangement everyone accepts without question; the burden of proof is not on why you go, but why anyone thinks there might be a reason for not going. The implication is that an 18-year-old is too young and confused to know what he wants to do, and that he should listen to those who know best and go to college.

I don't agree. I believe that college has to be judged not on what other 20 people think is good for students, but on how good it feels to the students themselves.

I believe that people have an inside view of what's good for them. If a child 21 doesn't want to go to school some morning, better let him stay at home, at least until you find out why. Maybe he knows something you don't. It's the same with college. If high-school graduates don't want to go, or if they don't want to go right away, they may perceive more clearly than their elders that college is not for them. It is no longer obvious that adolescents are best off studying a core curriculum that was constructed when all educated men could agree on what made them educated, or that professors, advisors, or parents can be of any particular help to young people in choosing a major or a career. High-school graduates see college graduates driving cabs and decide it's not worth going. College students find no intellectual stimulation in their studies and drop out.

If students believe that college isn't necessarily good for them, you can't 22 expect them to stay on for the general good of mankind. They don't go to school to beat the Russians to Jupiter, improve the national defense, increase the GNP, or create a new market for the arts—to mention some of the benefits taxpayers are supposed to get for supporting higher education.

Nor should we expect to bring about social equality by putting all young 23 people through four years of academic rigor. At best, it's a roundabout and expensive way to narrow the gap between the highest and lowest in our society anyway. At worst, it is unconsciously elitist. Equalizing opportunity through universal higher education subjects the whole population to the intellectual mode natural only to a few. It violates the fundamental egalitarian principle of respect for the differences between people.

Of course, most parents aren't thinking of the "higher" good at all. They 24 send their children to college because they are convinced young people benefit financially from those four years of higher education. But if money is the only goal, college is the dumbest investment you can make. I say this because a young banker in Poughkeepsie, New York, Stephen G. Necel, used a computer to compare college as an investment with other investments available in 1974, and college did not come out on top.

For the sake of argument, the two of us invented a young man whose rich 25 uncle gave him, in cold cash, the cost of a four-year education at any college he chose, but the young man didn't have to spend the money on college. After bales of computer paper, we had our mythical student write to his uncle: "Since you said I could spend the money foolishly if I wished, I am going to blow it all on Princeton."

The much respected financial columnist Sylvia Porter echoed the common 26 assumption when she said last year, "A college education is among the very best investments you can make in your entire life." But the truth is not quite so rosy, even if we assume that the Census Bureau is correct when it says that as of 1972, a man who completed four years of college would expect to earn $199,000 more between the ages of 22 and 64 than a man who had only a high-school diploma.

If a 1972 Princeton-bound high-school graduate had put the $34,181 that 27 his four years of college would have cost him into a savings bank at 7.5 percent interest compounded daily, he would have had at age 64 a total of $1,129,200, or $528,200 more than the earnings of a male college graduate, and more than five times as much as the $199,000 extra the more educated man could expect to earn between 22 and 64.

The big advantage of getting your college money in cash now is that you 28 can invest it in something that has a higher return than a diploma. For instance, a Princeton-bound high-school graduate of 1972 who liked fooling around with cars could have banked his $34,181, and gone to work at the local garage at close to $1,000 more per year than the average high-school graduate. Meanwhile, as he was learning to be an expert auto mechanic, his money would be ticking away in the bank. When he became 28, he would have earned $7,199 less on his job from age 22 to 28 than his college-educated friend, but he would have had $73,113 in his passbook — enough to buy out his boss, go into the used-car business, or acquire his own new-car dealership. If successful in business, he could expect to make more than the average college graduate. And if he had the brains to get into Princeton, he would be just as likely to make money without the four years spent on campus. Unfortunately, few college-bound high-school graduates get the opportunity to bank such a large sum of money and then wait for it to make them rich. And few parents are sophisticated enough to understand that in financial returns alone, their children would be better off with the money than with the education.

Rates of return and dollar signs on education are fascinating brain teasers, 29 but obviously there is a certain unreality to the game. Quite aside from the noneconomic benefits of college, and these should loom larger once the dollars are cleared away, there are grave difficulties in assigning a dollar value to college at all.

In fact there is no real evidence that the higher income of college graduates 30 is due to college. College may simply attract people who are slated to earn more money anyway; those with higher IQs, better family backgrounds, a more enterprising temperament. No one who has wrestled with the problem is prepared to attribute all of the higher income to the impact of college itself.

Christopher Jencks, author of *Inequality*, a book that assesses the effect of 31 family and schooling in America, believes that education in general accounts for less than half of the difference in income in the American population. "The biggest single source of income differences," writes Jencks, "seems to be the fact that men from high-status families have higher incomes than men from low-status families even when they enter the same occupations, have the same amount of education, and have the same test scores."

Jacob Mincer of the National Bureau of Economic Research and Colum- 32 bia University states flatly that of "20 to 30 percent of students at any level, the additional schooling has been a waste, at least in terms of earnings." College fails to work its income-raising magic for almost a third of those who go. More than half of those people in 1972 who earned $15,000 or more reached that comfortable bracket without the benefit of a college diploma. Jencks says that financial success in the U.S. depends a good deal on luck, and the most sophisticated regression analyses have yet to demonstrate otherwise.

But most of today's students don't go to college to earn more money anyway. 33 In 1968, when jobs were easy to get, Daniel Yankelovich made his first nationwide survey of students. Sixty-five percent of them said they "would welcome less emphasis on money." By 1973, when jobs were scarce, that figure jumped to 80 percent.

The young are not alone. Americans today are all looking less to the pay 34 of a job than to the work itself. They want "interesting" work that permits them "to make a contribution," express themselves" and "use their special abilities," and they think college will help them find it.

Jerry Darring of Indianapolis knows what it is to make a dollar. He worked 35 with his father in the family plumbing business, on the line at Chevrolet, and in the Chrysler foundry. He quit these jobs to enter Wright State University in Dayton, Ohio, because "in a job like that a person only has time to work, and after that he's so tired that he can't do anything else but come home and go to sleep."

Jerry came to college to find work "helping people." And he is perfectly 36 willing to spend the dollars he earns at dull, well-paid work to prepare for lower-paid work that offers the reward of service to others.

Jerry's case is not unusual. No one works for money alone. In order to deal 37 with the nonmonetary rewards of work, economists have coined the concept of "psychic income," which according to one economic dictionary means "income that is reckoned in terms of pleasure, satisfaction, or general feelings of euphoria."

Psychic income is primarily what college students mean when they talk 38 about getting a good job. During the most affluent years of the late 1960s and early 1970s college students told their placement officers that they wanted to be researchers, college professors, artists, city planners, social workers, poets, book publishers, archeologists, ballet dancers, or authors.

The psychic income of these and other occupations popular with students 39 is so high that these jobs can be filled without offering high salaries. According to one study, 93 percent of urban university professors would choose the same vocation again if they had the chance, compared with only 16 percent of unskilled auto workers. Even though the monetary gap between college professor and auto worker is now surprisingly small, the difference in psychic income is enormous.

But colleges fail to warn students that jobs of these kinds are hard to come 40 by, even for qualified applicants, and they rarely accept the responsibility of helping students choose a career that will lead to a job. When a young person says he is interested in helping people, his counselor tells him to become a psychologist. But jobs in psychology are scarce. The Department of Labor, for instance, estimates there will be 4,300 new jobs for psychologists in 1975 while colleges are expected to turn out 58,430 B.A.s in psychology that year.

Of thirty psych majors who reported back to Vassar what they were doing 41 a year after graduation in 1973, only five had jobs in which they could possibly use their courses in psychology, and two of these were working for Vassar.

The outlook isn't much better for students majoring in other psychic-pay 42 disciplines: sociology, English, journalism, anthropology, forestry, education. Whatever college graduates want to do, most of them are going to wind up doing what there is to do.

John Shingleton, director of placement at Michigan State University, ac- 43 cuses the academic community of outright hypocrisy. "Educators have never said, 'Go to college and get a good job,' but this has been implied, and now students expect it. . . . If we care what happens to students after college, then let's get involved with what should be one of the basic purposes of education: career preparation."

In the 1970s, some of the more practical professors began to see that jobs 44 for graduates meant jobs for professors too. Meanwhile, students themselves reacted to the shrinking job market, and a "new vocationalism" exploded on campus. The press welcomed the change as a return to the ethic of achievement and service. Students were still idealistic, the reporters wrote, but they now saw that they could best make the world better by healing the sick as physicians or righting individual wrongs as lawyers.

But there are no guarantees in these professions either. The American 45 Enterprise Institute estimated in 1971 that there would be more than the target ratio of 100 doctors for every 100,000 people in the population by 1980. And the odds are little better for would-be lawyers. Law schools are already graduating twice as many new lawyers every year as the Department of Labor thinks will be needed, and the oversupply is growing every year.

And it's not at all apparent that what is actually learned in a "professional" 46 education is necessary for success. Teachers, engineers, and others I talked to said they find that on the job they rarely use what they learned in school. In order to see how well college prepared engineers and scientists for actual paid work in their fields, The Carnegie Commission queried all the employees with degrees in these fields in two large firms. Only one in five said the work they were doing bore a "very close relationship" to their college studies, while almost a third saw "very little relationship at all." An overwhelming majority could think of many people who were doing their same work, but had majored in different fields.

Majors in nontechnical fields report even less relationship between their 47 studies and their jobs. Charles Lawrence, a communications major in college and now the producer of "Kennedy & Co.," the Chicago morning television show, says, "You have to learn all that stuff and you never use it again. I learned my job doing it." Others employed as architects, nurses, teachers, and other members of the so-called learned professions report the same thing.

Most college administrators admit that they don't prepare their graduates 48 for the job market. "I just wish I had the guts to tell parents that when you get out of this place you aren't prepared to do anything," the academic head of a famous liberal-arts college told us. Fortunately, for him, most people believe that you don't have to defend a liberal-arts education on those grounds. A liberal-arts education is supposed to provide you with a value system, a standard, a set of ideas, not a job. "Like Christianity, the liberal arts are seldom practiced and would probably be hated by the majority of the populace if they were," said one defender.

The analogy is apt. The fact is, of course, that the liberal arts are a religion 49 in every sense of that term. When people talk about them, their language becomes elevated, metaphorical, extravagant, theoretical and reverent. And faith in personal salvation by the liberal arts is professed in a creed intoned on ceremonial occasions such as commencements.

If the liberal arts are a religious faith, the professors are its priests. But 50 disseminating ideas in a four-year college curriculum is slow and most expensive. If you want to learn about Milton, Camus, or even Margaret Mead you can find them in paperback books, the public library, and even on television.

And when most people talk about the value of a college education, they 51 are not talking about great books. When at Harvard commencement, the president welcomes the new graduates into "the fellowship of educated men and women," what he could be saying is, "Here is a piece of paper that is a passport to jobs, power, and instant prestige." As Glenn Bassett, a personnel specialist at G.E. says, "In some parts of G.E., a college degree appears completely irrelevant to selection to, say, a manager's job. In most, however, it is a ticket of admission."

But now that we have doubled the number of young people attending col- 52 lege, a diploma cannot guarantee even that. The most charitable conclusion we can reach is that college probably has very little, if any, effect on people and things at all. Today, the false premises are easy to see:

First, college doesn't make people intelligent, ambitious, happy, or liberal. 53 It's the other way around. Intelligent, ambitious, happy, liberal people are attracted to higher education in the first place.

Second, college can't claim much credit for the learning experiences that 54 really change students while they are there. Jobs, friends, history, and most of all the sheer passage of time, have as big an impact as anything even indirectly related to the campus.

Third, colleges have changed so radically that a freshman entering in the 55 fall of 1974 can't be sure to gain even the limited value research studies assigned to colleges in the '60s. The sheer size of undergraduate campuses of the 1970s makes college even less stimulating now than it was 10 years ago. Today even motivated students are disappointed with their college courses and professors.

Finally, a college diploma no longer opens as many vocational doors. Em- 56 ployers are beginning to realize that when they pay extra for someone with a diploma, they are paying only for an empty credential. The fact is that most of the work for which employers now expect college training is now or has been capably done in the past by people without higher educations.

College, then, may be a good place for those few young people who are 57 really drawn to academic work, who would rather read than eat, but it has become too expensive, in money, time, and intellectual effort to serve as a holding pen for large numbers of our young. We ought to make it possible for those reluctant, unhappy students to find alternative ways of growing up and more realistic preparation for the years ahead.

QUESTIONS FOR READING AND REVISING

1. Beginning in her first paragraph and continuing throughout her essay, Bird mentions various "wrong" reasons why students attend college. What reasons, if any, does she identify as the "right" ones? How significant to her is the difference between being "in school" (paragraph 1), "getting an education" (paragraph 3), and "picking up a diploma" (paragraph 18)? Explain whether this distinction has to do more with values and ideals or with practicality.

2. In paragraph 7, Bird says of the antiwar protests in the late 1960s. "Few understood that the protests had tapped the basic discontent with college itself." What evidence does she present to support this idea of a fundamental incompatibility between students and college? Does her point seem to be that college

should not exist at all, as her essay's title suggests, or that students, administrators, and parents approach it with false expectations? Explain.

3. Bird *describes* college in paragraph 2 as "at worst a young folks' home or even a prison that keeps them out of the mainstream of economic life for a few more years." In the next paragraph she refers to "the premise . . . that college is the best place for all high-school graduates." What other comments in her essay indicate that Bird's objections to college relate specifically to four-year undergraduate degree programs aimed at young people entering straight from high school? How do you imagine her criticisms would change if she wrote about alternatives such as evening classes for working adults? two-year vocational schools? work-study programs?

4. In paragraph 11, Bird *describes* how she did the research that led to this essay. Which of these sources and types of information has she used most extensively? Which are most persuasive? How might her use of *evidence* have been different if she were a scholar or educator writing for a professional publication instead of a journalist addressing a general audience?

5. Bird uses a number of phrases that reflect her *thesis*, such as "students . . . hang around college" (paragraph 8); "we get them out of the way by sending them to college" (paragraph 12); "bad as it is, college is often preferable to a far worse fate" (paragraph 15). How do Bird's word choices affect your acceptance of the points she is making? What other examples of language can you find that reinforce her views about college and college students?

6. Bird addresses her readers both with the narrator's *I* and with a *we* that includes narrator and readers. What role do *we* play in this essay? Is it an active or a passive role? How does Bird imply that *we* should feel proud of ourselves? guilty? uninvolved? Based on Bird's first-person-plural statements, describe the *we* in this essay as an actual segment of the American population. Does that population segment include you?

QUESTIONS ON CONNECTIONS

1. Amber Kennish's essay, "Three Rounds with Dad" (p. 133), takes Caroline Bird's essay as its starting point. In her third paragraph, Kennish says, ". . . having brought forth every valid point in Bird's essay. . . ." Has Kennish in fact used all of Bird's valid points? Which does Kennish emphasize? If you were the protagonist in Kennish's fight with her dad, how would you present Bird's position differently? What counterarguments do you think Bird herself would make to her dad's winning punches?

2. A striking difference between Kennish's essay and Bird's is that Kennish presents a two-sided *argument*, whereas Bird emphasizes only her own case. How does

each writer's *purpose* influence the form, the argument, and the *evidence* each chooses to use — and not to use?

SUGGESTIONS FOR WRITING

1. Bird's essay is negative rather than positive in *tone* in that she focuses on criticizing the present system of higher education. If Bird had gone on to recommend changes that would cure the problems she diagnoses, what do you think those changes would be? Write an essay proposing solutions to the problems Bird diagnoses and show how your proposal would have a positive effect on individual students and society.

2. "College Is a Waste of Time and Money" was first published in 1975. Bird's *description* of how colleges market themselves to students (paragraph 6) and what students are like (paragraph 8) depicts a situation that existed more than ten years ago. How have the function of college and the needs of students changed since then? Write an argumentative essay that updates Bird's essay based on your own reasons for attending college, your expectations of how your education and your degree will help you in the future, and the relevance of Bird's arguments to college as it exists in the second half of the 1980s.

3. Amber Kennish's *argument* with her father suggests that the value of college may be more evident to someone who has spent twenty or thirty years in the work force than to someone still in school. Caroline Bird, in contrast, asserts that "college has to be judged not on what other people think is good for students, but on how good it feels to the students themselves." Which position do you find more persuasive? Write an argumentative essay defending your view.

PATRICK FENTON

"I've been identified as a working-class writer," muses Patrick Fenton, and adds, "It's not the worst thing that could happen to you." In a 1984 New York Times article he described his boyhood in Brooklyn's Irish tenements: "I slept in the back of our kitchen on the top floor of a cold-water flat. . . . Mice would make scratchy sounds with their nails as they ran across the Formica top of the kitchen table. Some mornings, I would wake up with a cockroach crushed across my shirt like a raisin."

Born in Brooklyn on St. Patrick's Day, 1941, Fenton dropped out of high school at sixteen. Although he had enjoyed reading and writing compositions in grammar school, expressing oneself was viewed as a mark of weakness by the street gangs he hung out with as a teenager, so he went to work in the local waterfront factories. He drove trucks in Manhattan's garment district; he got a job at the World's Fair. At nineteen he joined the army and spent two years in Germany. At twenty-one he signed on as a cargo loader at New York's John F. Kennedy Airport. With a wife and small children to support, Fenton had little time or energy for writing. He contributed a few pieces to the Park Slope News in Brooklyn, where a supportive editor pushed him to do more. His local features attracted the notice of a small magazine editor, who in turn drew the attention of New York magazine to Fenton's writing. The resulting interview led to New York's 1973 publication of "Confessions of a Working Stiff."

"I told [the New York editor] what type of work I was doing," Fenton relates, "and he said, 'Why don't you write a story about that?' It almost wrote itself. It came right out."

Suddenly Patrick Fenton was a writer. Editors wanted to see more of his work. David Susskind featured him on a television show. After eight gritty years as a cargo loader, Fenton quit to take a civil service job and to continue a freelance writing career that has brought him publication in books and periodicals, including Newsday, the New York Daily News, and the New York Times. He has appeared on radio as well as television, and sometimes speaks at schools and colleges. Fenton is determined to pass on to other struggling young writers the encouragement his Brooklyn neighbor, author Pete Hamill, gave him in his early days. He is also finishing the college degree he started under the G.I. Bill—though he has not taken any writing courses. His three years of moonlighting for the Park Slope News taught him to write, revise, and learn from criticism, he says —and to persevere. "Some days the stuff flows nice and easy. Other times I think, 'I'm never going to get this! Where do I get off, telling myself I'm a writer?' But then I sit down and do it."

Confessions of a Working Stiff

The Big Ben is hammering out its 5:45 alarm in the half-dark of another   1
Tuesday morning. If I'm lucky, my car down in the street will kick over for
me. I don't want to think about that now; all I want to do is roll over into
the warm covers that hug my wife. I can hear the wind as it whistles up and
down the sides of the building. Tuesday is always the worst day—it's the day
the drudgery, boredom, and fatigue start all over again. I'm off from work on
Sunday and Monday, so Tuesday is my blue Monday.

I make my living humping cargo for Seaboard World Airlines, one of the   2
big international airlines at Kennedy Airport. They handle strictly all cargo.
I was once told that one of the Rockefellers is the major stockholder for the
airline, but I don't really think about that too much. I don't get paid to think.
The big thing is to beat that race with the time clock every morning of your
life so the airline will be happy. The worst thing a man could ever do is to
make suggestions about building a better airline. They pay people $40,000 a
year to come up with better ideas. It doesn't matter that these ideas never
work; it's just that they get nervous when a guy from South Brooklyn or Ozone
Park acts like he actually has a brain.

I throw a Myadec high-potency vitamin into my mouth to ward off one of   3
the ten colds I get every year from humping mailbags out in the cold rain at
Kennedy. A huge DC-8 stretch jet waits impatiently for the 8,000 pounds of
mail that I will soon feed its empty belly. I wash the Myadec down with some
orange juice and grab a brown bag filled with bologna and cheese. Inside the
lunch bag there is sometimes a silly note from my wife that says, "I Love You
—Guess Who?" It is all that keeps me going to a job that I hate.

I've been going there for seven years now and my job is still the same. It's   4
weary work that makes a man feel used up and worn out. You push and you
pull all day long with your back. You tie down pallets loaded with thousands
of pounds of freight. You fill igloo-shaped containers with hundreds of boxes
that all look the same. If you're assigned to work the warehouse, it's really
your hard luck. This is the job all the men hate most. You stack box upon
box until the pallet resembles the exact shape of the inside of the plane. You
get the same monotonous feeling an adult gets when he plays with a child's
blocks. When you finish one pallet, you find another and start the whole dull
process over again.

The airline pays me $192 a week for this. After they take out taxes and   5
$5.81 for the pension, I go home with $142. Once a month they take out $10
for term life insurance, and $5.50 for union dues. The week they take out the
life insurance is always the worst: I go home with $132. My job will never

change. I will fill up the same igloos with the same boxes for the next 34 years of my life, I will hump the same mailbags into the belly of the plane, and push the same 8,000-pound pallets with my back. I will have to do this until I'm 65 years old. Then I'll be free, if I don't die of a heart attack before that, and the airline will let me retire.

In winter the warehouse is cold and damp. There is no heat. The large steel 6 doors that line the warehouse walls stay open most of the day. In the cold months, wind, rain and snow blow across the floor. In the summer the warehouse becomes an oven. Dust and sand from the runways mix with the toxic fumes of fork lifts, leaving a dry, stale taste in your mouth. The high windows above the doors are covered with a thick, black dirt that kills the sun. The men work in shadows with the constant roar of jet engines blowing dangerously in their ears.

Working the warehouse is a tedious job that leaves a man's mind empty. If 7 he's smart he will spend his days wool-gathering. He will think about pretty girls that he once knew, or some other daydream of warm, dry places where you never had a chill. The worst thing he can do is to think about his problems. If he starts to think about how he is going to pay the mortgage on the $30,000 home that he can't afford, it will bring him down. He will wonder why he comes to the cargo airline every morning of his life, and even on Christmas Day. He will start to wonder why he has to listen to the deafening sound of the jets as they rev up their engines. He will wonder why he crawls on his hands and knees, breaking his back a little bit more every day.

To keep his kids in that great place in the country in the summer, that 8 great place far away from Brooklyn and the South Bronx, he must work every hour of overtime that the airline offers him. If he never turns down an hour, if he works some 600 hours over, he can make about $15,000. To do this he must turn against himself, he must pray that the phone rings in the middle of the night, even though it's snowing out and he doesn't feel like working. He must hump cargo late into the night, eat meatball heroes for supper, drink coffee that starts to taste like oil, and then hope that his car starts when it's time to go home. If he gets sick — well, he better not think about that.

All over Long Island, Ozone Park, Brooklyn, and as far away as the Bronx, 9 men stir in the early morning hours as a new day begins. Every morning is the same as the last. Some of the men drink beer for breakfast instead of coffee. Way out in Bay Shore a cargoman snaps open a can of Budweiser. It's 6 A.M., and he covers the top of the can with his thumb in order to keep down the loud hiss as the beer escapes. He doesn't want to awaken his children as they dream away the morning in the next room. Soon he will swing his Pinto wagon up onto the crowded Long Island Expressway and start the long ride to the job. As he slips the car out of the driveway he tucks another can of beer between his legs.

All the men have something in common: they hate the work they are doing 10 and they drink a little too much. They come to work only to punch a timecard that has their last name on it. At the end of the week they will pick up a paycheck with their last name on it. They will never receive a bonus for a job well done, or even a party. At Christmastime a card from the president of the airline will arrive at each one of their houses. It will say Merry Christmas and have the president's name printed at the bottom of it. They know that the airline will be there long after they are dead. Nothing stops it. It runs nonstop, without sleep, through Christmas Day, New Year's Eve, Martin Luther King's birthday, even the deaths of presidents.

It's seven in the morning and the day shift is starting to drift in. Huge 11 tractors are backing up to the big-mouth doors of the warehouse. Cattle trucks bring tons of beef to feed its insatiable appetite for cargo. Smoke-covered trailers with refrigerated units packed deep with green peppers sit with their diesel engines idling. Names like White, Mack, and Kenworth are welded to the front of their radiators, which hiss and moan from the overload. The men walk through the factory-type gates of the parking lot with their heads bowed, oblivious of the shuddering diesels that await them.

Once inside the warehouse they gather in groups of threes and fours like 12 prisoners in an exercise yard. They stand in front of the two time clocks that hang below a window in the manager's office. They smoke and cough in the early morning hour as they await their work assignments. The manager, a nervous-looking man with a stomach that is starting to push out at his belt, walks out with the pink work sheets in his hand.

Eddie, a young Irishman with a mustache, has just bolted in through the 13 door. The manager has his timecard in his hand, holding it so no one else can hit Eddie in. Eddie is four minutes late by the time clock. His name will now go down in the timekeeper's ledger. The manager hands the card to him with a "you'll be up in the office if you don't straighten out" look. Eddie takes the card, hits it in, and slowly takes his place with the rest of the men. He has been out till four in the morning drinking beer in the bars of Ozone Park; the time clock and the manager could blow up, for all he cares. "Jesus," he says to no one in particular, "I hope to Christ they don't put me in the warehouse this morning."

Over in another group, Kelly, a tall man wearing a navy knit hat, talks to 14 the men. "You know, I almost didn't make it in this morning. I passed this green VW on the Belt Parkway. The girl driving it was singing. Jesus, I thought to myself, it must be great going somewhere at 6:30 in the morning that makes you want to sing." Kelly is smiling as he talks. "I often think, why the hell don't you keep on going, Kelly? Don't get off at the cargo exit, stay on. Go anywhere, even if it's only Brooklyn. Christ, if I was a single man I think I would do just that. Some morning I'd pass this damn place by and drive as far away as Riverhead. I don't know what I'd do when I got there — maybe I'd pick up a pound of beefsteak tomatoes from one of those roadside stands or something."

The men laugh at Kelly but they know he is serious. "I feel the same way 15 sometimes," the man next to him says. "I find myself daydreaming a lot lately; this place drives you to that. I get up in the morning and I just don't want to come to work. I get sick when I hit that parking lot. If it wasn't for the kids and the house I'd quit." The men then talk about how hard it is to get work on "the outside." They mention "outside" as if they were in a prison.

Each morning there is an Army-type roll call from the leads. The leads are 16 foremen who must keep the men moving; If they don't, it could mean their jobs. At one time they had power over the men but as time went by the company took away their little bit of authority. They also lost the deep interest, even enjoyment, for the hard work they once did. As the cargo airline grew, it beat this out of them, leaving only apathy. The ramp area is located in the backyard of the warehouse. This is where the huge jets park to unload their 70,000-pound payloads. A crew of men fall in behind the ramp lead as he mopes out of the warehouse. His long face shows the hopelessness of another day.

A brutal rain has started to beat down on the oil-covered concrete of the 17 ramp as the 306 screeches in off the runway. Its engines scream as they spit off sheets of rain and oil. Two of the men cover their ears as they run to put up a ladder to the front of the plane. The airline will give them ear covers only if they pay for half of them. A lot of men never buy them. If they want, the airline will give them two little plugs free. The plugs don't work and hurt the inside of the ears.

The men will spend the rest of the day in the rain. Some of them will set 18 up conveyor belts and trucks to unload the thousands of pounds of cargo that sit in the deep belly of the plane. Then they will feed the awkward bird until it is full and ready to fly again. They will crawl on their hands and knees in its belly, counting and humping hundreds of mailbags. The rest of the men will work up topside on the plane, pushing 8,000-pound pallets with their backs. Like Egyptians building a pyramid, they will pull and push until the pallet finally gives in and moves like a massive stone sliding through sand. They don't complain too much; they know that when the airline comes up with a better system some of them will go.

The old-timers at the airline can't understand why the younger men stay 19
on. They know what the cargo airline can do to a man. It can work him hard
but make him lazy at the same time. The work comes in spurts. Sometimes a
man will be pushed for three hours of sweat, other times he will just stand
around bored. It's not the hard work that breaks a man at the airline, it's the
boredom of doing the same job over and over again.

At the end of the day the men start to move in off the ramp. The rain is 20
still beating down at their backs but they move slowly. Their faces are red and
raw from the rain-soaked wind that has been snapping at them for eight hours.
The harsh wind moves in from the direction of the city. From the ramp you
can see the Manhattan skyline, gray- and blue-looking, as it peeks up from
the west wall of the warehouse. There is nothing to block the winter weather
as it rolls in like a storm across a prairie. They head down to the locker room,
heads bowed, like a football team that never wins.

With the workday almost over, the men move between the narrow, gray 21
rows of lockers. Up on the dirty walls that surround the lockers someone has
written a couple of four-letter words. There is no wit to the words; they just
say the usual. As they strip off their wet gear the men seem to come alive.

"Hey, Arnie! You want to stay four hours? They're asking for overtime 22
down in Export," one of the men yells over the lockers.

Arnie is sitting about four rows over, taking off his heavy winter clothing. 23
He thinks about this for a second and yells back, "What will we be doing?"

"Working the meat trailer." This means that Arnie will be humping huge 24
sides of beef off rows of hooks for four hours. Blood will drip down onto his
clothes as he struggles to the front of the trailer. Like most of the men, he
needs the extra money and knows that he should stay. He has Master Charge,
Korvettes, Times Square Stores, and Abraham & Straus to pay.

"Nah, I'm not staying tonight. Not if it's working the meat trailer. Don 25
wanted to stop for a few beers at The Owl; maybe I'll stay tomorrow night."

It's four o'clock in the afternoon now—the men have twelve minutes to 26
go before they punch out. The airline has stopped for a few seconds as the
men change shifts. Supervisors move frantically across the floor pushing the
fresh lot of new men who have just started to come in. They hand out work
sheets and yell orders: "Jack, get your men into their rain gear. Put three men
in the bellies to finish off the 300 flight. Get someone on the pepper trailers,
they've been here all morning."

The morning shift stands around the time clock with three minutes to go. 27
Someone says that Kevin Delahunty has just been appointed to the Fire Department. Kevin, a young Irishman from Ozone Park, has been working the
cargo airline for six years. Like most of the men, he has hated every minute
of it. The men are openly proud of him as they reach out to shake his hand.

Kevin has found a job on "the outside." "Ah, you'll be leaving soon," he tells Pat. "I never thought I'd get out of here either, but you'll see, you're going to make it."

The manager moves through the crowd handing out timecards and stops 28 when he comes to Kevin. Someone told him Kevin is leaving. "Is that right, Delahunty? Well I guess we won't expect you in tomorrow, will we? Going to become a fireman, eh? That means you'll be jumping out of windows like a crazy man. Don't act like you did around here," he adds as he walks back to his office.

The time clock hits 4:12 and the men pour out of the warehouse. Kevin 29 will never be back, but the rest of them will return in the morning to grind out another eight hours. Some of them will head straight home to the bills, screaming children, and a wife who tries to understand them. They'll have a Schaefer or two, then they'll settle down to a night of television.

Some of them will start to fill up the cargo bars that surround Kennedy 30 Airport. They will head to places like Gaylor's on Rockaway Boulevard or The Dew Drop Inn down near Farmers Boulevard. They will drink deep glasses of whiskey and cold mugs of Budweiser. The Dew Drop has a honky-tonk mood of the Old West to it. The barmaid moves around like a modern-day Katie Elder. Like Brandy, she's a fine girl, but she can out-curse any cargoman. She wears a low-cut blouse that reveals most of her breasts. The jukebox will beat out some Country & Western as she says, "Ah, hell, you played my song." The cargomen will hoot and holler as she substitutes some of her own obscene lyrics.

They will drink late into the night, forgetting time clocks, Master Charge, 31 First National City, Korvettes, mortgages, cars that don't start, and jet engines that hurt their ears. They will forget about damp, cold warehouses, winters that get longer and colder every year, minutes that drift by like hours, supervisors that harass, and the thought of growing old on a job they hate. At midnight they will fall dangerously into their cars and make their way up onto the Southern State Parkway. As they ride into the dark night of Long Island they will forget it all until 5:45 the next morning—when the Big Ben will start up the whole grind all over again.

QUESTIONS FOR READING AND REVISING

1. Fenton's description of his job as a cargo loader can be viewed as a *cause-and-effect* essay on two levels. First, what are the apparent causes of Fenton's taking this job and planning to stay in it until retirement? Second, looking at the job

as a cause, what are its effects on his life and the lives of his co-workers? If this essay were constructed as an *argument* instead of a combination of cause-and-effect and *description,* what do you think its thesis would be? Would the essay be more or less effective than it is now? Why?

2. This essay is narrated by the author, who speaks mainly in the first person. At what points does he switch to the second person? to the third person? What is the effect of each change? Compare Fenton's *description* of hypothetical workers — singular in paragraphs 7 – 8, plural in paragraphs 9 – 10 — with his description of real co-workers in paragraphs 13 – 15. How do these three different uses of the third person fulfill different functions in the essay?

3. One of the ways Fenton writes about a boring situation without boring his readers is by enriching his account with sensory details. The essay opens with a ringing alarm clock. What other sounds, smells, tastes, and physical sensations add to the vividness of Fenton's description?

4. Another of Fenton's techniques is careful use of language. What words and phrases help him to sound like the "working stiff" of his title? How do the references to men and to women in this essay contribute to its blue-collar tone? What words and phrases reveal that Fenton is more conscious of the effects of language than one might expect a cargo loader to be?

5. In addition to description, Fenton makes extensive use of *illustration,* and *analogy.* Look especially closely at his *similes* and *metaphors*: the airplane's "empty belly" (paragraph 3), "igloo-shaped containers" and "the same monotonous feeling an adult gets when he plays with a child's blocks" (paragraph 4). Find at least six other *figures of speech* in the essay. What is the dominant impression created by each one?

6. Fenton mentions a number of brand names and names of places as well as names of people. What contribution do these names make to his essay? What do they tell you about his characters? What do they imply about Fenton's conception of his probable *audience*?

QUESTIONS ON CONNECTIONS

1. Both Patrick Fenton and Linda Lavelle ("Confessions of a Blue-Collar Worker," p. 144) describe working in tedious jobs for the sake of a paycheck. Both writers mention the different perspectives of young and old workers. Why do you think Lavelle gives more emphasis to this aspect of her essay than Fenton does? What time-related words and phrases strengthen her focus on the transition from youth to age? How does each writer's use of verb tenses suit his or her viewpoint and purpose? What is the effect of Fenton's ending his essay in the future tense, compared with Lavelle's ending hers in the past tense?

2. Lavelle tells her readers several things she learned from working in a factory, most of them unpleasant. How would the impact of Fenton's essay change if he had included Lavelle's lessons in numbers operations, stolen goods, and fights among workers? How would the impact of Lavelle's essay change if she had chosen one of these incidents as her focus instead of giving a general overview of her life at the factory? Taking these two essays as they are, how would you characterize Lavelle's *tone* in comparison with Fenton's? On what evidence do you base your response?

SUGGESTIONS FOR WRITING

1. Fenton dramatizes his plight by giving a vivid, detailed *description* of it. Choose a job you have held, or a role you have played as a member of a sports team, club, or other group that dominated your life while you were in it. Write a *descriptive* essay about what it was like and how it affected you.

2. Fenton and Lavelle both got into boring jobs in order to meet their financial obligations and stayed because they wanted or needed the money. In neither essay does the writer mention any anger or frustration at having made choices that created this financial bind. Write a *cause-and-effect* essay showing how and why people get into such dead-end situations. Emphasize the negative effect on them, their families, and their culture, or ways of avoiding this predicament by recognizing other options, or both.

3. Both Patrick Fenton and Linda Lavelle paint a bleak picture of their jobs, suggesting that everyone involved in such work finds it tedious and dehumanizing. A similar portrait of mass-production work appears in James Taylor's song, "Millworker," which ends: "So may I work the mills just as long as I am able, / And never meet the man whose name is on the label." Imagine that either Fenton or Lavelle *did* meet the owner or a top manager at the place where they work. Presumably, this person knows relatively little about the job itself but views it from a political, historical, social, or economic perspective. Write a *comparison and contrast* essay in which the owner/manager either (a) presents a positive view of the job in opposition to the employee's negative one, or (b) tells the employee how lucky he or she is to work there instead of in some other job that the employer describes as worse.

SAMUEL G. FREEDMAN

The process of learning to write, says Samuel Freedman, occurs in three phases: "One, trying everything — different voices, purple prose — and making mistakes. Two, extreme asceticism — every rule taken to the extreme. I spent two years, for example, eliminating adjectives so I could learn to write without them. Three — and this is the stage all mature writers reach — knowing when to break the rules. If you use the only sentence fragment you've used in three years, it's got to be the perfect time for it. Or that one piece of the vernacular in an otherwise elegant essay — it's got to be just right. It's got to achieve just the right purpose."

Freedman, a staff writer for the New York Times *since 1981, returned to his hometown by a roundabout route. Born in New York in 1955, he majored in journalism and history at the University of Wisconsin at Madison, where he moonlighted as a stringer for the* Milwaukee Journal. *During the summers, Freedman worked for a printer, for the* Courier-News *in Bridgewater, New Jersey, and for the* Minneapolis Star. *After graduating in 1977, he went back to the* Courier-News, *then took a job at the* Suburban Trib, *a supplement of the* Chicago Tribune. *From there he moved to the* New York Times. *He has won various awards for news, feature, and investigative reporting. "Live Aid and the Woodstock Nation" originally appeared in the* New York Times *on July 18, 1985.*

The main thing he's learned in ten years of professional writing, says Freedman, is "the power of storytelling. We don't develop style; it's a natural and unconscious expression of our own minds. And rules of good writing are rules of good writing, regardless of the form — poetry, journalism, playwriting, fiction, nonfiction. Whatever makes one kind of writing good makes them all good. And one of the most important rules is 'show me, don't tell me'."

Live Aid and
the Woodstock Nation

It was the word on everybody's lips at the Live Aid concert last Saturday 1
in Philadelphia. "Woodstock II," said the rock star Neil Young. "It's your Woodstock," the singer Joan Baez told the crowd in John F. Kennedy Stadium. Seventeen-year-old Tom Teter of Vineland, N.J., agreed: "It's our Woodstock and it's just as good."

There was abundant reason for the comparison. The organizers of Live Aid 2
consciously harkened to the 1969 festival, a counterculture conclave that led Abbie Hoffman to coin the term "Woodstock Nation" for America's young.

And certainly Live Aid as an event, a spectacle, addressed the desire of many fans—people in their teens or 20s who know Woodstock as an icon of the decade they worship—to enact their vision of the 1960s.

But if Woodstock was the obvious point of reference for the mammoth Live 3 Aid shows in Philadelphia and London—seen by 162,000 fans in Kennedy and Wembley Stadiums and an estimated 1.5 billion on a worldwide television broadcast—it was not necessarily the right one. If anything, the distance from a rain-soaked dairy farm in Bethel, N.Y., to a state-of-the-art stage in Philadelphia is measured in much more than 16 years and a few hundred miles.

Between then and now, rock-and-roll has moved from the turbulent, youth- 4 ful fringe into the vast middle ground of American culture and commerce. Its audience—and in many cases, performers—has turned from social rebels to solid citizens. Woodstock was on the surface an apolitical event, promising merely "three days of music and peace," which took on enormous resonance more by what it represented than by what it said outright. Live Aid was a political event—in that it was created solely to raise money for African famine relief—that largely appealed to fans as a megaconcert.

"You've got to face the reality of the event," said Bill Graham, the promoter 5 of the Live Aid concert. "People are concerned about the plight in Africa, but if there was no famine, we'd have sold as many tickets." Whatever the motive, the harvest was handsome indeed. In a single day, Live Aid raised an estimated $70 million, far outstripping the figure from such renowned rock charity events as George Harrison's 1971 Concert for Bangladesh.

The differences between Woodstock and Live Aid, which is to say between 6 America in 1969 and America in 1985, show up in many specific ways, too. Woodstock was a chaotic, anarchic happening that sprawled over three days; Live Aid's 14-hour Philadelphia concert ran only three minutes overtime. Where hippie entrepreneurs sold hallucinogens at Woodstock—there were two drug-related deaths and hundreds of "bad trips" from LSD—the drug of choice at Live Aid was beer. The lasting images of Woodstock include skinny-dippers in a wallow called "Passion Puddle"; the crowd at Live Aid had short hair and waved the Stars and Stripes. One fan arrived in a limousine, from which his chauffeur watched the show on a built-in television.

Appeal for 40-Year-Olds

Live Aid was the kind of rock concert even a parent could like, especially 7 since the typical parent of teenage children today grew up on the Beatles, Bob Dylan, and Elvis Presley. And that was part of the point in the packaging of Live Aid.

"This show was designed to be most appreciated by a 40-year-old," said   8
Michael C. Mitchell, president of Worldwide Sports and Entertainment, the
company that produced the Live Aid telecast. "It's their music—Joan Baez,
Mick Jagger, Bob Dylan. We took a lot of performers from 1960 to 1980 and
very few since. If the show aimed only at the kids—the 16-, 17-, 18-year-
olds—we'd have a problem. They don't give money."

Besides individual performers with roots in the 1960s in general and Wood-   9
stock in particular, Live Aid offered the reunions of period bands such as the
Who, Led Zeppelin, and Crosby, Stills, Nash, and Young. These performances
added to the sense of a once-in-a-lifetime event, but they also threw the passage
of time into clear relief. David Crosby, Stephen Stills, Graham Nash, and
Neil Young played together in public for the first time ever at Woodstock. By
the time they reassembled for Live Aid, Mr. Nash was graying at the temples,
Mr. Stills had a double chin, Mr. Crosby has been convicted on drug- and
gun-possession charges and Mr. Young has endorsed Ronald Reagan for president.

"Longing for the 60s"

Such 1960s stars, though, continue to carry a mythological importance for   10
the teen-aged audience that filled Kennedy Stadium. "It might be that the
children of the 80s are longing for a Woodstock, longing for the 60s," Miss
Baez said. "The similarity I felt between Woodstock and Live Aid was that
desire for some unwritten solidarity, for a chance for their community to come
together." Another part of the nostalgia for the 60s is the desire for a sense
of commitment, and the African famine, like the campaign for American
institutions to divest themselves of their holdings in South Africa, provided
such a rallying point.

At the same time, Miss Baez said, she doubted how much Saturday's au-   11
dience really shared with the 500,000 at Woodstock. "I wondered what kind
of problems they have," she said of the Live Aid spectators. "At Woodstock,
you had the war, rebellion against parents, bad acid—a rainbow of things.
These kids in Philadelphia had cooled out to 'feel good about themselves.' It's
not easy to ruffle them."

Other observers attacked what they saw as the concert's calculated show of   12
conscience. "I think it's great if the money raised does save lives," said Greil
Marcus, author of *Mystery Train* and rock music columnist for *Art Forum*
magazine. "But it was an enormous orgy of self-satisfaction, self-congratula-
tion."

"It's good people wanted to do something about the famine and I'll be 13
gladder when the money gets to Africa," said Marshall Berman, a professor of
political science at the City University of New York and the author of *All
That Is Solid Melts Into Air: The Experience of Modernity.* "But a little humility
and wariness wouldn't hurt."

A Global Language

What seems indisputable, however, is that Live Aid deeply changed the 14
rules of what a rock concert is. While Woodstock ushered in the era of the
gargantuan outdoor festival—Altamont, Powder Ridge, and Watkins Glen
followed—Live Aid was a case of what Neil Young called "high tech meeting
the 60s." If the concert itself was modeled on Woodstock, the broadcast borrowed more from the 1984 Olympics and the Jerry Lewis telethon.

In place of Woodstock's communion on a soggy hillside, Live Aid's world- 15
wide audience overwhelmingly experienced the event through television. The
broadcast intercut footage from concerts in Philadelphia, London, and several
foreign countries with fund-raising appeals by prominent politicians, artists,
and sports stars. Even in Kennedy Stadium itself, the crowd did not watch the
performers as much as it watched their images on several huge video monitors.
It was the Marshall McLuhan "global village" prophecy come to pass.

The fact that rock-and-roll was the Esperanto of the "global village" was 16
itself significant. In 1969, Woodstock's promoters had to scramble to find
anybody willing to provide land for a festival. In 1985, Philadelphia officials
grabbed the Live Aid concert as a way of rehabilitating the city's image in the
aftermath of the Move tragedy. The concert in turn was carried by network
television, FM rock stations and a 24-hour rock cable station—manifestations
of a rock-based economy that was only in its infancy during Woodstock.

"Finally, the music industry was looked at on such a high level," said Mr. 17
Graham, who began promoting rock concerts 20 years ago and has organized
a number of charity shows. "And finally, the world at large realizes there are
people in our industry who do things about their beliefs. For the world I work
in, this was out finest hour. By far."

QUESTIONS FOR READING AND REVISING

1. Does Freedman's *comparison and contrast* of Live Aid and Woodstock suggest a
   preference for one event over the other, or does it depict each event as serving
   a different but valid purpose? Explain. What does Freedman identify as the

values represented by Woodstock? by Live Aid? From the evidence presented in this essay, how significant were these values to the organizers of each concert? to the performers? to the audience?

2. What are the main characteristics of Live Aid and Woodstock that Freedman compares? He states that in both cases, fans bought tickets primarily to hear the music; yet his essay includes almost no comment on the music at either event. Why? If Freedman had compared the types of bands at the two concerts, or the songs played in 1969 and 1985 by the same performers, or the dominant themes and sounds in rock-and-roll then and now, how would his *thesis* be different?

3. In paragraph 3 Freedman says, "But if Woodstock was the obvious point of reference for the mammoth Live Aid shows . . . it was not necessarily the right one." What alternative point of reference, if any, does Freedman suggest? What factors does he see as restricting the comparability of Live Aid and Woodstock? What is the effect of emphasizing contrast rather than similarity at this early stage in the essay?

4. In paragraph 16 Freedman notes, "The fact that rock-and-roll was the Esperanto of the 'global village' was itself significant." That is, an important aspect of Live Aid was its demonstration that rock-and-roll has become the common language of a worldwide community linked by mass communication. How is this "fact" significant to Freedman's comparison of Live Aid with Woodstock? Judging from the evidence and interpretations he presents, how does he see it as significant to international economics and politics?

5. Freedman's main quotations about Live Aid come from observers with a range of perspectives: a promoter, a producer, a performer, a music writer, and a professor of political science. What aspect of the event does each of these people pay most attention to? How does the variety of their concerns and views serve Freedman's comparison and contrast and strengthen his essay as a whole? How would the essay's impact be different if Freedman had quoted members of the audience rather than these specialists?

6. In the biographical note preceding this essay, Freedman states that one of the most important rules of good writing is "show me, don't tell me." What does he mean by this? How does he follow this rule in choosing what to include and leave out of "Live Aid and the Woodstock Nation"? What specific words and phrases in the essay function to "show" rather than "tell"?

QUESTIONS ON CONNECTIONS

1. A central theme in Freedman's essay is the transformation since Woodstock of rock-and-roll, its performers, and its audience "from social rebels to solid citizens." In 1969 the very idea of a large-scale rock concert was threatening to

many adults—"Woodstock's promoters had to scramble to find anybody willing to provide land for a festival." By 1985, Woodstock and its participants had become not only respectable but "an icon." How is this legitimizing of rock-and-roll reflected in Erik Field's *classification* and evaluation of his record collection in "Rock Around the World" (p. 83)? How might Field's comments on each geographic/musical category have been different if he were writing at the time these albums came out?

2. Whereas Freedman's essay is structured as a *comparison and contrast*, Field's is a *classification*. Field uses a contrast, however (Spam versus filet mignon), to introduce his classification. How does this image strengthen his essay? What problems would Field have faced if he had used Spam versus filet mignon as the central metaphor in a comparison-and-contrast essay about rock-and-roll? How would the effect of "Live Aid and the Woodstock Nation" change if Freedman had chosen to classify the types of music at the Live Aid concert instead of comparing the event as a whole with Woodstock?

3. Karen Kramer's *comparison* of drummers and percussionists in "The Little Drummer Boys" (p. 138) is written in a very different style from Freedman's comparison of Live Aid and Woodstock. What are the most significant stylistic differences? How does Kramer's style and approach to her subject enable her to use different types of evidence from Freedman? How is she able to use her evidence in different ways? Freedman's essay is aimed at *New York Times* readers; what kind of audience is Kramer's essay best suited for? Why?

SUGGESTIONS FOR WRITING

1. One point dramatized by the success of Live Aid is that rock-and-roll has gained not only legitimacy since Woodstock but political and economic clout as well. The power of the music industry to mobilize communications technology for a worldwide broadcast, to win support from prominent politicians, artists, and sports figures, to gain the cooperation of foreign governments, to draw a record-breaking global audience, and to raise $70 million in one day suggests some intriguing possibilities for the future. We already have a former movie star as president of the United States; will a rock star be next? If the music business can help alleviate famine in Africa, what might it accomplish for domestic problems? Is music — foreign tours and broadcasts by American bands — a strong potential weapon in the Cold War? Choose one plausible political or economic role rock-and-roll could play in the sixteen years after Live Aid, or one that it is already playing (for example, country music's Farm Aid benefit concerts, or Bruce Springsteen's donations to unemployed workers in the cities where he plays). Write an argumentative essay about why and how this would or would not be a desirable development, from the standpoint of the existing

political/economic structure, the music industry and musicians, or the benefi-
ciaries.

2. Both Karen Kramer's and Samuel Freedman's essays demonstrate that *comparison
and contrast* can be a useful form to use when writing about music and musicians.
Kramer compares qualities of two groups of performers, whereas Freedman makes
a comparison over time between two complex events. Select some other phenomenon in the arts or entertainment — the Japanese film *The Seven Samurai*
versus the American *The Magnificent Seven*; the effectiveness of television at
showing football versus basketball games; blockbuster shows at large museums
versus small local art exhibitions; or whatever else interests you — and write a
comparison-and-contrast essay about it explaining your idea about each subject.

3. At Woodstock, music was perceived as being of, for, and to some extent by
the people. Rock-and-roll was still close to its roots in the black musical tradition, in which anyone who had access to an instrument or the ingenuity to
make one could be a musician. At Live Aid, music was widely perceived as a
commodity produced by professionals who function as one part of a highly
specialized, profit-oriented, studio-based industry. Erik Field's "Rock Around
the World" can be seen as illustrating the consumer's perspective. Though
Field is more attentive to the substance of music than many record-buyers, his
essay says little about the direct, visceral connection between players and listeners that was originally the heart of rock-and-roll. How has the "rock-based
economy" cited by Freedman affected would-be musicians? successful musicians? their audiences? Was the role of rock-and-roll at Live Aid to stir up
listeners' sympathy and support for famine victims, or simply to make money?
Can this phenomenon — the specialization of performers and the dwindling of
authentic popular participation — be seen in other areas of modern democratic
culture? Write a *cause-and-effect* essay exploring one of these questions or some
other aspect of the widening gap between professionals and amateurs, actors
and spectators, in present-day society.

BOB GREENE

"I always wanted to be, and I basically consider myself to be, a storyteller," says Bob Greene. "I always wanted to tell stories, whatever format they were in." Perhaps it is not surprising, then, that by the age of thirty-four Greene found himself juggling a nationally syndicated daily newspaper column, a monthly piece in Esquire, *and periodic contributions to ABC-News's* Nightline. *A Midwesterner with a nationwide beat, Greene was born in Columbus, Ohio, in 1947, and in 1969 he took a B.S. degree at Northwestern University, where he also edited the student newspaper. He became a reporter and then a columnist for the* Chicago Sun-Times *until the* Chicago Tribune *lured him away in 1978. By then he had already published four books: two volumes of collected essays and two chronicles of life on the road with a major show. The first show was political; Greene wrote it up as* Running: A Nixon-McGovern Campaign Journal *(1973). The second was a tour with Alice Cooper's rock-and-roll band, which Greene covered not only from the sidelines but from a Santa Claus costume onstage.* Billion-Dollar Baby *was published in 1974. A decade later Greene's own baby — his daughter Amanda Sue — became the subject of* Good Morning, Merry Sunshine *(1984), a diary of first-time fatherhood. Though Greene still does four columns a week for the* Tribune, *his monthly "American Beat" feature for* Esquire, *and at least two taped segments each month for* Nightline, *his sense of proportion has changed. "It used to be that if* Nightline *called and said, 'Go to California,' I would get excited and think, 'Hey, this is pretty cool.' Now if* Nightline *calls and asks me to get on a plane quickly, I think, 'Hey, I'd rather be with Amanda.' " His most recent book is* Cheeseburgers *(1985).*

"How Unwritten Rules Circumscribe Our Lives" originally appeared as a column in the Chicago Tribune *in 1982.*

How Unwritten Rules
Circumscribe Our Lives

The restaurant was almost full. A steady hum of conversation hung over the room; people spoke with each other and worked on their meals.

Suddenly, from a table near the center of the room, came a screaming voice:

"Damn it, Sylvia. . . ."

The man was shouting at the top of his voice. His face was reddened, and he yelled at the woman sitting opposite him for about fifteen seconds. In the crowded restaurant, it seemed like an hour. All other conversation in the room stopped, and everyone looked at the man. He must have realized this, because as abruptly as he had started, he stopped; he lowered his voice and finished whatever it was he had to say in a tone the rest of us could not hear.

It was startling precisely because it almost never happens; there are no laws 5 against such an outburst, and with the pressures of our modern world you would almost expect to run into such a thing on a regular basis. But you don't; as a matter of fact, when I thought about it I realized that it was the first time in my life I had witnessed such a demonstration. In all the meals I have had in all the restaurants, I had never seen a person start screaming at the top of his lungs.

When you are eating among other people, you do not raise your voice; it 6 is just an example of the unwritten rules we live by. When you consider it, you recognize that those rules probably govern our lives on a more absolute basis than the ones you could find if you looked in the lawbooks. The customs that govern us are what make a civilization; there would be chaos without them, and yet for some reason — even in the disintegrating society of 1982 — we obey them.

How many times have you been stopped at a red light late at night? You 7 can see in all directions; there is no one else around — no headlights, no police cruiser idling behind you. You are tired and you are in a hurry. But you wait for the light to change. There is no one to catch you if you don't, but you do it anyway. Is it for safety's sake? No; you can see that there would be no accident if you drove on. Is it to avoid getting arrested? No; you are alone. But you sit and wait.

At major athletic events, it is not uncommon to find 80,000 or 90,000 or 8 100,000 people sitting in the stands. On the playing field are two dozen ath-letes; maybe fewer. There are nowhere near enough security guards on hand to keep the people from getting out of their seats and walking onto the field en masse. But it never happens. Regardless of the emotion of the contest, the spectators stay in their places, and the athletes are safe in their part of the arena. The invisible barrier always holds.

In restaurants and coffee shops, people pay their checks. A simple enough 9 concept. Yet it would be remarkably easy to wander away from a meal without paying at the end. Especially in these difficult economic times, you might expect that to become a common form of cheating. It doesn't happen very often. For whatever the unwritten rules of human conduct are, people auto-matically make good for their meals. They would no sooner walk out on a check than start screaming.

Rest rooms are marked "Men" and "Women." Often there are long lines 10 at one or another of them, but males wait to enter their own washrooms, and women to enter theirs. In an era of sexual egalitarianism, you would expect impatient people to violate this rule on occasion; after all, there are private stalls inside, and it would be less inconvenient to use them than to wait. . . . It just isn't done. People obey the signs.

Even criminals obey the signs. I once covered a murder which centered 11 around that rule being broken. A man wanted to harm a woman — which woman apparently didn't matter. So he did the simplest thing possible. He went to a public park and walked into a rest room marked "Women" — the surest place to find what he wanted. He found it. He attacked with a knife the first woman to come in there. Her husband and young child waited outside, and the man killed her. Such a crime is not commonplace, even in a world grown accustomed to nastiness. Even the most evil elements of our society generally obey the unspoken rule: If you are not a woman, you do not go past a door marked "Women."

I know a man who, when he pulls his car up to a parking meter, will put 12 change in the meter even if there is time left on it. He regards it as the right thing to do; he says he is not doing it just to extend the time remaining — even if there is sufficient time on the meter to cover whatever task he has to perform at the location, he will pay his own way. He believes that you are supposed to purchase your own time; the fellow before you purchased only his.

I knew another man who stole tips at bars. It was easy enough; when the 13 person sitting next to this man would depart for the evening and leave some silver or a couple dollars for the bartender, this guy would wait until he thought no one was looking and then sweep the money over in front of him. The thing that made it unusual is that I never knew anyone else who even tried this; the rules of civility stated that you left someone else's tip on the bar until it got to the bartender, and this man stood out because he refused to comply.

There are so many rules like these — rules we all obey — that we think about 14 them only when that rare person violates them. In the restaurant, after the man had yelled "Damn it, Sylvia" and had then completed his short tirade, there was a tentative aura among the other diners for half an hour after it happened. They weren't sure what disturbed them about what they had witnessed; they knew, though, that it violated something very basic about the way we were supposed to behave. And it bothered them — which in itself is a hopeful sign that things, more often than not, are well.

QUESTIONS FOR READING AND REVISING

1. At what points in his essay does Greene state his *thesis*? What is the effect of opening with an *illustration* and following with an interpretation and then a thesis, rather than the reverse? How would the effect be different if Greene had switched the order? Or if he had used a less informative title?

2. Which, if any, of the illustrations Greene uses are not really *examples* of un-written rules? Which are not as applicable now as they might have been when Greene wrote this essay? Which are the most effective? If you were revising the essay, what illustrations would you add or delete? Why?

3. In his closing paragraph, Greene suggests implications for his thesis that expand it from an observation about human conduct into a sociopolitical statement. What is he saying here? What does this implied thesis tell you about Greene's concept of his probable *audience*?

4. At what points and in what ways does Greene introduce values into this essay before its closing paragraph? What generalizations and specific word choices indicate his assumption that readers share his values? agree with his observa-tions about unwritten rules? To what extent do you think the credibility of Greene's thesis depends on readers finding his examples believable?

5. This essay starts in the third person, switches to the second person, and changes almost immediately to the first person. Greene continues to juggle all three as he progresses. How does his use of the second-person *you* strengthen his presen-tation? What is the function of the first-person singular *I*? the first-person plural *we*? What risks does Greene take by using the first and second person in the ways he does?

6. Is Greene's *tone* in this essay more formal or informal? What characteristics of his *style* help convey that tone? What word choices contribute to his tone? If Greene had chosen a different tone, what other aspects of the essay besides those you have just identified would he have needed to change?

QUESTIONS ON CONNECTIONS

1. Terry Burns's "The Blanket Party" (p. 39) describes a situation in which self-interest outweighs social responsibility. Most of the *examples* cited by Bob Greene illustrate a similar conflict, but here, social responsibility usually wins. In which of Greene's examples might the outcome be different if the person's self-interest were stronger or weaker—for instance, if the man who always pays his parking meter were down to his last dollar, or if the man who steals tips inherited a fortune? In Burns's essay, what changes in the situation could shift the balance between self-interest and social responsibility so that blanket parties no longer happened? Given the purpose of military training, how desirable would such a shift be?

2. Some of the details in Greene's and Burns's essays are similar—for example, the reluctance of individuals to break a consensus of silence. List at least three such parallels. Which of these details do Greene and Burns use in different ways to create opposite moods? How are these two writers' conclusions similar, and how are they different?

SUGGESTIONS FOR WRITING

1. Bob Greene takes a rather unusual view in this essay by (a) focusing on the majority who abide by social rules rather than the minority who break them and (b) suggesting that to have our lives circumscribed by rules is a good thing. Some social critics would agree with Greene on (b) but argue that "the disintegrating society of 1982" has degenerated into chaos since he wrote, and that the rules nowadays are more often flouted than followed. Others would agree with (a) but contend that mindless obedience to rules stifles individuality, undermining the ideals of active democracy by reducing people to automatons. (Henry David Thoreau's "On Civil Disobedience" offers an excellent example of this view.) Choose one of these positions and write an argumentative essay responding to Bob Greene's; or write an argumentative essay, using updated evidence, which defends Greene's position.

2. A common argument in favor of legalizing marijuana, and some other drugs and activities, is that, when the legal system prohibits a practice many or most people believe to be harmless, people lose respect for the law. Bob Greene writes about the unwritten rules most citizens obey even though they are not legally binding. Write an essay about a law or laws that many citizens break, examining what this reveals about the legal system and people's attitudes toward it.

3. Some of Bob Greene's *illustrations*, like Terry Burns's in "The Blanket Party," spark our curiosity about the characters involved. What kind of person was Burns's Airman Goodrich when he wasn't trying to make it in the military? Why didn't he drop out instead of persisting through two more blanket parties and endless failures? What was bothering Greene's fellow restaurant diner about his companion Sylvia? What sort of man is Greene's acquaintance who always pays the parking meter? who steals tips from bartenders? We have all encountered people who intrigue us by behaving unpredictably. Choose someone you have known whose surprising behavior made you want to understand her or him better. Write a descriptive or narrative essay indicating what first intrigued you about this person, and what you found out as the acquaintanceship progressed.

DONALD HALL

"Poets like me," says Donald Hall, *"who find performing nearly as attractive as writing, are in danger of becoming not poets but scriptwriters for our own one-man shows."* Born in New Haven, Connecticut, in 1928, Hall started on the road to poetry at fourteen. *"I worked very hard at it,"* he recalls. *"I'd go up to my room after school and write poetry. I began to write poems in order to be loved by women."* The main rival for Hall's affections, however, was sports: *"Like most boys I wanted desperately to be an athlete, but . . . I was wholly incompetent: I dropped the ball; I struck out; I practiced the airball layup."*

Hall eventually reconciled his two loves by becoming a poet and an essayist who is also a sports fan and who sometimes writes about sports. He graduated from Harvard in 1951 and went on to Oxford, where his first book of poems was published. He did further postgraduate work as a Creative Writing Fellow at Stanford, becoming poetry editor for the Paris Review in the same year. Hall taught at the University of Michigan from 1957 to 1977, during which period he published numerous books of poetry, prose, and criticism, as well as several widely used textbooks. He has edited several anthologies and served as a judge for some of the nation's most prestigious writing awards. Hall now lives on a farm in Danbury, New Hampshire, where he divides his time among writing projects, reading, and (*"to come down from this excitement"*) watching sports.

"A writer of bad prose, in order to become a writer of good prose, must alter his character," says Hall. *"He does not have to become good in terms of conventional morality, but he must become honest in the expression of himself, which means that he must know himself. . . . For some people, some of the time, this simply means not telling deliberate lies. For most people, it means learning when they are lying and when they are not."*

"Four Kinds of Reading" appeared originally in the New York Times on January 26, 1969.

Four Kinds of Reading

Everywhere one meets the idea that reading is an activity desirable in itself. 1 It is understandable that publishers and librarians—and even writers—should promote this assumption, but it is strange that the idea should have general currency. People surround the idea of reading with piety and do not take into account the purpose of reading or the value of what is being read. Teachers and parents praise the child who reads, and praise themselves, whether the text be *The Reader's Digest* or *Moby-Dick*. The advent of TV has increased the false values ascribed to reading, since TV provides a vulgar alternative. But this piety is silly; and most reading is no more cultural or intellectual or imaginative than shooting pool or watching *What's My Line.*

It is worth asking how the act of reading became something to value in 2 itself, as opposed for instance to the act of conversation or the act of taking a walk. Mass literacy is a recent phenomenon, and I suggest that the aura which decorates reading is a relic of the importance of reading to our great-great-grandparents. Literacy used to be a mark of a social distinction, separating a small portion of humanity from the rest. The farm laborer who was ambitious for his children did not daydream that they would become schoolteachers or doctors; he daydreamed that they would learn to read, and that a world would therefore open up to them in which they did not have to labor in the fields fourteen hours a day for six days a week in order to buy salt and cotton. On the next rank of society, ample time for reading meant that the reader was free from the necessity to spend most of his waking hours making a living of any kind. This sort of attitude shades into the contemporary man's boast of his wife's cultural activities. When he says that his wife is interested in books and music and pictures, he is not only enclosing the arts in a delicate female world; he is saying that he is rich enough to provide her with the leisure to do nothing. Reading is an inactivity, and therefore a badge of social class. Of course, these reasons for the piety attached to reading are never acknowledged. They show themselves in the shape of our attitudes toward books; reading gives off an air of gentility.

It seems to me possible to name four kinds of reading, each with a char- 3 acteristic manner and purpose. The first is reading for information—reading to learn about a trade, or politics, or how to accomplish something. We read a newspaper this way, or most textbooks, or directions on how to assemble a bicycle. With most of this sort of material, the reader can learn to scan the page quickly, coming up with what he needs and ignoring what is irrelevant to him, like the rhythm of the sentence, or the play of metaphor. Courses in speed-reading can help us read for this purpose, training the eye to jump quickly across the page. If we read the *New York Times* with the attention we should give a novel or a poem, we will have time for nothing else, and our mind will be cluttered with clichés and dead metaphor. Quick eye-reading is a necessity to anyone who wants to keep up with what's happening or learn much of what has happened in the past. The amount of reflection, which interrupts and slows down the reading, depends on the material.

But it is not the same activity as reading literature. There ought to be 4 another word. If we read a work of literature properly, we read slowly, and we hear all the words. If our lips do not actually move, it's only laziness. The muscles in our throats move and come together when we see the word "squeeze."

We hear the sounds so accurately that if a syllable is missing in a line of poetry we hear the lack, though we may not know what we are lacking. In prose we accept the rhythms and hear the adjacent sounds. We also register a track of feeling through the metaphors and associations of words. Careless writing prevents this sort of attention, and becomes offensive. But the great writers reward this attention. Only by the full exercise of our powers to receive language can we absorb their intelligence and their imagination. This kind of reading goes through the ear—though the eye takes in the print and decodes it into sound —to the throat and the understanding, and it can never be quick. It is slow and sensual, a deep pleasure that begins with touch and ends with the sort of comprehension that we associate with dream.

Too many intellectuals read in order to reduce images to abstractions. With 5 a philosopher one reads slowly, as if it were literature, but much time must be spent with the eyes turned away from the pages, reflecting on the text. To read literature this way is to turn it into something it is not—to concepts clothed in character, or philosophy sugar-coated. I think that most literary intellectuals read this way, including the brighter Professors of English, with the result that they miss literature completely, and concern themselves with a minor discipline called the history of ideas. I remember a course in Chaucer at my university in which the final exam largely required the identification of a hundred or more fragments of Chaucer, none as long as a line. If you liked poetry and read Chaucer through a couple of times slowly, you found yourself knowing them all. If you were a literary intellectual, well-informed about the great chain of being, chances are you had a difficult time. To read literature is to be intimately involved with the words on the page and never to think of them as the embodiments of ideas which can be expressed in other terms. On the other hand, intellectual writing—closer to mathematics on a continuum that has at its opposite pole lyric poetry—requires intellectual reading, which is slow because it is reflective and because the reader must pause to evaluate concepts.

But most of the reading which is praised for itself is neither literary nor 6 intellectual. It is narcotic. Novels, stories, and biographies—historical sagas, monthly regurgitations of book clubs, four- and five-thousand word daydreams of the magazines—these are the opium of the suburbs. The drug is not harmful except to the addict himself and is no more injurious to him than Johnny Carson or a bridge club, but it is nothing to be proud of. This reading is the automated daydream, the mild trip of the housewife and the tired businessman, interested not in experience and feeling but in turning off the possibilities of experience and feeling. Great literature, if we read it well, opens us up to the world, and makes us more sensitive to it, as if we acquired eyes that could see through things and ears that could hear smaller sounds. But by narcotic reading, one can reduce great literature to the level of *The Valley of the Dolls*. One can read *Anna Karenina* passively and inattentively, and float down the river of lethargy as if one were reading a confession magazine: "I Spurned My Husband for a Count."

I think that everyone reads for narcosis occasionally, and perhaps most 7 consistently in late adolescence, when great readers are born. I remember reading to shut the world out, away at a school where I did not want to be; I invented a word to name my disease: "bibliolepsy," on the analogy of narcolepsy. But after a while the books became a window on the world and not a screen against it. This change doesn't always happen. I think that late adolescent narcotic reading accounts for some of the badness of English departments. As a college student, the boy loves reading and majors in English because he would be reading anyway. Deciding on a career, he takes up English teaching for the same reason. Then in graduate school he is trained to be a scholar, which is painful and irrelevant, and finds he must write papers and publish them to be a Professor — and at about this time he no longer requires reading for narcosis, and he is left with nothing but a Ph.D. and the prospect of fifty years of teaching literature; and he does not even like literature.

Narcotic reading survives the impact of television, because this type of 8 reading has even less reality than melodrama; that is, the reader is in control: once the characters reach into the reader's feelings, he is able to stop reading, or glance away, or superimpose his own daydreams. The trouble with television is that it writes its own script. Literature is often valued precisely because of its distance from the tangible. Some readers prefer looking into the text of a play to seeing it performed. Reading a play, it is possible to stage it oneself by an imaginative act; but it is also possible to remove it from real people. Here is Virginia Woolf, who was lavish in her praise of the act of reading, talking about reading a play rather than seeing it: "Certainly there is a good deal to be said for reading *Twelfth Night* in the book if the book can be read in a garden, with no sound but the thud of an apple falling to the earth, or of the wind ruffling the branches of the trees." She sets her own stage; the play is called *Virginia Woolf Reads Twelfth Night in a Garden*. Piety moves into narcissism, and the high metaphors of Shakespeare's lines dwindle into the flowers of an English garden; actors in ruffles wither, while the wind ruffles branches.

QUESTIONS FOR READING AND REVISING

1. Which of Hall's four kinds of reading is the most appropriate way to read his essay?

2. Does Hall seem to feel that most people read in all four ways, or that they

should? Which type of reading does Hall suggest he himself values most? least? What are his standards for judging? Are these standards equally applicable to all readers? Why or why not?

3. In paragraph 1 Hall says, "Most reading is no more cultural or intellectual or imaginative than shooting pool or watching *What's My Line.*" How does Hall appear to be defining *cultural, intellectual,* and *imaginative?* Does he mean us to take this statement literally or figuratively? If you were to evaluate reading, shooting pool, and watching *What's My Line* with regard to these three qualities, which activity would you rate the highest in each?

4. What is the main rhetorical pattern of this essay? Why is this pattern particularly appropriate to Hall's *purpose* in this essay? What additional strategy does Hall implement in his first two paragraphs? How does he carry this strategy through the rest of the essay? Look both for types of statements and for specific words and phrases.

5. Several times Hall makes a point by means of a *comparison,* such as the comparison of "most reading" with shooting pool and watching *What's My Line* in paragraph 1. How could Hall have stated the same opinion about "most reading" without the comparison? Would such a statement have been more effective or less? Why? What other comparisons does Hall use for similar purposes? How do they enhance his essay?

6. What is the role of *evidence* in "Four Kinds of Reading"? Why does Hall cite no sources or data? What types of support does he rely on instead to substantiate his claims? Which of Hall's statements represent a logical *argument,* and which reflect an appeal to the reader's emotions? Choose one paragraph in this essay and list all the value-laden nouns, verbs, and adjectives in it which help Hall to convey his *thesis.*

7. Hall uses the first person extensively in this essay — both the singular *I* and the plural *we.* Whom does he mean by *we?* How would the effect of his *we* statements change if he substituted *people* and *they?* If he substituted *you?* Where and why does Hall switch to *you?* Where and why does he use the impersonal third-person singular *one?*

QUESTIONS ON CONNECTIONS

1. In "Thank You Miss Alice Walker" (p. 128), Earnestine Johnson tells about reading Walker's book, *The Color Purple.* Which kind(s) of reading did Johnson apparently do? What *evidence* in her essay helps you to evaluate her reading? If you were to revise Hall's essay on the basis of Johnson's, what information would you add, and where? What statements, if any, would you change?

2. David Christman's "Nietzsche and the Art of Tattooing" (p. 55) is based on

his reading of a Nietzsche essay on the Apollonian and Dionysian concepts. Based on Hall's categories, what kind of reading did Christman apparently do? Could he have written his own essay if he had approached Nietzsche in one of the other ways described by Hall? If so, which one(s)? If not, why not? What is the best way to read Christman's essay, and why?

SUGGESTIONS FOR WRITING

1. Donald Hall's *thesis*, that reading is not in itself a desirable activity, is a striking one because it challenges a widely held, time-honored view. Hall explains why he believes as he does and suggests some possible historical reasons for the opposing view. However, he does not refute or even state the possible arguments in favor of reading as innately valuable. Write a counterargument to Hall's essay supporting the position he attacks: that "reading is an activity desirable in itself."

2. Hall's *classification* of reading focuses on the activity rather than on the reader, the author, the subject, or the type of writing. Given the great variety of formats now available for written communication, many other classification schemes besides Hall's four kinds of reading are possible. Think about the kinds of reading and writing you do in the course of a typical week. Write a classification essay that examines reading in a framework different from Hall's—for instance, the varied roles one person might play as a writer of term papers, exams, letters to friends and family, poems, stories, a diary, or whatever.

3. Hall's essay raises the issue of values as a critical factor in people's decisions about how to spend time. Each of us faces the choice dozens of times every day: Should I read the newspaper? telephone a friend? get some exercise? wash the dishes? eat? go to bed? turn on the television? Many of these decisions are based largely on expediency, but we are also heavily influenced by our perception of some activities as more worthwhile than others. Based on your own experience, write a *comparison-and-contrast* essay about the relative value of two or more different ways of spending time; or write a *cause-and-effect* essay exploring the historical, cultural, and practical reasons why you value certain activities more than others.

WILLIAM HUMPHREY

William Humphrey is "an odd man out of current American literature," a New York Times book reviewer observed, "encompassing its extreme poles of rustic energy and refined sensibility." The contrasts in Humphrey's novels and short stories fit with the diversity of his life. Humphrey often writes about his birthplace — Clarksville, Texas — though he left there at the age of thirteen and has seldom returned. "I write from imagination, not observation," he says. In his teens Humphrey studied painting in Dallas, joined and later left the Communist party, and was introduced by a friendly bookstore owner to the works of E. M. Forster and Virginia Woolf. He attented Southern Methodist University and the University of Texas, but left in 1945 to become a dramatist in New York. Failing at this plan, and desperate to leave the city, Humphrey hired himself out as a goatherd in Brewster, New York. There he began writing stories, which were published in periodicals ranging from The Sewanee Review to Esquire, the Saturday Evening Post, and Harper's Bazaar, and collected in his first book, The Last Husband and Other Stories (1953).

Established as a writer, Humphrey took a teaching job at Bard College. His first novel, Home from the Hill (1958), became a motion picture starring Robert Mitchum. After that came The Ordways (1965), A Time and a Place: Stories (1968), The Spawning Run: A Fable (1970), Proud Flesh (1973), Ah, Wilderness: The Frontier in American Literature (1977), Farther off from Heaven (1977), from which "The Salmon Instinct" is taken, Hostages to Fortune (1984), and The Collected Stories of William Humphrey (1985). The Spawning Run grew out of a fishing trip to Wales; unlike his other novels, which generally take five or six years to write, it was completed in eleven days. Humphrey won a National Institute of Arts and Letters grant in 1962 and a Texas Literature Award for Hostages to Fortune.

"I have no regular writing time or place," says Humphrey, "and I can write anywhere, including a dentist's waiting room, when things are going well." He drafts scenes as they come to him and later links them together, rewriting heavily. He revised the first chapter of Home from the Hill eighty-eight times. His current home base is a 165-acre farm in upstate New York.

The Salmon Instinct

When James I, King of England, was asked why he was going back, after a 1
long absence, to visit his native Scotland, he replied, "The salmon instinct."

The salmon is in his early adolescence when he leaves his native stream, 2
impelled by an irresistible urge for something he has never known, the salt,

salt sea. There he stays for the rest of his life, until he feels another prompting equally irresistible, the urge to reproduce himself. This the salmon can do only in that same stream in which he was born. And so, from distances as great as fifteen hundred miles, the old salmon heads for home.

Many things can, and do, kill the salmon on his long voyage home, but 3 nothing can deter or detour him. Not the diseases and parasites he is prone to, not fishermen, commercial or sporting, not the highest falls. He endures them, he eludes them, he leaps them, impelled by his ardent homesickness. Though long an expatriate, he knows his nationality as a naturalized American knows his, and back to the country of his birth he goes, as though throughout all the years away he has kept his first passport. Through the pathless sea he finds his way unerringly to the river down which he came on his voyage out long ago, and past each of its tributaries, each more temptingly like the one he is seeking the nearer he gets to that special one, as towns in the same country are similar but not the same. When he get to his, he knows it — as I, for instance, know Clarksville, and would know it even if, like the salmon, I had but one sense to lead me to it. The name given the salmon in Latin is *Salmo salar:* the fish that will leap waterfalls to get back home. Some later Linnaeus of the human orders must have classed me at birth among the Humphreys: in Welsh the name means "One who loves his hearth and home."

But I began to doubt my homing instincts, to think I had wandered too far 4 away, stayed gone too long, when, after crossing the ocean, I went back those thirty-two years later.

I had spent a few days in Dallas first, as the homecoming salmon spends a 5 few days in the estuary to reaccustom himself to sweet water after all his years at sea before ascending to his native stream; for although that is what he now longs for, those uterine waters of his, too sudden a change from the salt is a shock to him. Dallas had always been brackish to me.

The nearer I got to Clarksville the farther from it I seemed to be. This was 6 not where I was spawned. Strange places had usurped the names of towns I used to know. It was like what the British during World War II, fearing an invasion, had done, setting real but wrong place-names and roadsigns around the countryside so that the enemy in, say, Kent would find himself in villages belonging to Lancashire.

Gone were the spreading cottonfields I remembered, though this was the 7 season when they should have been beginning to whiten. The few patches that remained were small and sparse, like the patches of snow lingering on in sunless spots in New England in March and April. The prairie grass that had been there before the fields were broken for cotton had reclaimed them. The woods were gone—even Sulphur Bottom, that wilderness into which my father had gone in pursuit of the fugitive gunman: grazing land now, nearly all of it. For in a move that reverses Texas history, a move totally opposite to what I knew in my childhood, one which all but turns the world upside down, which makes the sun set in the East, Red River County has ceased to be Old South and become Far West. I who for years had had to set my Northern friends straight by pointing out that I was a Southerner, not a Westerner, and that I had never seen a cowboy or for that matter a beefcow any more than they had, found myself now in that Texas of legend and the popular image which when I was a child had seemed more romantic to me than to a boy of New England precisely because it was closer to me than to him and yet still worlds away. Gone from the square were the bib overalls of my childhood when the farmers came to town on Saturday. Ranchers now, they came in high-heeled boots and rolled-brim hats, a costume that would have provoked as much surprise, and even more derision, there, in my time, as it would on Manhattan's Madison Avenue.

You can never ascend the same river twice, an early philosopher tells us.   8
Its course, its composition are ever changing. Even so, one of its natives knows it, even one, like the salmon, who has spent most of his life away. I had been away from Clarksville since my father's death, and although ever since then I had been surprised each day to find myself alive, I was not an older man than he had lived to be. In that time much had changed in Clarksville; still, it was where I belonged.

Just as the salmon must leave home when the time comes, so he must return   9
to round out his life. There where he was born, he dies.

QUESTIONS FOR READING AND REVISING

1. Humphrey opens his essay with an earlier and more famous expatriate's use of the salmon *analogy*. What are the effects of his including this one-sentence paragraph about James I of England before he describes the salmon instinct? Would you have been more or less engaged by Humphrey's observations about salmon if he had begun with a statement about his own pilgrimage homeward instead of the king's? Why or why not?

2. By the end of paragraph 3, Humphrey has alluded several times to the salmon's human counterparts without explicitly revealing his essay's *purpose*. After starting with a king of England, he mentions "a naturalized American," then himself and Clarksville, and finally his name and its Welsh origins. How did these references affect your interest in his *description* of the salmon's return to its

native stream? To what extent did you anticipate Humphrey's revelation, starting in paragraph 4, that this essay is really about his own return to Clarksville, Texas? By the time Humphrey made this disclosure, what picture did you have of him and his life?

3. Like all writers of analogies, Humphrey shapes his subject to fit his purposes. For example, he refers to the salmon as sharing his own gender, even though "the urge to reproduce himself" obviously would be pointless if it involved only male salmon. What specific characteristics of the salmon make it more apt than any other creature for Humphrey's analogy? What characteristics does Humphrey ignore that might have pushed his analogy beyond its limits of applicability? How does he extend the analogy into his own experience once he finishes discussing the salmon itself?

4. Returning to one's roots is a common theme in literature, and one that has been described in a variety of ways. In this essay, how does Humphrey's use of the salmon *analogy* limit what he tells us about his hometown? When you finished reading this essay, what sense did you have of Humphrey's childhood? his reasons for returning? his plans after his return? What kinds of details would you expect Humphrey to have included about his visit to Clarksville if he had written a straightforward account instead of using the salmon analogy?

5. *Analogy* enables a writer to depict something unknown to the reader by comparing it with something familiar. Humphrey underscores our familiarity with the salmon instinct not only by what he says but by how he says it. What *clichés* in Humphrey's second and third paragraphs contribute to this sense of familiarity? What phrases reflect the timelessness and rhythm of the salmon's journey rather than the most direct way of making a point? How does Humphrey's use of sentence structure and punctuation suit his subject?

6. What appear to have been Humphrey's main emotions upon reaching his hometown? Which rhetorical technique does he use in paragraph 7 to convey these emotions? What point is he trying to make by returning in paragraphs 8 and 9 to the salmon analogy? Do you think this point is aimed solely at the reader, or partly at Humphrey's own need to interpret and understand his homecoming? How can you tell?

QUESTIONS ON CONNECTIONS

1. In "Handing Down Grace" (p. 106), Brenda Jacobs, like William Humphrey, describes a return to Southern roots. How is the mood of Jacobs's essay different from Humphrey's? What does each writer include that the other does not which accounts for this difference? How do the endings of the two essays emphasize the authors' contrasting emotions about going back to places familiar from their childhoods?

2. Ravenel Boykin Curry's "A Small Town" (p. 63) offers still another perspective on the theme of returning to Southern roots. Unlike Jacobs and Humphrey, Curry is not the main character in his narrative. What is the effect of his focusing on the people who live in Chesterfield, South Carolina, rather than on himself? How is Curry's reaction to Chesterfield different from Humphrey's reaction to Clarksville? What can you infer about each writer's reasons for making his pilgrimage?

3. Humphrey's, Jacobs's, and Curry's essays all have the rural South as their set-ting. How does this choice of scene function in relation to each writer's *thesis*? Which, if any, of these three essays could have been just as successful if the narrator were returning to an urban apartment? a house in a wealthy suburb? In each essay, what would be the main disadvantages of a change in setting?

SUGGESTIONS FOR WRITING

1. "You can never ascend the same river twice," quotes Humphrey in paragraph 8. Do you agree? Choose a place you have returned to after a long absence, or a person with whom you were reunited after a long separation. Write a *com-parison-and-contrast* essay about the changes you perceived on seeing this person or place again; or write an essay defending the position that it is possible to go home again.

2. Humphrey's paragraph 7 suggests an *irony*: While he was away from Clarksville, it turned into "that Texas of legend . . . which when I was a child had seemed more romantic to me than to a boy of New England." Yet as an adult, Hum-phrey appears more disconcerted than pleased by this childhood fantasy come true. The granting of wishes — usually with mixed results — is a popular theme in fairy tales, from classic stories like *Cinderella* and *Pinocchio* to modern ones like *Play It Again, Sam* and *Back to the Future*. Think of a situation in which someone or some organization — you, a friend, a political lobby, the United States — has a wish come true. Using a well-known plot or character as an *analogy*, show how and why the outcome is not all that had been hoped for.

3. William Humphrey, Brenda Jacobs, and Ravenel Boykin Curry all write about Southern roots that exemplify certain traditional American values. Each writer uses *definition* to help convey these values: Humphrey's *Salmo salar* and his own name; Jacobs's "othermothers" and "mammaws," Brother Bill and Sister Mattie; Curry's Billy Boy and Billy Boy, Jr. Names of people, places, objects, and phenomena can be invaluable to a writer attempting to create a vivid setting. Write an essay about some particularly distinctive place you have been, using definition to help express its distinctiveness.

BARBARA HUTTMAN

Barbara Huttman is perhaps best known to readers as a nurse, and to nurses as a writer. Her success in both fields has been impressive. Born in Oakland, California, in 1935, Huttman was a housewife before she took her A.D. degree in nursing at Cypress Community College in 1976 and became a staff nurse at Anaheim Memorial Hospital. A B.S. in nursing administration from California State University at Fullerton followed in 1978, and with it, a move to Kaiser-Permanente Hospital in Martinez as Inpatient Nurse Supervisor. That same year Huttman's article, "Nancy Nurse or Crusdaer Rabbit?" was published in Supervisor Nurse, *and she received the California-American Journal of Nursing Excellence in Writing Award. Since then she has written numerous journal articles and several books, including* Code Blue: A Nurse's True-Life Story *(1982) and the following essay, which first appeared in* Newsweek *in 1983. Huttman is currently Associate Director of Nursing Services at Children's Hospital of San Francisco.*

Of her two vocations, says Huttman, writing is "by far the easiest. Things like what happened to Mac [the patient in her essay] happen all the time here; happened yesterday; in fact, will probably happen today." Her extensive and intensive experience as a nurse/ writer led to television appearances discussing the patient's right to die with dignity. It is a topic on which Huttman has strong feelings, related to both her professions, "The worst thing about writing about hospital subjects is that you relive the experience," she says. "While it's really happening, you have people around to share it with, share the pain. When you write it down, you're alone with the emotion because to write it at all you have to relive the naked emotion."

A Crime of Compassion

"Murderer," a man shouted. "God help patients who get *you* for a nurse." 1

"What gives you the right to play God?" another one asked. 2

It was the Phil Donahue show where the guest is a fatted calf and the 3 audience a 200-strong flock of vultures hungering to pick up the bones. I had told them about Mac, one of may favorite cancer patients. "We resuscitated him 52 times in just one month. I refused to resuscitate him again. I simply sat there and held his hand while he died."

There wasn't time to explain that Mac was a young, witty, macho cop who 4 walked into the hospital with 32 pounds of attack equipment, looking as if he could single-handedly protect the whole city, if not the entire state. "Can't get rid of this cough," he said. Otherwise, he felt great.

Before the day was over, tests confirmed that he had lung cancer. And 5
before the year was over, I loved him, his wife, Maura, and their three kids
as if they were my own. All the nurses loved him. And we all battled his
disease for six months without ever giving death a thought. Six months isn't
such a long time in the whole scheme of things, but it was long enough to see
him lose his youth, his wit, his macho, his hair, his bowel and bladder control,
his sense of taste and smell, and his ability to do the slightest thing for himself.
It was also long enought to watch Maura's transformation from a young woman
into a haggard, beaten old lady.

When Mac had wasted away to a 60-pound skeleton kept alive by liquid 6
food we poured down a tube, IV solutions we dripped into his veins, and
oxygen we piped to a mask on his face, he begged us: "Mercy . . . for God's
sake, please just let me go."

Miracles: The first time he stopped breathing, the nurse pushed the button 7
that calls a "code blue" throughout the hospital and sends a team rushing to
resuscitate the patient. Each time he stopped breathing, sometimes two or
three times in one day, the code team came again. The doctors and technicians
worked their miracles and walked away. The nurses stayed to wipe the saliva
that drooled from his mouth, irrigated the big craters of bedsores that covered
his hips, suction the lung fluids that threatened to drown him, clean the feces
that burned his skin like lye, pour the liquid food down the tube attached to
his stomach, put pillows between his knees to ease the bone-on-bone pain,
turn him every hour to keep the bedsores from getting worse, and change his
gown and linen every two hours to keep him from being soaked in perspiration.

At night I went home and tried to scrub away the smell of decaying flesh 8
that seemed woven into the fabric of my uniform. It was in my hair, the
upholstery of my car—there was no washing it away. And every night I prayed
that his agonized eyes would never again plead with me to let him die.

Every morning I asked the doctor for a "no code" order. Without that order, 9
we had to resuscitate every patient who stopped breathing. His doctor was one
of the several who believe we must extend life as long as we have the means
and knowledge to do it. To not do it is to be liable for negligence, at least in
the eyes of many people, including some nurses. I thought about what it would
be like to stand before a judge, accused of murder, if Mac stopped breathing
and I didn't call a code.

And after the 52nd code, when Mac was still lucid enough to beg for death 10
again, and Maura was crumbled in my arms again, and when no amount of
pain medication stilled his moaning and agony, I wondered about a spiritual

judge. Was all this misery and suffering supposed to be building character or infusing us all with the sense of humility that comes from impotence?

Had we, the whole medical community, become so arrogant that we be- 11 lieved in the illusion of salvation through science? Had we become so self-righteous that we thought meddling in God's work was our duty, our moral imperative, and our legal obligation? Did we really believe that we had the right to force "life" on a suffering man who had begged for the right to die?

Such questions haunted me more than ever early one morning when Maura 12 went home to change her clothes and I was bathing Mac. He had been still for so long, I thought he at last had the blessed relief of coma. Then he opened his eyes and moaned, "Pain . . . no more . . . Barbara . . . do something . . . God, let me go."

Death: The desperation in the eyes and voice riddled me with guilt. "I'll 13 stop," I told him as I injected the pain medication.

I sat on the bed and held Mac's hands in mine. He pressed his bony fingers 14 against my hand and muttered, "Thanks." Then there was the one soft sigh and I felt his hands go cold in mine. "Mac?" I whispered, as I waited for his chest to rise and fall again.

A clutch of panic banded my chest, drew my finger to the code button, 15 urged me to do something, anything . . . but sit there alone with death. I kept one finger on the button, without pressing it, as a waxen pallor slowly transformed his face from person to empty shell. Nothing I've ever done in my 47 years has taken so much effort as it took *not* to press that code button.

Eventually, when I was as sure as I could be that the code team would fail 16 to bring him back, I entered the legal twilight zone and pushed the button. The team tried. And while they were trying, Maura walked in the room and shrieked, "No . . . don't let them do this to him . . . for God's sake . . . please, no more."

Cradling her in my arms was like cradling myself, Mac, and all those patients 17 and nurses who had been in this place before who do the best they can in a death-denying society.

So a TV audience accused me of murder. Perhaps I am guilty. If a doctor 18 had written a no-code order, which is the only *legal* alternative, would he have felt any less guilty? Until there is legislation making it a criminal act to code a patient who has requested the right to die, we will all of us risk the same fate as Mac. For whatever reason, we developed the means to prolong life, and now we are forced to use it. We do not have the right to die.

QUESTIONS FOR READING AND REVISING

1. At the core of Huttman's narrative is the ethical argument about a patient's right to die. How would you summarize her position? What types of *evidence* does she present in defense of this view? What role do data play in the case she makes? What role do moral concepts play? What value-laden words and images does Huttman use to emphasize the morality of her position? to win readers' emotional support?

2. Most of Huttman's narrative occurs in *chronological order.* What are the effects of opening the essay with a paragraph about what happened last instead of first? What words in paragraphs 1 and 2 add to the story's dramatic impact, and in what ways? How does paragraph 3 both establish Huttman's role and change the mood of her narrative?

3. Usually a narrative involves both opposition and cooperation among characters. Who are the main characters in Huttman's essay? What is the role of each one? Who or what is Huttman's opponent in the story's central conflict? How does she bring her opponent to life as a participant?

4. Crucial to writing a successful narrative is knowing what to leave out. What characters does Huttman mention only in passing who at the time were probably vivid and important to her? What incidents, which do not appear in this brief account, might she have described in a longer version? Judging from the people and scenes she does show us, what is Huttman's main strategy in this essay?

5. To make her story clear to a general *audience,* Huttman must explain certain medical terms and procedures. Find the places where she does this — where you learn something about her job or Mac's treatment that is essential to your understanding of the narrative. How does Huttman integrate this information in a nondisruptive way? When you look at her techniques for weaving in medical facts, what do you notice about the relative importance of logical versus emotional appeal to Huttman's argument?

6. One way Huttman dramatizes her story's central dilemma is by using the same words in strikingly different contexts. For example, in paragraph 4, Mac is described as "young, witty, macho"; in paragraph 5 Huttman shows him six months later having lost "his youth, his wit, his macho." What other words and phrases are repeated to highlight a significant change in context? Why is this an especially appropriate technique for this particular essay?

7. From what common expression did Huttman draw her essay's title? What does that expression normally refer to? What values does it imply? How does Huttman's variation on it exemplify her *thesis*?

QUESTIONS ON CONNECTIONS

1. The medical profession's reason for being is to save people's lives and protect their health. "A Crime of Compassion," like Beverly Dipo's "No Rainbows, No Roses" (p. 70), reminds us that a nurse's job also has a darker side—not every patient can be saved. How are Dipo's and Huttman's situations and attitudes similar in the cases they describe? How does each writer let us know that her patient has ceased to be a functioning human being with hope of recovery? Why was the aftermath of these two patients' deaths so different?

2. Huttman's essay exemplifies a problem discussed at some length by Elisabeth Kübler-Ross in "On the Fear of Death." Suppose Kübler-Ross were to *compare and contrast* the hospital death of Huttman's Mac, Beverly Dipo's Mrs. Trane, and Richard Selzer's "discus thrower." What aspects of each case might she cite as illustrating desirable and undesirable attitudes and procedures related to death? What point would she be likely to raise about the impact of doctor-nurse relations on patients?

SUGGESTIONS FOR WRITING

1. One of the most difficult questions in the debate over the patient's right to die is who is qualified to decide? At present, responsibility for "pulling the plug" is partly established by law and partly assumed by doctors (see Huttman's paragraph 18). The recent increase in medical malpractice suits encourages this uneasy balance of power. Huttman suggests that the patient and his or her family should have more say—that there is a "right to die" that the medical and legal professions ought to respect. This view is reflected by the current trend toward "living wills," in which a person records his or her wish not to be kept alive by artificial means if the question should ever arise. However, a living will has no legal authority. What is your opinion? Write an argumentative essay recommending how this dilemma should best be resolved.

2. Beverly Dipo's "No Rainbows, No Roses" emphasizes the intense intimacy of death and the anticlimax of an obituary. Barbara Huttman's private experience of Mac's death was followed by "the legal twilight zone" that later became a media spotlight. Many of us have found that certain events in our lives have a long-range impact very different from what we anticipated, and different from our experience at the time. This is particularly true of rites of passage such as deaths, births, marriages, leaving home, and taking a first job. Write an essay about an incident in your life that examines it from more than one chronological vantage point. Emphasize the change in your perspective before and during the event, or during and after, or all three.

3. "We developed the means to prolong life," says Huttman in her closing paragraph, "and now we are forced to use it." A similar problem has sprung up in
   other areas of modern existence: Human beings create technology that has the
   power to change our lives, and once that power exists, we feel obliged to
   exercise it, whatever the ultimate results. Most of the scientists who developed
   the first atomic bomb assumed their work would make war obsolete — no government would actually *use* such a weapon, they believed — until the United
   States dropped the bomb on two Japanese cities. More recently, workers complain of being squeezed out of jobs by unnecessary automation and computer-
   ization. Choose one of these or some other instance of technology that may
   have outpaced people's capacity to apply it judiciously. Write a *cause-and-effect*
   essay indicating the actual or potential impact of this technological change.

GARRISON KEILLOR

"Writing is still a pleasure to me after all these years," Garrison Keillor *wrote recently to his high-school English teacher. "I've stuck an awful lot of paper into typewriters, but I still get a little thrill with each fresh sheet. One never knows what might result. It's usually dreary, but in writing, unlike teaching, we get to destroy the failures. In teaching, all the failures graduate anyway, as I well know, having been one of them."*

Keillor's modesty is typical. Born in Anoka, Minnesota, in 1942, his only noteworthy failure was his trip east to look for a writing job after he graduated from the University of Minnesota. Keillor had already introduced himself to radio as a disc jockey at the campus station. When no one in New York or Boston offered him a magazine staff position, he went home to Minnesota and a classical music show on public radio. Keillor alternated between radio and writing for several years, selling his first of many pieces to The New Yorker *in 1969. Five years later, an assignment for that magazine on the Grand Ole Opry inspired him to create "A Prairie Home Companion." The program — one of the few live variety shows on radio — is carried on National Public Radio by satellite to nearly two hundred stations across America. It is also the subject of Keillor's highly successful second book,* Lake Wobegon Days *(1985).*

Keillor still publishes in The New Yorker; *his first book,* Happy to Be Here *(1982), is a collection of his short pieces that includes "My Stepmother, Myself." And he still hosts his old early-morning show for Minneapolis Public Radio. But Keillor remains best known as the chronicler of small-town life in fictional Lake Wobegon, Minnesota. Populated with characters who seem as real as next-door neighbors and mythical sponsors such as Powdermilk Biscuits and Ralph's Pretty Good Grocery, Lake Wobegon has offered America's heartland back to Americans — and given Garrison Keillor his voice.*

My Stepmother, Myself

Recently in Weeseville, Pennsylvania, a woman was dismissed from her job 1
as a human-resources coordinator and driven over a cliff by an angry mob of villagers carrying flaming torches and hurling sharp rocks after they learned that she was married to a man who had custody of his three children by a previous marriage.

In California, soon after her marriage to a prince (her first marriage, his 2
seventh), a woman named Sharon Mittel was shut up in a dungeon under the provisions of that state's Cruel and Unnatural Parent Act, which allows the immediate imprisonment of a stepparent upon the complaint of a stepchild. The prince's oldest daughter accused Sharon of slapping her. She was later

freed after an appeal to a king, but she now faces a long series of tests to prove her innocence, such as finding a tree of pure gold and a seedless grapefruit. She also must answer some riddles.

Are these merely two isolated incidents? Or are they, as a new and exhaustive report on stepmothers clearly points out, fairly indicative?   3

"The myth of the evil stepmother is still with us," the report concludes.   4
"Stepmothers are still associated with the words *cruel* and *wicked,* which has made them easy targets for torture and banishment as well as severely limiting their employment, particularly in the so-called 'caring' professions such as nursing, social work, and education. The myth that stepmothers use poisons and potions has virtually barred them from the food and drug industries. In general, stepmothers are not only underpaid and underemployed but also feared and despised."

How cruel is the typical stepmother?   5

Not very, according to the report, which examines many cases of alleged   6
cruelty and finds almost all of them untrue. "The media have jumped on every little misunderstanding, and have blown it up to outlandish proportions," the report finds. Recently, three stepdaughters whose relationships with their stepmothers are well known agreed to speak out and set the record straight. Because each has suffered from publicity in the past and is trying to lead as normal a life as possible under the circumstances, only first names will be used.

Snow

The story the press told was that I was in a life-threatening situation as a   7
child and that the primary causal factor was my stepmother's envy. I can see now that there were other factors and that I didn't give *her* much reinforcement — but anyway, the story was that I escaped from her and was taken in by dwarves and she found me and poisoned me with an apple and I was dead and the prince fell in love with me and brought me back to life and we got married, et cetera, et cetera. And that is what I believed right up to the day I walked out on him. I felt like I owed my life to Jeff because he had begged the dwarves for my body and carried it away and so the apple was shaken loose from my throat. That's why I married him. Out of gratitude.

As I look back on it, I can see that that was a very poor basis for a rela-   8
tionship. I was traumatized, I had been lying in a coffin under glass for *years,* and I got up and married the first guy I laid eyes on. The big prince. My hero.

Now I can see how sick our marriage was. He was always begging me to lie   9
still and close my eyes and hold my breath. He could only relate to me as a

dead person. He couldn't accept me as a living woman with needs and desires of my own. It is terribly hard for a woman to come to terms with the fact that her husband is a necrophiliac, because, of course, when it all starts, you aren't aware of what's going on — you're dead.

In trying to come to terms with myself, I've had to come to terms with my 10 stepmother and her envy of my beauty, which made our relationship so destructive. She was a victim of the male attitude that prizes youth over maturity when it comes to women. Men can't dominate the mature woman, so they equate youth with beauty. In fact, she *was* beautiful, but the mirror (which, of course, reflected that male attitude) presented her with a poor self-image and turned her against me.

But the press never wrote the truth about me. 11

Or about the dwarves. All I can say is that they should have been named 12 Dopey, Sleepy, Slimy, Sleazy, Dirty, Disgusting, and Sexist. The fact is that I *knew* the apple was poisoned. For me, it was the only way out.

Gretel

When Hansel and I negotiated the sale of book rights to Grimm Bros., he 13 and I retained the right of final approval of the manuscript and agreed to split the proceeds fifty-fifty. We shook hands on it and I thought the deal was set, but then his lawyers put me under a spell, and when I woke up, they had rewritten the contract and the book too! I couldn't believe it! Not only did the new contract cut me out (under the terms, I was to get ten shiny baubles out of the first fortune the book earned and three trinkets for each additional fortune) but the book was pure fiction.

Suddenly he was portrayed as the strong and resourceful one, a regular little 14 knight, and I came off as a weak sister. Dad was shown as a loving father who was talked into abandoning us in the forest by Gladys, our "wicked" stepmother.

Nothing could be further from the truth. 15

My brother was a basket case from the moment the birds ate the bread 16 crumbs. He lay down in a heap and whimpered, and I had to slap him a couple times *hard* to make him walk. Now the little wiener makes himself out to be the hero who kept telling me, "Don't cry, Gretel." Ha! The only crying I did was from sheer exhaustion carrying him on my back.

As for Dad, he was no bleeding heart. He was very much into the whole 17 woodcutter/peasant/yeoman scene — cockfighting, bullbaiting, going to the village on Saturday to get drunk and watch a garroting or a boiling — don't kid

yourself, Gladys couldn't send us to our *rooms* without his say-so. The truth is
that he was in favor of the forest idea from the word go.

What I can't understand is why they had to lie about it. Many, *many* parents 18
left their children in the forest in those days. It was nothing unusual.

Nowadays, we tend to forget that famine can be a very difficult experience 19
for a family. For my parents, ditching the kids was not only a solution, it was
an act of faith. They believed that ravens would bring morsels of food in their
beaks, or that wolves would take care of the kids, or a frog would, or that the
fairies would step in. Dwarves, a hermit, a band of pilgrims, a kindly shepherd,
somebody. And they were right.

And that is why I was never seriously worried for one single moment while 20
we were there. Deep down, I always knew we would make it.

I don't mean to say that it wasn't a trying experience, an *emotional* expe- 21
rience. It was. And yet there isn't a single documented case of a child left in
the forest who suffered any lasting damage. You look at those children today
and you will find they are better people for having gone through it. Except for
my brother, that is. The little jerk. He and my father live in luxurious manors
with beautiful tapestries and ballrooms, and I live above an alchemist's shop
in a tiny garret they call a condo. As for Gladys, she was kicked out without
so much as a property settlement. She didn't even get half of the hut. I guess
she is the one who suffered most. Her and the witch.

I often think about the witch—I ask myself, Why did I give her the shove? 22
After all, it wasn't me she was after.

I guess that, back then, I wasn't prepared to understand her type of milit- 23
ance. I couldn't see that she was fattening up Hansel in order to make a very
radical statement. If only I had. Not that I necessarily would have joined her
in making that statement, but I would have seen that from her point of view
it has validity and meaning.

And I would have seen that Gladys, in proposing the forest as a viable 24
alternative, was offering me independence at a very early age.

I wish I had been able to thank her.   25

Cinderella

A woman in my position does not find it easy to "come out of the palace," 26
so to speak, and to provide intimate details of her personal life. I do so only
because I believe it is time to put the Cinderella myth to rest once and for
all—the myth that one can escape housework by marrying a prince.

The truth is that I am busier than ever. Supervising a large household 27
staff—cooks, maids, footmen, pages, ladies-in-waiting, minstrels and trou-

badours, a bard or two — is just plain hard work. Often I find myself longing for the "good old days" when my stepmother made me sweep the hearth.

We see each other almost every day — she comes up here and we play tennis   28 or I go down there for lunch — and we often reminisce and laugh about our little disagreements. She is one of my best friends. Other people treat me like royalty but she treats me like a real person. My husband won't let me touch a broom, but I go to her house and she puts me to work! I love it. I tell her, "Mother, you're the only one who yells at me. Don't ever stop." And I mean it. Anger is real. It's honest.

Honesty is a rare commodity in a palace, and that is why so many "fairy-   29 tale" marriages end up on the rocks. You wouldn't believe the amount of fawning and flattering that goes on! Between the courtiers bowing and scraping and the supplicants and petitioners wheedling and whining, and the scheming of bishops and barons, not to mention the sorcery and witchcraft, the atmosphere is such that it's terribly hard for a man and a woman to establish a loving, trusting, sharing type of relationship.

It's true that we lived happily ever after, but believe me, we have had to   30 work at it!

QUESTIONS FOR READING AND REVISING

1. Keillor is an expert at parody — mimicking something serious with which the audience is familiar. What is he parodying in this essay? What *evidence* does he use to create an impression of authenticity? How does the essay's overall structure make his presentation of evidence convincing?

2. What are the effects of the title, "My Stepmother, Myself"? What details in Keillor's first paragraph suggest that this may be a serious essay? What details give the opposite impression? How does Keillor use the same techniques in more exaggrated form in paragraph 2? At what point is it no longer possible to believe that he might be serious?

3. Two rhetorical patterns that strengthen the essay are *illustration* and *analogy*. Where does Keillor use illustration, and what does it contribute to the essay? What is his central analogy? What specific words and phrases enable him to identify the analogy clearly without naming it?

4. Why do you think Keillor put the story of "Snow" before "Gretel" and "Cinderella"? How does his style change when he switches from the "author's" voice to "Snow's"? Compare paragraphs 3 – 7 with paragraphs 8 – 13. What are the distinctive features of each of these two *voices*? Does Keillor's "author" style in

this essay represent his own writing style or that of a character like Snow and the others? How can you tell?

5. Keillor gives no biographical data about his three interviewees but lets them speak for themselves. On the basis of his "statements" from Snow White, Gretel, and Cinderella, write a paragraph describing the personality of each character. What specific clues in their statements distinguish these three heroines from each other? To what extent do their personalities as depicted by Keillor reflect their original fairy-tale personalities?

6. What is the ostensible *thesis* of "My Stepmother, Myself"? What opposing position does it refute? Which, if any, of the alleged facts, opinions, and conclusions Keillor presents seem to be accurate or to represent his true views? Which, if any, are utterly implausible? What is the real *purpose* of this essay?

QUESTIONS ON CONNECTIONS

1. "The myth of the evil stepmother is still with us," notes Keillor in paragraph 4. According to Judy Jennings's "Second-Class Mom" (p. 113), there is truth beneath Keillor's humor. Which of the stepmothers described in Keillor's essay might Jennings identify with? What points does she make that suggest reasons for the stepmother stereotype? Why do you think no comparable stereotype exists for stepchildren?

2. Jennings writes about stepmotherhood with the authority of experience. Keillor's narrations in the voices of Snow White, Gretel, and Cinderella strive to convey a similar authority. What features of Jennings's essay also characterize Keillor's? How are the author's purposes different? Given their purposes, how does Jennings sound believable, while Keillor's characters sound funny?

SUGGESTIONS FOR WRITING

1. Garrison Keillor's and Judy Jennings's observations about stepmothers remind us that nearly everyone winds up at some point in an intensely emotional relationship where expectations and reality clash. Keillor's characters describe conflict, disillusion, and anger not only between daughter and stepmother, but between husband and wife and brother and sister. Jennings talks about the strains of being involved in "the only type of mothering we do without choice" (paragraph 6) — strains that obviously affect every member of her family. Choose a relationship in which you have felt you were in a no-win situation, caught between ideals you could not give up and obstacles you could not overcome. Write a *narrative* or *illustrative* essay based on that experience.

2. Keillor creates humor by reporting old stories as if they were news, and linking familiar clichés with real human experience. Think of a fairy tale or some other widely known story, either classic (Faust, Romeo and Juliet, Frankenstein) or modern (Star Wars, ET, Rambo). Write a parody of the story or its characters by changing its context so as to connect fantasy with reality: Romeo and Juliet enter marriage counseling; Barbara Walters interviews Darth Vader; the Devil tries to negotiate a more advantageous interest rate for Faust's soul.

3. Keillor uses the *analogy* of fairy tale stepmothers in a comical way. Analogy is also a good tool for examining a serious situation; see, for example, William Humphrey's "The Salmon Instinct." Fairy tales are particularly apt for this purpose because they mirror universal human conflicts — in this case, the animosity between mother and daughter as the girl becomes a woman. Choose a fairy tale that reflects a social or psychological phenomenon you have experienced or witnessed. Write an extended analogy that uses the story to convey your interpretation of its real-life parallel.

STEPHEN KING

"People's appetites for terror seem insatiable," remarks Stephen King. As the author of ten successful horror novels in as many years, he should know. Born in Portland, Maine, in 1947, King took a Bachelor of Science degree from the University of Maine in 1970 and then taught English at Hampden Academy until Carrie *hit the best-seller lists three years later. After* Carrie *came* Salem's Lot *(1975),* The Shining *(1977),* The Stand *(1978),* The Dead Zone *(1979),* Firestarter *(1980),* Cujo *(1981),* Christine *(1983),* Pet Sematary *(1983), and* The Talisman *(1984), which he wrote with Peter Straub. King has also published* Night Shift *(1978), a collection of short stories, and a book of nonfiction essays called* Danse Macabre *(1981), from which "On the Horror in Horror Movies" is taken.*

Though King's ascent up the ladder of fame and fortune has been fast, it hasn't all been smooth. The boy who was always picked last for baseball teams, young Stephen took refuge in watching movies on television. After he graduated from college, the only summer job he could get was in a laundromat. During his short teaching career, he and his wife Tabby lived in a trailer, where he wrote with a child's desk propped on his knees. Now he suffers from high blood pressure, headaches, and insomnia as well as constant pressure from reporters, schools, and other organizations seeking interviews or appearances. Though he enjoys his forays into the glamorous world of publishing—"GWOP" as his editor calls it—his day-to-day life is the clamor of tending to his children in their lakefront Maine home and the solitude of his typewriter.

On the Horror in Horror Movies

If we say "art" is any piece of creative work from which an audience receives   1
more than it gives (a liberal definition of art, sure, but in this field it doesn't
pay to be too picky), then I believe that the artistic value the horror movie
most frequently offers is its ability to form a liaison between our fantasy fears
and our real fears. I've said and will reemphasize here that few horror movies
are conceived with "art" in mind; most are conceived only with "profit" in
mind. The art is not consciously created but rather thrown off, as an atomic
pile throws off radiation.

I do not contend by saying the above that every exploitation horror flick is   2
"art," however. You could walk down Forty-second Street in Times Square on
any given afternoon or evening and discover films with names like *The Bloody
Mutilators, The Female Butcher,* or *The Ghastly Ones*—a 1972 film [in which]
we are treated to the charming sight of a woman being cut open with a two-

handed bucksaw; the camera lingers as her intestines spew out onto the floor. These are squalid little films with no whiff of art in them, and only the most decadent filmgoer would try to argue otherwise. They are the staged equivalent of those 8- and 16-millimeter "snuff" movies which have reputedly oozed out of South America from time to time.

Another point worth mentioning is the great risk a filmmaker takes when   3
he/she decides to make a horror picture. In other creative fields, the only risk is failure — we can say, for instance, that the Mike Nichols film of *The Day of the Dolphin* "fails," but there is no public outcry, no mothers picketing the movie theaters. But when a horror movie fails, it often fails into painful absurdity or squalid porno-violence.

There are films which skate right up to the border where "art" ceases to   4
exist in any form and exploitation begins, and these films are often the field's most striking successes. *The Texas Chainsaw Massacre* is one of these; in the hands of Tobe Hooper, the film satisfies that definition of art which I have offered, and I would happily testify to its redeeming social merit in any court in the country. I would not do so for *The Ghastly Ones*. The difference is more than the difference between a chainsaw and a bucksaw; the difference is something like seventy million light-years. Hooper works in *Chainsaw Massacre*, in his own queerly apt way, with taste and conscience. *The Ghastly Ones* is the work of morons with cameras.[1]

So, if I'm going to keep this discussion in order, I'll keep coming back to   5
the concept of value — of art, of social merit. If horror movies have redeeming social merit, it is because of that ability to form liaisons between the real and unreal — to provide subtexts. And because of their mass appeal, these subtexts are often culturewide.

In many cases — particularly in the fifties and then again in the early sev-   6
enties — the fears expressed are sociopolitical in nature, a fact that gives such disparate pictures as Don Siegel's *Invasion of the Body Snatchers* and William Friedkin's *The Exorcist* a crazily convincing documentary feel. When the horror movies wear their various sociopolitical hats — the B-picture as tabloid editorial — they often serve as an extraordinarily accurate barometer of those things which trouble the night-thoughts of a whole society.

But horror movies don't always wear a hat which identifies them as disguised   7

---

[1]One success in skating over this thin ice does not necessarily guarantee that the filmmaker will be able to repeat such a success; while his innate talent saves Hooper's second film, *Eaten Alive*, from descending to *The Bloody Mutilators* category, it is still a disappointment. The only director I can think of who has explored this gray land between art and porno-exhibitionism successfully — even brilliantly — again and again with never a misstep is the Canadian filmmaker David Cronenberg.

comments on the social or political scene. . . . More often the horror movie points even further inward, looking for those deep-seated personal fears — those pressure points — we all must cope with. This adds an element of universality to the proceedings and may produce an even truer sort of art. It also explains, I think, why *The Exorcist* (a social horror film if there ever was one) did only so-so business when it was released in West Germany, a country which had an entirely different set of social fears at the time (they were a lot more worried about bomb-throwing radicals than about foul-talking young people), and why *Dawn of the Dead* went through the roof there.

This second sort of horror film has more in common with the Brothers 8
Grimm than with the op-ed page in a tabloid paper. It is the B-picture as fairy tale. This sort of picture doesn't want to score political points but to scare the hell out of us by crossing certain taboo lines. So if my idea about art is correct (it giveth more than it receiveth), this sort of film is of value to the audience by helping it to better understand what those taboos and fears are, and why it feels so uneasy about them.

A good example of this second type of horror movie is RKO's *The Body* 9
Snatcher (1945), liberally adapted — and that's putting it kindly — from a Robert Louis Stevenson story and starring Karloff and Lugosi. . . .

As an example of the art, *The Body Snatcher* is one of the forties' best. And 10
as an example of this second artistic "purpose" — that of breaking taboos — it positively shines.

I think we'd all agree that one of the great fears which all of us must deal 11
with on a purely personal level is the fear of dying; without good old death to fall back on, the horror movies would be in bad shape. A corollary to this is that there are "good" deaths and "bad" deaths; most of us would like to die peacefully in our beds at age eighty, . . . but very few of us are interested in finding out how it might feel to get slowly crushed under an automobile lift while crankcase oil drips slowly onto our foreheads.

Lots of horror films derive their best effects from this fear of the bad death 12
(as in *The Abominable Dr. Phibes,* where Phibes dispatches his victims one at a time using the Twelve Plagues of Egypt, slightly updated, a gimmick worthy of the Batman comics during their palmiest days). Who can forget the lethal binoculars in *Horrors of the Black Museum,* for instance? They came equipped with spring-loaded six-inch prongs, so that when the victim put them to her eyes and then attempted to adjust the field of focus . . . .

Others derive their horror simply from the fact of death itself and the decay 13
which follows death. In a society where such a great store is placed in the fragile commodities of youth, health, and beauty (and the latter, it seems to me, is very often defined in terms of the former two), death and decay become inevitably horrible and inevitably taboo. If you don't think so, ask yourself

why the second grade doesn't get to tour the local mortuary along with the police department, the fire department, and the nearest McDonald's — one can imagine, or I can in my more morbid moments, the mortuary and McDonald's combined; the highlights of the tour, of course, would be a viewing of the McCorpse.

No, the funeral parlor is taboo. Morticians are modern priests, working 14 their arcane magic of cosmetics and preservation in rooms that are clearly marked "off limits." Who washes the corpse's hair? Are the fingernails and toenails of the dear departed clipped one final time? Is it true that the dead are encoffined *sans* shoes? Who dresses them for their final star turn in the mortuary viewing room? How is a bullet hole plugged and concealed? How are strangulation bruises hidden?

The answers to all these questions are available, but they are not common 15 knowledge. And if you try to make the answers part of your store of knowledge, people are going to think you a bit peculiar. I know; in the process of researching a forthcoming novel about a father who tries to bring his son back from the dead, I collected a stack of funeral literature a foot high — and any number of peculiar glances from folks who wondered why I was reading *The Funeral: Vestige or Value?*

But this is not to say that people don't have a certain occasional interest 16 in what lies behind the locked door in the basement of the mortuary, or what may transpire in the local graveyard after the mourners have left . . . or at the dark of the moon. *The Body Snatcher* is not really a tale of the supernatural, nor was it pitched that way to its audience; it was pitched as a film (as was that notorious sixties documentary *Mondo Cane*) that would take us "beyond the pale," over that line which marks the edge of taboo ground.

"Cemeteries raided, children slain for bodies to dissect!" the movie poster 17 drooled. "Unthinkable realities and unbelievable FACTS of the dark days of early surgical research EXPOSED IN THE MOST DARING SHRIEK-AND-SHUDDER SHOCK SENSATION EVER BROUGHT TO THE SCREEN!" (All of this printed on a leaning tombstone.)

But the poster does not stop there; it goes on very specifically to mark out 18 the exact location of the taboo line and to suggest that not everyone may be adventurous enough to transgress this forbidden ground: "If You Can 'Take It' See GRAVES RAIDED! COFFINS ROBBED! CORPSES CARVED! MIDNIGHT MURDER! BODY BLACKMAIL! STALKING GHOULS! MAD REVENGE! MACABRE MYSTERY! And Dont Say We Didn't Warn You!"

All of it has sort of a pleasant, alliterative ring, doesn't it? 19

These "areas of unease" — the political-social-cultural and those of the more 20 mythic, fairy-tale variety — have a tendency to overlap, of course; a good horror picture will put the pressure on at as many points as it can. *They Came from Within*, for instance, is about sexual promiscuity on one level; on another level it's asking you how you'd like to have a leech jump out of a letter slot and fasten itself onto your face. These are not the same areas of unease at all.

But since we're on the subject of death and decay, we might look at a couple of films where this particular area of unease has been used well. The prime example, of course, is *Night of the Living Dead,* where our horror of these final states is exploited to a point where many audiences found the film well-nigh unbearable. Other taboos are also broken by the film: at one point a little girl kills her mother with a garden trowel . . . and then begins to eat her. How's that for taboo-breaking? Yet the film circles around to its starting-point again and again, and the key word in the film's title is not *living* but *dead.*

At an early point, the film's female lead, who has barely escaped being killed by a zombie in a graveyard where she and her brother have come to put flowers on their dead mother's grave (the brother is not so lucky), stumbles into a lonely farmhouse. As she explores, she hears something dripping . . . dripping . . . dripping. She goes upstairs, sees something, screams . . . and the camera zooms in on the rotting, weeks-old head of a corpse. It is a shocking, memorable moment. Later, a government official tells the watching, beleaguered populace that, although they may not like it (i.e., they will have to cross the taboo line to do it), they must burn their dead; simply soak them with gasoline and light them up. Later still, a local sheriff expresses our own uneasy shock at having come so far over the taboo line. He answers a reporter's question by saying, "Ah, they're dead . . . they're all messed up."

The good horror director must have a clear sense of where the taboo line lies, if he is not to lapse into unconscious absurdity, and a gut understanding of what the countryside is like on the far side of it. In *Night of the Living Dead*, George Romero plays a number of instruments, and he plays them like a virtuoso. A lot has been made of this film's graphic violence, but one of the film's most frightening moments comes near the climax, when the heroine's brother makes his reappearance, still wearing his driving gloves and clutching for his sister with the idiotic, implacable single-mindedness of the hungry dead. The film is violent, as is its sequel, *Dawn of the Dead*—but the violence has its own logic, and I submit to you that in the horror genre, logic goes a long way toward proving morality.

The crowning horror in Hitchcock's *Psycho* comes when Vera Miles touches that chair in the cellar and it spins lazily around to reveal Norman's mother at last — a wizened, shriveled corpse from which hollow eyesockets stare up blankly. She is not only dead; she has been stuffed like one of the birds which decorate Norman's office. Norman's subsequent entrance in dress and makeup is almost an anticlimax.

In AIP's *The Pit and the Pendulum* we see another facet of the bad death — 25 perhaps the absolute worst. Vincent Price and his cohorts break into a tomb through its brickwork, using pick and shovel. They discover that the lady, his late wife, has indeed been buried alive; for just a moment the camera shows us her tortured face, frozen in a rictus of terror, her bulging eyes, her clawlike fingers, the skin stretched tight and gray. Following the Hammer films, this becomes, I think, the most important moment in the post-1960 horror film, signaling a return to an all-out effort to terrify the audience . . . and a willingness to use any means at hand to do it.

Other examples abound. No vampire movie can be complete without a 26 midnight creep through the tombstones and the jimmying of a crypt door. The John Badham remake of *Dracula* has disappointingly few fine moments, but one rather good sequence occurs when Van Helsing (Laurence Olivier) discovers his daughter Mina's grave empty . . . and an opening at its bottom leading deeper into the earth.[2] This is English mining country, and we're told that the hillside where the cemetery has been laid out is honeycombed with old tunnels. Van Helsing nevertheless descends, and the movie's best passage follows — crawling, claustrophobic, and reminiscent of that classic Henry Kuttner story, "The Graveyard Rats." Van Helsing pauses at a pool for a moment, and his daughter's voice comes from behind him, begging for a kiss. Her eyes glitter unnaturally; she is still dressed in the cerements of the grave. Her flesh has decayed to a sick green color and she stands, swaying, in this passage under the earth like something from a painting of the Apocalypse. In this one moment Badham has not merely asked us to cross the taboo line with him; he has quite literally pushed us across it and into the arms of this rotting corpse — a corpse made more horrible because in life it conformed so perfectly to those conventional American standards of beauty: youth and health. It's only a moment, and the movie holds no other moment comparable to it, but it is a fine effect while it lasts.

[2]Van Helsing's *daughter?* I hear you saying with justifiable dismay. Yes indeed. Readers familiar with Stoker's novel will see that Badham's film (and the stage play from which it was drawn) has rung any number of changes on the novel. In terms of the tale's interior logic, these changes of plot and relationship seem to work, but to what purpose? The changes don't cause Badham to say anything new about either the Count or the vampire myth in general, and to my mind there was no coherent reason for them at all. As we have to far too often, we can only shrug and say, "That's showbiz."

QUESTIONS FOR READING AND REVISING

1. King opens his essay with an admittedly generous *definition* of art as "any piece of creative work from which an audience receives more than it gives." Do you agree or disagree with this definition? Why? To what degree would you expect other writers and filmmakers to accept it? What does King achieve by stressing art — which he tells us is seldom deliberate in horror movies if it occurs at all — instead of some less controversial quality such as social merit or therapeutic value?

2. Given King's reputation, do you think his *audience* would have been impressed or disappointed if he had not included so many blood-curdling examples in his essay? How would the essay's impact change if King had focused more on description and less on interpretation of horror movies? Which aspect of the essay do you think interested the author more when he wrote it? Which aspect did he expect would be of greater interest to his audience?

3. In paragraph 15 King mentions the peculiar glances he received while reading a book about funerals for his next novel. How might readers of this essay respond differently to it if the author were someone without Stephen King's special credentials? What steps, if any, does King take to assure his readers that their fascination (and his) with horror is legitimate rather than ghoulish?

4. King uses an informal and very personal style in this essay, referring frequently to his own opinions. Why do you think he chose this approach rather than a more detached *tone*? How does his *style* affect the credibility of his theme? How would you expect his style to change if he were addressing students in a film course where all the movies he cites were shown? How would it change if his audience consisted of film critics? sociologists or psychologists? Judging from his style, who has King identified as his main audience?

5. In paragraph 5 and throughout his essay, King stresses the universality of the fears and fantasies touched on by horror movies. What specific reference does he make to institutions or individuals that all his readers are likely to be familiar with? Why do these references include phenomena not directly related to horror movies?

QUESTIONS ON CONNECTIONS

1. In "Look Out Behind You!" (p. 101), Matthew Holicek examines the predictability and absurdity of the subgenre of horror movies known as slashers. What similar techniques do Holicek and King use in exploring their contrasting themes? Why are these techniques useful in any discussion of horror movies?

2. In King's essay, scenes from horror movies merely serve as *examples* to illustrate

his theoretical points, while in Holicek's essay, they are central to his *thesis.* Yet King's incidental scenes are scarier than Holicek's focal ones. What specific differences in choice of material and technique create this contrast in impact? How does each author's way of selecting, placing, and describing movie scenes in his essay suit his particular thesis?

3. Essential for a writer of thrillers is the ability to create suspense, surprise, and shock. How do King's and Holicek's manipulation of sentence length and structure, punctuation, and word choice reflect their experience and skill as writers?

SUGGESTIONS FOR WRITING

1. Stephen King's "On the Horror in Horror Movies" shows us how the central characteristic of a popular art form serves as a bridge between the real and unreal and as a touchstone for deep-seated emotions. Choose another popular art form — space films, macho films, films about interpersonal relationships, music videos, rock-and-roll, subway graffiti, or whatever interests you — and write an essay analyzing its social and psychological function for its *audience.*

2. In paragraph 8 King alludes to the similarity between certain horror movies and the Brothers Grimm — "the B-picture as fairy tale. This sort of picture doesn't want to score political points but to scare the hell out of us by crossing certain taboo lines." Most fairy tales do indeed contain scenes of violence and horror, though on a less terrifying level than the B-pictures King refers to. Write a *comparison-and-contrast* essay about one or more fairy tales that cross taboo lines. The contrast might be between fairy tales and horror movies, or between the outward sunniness and the inward violence of these children's stories.

3. Neither King nor Holicek, in their consideration of horror movies, mentions the blockbuster fright films made from Stephen King's novels. Write an essay which either (a) demonstrates how these movies illustrate the principles established in "On the Horror in Horror Movies," or (b) traces similar plot lines, shock tactics, and other predictable horror techniques in various King films, explaining why audiences accept or even welcome such predictability.

JEANE J. KIRKPATRICK

"My experience demonstrates to my satisfaction that it is both possible and feasible for women in our times to successfully combine traditional and professional roles, that it is not necessary to ape men's career patterns — starting early and keeping one's nose to a particular grindstone, but that, instead, one can do quite different things at different stages of one's life," says Jeane Kirkpatrick. "All that is required is a little luck and a lot of work."

The phenomenal variety of Kirkpatrick's achievements supports her view. Born in Duncan, Oklahoma, in 1926, she went east to attend Stephens College and then Barnard College, where she received a B.A. in 1948. She took her M.A. at Columbia University in 1950 and her Ph.D. there in 1967. In between, she was a French Government Fellow at the University of Paris Institute de Science Politique, a research analyst at the Department of State in Washington, a research associate at George Washington University, and an assistant professor of political science at Trinity College. Upon leaving Columbia, Kirkpatrick returned to Washington, where she taught at Georgetown University. She has subsequently served as an intermittent consultant for the Departments of State, HEW (Health, Education, and Welfare), and Defense; an officer of the Democratic National Committee; and a resident scholar at the conservative American Enterprise Institute.

In addition, Kirkpatrick has written, edited, and contributed to numerous books and articles. She served as the United States ambassador to the United Nations from 1981 to 1985. When President Reagan ordered an invasion of the Caribbean island of Grenada in October 1983, Kirkpatrick defended the action. The following essay, published in Strategic Review, Winter 1984, is a speech she prepared, but did not deliver, for the General Assembly's November 2 debate on a resolution condemning the United States for its "flagrant violation of international law."

The U.N. and Grenada:
A Speech Never Delivered

Mr. President: The United States did not oppose the inscription of "The Situation in Grenada" under Rule 15 as an additional item for consideration by the General Assembly during the current session. The United States does not object to debate of this issue. To the contrary, we welcome a full, judicious consideration of all the facts pertaining to the situation in Grenada, convinced that an understanding of the situation will support the actions of the Organization of Eastern Caribbean States and its associates, including the United States; that the use of force by the task force was lawful under international law and the U.N. Charter because it was undertaken to protect U.S. nationals from a clear and present danger, because it was a legitimate exercise of regional collective security, and because it was carried out with due concern for lawful procedures in the service of the values of the Charter—including the restoration of the rule of law, self-determination, sovereignty, democracy, and respect for the human rights of the people of Grenada.

We did object to giving special priority to the consideration of this item, 2 not because we do not deem it important—obviously we do—but because the situation that now prevails in Grenada is not *more* urgent than other matters still to be considered by the Assembly—matters that involve the same basic values of the Charter and even more human lives, such as the situation in Lebanon, Southern Africa, Central America, Afghanistan, the war between Iran and Iraq—or other issues that will not come before the Assembly at all, such as the aggression against Chad, or the repression of the Polish people, or the persecution of Andrei Sakharov, Anatoly Shcharansky, José Pujals, Ricardo Bofil, Eloy Gutierrez Menoyo and other beleaguered defenders of human rights. Moreover, we deemed it hypocritical and politically tendentious to turn the Assembly's urgent attention to the situation in Grenada only after the real emergency in that country had passed—which is to say, only after Grenada had been rescued from the murderous elements that had taken over the country, threatening the people of that country and the neighboring states as well.

"Application of Universal Norms"

But now the issue is before us, so let us consider it in all its aspects. Let us 3 consider all the issues raised in this resolution. Let us consider the situation that prevailed in Grenada before the intervention of October 25. Let us consider whether that situation was such as to warrant the use of force in a manner consistent with the Charter of the United Nations. Let us consider whether the principle of self-determination was violated or upheld. Let us consider whether the sovereignty of Grenada was destroyed or restored. Let us consider whether the people of Grenada were victimized or liberated. Let us consider whether the cause of peace was damaged or served.

These may appear to be difficult questions, but the difficulties disappear 4 when they are addressed not in the abstract, but in the context of the concrete circumstances that led small, peaceful, democratic island states of the Caribbean not merely to sanction the intervention but to request and to participate in it. The test of law lies not in the assertion of abstract principles, but in the application of universal norms to specific situations. A court that cannot distinguish between lawful and criminal use of force, between force used to protect the innocent and force used to victimize them, is not worthy to sit in judgment. The failure to draw such distinctions will not preserve law as an instrument of justice and peace, but will erode the moral and legal—and ultimately political —foundations of civilized existence.

"An Authentic Reign of Terror"

First there is the question of force. The intrusion of force into the public 5 life of Grenada did not begin with the intervention of October 25. From 1979 Grenada had been ruled by a government that came to power by coup, over-throwing a corrupt, though elected, predecessor. The government of Maurice Bishop was initially welcomed by Grenadians. Initially it promised to hold elections and respect basic human rights. These promises were honored in the breach, as the government attempted to impose a Castro-style dictatorship with Cuban and Soviet aid. Eventually, when Bishop sought to free himself from the Cuban-Soviet grip, he was arrested by his Cuban-trained deputy, Bernard Coard, and shot in cold blood on October 19 along with other mem-bers of his cabinet and political leaders. At least eighteen deaths were con-firmed and many more were reported, including those of women and children. There was no court, no trial, no judgment, only murder. Expressing "horror at these brutal and vicious murders," Prime Minister Tom Adams of Barbados said that the division in the Caribbean now went "far beyond ideological pluralism" and "is the difference between barbarians and human beings."

In the wake of these murders, the People's Revolutionary Army announced 6 the dissolution of the government and the formation of a 16-member Revo-lutionary Military Council with General Hudson Austin as the nominal head. This group was not a government—it indicated that it would subsequently announce a government—but literally a gang of murderers who imposed an authentic reign of terror upon the Grenadian people. It decreed a 24-hour curfew, warning that violators would be shot on sight, and closed the airport, thereby entrapping nearly one thousand U.S. citizens—each and every one a potential hostage. Although the Military Council gave assurances that the airport would be opened on October 24 and foreigners allowed to depart, it failed to fulfill that assurance. The threat of violence against these American citizens, and against the people of Grenada, was real and imminent.

"Infrastructure for Hostility Against Neighboring States"

Grenada's neighbors also feared for their security. During the period of his 7 rule, Bishop had permitted Grenada to be transformed into a base for the projection of Soviet and Cuban military power in the Western Hemisphere. The instruments of violence and deception assembled during Bishop's tenure now fell into the hands of Bishop's murderous successors, presumably even more pliant tools of Soviet and Cuban designs. Here is how this new threat was viewed by Prime Minister Edward Seaga of Jamaica, one of Grenada's Caribbean neighbors. The danger, he told the Jamaican Parliament on October 25, arose "from the capacity of the leadership which seized power to use the armed capabilities and military infrastructure of Grenada for acts of hostility against neighboring states." He went on:

> The size and sophistication of the armed force of Grenada can be measured by a comparison with those of Jamaica. Grenada, having only one-twentieth of the population of Jamaica, had mobilized an army that was one and a half times as large as the Jamaica Defense Force. Some of Grenada's neighbors have no army at all; others have armies of less than two hundred men.
>
> The new airstrip, in the final stages of completion by Cubans, added another capability which in the hands of sane men would have offered no threat, but against the background of the insanity of the past two weeks would be a logical staging area for countries whose interests are similar, and who have ambitions for using Grenada as a center for subversion, sabotage, and infiltration within the area and against member states of the Organization of Eastern Caribbean States.
>
> Again, the powerful broadcasting station in Grenada, standing on its own, although capable of reaching from one end of the Caribbean to the other and far exceeding the power of any station in Jamaica, would in itself not necessarily be a threat, but in the hands of extremists of a military or ideological nature, both of whom exist in Grenada, constitutes a potent weapon for subverting neighboring states.
>
> While Maurice Bishop was alive, there was some indication that these capabilities could and would be used in this subversive manner against neighboring states, as there were complaints regarding training of a paramilitary nature taking place in Grenada among citizens of neighboring countries known for their own subversive interests.
>
> However, whatever may have been the threat, it was minimal in the hands of Maurice Bishop, who was a moderate in comparison with the military and political leaders

of the regime which overthrew him. A totally different
picture emerges when this array of military and subversive
capability came to be at the disposal of one of the most
extremist groups of men to assume control of any country
in recent times. Few countries can have claimed the experience of having its entire cabinet wiped out in the manner in which that of Grenada was exterminated. Who then
can blame the Eastern Caribbean states for perceiving this
combination of awesome might and brutal men, who apparently had no concept of where to stop in taking human
life, as a prelude to hostile action being taken beyond their
own borders by those in power in Grenada?

"Warehouses Packed with Arms"

Prime Minister Seaga made these comments on the basis of the perceived 8
threat emanating from Grenada but *before* the full scope of the Soviet and
Cuban military capability on the island had been uncovered. These fears, as
he subsequently said, were amply confirmed by what was found on the island,
including "thousands of crates filled with millions of rounds of ammunition
and a large number of other crates of Russian AK-47 submachine guns. Heavy
artillery capable of firing 2,000 rounds per minute, antitank weapons and
antiaircraft installations . . . embedded in the hillside around Point Salines
have been uncovered. . . ." He went on:

> There is no longer any mystery, therefore, about what
> was going on at the Cuban-built airport at Point Salines.
> The airport has turned out to be nothing less than a so-
> phisticated military camp. All the signs and directions are
> in Spanish, none in English. Facilities are present through-
> out for the storage of arms, and there is no evidence of
> provision being made for any normal commercial or civilian
> traffic. The installation is filled with places to hang rifles
> — even in the sanitary conveniences. The six warehouses
> packed with arms and other discoveries speak more elo-
> quently than any words could of a Grenada that was being
> converted into a fortress and a base camp for hostile activ-
> ities against its neighbors and within the region.

The Prime Minister does not speak of the weapons found in the small island 9
of Carriacou adjoining Grenada, where only yesterday were uncovered 700
rifles and 38 Soviet-made AK-47s, rocket-propelled grenades, 150 cases of
ammunition, two jeeps, a truck, a generator, radio equipment and a dozen

cases of TNT. Less than a mile from Grenada's "tourist" airport, six warehouses were found which contained materiel of a similar variety, but in far larger numbers — enough to outfit two brigades, or 8,000 men, according to U.S. military officials.

"Secret Treaties for Covert Supply of Arms"

Mr. President, these discoveries revealed only what had already been em- 10 placed in Grenada. They do not speak of the buildup that was envisioned through 1985 and agreed to in five secret treaties, three with the Soviet Union, one with Cuba, and one with North Korea, which alone had agreed to supply $12 million worth of arms. These secret treaties provide for the covert supply of arms to Grenada from the Soviet Union, to be transshipped through Cuba — a pattern that is also being followed in Central America. The arms included millions of rounds of ammunition, sniper rifles, armored vehicles, naval patrol craft from North Korea, antiaircraft guns, antitank guns, mortars, thousands of automatic rifles, hand grenades and landmines, and 18,000 military uniforms — 18,000 military uniforms for a country with a population of only 100,000. In addition, the treaties provided for assistance in the creation of a force run by the Ministry of Interior and for surveillance equipment and other items used by the KGB. They also provided for training Grenadians in the Soviet Union.

Mr. President, the United Nations was established to beat swords into 11 plowshares. In Grenada, the Soviet Union and its proxies beat plowshares into AK-47s, machine guns and heavy artillery.

"Direct Appeal to the OECS"

Is there any reasonable basis for concluding that the fears of Grenada's 12 neighbors were unfounded? Can any prudent judgment question the urgent appeal from the Organization of Eastern Caribbean States for assistance in meeting this threat to their security?

The OECS, a subregional body established to promote regional cooperation 13 and collective security, determined that the collapse of government and the disintegration of public order in Grenada posed a threat to the security and stability of the region. As a consequence, the OECS members decided to take necessary measures in response to this threat, in accordance with Article 8 of the OECS Treaty. They sought the assistance of friendly foreign states to participate in a collective security force. The United States, together with Barbados and Jamaica, agreed with the OECS assessment of the gravity of the situation and offered to contribute forces to a collective action in support of this regional measure. The Governor General of Grenada made a confidential, direct appeal to the OECS to take action to restore order on the island. As the sole remaining authoritative representative of government in Grenada, his appeal for action carried exceptional moral and legal weight.

Listen to the Governor General's description of his request and his thoughts about it, as expressed in a BBC interview: 14

> Q: Does it not seem a little strange that the Governor General of a Commonwealth country should ask America to intervene rather than Britain?
>
> A: Well, I thought the Americans would do it much faster and more decisively. At first, I was against invasion of the country. But things deteriorated very rapidly. You see, when the military took over, they quickly came to me and acknowledged my authority as representative of the Queen, in the same way as the People's Revolutionary Government did when they overthrew the elected government. And at first I thought they were the right people. I was impressed. But within a very short time I thought things deteriorated rapidly. For example, I still need to know what became of the bodies of people who were killed on that day, including the bodies of Prime Minister Bishop and three cabinet ministers. I know that these bodies have never been handed over to relatives, and I am advised that these bodies were never taken to the hospital or any of the two undertakers in town.
>
> Q: What was the moment you decided that an invasion was necessary?
>
> A: I think I decided so on Sunday the 23rd, late Sunday evening.
>
> Q: But the British say that on that day you told them you still didn't want one; that was early in the day, was it?
>
> A: I did see somebody earlier in the day, and during that time I did see somebody and they said you know invasion was the last thing they wanted, and I said it in my speech. But if it came to that, I would give every support; and later on, as things deteriorated, I thought, because people were scared, you know, I had several calls from responsible people in Grenada that something should be done. "Mr. Governor General, we are depending on you [that] something be done. People in Grenada cannot do it,

you must get help from outside." What I did ask for was not an invasion, but help from outside.

Q: Do you regret that the British were not associated with America in coming in?

A: I would not like to comment on this. I'm afraid in my position I would not like to blame any country for anything or to express such regrets. But what I can say is that we were very, very grateful that these other countries came to our rescue and they came just on time.

Q: Did you invite Britain to take part?

A: No, I did not invite Britain to take part, and I asked for help from the OECS countries. I also asked the OECS to ask America whether they can help. And then I con-firmed this in writing myself to the President of the USA.

Q: How long, sir, do you think the Americans should remain here?

A: I would like — and I speak for the people who have to live and work in Grenada — I would like them to remain here as long as it is necessary. This I cannot say at the moment. I cannot say two weeks or three weeks or two months. I don't know.

And Governor General Scoon said, further, in his radio speech to the 15 people:

> Innocent men, women and children were also killed or injured. To say the least, I was deeply saddened, and I shall like to extend heartfelt sympathy to the bereaved families. The killing of Prime Minister Bishop and the subsequent control of our country by the People's Revolutionary Army so horrified not only Grenadians but the entire Caribbean, the Commonwealth and beyond that certain Caribbean states with the support of the United States of America decided to come to our aid in the restoration of peace and order. Of course, intervention by foreign troops is the last thing one would want for one's country. But in our case, it has happened in deteriorating circumstances, repugnant to the vast majority.

"Consistent with the Charter of the U.N. and of the OAS"

Mr. President, collective action in response to the kind of dangerous situ- 16 ation that existed in Grenada is consistent with the Charter of the United

Nations and with the Charter of the Organization of American States. Both Charters expressly recognize the competence of regional security bodies in ensuring peace and stability. The OECS states are not parties to the Rio Treaty, and the OECS Treaty, which concerns itself in part with matters of collective security, is their regional security arrangement.

Article 22 of the OAS Charter states that measures taken pursuant to 17 collective security agreements do not violate the OAS Charter provisions prohibiting intervention and the use of force. Similarly, Article 52 of the U.N. Charter expressly permits regional arrangements for the maintenance of peace and security consistent with the purposes and principles of the United Nations. The actions and objectives of the collective security force, in the circumstances I have described, are consistent with those purposes and principles.

The OECS states, in taking lawful collective action, were free to call upon 18 other concerned states, including the United States, for assistance in their effort to maintain the peace and security of the Caribbean. Assistance given in response to their request is itself lawful. Moreover, U.S. cooperation with the collective security force permitted the safe evacuation of endangered U.S. citizens. Such humanitarian action is justified by well-established principles of international law.

Mr. President, the extent of the danger faced by U.S. citizens in Grenada 19 was vividly illustrated by the numerous photographs of American students kissing the ground after deplaning in the United States. "We thought we could be potential hostages," said one. "We just wanted to get out if we could." Said another, who talked to Grenadians about leaving: "They said they were afraid and they would leave if they could. If they feel that way about their own government, I don't see how I could trust it." Let me also quote, if I may, from a letter that was sent to President Reagan by 65 students last Thursday:

> We the students of St. George's University School of Medicine at Kingstown Medical College, St. Vincent, would like to express our appreciation of your concern for the safety of our fellow students in Grenada . . . Having spent the past two years in Grenada and being in almost daily contact with American students there during the recent unrest, we support your decision. . . .

"An Intervention Popular Throughout the Region"

There is no question, Mr. President, that the intervention in Grenada was 20 immensely popular throughout the Caribbean region. The Prime Minister of

Barbados, Tom Adams, said: "There has seldom been in these islands such virtual unanimous support in the media and at political and popular levels for an action so potentially divisive." The Jamaican columnist and opinion analyst, Dr. Carl Stone, wrote that the intervention in Grenada "is both popular here in Jamaica and in the rest of the Caribbean because of the feelings about the murderous butchers of St. George's." James Nelson Goodsell, the Latin American correspondent for the *Christian Science Monitor*, reported: "At the recent Inter-American Press Association meeting in Lima, Peru, there was virtually unanimous backing by Caribbean editors for the combined U.S.-Caribbean invasion of Grenada."

Mr. Goodsell's finding was amply confirmed by reactions in the region to 21 the intervention. Mark A. Conyers, the managing editor of the *Trinidad Guardian*, said: "I thoroughly agree with the forces' landing. You have to protect Caribbean democracy. There must be an elected government in Grenada, and this landing should help bring that about." An editorial in the *Bridgetown Advocate* noted: "If we are really serious about the concept of sovereignty, what has been done has given the Grenadians a real chance to recapture their true sovereignty as a people." This point was echoed in *El Universal* of Caracas, which said that the action in Grenada was "taken to end totalitarian intervention in the Republic of Grenada, and it will guarantee that island's people the right to freedom and to elect their governments democratically." An editorial on October 27 in Colombia's leading daily, *Il Tiempo*, noted that the Cubans in Grenada were not simply workers and teachers "but a group armed to the teeth, capable of direct combat in a direct and efficient manner. . . . Now Fidel orders the Cubans dug in on the island to resist until the end, by which he virtually admits that they had already invaded the island by other means and that now they refuse to allow themselves to be pushed away."

"The Views of the People of Grenada"

I could go on citing regional opinion, but the views that count most are 22 the views of the people of Grenada. Let me quote from Alister Hughes, the Agence France Presse and CANA correspondent and the sole independent news link between Grenada and the outside world until his arrest on October 19: "I don't regard it as an invasion, but a rescue operation. I haven't met any Grenadian who had expressed any other view." He added: "Thank God they came. If someone had not come in and done something, I hesitate to say what the situation in Grenada would be now."

TV interviews conducted by the Canadian Broadcasting corporation found 23 the people in the streets of St. George's uniformly favorable to the intervention, a reaction also found by *Washington Post* reporter Ed Cody. The Governor General himself, Paul Scoon, said: "The people of Grenada, the people who live and work here, . . . I am well advised have welcomed the presence of these troops as a positive step forward in the restoration not only of peace and order but also of full sovereignty that's enabling our democratic institutions to function according to the expressed wishes of the Grenadian people at the earliest possible time."

"Self-Determination Involves Respect for Fundamental Freedoms"

The Governor General has, of course, raised here the central issue, the 24 issue of democracy, the issue that is at the heart of the principle of self-government and self-determination. It is the Governor General's intention, which we fully support, that the people of Grenada will exercise their right of self-government and self-determination through the instrumentalities of free elections and free institutions. How, then, has their right of self-determination been violated, as some claim?

The states which make this claim presumably believe that the Grenadian 25 people enjoyed self-determination before October 25, which is to say, when they were subjected to a brutal reign of terror. The fact that these states include the Soviet Union, Cuba, and Nicaragua and others of their imperial vocation should not be at all surprising, since they do not, in fact, see any contradiction between self-determination and totalitarianism, between self-determination and the seizure of power by armed minorities, between self-determination and the subversion of democratic neighbors, between self-determination and absorption into the Soviet Empire.

Self-determination involves respect for "human rights and fundamental free- 26 doms," as stated in Article 55 of the Charter, and it is expressed through "self-government" that takes due account, as Article 76 states, of "the freely expressed wishes of the peoples concerned." Is there anyone here who can reasonably believe and credibly assert that the prospect for the full enjoyment of this right by the Grenadian people was not immensely better after October 25 than it was before that date? The Grenadian people do not take that view, nor do their neighbors who are closest to their situation.

Life is already returning to usual in Grenada. People are moving freely on 27 the streets after having been confined for ten days.

The Governor General and the people of Grenada know precisely what it 28 plans and how it proposes to achieve its goals. The Governor General is planning for a nonpolitical interim administration to prepare elections and return to democracy.

In the same broadcast quoted earlier, the Governor General announced 29 that 400 soldiers and national policemen from the Eastern Caribbean countries that took part in the landing would be formed into a security force. The Governor General has ordered remaining members of the People's Revolutionary Army and the militia to stop fighting and has officially disbanded the armed forces.

The proof of the pudding, of course, is finally in the eating. It is one thing 30 to rescue people from murderers and another for those same people to hold free elections. The latter does not necessarily follow from the former, although surely free elections and democratic life can hardly exist under conditions of terror. But let there be no question that it is the profound hope of the people of the United States that the Grenadian people shall soon enjoy freedom, democracy and stability. We trust that this hope is shared by those who invoke the principle of self-determination in their objection to the means used to rescue the Grenadian people.

"Force Used to Liberate and Force Used to Impose Terror"

There are those who say — let us be blunt — that the use of force by the 31 United States in Grenada is equivalent to the use of force by the Soviet Union in Afghanistan or Eastern Europe. Let me just pose the following questions in response: Is there no distinction to be drawn between force used to liberate captive people from terror and force used to impose terror on captive people? Is Solidarnosc in Poland to be equated with the Revolutionary Military Council in Grenada? Is "socialism with a human face" in Czechoslovakia of the Prague Spring the same as communism armed to the teeth in the Grenada of Bishop's killers?

There is, let me say, a parallel to be drawn between Grenada and Afghan- 32 istan — a very meaningful parallel. Just as Maurice Bishop was murdered in Grenada because he tried to free himself from the Soviet stranglehold, so, too, was Mohammed Daud murdered in Afghanistan and after him Hafizollah Amin. Let me here also remind the representative of South Yemen that on June 26, 1978, the President of South Yemen, Selim Rubai Ali, and two of his followers were executed for precisely the same reason. They, too, discovered that the only thing more dangerous than embracing the Soviet bear is trying to break loose from its deadly grip. They, too, learned that the price of trying to reverse the course of history — the inexorable course of history, in the Soviet view — is violent death. This, and this alone, is the parallel between Grenada and Afghanistan. The difference is that the people of Grenada have now been spared the cruel fate of the people of Afghanistan.

Speaking before the OAS, the representative of St. Lucia said that the 33
United States is only "guilty of responding positively to a formal request for
assistance from some of the Eastern Caribbean states who wish only to maintain
their security and protect their people from the totalitarian grip which seeks
to place a stranglehold on the Caribbean." There are others in this world who,
if not now similarly threatened by the totalitarian grip of the Soviet Union
and its proxies—who specialize in gaining power through subversion and terror
and then consolidating totalitarian control—may well be so threatened in the
future. In voting on this resolution, we ask them to consider what they would
do were they to be in the position of the Eastern Caribbean states? What
would they want done were their country subjected to the kind of terror that
prevailed in Grenada? Would they, too, appeal for rescue? And if they would
—which would be entirely consistent with a desire to preserve and defend
one's nation—we ask just one more question: How can they reconcile that
position with a vote in favor of the resolution now before us?

"End of the Dreams and Hopes of the U.N.?"

Has it come to this: that this organization, founded in the wake of a great 34
war against tyrants, comprising from the moment of its birth nations liberated
by force from the troops and quisling governments of tyrants, should meet here
to deplore the rescue of the people of Grenada from the grip of a small band
of murderous men whose clear intention was to secure the permanent subjugation of Grenada and its people and put this small but strategically located
island at the disposal of foreign tyrants?

If yesterday's victims of yesterday's tyrants should join today in "deploring" 35
the liberation of today's victim from today's tyrants—and should do so in an
organization founded precisely to ensure that there be no more victims, no
more tyrants—it would surely mark the end of the dreams and hopes of the
United Nations.

QUESTIONS FOR READING AND REVISING

1. Kirkpatrick's *argument* is no mere exercise, but an attempt to influence world
   events. In representing one of the most powerful nations on earth before the
   United Nations, Kirkpatrick planned a speech that uses standard argumentative
   strategy: she presents a thesis, makes subclaims in support of her thesis, and
   documents her claims with evidence. What is the substance of Kirkpatrick's

thesis? What subclaims does she present with it in paragraph 1? What further claims does she add in paragraph 2? Where does Kirkpatrick's argument begin to shift from a strictly rational to a partly emotional appeal? What words and phrases signal this shift?

2. In addition to defending her thesis, Kirkpatrick devotes considerable space to a counterattack on the United States's main ideological adversary. What *logical fallacy* does this attack represent? At what points in her speech does Kirkpatrick raise it? What clues does she give in paragraph 2 of her intention to take the offensive in this way? Why do you think she chose to do so?

3. Notice Kirkpatrick's use of the first-person plural in her opening paragraphs. Whom does she mean by "we" in paragraph 2? Whom does she mean by "us" in paragraph 3? What is the effect of the switch? How does Kirkpatrick increase this effect?

4. After preparing her audience in paragraph 3 for a discussion of the U.S. intervention in Grenada, Kirkpatrick does not immediately proceed with that discussion. Instead, in paragraph 4 she alludes to the U.N. General Assembly as if it were a court of law. How does this characterization put a special set of obligations on her listeners? How does it pave the way for her condemnations of Soviet actions later in her speech?

5. Paragraphs 6–7 are phrased as a chronological summary of the events under discussion. What claims does Kirkpatrick make in support of her argument while presenting this summary? What words and phrases highlight the clash of values underlying the U.S. action? What two words in paragraph 6 emphasize the U.S. position by assuring us that Kirkpatrick's value-laden phrases are accurate?

6. In paragraph 5 Kirkpatrick introduces what will be a major element of her speech: testimony from other sources. Looking back to paragraph 4, how does Kirkpatrick's use of testimony fit with her approach to this General Assembly debate? Suppose her audience — including the Soviet representatives — were to accept the way Kirkpatrick is trying to define the debate. What would her "opponents" have to do to present a successful rebuttal? How does Kirkpatrick's choice of "witnesses" make such a rebuttal difficult?

7. Kirkpatrick's strategy of quoting Caribbean leaders not only provides support for her claims but also adds new claims that might have been less persuasive coming directly from the United States's representative. What inferences does Jamaican Prime Minister Seaga make in paragraphs 7 and 8 that bolster Kirkpatrick's case? How do Seaga's claims help Kirkpatrick's contentions in paragraph 10 to sound convincing? What other *evidence* does Kirkpatrick offer in support of these contentions?

8. Having established the need for intervention on Grenada, Kirkpatrick begins the next phase of her *argument* in favor of the U.S. invasion in paragraph 12

(see her overview in paragraph 1). What is the thrust and purpose of paragraphs 12–18? How does Kirkpatrick use the security of other neighboring countries as a bridge to her next important point in paragraph 19? How does she use that point in turn to lead to the claim she defends in paragraphs 20–23?

9. Paragraphs 24 and following raise a crucial issue, one that Kirkpatrick obviously feels obliged to handle at length and with great care. What is this keystone of the debate between the United States and its opponents? What strategies does Kirkpatrick use to defend her position in paragraphs 24–30? How and why does she shift from a defensive to an offensive stance in paragraphs 31–33? How does she use the groundwork she presented previously in paragraph 4 when she reaches her conclusion in paragraphs 33–35?

QUESTIONS ON CONNECTIONS

1. Steve West concludes his *argument* in "Evaluating U.S. Motives for the Grenada Invasion" (p. 236) by offering an interpretation very different from Kirkpatrick's of the Reagan administration's reasons for sending troops to Grenada. How would the impact of West's essay be changed if he had omitted this final paragraph and stopped after his rebuttal of Kirkpatrick's argument? What evidence does West present in support of his conclusion? What additional evidence in Kirkpatrick's essay might he have cited? If you were Kirkpatrick, how would you refute West's conclusion?

2. Which argument — Kirkpatrick's or West's — do you find more convincing? Why? If the order of the two were reversed — if West presented his views and Kirkpatrick rebutted them — how would you expect each writer's approach to change? Do you think the relative effectiveness of the arguments would be likely to shift significantly? Why or why not?

SUGGESTIONS FOR WRITING

1. A central issue in the debate over the U.S. intervention in Grenada was whether one nation ever has the right to overthrow the government of another, and if so, what constitutes sufficient reason. Taking both Jeane Kirkpatrick's and Steve West's arguments into consideration, write your own argumentative essay addressing this issue.

2. Kirkpatrick's extensive anti-Soviet rhetoric suggests that she and West might agree on one point: "taking a stand against Communism" was apparently an important motive behind the decision to invade Grenada. Kirkpatrick's entire speech reflects the Reagan administration's tendency to view the world, rightly

or wrongly, as a battleground between the United States and the Soviet Union. This adversarial attitude is a pervasive one in our culture. Our legal system centers on the idea that every breach of justice can be cast as one party versus another, and every case ends with a winner and a loser. Our political system operates the same way. Even our sports are set up competitively, from the Olympics to professional football to amateur volleyball. Is this the only realistic way to organize human affairs? Write a *cause-and-effect* or *comparison-and-contrast* essay exploring an alternative attitude.

3. Ethics are a perennial source of debate in politics, where the problems are usually complex and the solutions often elusive. Should we sell nuclear technology to Nation X? If we do, they may use it to build weapons, endangering our future safety and the world's. If we don't, probably the Soviets will, and we will lose international leverage. Should we support a government that is favorable to the United States but repressive of human rights? Should we boycott trade to show our disapproval of apartheid, political arrests, or civil war, or will the resulting shortages hurt the people we mean to help? Choose a political problem you have studied, or about which you are curious, which has a strong ethical aspect. Write an analysis of this political problem in which you include your proposal explaining how this problem should be handled.

ELISABETH KÜBLER-ROSS

"It is a challenge to share with a human being his most difficult hours — and sometimes his finest," writes Elisabeth Kübler-Ross. This Swiss-American psychiatrist became an expert on the terminally ill through her work at the University of Chicago in the late fifties and sixties. Born in 1926 in Zurich, where she completed medical school, Kübler-Ross came to the United States as an intern in 1958. Seven years later, while teaching psychiatry at the University of Chicago Medical School, she created a teaching seminar at the Billings Hospital that she described as "a series of conversations with the terminally ill which would make it possible for them to talk about their feelings and thoughts in this crisis situation . . . [and] others would learn too how better to work with the dying."

Kübler-Ross's blend of scientific training, compassion, and personal experience has helped her to become one of the world's foremost writers about dying and human attitudes toward death. She has written eight books on the subject; "On the Fear of Death" is taken from her first and most famous book, On Death and Dying *(1969). In 1976 she founded Shanti Nilaya (home of peace) north of Escondido, California, which she now heads.*

On the Fear of Death

Let me not pray to be sheltered from
dangers but to be fearless in facing
them.
Let me not beg for the stilling of
my pain but for the heart to conquer it.
Let me not look for allies in life's
battlefield but to my own strength.
Let me not crave in anxious fear to
be saved but hope for the patience to
win my freedom.
Grant me that I may not be a
coward, feeling your mercy in my
success alone; but let me find the grasp
of your hand in my failure.
 — Rabindranath Tagore, *Fruit-Gathering*

Epidemics have taken a great toll of lives in past generations. Death in infancy and early childhood was frequent and there were few families who didn't lose a member of the family at an early age. Medicine has changed greatly in the last decades. Widespread vaccinations have practically eradicated many illnesses, at least in western Europe and the United States. The use of chemotherapy, especially the antibiotics, has contributed to an ever-decreasing number of fatalities in infectious diseases. Better child care and education have effected a low morbidity and mortality among children. The many diseases that have taken an impressive toll among the young and middle-aged have been conquered. The number of old people is on the rise, and with this fact come the number of people with malignancies and chronic diseases associated more with old age.

Pediatricians have less work with acute and life-threatening situations as they have an ever-increasing number of patients with psychosomatic disturbances and adjustment and behavior problems. Physicians have more people in their waiting rooms with emotional problems than they have ever had before, but they also have more elderly patients who not only try to live with their decreased physical abilities and limitations but who also face loneliness and isolation with all its pains and anguish. The majority of these people are not seen by a psychiatrist. Their needs have to be elicited and gratified by other professional people, for instance, chaplains and social workers. It is for them that I am trying to outline the changes that have taken place in the last few decades, changes that are ultimately responsible for the increased fear of death, the rising number of emotional problems, and the greater need for understanding of and coping with the problems of death and dying.

When we look back in time and study old cultures and people, we are impressed that death has always been distasteful to man and will probably always be. From a psychiatrist's point of view this is very understandable and can perhaps best be explained by our basic knowledge that, in our unconscious, death is never possible in regard to ourselves. It is inconceivable for our unconscious to imagine an actual ending of our own life here on earth, and if this life of ours has to end, the ending is always attributed to a malicious intervention from the outside by someone else. In simple terms, in our unconscious mind we can only be killed; it is inconceivable to die of a natural cause or of old age. Therefore death in itself is associated with a bad act, a frightening happening, something that in itself calls for retribution and punishment.

One is wise to remember these fundamental facts as they are essential in understanding some of the most important, otherwise unintelligible communications of our patients.

The second fact that we have to comprehend is that in our unconscious mind we cannot distinguish between a wish and a deed. We are all aware of some of our illogical dreams in which two completely opposite statements can exist side by side—very acceptable in our dreams but unthinkable and illogical in our wakening state. Just as our unconscious mind cannot differentiate between the wish to kill somebody in anger and the act of having done so, the young child is unable to make this distinction. The child who angrily wishes his mother to drop dead for not having gratified his needs will be traumatized greatly by the actual death of his mother—even if this event is not linked closely in time with his destructive wishes. He will always take part or the whole blame for the loss of his mother. He will always say to himself—rarely to others—"I did it, I am responsible, I was bad, therefore Mommy left me." It is well to remember that the child will react in the same manner if he loses a parent by divorce, separation, or desertion. Death is often seen by a child as an impermanent thing and has therefore little distinction from a divorce in which he may have an opportunity to see a parent again.

Many a parent will remember remarks of their children such as, "I will bury   6
my doggy now and next spring when the flowers come up again, he will get up." Maybe it was the same wish that motivated the ancient Egyptians to supply their dead with food and goods to keep them happy and the old American Indians to bury their relatives with their belongings.

When we grow older and begin to realize that our omnipotence is really   7
not so omnipotent, that our strongest wishes are not powerful enough to make the impossible possible, the fear that we have contributed to the death of a loved one diminishes—and with it the guilt. The fear remains diminished, however, only so long as it is not challenged too strongly. Its vestiges can be seen daily in hospital corridors and in people associated with the bereaved.

A husband and wife may have been fighting for years, but when the partner   8
dies, the survivor will pull his hair, whine and cry louder and beat his chest in regret, fear and anguish, and will hence fear his own death more than before, still believing in the law of talion—an eye for an eye, a tooth for a tooth—"I am responsible for her death, I will have to die a pitiful death in retribution."

Maybe this knowledge will help us understand many of the old customs and   9
rituals which have lasted over the centuries and whose purpose is to diminish the anger of the gods or the people as the case may be, thus decreasing the anticipated punishment. I am thinking of the ashes, the torn clothes, the veil, the *Klage Weiber*[1] of the old days—they are all means to ask you to take pity on them, the mourners, and are expressions of sorrow, grief, and shame. If someone grieves, beats his chest, tears his hair, or refuses to eat, it is an attempt

[1]Weeping women.

at self-punishment to avoid or reduce the anticipated punishment for the blame that he takes on the death of a loved one.

This grief, shame, and guilt are not very far removed from feelings of anger 10 and rage. The process of grief always includes some qualities of anger. Since none of us likes to admit anger at a deceased person, these emotions are often disguised or repressed and prolong the period of grief or show up in other ways. It is well to remember that it is not up to us to judge such feelings as bad or shameful but to understand their true meaning and origin as something very human. In order to illustrate this I will again use the example of the child — and the child in us. The five-year-old who loses his mother is both blaming himself for her disappearance and being angry at her for having deserted him and for no longer gratifying his needs. The dead person then turns into something the child loves and wants very much but also hates with equal intensity for this severe deprivation.

The ancient Hebrews regarded the body of a dead person as something 11 unclean and not to be touched. The early American Indians talked about the evil spirits and shot arrows in the air to drive the spirits away. Many other cultures have rituals to take care of the "bad" dead person, and they all originate in this feeling of anger which still exists in all of us, though we dislike admitting it. The tradition of the tombstone may originate in the wish to keep the bad spirits deep down in the ground, and the pebbles that many mourners put on the grave are leftover symbols of the same wish. Though we call the firing of guns at military funerals a last salute, it is the same symbolic ritual as the Indian used when he shot his spears and arrows into the skies.

I give these examples to emphasize that man has not basically changed. 12 Death is still a fearful, frightening happening, and the fear of death is a universal fear even if we think we have mastered it on many levels.

What has changed is our way of coping and dealing with death and dying 13 and our dying patients.

Having been raised in a country in Europe where science is not so advanced, 14 where modern techniques have just started to find their way into medicine, and where people still live as they did in this country half a century ago, I may have had an opportunity to study a part of the evolution of mankind in a shorter period.

I remember as a child the death of a farmer. He fell from a tree and was 15 not expected to live. He asked simply to die at home, a wish that was granted without question. He called his daughters into the bedroom and spoke with each one of them alone for a few moments. He arranged his affairs quietly, though he was in great pain, and distributed his belongings and his land, none of which was to be split until his wife should follow him in death. He also asked each of his children to share in the work, duties, and tasks that he had carried on until the time of the accident. He asked his friends to visit him once more, to bid goodbye to them. Although I was a small child at the time, he did not exclude me or my siblings. We were allowed to share in the preparations of the family just as we were permitted to grieve with them until he died. When he did die, he was left at home, in his own beloved home which he had built, and among his friends and neighbors who went to take a last look at him where he lay in the midst of flowers in the place he had lived in and loved so much. In that country today there is still no make-believe slumber room, no embalming, no false makeup to pretend sleep. Only the signs of very disfiguring illnesses are covered up with bandages and only infectious cases are removed from the home prior to the burial.

Why do I describe such "old-fashioned" customs? I think they are an in-   16 dication of our acceptance of a fatal outcome, and they help the dying patient as well as his family to accept the loss of a loved one. If a patient is allowed to terminate his life in the familiar and beloved environment, it requires less adjustment for him. His own family knows him well enough to replace a sedative with a glass of his favorite wine; or the smell of a home-cooked soup may give him the appetite to sip a few spoons of fluid which, I think, is still more enjoyable than an infusion. I will not minimize the need for sedatives and infusions and realize full well from my own experience as a country doctor that they are sometimes life-saving and often unavoidable. But I also know that patience and familiar people and foods could replace many a bottle of intravenous fluids given for the simple reason that it fulfills the physiological need without involving too many people and/or individual nursing care.

The fact that children are allowed to stay at home where a fatality has   17 struck and are included in the talk, discussions, and fears gives them the feeling that they are not alone in their grief and gives them the comfort of shared responsibility and shared mourning. It prepares them gradually and helps them view death as part of life, an experience which may help them grow and mature.

This is in great contrast to a society in which death is viewed as taboo,   18 discussion of it is regarded as morbid, and children are excluded with the presumption and pretext that it would be "too much" for them. They are then sent off to relatives, often accompanied by some unconvincing lies of "Mother has gone on a long trip" or other unbelievable stories. The child senses that something is wrong, and his distrust in adults will only multiply if other relatives add new variations of the story, avoid his questions or suspicions, shower him with gifts as a meager substitute for a loss he is not permitted to deal with.

Sooner or later the child will become aware of the changed family situation and, depending on the age and personality of the child, will have an unresolved grief and regard this incident as a frightening, mysterious, in any case very traumatic experience with untrustworthy grownups, which he has no way to cope with.

It is equally unwise to tell a little child who lost her brother that God loved 19 little boys so much that he took little Johnny to heaven. When this little girl grew up to be a woman she never solved her anger at God, which resulted in a psychotic depression when she lost her own little son three decades later.

We would think that our great emancipation, our knowledge of science and 20 of man, has given us better ways and means to prepare ourselves and our families for this inevitable happening. Instead the days are gone when a man was allowed to die in peace and dignity in his own home.

The more we are making advancements in science, the more we seem to 21 fear and deny the reality of death. How is this possible?

We use euphemisms, we make the dead look as if they were asleep, we ship 22 the children off to protect them from the anxiety and turmoil around the house if the patient is fortunate enough to die at home, we don't allow children to visit their dying parents in the hospitals, we have long and controversial discussions about whether patients should be told the truth — a question that rarely arises when the dying person is tended by the family physician who has known him from delivery to death and who knows the weaknesses and strengths of each member of the family.

I think there are many reasons for this flight away from facing death calmly. 23 One of the most important facts is that dying nowadays is more gruesome in many ways, namely, more lonely, mechanical, and dehumanized; at times it is even difficult to determine technically when the time of death has occurred.

Dying becomes lonely and impersonal because the patient is often taken 24 out of his familiar environment and rushed to an emergency room. Whoever has been very sick and has required rest and comfort especially may recall his experience of being put on a stretcher and enduring the noise of the ambulance siren and hectic rush until the hospital gates open. Only those who have lived through this may appreciate the discomfort and cold necessity of such transportation which is only the beginning of a long ordeal — hard to endure when you are well, difficult to express in words when noise, light, pumps, and voices are all too much to put up with. It may well be that we might consider more the patient under the sheets and blankets and perhaps stop our well-meant efficiency and rush in order to hold the patient's hand, to smile, or to listen to a question. I include the trip to the hospital as the first episode in dying, as it is for many. I am putting it exaggeratedly in contrast to the sick man who is left at home — not to say that lives should not be saved if they can be saved by a hospitalization but to keep the focus on the patient's experience, his needs and his reactions.

When a patient is severely ill, he is often treated like a person with no 25 right to an opinion. It is often someone else who makes the decision if and when and where a patient should be hospitalized. It would take so little to remember that the sick person too has feelings, has wishes and opinions, and has — most important of all — the right to be heard.

Well, our presumed patient has now reached the emergency room. He 26 will be surrounded by busy nurses, orderlies, interns, residents, a lab technician perhaps who will take some blood, an electrocardiogram technician who takes the cardiogram. He may be moved to X-ray and he will overhear opinions of his condition and discussions and questions to members of the family. He slowly but surely is beginning to be treated like a thing. He is no longer a person. Decisions are made often without his opinion. If he tries to rebel he will be sedated and after hours of waiting and wondering whether he has the strength, he will be wheeled into the operating room or intensive treatment unit and become an object of great concern and great financial investment.

He may cry for rest, peace, and dignity, but he will get infusions, transfu- 27 sions, a heart machine, or tracheotomy if necessary. He may want one single person to stop for one single minute so that he can ask one single question — but he will get a dozen people around the clock, all busily preoccupied with his heart rate, pulse, electrocardiogram or pulmonary functions, his secretions or excretions but not with him as a human being. He may wish to fight it all but it is going to be a useless fight since all this is done in the fight for his life, and if they can save his life they can consider the person afterwards. Those who consider the person first may lose precious time to save his life! At least this seems to be the rationale or justification behind all this — or is it? Is the reason for this increasingly mechanical, depersonalized approach our own defensiveness? Is this approach our own way to cope with and repress the anxieties that a terminally or critically ill patient evokes in us? Is our concentration on equipment, on blood pressure, our desperate attempt to deny the impending death which is so frightening and discomforting to us that we displace all our knowledge onto machines, since they are less close to us than the suffering face of another human being which would remind us once more of our lack of omnipotence, our own limits and failures, and last but not least perhaps our own mortality?

Maybe the question has to be raised: Are we becoming less human or more 28
human? . . . it is clear that whatever the answer may be, the patient is suffering
more — not physically, perhaps, but emotionally. And his needs have not
changed over the centuries, only our ability to gratify them.

QUESTIONS FOR READING AND REVISING

1. Kübler-Ross introduces her essay with a quoted Eastern prayer about human
   values and individual strength, then opens with a paragraph on Western medicine. How does this dramatic switch constitute an appropriate beginning for
   her essay? How would the essay's thrust change if Kübler-Ross had left out
   either the prayer or her medical journal opening?

2. Kübler-Ross's one-sentence fourth paragraph stresses the importance of "these
   fundamental facts." What are the "facts" to which she refers? Based on her
   evidence, how convinced are you that they really are facts? Would you be more
   or less sympathetic with the case Kübler-Ross is making if she backed up her
   statements with data or examples or both? Explain why. Why do you think
   she has chosen not to do this?

3. In the explanatory section running from paragraph 3 to paragraph 12, Kübler-
   Ross uses the word *always* several times — "death has always been distasteful";
   "the ending is always attributed to a malicious intervention"; "he will always
   . . . take blame"; "grief always includes some qualities of anger." Why is her
   tone so emphatic here? What other words does she use in this section that serve
   the same purpose? How does your reaction to her observations change when
   she says *often* in paragraph 6 and *maybe* in paragraph 7?

4. Kübler-Ross refers to herself, her intentions, and her experiences in the first
   person throughout her essay. She also gives us the first-person viewpoint of
   various characters in her narrative. What is the effect of her use of *I* in each
   instance? Does Kübler-Ross's authorial voice remain the same or change over
   the course of her essay? How does her voice suit her subject, and how is it
   meant to affect her readers?

5. Kübler-Ross says in her second paragraph, "The majority of these people are
   not seen by a psychiatrist. Their needs have to be elicited and gratified by
   other professional people, for instance, chaplains and social workers. It is for
   them that I am trying to outline the changes that have taken place in the last
   few decades. . . ." Do you think "them" refers to chaplains and social workers,
   or to the troubled people who consult them, or both? What obligations as an
   author does Kübler-Ross take on, or reject, by identifying and limiting her
   audience in this way?

6. In writing about death and people's fear of it, Kübler-Ross is admittedly tackling a subject likely to touch off strong personal reactions in her readers. What techniques does she use to encourage her *audience* to interpret their experiences in accord with her views? How does she present her position in a positive light and show the alternatives to be undesirable in order to win sympathy from readers whose experience is different from hers? What common values (and prejudices) that all her readers are likely to share has Kübler-Ross succeeded in identifying? How has she done so?

7. In contrast to the declarative mode of most of her essay, Kübler-Ross ends with a string of questions. What is her *purpose* in asking us to examine the motives behind current approaches and attitudes toward health care? Notice that Kübler-Ross's questions cast her readers (*us*) on the side of medical technology, not in the role of patient (*him*). What does Kübler-Ross accomplish by this tactic?

QUESTIONS ON CONNECTIONS

1. One of Kübler-Ross's themes is that the family of a dying person benefits from sharing in the death and accepting it as an important event in their own lives. Beverly Dipo's "No Rainbows, No Roses" (p. 70) describes the solitary death of a woman who has sent her family home to spare them the pain of watching her die. What is Dipo's attitude toward her patient's decision? What evidence can you find in Dipo's essay that supports Kübler-Ross's position? What specific references in Kübler-Ross's last six paragraphs, about people dying in hospitals, apply to the relationship between Dipo and her patient?

2. Some of the specific medical technology mentioned in Kübler-Ross's essay also appears in Dipo's. Yet Kübler-Ross's depiction of a patient in a hospital (paragraphs 23 – 27) is predominantly negative, whereas Dipo's is predominantly positive. How do these two writers use medical details to create contrasting pictures of similar scenes? What other details contribute to the contrast?

SUGGESTIONS FOR WRITING

1. In her famous study, *The Neurotic Personality of Our Time* (1937), the psychiatrist Karen Horney draws a provocative distinction between anxiety and fear:

> When a mother is afraid that her child will die when it
> has only a pimple or a slight cold we speak of anxiety; but
> if she is afraid when the child has a serious illness we call
> her reaction fear. If someone is afraid whenever he stands

on a height or when he has to discuss a topic he knows well, we call his reaction anxiety; if someone is afraid when he loses his way high up in the mountains during a heavy thunderstorm we would speak of fear. Thus far we should have a neat distinction: fear is a reaction that is proportionate to the danger one has to face, whereas anxiety is a disproportionate reaction to danger, or even a reaction to imaginary danger.

Drawing on your own experience — or that of other people you know — write an expository essay in which you illustrate this distinction between fear and anxiety.

2. Reread Kübler-Ross's essay as well as Horney's distinction between fear and anxiety in the previous exercise, focusing on the nature of the distinction between fear and anxiety. When you feel comfortable with the distinction between these terms, consider another pair of words that are often used interchangeably: *courage* and *bravery*. Write an essay in which you compare and contrast the meanings of these words. Use incidents — either real or imagined — to underscore the distinctions you want to make between the *definitions* of these terms. Another way to approach this exercise is to focus on Mrs. Trane, the dying patient Beverly Dipo speaks of in her essay "No Rainbows, No Roses." Given what you know about "courage" and "bravery," which would you apply to Mrs. Trane? Why? If neither, explain why. Write an essay in which you defend the proposition that Mrs. Trane is either courageous or brave — or how neither term can be applied to her behavior in her final days.

DONALD M. MURRAY

"My work with students over the past sixteen years has made me much more confident in the potential that students bring to the writing class." So wrote Donald Murray in the preface to the second edition of his book, A Writer Teaches Writing *(1985). "The national hue and cry about the decline in writing skills may be demonstrated at the beginning of the course, but the potential for good writing—in many cases, excellent writing—is within every class."*

Born in 1924 in Boston, Massachusetts, Donald Murray graduated from the University of New Hampshire, where he now teaches. Murray worked for the Boston Herald after college and won a Pulitzer Prize for his editorials. Since then he has been an editor for Time *magazine and a full-time writer, selling several hundred magazine articles to* Reader's Digest *and the Saturday Evening Post, among others. He has written juvenile and adult nonfiction, short stories, novels, and poetry. His books include* The Man Who Had Everything *(1964),* Man Against Earth *and* The World of Sound Recording *(1965),* Learning by Teaching *(1982),* Writing for Your Readers *(1983), and* Write to Learn *(1984).*

In addition to his distinguished record as an English professor and department head at the University of New Hampshire, Murray has taught writing to professionals through corporate workshops, and for such newspapers as the Boston Globe, Providence Journal-Bulletin, *and* Raleigh Times. *His essay, "The Maker's Eye," originally appeared in* The Writer *in 1973 and has been revised several times since.*

The Maker's Eye:
Revising Your Own Manuscripts

When students complete a first draft, they consider the job of writing done 1 —and their teachers too often agree. When professional writers complete a first draft, they usually feel that they are at the start of the writing process. When a draft is complete, the job of writing can begin.

That difference in attitude is the difference between amateur and profes- 2 sional, inexperience and experience, journeyman and craftsman. Peter F. Drucker, the prolific business writer, calls his first draft "the zero draft"—after that he can start counting. Most writers share the feeling that the first draft, and all of those which follow, are opportunities to discover what they have to say and how best they can say it.

To produce a progression of drafts, each of which says more and says it more 3 clearly, the writer has to develop a special kind of reading skill. In school we are taught to decode what appears on the page as finished writing. Writers, however, face a different category of possibility and responsibility when they read their own first drafts. To them the words on the page are never finished. Each can be changed and rearranged, can set off a chain reaction of confusion or clarified meaning. This is a different kind of reading which is possibly more difficult and certainly more exciting.

Writers must learn to be their own best enemy. They must accept the 4 criticism of others and be suspicious of it; they must accept the praise of others and be even more suspicious of it. Writers cannot depend on others. They must detach themselves from their own pages so that they can apply both their caring and their craft to their own work.

Such detachment is not easy. Science fiction writer Ray Bradbury supposedly 5 puts each manuscript away for a year to the day and then rereads it as a stranger. Not many writers have the discipline or the time to do this. We must read when our judgment may be at its worst, when we are close to the euphoric moment of criticism.

Then the writer, counsels novelist Nancy Hale, "should be critical of every- 6 thing that seems to him most delightful in his style. He should excise what he most admires, because he wouldn't thus admire it if he weren't . . . in a sense protecting it from criticism." John Ciardi, the poet, adds, "The last act of the writing must be to become one's own reader. It is, I suppose, a schizo- phrenic process, to begin passionately and to end critically, to begin hot and to end cold; and, more important, to be passion-hot and critic-cold at the same time."

Most people think that the principal problem is that writers are too proud 7 of what they have written. Actually, a greater problem for most professional writers is one shared by the majority of students. They are overly critical, think everything is dreadful, tear up page after page, never complete a draft, see the task as hopeless.

The writer must learn to read critically but constructively, to cut what is 8 bad, to reveal what is good. Eleanor Estes, the children's book author, explains: "The writer must survey his work critically, coolly, as though he were a stranger to it. He must be willing to prune, expertly and hard-heartedly. At the end of each revision, a manuscript may look . . . worked over, torn apart, pinned together, added to, deleted from, words changed and words changed back. Yet the book must maintain its original freshness and spontaneity."

Most readers underestimate the amount of rewriting it usually takes to pro- 9 duce spontaneous reading. This is a great disadvantage to the student writer, who sees only a finished product and never watches the craftsman who takes the necessary step back, studies the work carefully, returns to the task, steps back, returns, steps back, again and again. Anthony Burgess, one of the most prolific writers in the English-speaking world, admits, "I might revise a page twenty times." Roald Dahl, the popular children's writer, states, "By the time I'm nearing the end of a story, the first part will have to be reread and altered and corrected at least 150 times. . . . Good writing is essentially rewriting. I am positive of this."

Rewriting isn't that virtuous. It isn't something that ought to be done. It 10 is simply something that most writers find they have to do to discover what they have to say and how to say it. It is a condition of the writer's life.

There are, however, a few writers who do little formal rewriting primarily 11 because they have the capacity and experience to create and review a large number of invisible drafts in their minds before they approach the page. And some writers slowly produce finished pages, performing all the tasks of revision simultaneously, page by page, rather than draft by draft. But it is still possible to see the sequence followed by most writers most of the time in rereading their own work.

Most writers scan their drafts first, reading as quickly as possible to catch 12 the larger problems of subject and form, then move in closer and closer as they read and write, reread and rewrite.

The first thing writers look for in their drafts is *information*. They know that 13 a good piece of writing is built from specific, accurate, and interesting information. The writer must have an abundance of information from which to construct a readable piece of writing.

Next writers look for *meaning* in the information. The specifics must build 14 to a pattern of significance. Each piece of specific information must carry the reader toward meaning.

Writers reading their own drafts are aware of *audience*. They put themselves 15 in the reader's situation and make sure that they deliver information which a reader wants to know or needs to know in a manner which is easily digested. Writers try to be sure that they anticipate and answer the questions a critical reader will ask when reading the piece of writing.

Writers make sure that the *form* is appropriate to the subject and the au- 16 dience. Form, or genre, is the vehicle which carries meaning to the reader, but form cannot be selected until the writer has adequate information to discover its significance and an audience which needs or wants that meaning.

Once writers are sure the form is appropriate, they must then look at the 17 *structure*, the order of what they have written. Good writing is built on a solid framework of logic, argument, narrative, or motivation which runs through the entire piece of writing and holds it together. This is the time when many writers find it most effective to outline as a way of visualizing the hidden spine on which the piece of writing is supported.

The element on which writers may spend a majority of their time is *devel-* 18 *opment*. Each section of a piece of writing must be adequately developed. It must give readers enough information so that they are satisfied. How much information is enough? That's as difficult as asking how much garlic belongs in a salad. It must be done to taste, but most beginning writers underdevelop, underestimating the reader's hunger for information.

As writers solve development problems, they often have to consider ques- 19 tions of *dimension*. There must be a pleasing and effective proportion among all the parts of the piece of writing. There is a continual process of subtracting and adding to keep the piece of writing in balance.

Finally, writers have to listen to their own voices. *Voice* is the force which 20 drives a piece of writing forward. It is an expression of the writer's authority and concern. It is what is between the words on the page, what glues the piece of writing together. A good piece of writing is always marked by a consistent, individual voice.

As writers read and reread, write and rewrite, they move closer and closer 21 to the page until they are doing line-by-line editing. Writers read their own pages with infinite care. Each sentence, each line, each clause, each phrase, each word, each mark of punctuation, each section of white space between the type has to contribute to the clarification of meaning.

Slowly the writer moves from word to word, looking through language to 22 see the subject. As a word is changed, cut, or added, as a construction is rearranged, all the words used before that moment and all those that follow that moment must be considered and reconsidered.

Writers often read aloud at this stage of the editing process, muttering or 23 whispering to themselves, calling on the ear's experience with language. Does this sound right — or that? Writers edit, shifting back and forth from eye to page and ear to page. I find I must do this careful editing in short runs, nor more than fifteen or twenty minutes at a stretch, or I become too kind myself. I begin to see what I hope is on the page, not what actually is on the page.

This sound tedious if you haven't done it, but actually it is fun. Making 24 something right is immensely satisfying, for writers begin to learn what they are writing about by writing. Language leads them to meaning, and there is the joy of discovery, of understanding, of making meaning clear as the writer employs the technical skills of language.

Words have double meanings, even triple and quadruple meanings. Each 25 word has its own potential for connotation and denotation. And when writers rub one word against the other, they are often rewarded with a sudden insight, an unexpected clarification.

The maker's eye moves back and forth from word to phrase to sentence to 26 paragraph to sentence to phrase to word. The maker's eye see the need for variety and balance, for firmer structure, for a more appropriate form. It peers into the interior of the paragraph, looking for coherence, unity, and emphasis, which make meaning clear.

I learned something about this process when my first bifocals were pre- 27 scribed. I had ordered a larger section of the reading portion of the glass because of my work, but even so, I could not contain my eyes within this new limit of vision. And I still find myself taking off my glasses and bending my nose toward the page, for my eyes unconsciously flick back and forth across the page, back to another page, forward to still another, as I try to see each evolving line in relation to every other line.

When does this process end? Most writers agree with the great Russian 28 writer Tolstoy, who said, "I scarcely ever reread my published writing. If by chance I come across a page, it always strikes me: all this must be rewritten; this is how I should have written it."

The maker's eye is never satisfied, for each word has the potential to ignite 29 new meaning. This article has been twice written all the way through the writing process, and it was published four years ago. Now it is to be republished in a book. The editors made a few small suggestions, and then I read it with my maker's eye. Now it has been re-edited, revised, reread, re-re-edited, for each piece of writing to the writer is full of potential and alternatives.

A piece of writing is never finished. It is delivered to a deadline, torn out 30 of the typewriter on demand, sent off with a sense of accomplishment and shame and pride and frustration. If only there were a couple more days, time for just another run at it, perhaps then . . .

QUESTIONS FOR READING AND REVISING

1. In this essay on the revision process, Murray devotes ten paragraphs to documenting the value of revising before he shifts to a step-by-step *process analysis*. How would you categorize these first ten paragraphs in terms of their rhetorical strategy? What is Murray's evident *purpose* here? What is the function of the quotations he includes from other experienced writers?

2. Who was Murray's *audience* when this essay was first published? Being a profes-

sional writer himself, talking about his craft to people who presumably have some familiarity with it, Murray could have used the first-person *I* or *we*, or the second-person *you*. Why do you think he chose the third-person *the writer* and *they* instead? In what way(s) does this choice limit or enlarge his potential audience? What type of reader would probably be most interested in this essay?

3. Murray does shift into the first person to bring in his own experience in paragraphs 23, 27, and 29 – 30. How is your response to these *anecdotes* different from the rest of the essay? How would the essay's total impact change if Murray phrased it all as one man's conclusions rather than as a set of universal facts about writing? Would it be more or less convincing? Interesting to read?

4. Murray analyzes the revision process by making general statements about what writers do. What absolute terms does he use in doing this besides *must* and *cannot* in paragraph 4? Compare Murray's *tone* with that of the statements he quotes from other writers. What differences do you notice? What are the probable reasons for these differences?

5. In Murray's opening paragraphs and throughout his essay he talks about "the job of writing." Considering how few people are able to earn a living from writing, it must be true, as Murray says in paragraph 24, that "this sounds tedious . . . but actually it is fun." In that paragraph he also echoes a statement he made in paragraph 2, which suggests *why* it is fun. What are those two statements? What quality do they reflect that links writing to the work of detectives, social scientists, and explorers?

6. Which of the statements in this essay correspond most vividly with your own experience of writing and revising? Which statements surprised and informed you? Which ones (if any) do you disagree with? Why?

QUESTIONS ON CONNECTIONS

1. Reread the section of Part I (Students on Writing) in which the student writers discuss their attitudes toward and strategies for revising. What specific similarities do you notice between Murray's account and those of the student writers? What specific differences? Which student writer's *tone* most closely resembles Murray's when talking about revision?

2. Reread Part III (Three Student Writers at Work). Given Donald Murray's attitude toward revision, how do you think he might respond to the revisions Barbara Seidel presents — and discusses — in that chapter? What additional advice — drawn from "The Maker's Eye" — might Murray offer Seidel to help her strengthen her essay?

SUGGESTIONS FOR WRITING

1. Find or recall an essay that you started to write at some point and never finished. Or choose a piece of writing you have done that could serve as the springboard for an essay—a letter, a diary entry, an answer on a questionnaire. Following the steps Murray outlines, revise or enlarge it into an essay you feel reasonably confident will be well-received by your classmates.

2. As Murray (and Tolstoy) note, one frustration of revising is that there are no final right answers—one can always think of better (or at least different) ways to say what one has already said. Think of another open-ended field of endeavor, such as getting into shape, painting a picture, understanding one's mate, or completing one's wardrobe. Write a *process-analysis* essay about this activity, including how to decide when to stop.

ROBERT NISBET

Called "one of our most original social critics" by the New York Times, Robert Nisbet has explored America from the inside for many decades. He was born in Los Angeles and received his bachelor's, master's, and doctorate from the University of California. He taught sociology at the University of California at Berkeley from 1939 to 1952, with a break in 1949 for a visiting professorship at Columbia University.

Nisbet was awarded a Guggenheim Fellowship for 1963 – 64 and a Rockefeller Foundation grant for 1975 – 78. He has a long list of resident scholar appointments to his credit, as well as over a dozen books. "Nostalgia" is taken from Prejudices: A Philosophical Dictionary (1982). He also has served on the board of editors of the American Journal of Sociology and the American Scholar. Among his other distinctions are fellowships in the American Academy of Arts and Sciences, the American Philosophical Society, and the Society of American Historians.

Nisbet has cited the works of Alexis de Tocqueville, among others, as having "permanently shaped my mind when I read them the first time . . . and I still draw heavily from them." The Times Literary Supplement has commented, "Professor Nisbet could well be seen as continuing where Tocqueville left off, in seeking in American experience the destiny of democracy itself."

Nostalgia

Living with the past is vital to individual and society alike. Prevention of what Eliot called "disowning the past" and what Plumb called "the death of the past" is a responsibility of scientist and humanist alike. Man is a time-binding creature, and commitment to the past is but the other side of devotion to the present. 1

Nostalgia is, however, a special and far from salutary approach to the past. It is even at best a rust of memory, often a disease. Nostalgia breaks the telescopic relation of past and present that is the essence of ritual. It makes of the past a cornucopia of anodynes and fancies to draw from at will. It seizes upon some period, decade, or century and bathes it in solutions of sentimentality. The past, so necessary to replenishment of the present when properly understood, takes the form of memorabilia, golden-oldies such as records, books, and movies which should not be wrenched from their ages. Rarely does any effusion of nostalgia last long, but on the evidence of modern times, one effusion will shortly be followed by another, however different. Now it is the 1890s, then the 1920s or 1930s, even, mirabile dictu, the 1950s. 2

One form of nostalgia invites special attention; it is what the French call 3
nostalgie de la boue, literally, nostalgia for the mud. Individuals reach a point
in their lives when they become preoccupied by warped memories of childhoods
spent in poverty, squalor, the gutter. In recapturing this "mud," the imagination filters it, driving out the evil and converting it into something that,
although crude and coarse by one's mature standards, nevertheless presents a
picture of straightforward honesty, of rugged health, in contrast to the present.
Much of the current fascination with "roots," with genealogical origins, has
nostalgie de la boue mixed with it. One re-creates an early Brownsville, Hell's
Kitchen, or Salt Flats, in part to remind oneself of how far one has come in
the world, but in equal part simply to return to the "mud" of childhood and
youth.

Such nostalgia is to be found in those who have served in war. No matter 4
how appalling and seemingly unbearable the actual experience of war may
have been at the time, the passage of a few years is usually enough to transfigure
the experience, to purge it of all that was terrifying or horrible. The mind goes
back with appreciation to battle episodes, to the inanition of garrison life, to
the special hardships and deprivations. Sometimes this nostalgia comes very
quickly once war is over. The contrast between the communalism one had
known in a military unit and the more impersonal civil life just returned to
can be sharp. Most war memoirs have this element of *nostalgie de la boue* in
them.

Spreading nostalgia for the Great Depression is a glittering example of *nos-* 5
talgie de la boue at the present time. Doubtless some of it is the consequence
of living in an age of inflation and soaring interest rates. But a larger part of
the Depression nostalgia is occupied by filtered memory of a simpler form of
life, of hardships met, suffered from, and overcome, of a higher standard or
morality, of closer cohesion of family, and of a smaller generation gap. There
is a special bond today among those old enough to have gone through the
Depression, and also a certain sense of snobbery toward those who were not
then born.

Nostalgia can overtake whole nations. One of Hitler's great talents was his 6
capacity for arousing sentimental memory of the times when *Deutschland über
Alles* was recognized by the whole world, until, as he tirelessly proclaimed,
Germany had been stabbed in the back in 1918. Germany is by no means
alone in its penchant for national nostalgia. One need think only of post-
Napoleonic France. In America at the present time there is a growing nostalgia
for the presidency of Franklin D. Roosevelt, even, somewhat more strangely,
that of John F. Kennedy. The image of Camelot has proved to be a successful
one. The politics of nostalgia is real in most elections and mass movements.

Nostalgia, like boredom, is difficult to measure, but that it is a force in   7
history is hardly to be doubted. It is a reasonable guess that nostalgia of all
types will play a larger role in the future. The greatest barrier to nostalgia, in
contrast to simple respect for the past, is a social structure in which the forces
of stable growth outweigh those of instability and perceived formlessness. Ritual — religious, political, and other — is a strong force against nostalgia. But,
as is evident enough, both the stable and the ritualized are diminishing in this
century. And there is nothing to suggest a reversal of this trend.

QUESTIONS FOR READING AND REVISING

1. Nisbet's approach in this extended *definition* is quite different from a dictionary's. Where does Nisbet begin to define nostalgia? Where does he come closest
   to making a straightforward statement of the term's meaning? How thorough
   and objective is Nisbet's explanation of nostalgia as we normally understand
   it? What aspects of nostalgia has he left out?

2. What do you think Nisbet means in paragraph 1 by "living with the past"? To
   what extent do the two phrases he quotes make his meaning clearer? How
   would their effect be different if Nisbet had identified their authors more fully?
   if he had explained more specifically what they refer to? How would the essay's
   impact be different without this paragraph?

3. In paragraph 2 Nisbet describes what nostalgia does, rather than what it is or
   what people do who engage in it. What *figures of speech* contribute to his
   description? What value-laden words convey Nisbet's opinion of nostalgia? Is
   his language in this paragraph derived more from the past or the present? How
   does this affect the paragraph's impact?

4. Why do you think Nisbet uses the French term, *nostalgie de la boue*, in paragraph
   3 and following instead of an English equivalent? How would the essay's effect
   change if he substituted "nostalgia for the mud"? if he substituted simply "nostalgia"? What other words in paragraph 3 indicate the values that are part of
   Nisbet's definition? What evidence does he give to support his idea that nostalgia — and particularly this type of nostalgia — has a negative effect on individuals or society?

5. Nisbet's focus throughout this essay is more on *what* than on *why*. On the basis
   of the examples he cites, write a sentence summarizing the reason(s) why people
   indulge in *nostalgie de la boue*. What reasons can you add that Nisbet does not
   suggest? Would his essay be more effective if he gave more consideration to
   these reasons? Why or why not?

6. Although nostalgia is a quintessentially human activity, human beings are

conspicuously absent from most of this essay. Look closely for places where another writer might have used *we* or *you* or *people* or the name of a person or group. What alternatives does Nisbet choose? How does this absence of human beings reflect Nisbet's focus as a sociologist rather than a psychologist, political scientist, or historian? How does it affect your response to what he is saying?

7. Nisbet ends his essay with a prediction for the future. Is it an optimistic or a pessimistic prediction? How do you know? What does Nisbet suggest as a means to a different future? To what extent is he recommending a course of action in this paragraph? In what ways do you think the diminishment of the stable and the ritualized encourage nostalgia?

QUESTIONS ON CONNECTIONS

1. In paragraph 3 Nisbet says that individuals "become preoccupied by warped memories of childhoods spent in poverty. . . . In recapturing this "mud," the imagination filters it . . . [into] a picture of straightforward honesty, of rugged health, in contrast to the present." Ann Louise Field's "The Sound of Angels" (p. 76) might be said to fit this description. In what ways does Field's essay contradict rather than confirm Nisbet's statements? If Field were to write a counterargument to Nisbet's essay, what do you think would be her *thesis*? her main subclaims?

2. Like Ann Louise Field, Julie Reardon in "The Unmarked Road" (p. 202) returns to the "mud" of past poverty. What aspects of each of these essays represent nostalgia as Nisbet defines it? Can you imagine a future for Field or for Reardon that would cause either to look back on her poverty as a healthier time in her life than the more successful present? If your answer is yes for either writer, describe what kind of future could have this effect. If your answer is no, why do you think Nisbet's *definition* breaks down for the writer in question?

3. Brenda Jacobs's "Handing Down Grace" (p. 106) follows a strategy similar to Nisbet's—using *definition* to contemplate roots in the past—but the two essays' moods and purposes are very different. To what extent does "Handing Down Grace" exemplify Nisbet's comment, "Much of the current fascination with roots, with genealogical origins, has *nostalgie de la boue* mixed with it"? Nisbet's next sentence in paragraph 3 gives his explanation of this phenomenon. Reread his sentence, and then write your own interpretation of Jacobs's exploration of her roots.

SUGGESTIONS FOR WRITING

1. Nisbet is a sociologist, and most of his generalized examples in this essay involve group experiences. He describes nostalgia as "far from salutary . . . often a disease"; but he says little about *why* he views the filtering of memories as unhealthy. Only in paragraph 6 does he move out of his reliance on value-oriented language into a real example of collective nostalgia endangering a society. Read closely paragraphs 4–6 and write an argumentative or cause-and-effect essay about the role of nostalgia in luring a nation, culture, or group back into a bad situation it has already undergone (and should have learned from) in the past.

2. Nisbet's essay implies that nostalgia is always ill-advised, whether for groups or for individuals. Erik Field's "Rock Around the World" (p. 83) and Patrick Kinder Lewis's "Five Minutes North of Redding" (p. 150) are both nostalgic essays which suggest that what one recalls with affection in the past can enrich one's appreciation of the present. Write an extended *definition* of nostalgia that takes a positive or a balanced attitude in contrast to Nisbet's negative one.

3. "Living with the past is vital to individual and society alike," writes Nisbet. Many of the essays in this book show people coming to terms with past hardships — Julie Reardon's "The Unmarked Road" (p. 202), Linda Lavelle's "Confessions of a Blue-Collar Worker" (p. 144), and Nelsy Massoud's "War in Paradise" (p. 175), for example. Write a *narrative* essay describing a difficult experience of your own, whether as part of a group, like Lavelle and Massoud, or as an isolated individual, like Reardon. Indicate the impact of this experience on your life in the present.

JO GOODWIN PARKER

Who is Jo Goodwin Parker? We don't know. She made her unusual first appearance as a writer when George Henderson, a professor at the University of Oklahoma, was preparing his book, America's Other Children: Public Schools Outside Suburbia *(1971). The following essay, from that book, arrived in Henderson's mail from West Virginia with Parker's name on it. Whether the author wrote it out of personal experience or as a spokesperson for America's rural poor, her voice is authentic.*

What Is Poverty?

You ask me what is poverty? Listen to me. Here I am, dirty, smelly, and with no "proper" underwear on and with the stench of my rotting teeth near you. I will tell you. Listen to me. Listen without pity. I cannot use your pity. Listen with understanding. Put yourself in my dirty, worn out, ill-fitting shoes, and hear me. 1

Poverty is getting up every morning from a dirt- and illness-stained mattress. The sheets have long since been used for diapers. Poverty is living in a smell that never leaves. This is a smell of urine, sour milk, and spoiling food sometimes joined with the strong smell of long-cooked onions. Onions are cheap. If you have smelled this smell, you did not know how it came. It is the smell of the outdoor privy. It is the smell of young children who cannot walk the long dark way in the night. It is the smell of the mattresses where years of "accidents" have happened. It is the smell of the milk which has gone sour because the refrigerator long has not worked, and it costs money to get it fixed. It is the smell of rotting garbage. I could bury it, but where is the shovel? Shovels cost money. 2

Poverty is being tired. I have always been tired. They told me at the hospital when the last baby came that I had chronic anemia caused from poor diet, a bad case of worms, and that I needed a corrective operation. I listened politely —the poor are always polite. The poor always listen. They don't say that there is no money for iron pills, or better food, or worm medicine. The idea of an operation is frightening and costs so much that, if I had dared, I would have laughed. Who takes care of my children? Recovery from an operation takes a long time. I have three children. When I left then with "Granny" the last time I had a job, I came home to find the baby covered with fly specks, and a diaper that had not been changed since I left. When the dried diaper came off, bits of my baby's flesh came with it. My other child was playing with a 3 sharp bit of broken glass, and my oldest was playing alone at the edge of a lake. I made twenty-two dollars a week, and a good nursery school costs twenty dollars a week for my three children. I quit my job.

Poverty is dirt. You say in your clean clothes coming from your clean house, 4 "Anybody can be clean." Let me explain about housekeeping with no money. For breakfast I give my children grits with no oleo or cornbread without eggs and oleo. This does not use up many dishes. What dishes there are, I wash in cold water and with no soap. Even the cheapest soap has to be saved for the baby's diapers. Look at my hands, so cracked and red. Once I saved for two months to buy a jar of Vaseline for my hands and the baby's diaper rash. When I had saved enough, I went to buy it and the price had gone up two cents. The baby and I suffered on. I have to decide every day if I can bear to put my cracked, sore hands into the cold water and strong soap. But you ask, why not hot water? Fuel costs money. If you have a wood fire it costs money. If you burn electricity, it costs money. Hot water is a luxury. I do not have luxuries. I know you will be surprised when I tell you how young I am. I look so much older. My back has been bent over the wash tubs for so long, I cannot remember when I ever did anything else. Every night I wash every stitch my school-age child has on and just hope her clothes will be dry by morning.

Poverty is staying up all night on cold nights to watch the fire, knowing 5 one spark on the newspaper covering the walls means your sleeping children die in flames. In summer poverty is watching gnats and flies devour your baby's tears when he cries. The screens are torn and you pay so little rent you know they will never be fixed. Poverty means insects in your food, in your nose, in your eyes, and crawling over you when you sleep. Poverty is hoping it never rains because diapers won't dry when it rains and soon you are using newspapers. Poverty is seeing your children forever with runny noses. Paper handkerchiefs cost money and all your rags you need for other things. Even more costly are antihistamines. Poverty is cooking without food and cleaning without soap.

Poverty is asking for help. Have you ever had to ask for help, knowing your 6 children will suffer unless you get it? Think about asking for a loan from a relative, if this is the only way you can imagine asking for help. I will tell you how it feels. You find out where the office is that you are supposed to visit. You circle that block four or five times. Thinking of your children, you go in. Everybody is very busy. Finally, someone comes out and you tell her that you need help. That never is the person you need to see. You go see another person, and after spilling the whole shame of your poverty all over the desk between you, you find that this isn't the right office after all—you must repeat the whole process, and it never is any easier at the next place.

You have asked for help, and after all it has a cost. You are again told to 7
wait. You are told why, but you don't really hear because of the red cloud of
shame and the rising black cloud of despair.

Poverty is remembering. It is remembering quitting school in junior high 8
because "nice" children had been so cruel about my clothes and my smell.
The attendance officer came. My mother told him I was pregnant. I wasn't,
but she thought that I could get a job and help out. I had jobs off and on, but
never long enough to learn anything. Mostly I remember being married. I was
so young then. I am still young. For a time, we had all the things you have.
There was a little house in another town, with hot water and everything. Then
my husband lost his job. There was unemployment insurance for a while and
what few jobs I could get. Soon, all our nice things were repossessed and we
moved back here. I was pregnant then. This house didn't look so bad when
we first moved in. Every week it gets worse. Nothing is ever fixed. We now
had no money. There were a few odd jobs for my husband, but everything
went for food then, as it does now. I don't know how we lived through three
years and three babies, but we did. I'll tell you something, after the last baby
I destroyed my marriage. It had been a good one, but could you keep on
bringing children in this dirt? Did you ever think how much it costs for any
kind of birth control? I knew my husband was leaving the day he left, but
there were no good-byes between us. I hope he has been able to climb out of
this mess somewhere. He never could hope with us to drag him down.

That's when I asked for help. When I got it, you know how much it was? 9
It was, and is, seventy-eight dollars a month for the four of us; that is all I
ever can get. Now you know why there is no soap, no needles and thread, no
hot water, no aspirin, no worm medicine, no hand cream, no shampoo. None
of these things forever and ever and ever. So that you can see clearly, I pay
twenty dollars a month rent, and most of the rest goes for food. For grits and
cornmeal, and rice and milk and beans. I try my best to use only the minimum
electricity. If I use more, there is that much less for food.

Poverty is looking into a black future. Your children won't play with my 10
boys. They will turn to other boys who steal to get what they want. I can
already see them behind the bars of their prison instead of behind the bars of
my poverty. Or they will turn to the freedom of alcohol or drugs, and find
themselves enslaved. And my daughter? At best, there is for her a life like
mine.

But you say to me, there are schools. Yes, there are schools. My children have 11
no extra books, no magazines, no extra pencils, or crayons, or paper and the most
important of all, they do not have health. They have worms, they have infections,
they have pink-eye all summer. They do not sleep well on the floor, or with me
in my one bed. They do not suffer from hunger, my seventy-eight dollars keeps

us alive, but they do suffer from malnutrition. Oh yes, I do remember what I was taught about health in school. It doesn't do much good. In some places there is a surplus commodities program. Not here. The county said it cost too much. There is a school lunch program. But I have two children who will already be damaged by the time they get to school.

But, you say to me, there are health clinics. Yes, there are health clinics 12 and they are in the towns. I live out here eight miles from town. I can walk that far (even if it is sixteen miles both ways), but can my little children? My neighbor will take me when he goes; but he expects to get paid, *one way or another*. I bet you know my neighbor. He is that large man who spends his time at the gas station, the barbershop, and the corner store complaining about the government spending money on the immoral mothers of illegitimate children.

Poverty is an acid that drips on pride until all pride is worn away. Poverty 13 is a chisel that chips on honor until honor is worn away. Some of you say that you would do *something* in my situation, and maybe you would, for the first week or the first month, but for year after year after year?

Even the poor can dream. A dream of a time when there is money. Money 14 for the right kinds of food, for worm medicine, for iron pills, for toothbrushes, for hand cream, for a hammer and nails and a bit of screening, for a shovel, for a bit of paint, for some sheeting, for needles and thread. Money to pay *in money* for a trip to town. And, oh, money for hot water and money for soap. A dream of when asking for help does not eat away the last bit of pride. When the office you visit is as nice as the offices of other governmental agencies, when there are enough workers to help you quickly, when workers do not quit in defeat and despair. When you have to tell your story to only one person, and that person can send you for other help and you don't have to prove your poverty over and over and over again.

I have come out of my despair to tell you this. Remember I did not come 15 from another place or another time. Others like me are all around you. Look at us with an angry heart, anger that will help you help me. Anger that will let you tell of me. The poor are always silent. Can you be silent too?

QUESTIONS FOR READING AND REVISING

1. Parker's essay is constructed as a *definition*; the phrase "Poverty is . . ." begins most paragraphs. What simple and obvious definition of poverty does Parker never give? How does she convey this definition without stating it? What specific words and phrases in her essay allude to the basic concept of poverty?

2. Make a list of Parker's "Poverty is . . ." sentences. What kind of progression do they show over the course of the essay? How would the effect be different if Parker began with the long-term impact of poverty on her family (see paragraphs 10–11) instead of with the sight and smell of herself and her house? How would it be different if she did not look into the future at the end but stayed with her description of the present?

3. Parker's opening sentence, and several of her other sentences throughout her essay, are ungrammatical or awkward. Find at least half a dozen examples of such grammatical "mistakes" — inconsistent tenses, lack of parallel structure, sentence fragments, and so on. Do these errors comprise a positive or negative feature? In what way(s)?

4. Parker phrases her essay as a sort of dialogue between herself and the reader, introducing herself forcefully in her first paragraph. What sentences and phrases does she use to reassert this uncomfortably close relationship as her essay progresses? What assumptions does she convey about her audience? What appears to be the goal of her essay?

5. Parker uses both the first and the second person in two different ways. *I* represents the narrator and also a character in the story; *you* represents the reader and also a character more or less synonymous with the narrator (see paragraphs 4–5). Which *you* do you find it easier to identify with? Why? Which *I* is easier to sympathize with? How does Parker's use of person help her to achieve the *purposes* indicated in her first and last paragraphs?

6. Short, bulletlike declarative sentences are one way Parker drives home her points; repetition is another. What are the most common effects of her three- and four-word sentences? What words and phrases besides *poverty* does she use repetitively, either within a paragraph or over the course of her essay? What are the effects of such repetition? How does it suit Parker's subject?

7. Although characters are important to Parker's narrative, she does not tell us the names of any of them. How does this anonymity—plus Parker's anonymity as an author — influence your response to her essay? How would the essay's impact be different if it were written in magazine form like Roger Rosenblatt's "Lebanon: A Legacy of Dreams and Guns," in which the narrator conducts interviews and presents data and interpretations?

QUESTIONS ON CONNECTIONS

1. Jo Goodwin Parker, Julie Reardon, and Ann Louise Field present three contrasting first-person accounts of being poor. Looking back through Parker's "What Is Poverty?" Reardon's "The Unmarked Road" (p. 202), and Field's "The Sound of Angels" (p. 76), how would you characterize each writer's attitude toward her poverty? (For example: bitter? hopeful? sad? angry? dis-

gusted? self-pitying? something else?) What factors in her past and present situation seem most responsible for each writer's attitude? Which of these depictions of poverty do you think you will remember the longest? Why?

2. Parker, Reardon, and Field all mention turning points in their lives, when they went from a comfortable life into poverty and unhappiness. What specific images does each writer use to dramatize this change? What role does the writer's "significant other" (husband or brother) play in her change in fortune? Who is the most vivid character in each essay, and why? What is this character's main function?

SUGGESTIONS FOR WRITING

1. Jo Goodwin Parker has turned one of the most basic facts of her existence into the topic of an intense and compelling essay. Choose some fundamental fact of your own life that has shaped your attitude toward yourself and the world. Write an extended *definition* that, like Parker's "What Is Poverty?" and Thu Hong Nguyen's "A Good Woman" (p. 188), demonstrates the profound impact of a single characteristic on an individual.

2. A well-known Beatles song avows, "I don't care too much for money — money can't buy me love." Earlier, before they became rich and famous, the Beatles sang, "Give me money — that's what I want!" No member of a modern industrialized society goes through life without being affected by money — how best to use it, how to get more of it, how much importance to give it, how to negotiate about it with other people. Think of a point at which money has played a pivotal role in your life. Write a *narrative* or *cause-and-effect* essay about the situation and its impact on you.

3. Parker, Field, and Reardon all show us their experience with poverty through their own eyes. Choose one of the other characters in one of their essays. Imagine a plausible future for this character in a different setting — keeping house in suburbia, dealing drugs in an urban ghetto, sitting behind a desk in an office, making license plates in prison, and the like. Write a *narrative* essay in which this character reminisces about his or her years of acquaintance with the writer, describing some of the same events but from a distinctly different point of view. Your essay may be humorous if you like, but it should be as realistic as possible, based on the probable effects of poverty on your chosen character as well as his or her relationship with the writer.

JAMES RACHELS

In the introduction to his book, Moral Problems *(1971), James Rachels wrote, "It is easy for the beginning student to conclude that, contrary to his expectations, moral philosophy has little relevance to actual moral problems." Rachels's concern has been to change that, as he does once again in the essay that follows.*

Now Dean of Humanities at the University of Alabama in Birmingham, Rachels was born in Columbus, Georgia, in 1941. He graduated from Mercer University and received his Ph.D, from the University of North Carolina in 1967. By then he had already been appointed an assistant professor at the University of Richmond (Virginia). Rachels went on to teach at New York University and the University of Miami before moving to the philosophy department at the University of Alabama. In addition to Moral Problems, *he has edited (with Frank Tillman)* Philosophical Issues: A Contemporary Introduction *(1972). A member of the American Philosophical Association, Rachels has published articles in several journals, including* Philosophical Quarterly *and the* Canadian Journal of Philosophy. *"Active and Passive Euthanasia" first appeared in the* New England Journal of Medicine *in 1975.*

Active and Passive Euthanasia

The distinction between active and passive euthanasia is thought to be crucial for medical ethics. The idea is that it is permissible, at least in some cases, to withhold treatment and allow a patient to die, but it is never permissible to take any direct action designed to kill the patient. This doctrine seems to be accepted by most doctors, and it is endorsed in a statement adopted by the House of Delegates of the American Medical Association on December 4, 1973.

> The intentional termination of the life of one human being by another — mercy killing — is contrary to that for which the medical profession stands and is contrary to the policy of the American Medical Association.
>
> The cessation of the employment of extraordinary means to prolong the life of the body when there is irrefutable evidence that biological death is imminent is the decision of the patient and/or his immediate family. The advice and judgment of the physician should be freely available to the patient and/or his immediate family.

However, a strong case can be made against this doctrine. In what follows I will set out some of the relevant arguments and urge doctors to reconsider their views on this matter.

To begin with a familiar type of situation, a patient who is dying of incurable　2 cancer of the throat is in terrible pain, which can no longer be satisfactorily alleviated. He is certain to die within a few days, even if present treatment is continued, but he does not want to go on living for those days since the pain is unbearable. So he asks the doctor for an end to it, and his family joins in the request.

Suppose the doctor agrees to withhold treatment, as the conventional doc-　3 trine says he may. The justification for his doing so is that the patient is in terrible agony, and since he is going to die anyway, it would be wrong to prolong his suffering needlessly. But now notice this. If one simply withholds treatment, it may take the patient longer to die, and so he may suffer more than he would if more direct action were taken and lethal injection given. This fact provides strong reason for thinking that, once the initial decision not to prolong his agony has been made, active euthanasia is actually preferable to passive euthanasia, rather than the reverse. To say otherwise is to endorse the option that leads to more suffering rather than less, and is contrary to the humanitarian impulse that prompts the decision not to prolong his life in the first place.

Part of my point is that the process of being "allowed to die" can be rela-　4 tively slow and painful, whereas being given a lethal injection is relatively quick and painless. Let me give a different sort of example. In the United States about one in 600 babies is born with Down's syndrome. Most of these babies are otherwise healthy—that is, with only the usual pediatric care, they will proceed to an otherwise normal infancy. Some, however, are born with congenital defects such as intestinal obstructions that require operations if they are to live. Sometimes, the parents and the doctor will decide not to operate, and let the infant die. Anthony Shaw describes what happens then:

> . . . When surgery is denied [the doctor] must try to keep the infant from suffering while natural forces sap the baby's life away. As a surgeon whose natural inclination is to use the scalpel to fight off death, standing by and watching a salvageable baby die is the most emotionally exhausting experience I know. It is easy at a conference, in a theoretical discussion, to decide that such infants should be allowed to die. It is altogether different to stand by in the nursery and watch as dehydration and infection wither

a tiny being over hours and days. This is a terrible ordeal
for me and the hospital staff—much more so than for the
parents who never set foot in the nursery.[1]

I can understand why some people are opposed to all euthanasia, and insist
that such infants must be allowed to live. I think I can also understand why
other people favor destroying these babies quickly and painlessly. But why
should anyone favor letting "dehydration and infection wither a tiny being
over hours and days?" The doctrine that says that a baby may be allowed to
dehydrate and wither but may not be given an injection that would end its
life without suffering, seems so patently cruel as to require no further refutation.
The strong language is not intended to offend but only to put the point in the
clearest possible way.

My second argument is that the conventional doctrine leads to decisions   5
concerning life and death made on irrelevant grounds.

Consider again the case of the infants with Down's syndrome who need   6
operations for congenital defects unrelated to the syndrome to live. Sometimes,
there is no operation, and the baby dies, but when there is no such defect,
the baby lives on. Now, an operation such as that to remove an intestinal
obstruction is not prohibitively difficult. The reason why such operations are
not performed in these cases is, clearly, that the child has Down's syndrome
and the parents and doctor judge that because of that fact it is better for the
child to die.

But notice that this situation is absurd, no matter what view one takes of   7
the lives and potentials of such babies. If the life of such an infant is worth
preserving, what does it matter if it needs a simple operation? Or, if one thinks
it better that such a baby should not live on, what difference does it make
that it happens to have an unobstructed intestinal tract? In either case, the
matter of life and death is being decided on irrelevant grounds. It is the Down's
syndrome, and not the intestines, that is the issue. The matter should be
decided, if at all, on that basis, and not be allowed to depend on the essentially
irrelevant question of whether the intestinal tract is blocked.

What makes this situation possible, of course, is the idea that when there   8
is an intestinal blockage, one can "let the baby die," but when there is no
such defect there is nothing that can be done, for one must not "kill" it. The
fact that this idea leads to such results as deciding life or death on irrelevant
grounds is another good reason why the doctrine should be rejected.

One reason why so many people think that there is an important moral   9

[1]A. Shaw, "Doctor, Do We Have a Choice?" New York Times Magazine, January 30, 1972,
p. 54. (Author's note.)

difference between active and passive euthanasia is that they think killing someone is morally worse than letting someone die. But is it? Is killing, in itself, worse than letting die? To investigate this issue, two cases may be considered that are exactly alike except that one involves killing whereas the other involves letting someone die. Then, it can be asked whether this difference makes any difference to the moral assessments. It is important that the cases be exactly alike, except for this one difference, since otherwise one cannot be confident that it is this difference and not some other that accounts for any variation in the assessments of the two cases. So, let us consider this pair of cases:

In the first, Smith stands to gain a large inheritance if anything should 10 happen to his six-year-old cousin. One evening while the child is taking his bath, Smith sneaks into the bathroom and drowns the child, and then arranges things so that it will look like an accident.

In the second, Jones also stands to gain if anything should happen to his 11 six-year-old cousin. Like Smith, Jones sneaks in planning to drown the child in his bath. However, just as he enters the bathroom Jones see the child slip and hit his head, and fall face down in the water. Jones is delighted; he stands by, ready to push the child's head back under if it is necessary, but it is not necessary. With only a little thrashing about, the child drowns all by himself, "accidentally," as Jones watches and does nothing.

Now Smith killed the child, whereas Jones "merely" let the child die. 12 That is the only difference between them. Did either man behave better, from a moral point of view? If the difference between killing and letting die were in itself a morally important matter, one should say that Jones's behavior was less reprehensible than Smith's. But does one really want to say that? I think not. In the first place, both men acted from the same motive, personal gain, and both had exactly the same end in view when they acted. It may be inferred from Smith's conduct that he is a bad man, although that judgment may be withdrawn or modified if certain further facts are learned about him — for example, that he is mentally deranged. But would not the very same thing be inferred about Jones from his conduct? And would not the same further considerations also be relevant to any modification of this judgment? Moreover, suppost Jones pleaded, in his own defense, "After all, I didn't do anything except just stand there and watch the child drown. I didn't kill him; I only let him die." Again, if letting die were in itself less bad than killing, this defense should have at least some weight. But it does not. Such a "defense" can only be regarded as a grotesque perversion of moral reasoning. Morally speaking, it is no defense at all.

Now, it may be pointed out, quite properly, that the cases of euthanasia 13
with which doctors are concerned are not like this at all. They do not involve
personal gain or the destruction of normal healthy children. Doctors are concerned only with cases in which the patient's life is of no further use to him,
or in which the patient's life has become or will soon become a terrible burden.
However, the point is the same in these cases: the bare difference between
killing and letting dies does not, in itself, make a moral difference. If a doctor
lets a patient die, for humane reasons, he is in the same moral position as if
he had given the patient a lethal injection for humane reasons. If his decision
was wrong — if, for example, the patient's illness was in fact curable — the
decision would be equally regrettable no matter which method was used to
carry it out. And if the doctor's decision was the right one, the method used
is not in itself important.

The AMA policy statement isolates the crucial issue very well; the crucial 14
issue is "the intentional termination of the life of one human being by another." But after identifying this issue, and forbidding "mercy killing," the
statement goes on to deny that the cessation of treatment is the intentional
termination of a life. This is where the mistake comes in, for what is the
cessation of treatment, in these circumstances, if it is not "the intentional
termination of the life of one human being by another"? Of course it is exactly
that, and if it were not, there would be no point to it.

Many people will find this judgment hard to accept. One reason, I think, 15
is that it is very easy to conflate the question of whether killing is, in itself,
worse than letting die, with the very different question of whether most actual
cases of killing are more reprehensible than most actual cases of letting die.
Most actual cases of killing are clearly terrible (think, for example, of all the
murders reported in the newspapers), and one hears of such cases every day.
On the other hand, one hardly ever hears of a case of letting die, except for
the actions of doctors who are motivated by humanitarian reasons. So one
learns to think of killing in a much worse light than of letting die. But this
does not mean that there is something about killing that makes it in itself
worse than letting die, for it is not the bare difference between killing and
letting die that makes the difference in these cases. Rather, the other factors
— the murderer's motive of personal gain, for example, contrasted with the
doctor's humanitarian motivation — account for different reactions to the different cases.

I have argued that killing is not in itself any worse than letting die; if my 16
contention is right, it follows that active euthanasia is not any worse than
passive euthanasia. What arguments can be given on the other side? The most
common, I believe, is the following:

"The important difference between active and passive euthanasia is that, 17 in passive euthanasia, the doctor does not do anything to bring about the patient's death. The doctor does nothing, and the patient dies of whatever ills already afflict him. In active euthanasia, however, the doctor does something to bring about the patient's death: he kills him. The doctor who gives the patient with cancer a lethal injection has himself caused his patient's death; whereas if he merely ceases treatment, the cancer is the cause of the death."

A number of points need to be made here. The first is that it is not exactly 18 correct to say that in passive euthanasia the doctor does nothing, for he does do one thing that is very important: he lets the patient die. "Letting someone die" is certainly different, in some respects, from other types of action—mainly in that it is a kind of action that one may perform by way of not performing certain other actions. For example, one may let a patient die by way of not giving medication, just as one may insult someone by way of not shaking his hand. But for any purpose of moral assessment, it is a type of action nonetheless. The decision to let a patient die is subject to moral appraisal in the same way that a decision to kill him would be subject to moral appraisal: it may be assessed as wise or unwise, compassionate or sadistic, right or wrong. If a doctor deliberately let a patient die who was suffering from a routinely curable illness, the doctor would certainly be to blame for what he had done, just as he would be to blame if he had needlessly killed the patient. Charges against him would then be appropriate. If so, it would be no defense at all for him to insist that he didn't "do anything." He would have done something very serious indeed, for he let his patient die.

Fixing the cause of death may be very important from a legal point of view, 19 for it may determine whether criminal charges are brought against the doctor. But I do not think that this notion can be used to show a moral difference between active and passive euthanasia. The reason why it is considered bad to be the cause of someone's death is that death is regarded as a great evil— and so it is. However, if it has been decided that euthanasia—even passive euthanasia—is desirable in a given case, it has also been decided that in this instance death is no greater an evil than the patient's continued existence. And if this is true, the usual reason for not wanting to be the cause of someone's death simply does not apply.

Finally, doctors may think that all of this is only of academic interest— 20 the sort of thing that philosophers may worry about but that has no practical bearing on their own work. After all, doctors must be concerned about the legal consequences of what they do, and active euthanasia is clearly forbidden by the law. But even so, doctors should also be concerned with the fact that the law is forcing upon them a moral doctrine that may well be indefensible, and has a considerable effect on their practices. Of course, most doctors are not now in the position of being coerced in this matter, for they do not regard themselves as merely going along with what the law requires. Rather, in statements such as the AMA policy statement that I have quoted, they are endorsing this doctrine as a central point of medical ethics. In that statement, active euthanasia is condemned not merely as illegal but as "contrary to that for which the medical profession stands," whereas passive euthanasia is approved. However, the preceding considerations suggest that there is really no moral difference between the two, considered in themselves (there may be important moral differences in some cases in their *consequences*, but, as I pointed out, these differences may make active euthanasia, and not passive euthanasia, the morally preferable option). So, whereas doctors may have to discriminate between active and passive euthanasia to satisfy the law, they should not do any more than that. In particular, they should not give the distinction any added authority and weight by writing it into official statements of medical ethics.

QUESTIONS FOR READING AND REVISING

1. How can you tell immediately that Rachels's essay is an *argument*? Is his main purpose to win agreement for a position of his own, to refute a position he opposes, or to *persuade* readers to take some kind of action? What evidence in his essay indicates which of these three goals is uppermost in his thinking and strategy planning?

2. Rachels is a philosopher whose foremost professional tool is logic, yet his topic is a highly emotional one. Is his argument about euthanasia primarily a logical or an emotional appeal? How can you tell? At what point(s) in his essay does he make use of the opposite type of appeal? How does this tactic increase or decrease the essay's impact?

3. The balance between logic and emotion is crucial throughout this essay. Just as the term *euthanasia* is an emotionally neutral substitute for *mercy killing*, Rachels has chosen his words with a careful eye to their emotional weight. What pairs of synonyms, carrying different emotional connotations, does he use in this essay? (One example: *death* versus *an end to it.*) In what instances would the impact of a statement change significantly if the alternate word or phrase were used?

4. Where Rachels is making a point by means of logic, he generally tries to minimize the emotions involved. Look closely at his description of a patient dying painfully of cancer in paragraphs 2–3. How does he downplay the innate drama of this situation through the words he chooses and the way he uses them?

Rewrite one or two sentences of this description to depict rather than merely to announce the patient's agony. How does your rewrite change the focus of these two paragraphs?

5. What preference does Rachels appear to be expressing in the first sentence of paragraph 4? Where in this paragraph does his real point begin to emerge? How does the quoted passage help him to make his point? What contrasts do you notice between this description of a dying patient and the one in paragraphs 2–3? How do the two sentences following the quotation clarify Rachels' own position?

6. "My second argument is that the conventional doctrine leads to decisions concerning life and death made on irrelevant grounds," writes Rachels in paragraph 5. What does he mean by "the conventional doctrine"? What is the effect of using this phrase instead of a more explicit one? What are the "irrelevant grounds" he refers to? What unstated assumption about the power of medical science underlies this argument? Does Rachels support this assumption? If so, how?

7. Rachels bases a good deal of his argument in paragraph 9 and following on an imaginary *example*. Suppose that Jones in paragraph 11 did not sneak into the bathroom planning to drown his cousin, but found the child unconscious in the water and chose not to try artificial respiration. How would such a change affect Rachels's argument?

8. In paragraph 13 Rachels says, "Now, it may be pointed out, quite properly, that the cases of euthanasia with which doctors are concerned are not like this at all. . . . However, the point is the same in these cases." What does this tell you about the basis on which Rachels is evaluating morality? Does he rely primarily on a personal or social standard of right and wrong, on logic, on the law, or on some other set of criteria to guide his judgments?

9. Rachels ends his essay with this statement: "So, whereas doctors may have to discriminate between active and passive euthanasia to satisfy the law, they should not . . . give the distinction any added authority and weight by writing it into official statements of medical ethics." What assumption do both Rachels and the law make about the individual human differences between euthanasia cases that is not shared by the AMA statement quoted in paragraph 1? To what extent is Rachels concerned with what doctors should do when faced with an actual decision regarding either active or passive euthanasia? In what respects could this essay be classified as an extended definition?

QUESTIONS ON CONNECTIONS

1. How does the opening of Beverly Dipo's "A Time to Die" (p. 321) let you know that the author is presenting a different type of *argument* from James Rachels? Aside from the rhetorical contrast, Rachels constructs his argument

as a rebuttal to the AMA's statement of ethics. What is Dipo's thesis? What or whose position is she rebutting? How is the basis of her approach to defining morality and determining the morality of euthanasia different from Rachels's?

2. To what extent to Dipo's and Rachels's concerns overlap? What issues related to euthanasia do both writers consider? What points does Rachels make that Dipo does not? What points does Dipo make that Rachels does not?

3. Both Rachels and Dipo use *examples* to support their claims. Dipo names the characters in her examples and shows them in highly individual situations, whereas Rachels makes his examples as generalized as possible. How would each essay's impact change if these two writers switched tactics? In Dipo's "Judy" example, what are the effects of Judy's being a nurse?

4. What is the intended *audience* for Rachels's essay? for Dipo's? What role does Rachels mean his readers to play as they read his essay? Does he address them as fellow professionals, or as experts in a different field? How can you tell? What role(s) does Dipo want her readers to play as they read her essay? Does she depend most on her professional expertise, the precision of her logic, her audience's fears about their own deaths, their sympathy with her characters, their objective concern about the issue, or some combination? How can you tell?

SUGGESTIONS FOR WRITING

1. Write an *argument* defending your own position on euthanasia, using James Rachels's and Beverly Dipo's essays as background. If you agree with Rachels that the distinction between active and passive euthanasia is a false one, explain why both types of euthanasia are ethical and should be legal, or why both are immoral and should be prohibited. If you agree with Dipo's view that patients have a right to die as well as a right to live, write a defense of the AMA statement of ethics (or some modification of it) and indicate how life-and-death decisions should be made. You may wish to draw additional ideas and information from other essays in this book, such as those by Barbara Huttman and Elisabeth Kübler-Ross.

2. James Rachels suggests that having the power to take action that might extend a human life is equivalent to having an obligation to take that action. He also suggests that for a doctor passively to let death claim any patient is morally the same as actively terminating that patient's life. In making these arguments, Rachels is using logic to establish universal rules. A similar logic motivated the Truman administration's decision to drop the atomic bomb on Japan in World War II: because we have the power to take an action that might hasten the end of the war, we have a duty to take that action. Rachels's logic could be

extended to other aspects of life and death on an international scale. Write *cause-and-effect* essay showing what might happen if this were done — if, for example, the United States government were to decide that passively allowing the overthrow of a foreign government is morally the same as actively participating in its takeover.

3. The moral issues raised by Rachels and Dipo center on patients with enough money or health insurance to put their lives in a doctor's hands. Many life-and-death decisions are made at home, when patients and their families stay out of the hospital for cost reasons. Some nations, such as Great Britain, have instituted socialized medical care to ensure that a person's chances of survival are not determined by his or her financial status. In others, like the United States, health insurance is available at little or no charge to many workers through their employers, but it is prohibitively expensive for many others who are self-employed or unemployed. Write an essay examining the morality of medical decisions that are dictated by income rather than ethics.

ROGER ROSENBLATT

Roger Rosenblatt is one of the rare writers capable of handling a wide variety of subjects in a limited amount of space without becoming either brusque or superficial. Readers of his columns as a senior writer for Time *have watched him step adroitly from slips of the tongue in international diplomacy to attempted assassination, from history's famous letter-writers to twentieth-century fiction and the effects of war on children. "Lebanon: A Legacy of Dreams and Guns" originally appeared in* Time *in January, 1982.*

Rosenblatt was born in New York City in 1940 and graduated from New York University. He took his M.A. and Ph.D. at Harvard, where he became an assistant professor of American and English literature in 1968, and director of the expository writing program in 1970. He moved to Washington, D.C., in 1973 to serve as director of education for the National Endowment for the Humanities. Separating finally from academia, Rosenblatt became a columnist and literary editor at the New Republic. *In 1978 he moved to the* Washington Post, *and then to* Time. *He has also been a Fulbright scholar, a member of the board of directors of the National Book Critics Circle, a contributor to* Harper's *and* Saturday Review, *and the author of two books,* Black Fiction *(1974) and* Children of War *(1983).*

Lebanon: A Legacy of Dreams and Guns

> You are the bows from which your children as living arrows are sent forth.
>
> — Kahlil Gibran

Palestine twitches on the small white mat, struggles to raise her head, and 1 failing, falls back again: she cries, then stops. Some slice of light has caught her attention. The nurse in bright pink carries a bird cage to the mat, and for a moment Palestine is pleased by two jumpy canaries — one black, one yellow. Now she rolls back and forth. Her legs, still bowed, kick out spasmodically. You cannot tell if she hears the music in the nursery or the murmurs of the other babies, stacked up in their double-decker box cribs. She acknowledges no one. But everyone knows Palestine — if not by her blue "Space Patrol" sleep suit, then by the dark brown bruise on her right heel and, of course, by the circumstances of her birth.

For want of a standard term, the doctor on the case called the delivery a 2

"Caesarean section by explosion." It occurred last July in Beirut, during an Israeli air raid on the Fakhani Street PLO offices, when Palestine's mother, nine months pregnant, rushed from her apartment house in an effort to escape the bombs. No one is certain what happened next, but when the bombing stopped, Mrs. Halaby was found dead in the rubble. Three meters away, still enveloped in the placenta, lay her new little girl.

Only a remarkable twist, like the birth of Palestine, distinguishes one explosion from another in Beirut. For the past seven years the city has known the unremitting violence of the Palestinians, Phalangists, Syrians, and Israelis; the high period was a full-scale civil war in 1975–76, which blotted out up to 60,000 lives, roughly the same number that the United States lost during fourteen years in Vietnam. For the past few years destruction has been confined to Israeli reprisals against the PLO; sporadic clashes of the Syrians, Phalangists, and Palestinians; and the ordinary run of the street bombings and assassinations. As the Hachette guidebook on Lebanon observes, the city of Beirut is "overflowing with activity and variety."

The odd thing is that either the Lebanese are the most durable people in the world, or they have achieved a nirvana of terror that allows them an unearthly jauntiness. The sight of a new bank in Beirut is as common as a bashed-in Mercedes. You cannot tell if a hole in the ground is the work of a bomb or a construction team. The distinguishing sound of Beirut is the car horn — not the Beethoven or Roadrunner horn, but the I-am-going-to-kill-you horn. The most popular Beirut outfits are fatigues and berets, signifying the forces of the Syrians, the Palestinians, and occasionally the Lebanese themselves.

This is the place that will make up Palestine's official home, but in her mind her true home is likely to lie elsewhere. That mind is not entirely her property even now, any more than is her story, which is told in leaflets distributed by the PLO as part of its public relations. A postcard showing Palestine in a respirator bears a printed message in French that may be mailed to friends and allies. It refers to *"Technologie Israélienne"* and swears that Palestine *"est déterminée à continuer la marche vers la liberté."* Whether or not the baby has such determination at the moment, she will probably have it in four or five years. By then she may be an instrument of determination herself, her very name a beacon to other Palestinian children who are raised in this country to inherit their parents' dreams and enemies.

The Institute of Tel Zaatar was founded to provide foster families and education for the 313 children who lost their parents in the Tel Zaatar massacre of 1976. A year before that, 27 Palestinian residents of the Tel Zaatar camp were slaughtered by Christian Phalangists as they returned by bus from a rally celebrating a terrorist attack on Qiryat Shemona. In 1976 the Phalangists used 75-mm and 155-mm howitzers for a seven-week siege of the camp in which 3,000 died. Tel Zaatar was demolished.

The orphanage is a large, serene house with a facade of balconies. There 7 are 160 children in it now, not all of them victims of Tel Zaatar. Like children elsewhere, they have rebounded quickly from their tragedies. A small boy whose mother was killed while bringing water from a well refused at first to take water from anyone, fearing that it augured death. But after a few weeks in the home he overcame his phobia. A boy of two, who was in his father's arms when the man was shot, made no sound during the first six months in the home; now he is prattling like his peers.

Jamila, Boutros, and Mona have been at the home since it opened. Now 8 16, 16, and 17, respectively, they are considered elders, and have assumed the responsibilities of parents to the younger ones. They are sitting on a bed in a "family room"—all beds and dressers. Jamila, though in pigtails and sneakers, looks older than the other two. Her parents were killed in an Israeli shelling of Tyre. Boutros' father was killed when the Phalangists raided his poultry farm. Mona's father was killed after Tel Zaatar was destroyed.

"I was with my entire family, which divided into two groups, my mother 9 taking shelter in one building, my father, my brother, my sister and I hiding in another. But the Phalangists found us and started to shoot again. I fainted. I did not know what was happening until I awoke the next day and found my father, and everyone, all dead in the room with me."

Jamila observes that by losing their parents they have lost their childhood 10 as well. Like the girls in Belfast, these three have had to grow up quickly. Asked if they believe that they have gained anything by such experiences, Boutros replies, "Power." His face seems amiable for the answer. What he means by power is something specific: "To regain our homeland." At that all three talk at once: "First we were driven from Palestine in 1948"; "The Israeli's tried to exterminate us." "It's not their land. It's *our* land," says Jamila. Her voice is urgent. As the questions continue, she notices that her American visitor is sitting in an uncomfortable position. Without a word she rises and slips a pillow behind his back.

Whom do they most admire in the world? "Beside our great chairman, 11 Arafat," says Boutros, "there are Ho Chi Minh and Castro." For Jamila it is Lenin: "Because he made a new world for his people. He made them like themselves and work together." The question of the future is raised, and the three of them talk of Palestine's certain glory. Jamila offers something more: "I would put an end to the use of all nuclear weapons."

"Do you all plan to marry and have children of your own?"　　　　12

"You mean in the future?" They laugh. Mona blushes. Boutros jumps in: 13 "When I was very young, my parents told me about their leaving Palestine. I will teach my children to be strong and to depend on themselves, as I depend on myself. I will teach them to love all those who love the Palestinians."

Much of the nationalistic fervor arises from what the children have seen 14 firsthand as well as what they have been taught — as Nabil pointed out in the West Bank — so it is not fair to regard them solely as their elder's tools. Also their indoctrination may be indirect. The normal conversation of parents will influence children in any circumstance, and it would be a lot to ask of Palestinian parents that they display a political evenhandedness they do not feel. It may even be that for children like those in the Tel Zaatar home, this single-mindedness is not all that harmful. If there can be a benign side to indoctrination, it is that it offers a purpose; and when one's family is destroyed, any purpose, however limited, may be spiritually useful.

But the intensity of the indoctrination does not necessarily destroy one's 15 charitable impulses either. At this stage, at least, the children are still gentler than their masters would prefer — even when their masters happen to be in the military. Samer's father is a lieutenant colonel in the PLO: he controls the joint Palestinian-Lebanese forces in the region of Tyre. At the moment, Colonel Azmi controls his forces from a grass hut on stilts standing over an area bombed out by Israel last summer. The hut is furnished with red leather chairs and a Swedish-modern desk, behind which Colonel Azmi, 40, smokes Winstons and makes pronouncements:

"We are ready. We will not stop our struggle. We are not fascists. Our 16 power is our arms. Kissinger caused this trouble. We are not Communists. Begin is a Nazi. We never intend to kill children. Till the last child we will struggle to regain our homeland." The colonel looks up. "Ah, Samer."

His son enters the hut. Samer is four years old, about 3½ ft. high, and 17 dressed in matching black-and-white checked shirt and pants and polished black laced shoes. He strides regimentally toward the Swedish-modern desk and stands before his father.

"They are so young," explains the colonel. "But they are so proud." Then 18 to Samer: "Who is Sadat?"

"Sadat sold Palestine to Israel," says the boy, rapid-fire.　　　　19

"Who is Jimmy Carter?"　　　　20

"Carter supported Israel."   21

"Who are you?" asks his father with mock severity.   22

"I am from Palestine—from Hebron!"   23

"What is Israel?"   24

"The real name for Israel is Palestine."   25

The colonel invites his visitor to ask questions of his son.   26

"Samer, have you thought of what you would like to do when you grow up?" 27

"I want to marry." The colonel's men who have been sitting solemnly 28
around the hut explode with laughter. The boy blushes with shame and confusion. His father consoles him with a gesture of the hand. Asked if he would
like to live in a world that does not need soldiers, Samer says, "Yes, I would
love that." At his father's signal he exits.

"Colonel, would you send Samer into war?"   29

"I don't want him to suffer. But he would give his blood to regain his 30
homeland. If I am killed, my son will carry my gun."

The legatee system in which guns are passed to the children may find its 31
pinnacle in Ahmed, a leader in a PLO youth group, the *ashbals*, and in the
Boy Scouts. Just 15, he has already made speeches for the PLO in Cyprus,
Egypt, East Germany, Czechoslovakia, Bulgaria, Cuba and Moscow. The PLO
youth organization to which Ahmed belongs trains guerrillas from the ages of
eight to sixteen, when they may graduate to the rank of full commando. The
reason that Ahmed participates in both groups, explains Mahmoud Labadi,
the head of the PLO press relations in Beirut, is that "he is so active, he
doesn't want to let anything get past him." Labadi raises a hint of a smile to
let Ahmed know that he is teasing him. Ahmed smiles back broadly. His red
beret rests precariously on a cushion of burgeoning hair. His eyes look both
inquisitive and pained. His moustache is coming along.

Ahmed is sitting at the far end of a couch in a room at the PLO press office 32
on Wafik Al Tibi Street. On quiet days, that office's routine is to pass out
public relations material, like the postcard of Baby Palestine, and display Israeli
weapons recovered from attacks: a rocket with Hebrew lettering, the contents
of a cluster bomb lying in a helmet like a nest of brown eggs. This is not a
quiet day. Twenty-four hours earlier, Wafik Al Tibi Street was almost totally
obliterated by a car bomb filled with 100 kilos of TNT and 80 liters of gasoline.
Eighty-three people were killed and 200 hundred wounded. Labadi avoided
the explosion only by uncharacteristically arriving late to work. Now he tries
to catch up at his desk in the one room of the office that is not overwhelmed
by the noise of the cleanup. From time to time he looks up to see if Ahmed

needs a clarification in translation. On the whole, Ahmed's English is excellent.

"In 1970, when I was a child, the war began. Our family was thrown out 33 of our house. We lived in a school for many days. Then we lived someplace else. Once the war began, every place was dangerous. No place seemed safer than another." Still, Ahmed says that he was not afraid, even at so young an age, because "I figured out that a man may only die once."

"How long do you think you will live?"   34

"No one can know. Maybe I'll die in a minute." There is an unnerving 35 crash of debris on the balcony.

Ahmed hopes to study medicine one day, "because my people need doctors." 36 Asked if he has a more personal impetus, he says that he loves science, and his expression shows it. "I love to see how the body works — the head, the stomach, the heart." Can he retain his politics and be a doctor too? "The first work of a doctor is not to be a political man." He is presented with a hypothetical situation: he is a doctor fighting in Israel; a wounded Israeli comes to him for help. "Are you a Palestinian or a doctor?"

"A doctor, he says, with no hesitation.   37

"What is the most beautiful thing you have ever seen?"   38

"Palestinian soldiers. Because they defend our people."   39

"Have you ever seen something beautiful that is a bit more peaceful?"   40

"Yes." He smiles. "My lovely girl Jomaneh." Asked to describe Jomaneh, 41 he considers with only mild embarrassment. "She is not black and not white. Her eyes are green, I suppose. Her hair is long and blond."

"Is she intelligent?"   42

He turns to Labadi. "What should I tell him?"   43

"The truth."   44

"Yes, she is intelligent. But no girls are *very* intelligent. Jomaneh is more 45 intelligent than most." Labadi smiles, but does not look up.

The saddest thing Ahmed has ever seen, he says, is the sight of children 46 without their parents. In the Fakhani Street air raid last summer, he came upon three such children wandering dazed in the streets. He took them to his house, where they lived until a home was found for them. Yes, he does feel older than 15. "Because I do a job greater than myself."

He is asked if he believes in God: his yes is awed. Is his faith at all shaken 47 when he sees something like the devastation of yesterday's explosion? "Do you think: How could God allow such a thing to happen?" His answer is like Elizabeth's in Belfast: "No. There is no relationship between God and the people who do such things. Man does his work, God his."

"How do you see the future?"   48

"I do not think that war will last forever. I will work for that day." One of 49
Labadi's assistants enters the room to curtail the interview. The funeral procession is about to begin.

Out on the street a small cannon mounted on a pickup truck shoots white 50
clouds of disinfectant into the hot morning air. Most of the bodies were removed by midday yesterday, but in the afternoon someone discovered a detached face lying in a stairwell. Now children linger in the doorways to watch
a bulldozer push along the broken bricks. The children are kept off the street
itself as huge slabs of debris are thrown down from the windows of damaged
buildings—glass hitting the pavement with the crash of brief, sudden applause.
A strange boy in a clay-orange T shirt skips along the sidewalk flirting with
danger as the glass falls. He is bald, lost in some private game. His eyes roll
back, showing only whites.

It was, they say, the worst destruction since last July's air raids. Everyone 51
is positive that the bomb was the work of either the Syrians, the Phalangists,
the Israelis, or a combination of the above. The one group to take "credit"
for the act is something called the Front for the Liberation of Lebanon from
Foreigners. Within the general destruction, the front could take particular
credit for the murders of Sami al-Ghoush, a member of a militant Palestinian
organization, and his wife, who when the bomb exploded were just pulling up
in their car, having let off their ten-year-old daughter Lara at school. The
front could thus also take indirect credit for the sight of Lara in the morning,
standing between, and partly held up by, two girls her size, at the head of the
funeral procession now about to commence.

She has been placed at the head of the procession deliberately to symbolize 52
the effect of the bombing, and for a while she holds her ground with courage.
She wears a brownish barrette in her white-blond hair, which has been parted
in the middle and drawn to the back. Her white dotted dress has short puffed
sleeves and a Peter Pan collar. It is well pressed. Clearly Lara has been crying
a great deal, but she is not crying now. Her eyes are hollowed with dark rings.
If the girl were a dowager, you would say of her face: how beautiful she must
have looked when she was young.

Then Lara breaks down again. She covers her forehead with her right hand, 53
as if stricken with a headache. Her companions lead her away to a metal chair
in front of a store, where she rests as the procession begins to move without
her. She rejoins it later at the rear, half hidden behind the lines of PLO
soldiers, and the antiaircraft guns, and the sound trucks blaring tinny martial
music. Photographs of her father and mother are displayed in the windows of
an ambulance that serves as a hearse. The red lights of the ambulance spin,

the siren wails at a steady pitch, and the procession of some 800 Palestinians makes its mile-long journey through the dusty market-place, where chickens squawk in hanging cages and children clap at the parade. Now the children. Now the women in black. Now a bagpipe band, a legacy of the years of British influence.

The procession halts at a dirt clearing, where the crowd encircles a hoarse 54 speaker: "We are following the great leader who has been killed by the ene-mies." Sami's coffin has been removed from the ambulance, and is borne by six soldiers in helmets. Their faces shine with sweat. The coffin is wood painted silver. At first it tilts and looks about to spill—the soldiers on one side holding it higher than the others—but immediately it is righted again and draped with the Palestinian flag. The crowd climbs mounds of earth around the speaker in order to see him better.

"He has been killed by the Phalangists and the Israelis and the CIA. Now 55 we swear for his family: we will continue his mission. We may give up our soil, but not our weapons."

Lara is said to be nearby, but no one has seen her since the march began. 56

"I wonder what she is thinking [to a soldier in the crowd]."   57

"She is thinking: get revenge."   58

QUESTIONS ON READING AND REVISING

1. As Rosenblatt observes in paragraph 3, Beirut has been besieged by violence for many years. In that same paragraph he compares the casualties in the 1975–76 civil war with American losses during fourteen years in Vietnam. This essay, written for *Time* magazine, reflects the author's awareness that his audience has been reading, hearing, and watching stories about war for so long, the subject no longer shocks, or perhaps even interests, them. What is Rosenblatt's strategy for making this story different? What kind of reader curiosity and bias does he exploit to induce them to read his account?

2. Where does Rosenblatt present his *thesis*? What does he accomplish by opening his essay with a quotation and then an *anecdote* rather than with a paragraph stating his purpose? How does the essay's structure reflect its thesis? How would its impact be different if Rosenblatt had switched his opening and closing scenes?

3. In paragraph 8, Rosenblatt refers to "parents" twice. What effect does he achieve by repeating this word in contrasting contexts? Notice also the refer-ences to marriage and children in paragraphs 12–13 and 28. Why do you think

the response of the listeners in both cases was laughter? What can you infer about Rosenblat's reasons for questioning children on their hopes for the future? What point is he making by telling us about these two incidents?

4. In paragraph 10 Rosenblatt describes a girl speaking urgently about the war, then making her visitor more comfortable with a pillow. In paragraph 15 he says explicitly that "the intensity of the indoctrination does not necessarily destroy one's charitable impulses." The *anecdote* that follows further illustrates this point. What is Rosenblatt saying about the difference in attitudes between children and "their masters" (paragraph 15)? What other clues in the essay hint at the conclusion he expects us to draw about the relative value of patriotism and compassion?

5. The horror of living through a war is difficult to make real to an *audience* that has not experienced it. One way in which Rosenblatt conveys this horror is by juxtaposing fearful or startling *images* of war with homely, ordinary images of peace. What examples can you find of this *contrast* — between paragraphs, within paragraphs, and even within sentences? What specific tactics does Rosenblatt use to characterize war? To characterize peace?

6. Rosenblatt follows the journalistic tradition of keeping his reader's attention on his subject rather than himself. On the rare occasions when he does refer to himself, it is from the viewpoint of his subjects: "her American visitor" (paragraph 10), "his visitor" (paragraph 26). What other stylistic devices help Rosenblatt to stay out of sight? What are the advantages of this strategy? How does Rosenblatt put his imprint on his story without showing himself or addressing his *audience* directly?

QUESTIONS ON CONNECTIONS

1. Nelsy Massoud's role in "War in Paradise" (p. 175) is much more overt than Roger Rosenblatt's in "Lebanon: A Legacy of Dreams and Guns." Massoud is an insider whose personal experience provides the evidence for her thesis. On the basis of Massoud's essay, how does her indoctrination seem to have been different from that of the militant children in Rosenblatt's essay? How is the Lebanese adults' attitude toward war described in paragraphs 2 and 12 of Massoud's essay different from that of the adults in Rosenblatt's essay? How does Massoud's experience conflict with or confirm Rosenblatt's fears for the children now growing up in Beirut?

2. Massoud's main tactic for contrasting war and peace is the flashback: A violent incident interrupts her otherwise peaceful existence in New York, reminding her of a worse incident in Lebanon. Similarly, Max Ramsey's "For Myself" (p. 197) is a flashback from the present to the author's past experiences in Lebanon.

Why would Rosenblatt's essay be less effective if he had written his interviews as flashbacks after his safe return to the United States? What does he achieve by using a consistent present-tense time frame?

3. Rosenblatt puts more emphasis on showing his readers the effects of war than telling about them. Why didn't he include an explanation of his theme, like Massoud's paragraph 10, saying explicitly that war "kills all valuable principles in one's heart and mind"? How would such a statement change his essay's impact?

SUGGESTIONS FOR WRITING

1. The writer Walker Percy has observed that people often seem to feel most alive, most fully themselves, when the security of their lives is threatened. This may be one reason why Roger Rosenblatt and other journalists travel to danger zones like Lebanon and Vietnam. Based on your own experience or on the experience of people like Rosenblatt and Massoud, write an essay about the positive effects of surviving a threatening situation such as war, a natural disaster, or a violent crime.

2. We sometimes perceive our surroundings quite differently when we look at them though someone else's eyes. Rosenblatt's *description* of adults speaking for Baby Palestine and the ten-year-old Lara shows that such shifts in perception are not always accurate. Have you ever talked over a shared experience with a friend or family member and discovered that the two of you have conflicting memories? Have you ever participated in some activity in a foreign country, or some other unfamiliar setting, where you realize that your reaction was unlike that of everyone else around you? Write an essay describing such an experience, directly or indirectly contrasting your interpretation of the event and that of another participant.

3. Roger Rosenblatt, Nelsy Massoud, and Max Ramsey all emphasize that, as the poet William Wordsworth asserted, "The child is father of the man." A common proverb makes the same point in another way: "As the twig is bent, so grows the tree." Though few people would use the word "indoctrination" to describe their own culture's child-rearing practices, most of us are aware of beliefs or habits in ourselves and others that were drummed in at an early age. Among these are racial and religious prejudices, attitudes about sex roles and practices, treatment of the elderly, awe of prominent people, food preferences, etiquette, and trust in the printed word, to name only a few. Choose a habit or belief that you find particularly praiseworthy or irritating. Write a *cause-and-effect* essay either tracing its origins back to childhood training, or (if its origins are obvious) recommending a change in child-rearing practices that would encourage or eliminate it.

RICHARD SELZER

"Selzer is one of the few medical writers who takes a hard look at the actual subjects of medicine: disease, deformity and the human body with all its frailties. He is also one of the few who honestly notes the ambivalent reactions of doctors to these disturbing realities." These comments from a reviewer of Letters to a Young Doctor *(1982) reflect the complexity of Richard Selzer's dual insight as a physician and a writer. Born in Troy, New York, in 1928, Selzer graduated from Union College and went on to Albany Medical College. After postdoctoral study at Yale from 1957–60, he became an associate professor of surgery at Yale Medical School. His writing career has been simultaneous and illustrious: articles and stories in* Harper's, Esquire, Redbook, Mademoiselle, American Review, *and* Antaeus; *several books, including the volume of short stories* Rituals of Surgery *(1974) and two essay collections,* Mortal Lessons *(1977) and* Confessions of a Knife *(1979), from which "The Discus Thrower" is taken. In 1975 Selzer won the Columbia School of Journalism's National Magazine Award for essays published in* Esquire. *Now living in New Haven, Connecticut, he plans to augment his medical writing with a mythological treatment of the Civil War.*

The Discus Thrower

I spy on my patients. Ought not a doctor to observe his patients by any means and from any stance, that he might the more fully assemble evidence? So I stand in the doorways of hospital rooms and gaze. Oh, it is not all that furtive an act. Those in bed need only look up to discover me. But they never do.

From the doorway of Room 542 the man in the bed seems deeply tanned. Blue eyes and close-cropped white hair give him the appearance of vigor and good health. But I know that his skin is not brown from the sun. It is rusted, rather, in the last stage of containing the vile repose within. And the blue eyes are frosted, looking inward like the windows of a snowbound cottage. This man is blind. This man is also legless — the right leg missing from mid-thigh down, the left from just below the knee. It gives him the look of a bonsai, roots and branches pruned into the dwarfed facsimile of a great tree.

Propped on pillows, he cups his right thigh in both hands. Now and then he shakes his head as though acknowledging the intensity of his suffering. In all of this he makes no sound. Is he mute as well as blind?

The room in which he dwells is empty of all possessions — no get-well cards, small, private caches of food, day-old flowers, slippers, all the usual kickshaws of the sickroom. There is only the bed, a chair, a nightstand, and a tray on wheels that can be swung across his lap for meals.

"What time is it?" he asks.   5
"Three o'clock."   6
"Morning or afternoon?"   7
"Afternoon."   8
He is silent. There is nothing else he wants to know.   9
"How are you?" I say.   10
"Who is it?" he asks.   11
"It's the doctor. How do you feel?"   12
He does not answer right away.   13
"Feel?" he says.   14
"I hope you feel better," I say.   15
I press the button at the side of the bed.   16
"Down you go," I say.   17
"Yes, down," he says.   18
He falls back upon the bed awkwardly. His stumps, unweighted by legs and 19 feet, rise in the air, presenting themselves. I unwrap the bandages from the stumps, and begin to cut away the black scabs and the dead, glazed fat with scissors and forceps. A shard of white bone comes loose. I pick it away. I wash the wounds with disinfectant and redress the stumps. All this while, he does not speak. What is he thinking behind those lids that do not blink? Is he remembering a time when he was whole? Does he dream of feet? Of when his body was not a rotting log?

He lies solid and inert. In spite of everything, he remains impressive, as 20 though he were a sailor standing athwart a slanting deck.

"Anything more I can do for you?" I ask.   21
For a long moment he is silent.   22
"Yes," he says at last and without the least irony. "You can bring me a pair 23 of shoes."

In the corridor, the head nurse is waiting for me.   24

"We have to do something about him," she says. "Every morning he orders 25 scrambled eggs for breakfast, and, instead of eating them, he picks up the plate and throws it against the wall."

"Throws his plate?"   26

"Nasty. That's what he is. No wonder his family doesn't come to visit. They 27 probably can't stand him any more than we can."

She is waiting for me to do something.   28

"Well?"   29

"We'll see," I say.   30

The next morning I am waiting in the corridor when the kitchen delivers 31
his breakfast. I watch the aide place the tray on the stand and swing it across
his lap. She presses the button to raise the head of the bed. Then she leaves.

In time the man reaches to find the rim of the tray, then on to find the 32
dome of the covered dish. He lifts off the cover and places it on the stand.
He fingers across the plate until he probes the eggs. He lifts the plate in both
hands, sets it on the palm of his right hand, centers it, balances it. He hefts
it up and down slightly, getting the feel of it. Abruptly, he draws back his
right arm as far as he can.

There is the crack of the plate breaking against the wall at the foot of his 33
bed and the small wet sound of the scrambled eggs dropping to the floor.

And then he laughs. It is a sound you have never heard. It is something 34
new under the sun. It could cure cancer.

Out in the corridor, the eyes of the head nurse narrow.   35

"Laughed, did he?"   36

She writes something down on her clipboard.   37

A second aide arrives, brings a second breakfast tray, puts it on the night- 38
stand, out of his reach. She looks over at me shaking her head and making
her mouth go. I see that we are to be accomplices.

"I've got to feed you," she says to the man.   39

"Oh, no you don't," the man says.   40

"Oh, yes I do," the aide says, "after the way you just did. Nurse says so." 41

"Get me my shoes," the man says.   42

"Here's oatmeal," the aide says. "Open." And she touches the spoon to his 43
lower lip.

"I ordered scrambled eggs," says the man.   44

"That's right," the aide says.   45

I step forward.   46

"Is there anything I can do?" I say.   47

"Who are you?" the man asks.   48

In the evening I go once more to that ward to make my rounds. The head 49
nurse reports to me that Room 542 is deceased. She has discovered this quite
by accident, she says. No, there had been no sound. Nothing. It's a blessing,
she says.

I go into his room, a spy looking for secrets. He is still there in his bed. 50 His face is relaxed, grave, dignified. After a while, I turn to leave. My gaze sweeps the wall at the foot of the bed, and I see the place where it has been repeatedly washed, where the wall looks very clean and very white.

QUESTIONS FOR READING AND REVISING

1. What *thesis* is Selzer's essay intended to illustrate? What specific statements in the essay help to convey this thesis?

2. In his opening paragraph, Selzer refers to assembling *evidence.* What types of evidence does he use to support his position? Is his goal to present a rational *argument* or to win his reader's emotional sympathy? How can you tell?

3. Selzer implies in his first paragraph that he is the physician in charge of the patient in Room 542. How does he confirm this impression elsewhere in the essay? What is the effect of his credibility when the patient fails to recognize him as "the doctor"? How would the essay's impact be different if Selzer had included a scene showing himself giving medical treatment to the patient?

4. How does the thrust of "The Discus Thrower" change when the nurse and aides enter the essay? Notice the ways that Selzer, who is the narrator as well as a character in this story, conveys each character's attitude toward the others. What words and phrases tell us that Selzer's perspective is different from the nursing staff's? To what extent might the characters' attitudes toward the patient be influenced by their professional relationships to him and to each other? How would your reaction to the essay be different if you did not know that Selzer really is a doctor?

5. A well-known principle of writing is that we learn about characters from what they say about themselves, what other characters say about them, and what the narrator tells us. Which of these approaches does Selzer use most effectively? What do the various dialogues between characters add to our understanding of them and of Selzer's *purpose* in writing this essay?

6. Selzer tells us relatively little about his patient's medical history and condition. Instead, his depiction of the man in Room 542 leans heavily on descriptive adjectives and *figures of speech.* What words and phrases provide clues to the patient's health? How does Selzer's behavior toward this man help to prepare readers for his death and the nurse's — but not the doctor's — surprise at the end of the essay?

QUESTIONS ON CONNECTIONS

1. Selzer's essay, like Beverly Dipo's "No Rainbows, No Roses" (p. 70), ends with a close-up shot. Dipo shows us her patient's hands; Selzer shows us the wall at which his patient hurled scrambled eggs. What is the significance of this difference? How does it reflect a difference in the two authors' themes? How would the impact of Selzer's essay change if he left us looking at his patient's hands or stumpy legs instead of the wall?

2. Selzer, like Dipo, writes in the first person. Both authors begin with their own *point of view* and then withdraw to give us a look at the patient. However, whereas Dipo introduces herself as a nurse, Selzer calls himself a spy. How does the rest of each essay justify this difference in roles? How would Selzer have needed to change his story later on if he had started it by walking into Room 542 as Dipo does, preparing to treat a patient he knows is about to die?

3. Unlike Dipo, Selzer never tells us the name of his patient. What effect does this strategy have on our perceptions of "the discus thrower," the hospital staff involved in his case, and Selzer's view of the situation? Does Selzer's attitude toward hospital patients appear to have more in common with Dipo's or with Elisabeth Kübler-Ross's? What specific statements and tactics in his essay reveal his attitude?

SUGGESTIONS FOR WRITING

1. An essay that uses characters to help convey its theme creates the possibility for opposition, sympathy, or both. In "The Discus Thrower," Selzer uses the opposition between some of his characters (the patients, the nurses, and the aides) to highlight the sympathy between others (the patient and the doctor). Write a *comparison-and-contrast* essay using real or imaginary characters to represent your *point of view* and a conflicting one that addresses the same issue. Show people in similar situations (such as a doctor and a nurse) responding in sharply different ways, or people in contrasting situations (such as a doctor and a patient) sharing a position.

2. People who work with the ill or incapacitated are often forced to overrule their charges' wishes. Problems such as inadequate training, staffing, or funding sometimes create pressure to make decisions based on expediency rather than the most desirable outcome for all concerned. Choose a situation involving a person or group in authority and others who must abide by his, her, or their judgment — for example, a family argument, an organizational policy issue, or a political conflict. Write an *expository* essay in which you identify what you believe is the right decision, and explain the factors likely to help or hinder those in charge from reaching it.

3. Selzer gives us his view as a "spy" in "The Discus Thrower" — someone who observes but does not influence events. Imagine that you are one of the other characters in this essay — a nurse, an aide, a family member, or the patient himself. Select one of the issues raised by the man in Room 542 and write an argumentative essay in which you present a participant's viewpoint on that issue.

LEWIS THOMAS

Lewis Thomas has distinguished himself in both of his chosen fields: medicine and writing. Born in Flushing, New York, in 1913, he was first spurred toward medicine as the son of a general practitioner. Thomas entered Princeton University planning to concentrate on medicine, but he also discovered T. S. Eliot and Ezra Pound and began to publish poems of his own in the campus literary magazine. He completed Harvard Medical School and interned at Boston City Hospital; while there, he wrote a poem that was accepted by the Atlantic Monthly. During World War II, Thomas served in the navy as a lieutenant commander doing research in tropical diseases and also participated in the landing in Okinawa. In 1946 he returned to academic research, teaching, and administration at Johns Hopkins, then Tulane, and then the University of Minnesota. In 1954 he moved to New York University and in 1969 to Yale. He became president and chief executive officer of Memorial Sloan-Kettering Cancer Center in New York in 1973, where he is now chancellor.

While serving as dean of the medical school at Yale, Thomas was invited by a friend to contribute a monthly column to the New England Journal of Medicine. *He welcomed the chance to try his hand at essays — "Good bad verse was what I was pretty good at," he recalls. "The only other writing I'd done was scientific papers . . . in the relentlessly flat style required for absolute unambiguity." The column was a success: "After six months I'd had six essays published and thought that was enough. . . . I got a letter back saying no, I had to keep it up, they were getting letters from readers expressing interest." Prodded partly by an admiring letter from Joyce Carol Oates, Thomas eventually published twenty-nine of his "Notes of a Biology-Watcher" columns as a book. That collection,* The Lives of a Cell, *in which "The Iks" appears, not only became a best-seller but won the 1974 National Book Award for Arts and Letters. It was followed by* The Medusa and the Snail: More Notes of a Biology Watcher *(1979),* Late Night Thoughts on Listening to Mahler's Ninth Symphony *(1980), and an autobiography,* The Youngest Science *(1983).*

The Iks

The small tribe of Iks, formerly nomadic hunters and gatherers in the mountain valleys of northern Uganda, have become celebrities, literary symbols for the ultimate fate of disheartened, heartless mankind at large. Two disastrously conclusive things happened to them: the government decided to have a national park, so they were compelled by law to give up hunting in the valleys and become farmers on poor hillside soil, and then they were visited for two years by an anthropologist who detested them and wrote a book about them.

The message of the book is that the Iks have transformed themseves into 2 an irreversibly disagreeable collection of unattached, brutish creatures, totally selfish and loveless, in response to the dismantling of their traditional culture, Moreover, this is what the rest of us are like in our inner selves, and we will all turn into Iks when the structure of our society comes all unhinged.

The argument rests, of course, on certain assumptions about the core of 3 human beings and is necessarily speculative. You have to agree in advance that man is fundamentally a bad lot, out for himself alone, displaying such graces as affection and compassion only as learned habits. If you take this view, the story of the Iks can be used to confirm it. These people seem to be living together, clustered in small, dense villages, but they are really solitary, unrelated individuals with no evident use for each other. They talk, but only to make ill-tempered demands and cold refusals. They share nothing. They never sing. They turn the children out to forage as soon as they can walk, and desert the elders to starve whenever they can and the foraging children snatch food from the mouths of the helpless elders. It is a mean society.

They breed without love or even casual regard. They defecate on each 4 other's doorsteps. They watch their neighbors for signs of misfortune and only then do they laugh. In the book they do a lot of laughing, having so much bad luck. Several times they even laughed at the anthropologist, who found this especially repellent (one senses, between the lines, that the scholar is not himself the world's luckiest man). Worse, they took him into the family, snatched his food, defecated on his doorstep, and hooted dislike at him. They gave him two bad years.

It is a depressing book. If, as he suggests, there is only Ikness at the center 5 of each of us, our sole hope for hanging on to the name of humanity will be in endlessly mending the structure of our society, and it is changing so quickly and completely that we may never find the threads in time. Meanwhile, left to ourselves alone, solitary, we will become the same joyless, zestless, untouching lone animals.

But this may be too narrow a view. For one thing, the Iks are extraordinary. 6 They are absolutely astonishing, in fact. The anthropologist has never seen people like them anywhere, nor have I. You'd think, if they were simply examples of the common essence of mankind, they'd seem more recognizable. Instead, they are bizarre, anomalous. I have known my share of peculiar, difficult, nervous, grabby people, but I've never encountered any genuinely, consistently detestable human beings in all my life. The Iks sound more like abnormalities, maladies.

I cannot accept it. I do not believe that the Iks are representative of isolated, 7 revealed man, unobscured by social habits. I believe their behavior is something extra, something laid on. This unremitting, compulsive repellence is a kind of complicated ritual. They must have learned to act this way; they copied it, somehow.

I have a theory, then. The Iks have gone crazy.   8

The solitary Ik, isolated in the ruins of an exploded culture, has built a new 9 defense for himself. If you live in an unworkable society you can make up one of your own, and this is that the Iks have done. Each Ik has become a group, a one-man tribe of its own, a constituency.

Now everything falls into place. This is why they do seem, after all, vaguely 10 familiar to all of us. We've seen them before. This is precisely the way groups of one size or another, ranging from committees to nations, behave. It is, of course, this aspect of humanity that has lagged behind the rest of evolution, and this is why the Ik seems so primitive. In his absolute selfishness, his capacity to give anything away, no matter what, he is a successful committee. When he stands at the door of his hut, shouting insults at his neighbors in a loud harangue, he is city addressing another city.

Cities have all the Ik characteristics. They defecate on the doorsteps, in 11 rivers and lakes, their own or anyone else's. They leave rubbish. They detest all neighboring cities, give nothing away. They even build institutions for deserting elders out of sight.

Nations are the most Iklike of all. No wonder the Iks seem familiar. For 12 total greed, rapacity, heartlessness, and irresponsibility, there is nothing to match a nation. Nations, by law, are solitary, self-centered, withdrawn into themselves. There is no such thing as affection between nations, and certainly no nation ever loved another. They bawl insults from their doorsteps, defecate into whole oceans, snatch all the food, survive by detestation, take joy in the bad luck of others, celebrate the death of others, live for the death of others.

That's it, and I shall stop worrying about the book. It does not signify that 13 man is a sparse, inhuman thing at his center. He's all right. It only says what we've always known and never had enough time to worry about, that we haven't yet learned how to stay human when assembled in masses. The Ik, in his despair, is acting out this failure, and perhaps we should pay closer attention. Nations have themselves become too frightening to think about, but we might learn some things by watching these people.

QUESTIONS FOR READING AND REVISING

1. Thomas uses three rhetorical patterns in his essay. Find specific sentences or paragraphs that let you know "The Iks" is (1) a *cause-and-effect* essay, (2) an *argument,* and (3) an *analogy.* In Thomas's view, what cause has created what effect? What argument is he making or rebutting? What two phenomena does he perceive as analogous?

2. To characterize the Iks, Thomas both shows us and tells us what they are like. Which approach is he taking in paragraph 2? What parts of speech does he rely on most heavily in this *description?* Which approach is he taking in paragraphs 3 – 4? What parts of speech are most significant here? Which of these two descriptions gives you a more visual sense of the Iks? Which one is more openly judgmental?

3. Thomas uses repetition to emphasize the Iks' repellant qualities and to present his own position in the latter part of his essay. In what paragraphs does he introduce the Iks' key faults, which will become the basis of his *analogy?* In what paragraphs does he repeat those faults in new contexts? What qualities or behaviors, if any, does he include in his analogy that were not part of his original description? What stylistic techniques and word choices make Thomas's last catalog of obnoxious Ik-type behavior the most vivid and extreme?

4. After his climactic paragraph 12, Thomas's concluding paragraph 13 is surprisingly optimistic. What three statements in this paragraph tie off the essay's three rhetorical patterns? Suppose Thomas had used only one pattern and therefore needed to draw only one conclusion. How might he have ended more specifically? Less cheerfully? Write a short concluding paragraph for each pattern, giving careful thought to the implications Thomas glosses over when he concludes, "We might learn some things by watching these people."

5. What is the role of *evidence* in this essay? How important to Thomas's *purpose* is the accuracy of the anthropological research he mentions? The accuracy of his summary of that research? Why and how can you tell? What is the nature of Thomas's concern about the Iks?

6. In paragraphs 7 – 9, Thomas proposes three apparently different theories about the Iks. First, their repellence is a learned ritual: "they copied it, somehow." At what point in their history, and from whom or what, might the Iks have picked up their bizarre behavior? Second, "the Iks have gone crazy." *Crazy* is an unusual word choice for someone with Thomas's medical background. Is he treating craziness here as a cause (the Iks' behavior makes no sense, therefore they must be crazy) or as an effect (the Iks' social dislocation has turned into psychological dislocation)? Third, to defend themselves against "an unworkable society" the Iks have invented their own. Is this a "crazy" or rational act? Write a short paragraph integrating Thomas's three theories into a single explanation of the Iks' behavior.

QUESTIONS ON CONNECTIONS

1. Julie Reardon's "The Unmarked Road" (p. 202) could be viewed as an anthropological foray within America. What qualities do Reardon's characters have in common with the Iks? What factors in the backgrounds of Reardon's characters appear to have caused their present problems? In what ways are these people notably different from the Iks and why? How are Reardon's position and her response to her subjects different from those of the anthropologist in Thomas's essay?

2. What central concept about human behavior does Johnna Lynn Benson's "Rotten at the Core" (p. 31) share with Lewis Thomas's "The Iks"? Whereas Thomas focuses on a bizarre group of isolated individuals, Benson focuses on an individual who would like to feel more bizarre and isolated than she does. What ideas in her *cause-and-effect* analysis might help to explain the Iks' self-centeredness.

SUGGESTIONS FOR WRITING

1. "The Iks are extraordinary," writes Thomas. "You'd think, if they were simply examples of the common essence of mankind, they'd seem more recognizable. Instead, they are bizarre, anomalous." In this statement he alludes to the human tendency to interpret others in terms of ourselves, to sympathize with what we recognize, and to fear what we cannot understand. Thomas disarms the threat posed by the Iks by classifying them in familiar, comprehensible terms as "one-man tribes." Writers of horror stories use the opposite tactic: normal-looking people become threatening when they defy our expectations. (See, for example, Stephen King's "The Horror in Horror Movies.") This is also a favorite tactic of propagandists. Think of a political or social controversy that you feel has been distorted by one side's depicting its opponents or their practices as "bizarre, anomalous" — in short, inhuman. Write an essay showing how the real issue has been obscured by a manipulation of people's fears.

2. The message of the Iks, says Thomas, is not "that man is a sparse, inhuman thing at his center . . . [but] that we haven't yet learned how to stay human when assembled in masses." Choose a group of people who, acting en masse, illustrates this idea: Hitler's Germany, the Hell's Angels, upscale young professionals at a cocktail party, heavy-metal rock fans, your local police force. Write a description essay about one such group, or an *analogy* involving two of them.

3. A comparison of Lewis Thomas's, Julie Reardon's, and Johnna Lynn Benson's essays suggests that it is easy to analyze humankind in general or a large group of people we have never met, a bit more complicated to understand a few people we know slightly, and almost impossible to reach a full comprehension

of ourselves. In Thomas's essay, the principal source of information is an anthropologist; in Reardon's, an outside observer; and in Benson's, an insider collaborating with a psychologist. Imagine that your local culture, your family, or you yourself are the subject of a research investigation. Write an essay in the form of a report that evaluates the chosen subject from a professional viewpoint.

CALVIN TRILLIN

Calvin Trillin is a writer of many talents, none more uniquely appealing than his ability to turn eating into an adventure. Trillin's reputation as a devotee of food grew out of his "U.S. Journal" columns for The New Yorker. *His assignment was to cover America, but not on a political level. "You are what you eat," the saying goes; and Trillin found that the route to America's heart was through its stomach. "It was a way to write about the country in a cheerful glutton persona," he said in a* Writer's Digest *interview. "I don't think I could have gone from a murder to a racial dispute every three weeks."*

Trillin was born in Kansas City, Missouri — one of the nation's foremost barbecue centers — in 1935. When he was thirteen, the public schools closed temporarily, and his father sent him to secretarial school. After graduating from Yale in 1957, he became a reporter and writer at Time *magazine, where he worked with "some enormously talented people," including John Gregory Dunne and John McPhee. He joined* The New Yorker *as a staff writer in 1973 and added a regular column for* The Nation *in 1978 for a fee "somewhere in the high two figures." Trillin thinks of himself mainly as a magazine writer: "I don't write fiction naturally. And the hardest thing for me is a serious nonfiction piece on a controversy." Nevertheless, he has published almost a dozen books, some of them laced with controversy:* An Education in Georgia *(1964),* Barnett Frummer Is an Unbloomed Flower *(1969),* U.S. Journal *(1971),* American Fried *(1974),* Runestruck *(1977),* Alice, Let's Eat *(1978),* Floater *(1980),* Uncivil Liberties *(1982),* Third Helpings *(1983), in which "Ordering in Japanese" appears,* Killings *(1984), and* With All Disrespect *(1985).*

Trillin currently lives in Greenwich Village with his wife Alice and their two daughters. He says he has no regular daily writing schedule; instead, there are "old guys with long beards, called The Committee of National Goals, who meet in my head. They tell me just what I have to do every day, and they're absolutely intractable. You can't talk to them at all."

Ordering in Japanese

All in all, I spend a lot of time — time other people might spend worrying 1
about their tax situation or the Bomb — worrying about the possibility that I
might go right through a meal somewhere and still miss the good stuff. That's
what worried me about going to Tokyo. How was somebody who couldn't seem
to master a few wall signs in an American Chinatown going to figure out what
the special of the day was in Tokyo? Talk about the Mysteries of the East!
Even in European countries that are thoughtful enough to conduct their busi-

ness in the Roman alphabet, I often get edgy during meals because of a suspicion that the regulars are enjoying some local specialty that the management
has hidden from travelers by listing it on the menu in a foreign language.
Once, while Alice and I were eating lunch in a Sicilian city called Piazza
Armerina, I became nearly frantic at not being able to figure out what was
meant by the special of the day listed as Bocca di Lupo—a dish my high-
school Latin led me to believe was called Mouth of the Wolf. Before placing
an order, I thought it prudent to confirm my assumption that the phrase was
not meant literally, but no such dish was listed in the dictionary of menu terms
that I keep with me at all times in a foreign country—the way some travelers
always carry their passport and a carefully hidden American fifty-dollar bill.
The waiter spoke no English, and he just looked puzzled when I, having quickly
exhausted my Italian, cleared my throat and did what seemed to me a passable
wolf imitation. We never did order the special of the day, and I have assumed
ever since that it is only a matter of time before we run into some old Sicilian
hand who says, "I hope you got to Piazza Armerina for some of that marvelous
Bocca di Lupo."

I was thinking of Bocca di Lupo as Alice and I flew over the Pacific on the   2
way to our first stay in Tokyo. I like the Japanese food served in New York,
even though I have sometimes heard Alice discuss the purity of Japanese
ingredients—the sort of talk that can ordinarily put me off my feed. What
was to be found in Tokyo would presumably be even better, but how were we
meant to find it? "How am I going to get along in a place as foreign as Japan
when even an Italian menu can cause me to bay in a public place?" I asked
Alice.

"Where's your spirit of adventure?" Alice said. She reminded me what I   3
had said about pushing out frontiers in the interest of pure research—and
conveniently forgot that she had not been eager to take a flyer on Bocca di
Lupo herself.

I settled down to my airline reading—a book that displayed colored pictures   4
of Japanese dishes and explained what they were. "The word for noodles is
udon," I announced right away. I always take the precaution of learning the
word for noodles before entering any country, just in case. "Unless you want
the polite form," I went on, "which is *o-udon.* That's what I mean about
mystery: why would anyone want to be anything but polite about noodles?"

My precaution turned out to be well taken. "O-udon!" I was able to shout,   5
politely, during a stroll on our very first morning in Tokyo, as I stopped Alice
in her tracks and pointed to a store window beyond which someone was rolling
out noodle dough. By then, I was already feeling much less concerned about
the possibility that the language barrier could lead to my starvation. Having

arrived in Tokyo the previous evening tired from the flight, we had gone no
further for dinner than the hotel's sushi restaurant—where it became apparent
that someone sitting at a sushi bar, rather than at a table, can get his fill
simply by pointing at the fish on display. Sitting at the bar is the best place
to eat sushi anyway, since a good sushi chef puts on a good show—responding
to any order with an almost military "Hai!", a couple of taps with his knife to
get the rhythm, some quick strokes at the raw fish, an abrupt jab to plant the
fish in a ball of rice, and a flick of the wrist as he places the finished product
on the bar in front of you. According to a pocket-size sushi-identification chart
we picked up on the way in, we managed, without saying a word, to eat tuna,
belly of tuna (I thought I might like a country that troubles to distinguish
among cuts of tuna), abalone, salmon roe, sea urchin, "interior of arch shell,"
and, finally, some mysterious but fantastic mixture of fish and herbs that we
ordered by displaying enthusiasm as it was being prepared for someone else.

   "Aji no tataki," I had said the next morning, after a long session with my   6
food-picture book.

   "Does that mean 'I ate too much' in Japanese?" Alice asked.   7

   "It's what we had last night at the end of the meal," I said. I read from the   8
text: " 'Small pieces of pompano chopped and mixed with onions, ginger, and
sometimes leeks.' " My confidence was growing, and it wasn't depleted by
noticing that other sources identified aji as horse mackerel or a type of herring.
I felt that I had broken the code.

   By the time we stood in front of the store window admiring the technique   9
of the noodle maker, it had also become apparent that we had another great
demystification device at our disposal—the Japanese custom of restaurants
displaying in their windows full-size, absolutely realistic models of whatever
dishes they're offering. We had spent the morning wandering around Asakasa,
a neighborhood of small shops and a serious temple and a pleasant little amusement park where I had lost badly in hand-wrestling to a mechanical suma
wrestler, and a lot of what we had paused to admire had been models of sushi
and sashimi and tempura and noodles and lightly fried fish—my idea of win-
dow-shopping. When we reached the noodle shop, I realized that I was fam-
ished. One of the models it displayed looked particularly tempting—a large
bowlful of soup with thick white noodles and two huge mushrooms and a bean-
curd cake. We marched into the restaurant—a small, immaculate place—
and I beckoned the proprietor to come with me. He was polite but hesitant.
Did he think that I may have once suffered some slight at his hands which he
had long ago forgotten and was now, as they say in the saloons, inviting him
to step outside? Had some recent article comparing Japanese and American
crime statistics put him on his guard to the point where he suspected that

going outside with me might give Alice a shot at the cash register? Could he possibly have mistaken me for some sort of exchange-program public-health inspector who might object to noodles being made in the window? I could reassure him on that point by informing him that, quite the contrary, I had once offered to establish a defense fund for a barbecue man on the west coast of Florida who had allegedly assaulted a public-health inspector for suggesting that he clean his grill more than once a year — except that I don't know how to reassure in Japanese.

Whatever misgivings the noodle-shop proprietor had, though, were over- 10 come by his courtesy. He stepped outside. We studied the window together. As I tried to indicate what I wanted, I realized that my menu dictionary was remiss in offering me translations only for words like "grilled" and "well done." What I needed to know how to say in Japanese was "No, not that one — the one just behind it, near the corner." In a moment, though, he gave a quick nod, we went back inside, and a waitress brought to the table a precise replica of the replica. It was delicious. It cost the equivalent of two dollars.

"No wonder the crime rate is so low in Japan," I said to Alice. "Everybody 11 must be very, very happy."

"Tako yaki," I said to Alice, as we stood in front of a street vender and 12 watched him pour batter into the rows of half-circle indentations of an iron griddle — like one of those college kids at Williamsburg demonstrating how musket balls were made. "It's listed right here in the book under Street and Festival Foods." What we were attending was not a festival but an astonishing ritual that happens with enough regularity to draw a few dozen street venders. Every Sunday aftrernoon, a boulevard near the Olympic stadium becomes filled with thousands of Japanese teenagers who arrive in groups of a dozen or so, the members of each group dressed identically in costumes of the fifties. Each group gathers in a circle around a huge tape recorder that is playing songs like "Rock Around the Clock" and "Let's Go to the Hop," dances a carefully choreographed version of the twist in unison, and somehow seems very Japa-nese doing it. Naturally, I tried a tako yaki, but then I discovered a problem with eating completely foreign foods which I hadn't anticipated: was it possible that I didn't like tako yaki or had I stumbled across the one tako yaki stand that knowing tako-yaki eaters always avoid? I had to have several versions of tako yaki to settle that question — as it turns out, I don't like tako yaki — but then I fell into the same trap with four or five other street foods. By the time I could announce with certainty that I liked the fried buckwheat noodles being sold at half a dozen stands, I felt I had rocked several times around the clock. "There's no substitute for an adequate sample," I said to Alice.

My confidence continued to grow. At a sushi bar near the central fish 13
market, I realized that I did not have to remain silent when I pointed at a
delectable-looking piece of tuna. I could point and say anything I wanted to
— "Tippecanoe and Tyler too" or, 'Où se trouve la plage?" The results were
the same. "Hai!" the sushi chef would bark, and tap his knife a couple of times
on the cutting board in anticipation. All sorts of Japanese restaurants tend to
display their food, so we found that at, say, a yaki-tori restaurant—a restaurant
that specializes in grilling various parts of a chicken and various vegetables
over charcoal—we could get whatever we wanted grilled by simply pointing
to it and saying "Semper fidelis" or "You wanna buy a duck?"

Also, we discovered the food halls of the department stores. All of the large 14
department stores devote their bottom floor or two to food—not just packaged
food but fish and produce and salads and pastry and just about anything else
anybody could think of to eat. Not only that—they give samples. "I can't
believe it," I said to Alice, as we walked through the ground floor of a department store on the Ginza, politely trying out the shrimps and the dumplings
and the salmon and the rice cakes. "It's a Japanese bar mitzvah. A person
could have lunch here."

"I think you just did," Alice said.   15

I would maintain that I had not actually eaten lunch—I offer as proof the 16
fact that just a few minutes later I ate lunch at a little yaki-tori place called
Torigin, around the corner—but Alice may have been right in remarking that
I had attracted the attention of some salesclerks. If I lived in Tokyo, I suppose
that could get to be problem: I can imagine the clerks whispering to each
other as I walked off the escalator around the middle of some pleasant weekday,
"He's here—the foreign one who eats." They would snatch their toothpicks
off the sample tables. An assistant manager would approach me, smiling broadly,
and lead me firmly toward the elevator, with a grip like a mechanical suma
wrestler. Smiling, he would say, "How nice to see you again. Perhaps you
would like to visit our fine selection of notions and gifts on the fifth floor."

Of course, some mysteries remained unsolved. On a trip to Kyoto, we went 17
directly from a traditional breakfast at a Japanese inn to the garden of the
Ryonaji Temple, a garden whose simple perfection inspires people to contemplate all sorts of profundities as they gaze upon it, and all I could think of as
we stood there was "What could that orange thing next to the fish possibly
have been?" Of course, errors were made. Occasionally, we would point to
something being greatly enjoyed by some diners a few tables away only to find
when it arrived that it fell in that category of small sea creatures and odd

weeds that a longtime Tokyo resident named Ellen Reingold has summed up evocatively as "low-tide stuff."

Usually, though, a mistake did not mean disaster. On the morning I visited 18 the central fish market, for instance, I made a mistake while ordering my third breakfast. My first two breakfasts had gone off without a hitch. I had started eating at about seven-thirty, with some very good noodles in broth. By then, I had spent a couple of hours wandering around the market, a place I found almost as astounding as the boulevard of dancing teenagers. In what seemed to be acres of market-shed, thousands of fish were arranged with military precision for inspection by the people who would bid for them. Most of the fish were displayed in neat stacks of white Styrofoam boxes — so that, depending on size, a box might contain one mackerel or twenty-four perfectly aligned smelts. The huge tuna were lined up outside in precise rows, with a steak-size flap pulled back on each fish for inspection of the meat. The place was so clean and the fish so fresh that I suppose it might have struck some people as a confirmation of the purity of Japanese ingredients, but it just made me hungry.

After my noodle breakfast and sushi breakfast, I pressed my face against the 19 window of a tiny lunch counter where the short-order man started what seemed to be an onion stew in a frying pan, dropped what I took to be a breaded halibut steak into a deep-fat fryer, switched the steak to the frying pan after a while, broke an egg on top, and then put a cover on the frying pan to let the whole concoction cook together. It looked so good that I went in pointing. The halibut steak turned out to taste a lot like a pork cutlet. Tongetsu! After some consultation with my portable research library, I finally realized I was eating a version of tongetsu — a pork dish popular in inexpensive Japanese restaurants. "And excellent tongetsu at that," I said, drawing some of the same sort of looks that I had provoked in Sicily with my wolf imitation. "My compliments to the chef."

The most serious problem was in restaruants that were too sophisticated to 20 have food models in the window but too Japanese to have a menu in English. One evening, we wandered into a restaurant whose specialty seemed to be a fish stew that was cooked at the table — a sort of marine sukiyaki. Nobody spoke English. We went with the specialty — although I could see from observing some other diners that it was going to involve having someone hover around the table, picking bits out of the bubbling pot and encouraging us to eat. We had just had two straight meals like that — a constantly attended dinner at a Japanese inn followed by lunch at a fine sukiyaki place near the restaurant-supply area, where we had gone to buy some sushi models — and I was beginning to feel like a college freshman who arrives home late one night for his first Christmas vacation and is not allowed to go to sleep until he sits at the kitchen table eating some of his mother's specialties under the watchful eye of his mother ("You don't want any Swedish meatballs? You've always loved my Swedish meatballs. Here, have some Swedish meatballs"). Some of the fish in the pot looked very mysterious. Alice picked up a roundish lump with a black appendage on it, and peered at it suspiciously.

"A pure ingredient," I said helpfully.   21

She tried the black appendage.   22

"Shrewd of you to bite off the toe before you start on the body," I said.   23

Alice picked carefully at the remainder of the beast. "It's not bad," she 24 said, "although I wish I knew what it was."

"Well, this is strictly a fish restaurant," I said. "Otherwise, I might conclude 25 that we'd found, at long last, Mouth of the Wolf."

QUESTIONS FOR READING AND REVISING

1. Judging from this essay's title and its opening and closing paragraphs, what is Trillin's *thesis*? What themes and *images* does he introduce early in his essay and reintroduce toward the end to convey his thesis? How would the essay's effect be different if he had included an explicit thesis statement in his first paragraph or a sentence foreshadowing his ending?

2. What features of this essay qualify it as a *process analysis*? What process is Trillin analyzing? How would you summarize the steps it comprises? What is the essay's other main rhetorical pattern?

3. Writers about food often set themselves apart from the general public by using exotic language to describe expensive meals in exclusive restaurants. What strategies of content and style does Trillin use to establish in his first paragraph that he is no rarefied restaurant critic? What two groups of people does he set himself apart from in this paragraph? What persona does he thereby establish for himself?

4. In the world of entertainment, comics have straight men, cowboys have side-kicks, and Trillin has Alice. What crucial functions does Alice fill in "Ordering in Japanese"? In what ways would Trillin have had to change the essay's structure if she were not in it? How would its impact be different without her?

5. Trillin describes food in affectionate detail, but he says little about what the people in his essay look like. Reread his encounter with the noodle-shop proprietor in paragraphs 9–10 and with the salesclerks in paragraph 16. What is

his main technique for characterizing these people? How does Trillin's mini-mizing of their physical qualities and actual dialogue suit his essay's purposes?

6. Trillin's capacity to interpret almost anything in terms of food is a central source of humor in his essay. Find half a dozen places where Trillin responds to a situation differently from other people because of his focus on food — for example, in paragraph 1, taking "the Mysteries of the East" to refer to ordering meals in Japanese. What other qualities besides obsessiveness about food do these instances reveal about Trillin as a character in his own essay?

7. American tourists are commonly stereotyped as self-centered, loud, and insen-sitive, among other unflattering qualities. What statements and actions by Trillin show that he is not an "ugly American"? How would you describe his attitude toward Japanese customs? Point out specific word choices, phrasing, and sentence structure that reflect this attitude.

QUESTIONS ON CONNECTIONS

1. Sandra Casillas's "Cha-No-Yu, the Japanese Tea Ceremony" (p. 47) creates a very different mood from Calvin Trillin's "Ordering in Japanese." At the heart of the contrast is Casillas's emphasis on strangeness and ritual, versus Trillin's emphasis on informality and familiarity. What verbs does Trillin use in nar-rating his exploration of Tokyo, and particularly his entrance into Japanese restaurants, which dispel any sense of ritual? How do Casillas and Trillin in-corporate foreign words into their essays in keeping with their contrasting moods?

2. Both Petrea Galloway's "How to Fill a Car or Freezer with Meat" (p. 89) and John Siegrist's "Rattlesnake: A Palatable Experience" (p. 217) are, like Trillin's essay, narrative process analyses about strange foods. What aspect of the process in each case makes it strange, and therefore worth writing and reading about? Which essay is the most directive — that is, phrased as a set of instructions — and which one is least directive? To what extent does the writer's directiveness correspond with the likelihood that readers might actually try the process? What can you infer from these three essays about the possible functions of *process analysis* as a writing strategy?

SUGGESTIONS FOR WRITING

1. Trillin's essay shows a foreign traveler discovering that his fears about the language barrier were groundless. Most of us have found ourselves in similar situations, in which we approached a strange scene timidly and wound up

enjoying it. Write a narrative essay describing some experience of your own in which you confronted an unfamiliar culture — foreign or domestic — and established common ground more easily than you had expected.

2. Calvin Trillin, John Siegrist, and Petrea Galloway analyze the process of procuring food. This is a popular topic for *process analyses*: we are all familiar with recipes, and we all must eat every day. Indeed, psychologists classify feeding as one of the most basic animal activities, along with fighting, fleeing, and sexual behavior. Choose an aspect of one of these other activities that you deal with frequently — fighting for a good seat in a bus, concert, or cafeteria; dodging someone you don't want to talk to; thinking up ways to "accidentally" run into someone you do want to talk to. Write a process analysis of your methods.

3. Calvin Trillin and Sandra Casillas both highlight the elaborate rituals that have grown up around eating and drinking. Trillin treats food almost like a language: we all depend on it, we learn our own culture's approach to it in childhood, and we must adjust to other cultures' usages of it when we travel. Within many households, food functions as both a ritual and a language among family members, as parents and children jockey for power, attention, approval, and credibility around the dinner table. Write an extended *definition* or *analogy* showing how food in the home (or club or dormitory or restaurant) can become an important means of communication and expression.

EUDORA WELTY

"I think I became a writer because I love stories," says Eudora Welty. *"I never had any idea that I could be a professional writer. I'm now realizing, maybe the reason I first sent stories out to magazines was that I was too shy to show them to anybody I knew."* As the following essay richly demonstrates, Welty's subject matter and her context are the people she has known since childhood, moving in the landscape around Jackson, Mississippi, where she grew up. At seventy-six she still lives and works in the house on Pinehurst Street where she and her two brothers were born.

Welty attended Mississippi State College for Women but finished up at the University of Wisconsin and did postgraduate work at the Columbia School of Advertising. During the Depression she worked for newspapers, radio stations, and as a publicity agent photographing Mississippi towns for the Works Progress Administration. Her first book of stories, A Curtain of Green, was published in 1941. The Robber Bridegroom followed in 1942. Welty won a Guggenheim fellowship that year, as well as the O. Henry Award for fiction, which she won again in 1943. Her other books — novels, essays, and story collections — include The Wide Net (1943), Delta Wedding (1946), The Golden Apples (1949), The Ponder Heart (1954), The Bride of the Innisfallen (1955), The Shoe Bird (1964), Losing Battles (1970), One Time, One Place (1971), The Optimist's Daughter (1972, with a Pulitzer Prize the following year), The Eye of the Story (1978), in which "The Little Store" appears, The Collected Stories of Eudora Welty (1980), and One Writer's Beginnings (1984).

"I love writing," says Welty. *"Oh, I've often found it difficult, but I think the difficulties are pleasures. . . . In fact, I wouldn't be very interested in writing a story that didn't pose something that had to be solved."*

William Maxwell, Welty's editor at The New Yorker, has said of her, *"I can't think of any American writer more universally acknowledged to be a great writer. Everybody — every cat — knows that Eudora Welty is a great writer."*

The winner of a National Institute of Arts and Letters Gold Medal, National Medal for Literature, and Presidential Medal of Freedom, Welty remains modest. Her ears are tuned not to critics and reviewers but to the conversations going on around her. *"It is a mystery,"* she says. *"When I'm not writing, I can't imagine writing. And when I am writing, it doesn't occur to me to wonder."* When Welty is not writing, she is usually reading. *"In fact, the only advice I give young writers . . . is to read. It never occurs to them. I say, 'If you love to write, how can you miss what has been written? How can you do without that great pleasure and wonder of what other people have written?'"*

The Little Store

Two blocks away from the Mississippi State Capitol, and on the same street   1
with it, where our house was when I was a child growing up in Jackson, it was
possible to have a little pasture behind your backyard where you could keep a
Jersey cow, which we did. My mother herself milked her. A thrifty homemaker,
wife, mother of three, she also did all her own cooking. And as far as I can
recall, she never set foot inside a grocery store. It wasn't necessary.

For her regular needs, she stood at the telephone in our front hall and   2
consulted with Mr. Lemly, of Lemly's Market and Grocery downtown, who
took her order and sent it out on his next delivery. And since Jackson at the
heart of it was still within very near reach of the open country, the blackberry
lady clanged on her bucket with a quart measure at your front door in June
without fail, the watermelon man rolled up to your house exactly on time for
the Fourth of July, and down through the summer, the quiet of the early
morning streets was pierced by the calls of farmers driving in with their plenty.
One brought his with a song, so plaintive we would sing it with him:

> "Milk, milk,
> Buttermilk;
> Snap beans — butterbeans —
> Tender okra — fresh greens . . .
> And buttermilk."

My mother considered herself pretty well prepared in her kitchen and pantry   3
for any emergency that, in her words, might choose to present itself. But if
she should, all of a sudden, need another lemon or find she was out of bread,
all she had to do was call out, "Quick! Who'd like to run to the Little Store
for me?"

I would.   4

She'd count out the change into my hand, and I was away. I'll bet the   5
nickel that would be left over that all over the country, for those of my day,
the neighborhood grocery played a similar part in our growing up.

Our store had its name — it was that of the grocer who owned it, whom   6
I'll call Mr. Sessions — but "the Little Store" is what we called it at home. It
was a block down our street toward the capitol and half a block further, around
the corner, toward the cemetery. I knew even the sidewalk to it as well as I
knew my own skin. I'd skipped my jumping-rope up and down it, hopped its
length through mazes of hopscotch, played jacks in its islands of shade, ser-
pentined along it on my Princess bicycle, skated it backward and forward. In
the twilight I had dragged my steamboat by its string (this was homemade out

of every new shoebox, with candle in the bottom lighted and shining through colored tissue paper pasted over windows scissored out in the shapes of the sun, moon and stars) across every crack of the walk without letting it bump or catch fire. I'd "played out" on that street after supper with my brothers and friends as long as "first-dark" lasted; I'd caught its lightening bugs. On the first Armistice Day (and this will set the time I'm speaking of) we made our own parade down that walk on a single velocipede—my brother pedaling, our little brother riding the handlebars, and myself standing on the back, all with arms wide, flying flags in each hand. (My father snapped that picture as we raced by. It came out blurred.)

As I set forth for the Little Store, a tune would float toward me from the   7 house where there lived three sisters, girls in their teens, who ratted their hair over their ears, wore headbands like gladiators, and were considered to be very popular. They practiced for this in the daytime; they'd wind up the Victrola, leave the same record on they'd played before, and you'd see them bobbing past their dining-room windows while they danced with each other. Being three, they could go all day, cutting in:

> "Everybody ought to know-oh
> How to do the Tickle-Toe
> (how to do the Tickle-Toe)"—

they sang it and danced to it, and as I went by to the same song, I believed it.

A little further on, across the street, was the house where the principal of   8 our grade school lived—lived on, even while we were having vacation. What if she would come out? She would halt me in my tracks—she had a very carrying and well-known voice in Jackson, where she'd taught almost every-body—saying, "Eudora Alice Welty, spell OBLIGE." OBLIGE was the word that she of course knew had kept me from making 100 on my spelling exam. She'd make me miss it again now, by boring her eyes through me from across the street. This was my vacation fantasy, one good way to scare myself on the way to the store.

Down near the corner waited the house of a little boy named Lindsey. The   9 sidewalk here was old brick, which the roots of a giant chinaberry tree had humped up and tilted this way and that. On skates, you took it fast, in a series of skittering hops, trying not to touch ground anywhere. If the chinaberries had fallen and rolled in the cracks, it was like skating through a whole shooting match of marbles. I crossed my fingers that Lindsey wouldn't be looking.

During the big flu epidemic he and I, as it happened, were being nursed   10 through our sieges at the same time. I'd hear my father and mother murmuring to each other, at the end of a long day, "And I wonder how poor little *Lindsey* got along today?" Just as, down the street, he no doubt would have to hear his family saying, "And I wonder how is poor *Eudora* by now?" I got the idea that a choice was going to be made soon between poor little Lindsey and poor Eudora, and I came up with a funny poem. I wasn't prepared for it when my father told me it wasn't funny and my mother cried that if I couldn't be ashamed for myself, she'd have to be ashamed for me:

> There was a little boy and his name was Lindsey.
> He went to heaven with the influinzy.

He didn't, he survived it, poem and all, the same as I did. But his chinaberries could have brought me down in my skates in a flying act of contrition before his eyes, looking pretty funny myself, right in front of his house.

Setting out in this world, a child feels so indelible. He only comes to find 11 out later that it's all the others along his way who are making themselves indelible to him.

Our Little Store rose right up from the sidewalk; standing in a street of 12 family houses, it alone hadn't any yard in front, any tree or flowerbed. It was a plain frame building covered over with brick. Above the door, a little railed porch ran across on an upstairs level and four windows with shades were looking out. But I didn't catch on to those.

Running in out of the sun, you met what seemed total obscurity inside. 13 There were almost tangible smells—licorice recently sucked in a child's cheek, dill-pickle brine that had leaked through a paper sack in a fresh trail across the wooden floor, ammonia-loaded ice that had been hoisted from wet croker sacks and slammed into the icebox with its sweet butter at the door, and perhaps the smell of still-untrapped mice.

Then through the motes of cracker dust, cornmeal dust, the Gold Dust of 14 the Gold Dust Twins that the floor had been swept out with, the realities emerged. Shelves climbed to high reach all the way around, set out with not too much of any one thing but a lot of things—lard, molasses, vinegar, starch, matches, kerosene, Octagon soap (about a year's worth of octagon-shaped coupons cut out and saved brought a signet ring addressed to you in the mail. Furthermore, when the postman arrived at your door, he blew a whistle). It was up to you to remember what you came for, while your eye traveled from cans of sardines to ice cream salt to harmonicas to fly-paper (over your head, batting around on a thread beneath the blades of the ceiling fan, stuck with its testimonial catch).

Its confusion may have been in the eye of its beholder. Enchantment is cast 15 upon you by all those things you weren't supposed to have need for, it lures you close to wooden tops you'd outgrown, boy's marbles and agates in little net pouches, small rubber balls that wouldn't bounce straight, frazzly kite-string, clay bubble-pipes that would snap off in your teeth, the stiffest scissors. You could contemplate those long narrow boxes of sparklers gathering dust while you waited for it to be the Fourth of July or Christmas, and noisemakers in the shape of tin frogs for somebody's birthday party you hadn't been invited to yet, and see that they were all marvelous.

You might not have even looked for Mr. Sessions when he came around 16 his store cheese (as big as a doll's house) and in front of the counter looking for you. When you'd finally asked him for, and received from him in its paper bag, whatever single thing it was that you had been sent for, the nickel that was left over was yours to spend.

Down at a child's eye level, inside those glass jars with mouths in their sides 17 through which the grocer could run his scoop or a child's hand might be invited to reach for a choice, were wineballs, all-day suckers, gumdrops, peppermints. Making a row under the glass of a counter were the Tootsie Rolls, Hershey Bars, Goo-Goo Clusters, Baby Ruths. And whatever was the name of those pastilles that came stacked in a cardboard cylinder with a cardboard lid? They were thin and dry, about the size of tiddlywinks, and in the shape of twisted rosettes. A kind of chocolate dust came out with them when you shook them out in your hand. Were they chocolate? I'd say rather they were brown. They didn't taste of anything at all, unless it was wood. Their attraction was the number you got for a nickel.

Making up your mind, you circled the store around and around, around the 18 pickle barrel, around the tower of Cracker Jack Boxes; Mr. Sessions had built it for us himself on top of a packing case, like a house of cards.

If it seemed too hot for Cracker Jacks, I might get a cold drink. Mr. Sessions 19 might have already stationed himself by the cold-drinks barrel, like a mind reader. Deep in ice water that looked black as ink, murky shapes that would come up as Coca-Colas, Orange Crushes, and various flavors of pop, were all swimming around together. When you gave the word, Mr. Sessions plunged his bare arm in to the elbow and fished out your choice, first try. I favored a locally bottled concoction called Lake's Celery. (What else could it be called? It was made by a Mr. Lake out of celery. It was a popular drink here for years but was not known universally, as I found out when I arrived in New York and ordered one in the Astor bar.) You drank on the premises, with feet set wide apart to miss the drip, and gave him back his bottle.

But he didn't hurry you off. A standing scales was by the door, with a stack 20 of iron weights and a brass slide on the balance arm, that would weigh you up to three hundred pounds. Mr. Sessions, whose hands were gentle and smelled of carbolic, would lift you up and set your feet on the platform, hold your loaf of bread for you, and taking his time while you stood still for him, he would make certain of what you weighed today. He could even remember what you weighed the last time, so you could subtract and announce how much you'd gained. That was goodbye.

Is there always a hard way to go home? From the Little Store, you could 21 go partway through the sewer. If your brothers had called you a scarecat, then across the next street beyond the Little Store, it was possible to enter this sewer by passing through a privet hedge, climbing down into the bed of a creek, and going into its mouth on your knees. The sewer — it might have been no more than a "storm sewer" — came out and emptied here, where Town Creek, a sandy, most often shallow little stream that ambled through Jackson on its way to the Pearl River, ran along the edge of the cemetery. You could go in darkness through this tunnel to where you next saw light (if you ever did) and climb out through the culvert at your own street corner.

I was a scarecat, all right, but I was a reader with my own refuge in story- 22 books. Making my way under the sidewalk, under the street and the streetcar track, under the Little Store, down there in the wet dark by myself, I could be Persephone entering into my six-month sojourn underground — though I didn't suppose Persephone had to crawl, hanging onto a loaf of bread, and come out through the teeth of an iron grating. Mother Ceres would indeed be wondering where she could find me, and mad when she knew. "Now am I going to have to start marching to the Little Store for *myself?*"

I couldn't picture it. Indeed, I'm unable today to picture the Little Store 23 with a grown person in it, except for Mr. Sessions and the lady who helped him, who belonged there. We children thought it was ours. The happiness of errands was in part that of running for the moment away from home, a free spirit. I believed the Little Store to be a center of the outside world, and hence of happiness — as I believed what I found in the Cracker Jack box to be a genuine prize, which was as simply as I believed in the Golden Fleece.

But a day came when I ran to the store to discover, sitting on the front 24 step, a grown person, after all — more than a grown person. It was the Monkey Man, together with his monkey. His grinding-organ was lowered to the step beside him. In my whole life so far, I must have laid eyes on the Monkey Man no more than five or six times. An itinerant of rare and wayward appearances, he was not punctual like the Gipsies, who every year with the first cool days of fall showed up in the aisles of Woolworth's. You never knew when the Monkey Man might decide to favor Jackson, or which way he'd go. Sometimes you heard him as close as the next street, and then he didn't come up yours.

But now I saw the Monkey Man at the Little Store, where I'd never seen 25 him before. I'd never seen him sitting down. Low on that familiar doorstep, he was not the same any longer, and neither was his monkey. They looked just like an old man and an old friend of his that wore a fez, meeting quietly together, tired, and resting with their eyes fixed on some place far away, and not the same place. Yet their romance for me didn't have it in its power to waver. I wavered. I simply didn't know how to step around them, to proceed on into the Little Store for my mother's emergency as if nothing had happened. If I could have gone in there after it, whatever it was, I would have given it to them — putting it into the monkey's cool little fingers. I would have given them the Little Store itself.

In my memory they are still attached to the store — so are all the others. 26 Everyone I saw on my way seemed to me then part of my errand, and in a way they were. As I myself, the free spirit, was part of it too.

All the years we lived in that house where we children were born, the same 27 people lived in the other houses on our street too. People changed through the arithmetic of birth, marriage, and death, but not by going away. So families just accrued stories, which through the fullness of time, in those times, their own lives made. And I grew up in those.

But I didn't know there'd ever been a story at the Little Store, one that 28 was going on while I was there. Of course, all the time the Sessions family had been living right overhead there, in the upstairs rooms behind the little railed porch and the shaded windows; but I think we children never thought of that. Did I fail to see them as a family because they weren't living in an ordinary house? Because I so seldom saw them close together, or having anything to say to each other? She sat in the back of the store, her pencil over a ledger, while he stood and waited on children to make up their minds. They worked in twin black eyeshades, held on their gray heads by elastic bands. It may be harder to recognize kindness — or unkindness, either — in a face whose eyes are in shadow. His face underneath his shade was as round as the little wooden wheels in the Tinker Toy box. So was her face, I didn't know, perhaps didn't even wonder: were they husband and wife or brother and sister? Were they father and mother? There were a few other persons, of various ages, wandering singly in by the back door and out. But none of their relationships could I imagine, when I'd never seem them sitting down together around their own table.

The possibility that they had any other life at all, anything beyond what 29 we could see within the four walls of the Little Store, occurred to me only when tragedy struck their family. There was some act of violence. The shock to the neighborhood traveled to the children, of course; but I couldn't find out from my parents what had happened. They held it back from me, as they'd already held back many things, "until the time comes for you to know."

You could find out some of these things by looking in the unabridged dic- 30 tionary and the encyclopedia — kept to hand in our dining room — but you couldn't find out there what had happened to the family who for all the years of your life had lived upstairs over the Little Store, who had never been anything but patient and kind to you, who never once had sent you away. All I ever knew was its aftermath: they were the only people ever known to me who simply vanished. At the point where their life overlapped into ours, the story broke off.

We weren't being sent to the neighborhood grocery for facts of life, or death. 31 But of course those are what we were on the track of, anyway. With the loaf of bread and the Cracker Jack prize, I was bringing home the intimations of pride and disgrace, and rumors and early news of people coming to hurt one another, while others practiced for joy — storing up a portion for myself of the human mystery.

QUESTIONS FOR READING AND REVISING

1. Welty's title indicates that this essay is about a store, but her first paragraph suggests it may be about her mother instead. Who or what is the real subject of "The Little Store"? In what paragraph does Welty draw back from the first long narrative section of her essay and explain why she has been shifting focus from character to character down the street toward the store?

2. This descriptive essay shows us people, places, objects, and ideas. What does Welty accomplish by opening with a sentence that establishes her geographic location? How do the sentences that follow about her mother help to set the essay's mood? What is the effect of Welty's describing her mother in terms of what she does rather than what she looks like?

3. What specific words in paragraph 1 locate Welty's essay in time? What details in paragraphs 2 – 5 establish a convincing child's-eye viewpoint? What details emphasize that Welty is writing about her childhood from an adult's perspective many years later? How would the essay's impact be different if Welty used a child's present-tense voice instead of an adult's reminiscence to tell her story? How would it be different if she made her adult self a character in the narrative and turned her childhood scenes into flashbacks?

4. What does the Lindsey incident in paragraphs 9 – 10 tell you about Welty's

relationship with her parents? Why do you think she wrote her funny poem? How would the effect of this incident change if Welty substituted "I hoped and prayed" for "I crossed my fingers" in paragraph 9, and substituted "feeling mortified" for "looking pretty funny myself" in paragraph 10?

5. In paragraph 12 Welty approaches her target possessively ("Our Little Store"), and then reiterates her first-person child's-eye view ("But I didn't catch on to those"). Once inside the store, however, she switches to *you*. What is the effect of the second person in paragraphs 13–16? What technique does Welty use to bring her readers more deeply into her story in paragraph 17? How does she then create a transition from *you* back to *I* in paragraphs 18–19?

6. In paragraphs 23 and 26–27, as in paragraph 11, Welty steps back from her child to her adult persona. How do these paragraphs enrich the incidents, people, and places she describes? What do they tell you about Welty's dominant mood and attitude in childhood, and about her perception of her childhood as an adult? What is the structural function of these paragraphs?

7. How would the impact of "The Little Store" be different if Welty had ended with paragraph 27 instead of adding the Sessions mystery? Does this last section make the essay's organization more parallel to that of childhood, or less? In what way(s)? Welty opens paragraph 28 with, "But I didn't know there'd ever been a story at the Little Store, one that was going on while I was there." What does this introduction, and the narrative that follows, tell you about Welty's ideas of what comprises a story?

QUESTIONS ON CONNECTIONS

1. In what ways does Barbara Carter's essay, "Momma's Cupboard" (p. 43), convey a theme similar to Welty's by means of a similar structure? How does each of these two writers characterize her mother? What set of values, positive and negative, is represented by each mother? How do Welty and Carter carry over these values into their essays as a whole?

2. Neither Welty nor Carter describes her siblings, but both writers give us a sense of what their siblings are like. In what two places does Welty do this? What technique(s) does she use? What impression do you get of her brothers? Where and how does Carter characterize her brothers and sisters? How does Carter's relationship with her siblings appear to have been different from Welty's?

3. Like Eudora Welty, Brenda Jacobs in "Handing Down Grace" (p. 106) writes about her Mississippi family roots. How do these two writers' perspectives on the South contrast with each other and why? In what respects are they similar? After rereading Jacobs's essay, what do you notice about the way Welty uses her Southern setting?

4. Ann Louise Field's "The Sound of Angels" (p. 76) shows that southern California is in some ways not so far from Mississippi. What specific childhood passions, fears, and pastimes are featured in both of these descriptive essays? What are the most striking similarities and differences in their endings?

SUGGESTIONS FOR WRITING

1. Eudora Welty's mother milked her own cow, did all her own cooking, and never set foot inside a grocery store. Fresh fruit and vegetables were bought at the door from the farmers who grew them or the "blackberry lady" who picked them. Nowadays milk, fruit and vegetables, even multi-course meals, are available from the supermarket in plastic containers; and many children are suspicious of food found growing outdoors on plants. Based on your own experience, write a *descriptive* or *comparison/contrast* essay about modern perspectives on food — for example, how it feels to catch, clean, and cook a fish after years of Big Macs; the dilemma of choosing a cold drink with or without caffeine, calories, and chemicals; revisiting a childhood berry patch; helping your mother bake a loaf of homemade bread.

2. Eudora Welty talks of the games she played en route to the neighborhood market nicknamed "the Little Store," and the awe-inspiring Monkey Man who occasionlly passed through town. Ann Field reminisces about the sankies where she and her brother hid, and their private doughnut breakfasts. Nicknames, secret codes, and rituals are a central feature of childhood, a way of redesigning reality as well as learning to live in it. Write an essay about some aspect of your childhood that was transformed by imagination. Blend your perception at the time with your perspective looking back.

3. Welty still remembers the farmer's song to sell his produce, "so plaintive we would sing it with him." In Brenda Jacobs's Mississippi, "a community gathering where music, usually gospel music, is played and sung is to the participants a 'sang'." Rock musician Robbie Robertson once commented of the South, "You can actually drive down the highway at night, and if you listen, you hear music. I don't know if it's coming from the people or if it's coming from the air. It lives, and it's rooted there." Sharing music is a rich American tradition. Many adults have vivid memories of the lullaby Mother used to sing, the funny songs Dad taught on car trips, or the harmonies learned in church choir. Write an essay explaining how music enriched your sense of community and communication when you were growing up.

4. One of the most popular topics in literature is the painful transition from childhood innocence to adult knowledge. Very often parents try to shield their children: "They held it back from me," says Eudora Welty of the Sessions tragedy, "as they'd already held back many things, 'until the time comes for

you to know'." Barbara Carter represents her turning point with her brother's passing around a bottle of vanilla flavoring from the forbidden cupboard. Ann Louise Field's disillusionment began with her brother's ordering her in tears to steal oranges and culminated in her mother's attempted suicide. Write an essay about such a rite of passage in your own life, indicating what kind of consciousness you moved out of and into.

TOM WICKER

If Tom Wicker's life has been steadfast, it illustrates that adjective with a good deal more dramatic flair than the life he describes in the following essay, which originally appeared in the New York Times on October 17, 1983. Wicker's career as a writer has been diverse both geographically and generically. Born in Hamlet, North Carolina, in 1926, Wicker took a journalism degree at the University of North Carolina and then went north to Harvard on a Neiman Fellowship. He returned to North Carolina as a newspaper editor, became publishing information director for the Board of Public Welfare, and wrote his first novel, Get Out of Town (1951), under the pseudonym Paul Connolly. While Paul Connolly became the author of two more novels, Tears Are for Angels (1952) and So Fair, So Evil (1955), Tom Wicker wrote a few of his own: The Kingpin (1953), The Devil Must (1957), The Judgment (1961), and Facing the Lions (1973).

Meanwhile, Wicker's newspaper career took him to the Winston-Salem (North Carolina) Journal, where he filled half a dozen positions, including Washington correspondent. From 1952–54 he also served in the U.S. Naval Reserve. In 1959 Wicker became an associate editor at the Nashville Tennesseean, and a year later joined the New York Times as a member of its Washington bureau staff. After a promotion to bureau chief in 1964, he moved up in 1968 to the associate editorship he still holds. In addition to his novels and pieces for the Times, Tom Wicker has written five books of nonfiction: Kennedy Without Tears (1964), JFK and LBJ: The Influence of Personality upon Politics (1968), A Time to Die (1975), On Press (1978), and Unto This Hour (1984).

A Steadfast Life

Esta Cameron Wicker was 89 years old when they buried her beneath the long-leaf pines in Mary Love Cemetery. She had lived, it was commonly said of her, a long, good, full life in which she had exemplified the words of the hymn they sang at her funeral.

> Faith of our fathers,
> Living faith,
> We will be true
> To thee til death.

Those at the graveside thought it a splendid final touch that the rumble of a train passing made it hard to hear the words of the Rev. William Simpson. For Hamlet is a railroad town, over which the lonely wail of the steam engine used to fall in the hot summer nights; and where even in the declining years of railroading the sounds of diesel locomotives and iron wheels on rails still dominate. And Esta Wicker's husband, beside whom she now lies again, spent all his adult life in the service of what he used to call "the road."

As Mr. Simpson noted, it was fitting, too, that final services were held in the Fellowship building of the First Methodist Church—where, he said, "Every time the doors opened, she was there." But the church is undergoing repairs, so the funeral was moved to the building where for countless church suppers and other festivities she had served up chicken and dumplings and baked the rolls no one else, by common consent, could make quite so well.

But it was not just for her considerable kitchen and household skills— though in her time these were too much the measure of women—that Esta Wicker was remembered here where she lived for more than 60 years, most of them in the same small house on Hamlet Avenue. Though many of her contemporaries had preceded her to Mary Love Cemetery, many of all ages remained to recall her warmth and friendship, her unfailing joviality.

She had power, too—an indomitable strength of will, not always easy on those around her, that derived not from position but character. She had her principles—duty, work, honor, integrity—and asserted them; she had her loyalties—to family, church, friends and the Democratic Party of Franklin D. Roosevelt that she firmly believed had saved her house and family when the banks were closed and the men were out of work—and never deserted them. Nor did she have much patience with those less firmly committed.

Perhaps, too, some saw her as the personification of timeless values. She powerfully represented, for example, the American faith in future generations. The circumstances of her youth had denied her the educational opportunity now taken for granted; and in her prime the struggle to keep a family going in the Depression years was her preoccupation. Yet she never doubted things could be better for her children, whose need for education she relentlessly preached, and whose intellectual curiosity she cultivated—not least by her own example—and defended against all pressures to conform.

And if, in her religion, Esta Wicker never questioned the great Christian virtues of faith, hope, and charity, in her daily life she took them seriously. She could succumb to the sin of pride; confident in her own strength, she was sometimes bitter about people, not so much because they had more than she, but because she thought they deserved less. But she actively practiced generosity to the many not so fortunate as she was; and at her death the friends who filled her house with kindness and love were only following in the old time-tested tradition she had herself so faithfully honored.

She represented something steadfast and unchanging, too. Mind and memory betrayed her before that vigorous body that once never seemed to tire, and in her last years she had gone to live with a loving daughter in Virginia. There, with increasing frequency, she would slip back, back into the timeless calls of memory, to days earlier than her children had known, to the larger family in which she had grown up, in Moore County, N.C., in a time all but unimaginable now.

Her life had stretched from the 19th far into the 20th century, encompassing   9
its swift and bewildering change. Yet, in all that time, as life and her surroundings changed and changed again, as she adapted to necessity and dealt with new conditions, she saw nothing that caused her to lose faith in basic values, in those verities of heart and character that guided her home.

And it *was* a homecoming that brought her back to Hamlet, to the com-   10
panion of her life, the friends of her years, the children of her hopes, the grandchildren of her faith, finally to the abiding earth. Under the pines, in the rumble of the train, in the old comforting cadences of the service, it was even possible to believe as she did in a better future, that there might even be a future.

For her son, at least, Esta Wicker had spoken her own epitaph. In a con-   11
versation about the changes in recent years in racial attitudes and customs in the South she was proud to call home, she recalled of his childhood:

"In our house, you were never taught all that hate some people had. I never   12
taught you to hate anybody."

QUESTIONS FOR READING AND REVISING

1. Tom Wicker praises his mother for a type of "good, full life" that he himself has not chosen to emulate. What qualities in Esta Wicker suggest why this eulogy was deemed worthy of a column in the *New York Times?* Which of her characteristics and achievements might many *Times* readers share or envy, although her journalist son does not? Which of her virtues does Wicker seem to hope he shares?

2. Is this essay more like a snapshot or a home movie of a real person, or a memorial portrait? If Esta Wicker were still alive, what aspects of her life would you expect Wicker to describe that he has omitted here? What words and phrases does he use that create a sense of timelessness? What *purpose* do you think this kind of depiction serves for Wicker as a bereaved son?

3. Esta Wicker was buried near the house she lived in for more than sixty years in Hamlet, North Carolina. To what extent does Wicker's *thesis* depend on his mother's having spent almost her whole life in the small town? How would the essay's structure and effect be different if Mrs. Wicker had died in New York? in a retirement village? in a nursing home?

4. Presumably many people who read this essay in the *New York Times* were motivated by their admiration of and interest in Tom Wicker. Yet he never mentions himself in the first person or appears at all until the final paragraphs. Judging from the substance of the essay, the way Wicker writes, and the biographical information preceding the essay, what can you infer about his relationship with his mother? What appear to be her main contributions to his professional success? Why do you think Wicker avoids directly satisfying his readers' curiosity on these questions?

5. Wicker gives us no physical description of his mother. Why do you think he chose to omit such information? What sensory details does his essay contain? What do they tell us about Esta Wicker? about Tom Wicker?

6. One of the comforting aspects of "rites of passage" such as funerals is their universality and familiarity. Wicker depicts his late mother as a sort of maternal Everywoman, mentioning in paragraph 7 "the old time-tested tradition she had herself so faithfully honored." What other clichéd language besides "time-tested tradition" helps to convey the sense of Esta Wicker as a traditionalist and a model of traditional values?

QUESTIONS ON CONNECTIONS

1. Barbara Seidel's "A Tribute to My Father" (p. 212) is a portrait of a man who is still alive. In what ways is Seidel's depiction like Wicker's? What are its most significant differences? How do these two characterizations reflect a contrast between Seidel's and Wicker's purposes?

2. Neither Seidel's nor Wicker's essay follows a *chronological order* or attempts to trace its subject's whole life from birth to death. How would the effect of Wicker's eulogy change if he went farther back in time, as Seidel does, and talked about his mother's youth and courtship? How would it change if Wicker, like Seidel, began instead of ended with a scene between him and his mother on the subject of values handed down from one generation to the next?

3. To what extent do you think Seidel's father and Wicker's mother would have perceived themselves as similar people? What words do both Seidel and Wicker use to describe their parents? What words used by each author would be out of place in the other's essay?

SUGGESTIONS FOR WRITING

1. Both Tom Wicker and Barbara Seidel depict their parents as mainstream Americans, committed to traditional values, content to be known only within their own sphere. Such a parent might be irksome to live with at times but relatively

easy to memorialize with respect and appreciation. Parents who are more ambitious or flamboyant often pose a greater challenge. Choosing one of your own parents, some other family member, or a parent outside your family, write a *cause-and-effect* essay about that person's impact on his or her offspring.

2. Does Tom Wicker's eulogy to his mother comprise the kind of memoir you would want your children to write about you? Envision yourself at the age of eighty-nine and write your own eulogy summarizing the outstanding features of your life from the viewpoint of a child, friend, or potential biographer.

3. As Americans, we tend to think of small-town living and homespun virtue as part of our heritage, like apple pie and ice cream. Given the present trend toward urban condos, tax shelters, and the pursuit of self-actualization, Wicker's essay appeals to us partly because the existence it describes is so foreign to what we may see around us. In his work as a journalist, Wicker himself constantly confronts issues like freedom of the press, the threat of nuclear war, and political maneuvering and infighting. Imagine a discussion between him and his mother—or any child and parent with different lifestyles and views—on a subject about which the participants strongly disagree. Write an expository essay that analyzes the reasons why each person takes the stand he or she does, and explain why one position is ultimately more persuasive than the other.

GEORGE F. WILL

"His much-praised wit is only the most noticeable feature of his precise and elegant style," remarked a Commentary *reviewer of George Will's book,* The Pursuit of Virtue and Other Tory Notions *(1982). In that same year a* National Review *writer took a different view of* Statecraft as Soulcraft: What Government Does: *"Even an audience at Mt. Olympus would probably find it a mite stuffy." Controversy is a keynote in Will's work as a political columnist for* Newsweek *and the* Washington Post, *provoking arguments as well as presenting them.*

George Will was born in Champaign, Illinois, in 1941. He attended Oxford University and Princeton and has taught at Michigan State University, the University of Illinois, and the University of Toronto. After serving as a congressional aide, he became Washington editor of the National Review *and in 1977 won the Pulitzer Prize for Commentary.*

"A column is not an adequate format for the full, orderly deployment and defense of a political philosophy," wrote Will in the introduction to The Pursuit of Happiness and Other Sobering Thoughts *(1979). "But it is a fine format for an argument." The argument that follows originally appeared as a column in the June 7, 1982 issue of* Newsweek.

Opposing Prefab Prayer

I stand foursquare with the English ethicist who declared: "I am fully convinced that the highest life can only be lived on a foundation of Christian belief — or some substitute for it." But President Reagan's constitutional amendment concerning prayer in public schools is a mistake.

His proposal reads: "Nothing in this Constitution shall be construed to prohibit individual or group prayer in public schools or other public institutions. No person shall be required by the United States or by any state to participate in prayer." This would restore the status quo ante the 1962 Supreme Court ruling that public-school prayers violate the ban on "establishment" of religion. The amendment would not settle the argument about prayer; it would relocate the argument. All fifty states, or perhaps, all 3,041 county governments, or all 16,214 school districts would have to decide whether to have "voluntary" prayers. But the issue is not really voluntary prayers for individuals. The issue is organized prayers for groups of pupils subject to compulsory school-attendance laws. In a 1980 resolution opposing "government authored or sponsored religious exercises in public schools," the Southern Baptist Convention noted that "the Supreme Court has not held that it is illegal for any individual to pray or read his or her Bible in public schools."

The Question: This nation is even more litigious than religious, and the   3
school-prayer issue has prompted more, and more sophsiticated, arguments about constitutional law than about the nature of prayer. But fortunately Sen. Jack Danforth is an ordained Episcopal priest and is the only person ever to receive degrees from the Yale Law School and the Yale Divinity School on the same day. Danforth is too polite to pose the question quite this pointedly, but the question is: is public-school prayer apt to serve authentic religion, or is it apt to be mere attitudinizing, a thin gruel of vague religious vocabulary? Religious exercises should arise from a rich tradition and reflect that richness. Prayer, properly understood, arises from the context of the praying person's particular faith. So, Danforth argues, "for those within a religious tradition, it simply is not true that one prayer is as good as any other."

One person's prayer may not be any sort of prayer to another person whose   4
devotion is to a different tradition. To children from certain kinds of Christian families, a "nondenominational" prayer that makes no mention of Jesus Christ would be incoherent. The differences between Christian and Jewish expressions of piety are obvious: the differences between Protestants and Roman Catholics regarding, for example, Mary and the saints are less obvious, but they are not trivial to serious religious sensibilities. And as Danforth says, a lowest-common-denominator prayer would offend all devout persons. "Prayer that is so general and so diluted as not to offend those of most faiths is not prayer at all. True prayer is robust prayer. It is bold prayer. It is almost by definition sectarian prayer."

Liturgical reform in the Roman Catholic and Episcopal churches has oc-   5
casioned fierce controversies that seem disproportionate, if not unintelligible, to persons who are ignorant of or indifferent about those particular religious traditions. But liturgy is a high art and a serious business because it is designed to help turn minds from worldly distractions, toward transcendent things. Collective prayer should express a shared inner state, one that does not occur easily and spontaneously. A homogenized religious recitation, perfunctorily rendered by children who have just tumbled in from a bus or playground, is not apt to arise from the individual wills, as real prayer must.

Buddhists are among the almost ninety religious organizations in America   6
that have at least 50,000 members. Imagine. Danforth urges, the Vietnamese Buddhist in a fourth-grade class in, say, Mississippi. How does that child deal with a "voluntary" prayer that is satisfactory to the local Baptists? Or imagine a child from America's growing number of Muslims, for whom prayer involves turning toward Mecca and prostrating oneself. Muslim prayer is adoration of

Allah; it involves no requests and asks no blessing, as most Christian prayers do. Reagan says: "No one will ever convince me that a moment of voluntary prayer will harm a child." . . . Danforth asks: how is America—or religion —served by the embarrassment of children who must choose between insincere compliance with, or conscientious abstention from, a ritual?

A Suggestion: In a nation where millions of adults (biologically speaking) 7 affect the Jordache look or whatever designer's whim is *de rigueur,* peer pressure on children is not a trivial matter. Supporters of Reagan's amendment argue that a 9-year-old is "free" to absent himself or otherwise abstain from a "voluntary" prayer—an activity involving his classmates and led by that formidable authority figure, his teacher. But that argument is akin to one heard a century ago from persons who said child-labor laws infringed the precious freedom of children to contract to work ten-hour days in coal mines.

To combat the trivializing of religion and the coercion of children who take 8 their own religious traditions seriously, Danforth suggests enacting the following distinction: "The term 'voluntary prayer' shall not include any prayer composed, prescribed, directed, supervised, or organized by an official or employee of a state or local government agency, including public school principals and teachers." When religion suffers the direct assistance of nervous politicians, the result is apt to confirm the judgment of the child who prayed not to God but for God because "if anything happens to him, we're properly sunk."

It is, to say no more, curious that, according to some polls, more Americans 9 favor prayers in schools than regularly pray in church. Supermarkets sell processed cheese and instant mashed potatoes, so many Americans must like bland substitutes for real things. But it is one thing for the nation's palate to tolerate frozen waffles; it is another and more serious thing for the nation's soul to be satisfied with add-water-and-stir instant religiosity. When government acts as liturgist for a pluralistic society, the result is bound to be a purée that is tasteless, in several senses.

QUESTIONS ON READING AND REVISING

1. Will makes it clear in his opening paragraph what he is against: President Reagan's proposed constitutional amendment permitting prayer in public schools. What, if anything, is he for in this essay? If Will had written a concluding paragraph summarizing his national policy recommendations on school prayer, what would it say? Why do you think Will did not add such a paragraph?

2. Will's *argument* leans heavily on the statements of other people: the English

ethicist quoted in paragraph 1, President Reagan, and Senator Jack Danforth. Does he share or oppose any of their positions unequivocally? What is Will saying when he tells us he stands foursquare with the unidentified ethicist? Why is the ethicist's name unimportant?

3. The amendment Will opposes does not mandate prayer in schools. It is phrased negatively: "Nothing in this Constitution shall be construed to prohibit. . . ." Yet Will assumes that the inevitable result would require some public-school students to say a specified prayer. By what logical steps does he reach this conclusion? Whose views is he expressing when he says "the issue is" in paragraph 2 and "the question is" in paragraph 3?

4. Throughout his essay, Will reminds us in subtle ways that what is said is not always what is meant. Sometimes he uses *irony* to make this point, as in paragraph 7, where he compares children's freedom to abstain from prayer with their freedom a century earlier to contract for ten-hour workdays. How does Will's irony create a context for the child's prayer he quotes at the end of paragraph 8? When he refers to "nervous politicians" earlier in that sentence, does he mean Senator Danforth or the public officials Danforth has listed?

5. Will concludes his essay by condemning the proposed constitutional amendment for making prayer "tasteless." This is a rather frivolous adjective to describe an alteration to the nation's most important legal document. Is Will attacking the amendment, the controversy, the Americans who favor prayer in schools, Americans in general, or all four? What is the effect of this conclusion on Will's *thesis* as stated in paragraph 1, and on the more substantive argument he presents earlier in the essay?

6. Aside from quotations, Will's shortest sentence in this essay is ten words long. Nearly all his other sentences are considerably longer; many are compound or complex or both. What does Will's sentence length and sentence structure tell us about how he means us to read his essay? On the basis of his style, what kind of *audience* does he expect will be most sympathetic to his arguments? What other aspects of the essay provide clues to its intended audience?

QUESTIONS ON CONNECTIONS

1. Pamela Garrettson's "Prayer in America's Public Schools: Let's Not Start a Religious War" (p. 96) takes essentially the same position and offers many of the same arguments as Will's essay. How do these two writers' goals and approaches differ? Which essay is more comprehensive? Which one is more pragmatic? How does Garrettson's intended *audience* apparently differ from Will's?

2. Garrettson's presentation depends more on her own experience than Will's does. How would the impact of Will's essay change if he did not quote President

Reagan and Senator Jack Danforth, but simply made his case in his own words? How would the impact of Garrettson's essay change if she were a senator?

SUGGESTIONS FOR WRITING

1. Both Will and Garrettson oppose President Reagan's proposed constitutional amendment legalizing organized prayer in the public schools, and for similar reasons. This amendment, however, is by no means the only way to address the issue of students' freedom of religious expression. If you were the president of the United States, what course would you take to act in accord with your own convictions and also respect the convictions of your diverse constituency? If you believe that President Reagan's amendment is the best answer, write an *argumentative* essay refuting Will and Garrettson. If you support students' right to pray but not this constitutional amendment, propose an alternate course of action, explaining your reasons. If you believe no action is the best solution, write an essay justifying your view to proponents of the amendment as altered by Senator Danforth.

2. Religious beliefs have become an issue in other areas of American life besides prayer in the public schools. One student sparked heated controversy by refusing to stand for her class's pledge to the flag, which includes the phrase, "one nation under God." American currency is engraved "In God We Trust." "Creationists" insist that the biblical theory of creation should be given equal time with the explanations offered by science. The central argument in the abortion debate also relates to religious convictions. Choose one of these issues and write an essay explaining its relation to the First Amendment's guarantee of separation between church and state, and explaining how the problem should be resolved.

3. The idea of compulsory public education is based on the assumption that certain skills and information — most notably the "three Rs," reading, writing, and 'rithmetic — are so valuable to every citizen that all citizens should have access to them. In our era, public education goes way beyond these basics. Modern students are exposed to literature, languages, science and social science, higher mathematics, the arts, practical and vocational programs, sports, and numerous extracurricular opportunities, including religious instruction and expression. Write a *comparison-and-contrast* essay suggesting how a different educational policy or system would provide more effective preparation for informed, involved citizens.

RICHARD WRIGHT

Richard Wright is widely recognized as one of the foremost literary talents in twentieth century America. As the following excerpt from his autobiography Black Boy *(1945) demonstrates, his path to success was long and uphill. Wright was born near Natchez, Mississippi, in 1908. His formal education was sporadic because he moved a number of times, and at fifteen he left school. He worked at odd jobs in the South, reading voraciously in his spare time. Eventually he was able to move to Chicago, where he clerked at the U.S. Post Office during the late 1920s.*

In 1932 Wright joined the Communist party. Though he adopted a Marxist perspective in the poems and short stories he was writing by then, and published only in left-wing periodicals, he was too individualistic for some party members and quit the party in 1944. Meanwhile, he became associated with the Works Progress Administration Federal Writers' Project in Chicago and New York from 1935 to 1937. In 1938 he won Story *magazine's prize for the best book-length manuscript for four long stories, which were subsequently published as* Uncle Tom's Children. *Though the book was well received, Wright later wrote, "I swore to myself that if I ever wrote another book, no one would weep over it; that it would be so hard and deep that they would have to face it without the consolation of tears." His next book was the powerful* Native Son *(1940), the story of a young black man in Chicago who commits two murders. Wright turned it into a play for Broadway a year later and continued publishing articles, essays, short stories, and poems in magazines and newspapers including* Atlantic Monthly, Saturday Review, New Republic, Negro Digest, Daily Worker, New Work World Telegram, *and* New Masses.

In 1946 Wright accepted the French government's invitation to visit France; the next year he, his second wife, and his two daughters returned to Paris to live permanently. There Wright became acquainted with Jean-Paul Sartre, Simone de Beauvoir, and the other writers in the existentialist circle. Among his later works are The Outsider *(1953),* Savage Holiday *(1954),* Black Power *(1954),* The Color Curtain *(1956),* Pagan Spain *(1957),* White Man, Listen! *(1957), and* The Long Dream *(1958). Wright died in Paris of a heart attack in 1960. Several more books were published posthumously, including the story collections* Quintet *and* Eight Men *(1961), the novel* Lawd Today *(1963), the play* Daddy Goodness *(1968), and the novella* The Man Who Lived Underground *(1971).*

Discovering Books

One morning I arrived early at work and went into the bank lobby where 1
the Negro porter was mopping. I stood at a counter and picked up the Memphis
Commercial Appeal and began my free reading of the press. I came finally to
the editorial page and saw an article dealing with one H.L. Mencken. I knew
by hearsay that he was the editor of the *American Mercury*, but aside from that
I knew nothing about him. The article was a furious denunciation of Mencken,
concluding with one, hot, short sentence: Mencken is a fool.

I wondered what on earth this Mencken had done to call down upon him 2
the scorn of the South. The only people I had ever heard denounced in the
South were Negroes, and this man was not a Negro. Then what ideas did
Mencken hold that made a newspaper like the *Commercial Appeal* castigate
him publicly? Undoubtedly he must be advocating ideas that the South did
not like. Were there, then, people other than Negroes who criticized the
South? I knew that during the Civil War the South had hated northern whites,
but I had not encountered such hate during my life. Knowing no more of
Mencken than I did at that moment, I felt a vague sympathy for him. Had
not the South, which had assigned me the role of a nonman, cast at him its
hardest words?

Now, how could I find out about this Mencken? This was a huge library 3
near the riverfront, but I knew that negroes were not allowed to patronize its
shelves any more than they were the parks and playgrounds of the city. I had
gone into the library several times to get books for the white men on the job.
Which of them would now help me to get books? And how could I read them
without causing concern to the white men with whom I worked? I had so far
been successful in hiding my thoughts and feelings from them, but I knew that
I would create hostility if I went about this business of reading in a clumsy
way.

I weighed the personalities of the men on the job. There was Don, a Jew; 4
but I distrusted him. His position was not much better than mine and I knew
that he was uneasy and insecure; he had always treated me in an offhand,
bantering way that barely concealed his contempt. I was afraid to ask him to
help me to get books; his frantic desire to demonstrate a racial solidarity with
the whites against Negroes might make him betray me.

Then how about the boss? No, he was a Baptist and I had the suspicion 5
that he would not be quite able to comprehend why a black boy would want
to read Mencken. There were other white men on the job whose attitudes
showed clearly that they were Kluxers or sympathizers, and they were out of
the question.

There remained only one man whose attitude did not fit into an anti-Negro   6
category, for I had heard the white men refer to him as a "Pope lover." He
was an Irish Catholic and was hated by the white Southerners. I knew that
he read books, because I had got him volumes from the library several times.
Since he, too, was an object of hatred, I felt that he might refuse me but
would hardly betray me. I hesitated, weighing and balancing the imponderable
realities.

One morning I paused before the Catholic fellow's desk.   7
"I want to ask you a favor," I whispered to him.   8
"What is it?"   9
"I want to read. I can't get books from the library. I wonder if you'd let me   10
use your card?"
He looked at me suspiciously.   11
"My card is full most of the time," he said.   12
"I see," I said and waited, posing my question silently.   13
"You're not trying to get me into trouble, are you, boy?" he asked, staring   14
at me.
"Oh, no, sir."   15
"What book do you want?"   16
"A book by H. L. Mencken."   17
"Which one?"   18
"I don't know. Has he written more than one?"   19
"He has written several."   20
"I didn't know that."   21
"What makes you want to read Mencken?"   22
"Oh, I just saw his name in the newspaper," I said.   23
"It's good of you to want to read," he said. "But you ought to read the right   24
things."
I said nothing. Would he want to supervise my reading?   25
"Let me think," he said. "I'll figure out something."   26
I turned from him and he called me back. He stared at me quizzically.   27
"Richard, don't mention this to the other white men," he said.   28
"I understand," I said. "I won't say a word."   29
A few days later he called me to him.   30
"I've got a card in my wife's name," he said. "Here's mine."   31
"Thank you, sir."   32
"Do you think you can manage it?"   33
"I'll manage fine," I said.   34
"If they suspect you, you'll get in trouble," he said.   35
"I'll write the same kind of notes to the library that you wrote when you   36
sent me for books," I told him. "I'll sign your name."

He laughed.　　　　　　　　　　　　　　　　　　　　　　　　　37

"Go ahead. Let me see what you get," he said.　　　　　　　　　38

That afternoon I addressed myself to forging a note. Now, what were the　39
names of books written by H. L. Mencken? I did not know any of them. I
finally wrote what I thought would be a foolproof note: *Dear Madam: Will you
please let this nigger boy*—I used the word "nigger" to make the librarian feel
that I could not possibly be the author of the note—*have some books by H.
L. Mencken?* I forged the white man's name.

I entered the library as I had always done when on errands for whites, but　40
I felt that I would somehow slip up and betray myself. I doffed my hat, stood
a respectful distance from the desk, looked as unbookish as possible, and waited
for the white patrons to be taken care of. When the desk was clear of people,
I still waited. The white librarian looked at me.

"What do you want, boy?"　　　　　　　　　　　　　　　　41

As though I did not possess the power of speech, I stepped forward and　42
simply handed her the forged note, not parting my lips.

"What books by Mencken does he want?" she asked.　　　　　43

"I don't know, ma'am," I said, avoiding her eyes.　　　　　　　44

"Who gave you this card?"　　　　　　　　　　　　　　　45

"Mr. Falk," I said.　　　　　　　　　　　　　　　　　　　46

"Where is he?"　　　　　　　　　　　　　　　　　　　　47

"He's at work, at the M——— Optical Company," I said. "I've been in　48
here for him before."

"I remember," the woman said. "But he never wrote notes like this."　49

Oh, God, she's suspicious. Perhaps she would not let me have the books?　50
If she had turned her back at that moment, I would have ducked out the door
and never gone back. Then I thought of a bold idea.

"You can call him up, ma'am," I said, my heart pounding.　　　　51

"You're not using these books, are you?" she asked pointedly.　　　52

"Oh, no, ma'am. I can't read."　　　　　　　　　　　　　　53

"I don't know what he wants by Mencken," she said under her breath.　54

I knew now that I had won; she was thinking of other things and the race　55
question had gone out of her mind. She went to the shelves. Once or twice
she looked over her shoulder at me, as though she was still doubtful. Finally
she came forward with two books in her hand.

"I'm sending him two books," she said. "But tell Mr. Falk to come in next　56
time, or send me the names of the books he wants. I don't know what he
wants to read."

I said nothing. She stamped the card and handed me the books. Not daring　57
to glance at them, I went out of the library, fearing that the woman would
call me back for further questioning. A block away from the library I opened

one of the books and read a title: *A Book of Prefaces*. I was nearing my nineteenth birthday and I did not know how to pronounce the word *preface*. I
thumbed the pages and saw strange words and strange names. I shook my head,
disappointed. I looked at the other book; it was called *Prejudices*. I knew what
that word meant; I had heard it all my life. And right off I was on guard
against Mencken's books. Why would a man want to call a book *Prejudices?*
The word was so stained with all my memories of racial hate that I could not
conceive of anybody using it for a title. Perhaps I had made a mistake about
Mencken? A man who had prejudices must be wrong.

When I showed the books to Mr. Falk, he looked at me and frowned.   58
"That librarian might telephone you," I warned him.   59
"That's all right," he said. "But when you're through reading those books, 60
I want to tell me what you get out of them."

That night in my rented room, while letting the hot water run over my can 61
of pork and beans in the sink. I opened *A Book of Prefaces* and began to read.
I was jarred and shocked by the style, the clear, clean, sweeping sentences.
Why did he write like that? And how did one write like that? I pictured the
man as a raging demon, slashing with his pen, consumed with hate, de-
nouncing everything American, extolling everything European or German,
laughing at the weaknesses of people, mocking God, authority. What was this?
I stood up, trying to realize what reality lay behind the meaning of the words. . . .
Yes, this man was fighting, fighting with words. He was using words as a
weapon, using them as one would use a club. Could words be weapons? Well,
yes, for here they were. Then, maybe, perhaps, I could use them as a weapon?
No. It frightened me. I read on and what amazed me was not what he said,
but how on earth anybody had the courage to say it.

Occasionally I glanced up to reassure myself that I was alone in the room. 62
Who were these men about whom Mencken was talking so passionately? Who
was Anatole France? Joseph Conrad? Sinclair Lewis, Sherwood Anderson,
Dostoevski, George Moore, Gustave Flaubert, Maupassant, Tolstoy, Frank
Harris, Mark Twain, Thomas Hardy, Arnold Bennett, Stephen Crane, Zola,
Norris, Gorky, Bergson, Ibsen, Balzac, Bernard Shaw, Dumas, Poe, Thomas
Mann, O. Henry, Dreiser, H. G. Wells, Gogol, T. S. Eliot, Gide, Baudelaire,
Edgar Lee Masters, Stendhal, Turgenev, Huneker, Nietzsche, and scores of
others? Were these men real? Did they exist or had they existed? And how
did one pronounce their names?

I ran across many words whose meanings I did not know, and I either looked 63
them up in a dictionary or, before I had a chance to do that, encountered the
word in a context that made its meaning clear. But what strange world was
this? I concluded the book with the conviction that I had somehow overlooked

something terribly important in life. I had once tried to write, had once reveled
in feeling, had let my crude imagination roam, but the impulse to dream had
been slowly beaten out of me by experience. Now it surged up again and I
hungered for books, new ways of looking and seeing. It was not a matter of
believing or disbelieving what I read, but of feeling something new, of being
affected by something that made the look of the world different.

As dawn broke I ate my pork and beans, feeling dopey, sleepy. I went to 64
work, but the mood of the book would not die; it lingered, coloring everything
I saw, heard, did. I now felt that I knew what the white men were feeling.
Merely because I had read a book that had spoken of how they lived and
thought, I identified myself with that book. I felt vaguely guilty. Would I,
filled with bookish notions, act in a manner that would make the whites dislike
me?

I forged more notes and my trips to the library became frequent. Reading 65
grew into a passion. My first serious novel was Sinclair Lewis's *Main Street*. It
made me see my boss, Mr. Gerald, and identify him as an American type. I
would smile when I saw him lugging his golf bags into the office. I had always
felt a vast distance separating me from the boss, and now I felt closer to him,
though still distant. I felt now that I knew him, that I could feel the very
limits of his narrow life. And this had happened because I had read a novel
about a mythical man called George F. Babbitt.

The plots and stories in the novels did not interest me so much as the point 66
of view revealed. I gave myself over to each novel without reserve, without
trying to criticize it; it was enough for me to see and feel something different.
And for me, everything was something different. Reading was like a drug, a
dope. The novels created moods in which I lived for days. But I could not
conquer my sense of guilt, my feeling that the white men around me knew
that I was changing, that I had begun to regard them differently.

Whenever I brought a book to the job, I wrapped it in newspaper—a habit 67
that was to persist for years in other cities and under other circumstances. But
some of the white men pried into my packages when I was absent and they
questioned me.

"Boy, what are you reading those books for?"   68

"Oh, I don't know, sir."   69

"That's deep stuff you're reading, boy."   70

"I'm just killing time, sir."   71

"You'll addle your brains if you don't watch out."   72

I read Dreiser's *Jennie Gerhardt* and *Sister Carrie* and they revived in me a 73
vivid sense of my mother's suffering; I was overwhelmed, I grew silent, wondering about the life around me. It would have been impossible for me to have

told anyone what I derived from these novels, for it was nothing less than a sense of life itself. All my life had shaped me for the realism, the naturalism of the modern novel, and I could not read enough of them.

Steeped in new moods and ideas, I bought a ream of paper and tried to 74 write; but nothing would come, or what did come was flat beyond telling. I discovered that more than desire and feeling were necessary to write and I dropped the idea. Yet I still wondered how it was possible to know people sufficiently to write about them? Could I ever learn about life and people? To me, with my vast ignorance, my Jim Crow station in life, it seemed a task impossible of achievement. I now knew what being a Negro meant. I could endure the hunger. I had learned to live with hate. But to feel that there were feelings denied me, that the very breath of life itself was beyond my reach, that more than anything else hurt, wounded me. I had a new hunger.

In buoying me up, reading also cast me down, made me see what was 75 possible, what I had missed. My tension returned, new, terrible, bitter, surging, almost too great to be contained. I no longer *felt* that the world about me was hostile, killing; I *knew* it. A million times I asked myself what I could do to save myself, and there were no answers. I seemed forever condemned, ringed by walls.

I did not discuss my reading with Mr. Falk, who had lent me his library 76 card; it would have meant talking about myself and that would have been too painful. I smiled each day, fighting desperately to maintain my old behavior, to keep my disposition seemingly sunny. But some of the white men discerned that I had begun to brood.

"Wake up there, boy!" Mr. Olin said one day.   77

"Sir!" I answered for the lack of a better word.   78

"You act like you've stolen something," he said.   79

I laughed in the way I knew he expected me to laugh, but I resolved to be 80 more conscious of myself, to watch my every act, to guard and hide the new knowledge that was dawning within me.

If I went north, would it be possible for me to build a new life then? But 81 how could a man build a life upon vague, unformed yearnings? I wanted to write and I did not even know the English language. I bought English grammars and found them dull. I felt that I was getting a better sense of the language from novels than grammars. I read hard, discarding a writer as soon as I felt that I had grasped his point of view. At night the printed page stood before my eyes in sleep.

Mrs. Moss, my landlady, asked me one Sunday morning: 82

"Son, what is this you keep on reading?"   83

"Oh, nothing. Just novels." 84

"What you get out of 'em?" 85

"I'm just killing time," I said. 86

"I hope you know your own mind," she said in a tone which implied that 87 she doubted if I had a mind.

I knew of no Negroes who read the books I liked and I wondered if any 88 Negroes ever thought of them. I knew that there were Negro doctors, lawyers, newspapermen, but I never saw any of them. When I read a Negro newspaper I never caught the faintest echo of my preoccupation in its pages. I felt trapped and occasionally, for a few days, I would stop reading. But a vague hunger would come over me for books, books that opened up new avenues of feeling and seeing, and again I would forge another note to the white librarian. Again I would read and wonder as only the naive and unlettered can read and wonder, feeling that I carried a secret, criminal burden about with me each day.

That winter my mother and brother came and we set up housekeeping, 89 buying furniture on the installment plan, being cheated and yet knowing no way to avoid it. I began to eat warm food and to my surprise found the regular meals enabled me to read faster. I may have lived through many illnesses and survived them, never suspecting that I was ill. My brother obtained a job and we began to save toward the trip north, plotting our time, setting tentative dates for departure. I told none of the white men on the job that I was planning to go north; I knew that the moment they felt I was thinking of the North they would change toward me. It would have made them feel that I did not like the life I was living, and because my life was completely conditioned by what they said or did, it would have been tantamount to challenging them.

I could calculate my chances for life in the South as a Negro fairly clearly 90 now.

I could fight the southern whites by organizing with other Negroes, as my 91 grandfather had done. But I knew that I could never win that way; there were many whites and there were but few blacks. They were strong and we were weak. Outright black rebellion could never win. If I fought openly I would die and I did not want to die. News of lynchings were frequent.

I could submit and live the life of a genial slave, but that was impossible. 92 All of my life had shaped me to live by my own feelings and thoughts. I could make up to Bess and marry her and inherit the house. But that, too, would be the life of a slave; if I did that, I would crush to death something within me, and I would hate myself as much as I knew the whites already hated those who had submitted. Neither could I ever willingly present myself to be kicked, as Shorty had done. I would rather have died than do that.

I could drain off my restlessness by fighting with Shorty and Harrison. I had 93
seen many Negroes solve the problem of being black by transferring their hatred
of themselves to others with a black skin and fighting them. I would have to
be cold to do that, and I was not cold and I could never be.

I could, of course, forget what I had read, thrust the whites out of my mind, 94
forget them; and find release from anxiety and longing in sex and alcohol. But
the memory of how my father had conducted himself made that course repug-
nant. If I did not want others to violate my life, how could I voluntarily violate
it myself?

I had no hope whatever of being a professional man. Not only had I been 95
so conditioned that I did not desire it, but the fulfillment of such an ambition
was beyond my capabilities. Well-to-do Negroes lived in a world that was
almost as alien to me as the world inhabited by whites.

What, then, was there? I held my life in my mind, in my consciousness 96
each day, feeling at times that I would stumble and drop it, spill it forever.
My reading had created a vast sense of distance between me and the world in
which I lived and tried to make a living, and that sense of distance was
increasing each day. My days and nights were one long, quiet, continuously
contained dream of terror, tension, and anxiety. I wondered how long I could
bear it.

QUESTIONS FOR READING AND REVISING

1. How does Wright establish his role in the first paragraph as that of a man in
   control of his destiny, not a passive victim of racial discrimination? Where and
   how does he first reveal that he is black? In what context does he introduce
   the discrimination he faces? What is his *tone* when mentioning it?

2. In his first three paragraphs, Wright sets up both the immediate and the longer-
   term problem that will keep us intrigued through his essay. What is his immediate problem? What larger conflict in his life does it reflect? How does
   Wright indirectly introduce in paragraph 2 the major challenge that will become dominant by the end of his essay? What is that challenge? What technique does Wright use to depict the South as more like a hostile individual
   than a geographic region?

3. In what ways is Wright's evaluation of the men he works with shaped by his
   experience as the wearer of a racial label? At what point in the essay do we
   first see Wright as these men see him? How would the impact of the library-
   card scene (paragraphs 7–38) be different if he had merely told us what happened instead of showing it to us in dialogue? How is your response to this

scene influenced by having met Wright in his private persona before seeing him in his public one?

4. In each scene involving dialogue, Wright uses the same strategies to avoid giving himself away to the other speaker(s). What are these strategies? In what other ways does he apply them to his contact with the world? What aspects of himself is Wright hiding, and why?

5. In paragraphs 73 – 76 Wright describes his inner turmoil as he enters a new realm of existence through reading, yet cannot fully share it. "I bought a ream of paper and tried to write," he relates, "but nothing would come, or what did come was flat beyond telling." What *cause-and-effect* chain is Wright discovering between his reading, the awakening of his feelings, his awareness of the world's hostility, his need to pretend no such hostility exists, and his inability to write? What is the effect of his encounter with Mr. Olin in paragraphs 77 – 80? Why does Wright's first question in paragraph 81 follow inevitably from paragraph 80?

6. In paragraphs 90 – 95 Wright presents a chilling catalog of his options. What does he convey about himself by not expressing hatred for his oppressors, not using negative adjectives to characterize them, and indeed, barely mentioning them? The reality of this list of repellent possibilities is sharpened by all the scenes that have preceded it. Where and how in the essay has Wright shown himself trying, at least indirectly, each of the options he mentions?

7. Wright emphasizes the *contrast* between his inner and outer worlds by using contrasting styles to describe them. Compare, for example, paragraph 57 with paragraph 61. What techniques of sentence structure, word choice, and usage are most striking in each one? What single verb in paragraph 57 gives a hint of the language to come in paragraph 61? Find at least two more paragraphs where Wright describes his reactions to reading, and note the words and phrases with which his prose, like his mind, comes to life.

QUESTIONS ON CONNECTIONS

1. In what ways is Earnestine Johnson's experience with *The Color Purple*, described in "Thank You Miss Alice Walker" (p. 128), similar to Richard Wright's discovery of the world of fiction? In what ways are these two writers' situations, and therefore their experiences, significantly different? Johnson uses the words *shame* and *embarrass* several times in her essay. How does her application of these words, and her self-concept in general, appear to relate to Wright's sense of himself as a black in a white-dominated world?

2. Both Wright's and Johnson's essays center on encounters with books their audience may or may not have read. How does each writer characterize the books in question so as to compensate for this potential gap? What aspects of

the books they discuss are most impressive and important to each writer? From their approach to the novels they read, what can you deduce about Wright's assumptions about, experience with, and expectations of other blacks versus Johnson's?

SUGGESTIONS FOR WRITING

1. Richard Wright describes an existence that requires as cool a head and as much skill at deception as any international spy or alien invader. Wright's straightforward narrative emphasizes that living in disguise may be fraught with drama, but it is by no means glamorous or romantic. For Americans today, pretending to be someone you are not remains a fairly common experience, though usually less serious and much less agonizing than it was for Wright. Think of an occasion in your life when you had to play a role in which you felt uncomfortable or fearful, or when you realized that someone you encountered was playing such a role. Write a *narrative* or *cause-and-effect* essay about that experience.

2. Wright's difficulty in getting hold of books and his soul-shaking reaction to them once he did is a reminder that we often appreciate most what costs us most — whether it is a relationship, an object, an opportunity, or an achievement. Similarly, we are likely to resent deeply anyone who squanders or takes for granted something we have craved and fought for. Write an essay about a hard-won prize or privilige in your life, or a rivalry that arose from jealousy or envy, paying attention to the social or political arrangement that is responsible for inequity of access.

3. "There is no Frigate like a Book," wrote Emily Dickinson in the 1870s, "to take us Lands away." Richard Wright and Earnestine Johnson confirm Dickinson's observation. Most of us who enjoy reading can remember hours that were transformed by a book: when we looked up from its pages and could barely remember where we were; when we balked at the demands of parents, friends, and obligations to stop reading and come back to reality; or when we returned to earth blinking at the change in our vision. Write an essay about a book or an experience with reading that deeply affected you.

DORIS LESSING

Doris Lessing reports having grown up "alone in a landscape with very few human things to dot it. At the time it was hellishly lonely, but now I realize how extraordinary it was, and how very lucky I was." Born in Persia (now Iran) in 1919, Lessing spent much of her childhood in transit between her birthplace and England before her family settled on a farm in Southern Rhodesia (now Zimbabwe). There they struggled to eke out a living in the face of natural disasters and with low crop prices. Her family's mud and thatch house "overlooked in all directions a great system of mountains, rivers, valleys, while overhead the sky arched from horizon to empty horizon." Her life there, with access only to her parents, a younger brother, a few distant neighbors, and the native workers her family hired, is amply evident in such stories as "The Old Chief Mshlanga" as well as in such semiautobiographical novels as Martha Quest *(1952)* Proper Marriage *(1954), and* Landlocked *(1965).*

Forced to abandon school at age fourteen, Lessing educated herself by reading "the classics of European and American literature." "There was no one to talk to," she reports, "so I read." After a brief stint as a secretary in Salisbury and two unsuccessful marriages, Lessing arrived in London in 1949 with little money, a child, and a manuscript for her first novel, The Grass Is Singing *(1950). The success of this novel enabled her to devote herself to writing. In 1951 she published a collection of her African stories,* This Was the Old Chief's Country. *She returned to Rhodesia in 1956, published her impressions in* Going Home *(1957), left the country once again, and was subsequently barred from returning because of her liberal racial views. Lessing's most famous work is* The Golden Notebook *(1962), a compelling synthesis of her main concerns as a writer: racism, sexual politics, and "individual conscience in its relation with the collective." In Lessing's vision of art, the writer "talks, as an individual to individuals, in a small personal voice. In an age of committee art, public art, people may begin to feel again a need for the small personal voice; and this will feed confidence into writers and, with confidence because of the knowledge of being needed, the warmth and humanity and love of people which is essential for a great age of literature." Lessing's commitment to writing short stories remains fervent: "Some writers I know have stopped writing short stories because, as they say, 'there is no market for them.' Others, like myself, the addicts, go on, and I suspect I would go on even if there really wasn't any home for them but a private drawer."*

The Old Chief Mshlanga

They were good, the years of ranging the bush over her father's farm which,   1
like every white farm, was largely unused, broken only occasionally by small
patches of cultivation. In between, nothing but trees, the long sparse grass,
thorn and cactus and gully, grass and outcrop and thorn. And a jutting piece
of rock which had been thrust up from the warm soil of Africa unimaginable
eras of time ago, washed into hollows and whorls by sun and wind that had
travelled so many thousands of miles of space and bush, would hold the weight
of a small girl whose eyes were sightless for anything but a pale willowed river,
a pale gleaming castle — a small girl singing: "Out flew the web and floated
wide, the mirror cracked from side to side. . . ."

Pushing her way through the green aisles of the mealie[1] stalks, the leaves   2
arching like cathedrals veined with sunlight far overhead, with the packed red
earth underfoot, a fine lace of red-starred witchweed would summon up a black
bent figure croaking premonitions: the Northern witch, bred of cold northern
forests, would stand before her among the mealie fields, and it was the mealie
fields that faded and fled, leaving her among the gnarled roots of an oak, snow
falling thick and soft and white, the woodcutter's fire glowing red welcome
through crowding tree trunks.

A white child, opening its eyes curiously on a sun-suffused landscape, a   3
gaunt and violent landscape, might be supposed to accept it as her own, to
take the msasa trees and the thorn trees as familiars, to feel her blood running
free and responsive to the swing of the seasons.

This child could not see a msasa tree, or the thorn, for what they were.   4
Her books held tales of alien fairies, her rivers ran slow and peaceful, and she
knew the shape of the leaves of an ash or an oak, the names of the little
creatures that lived in English streams, when the words "the veld" meant
strangeness, though she could remember nothing else.

Because of this, for many years, it was the veld that seemed unreal; the sun   5
was a foreign sun, and the wind spoke a strange language.

The black people on the farm were as remote as the trees and the rocks.   6
They were an amorphous black mass, mingling and thinning and massing like
tadpoles, faceless, who existed merely to serve, to say "Yes, Baas,"[2] take their
money and go. They changed season by season, moving from one farm to the
next, according to their outlandish needs, which one did not have to understand, coming from perhaps hundreds of miles north or east, passing on after

---

[1]Corn, maize.
[2]Boss, sir.

a few months — where? Perhaps even as far away as the fabled gold mines of Johannesburg, where the pay was so much better than the few shillings a month and the double handful of mealie meal twice a day which they earned in that part of Africa.

The child was taught to take them for granted: the servants in the house 7 would come running a hundred yards to pick up a book if she dropped it. She was called "Nkosikaas" — Chieftainess, even by the black children her own age.

Later, when the farm grew too small to hold her curiosity, she carried a 8 gun in the crook of her arm and wandered miles a day, from vlei[3] to vlei, from kopje[4] to kopje, accompanied by two dogs: the dogs and the gun were an armour against fear. Because of them she never felt fear.

If a native came into sight along the kaffir[5] paths half a mile away, the dogs 9 would flush him up a tree as if he were a bird. If he expostulated (in his uncouth language which was by itself ridiculous) that was cheek.[6] If one was in a good mood, it could be a matter for laughter. Otherwise one passed on, hardly glancing at the angry man in the tree.

On the rare occasions when white children met together they could amuse 10 themselves by hailing a passing native in order to make a buffoon of him; they could set the dogs on him and watch him run; they could tease a small black child as if he were a puppy — save that they would not throw stones and sticks at a dog without a sense of guilt.

Later still, certain questions presented themselves in the child's mind; and 11 because the answers were not easy to accept, they were silenced by an even greater arrogance of manner.

It was even impossible to think of the black people who worked about the 12 house as friends, for if she talked to one of them, her mother would come running anxiously: "Come away; you mustn't talk to natives."

It was this instilled consciousness of danger, of something unpleasant, that 13 made it easy to laugh out loud, crudely, if a servant made a mistake in his English or if he failed to understand an order — there is a certain kind of laughter that is fear, afraid of itself.

One evening, when I was about fourteen, I was walking down the side of 14 a mealie field that had been newly ploughed, so that the great red clods showed fresh and tumbling to the vlei beyond, like a choppy red sea; it was that hushed

---

[3]A shallow lake or a low-lying swamp ground.
[4]Knoll, hill.
[5]Native Bantu.
[6]Impudence, arrogance.

and listening hour, when the birds send long sad calls from tree to tree, and all the colors of earth and sky and leaf are deep and golden. I had my rifle in the curve of my arm, and the dogs were at my heels.

In front of me, perhaps a couple of hundred yards away, a group of three 15 Africans came into sight around the side of a big antheap. I whistled the dogs close in to my skirts and let the gun swing in my hand, and advanced, waiting for them to move aside, off the path, in respect for my passing. But they came on steadily, and the dogs looked up at me for the command to chase. I was angry. It was "cheek" for a native not to stand off a path, the moment he caught sight of you.

In front walked an old man, stooping his weight on to a stick, his hair 16 grizzled white, a dark red blanket slung over his shoulders like a cloak. Behind him came two young men, carrying bundles of pots, assegais,[7] hatchets.

The group was not a usual one. They were not natives seeking work. These 17 had an air of dignity, of quietly following their own purpose. It was the dignity that checked my tongue. I walked quietly on, talking softly to the growling dogs, till I was ten paces away. Then the old man stopped, drawing his blanket close.

" 'Morning, Nkosikaas," he said, using the customary greeting for any time 18 of the day.

"Good morning," I said, "Where are you going?" My voice was a little 19 truculent.

The old man spoke in his own language, then one of the young men stepped 20 forward politely and said in careful English: "My Chief travels to see his brothers beyond the river."

A Chief! I thought, understanding the pride that made the old man stand 21 before me like an equal — more than an equal, for he showed courtesy, and I showed none.

The old man spoke again, wearing dignity like an inherited garment, still 22 standing ten paces off, flanked by his entourage, not looking at me (that would have been rude) but directing his eyes somewhere over my head at the trees.

"You are the little Nkosikaas from the farm of Baas Jordan?"   23

"That's right," I said.   24

"Perhaps your father does not remember," said the interpreter for the old 25 man, "but there was an affair with some goats. I remember seeing you when you were. . . ." The young man held his hand at knee level and smiled.

We all smiled.   26

"What is your name?" I asked.   27

[7]Spears.

"This is Chief Mshlanga," said the young man.   28

"I will tell my father that I met you," I said.   29

The old man said: "My greetings to your father, little Nkosikaas."   30

"Good morning," I said politely, finding the politeness difficult, from lack 31
of use.

" 'Morning, little Nkosikaas," said the old man, and stood aside to let me 32
pass.

I went by, my gun hanging awkwardly, the dogs sniffing and growling, 33
cheated of their favourite game of chasing natives like animals.

Not long afterwards I read in an old explorer's book the phrase: "Chief 34
Mshlanga's country." It went like this: "Our destination was Chief Mshlanga's
country, to the north of the river; and it was our desire to ask his permission
to prospect for gold in his territory."

The phrase "ask his permission" was so extraordinary to a white child, 35
brought up to consider all natives as things to use, that it revived those questions, which could not be suppressed: they fermented slowly in my mind.

On another occasion one of those old prospectors who still move over Africa 36
looking for neglected reef, with their hammers and tents, and pans for sifting
gold from crushed rock, came to the farm and, in talking of the old days, used
that phrase again: "This was the Old Chief's country," he said. "It stretched
from those mountains over there way back to the river, hundreds of miles of
country." That was his name for our district: "The Old Chief's Country"; he
did not use our name for it—a new phrase which held no implication of
usurped ownership.

As I read more books about the time when this part of Africa was opened 37
up, not much more than fifty years before, I found Old Chief Mshlanga had
been a famous man, known to all the explorers and prospectors. But then he
had been young; or maybe it was his father or uncle they spoke of—I never
found out.

During that year I met him several times in the part of the farm that was 38
traversed by natives moving over the country. I learned that the path up the
side of the big red field where the birds sang was the recognized highway for
migrants. Perhaps I even haunted it in the hope of meeting him: being greeted
by him, the exchange of courtesies, seemed to answer the questions that troubled me.

Soon I carried a gun in a different spirit; I used it for shooting food and not 39
to give me confidence. And now the dogs learned better manners. When I
saw a native approaching, we offered and took greetings; and slowly that other
landscape in my mind faded, and my feet struck directly on the African soil,
and I saw the shapes of tree and hill clearly, and the black people moved back,

as it were, out of my life; it was as if I stood aside to watch a slow intimate dance of landscape and men, a very old dance, whose steps I could not learn.

But I thought: this is my heritage, too; I was bred here; it is my country as well as the black man's country; and there is plenty of room for all of us, without elbowing each other off the pavements and roads.   40

It seemed it was only necessary to let free that respect I felt when I was talking with old Chief Mshlanga, to let both black and white people meet gently, with tolerance for each other's differences: it seemed quite easy.   41

Then, one day, something new happened. Working in our house as servants were always three natives: cook, houseboy, garden boy. They used to change as the farm natives changed: staying for a few months, then moving on to a new job, or back home to their kraals.[8] They were thought of as "good" or "bad" natives; which meant: how did they behave as servants? Were they lazy, efficient, obedient, or disrespectful? If the family felt good-humoured, the phrase was: "What can you expect from raw black savages?" If we were angry, we said: "These damned niggers, we would be much better off without them."   42

One day, a white policeman was on his rounds of the district, and he said laughingly: "Did you know you have an important man in your kitchen?"   43

"What!" exclaimed my mother sharply. "What do you mean?"   44

"A Chief's son." The policeman seemed amused. "He'll boss the tribe when the old man dies."   45

"He's better not put on a Chief's son act with me," said my mother.   46

When the policeman left, we looked with different eyes at our cook: he was a good worker, but he drank too much at weekends — that was how we knew him.   47

He was a tall youth, with very black skin, like black polished metal, his tightly growing black hair parted white man's fashion at one side, with a metal comb from the store stuck into it; very polite, very distant, very quick to obey an order. Now it had been pointed out, we said: "Of course, you can see. Blood always tells."   48

My mother became strict with him now she knew about his birth and prospects. Sometimes, when she lost her temper, she would say: "You aren't the Chief yet, you know." And he would answer her very quietly, his eyes on the ground: "Yes, Nkosikaas."   49

One afternoon he asked for a whole day off, instead of the customary half-day, to go home next Sunday.   50

"How can you go home in one day?"   51

"It will take me half an hour on my bicycle," he explained.   52

[8]Tribal villages.

I watched the direction he took; and the next day I went off to look for 53
this kraal; I understood he must be Chief Mshlanga's successor: there was no
other kraal near enough our farm.

Beyond our boundaries on that side the country was new to me. I followed 54
unfamiliar paths past kopjes that till now had been part of the jagged horizon,
hazed with distance. This was Government land, which had never been cultivated by white men; at first I could not understand why it was that it appeared, in merely crossing the boundary, I had entered a completely fresh type
of landscape. It was a wide green valley, where a small river sparkled, and
vivid waterbirds darted over the rushes. The grass was thick and soft to my
calves, the trees stood tall and shapely.

I was used to our farm, whose hundreds of acres of harsh eroded soil bore 55
trees that had been cut for the mine furnaces and had grown thin and twisted,
where the cattle had dragged the grass flat, leaving innumerable crisscrossing
trails that deepened each season into gullies, under the force of the rains.

This country had been left untouched, save for prospectors whose picks had 56
struck a few sparks from the surface of the rocks as they wandered by; and for
migrant natives whose passing had left, perhaps, a charred patch on the trunk
of a tree where their evening fire had nestled.

It was very silent: a hot morning with pigeons cooing throatily, the midday 57
shadows lying dense and thick with clear yellow spaces of sunlight between
and in all that wide green parklike valley, not a human soul but myself.

I was listening to the quick regular tapping of a woodpecker when slowly a 58
chill feeling seemed to grow up from the small of my back to my shoulders, in
a constricting spasm like a shudder, and at the roots of my hair a tingling
sensation began and ran down over the surface of my flesh, leaving me goose-
fleshed and cold, though I was damp with sweat. Fever? I thought; then uneasily, turned to look over my shoulder; and realized suddenly that this was fear.
It was extraordinary, even humiliating. It was a new fear. For all the years I
had walked by myself over this country I had never known a moment's uneasiness; in the beginning because I had been supported by a gun and the dogs,
then because I had learnt an easy friendliness for the Africans I might encounter.

I had read of this feeling, how the bigness and silence of Africa, under the 59
ancient sun, grows dense and takes shape in the mind, till even the birds seem
to call menacingly, and a deadly spirit comes out of the trees and the rocks.
You move warily, as if your very passing disturbs something old and evil,
something dark and big and angry that might suddenly rear and strike from
behind. You look at groves of entwined trees, and picture the animals that
might be lurking there; you look at the river running slowly, dropping from

level to level through the vlei, spreading into pools where at night the buck come to drink, and the crocodiles rise and drag them by their soft noses into underwater caves. Fear possessed me. I found I was turning round and round, because of that shapeless menace behind me that might reach out and take me; I kept glancing at the files of kopjes which, seen from a different angle, seemed to change with every step so that even known landmarks, like a big mountain that had sentineled my world since I first became conscious of it, showed an unfamiliar sunlit valley among its foothills. I did not know where I was. I was lost. Panic seized me. I found I was spinning round and round, staring anxiously at this tree and that, peering up at the sun which appeared to have moved into an eastern slant, shedding the sad yellow light of sunset. Hours must have passed! I looked at my watch and found that this state of meaningless terror had lasted perhaps ten minutes.

The point was that it was meaningless. I was not ten miles from home: I 60 had only to take my way back along the valley to find myself at the fence; away among the foothills of the kopjes gleamed the roof of a neighbour's house, and a couple of hours walking would reach it. This was the sort of fear that contracts the flesh of a dog at night and sets him howling at the full moon. It had nothing to do with what I thought or felt; and I was more disturbed by the fact that I could become its victim than of the physical sensation itself: I walked steadily on, quietened, in a divided mind, watching my own pricking nerves and apprehensive glances from side to side with a disgusted amusement. Deliberately I set myself to think of this village I was seeking, and what I should do when I entered it — if I could find it, which was doubtful, since I was walking aimlessly and it might be anywhere in the hundreds of thousands of acres of bush that stretched about me. With my mind on that village, I realized that a new sensation was added to the fear: loneliness. Now such a terror of isolation invaded me that I could hardly walk; and if it were not that I came over the crest of a small rise and saw a village below me, I should have turned and gone home. It was a cluster of thatched huts in a clearing among trees. There were neat patches of mealies and pumpkins and millet, and cattle grazed under some trees at a distance. Fowls scratched among the huts, dogs lay sleeping on the grass, and goats friezed a kopje that jutted up beyond a tributary of the river lying like an enclosing arm round the village.

As I came close I saw the huts were lovingly decorated with patterns of 61 yellow and red and ochre mud on the walls; and the thatch was tied in place with plaits of straw.

This was not at all like our farm compound, a dirty and neglected place, a 62 temporary home for migrants who had no roots at all.

And now I did not know what to do next. I called a small black boy, who 63
was sitting on a log playing a stringed gourd, quite naked except for the strings
of blue beads round his neck, and said: "Tell the Chief I am here." The child
stuck his thumb in his mouth and stared shyly back at me.

For minutes I shifted my feet on the edge of what seemed a deserted village, 64
till at last the child scuttled off, and then some women came. They were
draped in bright cloths, with brass glinting in their ears and on their arms.
They also stared, silently; then turned to chatter among themselves.

I said again: "Can I see Chief Mshlanga?" I saw they caught the name; they 65
did not understand what I wanted. I did not understand myself.

At last I walked through them and came past the huts and saw a clearing 66
under a big shady tree, where a dozen old men sat cross-legged on the ground,
talking. Chief Mshlanga was leaning back against the tree, holding a gourd in
his hand, from which he had been drinking. When he saw me, not a muscle
of his face moved, and I could see he was not pleased: perhaps he was afflicted
with my own shyness, due to being unable to find the right forms of courtesy
for the occasion. To meet me, on our own farm, was one thing; but I should
not have come here. What had I expected? I could not join them socially: the
thing was unheard of. Bad enough that I, a white girl, should be walking the
veld alone as a white man might: and in this part of the bush where only
Government officials had the right to move.

Again I stood, smiling foolishly, while behind me stood the groups of brightly 67
clad, chattering women, their faces alert with curiosity and interest, and in
front of me sat the old men, with old lined faces, their eyes guarded, aloof. It
was a village of ancients and children and women. Even the two young men
who kneeled beside the Chief were not those I had seen with him previously:
the young men were all away working on the white men's farms and mines,
and the Chief must depend on relatives who were temporarily on holiday for
his attendants.

"The small white Nkosikaas is far from home," remarked the old man at 68
last.

"Yes," I agreed, "it is far." I wanted to say: "I have come to pay you a 69
friendly visit, Chief Mshlanga." I could not say it. I might now be feeling an
urgent helpless desire to get to know these men and women as people, to be
accepted by them as a friend, but the truth was I had set out in a spirit of
curiosity: I had wanted to see the village that one day our cook, the reserved
and obedient young man who got drunk on Sundays, would one day rule over.

"The child of Nkosi Jordan is welcome," said Chief Mshlanga. 70

"Thank you," I said, and could think of nothing more to say. There was a 71 silence, while the flies rose and began to buzz around my head; and the wind shook a little in the thick green tree that spread its branches over the old men.

"Good morning," I said at last. "I have to return now to my home."   72

" 'Morning, little Nkosikaas," said Chief Mshlanga.   73

I walked away from the indifferent village, over the rise past the staring   74
amber-eyed goats, down through the tall stately trees into the great rich green valley where the river meandered and the pigeons cooed tales of plenty and the woodpecker tapped softly.

The fear had gone; the loneliness had set into stiff-necked stoicism; there   75
was now a queer hostility in the landscape, a cold, hard, sullen indomitability that walked with me, as strong as a wall, as intangible as smoke; it seemed to say to me: you walk here as a destroyer. I went slowly homewards, with an empty heart: I had learned that if one cannot call a country to heel like a dog, neither can one dismiss the past with a smile in an easy gush of feeling, saying: I could not help it, I am also a victim.

I only saw Chief Mshlanga once again.   76

One night my father's big red land was trampled down by small sharp   77
hooves, and it was discovered that the culprits were goats from Chief Mshlanga's kraal. This had happened once before, years ago.

My father confiscated all the goats. Then he sent a message to the old Chief   78
that if he wanted them he would have to pay for the damage.

He arrived at our house at the time of sunset one evening, looking very old   79
and bent now, walking stiffly under his regally draped blanket, leaning on a big stick. My father sat himself down in his big chair below the steps of the house; the old man squatted carefully on the ground before him, flanked by his two young men.

The palaver was long and painful, because of the bad English of the young   80
man who interpreted and because my father could not speak dialect, but only kitchen kaffir.

From my father's point of view, at least two hundred pounds worth of   81
damage had been done to the crop. He knew he could not get the money from the old man. He felt he was entitled to keep the goats. As for the old Chief, he kept repeating angrily: "Twenty goats! My people cannot lose twenty goats! We are not rich, like the Nkosi Jordan, to lose twenty goats at once."

My father did not think of himself as rich, but rather as very poor. He   82
spoke quickly and angrily in return, saying that the damage done meant a great deal to him, and that he was entitled to the goats.

At last it grew so heated that the cook, the Chief's son, was called from   83
the kitchen to be interpreter, and now my father spoke fluently in English, and our cook translated rapidly so that the old man could understand how

very angry my father was. The young man spoke without emotion, in a mechanical way, his eyes lowered, but showing how he felt his position by a hostile uncomfortable set of the shoulders.

It was now in the late sunset, the sky a welter of colors, the birds singing 84 their last songs, and the cattle, lowing peacefully, moving past us towards their sheds for the night. It was the hour when Africa is most beautiful; and here was this pathetic, ugly scene, doing no one any good.

At last my father stated finally: "I'm not going to argue about it. I am 85 keeping the goats."

The old Chief flashed back in his own language: "That means that my 86 people will go hungry when the dry season comes."

"Go to the police, then," said my father, and looked triumphant. 87

There was, of course, no more to be said. 88

The old man sat silent, his head bent, his hands dangling helplessly over 89 his withered knees. Then he rose, the young men helping him, and he stood facing my father. He spoke once again, very stiffly; and turned away and went home to his village.

"What did he say," asked my father of the young man, who laughed un- 90 comfortably and would not meet his eyes.

"What did he say," insisted my father. 91

Our cook stood straight and silent, his brows knotted together. Then he 92 spoke. "My father says: All this land, this land you call yours, is his land, and belongs to our people."

Having made this statement, he walked off into the bush after his father, 93 and we did not see him again.

Our next cook was a migrant from Nyasaland, with no expectations of 94 greatness.

Next time the policeman came on his rounds he was told this story. He 95 remarked: "That kraal has no right to be there; it should have been moved long ago. I don't know why no one has done anything about it. I'll have a chat to the Native Commissioner next week. I'm going over for tennis on Sunday, anyway."

Some time later we heard that Chief Mshlanga and his people had been 96 moved two hundred miles east, to a proper native reserve; the Government land was going to be opened up for white settlement soon.

I went to see the village again, about a year afterwards. There was nothing 97 there. Mounds of red mud, where the huts had been, had long swathes of rotting thatch over them, veined with the red galleries of the white ants. The pumpkin vines rioted everywhere, over the bushes, up the lower branches of trees so that the great golden balls rolled underfoot and dangled overhead: it was a festival of pumpkins. The bushes were crowding up, the new grass sprang vivid green.

The settler lucky enough to be allotted the lush warm valley (if he chose 98 to cultivate this particular section) would find, suddenly, in the middle of a mealie field, the plants were growing fifteen feet tall, the weight of the cobs dragging at the stalks, and wonder what unsuspected vein of richness he had struck.

QUESTIONS FOR READING

1. Identify the narrator's *point of view* in the first paragraph. What does Lessing gain by presenting the opening of the story from this perspective? What does the sound of the narrator's voice in the opening paragraph remind you of? Where have you heard this kind of language before?

2. When does the *point of view* shift in this story? To what? With what effect? In terms of the potential impact of her story, what does Lessing gain by this shift in point of view?

3. How does the narrator characterize "the black people on the farm" (paragraph 6)? What is the young girl's initial reaction to them? How were young whites trained to respond to blacks? When does the young girl first question that training? with what effect?

4. What initial impression of the Old Chief Mshlanga does the narrator present? What attitude toward the Old Chief does the narrator convey in this first *description*? Explain how this encounter alters the young girl's perception of blacks.

5. What is the nature of white "fear" of blacks? Discuss the importance of the young girl's gun in relation to that fear. At what point does she recognize the connection between her attitude toward the gun and her relationship with the blacks? What "new fear," what "larger terror," does the young girl experience? (See specifically paragraphs 58 and following.)

6. Reread the section of the story (paragraphs 58–60) in which the young girl loses her way. What stylistic devices does Lessing use to reinforce the child's physical and psychological sense of being lost? What does she notice as she enters the native village? What codes of behavior does she violate during her "friendly visit" to the Old Chief? What does she learn from her visit? In what sense is she "also a victim"?

7. Reread the last two paragraphs of the story. What general point does Lessing emphasize in the young girl's final visit to the village? Comment on Lessing's use of *irony* here. How, for example, does Lessing encourage her readers to respond to such phrases as "festival of pumpkins" and "unsuspected vein of richness"?

QUESTIONS ON CONNECTIONS

1. In her essay, "The Unmarked Road" (p. 202), Julie Reardon reports on her encounters with impoverished Americans. What stylistic similarities can you identify linking it with Lessing's depiction of the relationship between her narrator and black Africans? What inferences can you draw about each writer's *purpose*? In what specific respects is the impact of the story similar to that of the essay? What other connections can you identify between them? Apply the same questions to Lewis Thomas's essay, "The Iks."

2. *Compare and contrast* the sense of isolation the narrator experiences in Lessing's story with the sense of isolation Brenda Jacobs describes in her essay, "Handing Down Grace" (p. 106). In what specific ways does unfamiliarity with language and cultural difference lead to greater sensitivity and awareness in both Jacobs's and Lessing's narrators.

SUGGESTIONS FOR WRITING

1. Doris Lessing's stories of life in Africa have earned her great critical acclaim. One reviewer suggests that on the basis of these stories alone "Doris Lessing must be counted as one of the most important fiction writers of our time." The social and political commentary in Lessing's African stories, another critic contends, "confirm in precise and painful detail, like stitches in a wound the abuse of the native population of Southern Rhodesia by the white settlers of British descent . . . . Doris Lessing's work is an uninterrupted study of loneliness, but here it is particularly the isolation of a few white exiles, claiming vast strange land." Reread "The Old Chief Mshlanga" and write an essay in which you show how the story may be read as an "uninterrupted study of loneliness."

2. Much of the impact of Lessing's story derives from the young girl's recognition — and appreciation — of the dignity and cultural richness of a people she had previously taken for granted. Examine your own experience. Write a *narrative* or *descriptive* essay in which you present the consequences of finding yourself in an alien culture. What prompted you to appreciate the distinctiveness of these "strangers"? What did you learn about yourself as a result of this encounter.

YUKIO MISHIMA

When Yukio Mishima took his own life in 1970 by performing the ritual seppuku, *he was an internationally renowned writer of novels, short stories, plays, and essays as well as a cult figure in his own land. Born in Tokyo in 1925, the son of a government official, Mishima grew up as a frail child in a protective environment. His rejection as unfit for military service during World War II humiliated him and led him to dedicate himself to rebuilding his body and to serving the samurai ideal. He graduated from Tokyo University in 1947 with a law degree, and after a year in government service, he turned to writing full-time. Influenced by the celebrated novelist Yasunari Kawabata, Mishima turned to medieval Japanese classics for both the inspiration and the subjects for such novels as* Confessions of a Mask *(1948),* The Temple of the Golden Pavilion *(1959),* The Sailor Who Fell from Grace with the Sea *(1965), and the four-volume* The Sea of Fertility *(1970) as well as in short stories, collected in* Death in Midsummer and Other Stories *(1966). "Patriotism" was translated by Geoffrey W. Sargent.*

Mishima expressed his obsession with returning to the values of a feudal Japan, controlled by samurai loyal to the emperor, in both fiction and reality. When his effort to enlist the aid of the military in combating Japanese materialism failed, he responded by turning to the traditional samurai ritual of seppuku.

Patriotism

1

On the twenty-eighth of February, 1936 (on the third day, that is, of the February 26 incident), Lieutenant Shinji Takeyama of the Konoe Transport Battalion — profoundly disturbed by the knowledge that his closest colleagues had been with the mutineers from the beginning, and indignant at the imminent prospect of Imperial troops attacking Imperial troops — took his officer's sword and ceremonially disemboweled himself in the eight-mat room of his private residence in the sixth block of Aoba-chō, in Yotsuya Ward. His wife, Reiko, followed him, stabbing herself to death. The lieutenant's farewell note consisted of one sentence: "Long live the Imperial Forces." His wife's, after apologies for her unfilial conduct in thus preceding her parents to the grave, concluded: "The day which, for a soldier's wife, had to come, has come . . . ." The last moments of this heroic and dedicated couple were such as to make the gods themselves weep. The lieutenant's age, it should be noted, was thirty-one, his wife's twenty-three; and it was not half a year since the celebration of their marriage.

1

2

Those who saw the bride and bridegroom in the commemorative photograph 2 —perhaps no less than those actually present at the lieutenant's wedding— had exclaimed in wonder at the bearing of this handsome couple. The lieutenant, majestic in military uniform, stood protectively beside his bride, his right hand resting upon his sword, his officer's cap held at his left side. His expression was severe, and his dark brows and wide-gazing eyes well conveyed the clear integrity of their youth. For the beauty of the bride in her white overrobe no comparisons were adequate. In the eyes, round beneath soft brows, in the slender, finely shaped nose, and in the full lips, there was both sensuousness and refinement. One hand, emerging shyly from a sleeve of the overrobe, held a fan, and the tips of the fingers, clustering delicately, were like the bud of a moonflower.

After the suicide, people would take out this photograph and examine it, 3 and sadly reflect that too often there was a curse on these seemingly flawless unions. Perhaps it was no more than imagination, but looking at the picture after the tragedy it almost seemed as if the two young people before the gold-lacquered screen were gazing, each with equal clarity, at the deaths which lay before them.

Thanks to the good offices of their go-between, Lieutenant General Ozeki, 4 they had been able to set themselves up in a new home at Aoba-chō in Yotsuya. "New home" is perhaps misleading. It was an old three-room rented house backing onto a small garden. As neither the six- nor the four-and-a-half-mat room downstairs was favored by the sun, they used the upstairs eight-mat room as both bedroom and guest room. There was no maid, so Reiko was left alone to guard the house in her husband's absence.

The honeymoon trip was dispensed with on the grounds that these were 5 times of national emergency. The two of them had spent the first night of their marriage at this house. Before going to bed, Shinji, sitting erect on the floor with his sword laid before him, had bestowed upon his wife a soldierly lecture. A woman who had become the wife of a soldier should know and resolutely accept that her husband's death might come at any moment. It could be tomorrow. It could be the day after. But, no matter when it came— he asked—was she steadfast in her resolve to accept it? Reiko rose to her feet, pulled open a drawer of the cabinet, and took out what was the most prized of her new possessions, the dagger her mother had given her. Returning to her place, she laid the dagger without a word on the mat before her, just as her husband had laid his sword. A silent understanding was achieved at once, and the lieutenant never again sought to test his wife's resolve.

In the first few months of her marriage Reiko's beauty grew daily more   6
radiant, shining serene like the moon before the rain.

As both were possessed of young, vigorous bodies, their relationship was   7
passionate. Nor was this merely a matter of the night. On more than one
occasion, returning home straight from manuevers, and begrudging even the
time it took to remove his mud-splashed uniform, the lieutenant had pushed
his wife to the floor almost as soon as he had entered the house. Reiko was
equally ardent in her response. For a little more or a little less than a month,
from the first night of their marriage Reiko knew happiness, and the lieutenant,
seeing this, was happy, too.

Reiko's body was white and pure, and her swelling breasts conveyed a firm   8
and chaste refusal; but, upon consent, those breasts were lavish with their
intimate, welcoming warmth. Even in bed these two were frighteningly and
awesomely serious. In the very midst of wild, intoxicating passions, their hearts
were sober and serious.

By day the lieutenant would think of his wife in the brief rest periods   9
between training; and all day long, at home, Reiko would recall the image of
her husband. Even when apart, however, they had only to look at the wedding
photograph for their happiness to be once more confirmed. Reiko felt not the
slightest surprise that a man who had been a complete stranger until a few
months ago should now have become the sun about which her whole world
revolved.

All these things had a moral basis and were in accordance with the Edu-   10
cation Rescript's injunction that "husband and wife should be harmonious."
Not once did Reiko contradict her husband, nor did the lieutenant ever find
reason to scold his wife. On the god shelf below the stairway, alongside the
tablet from the Great Ise Shrine, were set photographs of their Imperial Ma-
jesties, and regularly every morning, before leaving for duty, the lieutenant
would stand with his wife at this hallowed place, and together they would bow
their heads low. The offering water was renewed each morning, and the sacred
sprig of *sasaki* was always green and fresh. Their lives were lived beneath the
solemn protection of the gods and were filled with an intense happiness which
set every fiber in their bodies trembling.

3

Although Lord Privy Seal Saitō's house was in their neighborhood, neither   11
of them heard any noise of gunfire on the morning of February 26. It was a
bugle, sounding muster in the dim, snowy dawn, when the ten-minute tragedy
had already ended, which first disrupted the lieutenant's slumbers. Leaping at

once from his bed, and without speaking a word, the lieutenant donned his uniform, buckled on the sword held ready for him by his wife, and hurried swiftly out into the snow-covered streets of the still darkened morning, He did not return until the evening of the twenty-eighth.

Later, from the radio news, Reiko learned the full extent of this sudden 12 eruption of violence. Her life throughout the subsequent two days was lived alone, in complete tranquility, and behind locked doors.

In the lieutenant's face, as he hurried silently out into the snowy morning, 13 Reiko had read the determination to die. If her husband did not return, her own decision was made: she too would die. Quietly she attended to the disposition of her personal possessions. She chose her sets of visiting kimonos as keepsakes for friends of her schooldays, and she wrote a name and address on a stiff paper wrapping in which each was folded. Constantly admonished by her husband never to think of the morrow, Reiko had not even kept a diary and was now denied the pleasure of assiduously rereading her record of the happiness of the past few months and consigning each page to the fire as she did so. Ranged across the top of the radio were a small china dog, a rabbit, a squirrel, a bear, and a fox. There were also a small vase and a water pitcher. These comprised Reiko's one and only collection. But it would hardly do, she imagined, to give such things as keepsakes. Nor again would it be quite proper to ask specifically for them to be included in the coffin. It seemed to Reiko, as these thoughts passed through her mind, that the expressions on the small animals' faces grew even more lost and forlorn.

Reiko took the squirrel in her hand and looked at it. And then, her thoughts 14 turning to a realm far beyond these childlike affections, she gazed up into the distance at the great sunlike principle which her husband embodied. She was ready, and happy, to be hurtled along to her destruction in that gleaming sun chariot — but now, for these few moments of solitude she allowed herself to luxuriate in this innocent attachment to trifles. The time when she had genuinely loved these things, however, was long passed. Now she merely loved the memory of having once loved them, and their place in her heart had been filled by more intense passions, by a more frenzied happiness . . . . For Reiko had never, even to herself, thought of those soaring joys of the flesh as a mere pleasure. The February cold, and the icy touch of the china squirrel, had numbed Reiko's slender fingers; yet, even so, in her lower limbs, beneath the ordered repetition of the pattern which crossed the skirt of her trim *meisen* kimono, she could feel now, as she thought of the lieutenant's powerful arms reaching out toward her, a hot moistness of the flesh which defied the snows.

She was not in the least afraid of the death hovering in her mind. Waiting 15 alone at home, Reiko firmly believed that everything her husband was feeling or thinking now, his anguish and distress, was leading her — just as surely as the power in his flesh—to a welcome death. She felt as if her body could melt away with ease and be transformed to the merest fraction of her husband's thought.

Listening to the frequent announcements on the radio, she heard the names ⟨16⟩ of several of her husband's colleagues mentioned among those of the insurgents. This was the news of death. She followed the developments closely, wondering anxiously, as the situation became daily more irrevocable, why no Imperial ordinance was sent down, and watching what had at first been taken as a movement to restore the nation's honor come gradually to be branded with the infamous name of mutiny. There was no communication from the regiment. At any moment, it seemed, fighting might commence in the city streets, where the remains of the snow still lay.

Toward sundown in the twenty-eighth Reiko was startled by a furious ⟨17⟩ pounding on the front door. She hurried downstairs. As she pulled with fumbling fingers at the bolt, the shape dimly outlined beyond the frosted-glass panel made no sound, but she knew it was her husband. Reiko had never known the bolt of the sliding door to be so stiff. Still it resisted. The door just would not open.

In a moment, almost before she knew she had succeeded, the lieutenant ⟨18⟩ was standing before her on the cement floor inside the porch, muffled in a khaki greatcoat, his top boots heavy with slush from the street. Closing the door behind him, he returned the bolt once more to its socket. With what significance, Reiko did not understand.

"Welcome home."   ⟨19⟩

Reiko bowed deeply, but her husband made no response. As he had already ⟨20⟩ unfastened his sword and was about to remove his greatcoat, Reiko moved around behind to assist. The coat, which was cold and damp had lost the odor of horse dung it normally exuded when exposed to the sun, weighed heavily upon her arm. Draping it across a hanger, and cradling the sword and leather belt in her sleeves, she waited while her husband removed his top boots and them followed behind him into the "living room." This was the six-mat room downstairs.

Seen in the clear light from the lamp, her husband's face, covered with a ⟨21⟩ heavy growth of bristle, was almost unrecognizably wasted and thin. The cheeks were hollow, their luster and resilience gone. In his normal good spirits he would have changed into old clothes as soon as he was home and have pressed her to get supper at once, but now he sat before the table still in his uniform, his head drooping dejectedly. Reiko refrained from asking whether she should prepare the supper.

After an interval the lieutenant spoke.   ⟨22⟩

"I knew nothing. They hadn't asked me to join. Perhaps out of consider- 23
ation, because I was newly married. Kanō, and Homma too, and Yamaguchi."

Reiko recalled momentarily the faces of high-spirited young officers, friends 24
of her husband, who had come to the house occasionally as guests.

"There may be an Imperial ordinance sent down tomorrow. They'll be 25
posted as rebels, I imagine. I shall be in command of a unit with orders to
attack them . . . . I can't do it. It's impossible to do a thing like that."

He spoke again. 26

"They've taken me off guard duty, and I have permission to return home 27
for one night. Tomorrow morning, without question, I must leave to join the
attack. I can't do it, Reiko."

Reiko sat erect with lowered eyes. She understood that her husband had 28
spoken of his death. The lieutenant was resolved. Each word, being rooted in
death, emerged sharply and with powerful significance against this dark, un-
movable background. Although the lieutenant was speaking of his dilemma,
already there was no room in his mind for vacillation.

However, there was a clarity, like the clarity of the stream fed from melting 29
snows, in the silence which rested between them. Sitting in his own home
after the long two-day ordeal, and looking across at the face of his beautiful
wife, the lieutenant was for the first time experiencing true piece of mind. For
he had at once known, though she said nothing, that his wife divined the
resolve which lay beneath his words.

"Well, then. . . . " The lieutenant's eyes opened wide. Despite his ex- 30
haustion they were strong and clear, and now for the first time they looked
straight into the eyes of his wife. "Tonight I shall cut my stomach."

Reiko did not flinch. 31

Her round eyes showed tension, as taut as the clang of bell. 32

"I am ready," she said. "I ask permission to accompany you." 33

The lieutenant felt almost mesmerized by the strength in those eyes. His 34
words flowed swiftly and easily, like the utterances of a man in delirium, and
it was beyond his understanding how permission in a matter of such weight
could be expressed so casually.

"Good. We'll go together. But I want you as a witness, first, for my own 35
suicide. Agreed?"

When this was said a sudden release of abundant happiness welled up in 36
both of their hearts. Reiko was deeply affected by the greatness of her husband's
trust in her. It was vital for the lieutenant, whatever else might happen, that
there should be no irregularity in his death. For that reason there had to be a
witness. The fact that he had chosen his wife for this was the mark of his
trust. The second, and even greater mark, was that though he had pledged

that they should die together he did not intend to kill his wife first — he had deferred her death to a time when he would no longer be there to verify it. If the lieutenant had been a suspicious husband, he would doubtless, as in the usual suicide pact, have chosen to kill his wife first.

When Reiko said, "I ask permission to accompany you," the lieutenant felt   37 these words to be the final fruit of the education which he had himself given his wife, starting on the first night of their marriage, and which had schooled her, when the moment came, to say what had to be said without a shadow of hesitation. This flattered the lieutenant's opinion of himself as a self-reliant man. He was not so romantic or conceited as to imagine that the words were spoken spontaneously, out of love for her husband.

With happiness welling almost too abundantly in their hearts, they could not   38 help smiling at each other. Reiko felt as if she had returned to her wedding night.

Before her eyes was neither pain nor death. She seemed to see only a free   39 and limitless expanse opening out into vast distances.

"The water is hot. Will you take your bath now?"   40

Ah yes, of course."   41

"And supper . . . ?"   42

The words were delivered in such level, domestic tones that the lieutenant   43 came near to thinking, for the fraction of a second, that everything had been a hallucination.

"I don't think we'll need supper. But perhaps you could warm some sake?"   44

"As you wish."   45

As Reiko rose and took a *tanzen* gown from the cabinet for after the bath,   46 she purposely directed her husband's attention to the opened drawer. The lieutenant rose, crossed to the cabinet, and looked inside. From the ordered array of paper wrappings he read, one by one, the addresses of the keepsakes. There was no grief in the lieutenant's response to this demonstration of heroic resolve. His heart was filled with tenderness. Like a husband who is proudly shown the childish purchases of a young wife, the lieutenant, overwhelmed by affection, lovingly embraced his wife from behind and implanted a kiss upon her neck.

Reiko felt the roughness of the lieutenant's unshaven skin against her neck.   47 This sensation, more than being just a thing of this world, was for Reiko almost the world itself, but now — with the feeling that it was soon to be lost forever — it had freshness beyond all her experience. Each moment had its own vital strength, and the senses in every corner of her body were reawakened. Accepting her husband's caresses from behind, Reiko raised herself on the tips of her toes, letting the vitality seep through her entire body.

"First the bath, and then, after some sake . . . lay out the bedding upstairs, 48
will you?"

The lieutenant whispered the words into his wife's ear. Reiko silently nod- 49
ded.

Flinging off his uniform, the lieutenant went to the bath. To faint back- 50
ground noises of slopping water Reiko tended the charcoal brazier in the living
room and began the preparations for warming the sake.

Taking the *tanzen*, a sash, and some underclothes, she went to the bathroom 51
to ask how the water was. In the midst of a coiling cloud of steam the lieutenant
was sitting cross-legged on the floor, shaving, and she could dimly discern the
rippling movements of the muscles on his damp, powerful back as they responded to the movement of his arms.

There was nothing to suggest a time of any special significance. Reiko, 52
going busily about her tasks, was preparing side dishes from odds and ends in
stock. Her hands did not tremble. If anything, she managed even more effi-
ciently and smoothly than usual. From time to time, it is true, there was a
strange throbbing deep within her breast. Like distant lightning, it had a
moment of sharp intensity and then vanished without trace. Apart from that,
nothing was in any way out of the ordinary.

The lieutenant, shaving in the bathroom, felt his warmed body miraculously 53
healed at last of the desperate tiredness of the days of indecision and filled —
in spite of the death which lay ahead — with pleasurable anticipation. The
sound of his wife going about her work came to him faintly. A healthy physical
craving, submerged for two days, reasserted itself.

The lieutenant was confident there had been no impurity in that joy they 54
had experienced when resolving upon death. They had both sensed at that
moment — though not, of course, in any clear and conscious way — that those
permissible pleasures which they shared in private were once more beneath
the protection of Righteousness and Divine Power, and of a complete and
unassailable morality. On looking into each other's eyes and discovering there
an honorable death, they had felt themselves safe once more behind steel walls
which none could destroy, encased in an impenetrable armor of Beauty and
Truth. Thus, so far from seeing any inconsistency or conflict between the urges
of his flesh and the sincerity of his patriotism, the lieutenant was even able to
regard the two as parts of the same thing.

Thrusting his face close to the dark, cracked, misted wall mirror, the lieu- 55
tenant shaved himself with great care. This would be his death face. There
must be no unsightly blemishes. The clean-shaven face gleamed once more
with a youthful luster, seeming to brighten the darkness of the mirror. There

was a certain elegance, he even felt, in the association of death with this radiantly healthy face.

Just as it looked now, this would become his death face! Already, in fact, 56 it had half departed from the lieutenant's personal possession and had become the bust above a dead soldier's memorial. As an experiment he closed his eyes tight. Everything was wrapped in blackness, and he was no longer a living, seeing creature.

Returning from the bath, the traces of the shave glowing faintly blue be- 57 neath his smooth cheeks, he seated himself beside the now well-kindled charcoal brazier. Busy though Reiko was, he noticed, she had found time lightly to touch up her face. Her cheeks were gay and her lips moist. There was no shadow of sadness to be seen. Truly, the lieutenant felt, as he saw this mark of his young wife's passionate nature, he had chosen the wife he ought to have chosen.

As soon as the lieutenant had drained his sake cup he offered it to Reiko. 58 Reiko had never before tasted sake, but she accepted without hesitation and sipped timidly.

"Come here," the lieutenant said. 59

Reiko moved to her husband's side and was embraced as she leaned back- 60 ward across his lap. Her breast was in violent commotion, as if sadness, joy, and the potent sake were mingling and reacting within her. The lieutenant looked down into his wife's face. It was the last face he would see in this world, the last face he would see of his wife. The lieutenant scrutinized the face minutely, with the eyes of a traveler bidding farewell to splendid vistas which he will never revisit. It was a face he could not tire of looking at—the features regular yet not cold, the lips lightly closed with a soft strength. The lieutenant kissed those lips, unthinkingly. And suddenly, though there was not the slightest distortion of the face into the unsightliness of sobbing, he noticed that tears were welling slowly from beneath the long lashes of the closed eyes and brimming over into a glistening stream.

When, a little later, the lieutenant urged that they should move to the 61 upstairs bedroom, his wife replied that she would follow after taking a bath. Climbing the stairs alone to the bedroom, where the air was already warmed by the gas heater, the lieutenant lay down on the bedding with arms outstretched and legs apart. Even the time at which he lay waiting for his wife to join him was no later and no earlier than usual.

He folded his hands beneath his head and gazed at the dark boards of the 62 ceiling in the dimness beyond the range of the standard lamp. Was it death he was now waiting for? Or a wild ecstasy of the senses? The two seemed to overlap, almost as if the object of this bodily desire was death itself. But, however that might be, it was certain that never before had the lieutenant tasted such total freedom.

There was the sound of a car outside the window. He could hear the screech 63 of its tires skidding in the snow piled at the side of the street. The sound of its horn reechoed from nearby walls. . . . Listening to these noises he had the feeling that this house rose like a solitary island in the ocean of a society going as restlessly about its business as ever. All around, vastly and untidily, stretched the country for which he grieved. He was to give his life for it. But would that great country, with which he was prepared to remonstrate to the extent of destroying himself, take the slightest heed of his death? He did not know; and it did not matter. His was a battlefield without glory, a battlefield where none could display deeds of valor: it was the front line of the spirit.

Reiko's footsteps sounded on the stairway. The steep stairs in this old house 64 creaked badly. There were fond memories in that creaking, and many a time, while waiting in bed, the lieutenant had listened to its welcome sound. At the thought that he would hear it no more he listened with intense concentration, striving for every corner of every moment of this precious time to be filled with the sound of those soft footfalls on the creaking stairway. The moments seemed transformed to jewels, sparkling with inner light.

Reiko wore a Nagoya sash about the waist of her *yukata*, but as the lieu- 65 tenant reached toward it, its redness sobered by the dimness of the light, Reiko's hand moved to his assistance and the sash fell away, slithering swiftly to the floor. As she stood before him, still in her *yukata*, the lieutenant inserted his hands through the side slits beneath each sleeve, intending to embrace her as she was; but at the touch of his finger tips upon the warm naked flesh, and as the armpits closed gently about his hands, his whole body was suddenly aflame.

In a few moments the two lay naked before the glowing gas heater. 66

Neither spoke the thought, but their hearts, their bodies, and their pound- 67 ing breasts blazed with the knowledge that this was the very last time. It was as if the words "The Last Time" were spelled out, in invisible brushstrokes, across every inch of their bodies.

The lieutenant drew his wife close and kissed her vehemently. As their 68 tongues explored each other's mouths, reaching out into the smooth, moist interior, they felt as if the still-unknown agonies of death had tempered their senses to the keenness of red-hot steel. The agonies they could not yet feel, the distant pains of death, had refined their awareness of pleasure.

"This is the last time I shall see your body," said the lieutenant. "Let me 69 look at it closely." And, tilting the shade on the lampstand to one side, he directed the rays along the full length of Reiko's outstretched form.

Reiko lay still with her eyes closed. The light from the low lamp clearly 70
revealed the majestic sweep of her white flesh. The lieutenant, not without a
touch of egocentricity, rejoiced that he would never see this beauty crumble
in death.

At his leisure, the lieutenant allowed the unforgettable spectacle to engrave 71
itself upon his mind. With one hand he fondled the hair, with the other he
softly stroked the magnificent face, implanting kisses here and there where his
eyes lingered. The quiet coldness of the high, tapering forehead, the closed
eyes with their long lashes beneath faintly etched brows, the set of the finely
shaped nose, the gleam of teeth glimpsed between full, regular lips, the soft
cheeks and the small, wise chin . . . these things conjured up in the lieutenant's mind the vision of a truly radiant death face, and again and again he
pressed his lips tight against the white throat—where Reiko's own hand was
soon to strike—and the throat reddened faintly beneath his kisses. Returning
to the mouth he laid his lips against it with the gentlest of pressures, and
moved them rhythmically over Reiko's with the light rolling motion of a small
boat. If he closed his eyes, the world became a rocking cradle.

Wherever the lieutenant's eyes moved his lips faithfully followed. The high, 72
swelling breasts, surmounted by nipples like the buds of a wild cherry, hardened
as the lieutenant's lips closed about them. The arms flowed smoothly downward
from each side of the breast, tapering toward the wrists, yet losing nothing of
their roundness or symmetry, and at their tips were those delicate fingers which
had held the fan at the wedding ceremony. One by one, as the lieutenant
kissed them, the fingers withdrew behind their neighbor as if in shame. . . .
The natural hollow curving between the bosom and the stomach carried in its
lines a suggestion not only of softness but of resilient strength, and while it
gave forewarning of the rich curves spreading outward from here to the hips
it had, in itself, an appearance only of restraint and proper discipline. The
whiteness and richness of the stomach and hips was like milk brimming in a
great bowl, and the sharply shadowed dip of the navel could have been the
fresh impress of a raindrop, fallen there that very moment. Where the shadows
gathered more thickly, hair clustered, gentle and sensitive, and as the agitation
mounted in the now no longer passive body there hung over this region a
scent like the smoldering of fragrant blossoms, growing steadily more pervasive.

At length, in a tremulous voice, Reiko spoke. 73

"Show me. . . . Let me look too, for the last time." 74

Never before had he heard from his wife's lips so strong and unequivocal a 75
request. It was as if something which her modesty had wished to keep hidden
to the end had suddenly burst its bonds of constraint. The lieutenant obedi-
ently lay back and surrendered himself to his wife. Lithely she raised her white,
trembling body, and—burning with an innocent desire to return to her hus-

band what he had done for her—placed two white fingers on the lieutenant's eyes, which gazed fixedly up at her, and gently stroked them shut.

Suddenly overwhelmed by tenderness, her cheeks flushed by a dizzying uprush 76 of emotion, Reiko threw her arms about the lieutenant's close-cropped head. The bristly hairs rubbed painfully against her breast, the prominent nose was cold as it dug into her flesh, and his breath was hot. Relaxing her embrace, she gazed down at her husband's masculine face. The severe brows, the closed eyes, the splendid bridge of the nose, the shapely lips drawn firmly together . . . the blue, clean-shaven cheeks reflected the light and gleaming smoothly. Reiko kissed each of these. She kissed the broad nape of the neck, the strong, erect shoulders, the powerful chest with its twin circles like shields and its russet nipples. In the armpits, deeply shadowed by the ample flesh of the shoulders and chest, a sweet and melancholy odor emanated from the growth of hair, and in the sweetness of this odor was contained, somehow, the essence of young death. The lieutenant's naked skin glowed like a field of barley, and everywhere the muscles showed in sharp relief, converging on the lower abdomen about the small, unassuming navel. Gazing at the youthful, firm stomach, modestly covered by a vigorous growth of hair, Reiko thought of it as it was soon to be, cruelly cut by the sword, and she laid her head upon it, sobbing in pity, and bathed it with kisses.

At the touch of his wife's tears upon his stomach the lieutenant felt ready 77 to endure with courage the cruelest agonies of his suicide.

What ecstasies they experienced after these tender exchanges may well be 78 imagined. The lieutenant raised himself and enfolded his wife in a powerful embrace, her body now limp with exhaustion after her grief and tears. Passionately they held their faces close, rubbing cheek against cheek. Reiko's body was trembling. Their breasts, moist with sweat, were tightly joined, and every inch of the young and beautiful bodies had become so much one with the other that it seemed impossible there should ever again be a separation. Reiko cried out. From the heights they plunged into the abyss, and from the abyss they took wing and soared once more to dizzying heights. The lieutenant panted like the regimental standard-bearer on a route march. . . . As one cycle ended, almost immediately a new wave of passion would be generated, and together—with no trace of fatigue—they would climb again in a single breathless movement to the very summit.

4

When the lieutenant at last turned away, it was not from weariness. For 79 one thing, he was anxious not to undermine the considerable strength he

would need in carrying out his suicide. For another, he would have been sorry
to mar the sweetness of these last memories by overindulgence.

Since the lieutenant had clearly desisted, Reiko too, with her usual 80
compliance, followed his example. The two lay naked on their backs, with
fingers interlaced, staring fixedly at the dark ceiling. The room was warm
from the heater, and even when the sweat had ceased to pour from their
bodies they felt no cold. Outside, in the hushed night, the sounds of
passing traffic had ceased. Even the noises of the trains and streetcars
around Yotsuya station did not penetrate this far. After echoing through the
region bounded by the moat, they were lost in the heavily wooded park
fronting the broad driveway before Akasaka Palace. It was hard to believe
in the tension gripping this whole quarter, where the two factions of the
bitterly divided Imperial Army now confronted each other, poised for battle.

Savoring the warmth glowing within themselves, they lay still and re- 81
called the ecstasies they had just known. Each moment of the experience
was relived. They remembered the taste of kisses which had never wear-
ied, the touch of naked flesh, episode after episode of dizzying bliss. But
already, from the dark boards of the ceiling, the face of death was peering down. These joys had been final, and their bodies would never know
them again. Not that joy of this intensity — and the same thought had
occurred to them both — was ever likely to be reexperienced, even if they
should live on to old age.

The feel of their fingers intertwined — this too would soon be lost. Even 82
the wood-grain patterns they now gazed at on the dark ceiling boards would
be taken from them. They could feel death edging in, nearer and nearer. There
could be no hesitation now. They must have the courage to reach out to death
themselves, and to seize it.

"Well, let's make our preparations," said the lieutenant. The note of de- 83
termination in the words was unmistakable, but at the same time Reiko had
never heard her husband's voice so warm and tender.

After they had risen, a variety of tasks awaited them. 84

The lieutenant, who had never once before helped with the bedding, now 85
cheerfully slid back the door of the closet, lifted the mattress across the room
by himself, and stowed it away inside.

Reiko turned off the gas heater and put away the lamp standard. During 86
the lieutenant's absence she had arranged this room carefully, sweeping and
dusting it to a fresh cleanness, and now — if one overlooked the rosewood
table drawn into one corner — the eight-mat room gave all the appearance of
a reception room ready to welcome an important guest.

"We've seen some drinking here, haven't we? With Kanō and Homma and 87
Noguchi. . . ."

"Yes, they were great drinkers, all of them." 88

"We'll be meeting them before long, in the other world. They'll tease us, 89
I imagine, when they find I've brought you with me."

Descending the stairs, the lieutenant turned to look back into this calm, 90
clean room, now brightly illuminated by the ceiling lamp. There floated across
his mind the faces of the young officers who had drunk there, and laughed,
and innocently bragged. He had never dreamed then that he would one day
cut open his stomach in this room.

In the two rooms downstairs husband and wife busied themselves smoothly 91
and serenely with their respective preparations. The lieutenant went to the
toilet, and then to the bathroom to wash. Meanwhile Reiko folded away her
husband's padded robe, placed his uniform tunic, his trousers, and a newly cut
bleached loincloth in the bathroom, and set out sheets of paper on the living-
room table for the farewell notes. Then she removed the lid from the writing
box and began rubbing ink from the ink tablet. She had already decided upon
the wording of her own note.

Reiko's fingers pressed hard upon the cold gilt letters of the ink tablet, and 92
the water in the shallow well at once darkened, as if a black cloud had spread
across it. She stopped thinking that this repeated action, this pressure from
her fingers, this rise and fall of faint sound, was all and solely for death. It was
a routine domestic task, a simple paring away of time until death should finally
stand before her. But somehow, in the increasingly smooth motion of the
tablet rubbing on the stone, and in the scent from the thickening ink, there
was unspeakable darkness.

Neat in his uniform, which he now wore next to his skin, the lieutenant 93
emerged from the bathroom. Without a word he seated himself at the table,
bolt upright, took a brush in his hand, and stared undecidedly at the paper
before him.

Reiko took a white silk kimono with her and entered the bathroom. When 94
she reappeared in the living room, clad in the white kimono and with her face
lightly made up, the farewell note lay completed on the table beneath the
lamp. The thick black brushstrokes said simply:

"Long Live the Imperial Forces — Army Lieutenant Takeyama Shinji." 95

While Reiko sat opposite him writing her own note, the lieutenant gazed 96
in silence, intensely serious, at the controlled movement of his wife's pale
fingers as they manipulated the brush.

With their respective notes in their hands — the lieutenant's sword strapped 97
to his side, Reiko's small dagger thrust into the sash of her white kimono —

the two of them stood before the god shelf and silently prayed. Then they put out all the downstairs lights. As he mounted the stairs the lieutenant turned his head and gazed back at the striking, white-clad figure of his wife, climbing behind him, with lowered eyes, from the darkness beneath.

The farewell notes were laid side by side in the alcove of the upstairs room. 98 They wondered whether they ought not to remove the hanging scroll, but since it had been written by their go-between, Lieutenant General Ozeki, and consisted, moreover, of two Chinese characters signifying "Sincerity," they left it where it was. Even if it were to become stained with splashes of blood, they felt that the lieutenant general would understand.

The lieutenant, sitting erect with his back to the alcove, laid his sword on 99 the floor before him.

Reiko sat facing him, a mat's width away. With the rest of her so severely 100 white the touch of rouge on her lips seemed remarkably seductive.

Across the dividing mat they gazed intently into each other's eyes. The 101 lieutenant's sword lay before his knees. Seeing it, Reiko recalled their first night and was overwhelmed with sadness. The lietenant spoke, in a hoarse voice:

"As I have no second to help me I shall cut deep. It may look unpleasant, 102 but please do not panic. Death of any sort is a fearful thing to watch. You must not be discouraged by what you see. Is that all right?"

"Yes."   103

Reiko nodded deeply.   104

Looking at the slender white figure of his wife the lieutenant experienced 105 a bizarre excitement. What he was about to perform was an act in his public capacity as a soldier, something he had never previously shown his wife. It called for a resolution equal to the courage to enter battle; it was a death of no less degree and quality than death in the front line. It was his conduct on the battlefield that he was now to display.

Momentarily the thought led the lieutenant to a strange fantasy. A lonely 106 death on the battlefield, a death beneath the eyes of his beautiful wife . . . in the sensation that he was now to die in these two dimensions, realizing an impossible union of them both, there was sweetness beyond words. This must be the very pinnacle of good fortune, he thought. To have every moment of his death observed by those beautiful eyes — it was like being borne to death on a gentle, fragrant breeze. There was some special favor here. He did not understand precisely what it was, but it was a domain unknown to others: a dispensation granted to no one else had been permitted to himself. In the radiant, bridelike figure of his white-robed wife the lieutenant seemed to see a vision of all those things he had loved and for which he was to lay down his life — the Imperial Household, the Nation, the Army Flag. All these, no less than the wife who sat before him, were presences observing him closely with clear and never-faltering eyes.

Reiko too was gazing intently at her husband, so soon to die, and she 107 thought that never in this world had she seen anything so beautiful. The lieutenant always looked well in uniform, but now, as he contemplated death with severe brows and firmly closed lips, he revealed what was perhaps masculine beauty at its most superb.

"It's time to go," the lieutenant said at last. 108

Reiko bent her body low to the mat in a deep bow. She could not raise her 109 face. She did not wish to spoil her makeup with tears, but the tears could not be held back.

When at length she looked up she saw hazily through the tears that her 110 husband had wound a white bandage around the blade of his now unsheathed sword, leaving five or six inches of naked steel showing at the point.

Resting the sword in its cloth wrapping on the mat before him, the lieu- 111 tenant rose from his knees, resettled himself crosslegged, and unfastened the hooks of his uniform collar. His eyes no longer saw his wife. Slowly, one by one, he undid the flat brass buttons. The dusky brown chest was revealed, and then the stomach. He unclasped his belt and undid the buttons of his trousers. The pure whiteness of the thickly coiled loincloth showed itself. The lieutenant pushed the cloth down with both hands, further to ease his stomach, and then reached for the white-bandaged blade of his sword. With his left hand he massaged his abdomen, glancing downward as he did so.

To reassure himself on the sharpness of his sword's cutting edge the lieu- 112 tenant folded back the left trouser flap, exposing a little of his thigh, and lightly drew the blade across the skin. Blood welled up in the wound at once, and several streaks of red trickled downward, glistening in the strong light.

It was the first time Reiko had ever seen her husband's blood, and she felt 113 a violent throbbing in her chest. She looked at her husband's face. The lieutenant was looking at the blood with calm appraisal. For a moment — though thinking at the same time that it was hollow comfort — Reiko experienced a sense of relief.

The lieutenant's eyes fixed his wife with an intense, hawklike stare. Moving 114 the sword around to his front, he raised himself slightly on his hips and let the upper half of his body lean over the sword point. That he was mustering his whole strength was apparent from the angry tension of the uniform at his shoulders. The lieutenant aimed to strike deep into the left of his stomach. His sharp cry pierced the silence of the room.

Despite the effort he had himself put into the blow, the lieutenant had the 115 impression that someone else had struck the side of his stomach agonizingly with a thick rod of iron. For a second or so his head reeled and he had no idea what had happened. The five or six inches of naked point had vanished completely into his flesh, and the white bandage, gripped in his clenched fist, pressed directly against his stomach.

He returned to consciousness. The blade had certainly pierced the wall of 116 the stomach, he thought. His breathing was difficult, his chest thumped violently, and in some far deep region, which he could hardly believe was a part of himself, a fearful and excruciating pain came welling up as if the ground had split open to disgorge a boiling stream of molten rock. The pain came suddenly nearer, with terrifying speed. The lieutenant bit his lower lip and stifled an instinctive moan.

Was this *seppuku?* — he was thinking. It was a sensation of utter chaos, as 117 if the sky had fallen on his head and the world was reeling drunkenly. His will power and courage, which had seemed so robust before he made the incision, had now dwindled to something like a single hairlike thread of steel, and he was assailed by the uneasy feeling that he must advance along this thread, clinging to it with desperation. His clenched fist had grown moist. Looking down, he saw that both his hand and the cloth about the blade were drenched in blood. His loincloth too was dyed a deep red. It struck him as incredible that, amidst this terrible agony, things which could be seen could still be seen, and existing things existed still.

The moment the lieutenant thrust the sword into his left side and she saw 118 the deathly pallor fall across his face, like an abruptly lowered curtain, Reiko had to struggle to prevent herself from rushing to his side. Whatever happened, she must watch. She must be a witness. That was the duty her husband had laid upon her. Opposite her, a mat's space away, she could clearly see her husband biting his lip to stifle the pain. The pain was there, with absolute certainty, before her eyes. And Reiko had no means of rescuing him from it.

The sweat glistened on her husband's forehead. The lieutenant closed his 119 eyes, and then opened them again, as if experimenting. The eyes had lost their luster, and seemed innocent and empty like the eyes of a small animal.

The agony before Reiko's eyes burned as strong as the summer sun, utterly 120 remote from the grief which seemed to be tearing herself apart within. The pain grew steadily in stature, stretching upward. Reiko felt that her husband had already become a man in a separate world, a man whose whole being had been resolved into pain, a prisoner in a cage of pain where no hand could reach out to him. But Reiko felt no pain at all. Her grief was not pain. As she thought about this, Reiko began to feel as if someone had raised a cruel wall of glass high between herself and her husband.

Ever since her marriage her husband's existence had been her own existence, 121 and every breath of his had been a breath drawn by herself. But now, while her husband's existence in pain was a vivid reality, Reiko could find in this grief of hers no certain proof at all of her own existence.

With only his right hand on the sword the lieutenant began to cut sideways 122 across his stomach. But as the blade became entangled with the entrails it was pushed constantly outward by their soft resilience; and the lieutenant realized that it would be necessary, as he cut, to use both hands to keep the point pressed deep into his stomach. He pulled the blade across. It did not cut as easily as he had expected. He directed the strength of his whole body into his right hand and pulled again. There was a cut of three or four inches.

The pain spread slowly outward from the inner depths until the whole 123 stomach reverberated. It was like the wild clanging of a bell. Or like a thousand bells which jangled simultaneously at every breath he breathed and every throb of his pulse, rocking his whole being. The lieutenant could no longer stop himself from moaning. But by now the blade had cut its way through to below the navel, and when he noticed this he felt a sense of satisfaction, and a renewal of courage.

The volume of blood had steadily increased, and now it spurted from the 124 wound as if propelled by the beat of the pulse. The mat before the lieutenant was drenched red with splattered blood, and more blood overflowed onto it from pools which gathered in the folds of the lieutenant's khaki trousers. A spot, like a bird, came flying across to Reiko and settled on the lap of her white silk kimono.

By the time the lieutenant had at last drawn the sword across to the right 125 side of his stomach, the blade was already cutting shallow and had revealed its naked tip, slippery with blood and grease. But, suddenly stricken by a fit of vomiting, the lieutenant cried out hoarsely. The vomiting made the fierce pain fiercer still, and the stomach, which had thus far remained firm and compact, now abruptly heaved, opening wide its wound, and the entrails burst through, as if the wound too were vomiting. Seemingly ignorant of their master's suffering, the entrails gave an impression of robust health and almost disagreeable vitality as they slipped smoothly out and spilled over into the crotch. The lieutenant's head drooped, his shoulders heaved, his eyes opened to narrow slits, and a thin trickle of saliva dribbled from his mouth. The gold markings on his epaulettes caught the light and glinted.

Blood was scattered everywhere. The lieutenant was soaked in it to his 126 knees, and he sat now in a crumpled and listless posture, one hand on the floor. A raw smell filled the room. The lieutenant, his head drooping, retched repeatedly, and the movement showed vividly in his shoulders. The blade of the sword, now pushed back by the entrails and exposed to its tip, was still in the lieutenant's right hand.

It would be difficult to imagine a more heroic sight than that of the lieu- 127
tenant at this moment, as he mustered his strength and flung back his head.
The movement was performed with sudden violence, and the back of his head
struck with a sharp crack against the alcove pillar. Reiko had been sitting until
now with her face lowered, gazing in fascination at the tide of blood advancing
toward her knees, but the sound took her by surprise and she looked up.

The lieutenant's face was not the face of a living man. The eyes were 128
hollow, the skin parched, the once so lustrous cheeks and lips the color of
dried mud. The right hand alone was moving. Laboriously gripping the sword,
it hovered shakily in the air like the hand of a marionette and strove to direct
the point at the base of the lieutenant's throat. Reiko watched her husband
make this last, most heart-rending, futile exertion. Glistening with blood and
grease, the point was thrust at the throat again and again. And each time it
missed its aim. The strength to guide it was no longer there. The straying
point struck the collar and the collar badges. Although its hooks had been
unfastened, the stiff military collar had closed together again and was protecting the throat.

Reiko could bear the sight no longer. She tried to go to her husband's help, 129
but she could not stand. She moved through the blood on her knees, and her
white skirts grew deep red. Moving to the rear of her husband, she helped no
more than by loosening the collar. The quivering blade at last contacted the
naked flesh of the throat. At that moment Reiko's impression was that she
herself had propelled her husband forward; but that was not the case. It was
a movement planned by the lieutenant himself, his last exertion of strength.
Abruptly he threw his body at the blade, and the blade pierced his neck,
emerging at the nape. There was a tremendous spurt of blood and the lieutenant lay still, cold blue-tinged steel protruding from his neck at the back.

5

Slowly, her socks slippery with blood, Reiko descended the stairway. The 130
upstairs room was now completely still.

Switching on the ground-floor lights, she checked the gas jet and the main 131
gas plug and poured water over the smoldering, half-buried charcoal in the
brazier. She stood before the upright mirror in the four-and-a-half-mat room
and held up her skirts. The bloodstains made it seem as if a bold, vivid pattern
was printed across the lower half of her white kimono. When she sat down
before the mirror, she was conscious of the dampness and coldness of her
husband's blood in the region of her thighs, and she shivered. Then, for a

long while, she lingered over her toilet preparations. She applied the rouge generously to her cheeks, and her lips too she painted heavily. This was no longer makeup to please her husband. It was makeup for the world which she would leave behind and there was a touch of the magnificent and the spectacular in her brushwork. When she rose, the mat before the mirror was wet with blood. Reiko was not concerned about this.

Returning from the toilet, Reiko stood finally on the cement floor of the porchway. When her husband had bolted the door here last night it had been in preparation for death. For a while she stood immersed in the consideration of a simple problem. Should she now leave the bolt drawn? If she were to lock the door, it could be that the neighbors might not notice their suicide for several days. Reiko did not relish the thought of their two corpses putrifying before discovery. After all, it seemed, it would be best to leave it open. . . . She released the bolt, and also drew open the frosted-glass door a fraction. . . . At once a chill wind blew in. There was no sight of anyone in the midnight streets, and stars glittered ice-cold through the trees in the large house opposite.

Leaving the door as it was, Reiko mounted the stairs. She had walked here and there for some time and her socks were no longer slippery. About halfway up, her nostrils were already assailed by a peculiar smell.

The lieutenant was lying on his face in a sea of blood. The point protruding from his neck seemed to have grown even more prominent than before. Reiko walked heedlessly across the blood. Sitting beside the lieutenant's corpse, she stared intently at the face, which lay on one cheek on the mat. The eyes were opened wide, as if the lieutenant's attention had been attracted by something. She raised the head, folding it in her sleeve, wiped the blood from the lips, and bestowed a last kiss.

Then she rose and took from the closet a new white blanket and a waist cord. To prevent any derangement of her skirts, she wrapped the blanket about her waist and bound it there firmly with the cord.

Reiko sat herself on a spot about one foot distant from the lieutenant's body. Drawing the dagger from her sash, she examined its dully gleaming blade intently, and held it to her tongue. The taste of the polished steel was slightly sweet.

Reiko did not linger. When she thought how the pain which had previously opened such a gulf between herself and her dying husband was now to become a part of her own experience, she saw before her only the joy of herself entering a realm her husband had already made his own. In her husband's agonized face there had been something inexplicable which she was seeing for the first time. Now she would solve that riddle. Reiko sensed that at last she too would be able to taste the true bitterness and sweetness of that great moral principle in which her husband believed. What had until now been tasted only faintly through her husband's example she was about to savor directly with her own tongue.

Reiko rested the point of the blade against the base of her throat. She thrust 138 hard. The wound was only shallow. Her head blazed, and her hands shook uncontrollably. She gave the blade a strong pull sideways. A warm substance flooded into her mouth, and everything before her eyes reddened, in a vision of spouting blood. She gathered her strength and plunged the point of the blade deep into her throat.

QUESTIONS FOR READING

1. Define *seppuku*. What motivates Lieutenant Shinji Takeyama to commit this act? Why does his wife Reiko, follow him? Why does the narrator announce in paragraph 1 that "the last moments of this heroic and dedicated couple were such as to make the gods themselves weep." What value in Japanese society does the narrator refer to when he calls this couple "heroic" and "dedicated" in their last moments? To what larger set of beliefs is the act of *seppuku* attached?

2. "Patriotism" is divided into five distinct sections. Summarize what takes place in each section and identify the thematic focus of each. Given this structure, would you infer that Mishima seems more interested in character than in events? Explain. What does section 2, in which Mishima describes the relationship of the newly married couple, contribute to the overall impact of the story?

3. Section 3 presents in painstaking detail the couple's elaborate preparations for both lovemaking and *seppuku*. What does the explicit account of their sexual love contribute to the story? As a writer, what does Mishima do to prevent this scene from being viewed as indelicate or obscene? In what respect is their lovemaking connected to the ritual of *seppuku*?

4. Consider *point of view* in section 4. How does it shift? How does Mishima finally reconcile these differences? Summarize Reiko's response to her husband's death. What does Mishima suggest when he reports: "Ever since her marriage her husband's existence had been her own existence, and every breath of his had been a breath drawn by herself. But now, while her husband's existence in pain was a vivid reality, Reiko could find in this grief of hers no certain proof at all of her own existence" (paragraph 121)?

5. Section 5 focuses on Reiko's suicide. How does Mishima lead the reader back to a world larger than that bounded by Shinji and Reiko? What is the "inexplicable" something that Reiko now recognizes for the first time in her hus-

band's "agonized face"? To what concerns does she devote herself in her own last few moments? How do these concerns detract from or add to the dramatic impact of Reiko's suicide? Explain.

6. Consider the nature of ritual in the United States. In what specific ways are American rituals similar to or different from rituals in Japan? Identify one American military ritual and discuss the beliefs that underpin it. How is that ritual — and the beliefs that inform it — similar to the one described in "Patriotism"?

QUESTIONS ON CONNECTIONS

1. Read Sandra Casillas's essay, "Cha-No-Yu, the Japanese Tea Ceremony" (p. 47). What role does ritual play in the events Casillas reports? How is it similar to that presented by Mishima's story? Show how the nature of ritual in these two instances is deeply rooted in traditional patterns of behavior in Japanese culture.

2. For a contrasting view of ritual, read Michael Arlen's essay, "Ode to Thanksgiving." In what respects has the Thanksgiving ritual become trivialized in America? What evidence in Arlen's essay documents his attitude toward ritual? *Compare and contrast* Arlen's view of ritual to those of Mishima and Casillas. (For a humorous view of another Japanese ritual, see Calvin Trillin's essay, "Ordering in Japanese.")

3. Comment on the nature of the violence in "Patriotism." How does the violence depicted in this story bear significance beyond that of an individual's adherence to a military code of behavior? With this theme in mind, read Terry Burns's essay, "The Blanket Party" (p. 39). What similarities or differences do you notice in Mishima's and Burns's treatment of their characters' expectation of — and preparedness for — violence in military life?

4. *Compare and contrast* Mishima's portrait of Reiko with the "good woman" described in Thu Hong Nguyen's essay, "A Good Woman" (p. 188). What role does ritual play in a Vietnamese's woman's life? What characteristics do Reiko and the "good woman" in Vietnam share? What do the expectations placed on women's behavior reveal about each culture?

SUGGESTIONS FOR WRITING

1. Think about the title of Mishima's story. What, exactly, is the meaning of *patriotism* in this story? Now consider the following *definition* of *patriotism* offered

in the nineteenth century by England's Lord Acton: "Patriotism is in political life what faith is in religion." Write an essay in which you clarify Acton's definition and apply it to Mishima's "Patriotism." Show how the actions reported in Mishima's story—and the beliefs on which they are based—serve to confirm or challenge Acton's definition.

2. Reread Mishima's story, focusing this time on Reiko's character and actions. With Reiko in mind, read Thu Hong Nguyen's essay "A Good Woman." Write an essay in which you *compare and contrast* what constitutes a "good woman" in the Vietnamese and Japanese cultures presented in these two pieces. In what specific ways are Vietnamese and Japanese women expected to behave in similar ways? Different ways? What conclusion can you draw about women's identities and responsibilities in each culture?

FRANK O'CONNOR

"Storytelling is the nearest thing one can get to the quality of a pure lyric poem," Frank O'Connor observed. "It doesn't deal with problems; it doesn't have any solutions to offer; it just states the human condition." O'Connor often acknowledged his preference for that form of fiction: "A novel actually requires far more logic and far more knowledge of circumstances, whereas a short story can have the sort of detachment from circumstances that lyric poetry has."

The only son of a hard-working, hard-drinking laborer, Frank O'Connor was born Michael O'Donovan in Cork, Ireland, in 1903. He adopted his beloved mother's maiden name as a way of dealing with what he called his Oedipus complex, a subject he addressed in several stories and novels as well as in his autobiographical An Only Child (1961) and My Father's Son (1969). Unable to afford a formal education, O'Connor trained himself in the major European languages and literatures. "I had to content myself," he has explained, "with a make-believe education, and the curious thing is that it was the make-believe that succeeded." He began writing at an early age, and by twelve he had produced his first work — some poems, biographical sketches, and essays on historical subjects. "I was intended by God to be a painter," O'Connor later noted, "but I was very poor and paper and pencil were the cheapest. Music was out for that reason as well. Literature is the poor man's art."

As a teenager, O'Connor joined the Irish Republican Army and fought in the Irish Civil War from 1919 to 1921. He was captured and interned for nearly a year, an experience that made him skeptical of both Irish patriotism and the Catholic Church's promotion of personal sacrifice. O'Connor's work as a librarian in Cork and Dublin eventually brought him into contact with several of the leading figures in the Irish Literary Renaissance of the 1920s, including friendships with George Russell (who wrote under the pseudonym AE) and William Butler Yeats, who said of O'Connor: "He's doing for Ireland what Chekhov did for Russia." During the 1930s, O'Connor served as the director of Dublin's famous Abbey Theatre. Soon after the outbreak of World War II, he circumvented Ireland's official neutrality by moving to London and working as a broadcaster for the Ministry of Information. After the war, O'Connor devoted himself to writing, working in the theater, and teaching at various universities in Ireland and the United States. At the time of his death in 1966, his writings included fifteen novels and collections of short stories, a good deal of poetry, translations from Old Irish, five plays, and several volumes of memoirs.

O'Connor's theories on the short story are gathered in The Lonely Voice (1963), in which he notes that the short story "began, and continues to function, as a private art intended to satisfy the standards of the individual, solitary, critical reader."

Guests of the Nation

At dusk the big Englishman Belcher would shift his long legs out of the 1
ashes and ask, "Well, chums, what about it?" and Noble or me would say,
"As you please, chum" (for we had picked up some of their curious expressions), and the little Englishman 'Awkins would light the lamp and produce
the cards. Sometimes Jeremiah Donovan would come up of an evening and
supervise the play, and grow excited over 'Awkins's cards (which he always
played badly), and shout at him as if he was one of our own, "Ach, you divil
you, why didn't you play the tray?" But, ordinarily, Jeremiah was a sober and
contented poor devil like the big Englishman Belcher, and was looked up to
at all only because he was a fair hand at documents, though slow enough at
these, I vow. He wore a small cloth hat and big gaiters over his long pants,
and seldom did I perceive his hands outside the pockets of his pants. He
reddened when you talked to him, tilting from toe to heel and back and looking
down all the while at his big farmer's feet. His uncommon broad accent was
a great source of jest to me, I being from the town as you may recognize.

I couldn't at the time see the point of me and Noble being with Belcher 2
and 'Awkins at all, for it was and is my fixed belief you could have planted
that pair in any untended spot from this to Claregalway and they'd have stayed
put and flourished like a native weed. I never seen in my short experience two
men that took to the country as they did.

They were handed on to us by the Second Battalion to keep when the 3
search for them became too hot, and Noble and myself, being young, took
charge with a natural feeling of responsibility. But little 'Awkins made us look
right fools when he displayed he knew the countryside as well as we did and
something more. "You're the bloke they calls Bonaparte?" he said to me.
"Well, Bonaparte, Mary Brigid Ho'Connell was arskin abaout you and said
'ow you'd a pair of socks belonging to 'er young brother." For it seemed, as
they explained it, that the Second used to have little evenings of their own,
and some of the girls of the neighborhood would turn in, and seeing they were
such decent fellows, our lads couldn't well ignore the two Englishmen, but
invited them in and were hail-fellow-well-met with them. 'Awkins told me he
learned to dance "The Walls of Limerick" and "The Siege of Ennis" and "The
Waves of Tory" in a night or two, though naturally he could not return the
compliment, because our lads at that time did not dance foreign dances on
principle.

So whatever privileges and favors Belcher and 'Awkins had with the Second 4
they duly took with us, and after the first evening we gave up all pretense of
keeping a close eye on their behavior. Not that they could have got far, for

they had a notable accent and wore khaki tunics and overcoats with civilian pants and boots. But it's my belief they never had an idea of escaping and were quite contented with their lot.

Now, it was a treat to see how Belcher got off with the old woman of the house we were staying in. She was a great warrant to scold, and crotchety even with us, but before ever she had a chance of giving our guests, as I may call them, a lick of her tongue, Belcher had made her his friend for life. She was breaking sticks at the time, and Belcher, who hadn't been in the house for more than ten minutes, jumped up out of his seat and went across to her.

"Allow me, madam," he says, smiling his queer little smile; "please allow me," and takes the hatchet from her hand. She was struck too parlatic to speak, and ever after Belcher would be at her heels carrying a bucket, or basket, or load of turf, as the case might be. As Noble wittily remarked, he got into looking before she leapt, and hot water or any little thing she wanted Belcher would have it ready for her. For such a huge man (and though I am five foot ten myself I had to look up to him) he had an uncommon shortness — or should I say lack — of speech. It took us some time to get used to him walking in and out like a ghost, without a syllable out of him. Especially because 'Awkins talked enough for a platoon, it was strange to hear big Belcher with his toes in the ashes come out with a solitary "Excuse me, chum," or "That's right, chum." His one and only abiding passion was cards, and I will say for him he was a good cardplayer. He could have fleeced me and Noble many a time; only if we lost to him, 'Awkins lost to us, and 'Awkins played with the money Belcher gave him.

'Awkins lost to us because he talked too much, and I think now we lost to Belcher for the same reason. 'Awkins and Noble would spit at one another about religion into the early hours of the morning; the little Englishman as you could see worrying the soul out of young Noble (whose brother was a priest) with a string of questions that would puzzle a cardinal. And to make it worse, even in treating of these holy subjects, 'Awkins had a deplorable tongue; I never in all my career struck across a man who could mix such a variety of cursing and bad language into the simplest topic. Oh, a terrible man was little 'Awkins, and a fright to argue! He never did a stroke of work, and when he had no one else to talk to he fixed his claws into the old woman.

I am glad to say that in her he met his match, for one day when he tried to get her to complain profanely of the drought she gave him a great comedown by blaming the drought upon Jupiter Pluvius[1] (a deity neither 'Awkins nor I had ever even heard of, though Noble said among the pagans he was held to

[1]The Roman god Jupiter, the bringer of rain.

have something to do with rain). And another day the same 'Awkins was swearing at the capitalists for starting the German war,[2] when the old dame laid down her iron, puckered up her little crab's mouth and said, "Mr. 'Awkins, you can say what you please about the war, thinking to deceive me because I'm an ignorant old woman, but I know well what started the war. It was that Italian count that stole the heathen divinity out of the temple in Japan, for believe me, Mr. 'Awkins, nothing but sorrow and want follows them that disturbs the hidden powers!" Oh, a queer old dame, as you remark!

So one evening we had our tea together, and 'Awkins lit the lamp and we   9 all sat in to cards. Jeremiah Donovan came in too, and sat down and watched us for a while. Though he was a shy man and didn't speak much, it was easy to see he had no great love for the two Englishmen, and I was surprised it hadn't struck me so clearly before. Well, like that in the story, a terrible dispute blew up late in the evening between 'Awkins and Noble, about capitalists and priests and love for your own country.

"The capitalists," says 'Awkins, with an angry gulp, "the capitalists pays   10 the priests to tell you all abaout the next world, so's you won't notice what they do in this!"

"Nonsense, man," says Noble, losing his temper, "before ever a capitalist   11 was thought of people believed in the next world."

'Awkins stood up as if he was preaching a sermon. "Oh, they did, did   12 they?" he says with a sneer. "They believed all the things you believe, that's what you mean? And you believe that God created Hadam and Hadam created Shem and Shem created Jehoshophat? You believe all the silly hold fairy tale abaout Heve and Heden and the happle? Well, listen to me, chum. If you're entitled to 'old to a silly belief like that, I'm entitles to 'old to my own silly belief—which is, that the fust thing your God created was a bleedin' capitalist with mirality and Rolls Royce complete. Am I right, chum?" he says then to Belcher.

"You're right, chum," says Belcher, with his queer smile, and gets up from   13 the table to stretch his long legs into the fire and stroke his mustache. So, seeing that Jeremiah Donovan was going, and there was no knowing when the conversation about religion would be over, I took my hat and went out with him. We strolled down towards the village together and then he suddenly stopped, and blushing and mumbling, and shifting, as his way was, from toe to heel, he said I ought to be behind keeping guard on the prisoners. And I, having it put to me so suddenly, asked him what the hell he wanted a guard

[2]World War I.

on the prisoners at all for, and he said that so far as Noble and me were concerned we had talked it over and would rather be out with a column. "What use is that pair to us?" I asked him.

He looked at me for a spell and said, "I thought you knew we were keeping them as hostages." "Hostages — ?" says I, not quite understanding. "The enemy," he says in his heavy way, "have prisoners belong' to us, and now they talk of shooting them. If they shoot our prisoners we'll shoot theirs, and serve them right." "Shoot them?" said I, the possibility just beginning to dawn on me. "Shoot them exactly," said he. "Now," said I, "wasn't it very unforseen of you not to tell me and Noble that?" "How so?" he asks. "Seeing that we were acting as guards upon them, of course." "And hadn't you reason enough to guess that much?" "We had not, Jeremiah Donovan, we had not. How were we to know when the men were on our hands so long?" "And what difference does it make? The enemy have our prisoners as long or longer, haven't they?" "It makes a great difference," said I. "How so?" said he sharply; but I couldn't tell him the difference it made, for I was struck too silly to speak. "And when may we expect to be released from this anyway?" said I. "You may expect it tonight," says he. "Or tomorrow or the next day at the latest. So if it's hanging round here that worries you, you'll be free soon enough."

I cannot explain it even now, how sad I felt, but I went back to the cottage, a miserable man. When I arrived the discussion was still on, 'Awkins holding forth to all and sundry that there was no next world at all and Noble answering in his best canonical style that there was. But I saw 'Awkins was after having the best of it. "Do you know what, chum?" he was saying, with his saucy smile. "I think you're jest as big a bleedin' hunbeliever as I am. You say you believe in the next world and you know jest as much abaout the next world as I do, which is sweet damn-all. What's 'Eaven? You dunno. Where's 'Eaven? You dunno. Who's in 'Eaven? You dunno. You know sweet damn-all! I ask you again, do they wear wings?"

"Very well then," says Noble, "they do; is that enough for you? They do wear wings." "Where do they get them then? Who makes them? 'Ave they a fact'ry for wings? 'Ave they a sort of store where you 'ands in your chit and tikes your bleedin' wings? Answer me that."

"Oh, you're an impossible man to argue with," says Noble. "Now listen to me —" And off the pair of them went again.

It was long after midnight when we locked up the Englishmen and went to bed ourselves. As I blew out the candle I told Noble what Jeremiah Donovan had told me. Noble took it very quietly. After we had been in bed about an hour he asked me did I think we ought to tell the Englishmen. I having thought of the same thing myself (among many others) said no, because it was more than likely the English wouldn't shoot our men, and anyhow it wasn't to be supposed the Brigade who were always up and down with the Second Battalion and knew the Englishmen well would be likely to want them bumped off. "I think so," says Noble. "It would be sort of cruelty to put the wind up them now." "It was very unforeseen of Jeremiah Donovan anyhow," says I, and by Noble's silence I realized he took my meaning.

So I lay there half the night, and thought and thought, and picturing myself 19 and young Noble trying to prevent the Brigade from shooting 'Awkins and Belcher sent a cold sweat out through me. Because there were men on the Brigade you daren't let nor hinder without a gun in your hand, and at any rate, in those days disunion between brothers seemed to me an awful crime. I knew better after.

It was next morning we found it so hard to face Belcher and 'Awkins with 20 a smile. We went about the house all day scarcely saying a word. Belcher didn't mind us much; he was stretched into the ashes as usual with his usual look of waiting in quietness for something unforeseen to happen, but little 'Awkins gave us a bad time with his audacious gibing and questioning. He was disgusted at Noble's not answering him back. "Why can't you tike your beating like a man, chum?" he says. "You with your Hadam and Heve! I'm a Communist — or an Anarchist. An Anarchist, that's what I am." And for hours after he went round the house, mumbling when the fit took him "Hadam and Heve! Hadam and Heve!"

I don't know clearly how we got over that day, but get over it we did, and 21 a great relief it was when the tea things were cleared away and Belcher said in his peaceable manner, "Well, chums, what about it?" So we all sat round the table and 'Awkins produced the cards, and at that moment I heard Jeremiah Donovan's footsteps up the path, and a dark presentiment crossed my mind. I rose quietly from the table and laid my hand on him before he reached the door. "What do you want?" I asked him. "I want those two soldier friends of yours," he says reddening. "Is that the way it is, Jeremiah Donovan?" I ask. "That's the way. There were four of our lads went west this morning, one of them a boy of sixteen." "That's bad, Jeremiah," says I.

At that moment Noble came out, and we walked down the path together 22 talking in whispers. Feeney, the local intelligence officer, was standing by the gate. "What are you going to do about it?" I asked Jeremiah Donovan. "I want you and Noble to bring them out: you can tell them they're being shifted again; that'll be the quietest way." "Leave me out of that," says Noble suddenly. Jeremiah Donovan looked at him hard for a minute or two. "All right so," he said peaceably. "You and Feeney collect a few tools from the shed and dig a hole by the far end of the bog. Bonaparte and I'll be after you in about twenty minutes. But whatever else you do, don't let anyone see you with the tools. No one must know but the four of ourselves."

We saw Feeney and Noble go round to the houseen where the tools were 23 kept, and sidled in. Everything if I can so express myself was tottering before my eyes, and I left Jeremiah Donovan to do the explaining as best he could, while I took a seat and said nothing. He told them they were to go back to the Second. 'Awkins let a mouthful of curses out of him at that, and it was plain that Belcher, though he said nothing, was duly perturbed. The old woman was for having them stay in spite of us, and she did not shut her mouth until Jeremiah Donovan lost his temper and said some nasty things to her. Within the house by this time it was pitch dark, but no one thought of lighting the lamp, and in the darkness the two Englishmen fetched their khaki topcoats and said good-bye to the woman of the house. "Just as a man mikes a 'ome of a bleedin' place," mumbles 'Awkins, shaking her by the hand, "some bastard at Headquarters thinks you're too cushy and shunts you off." Belcher shakes her hand very hearty. "A thousand thanks, madam," he says, "a thousand thanks for everything . . ." as though he'd made it all up.

We go round to the back of the house and down towards the fatal bog. 24 Then Jeremiah Donovan comes out with what is in his mind. "There were four of our lads shot by your fellows this morning so now you're to be bumped off." "Cut that stuff out," says 'Awkins, flaring up. "It's bad enough to be mucked about such as we are without you plying at soldiers." "It's true," says Jeremiah Donovan, "I'm sorry, 'Awkins, but 'tis true," and comes out with the usual rigmarole about doing our duty and obeying our superiors. "Cut it out," says 'Awkins irritably. "Cut it out!"

Then, when Donovan sees he is not being believed he turns to me, "Ask 25 Bonaparte here," he says. "I don't need to arsk Bonaparte. Me and Bonaparte are chums." "Isn't it true, Bonaparte?" says Jeremiah Donovan solemnly to me. "It is," I say sadly, "it is." 'Awkins stops. "Now, for Christ's sike. . . ." "I mean it, chum," I say. "You daon't saound as if you mean it. You knaow well you don't mean it." "Well, if he don't I do," says Jeremiah Donovan, "Why the 'ell sh'd you want to shoot me, Jeremiah Donovan?" "Why the hell should your people take out four prisoners and shoot them in cold blood upon a barrack square?" I perceive Jeremiah Donovan is trying to encourage himself with hot words.

Anyway, he took little 'Awkins by the arm and dragged him on, but it was 26 impossible to make him understand that we were in earnest. From which you will perceive how difficult it was for me, as I kept feeling my Smith and

Wesson[3] and thinking what I would do if they happened to put up a fight or ran for it, and wishing in my heart they would. I knew if only they ran I would never fire on them. "Was Noble in this?" 'Awkins wanted to know, and we said yes. He laughed. But why should Noble want to shoot him? Why should we want to shoot him? What had he done to us? Weren't we chums (the word lingers painfully in my memory)? Weren't we? Didn't we understand him and didn't he understand us? Did either of us imagine for an instant that he'd shoot us for all the so-and-so brigadiers in the so-and-so British Army? By this time I began to perceive in the dusk the desolate edges of the bog that was to be their last earthly bed, and, so great a sadness overtook my mind, I could not answer him. We walked along the edge of it in the darkness, and every now and then 'Awkins would call a halt and begin again, just as if he was wound up, about us being chums, and I was in despair that nothing but the cold and open grave made ready for his presence would convince him that we meant it all. But all the same, if you can understand, I didn't want him to be bumped off.

At last we saw the unsteady glint of a lantern in the distance and made 27 towards it. Noble was carrying it, and Feeney stood somewhere in the darkness behind, and somehow the picture of the two of them so silent in the boglands was like the pain of death in my heart. Belcher on recognizing Noble, said " 'Allo, chum" in his usual peaceable way, but 'Awkins flew at the poor boy immediately, and the dispute began all over again, only that Noble hadn't a word to say for himself, and stood there with the swaying lantern between his gaitered legs.

It was Jeremiah Donovan who did the answering. 'Awkins asked for the 28 twentieth time (for it seemed to haunt his mind) if anybody thought he'd shoot Noble. "You would," says Jeremiah Donovan shortly. "I wouldn't, damn you!" "You would if you knew you'd be shot for not doing it." "I wouldn't, not if I was to be shot twenty times over; he's my chum. And Belcher wouldn't— isn't that right, Belcher?" "That's right chum," says Belcher peaceable. "Damned if I would. Anyway, who says Noble'd be shot if I wasn't bumped off? What d'you think I'd do if I was in Noble's place and we were out in the middle of a blasted bog?" "What would you do?" "I'd go with him wherever he was going. I'd share my last bob with him and stick by 'im through thick and thin."

"We've had enough of this," says Jeremiah Donovan, cocking his revolver. 29 "Is there any message you want to send before I fire?" "No, there isn't, but . . . ." "Do you want to say your prayers?" 'Awkins came out with a cold-blooded remark that shocked even me and turned to Noble again. "Listen to me,

[3]Pistol.

Noble," he said. "You and me are chums. You won't come over to my side, so I'll come over to your side. Is that fair? Just you give me a rifle and I'll go with you wherever you want."

Nobody answered him. 30

"Do you understand?" he said. "I'm through with it all. I'm a deserter or 31 anything else you like, but from this on I'm one of you. Does that prove to you that I mean what I say?" Noble raised his head, but as Donovan began to speak he lowered it again without answering. "For the last time have you any messages to send?" says Donovan in a cold and excited voice.

"Ah, shut up, you, Donovan; you don't understand me, but these fellows 32 do. They're my chums; they stand by me and I stand by them. We're not the capitalist tools you seem to think us."

I alone of the crowd saw Donovan raise his Webley to the back of 'Awkins's 33 neck, and as he did so I shut my eyes and tried to say a prayer. 'Awkins had begun to say something else when Donovan let fly, and, as I opened my eyes at the bang, I saw him stagger at the knees and lie out flat at Noble's feet, slowly, and as quiet as a child, with the lantern light falling sadly upon his lean legs and bright farmer's boots. We all stood very still for a while watching him settle out in the last agony.

Then Belcher quietly takes out a handkerchief, and begins to tie it about 34 his own eyes (for in our excitement we had forgotten to offer the same to 'Awkins), and, seeing it is not big enough, turns and asks for a loan of mine. I give it to him and as he knots the two together he points with his foot at 'Awkins. " 'E's not quite dead," he says, "better give 'im another.' Sure enough, 'Awkins's left knee as we see it under the lantern is rising again. I bend down and put my gun to his ear; then, recollecting myself and the company of Belcher, I stand up again with a few hasty words. Belcher understands what is in my mind. "Give 'im 'is first," he says. "I don't mind. Poor bastard, we dunno what's 'appening to 'im now." As by this time I am beyond all feeling I kneel down again and skilfully give 'Awkins the last shot so as to put him forever out of pain.

Belcher who is fumbling a bit awkwardly with the handkerchiefs comes out 35 with a laugh when he hears the shot. It is the first time I have heard him laugh, and it sends a shiver down my spine, coming as it does so inappropriately upon the tragic death of his old friend. "Poor blighter, he says quietly, "and last night he was so curious abaout it all. It's very queer, chums, I always think. Naow, 'e knows as much about it as they'll ever let 'im know, and last night 'e was all in the dark."

Donovan helps him to tie the handkerchiefs about his eyes. "Thanks, chum," 36 he says. Donovan asks him if there are any messages he would like to send. "Naow, chum," he says, "none for me. If any of you likes to write to 'Awkins mother you'll find a letter from 'er in 'is pocket. But my missus left me eight years ago. Went away with another fellow and took the kid with her. I likes the feelin' of a 'ome (as you may 'ave noticed) but I couldn't start again after that."

We stand around like fools now that he can no longer see us. Donovan 37 looks at Noble and Noble shakes his head. Then Donovan raises his Webley[4] again and just at that moment Belcher laughs his queer nervous laugh again. He must think we are talking of him; anyway, Donovan lowers his gun. " 'Scuse me, chums," says Belcher, "I feel I'm talking the 'ell of a lot . . . and so silly . . . abaout me being so 'andy about a 'ouse. But this thing come on me so sudden. You'll forgive me, I'm sure." "You don't want to say a prayer?" asks Jeremiah Donovan. "No, chum," he replies, "I don't think that'd 'elp. I'm ready if you want to get it over." "You understand," says Jeremiah Donovan, "it's not so much our doing. It's our duty, so to speak." Belcher's head is raised like a real blind man's, so that you can only see his nose and chin in the lamplight. "I never could make out what duty was myself," he said, "but I think you're all good lads, if that's what you mean. I'm not complaining." Noble, with a look of desperation, signals to Donovan, and in a flash Donovan raises his gun and fires. The big man goes over like a sack of meal, and this time there is no need of a second shot.

I don't remember much about the burying, but that it was worse than all 38 the rest, because we had to carry the warm corpses a few yards before we sunk them in the windy bog. It was all mad lonely, with only a bit of lantern between ourselves and the pitch blackness, and birds hooting and screeching all round disturbed by the guns. Noble had to search 'Awkins first to get the letter from his mother. Then having smoothed all signs of the grave away, Noble and I collected our tools, said good-bye to the others, and went back along the desolate edge of the treacherous bog without a word. We put the tools in the houseen and went into the house. The kitchen was pitch black and cold, just as we left it, and the old woman was sitting over the hearth telling her beads. We walked past her into the room, and Noble struck a match to light the lamp. Just then she rose quietly and came to the doorway, being not at all so bold or crabbed as usual.

"What did ye do with them?" she says in a sort of whisper, and Noble took 39 such a mortal start the match quenched in his trembling hand. "What's that?" he asks without turning round. "I heard ye," she said. "What did you hear?" asks Noble, but sure he wouldn't deceive a child the way he said it. "I heard ye. Do you think I wasn't listening to ye putting the things back in the

[4]Pistol.

houseen?" Noble struck another match and this time the lamp lit for him.
"Was that what ye did with them?" she said, and Noble said nothing—after
all what could he say?

So then, by God, she fell on her two knees by the door, and began telling 40
her beads, and after a minute or two Noble went on his knees by the fireplace,
so I pushed my way out past her, and stood at the door, watching the stars
and listening to the damned shrieking of the birds. It is so strange what you
feel at such moments, and not to be written afterwards. Noble says he felt he
seen everything ten times as big, perceiving nothing around him but the little
patch of black bog with the two Englishmen stiffening into it; but with me it
was the other way, as though the patch of bog where the two Englishmen were
was a thousand miles away from me, and even Noble mumbling just behind
me and the old woman and the birds and the bloody stars were all far away,
and I was somehow very small and very lonely. And anything that ever happened me after I never felt the same about again.

QUESTIONS FOR READING

1. The host/guest relationship forms the thematic center of O'Connor's story.
   What details does O'Connor use to reinforce the sense that Hawkins and
   Belcher, the British prisoners, are "guests of the nation"? Identify—and comment on—other aspects of the host/guest theme in the story. In what specific
   ways does O'Connor treat this theme ironically? Identify and discuss the effectiveness of other instances of *irony* in this story.

2. What is the effect of O'Connor's abrupt opening? What is the function of the
   scene in which he presents the message from Mary Brigid O'Connell, asking
   about Bonaparte as well as about her brother's socks?

3. How does O'Connor characterize Hawkins and Belcher? What traits does he
   emphasize in each? In what ways are they different? similar? How would you
   describe Hawkins's political beliefs? How, and for what *purpose*, does O'Connor
   connect those beliefs to the action of the story? What is the dramatic effect of
   Hawkins's debates with Noble about religion? Why are Hawkins's Irish guards
   shocked when he proposes that he desert and join the Irish cause? What belief
   does Hawkins express in making that proposal?

4. Contrast Belcher's response to his impending execution with that of Hawkins.
   What is the effect of his last-minute disclosures about Hawkins and himself?
   How does he use the word *chums* here? Contrast Belcher's behavior immediately
   before his execution with his behavior at the beginning of the story. How are
   the differences significant?

5. How does O'Connor first present Bonaparte in the story? Describe the transformation Bonaparte undergoes as the story unfolds. How "responsible" does Bonaparte feel about the executions? What is his response to them?

6. Comment on the function of the old woman and the cottage in the story. What importance does O'Connor attribute to Jeremiah Donovan? How is Donovan's attitude toward Belcher and Hawkins different from Noble's and Bonaparte's? How is that difference significant in developing the theme of the story?

7. Comment on the importance of the final scene. Contrast the nature of Noble's and Bonaparte's responses to the executions. What is the effect of each response on the reader? Why does Bonaparte "push" his way out past the old woman and Noble while they are praying? What does his literal position in the final scene signify?

8. Here is a later version of the final paragraph of "Guests of the Nation":

> Then, by God, in the very doorway, she fell on her knees and began praying, and after looking at her for a minute or two Noble did the same by the fireplace. I pushed my way out past her and left them at it. I stood at the door, watching the stars and listening to the shrieking of the birds dying out over the bogs. It is so strange what you feel at times like that you can't describe it. Noble says he saw everything ten times the size, as though there were nothing in the whole world but that little patch of bog with the two Englishmen stiffening into it, but with me it was as if the patch of bog where the Englishmen were was a million miles away, and even Noble and the old woman, mumbling behind me, and the birds and the bloody stars were all far away, and I was somehow very small and very lost and lonely like a child astray in the snow. And anything that happened me afterwards, I never felt the same about again.

Which version is more effective? Why?

QUESTIONS ON CONNECTIONS

1. O'Connor's story and Terry Burns's essay, "The Blanket Party" (p. 39), both examine violence within military contexts. How does the perspective of the narrator in each differ? How is it similar? Contrast the sense of justice implicit in Burns's essay with Bonaparte's view of that idea. How are the overall effects of the story and essay similar? different?

2. Max Ramsey's essay, "For Myself" (p. 197), offers another personal view of wartime suffering. Compare Ramsey's attitude toward war with Bonaparte's. What view of justice does each subscribe to? Identify the convergences in Ramsey and Bonaparte's views of "duty." How does each respond to the conflict between duty and belief?

3. Contrast O'Connor's attitude toward war to Thomas Hardy's in "Channel Firing," Roger Rosenblatt's in "Lebanon: A Legacy of Dreams and Guns," and Nelsy Massoud's in "War in Paradise" (p. 175). What common elements can you identify in their respective accounts of war?

SUGGESTIONS FOR WRITING

1. "Guests of the Nation" is in many respects a story about initiation, about a shift in Bonaparte's view of the world. Write an essay in which you trace Bonaparte's movement from innocence to experience. Show how O'Connor introduces and develops this transformation in Bonaparte's consciousness in the scenes leading up to the executions. How does O'Connor bring this theme to a climax in the story's final scene?

2. Another issue in O'Connor's story is the conflict between personal and institutional forms of justice. Write an essay focusing on the conflicting views of justice in the story. What idea does this conflict suggest to you? Your essay should explain that idea. Remember to support each of the points you make with detailed references to the language of the story.

KATHERINE ANNE PORTER

"My whole attempt," Katherine Anne Porter observed, "has been to discover and understand human motives, human feelings, to make a distillation of what human relations and experiences my mind has been able to absorb. I have never known an uninteresting human being, and I have never known two alike; there are broad classifications and deep similarities, but I am interested in the thumbprint." From the publication of her first short story at the age of thirty to her death at ninety in 1980, Katherine Anne Porter has focused in her fiction on the psychological dimensions of personal relations, a theme she has treated with great technical skill in numerous short stories and novellas.

A descendant of Daniel Boone and a distant cousin of William Sidney Porter (O. Henry), Katherine Anne Porter was born in Indian Creek, Texas, and studied at home and in convent schools. After an unsuccessful teenage marriage, Porter supported herself as a reporter and reviewer for various newspapers, as an extra in movies, and as an entertainer. She began her literary career while living in Mexico, and her first collection of short stories, Flowering Judas (1930), earned her recognition in her native land. After a trip to Europe, which later served as the basis for her best-selling novel Ship of Fools (1962), and a second brief marriage, Porter settled in New Orleans and published her celebrated novellas Old Mortality, Noon Wine, and Pale Horse, Pale Rider (1939). A third marriage and a second collection of stories, The Leaning Tower (1944), followed, along with the critical acclaim and financial success that enabled her to devote herself to writing and teaching. Her later publications include Collected Stories (1965), for which she earned a Pulitzer Prize and a National Book Award, Collected Essays (1970), and The Never-Ending Wrong (1972), an account of her involvement in the protests surrounding the Sacco-Vanzetti trial. Throughout her distinguished career, Porter steadfastly remained committed to the dignity and significance of individual lives: "Nothing is pointless, and nothing is meaningless if the artist will face it. And it's his business to face it. He hasn't got the right to sidestep it. . . . Human life itself may be almost pure chaos, but the work of the artist — the only thing he's good for — is to take these handfuls of confusion and disparate things, things that seem to be irreconcilable, and put them together in a frame to give them some kind of shape and meaning."

The Jilting of Granny Weatherall

She flicked her wrist neatly out of Doctor Harry's pudgy careful fingers and 1
pulled the sheet up to her chin. The brat ought to be in knee breeches. Doctoring around the country with spectacles on his nose! "Get along now, take your schoolbooks and go. There's nothing wrong with me."

Doctor Harry spread a warm paw like a cushion on her forehead where the 2
forked green vein danced and made her eyelids twitch. "Now, now, be a good girl, and we'll have you up in no time."

"That's no way to speak to a woman nearly eighty years old just because   3
she's down. I'd have you respect your elders, young man."

"Well, Missy, excuse me." Doctor Harry patted her cheek. "But I've got to   4
warn you, haven't I? You're a marvel, but you must be careful or you're going
to be good and sorry."

"Don't tell me what I'm going to be. I'm on my feet now, morally speaking.   5
It's Cornelia. I had to go to bed to get rid of her."

Her bones felt loose, and floated around in her skin, and Doctor Harry   6
floated like a balloon around the foot of the bed. He floated and pulled down
his waistcoat and swung his glasses on a cord. "Well, stay where you are, it
certainly can't hurt you."

"Get along and doctor your sick," said Granny Weatherall. "Leave a well   7
woman alone. I'll call for you when I want you. . . . Where were you forty
years ago when I pulled through milk-leg and double pneumonia? You weren't
even born. Don't let Cornelia lead you on," she shouted, because Doctor Harry
appeared to float up to the ceiling and out. "I pay my own bills, and I don't
throw my money away on nonsense!"

She meant to wave good-by, but it was too much trouble. Her eyes closed   8
of themselves, it was like a dark curtain drawn around the bed. The pillow
rose and floated under her, pleasant as a hammock in a light wind. She listened
to the leaves rustling outside the window. No, somebody was swishing newspapers: no, Cornelia and Doctor Harry were whispering together. She leaped
broad awake, thinking they whispered in her ear.

"She was never like this, *never* like this!" "Well, what can we expect?"   9
"Yes, eighty years old. . . ."

Well, and what if she was? She still had ears. It was like Cornelia to whisper   10
around doors. She always kept things secret in such a public way. She was
always being tactful and kind. Cornelia was dutiful; that was the trouble with
her. Dutiful and good: "So good and dutiful," said Granny, "that I'd like to
spank her." She saw herself spanking Cornelia and making a fine job of it.

"What'd you say, Mother?"   11

Granny felt her face tying up in hard knots.   12

"Can't a body think, I'd like to know?"   13

"I though you might want something."   14

"I do. I want a lot of things. First off, go away and don't whisper."   15

She lay and drowsed, hoping in her sleep that the children would keep out   16
and let her rest a minute. It had been a long day. Not that she was tired. It
was always pleasant to snatch a minute now and then. There was always so
much to be done, let me see: tomorrow.

Tomorrow was far away and there was nothing to trouble about. Things   17
were finished somehow when the time came; thank God there was always a

little margin over for peace: then a person could spread out the plan of life and tuck in the edges orderly. It was good to have everything clean and folded away, with the hair brushes and tonic bottles sitting straight on the white embroidered linen: the day started without fuss and the pantry shelves laid out with rows of jelly glasses and brown jugs and white stone-china jars with blue whirligigs and words painted on them: coffee, tea, sugar, ginger, cinnamon, allspice: and the bronze clock with the lion on top nicely dusted off. The dust that lion could collect in twenty-four hours! The box in the attic with all those letters tied up, well she'd have to go through that tomorrow. All those letters — George's letters and John's letters and her letters to them both — lying around for the children to find afterwards made her uneasy. Yes, that would be tomorrow's business. No use to let them know how silly she had been once.

While she was rummaging around she found death in her mind and it felt 18 clammy and unfamiliar. She had spent so much time preparing for death there was no need for bringing it up again. Let it take care of itself now. When she was sixty she had felt very old, finished, and went around making farewell trips to see her children and grandchildren, with a secret in her mind: this is the very last of your mother, children! Then she made her will and came down with a long fever. That was all just a notion like a lot of other things, but it was lucky too, for she had once for all got over the idea of dying for a long time. Now she couldn't be worried. She hoped she had better sense now. Her father had lived to be one hundred and two years old and had drunk a noggin of strong hot toddy on his last birthday. He told the reporters it was his daily habit, and he owed his long life to that. He had made quite a scandal and was very pleased about it. She believed she'd just plague Cornelia a little.

"Cornelia! Cornelia!" No footsteps, but a sudden hand on her cheek. "Bless 19 you, where have you been?"

"Here, mother." 20

"Well, Cornelia, I want a noggin of hot toddy." 21

"Are you cold, darling?" 22

"I'm chilly, Cornelia. Lying in bed stops the circulation. I must have told 23 you that a thousand times."

Well, she could just hear Cornelia telling her husband that Mother was 24 getting childish and they'd have to humor her. The thing that most annoyed her was that Cornelia thought she was deaf, dumb, and blind. Little hasty glances and tiny gestures tossed around her and over her head saying, "Don't cross her, let her have her way, She's eighty years old," and she sitting there as if she lived in a thin glass cage. Sometimes Granny almost made up her mind to pack up and move back to her own house where nobody could remind her every minute that she was old. Wait, wait, Cornelia, till your own children whisper behind your back!

In her day she had kept a better house and had got more work done. She 25 wasn't too old yet for Lydia to be driving eighty miles for advice when one of the children jumped the track, and Jimmy still dropped in and talked things over: "Now, Mammy, you've a good business head, I want to know what you think of this. . . ?" Old Cornelia couldn't change the furniture around without asking. Little things, little things! They had been so sweet when they were little. Granny wished the old days were back again with the children young and everything to be done over. It had been a hard pull, but not too much for her. When she thought of all the food she had cooked, and all the clothes she had cut and sewed, and all the gardens she had made—well, the children showed it. There they were, made out of her, and they couldn't get away from that. Sometimes she wanted to see John again and point to them and say, Well, I didn't do so badly, did I? But that would have to wait. That was for tomorrow. She used to think of him as a man, but now all the children were older than their father, and he would be a child beside her if she saw him now. It seemed strange and there was something wrong in the idea. Why, he couldn't possibly recognize her. She had fenced in a hundred acres once, digging the postholes herself and clamping the wires with just a negro boy to help. That changed a woman. John would be looking for a young woman with the peaked Spanish comb in her hair and the painted fan. Digging post holes changed a woman. Riding country roads in the winter when women had their babies was another thing: sitting up nights with sick horses and sick negroes and sick children and hardly ever losing one. John, I hardly ever lost one of them! John would see that in a minute, that would be something he could understand, she wouldn't have to explain anything!

It made her feel like rolling her her sleeves and putting the whole place to 26 rights again. No matter if Cornelia was determined to be everywhere at once, there were a great many things left undone on this place. She would start tomorrow and do them. It was good to be strong enough for everything, even if all you made melted and changed and slipped under your hands, so that by the time you finished you almost forgot what you were working for. What was it I set out to do? she asked herself intently, but she could not remember. A fog rose over the valley, she saw it marching across the creek swallowing the trees and moving up the hill like an army of ghosts. Soon it would be at the near edge of the orchard, and then it was time to go in and light the lamps. Come in, children, don't stay out in the night air.

Lighting the lamps had been beautiful. The children huddled up to her and 27 breathed like little calves waiting at the bars in the twilight. Their eyes followed the match and watched the flame rise and settle in a blue curve, then they moved away from her. The lamp was lit, they didn't have to be scared and hang on to mother any more. Never, never, never more. God, for all my life I thank Thee. Without Thee, my God, I could never have done it. Hail, Mary, full of grace.

I want you to pick all the fruit this year and see that nothing is wasted. 28 There's always someone who can use it. Don't let good things rot for want of using. You waste life when you waste good food. Don't let things get lost. It's bitter to lose things. Now, don't let me get to thinking, not when I am tired and taking a little nap before supper. . . .

The pillow rose about her shoulders and pressed against her heart and the 29 memory was being squeezed out of it: oh, push down the pillow, somebody: it would smother her if she tried to hold it. Such a fresh breeze blowing and such a green day with no threats in it. But he had not come, just the same. What does a woman do when she has put on the white veil and set out the white cake for a man and he doesn't come? She tried to remember. No, I swear he never harmed me but in that. He never harmed me but in that . . . and what if he did? There was the day, the day, but a whirl of dark smoke rose and covered it, crept up and over into the bright field where everything was planted so carefully in orderly rows. That was hell, she knew hell when she saw it. For sixty years she had prayed against remembering him and against losing her soul in the deep pit of hell, and now the two things were mingled in one and the thought of him was a smoky cloud from hell that moved and crept in her head when she had just got rid of Doctor Harry and was trying to rest a minute. Wounded vanity, Ellen, said a sharp voice in the top of her mind. Don't let your wounded vanity get the upper hand of you. Plenty of girls get jilted. You were jilted, weren't you? Then stand up to it. Her eyelids wavered and let in streamers of blue-gray light like tissue paper over her eyes. She must get up and pull the shades down or she'd never sleep. She was in bed again and the shades were not down. How could that happen? Better turn over, hide from the light, sleeping in the light gave you nightmares. "Mother, how do you feel now?" and a stinging wetness on her forehead. But I don't like having my face washed in cold water!

Hapsy? George? Lydia? Jimmy? No, Cornelia, and her features were swollen 30 and full of little puddles. "They're coming, darling, they'll all be here soon." Go wash your face, child, you look funny.

Instead of obeying, Cornelia knelt down and put her head on the pillow. 31 She seemed to be talking but there was no sound. "Well, are you tongue-tied? Whose birthday is it? Are you going to give a party?"

Cornelia's mouth moved urgently in strange shapes. "Don't do that, you 32
bother me, daughter."

Oh, no, Mother. Oh, no. . . ."   33

Nonsense. It was strange about children. They disputed your every word. 34
"No what, Cornelia?"

"Here's Doctor Harry."   35

"I won't see that boy again. He just left five minutes ago."   36

"That was this morning, Mother. It's night now. Here's the nurse."   37

"This is Doctor Harry, Mrs. Weatherall. I never saw you look so young and 38
happy!"

"Ah, I'll never be young again — but I'd be happy if they'd let me lie in 39
peace and get rested."

She thought she spoke up loudly, but no one answered. A warm weight on 40
her forehead, a warm bracelet on her wrist, and a breeze went on whispering,
trying to tell her something. A shuffle of leaves in the everlasting hand of
God. He blew on them and they danced and rattled. "Mother, don't mind,
we're going to give you a little hypodermic." "Look here, daughter, how do
ants get in this bed? I saw sugar ants yesterday." Did you send for Hapsy too?

It was Hapsy she really wanted. She had to go a long way back through a 41
great many rooms to find Hapsy standing with a baby on her arm. She seemed
to herself to be Hapsy also, and the baby on Hapsy's arm was Hapsy and
himself and herself, all at once, and there was no surprise in the meeting.
Then Hapsy melted from within and turned flimsy as gray gauze and the baby
was a gauzy shadow, and Hapsy came up close and said, "I thought you'd never
come," and looked at her very searchingly and said, "You haven't changed a
bit!" They leaned forward to kiss, when Cornelia began whispering from a
long way off, "Oh, is there anything you want to tell me? Is there anything I
can do for you?"

Yes, she had changed her mind after sixty years and she would like to see 42
George. I want you to find George. Find him and be sure to tell him I want
him to know I had my husband just the same and my children and my house
like any other woman. A good house too and a good husband that I loved and
fine children out of him. Better than I hoped for even. Tell him I was given
back everything he took away and more. Oh, no, oh, God, no, there was
something else besides the house and the man and the children. Oh, surely
they were not all? What was it? Something not given back. . . . Her breath
crowded down under her ribs and grew into a monstrous frightening shape
with cutting edges; it bored up into her head, and the agony was unbelievable:
Yes, John, get the doctor now, no more talk, my time has come.

When this one was born it should be the last. The last. It should have 43
been born first, for it was the one she had truly wanted. Everything came in
good time. Nothing left out, left over. She was strong, in three days she
would be as well as ever. Better. A woman needed milk in her to have her
full health.

"Mother, do you hear me?"   44

"I've been telling you—"   45

"Mother, Father Connolly's here."   46

"I went to Holy Communion only last week. Tell him I'm not so sinful as 47
all that."

"Father just wants to speak to you."   48

He could speak as much as he pleased. It was like him to drop in and inquire 49
about her soul as if it were a teething baby, and then stay on for a cup of tea
and a round of cards and gossip. He always had a funny story of some sort,
usually about an Irishman who made his little mistakes and confessed them,
and the point lay in some absurd thing he would blurt out in the confessional
showing his struggles between native piety and original sin. Granny felt easy
about her soul. Cornelia, where are your manners? Give Father Connolly a
chair. She had her secret comfortable understanding with a few favorite saints
who cleared a straight road to God for her. All as surely signed and sealed as
the papers for the new Forty Acres. Forever . . . heirs and assigns forever.
Since the day the wedding cake was not cut, but thrown out and wasted. The
whole bottom dropped out of the world, and there she was blind and sweating
with nothing under her feet and the walls falling away. His hand had caught
her under the breast, she had not fallen, there was the freshly polished floor
with the green rug on it, just as before. He had cursed like a sailor's parrot
and said, "I'll kill him for you." Don't lay a hand on him, for my sake leave
something to God. "Now, Ellen, you must believe what I tell you. . . ."

So there was nothing, nothing to worry about any more, except sometimes 50
in the night one of the children screamed in a nightmare, and they both
hustled out shaking and hunting for the matches and calling, "There, wait a
minute, here we are!" John, get the doctor now, Hapsy's time has come. But
there was Hapsy standing by the bed in a white cap. "Cornelia, tell Hapsy to
take off her cap. I can't see her plain."

Her eyes opened very wide and the room stood out like a picture she had 51
seen somewhere. Dark colors with the shadows rising toward the ceiling in
long angles. The tall black dresser gleamed with nothing on it but John's
picture, enlarged from a little one, with John's eyes very black when they
should have been blue. You never saw him, so how do you know how he
looked? But the man insisted the copy was perfect, it was very rich and hand-

some. For a picture, yes, but it's not my husband. The table by the bed had a linen cover and a candle and a cruxifix. The light was blue from Cornelia's silk lampshades. No sort of light at all, just frippery. You had to live forty years with kerosene lamps to appreciate honest electricity. She felt very strong and she saw Doctor Harry with a rosy nimbus around him.

"You look like a saint, Doctor Harry, and I vow that's as near as you'll ever 52 come to it."

"She's saying something." 53

"I heard you, Cornelia. What's all this carrying-on?" 54

"Father Connolly's saying—" 55

Cornelia's voice staggered and bumped like a cart in a bad road. It rounded 56 corners and turned back again and arrived nowhere. Granny stepped up in the cart very lightly and reached for the reins, but a man sat beside her and she knew him by his hands, driving the cart. She did not look in his face, for she knew without seeing, but looked instead down the road where the trees leaned over and bowed to each other and a thousand birds were singing a Mass. She felt like singing too, but she put her hand in the bosom of her dress and pulled out a rosary, and Father Connolly murmured Latin in a very solemn voice and tickled her feet. My God, will you stop that nonsense? I'm a married woman. What if he did run away and leave me to face the priest by myself? I found another a whole world better. I wouldn't have exchanged my husband for anybody except St. Michael himself, and you may tell him that for me with a thank you in the bargain.

Light flashed on her closed eyelids, and a deep roaring shook her. Cornelia, 57 is that lightning? I hear thunder. There's going to be a storm. Close all the windows. Call the children in. . . . "Mother, here we are, all of us." "Is that you, Hapsy?" "Oh no, I'm Lydia. We drove as fast as we could." Their faces drifted above her, drifted away. The rosary fell out of her hands and Lydia put it back. Jimmy tried to help, their hands fumbled together, and Granny closed two fingers around Jimmy's thumb. Beads wouldn't do, it must be something alive. She was so amazed her thoughts ran round and round. So, my dear Lord, this is my death and I wasn't even thinking about it. My children have come to see me die. But I can't, it's not time. Oh, I always hated surprises. I wanted to give Cornelia the amethyst set—Cornelia, you're to have the amethyst set, but Hapsy's to wear it when she wants, and, Doctor Harry, do shut up. Nobody sent for you. Oh, my dear Lord, do wait a minute. I meant to do something about the Forty Acres, Jimmy doesn't need it and Lydia will later on, with that worthless husband of hers. I meant to finish the altar cloth and send six bottles of wine to Sister Borgia for her dyspepsia. I want to send six bottles of wine to Sister Borgia, Father Connolly, now don't let me forget.

Cornelia's voice made short turns and tilted over and crashed. "Oh, Mother, 58 oh, Mother, oh, Mother. . . ."

"I'm not going, Cornelia. I'm taken by surprise. I can't go." 59

You'll see Hapsy again. What about her? "I thought you'd never come." 60 Granny made a long journey outward, looking for Hapsy. What if I don't find her? What then? Her heart sank down and down, there was no bottom to death, she couldn't come to the end of it. The blue light from Cornelia's lampshade drew into a tiny point in the center of her brain, it flickered and winked like an eye, quietly it fluttered and dwindled. Granny lay curled down within herself, amazed and watchful, staring at the point of light that was herself; her body was now only a deeper mass of shadow in an endless darkness and this darkness would curl around the light and swallow it up. God, give a sign!

For the second time there was no sign. Again no bridegroom and the priest 61 in the house. She could not remember any other sorrow because this grief wiped them all away. Oh, no, there's nothing more cruel than this—I'll never forgive it. She stretched herself with a deep breath and blew out the light.

QUESTIONS FOR READING

1. "The Jilting of Granny Weatherall" contains two narrative threads: an account of Granny Weatherall's last hour and an account of the events of her past as they pour into her mind on her deathbed. Reread the story and distinguish between these two narratives. What specific stylistic strategies does Porter use to separate the two? to weave them together?

2. Consider the story's title. What is the "jilting" that Granny experienced years earlier? On her deathbed, Granny worries about another "jilting." What is this "final" jilting, and who besides Granny is involved? What distinctions does Granny draw between these two jiltings? What is the significance of the name "Weatherall" in the story?

3. What details does Porter emphasize in her description of Granny Weatherall at the beginning of the story? Why, for example, does Porter note that Granny's "bones felt loose, and floated around in her skin, and Doctor Harry floated like a balloon around the foot of the bed" (paragraph 6)? Identify other moments when people and objects seem to "float." What do these moments reveal about Granny? What other characteristics does Porter emphasize in her description of Granny Weatherall?

4. In *A Reader's Guide to Literary Terms*, Karl Beckson and Arthur Ganz define

stream of consciousness as "the depiction of the thoughts and feelings which flow, with no apparent logic, through the mind of a character." In what specific ways is this story an example of stream of consciousness? In what ways does the story's effectiveness depend on additional narrative techniques?

5. Comment on the significance of Hapsy's role in the story. Why does she figure prominently in Granny's consciousness? Why doesn't Hapsy visit Granny on her deathbed? What distinction can you draw between Porter's depiction of Hapsy and Cornelia? Of Granny and Doctor Harry? With what effect?

QUESTIONS ON CONNECTIONS

1. *Compare and contrast* Katherine Anne Porter's depiction of Granny Weatherall with Beverly Dipo's portrait of Mrs. Trane in "No Rainbows, No Roses" (p. 70). What, for example, are the distinctive quirks and mannerisms of each? In what ways are they alike? different? Compare their attitudes toward death, their families, and doctors.

2. *Contrast* Doctor Harry's attitude toward patients with Richard Selzer's in "The Discus Thrower." How would you characterize the doctor/patient relationship in each?

3. Granny Weatherall spends a good deal of time preparing for her death. (See especially paragraphs 17–18 and following where she says, "Things were finished somehow when the time came . . . then a person could spread out the plan of life and tuck in the edges orderly.") Read Emily Dickinson's poem, "I Heard a Fly Buzz—When I Died." What is the nature of the character's "readiness" for death in Dickinson's poem, and how is that readiness similar to— and different from—Granny Weatherall's? With what consequences?

SUGGESTIONS FOR WRITING

1. In paragraph 10, Granny comments on the meaning of *dutiful* in the context of her own death: "Cornelia was dutiful; that was the trouble with her. Dutiful and good: 'So good and dutiful,' said Granny, 'that I'd like to spank her.' " Analyze the meaning of *dutiful* in this context and write an expository essay in which you explain the term's appropriateness in the context of a less traumatic family gathering. Remember that you are using *description* or *narration* to create a context for your analysis and not as an end in itself.

2. From the outset of the story, Porter relies on figurative language to convey and underscore her story's dramatic impact; for example, the opening of paragraph 2: "Doctor Harry spread a warm paw like a cushion on her forehead where the

forked green vein danced and made her eyelids twitch." As you reread the story, notice what kinds of *images* are repeated frequently enough to form a pattern (religious images offer one such example, as do images of light and dark, but do not restrict yourself to these two possibilities). Choose one such pattern of imagery and write an essay in which you explain the importance of that *image* in reinforcing the meaning of Porter's story.

ALICE WALKER

Black women in relation to their families, to their mothers, to each other, and to the world at large are recurring themes in Alice Walker's writing. In a recent interview, she explained that she has always been "curious to know why people in families (specifically black families) are often cruel to each other and how much of this cruelty is caused by outside forces, such as various social injustices, segregation, unemployment, etc." For Walker, "family relationships are sacred. No amount of outside pressure and injustice must make us lose sight of that fact. . . . In the black family, love, cohesion, support, and concern are crucial since a racist society constantly acts to destroy the black individual, the black family unit, the black child. In America, black people have only themselves and each other." Alice Walker has explored the richness and complexity of black American identity in her poems, stories, and novels, and in a broad range of nonfiction, including essays, introductions to the work of black writers, and a biography of Langston Hughes (1973).

Born in Eatonton, Georgia, in 1944, Alice Walker attended Spelman College in Atlanta for two years before graduating from Sarah Lawrence College in 1965. She has taught writing and black literatuare at Jackson State, Tougaloo, and Wellesley colleges as well as the University of Massachusetts, Boston, and Yale. She also worked as an editor of Ms. magazine before devoting herself full-time to writing. Collections of her poems include Once *(1968),* Revolutionary Petunias and Other Poems *(1973), and* Good Night, Willie Lee, I'll See You in the Morning *(1979). Her short fiction has been collected in* You Can't Keep a Good Woman Down *and* In Love and Trouble *(1973), from which* "Everyday Use" *is drawn. Her novels include* The Third Life of Grange Copeland *(1970),* Meridian *(1976), and* The Color Purple *(1982), for which she won the American Book Award and the Pulitzer Prize. Her most recent books are* In Search of Our Mothers' Gardens *(1983), a collection of her nonfiction, and* Horses Make a Landscape Look More Beautiful *(1984), a collection of her poetry.*

Everyday Use

for your grandmama

I will wait for her in the yard that Maggie and I made so clean and wavy 1
yesterday afternoon. A yard like this is more comfortable than most people
know. It is not just a yard. It is like an extended living room. When the hard
clay is swept clean as a floor and the fine sand around the edges lined with
tiny, irregular grooves anyone can come and sit and look up into the elm tree
and wait for the breezes that never come inside the house.

Maggie will be nervous until after her sister goes: she will stand hopelessly 2
in corners homely and ashamed of the burn scars down her arms and legs,
eyeing her sister with a mixture of envy and awe. She thinks her sister has
held life always in the palm of one hand, that "no" is a word the world never
learned to say to her.

You've no doubt seen those TV shows where the child who had "made it" 3
is confronted, as a surprise, by her own mother and father, tottering in weakly
from backstage. (A pleasant surprise, of course: what would they do if parent
and child came on the show only to curse out and insult each other?) On TV
mother and child embrace and smile into each other's faces. Sometimes the
mother and father weep, the child wraps them in her arms and leans across
the table to tell how she would not have made it without their help. I have
seen these programs.

Sometimes I dream a dream in which Dee and I are suddenly brought 4
together on a TV program of this sort. Out of a dark and soft-seated limousine
I am ushered into a bright room filled with many people. There I meet a
smiling, gray, sporty man like Johnny Carson who shakes my hand and tells
me what a fine girl I have. Then we are on the stage and Dee is embracing
me with tears in her eyes. She pins on my dress a large orchid, even though
she has told me once that she thinks orchids are tacky flowers.

In real life I am a large, big-boned woman with rough, man-working hands. 5
In the winter I wear flannel nightgowns to bed and overalls during the day. I
can kill and clean a hog as mercilessly as a man. My fat keeps me hot in zero
weather. I can work all day, breaking ice to get water for washing. I can eat
pork liver cooked over the open fire minutes after it comes steaming from the
hog. One winter I knocked a bull calf straight in the brain between the eyes
with a sledge hammer and had the meat hung up to chill before nightfall. But
of course all this does not show on television. I am the way my daughter would
want me to be: a hundred pounds lighter, my skin like an uncooked barley
pancake. My hair glistens in the hot bright lights. Johnny Carson has much
to do to keep up with my quick and witty tongue.

But that is a mistake. I know even before I wake up. Who ever knew a 6
Johnson with a quick tongue? Who can even imagine me looking a strange
white man in the eye? It seems to me I have talked to them always with one
foot raised in flight, with my head turned in whichever way is farthest from
them. Dee, though. She would always look anyone in the eye. Hesitation was
no part of her nature.

"How do I look, Mama?" Maggie says, showing just enough of her thin 7
body enveloped in pink skirt and red blouse for me to know she's there, almost
hidden by the door.

"Come out into the yard," I say. 8

Have you ever seen a lame animal, perhaps a dog run over by some careless 9
person rich enough to own a car, sidle up to someone who is ignorant enough
to be kind to him? That is the way my Maggie walks. She has been like this,
chin on chest, eyes on ground, feet in shuffle, ever since the fire that burned
the other house to the ground.

Dee is lighter than Maggie, with nicer hair and a fuller figure. She's a woman 10
now, though sometimes I forget. How long ago was it that the other house
burned? Ten, twelve years? Sometimes I can still hear the flames and feel
Maggie's arm sticking to me, her hair smoking and her dress falling off her in
little black papery flakes. Her eyes seemed stretched open, blazed open by the
flames reflected in them. And Dee. I see her standing off under the sweet gum
tree she used to dig gum out of; a look of concentration on her face as she
watched the last dingy gray board of the house fall in toward the red-hot brick
chimney. Why don't you do a dance around the ashes? I'd wanted to ask her.
She had hated the house that much.

I used to think she hated Maggie, too. But that was before we raised the 11
money, the church and me, to send her to Augusta to school. She used to
read to us without pity; forcing words, lies, other folks' habits, whole lives
upon us two, sitting trapped and ignorant underneath her voice. She washed
us in a river of make-believe, burned us with a lot of knowledge we didn't
necessarily need to know. Pressed us to her with the serious way she read, to
shove us away at just the moment, like dimwits, we seemed about to understand.

Dee wanted nice things. A yellow organdy dress to wear to her graduation 12
from high school; black pumps to match a green suit she'd made from an old
suit somebody gave me. She was determined to stare down any disaster in her
efforts. Her eyelids would not flicker for minutes at a time. Often I fought off
the temptation to shake her. At sixteen she had a style of her own: and knew
what style was.

I never had an education myself. After second grade the school was closed 13
down. Don't ask me why: in 1927 colored asked fewer questions than they do
now. Sometimes Maggie reads to me. She stumbles along good-naturedly but
can't see well. She knows she is not bright. Like good looks and money,
quickness passed her by. She will marry John Thomas (who has mossy teeth

in an earnest face) and then I'll be free to sit here and I guess just sing church
songs to myself. Although I never was a good singer. Never could carry a tune.
I was always better at a man's job. I used to love to milk till I was hoofed in
the side in '49. Cows are soothing and slow and don't bother you, unless you
try to milk them the wrong way.

I have deliberately turned my back on the house. It is three rooms, just like   14
the one that burned, except the roof is tin; they don't make shingle roofs any
more. There are no real windows, just some holes cut in the sides, like the
portholes in a ship, but not round and not square, with rawhide holding the
shutters up on the outside. This house is in a pasture, too, like the other one.
No doubt when Dee sees it she will want to tear it down. She wrote me once
that no matter where we "choose" to live, she will manage to come see us.
But she will never bring her friends. Maggie and I thought about this and
Maggie asked me, "Mama, when did Dee ever *have* any friends?"

She had a few. Furtive boys in pink shirts hanging about on washday after   15
school. Nervous girls who never laughed. Impressed with her they worshiped
the well-turned phrase, the cute shape, the scalding humor that erupted like
bubbles in lye. She read to them.

When she was courting Jimmy T she didn't have much time to pay to us,   16
but turned all her faultfinding power on him. He *flew* to marry a cheap gal
from a family of ignorant flashy people. She hardly had time to recompose
herself.

When she comes I will meet — but there they are!   17

Maggie attempts to make a dash for the house, in her shuffling way, but I   18
stay her with my hand. "Come back here," I say. And she stops and tries to
dig a well in the sand with her toe.

It is hard to see them clearly through the strong sun. But even the first   19
glimpse of leg out of the car tells me it is Dee. Her feet were always neat-
looking, as if God himself had shaped them with a certain style. From the
other side of the car comes a short, stocky man. Hair is all over his head a
foot long and hanging from his chin like a kinky mule tail. I hear Maggie suck
in her breath. "Uhnnnh," is what it sounds like. Like when you see the
wriggling end of a snake just in front of your foot on the road. "Uhnnnh."

Dee next. A dress down to the ground, in this hot weather. A dress so loud   20
it hurts my eyes. There are yellows and oranges enough to throw back the
light of the sun. I feel my whole face warming from the heat waves it throws
out. Earrings, too, gold and hanging down to her shoulders. Bracelets dangling
and making noises when she moves her arm up to shake the folds of the dress
out of her armpits. The dress is loose and flows, and as she walks closer, I like
it. I hear Maggie go "Uhnnnh" again. It is her sister's hair. It stands straight

up like the wool on a sheep. It is black as night and around the edges are two long pigtails that rope about like small lizards disappearing behind her ears.

"Wa-su-zo-Tean-o!" she says, coming on in that gliding way the dress makes 21 her move. The short stocky fellow with the hair to his navel is all grinning and he follows up with "Asalamalakim, my mother and sister!" He moves to hug Maggie but she falls back, right up against the back of my chair. I feel her trembling there and when I look up I see the perspiration falling off her chin.

"Don't get up," says Dee. Since I am stout it takes something of a push. 22 You can see me trying to move a second or two before I make it. She turns, showing white heels through her sandals, and goes back to the car. Out she peeks next with a Polaroid. She stoops down quickly and lines up picture after picture of me sitting there in front of the house with Maggie cowering behind me. She never takes a shot without making sure the house is included. When a cow comes nibbling around the edge of the yard she snaps it and me and Maggie *and* the house. Then she puts the Polaroid in the back seat of the car, and comes up and kisses me on the forehead.

Meanwhile Asalamalakim is going through the motions with Maggie's hand. 23 Maggie's hand is as limp as a fish, and probably as cold, despite the sweat, and she keeps trying to pull it back. It looks like Asalamalakim wants to shake hands but wants to do it fancy. Or maybe he don't know how people shake hands. Anyhow, he soon gives up on Maggie.

"Well," I say. "Dee." 24

"No, Mama," she says. "Not 'Dee,' Wangero Leewanika Kemanjo!" 25

"What happened to 'Dee'?" I wanted to know. 26

"She'd dead." Wangero said. "I couldn't bear it any longer being named 27 after the people who oppress me."

"You know as well as me you was named after your aunt Dicie," I said. 28 Dicie is my sister. She named Dee. We called her "Big Dee" after Dee was born.

"But who was *she* named after?" asked Wangero. 29

"I guess after Grandma Dee," I said. 30

"And who was she named after?" asked Wangero. 31

"Her mother," I said, and saw Wangero was getting tired. "That's about as 32 far back as I can trace it," I said. Though, in fact, I probably could have carried it back beyond the Civil War through the branches.

"Well," said Asalamalakim, "there you are." 33

"Uhnnnh," I heard Maggie say. 34

"There I was not," I said, "before 'Dicie' cropped up in our family, so why 35 should I try to trace it that far back?"

He just stood there grinning, looking down on me like somebody inspecting 36
a Model A car. Every once in a while he and Wangero sent eye signals over
my head.

"How do you pronounce this name?" I asked.   37

"You don't have to call me by it if you don't want to," said Wangero.   38

"Why should't I?" I asked. "If that's what you want us to call you, we'll   39
call you."

"I know it might sound awkward at first," said Wangero.   40

"I'll get used to it," I said. "Ream it out again."   41

Well, soon we got the name out of the way. Asalamalakim had a name   42
twice as long and three times as hard. After I tripped over it two or three
times he told me to just call him Hakim-a-barber. I wanted to ask him was he
a barber, but I didn't really think he was, so I didn't ask.

"You must belong to those beef-cattle people down the road," I said. They   43
said "Asalamalakim" when they met you, too, but they didn't shake hands.
Always too busy: feeding the cattle, fixing the fences, putting up salt-lick
shelters, throwing down hay. When the white folks poisoned some of the herd
the men stayed up all night with rifles in their hands. I walked a mile and a
half just to see the sight.

Hakim-a-barber said, "I accept some of their doctrines, but farming and   44
raising cattle is not my style." (They didn't tell me, and I didn't ask, whether
Wangero [Dee] had really gone and married him.)

We sat down to eat and right away he said he didn't eat collards and pork   45
was unclean. Wangero, though, went on through the chitlins and corn bread,
the greens and everything else. She talked a blue streak over the sweet potatoes. Everything delighted her. Even the fact that we still used the benches
her daddy made for the table when we couldn't afford to buy chairs.

"Oh, Mama!" she cried. Then turned to Hakim-a-barber. "I never knew   46
how lovely these benches are. You can feel the rump prints," she said, running
her hands underneath her and along the bench. Then she gave a sigh and her
hand closed over Grandma Dee's butter dish. "That's it!" she said. "I knew
there was something I wanted to ask you if I could have." She jumped up from
the table and went over in the corner where the churn stood, the milk in its
clabber by now. She looked at the churn and looked at it.

"This churn top is what I need," she said. "Didn't Uncle Buddy whittle it   47
out of a tree you all used to have?"

"Yes," I said.   48

"Uh huh," she said happily. "And I want the dasher, too."   49

"Uncle Buddy whittle that, too?" asked the barber.   50

Dee (Wangero) looked up at me.   51

"Aunt Dee's first husband whittled the dash," said Maggie so low you almost   52
couldn't hear her. "His name was Henry, but they called him Stash."

"Maggie's brain is like an elephant's," Wangero said, laughing. "I can use   53
the churn top as a centerpiece for the alcove table," she said, sliding a plate
over the churn, "and I'll think of something artistic to do with the dasher."

When she finished wrapping the dasher the handle stuck out. I took it for   54
a moment in my hands. You didn't even have to look close to see where hands
pushing the dasher up and down to make butter had left a kind of sink in the
wood. In fact, there were a lot of small sinks; you could see where thumbs and
fingers had sunk into the wood. It was beautiful light yellow wood, from a tree
that grew in the yard where Big Dee and Stash had lived.

After dinner Dee (Wangero) went to the trunk at the foot of my bed and   55
started rifling through it. Maggie hung back in the kitchen over the dishpan.
Out came Wangero with two quilts. They had been pieced by Grandma Dee
and then Big Dee and me had hung them on the quilt frames on the front
porch and quilted them. One was in the Lone Star pattern. The other was
Walk Around the Mountain. In both of them were scraps of dresses Grandma
Dee had worn fifty and more years ago. Bits and pieces of Grandpa Jarrell's
paisley shirts. And one teeny faded blue piece, about the size of a penny
matchbox, that was from Great Grandpa Ezra's uniform that he wore in the
Civil War.

"Mama," Wangero said sweet as a bird. "Can I have these old quilts?"   56

I heard something fall in the kitchen, and a minute later the kitchen door   57
slammed.

"Why don't you take one or two of the others?" I asked. "These old things   58
was just done by me and Big Dee from some tops your grandma pieced before
she died."

"No," said Wangero. "I don't want those. They are stitched around the   59
borders by machine."

"That'll make them last better," I said.   60

"That's not the point," said Wangero. "These are all pieces of dresses Grandma   61
used to wear. She did all this stitching by hand. Imagine!" She held the quilts
securely in her arms, stroking them.

"Some of the pieces, like those lavender ones, come from old clothes her   62
mother handed down to her," I said, moving up to touch the quilts. Dee
(Wangero) moved back just enough so that I couldn't reach the quilts. They
already belonged to her.

"Imagine!" she breathed again, clutching them closely to her bosom.   63

"The truth is," I said, "I promised to give them quilts to Maggie, for when 64 she marries John Thomas."

She gasped like a bee had stung her.   65

"Maggie can't appreciate these quilts!" she said. "She'd probably be back- 66 ward enough to put them to everyday use."

"I reckon she would," I said. "God knows I been saving 'em for long enough 67 with nobody using 'em. I hope she will!" I didn't want to bring up how I had offered Dee (Wangero) a quilt when she went away to college. Then she had told me they were old-fashioned, out of style.

"But they're *priceless!*" she was saying now, furiously; for she has a temper. 68 "Maggie would put them on the bed and in five years they'd be in rags. Less than that!"

"She can always make some more," I said. "Maggie knows how to quilt." 69

Dee (Wangero) looked at me with hatred. "You just will not understand. 70 The point is these quilts, *these* quilts!"

"Well," I said, stumped. "What would *you* do with them?" 71

"Hang them," she said. As if that was the only thing you *could* do with 72 quilts.

Maggie by now was standing in the door. I could almost hear the sound her 73 feet made as they scraped over each other.

"She can have them, Mama," she said, like somebody used to never winning 74 anything, or having anything reserved for her. "I can 'member Grandma Dee without the quilts."

I looked at her hard. She had filled her bottom lip with checkerberry snuff 75 and it gave her face a kind of dopey, hangdog look. It was Grandma Dee and Big Dee who taught her how to quilt herself. She stood there with her scarred hands hidden in the folds of her skirt. She looked at her sister with something like fear but she wasn't mad at her. This was Maggie's portion. This was the way she knew God to work.

When I looked at her like that something hit me in the top of my head 76 and ran down to the soles of my feet. Just like when I'm in church and the spirit of God touches me and I get happy and shout. I did something I never had done before: hugged Maggie to me, then dragged her on into the room, snatched the quilts out of Miss Wangero's hands and dumped them into Maggie's lap. Maggie just sat there on my bed with her mouth open.

"Take one or two of the others," I said to Dee. 77

But she turned without a word and went out to Hakim-a-barber. 78

"You just don't understand," she said, as Maggie and I came out to the car. 79

"What don't I understand?" I wanted to know. 80

"Your heritage," she said. And then she turned to Maggie, kissed her, and 81 said, "You ought to try to make something of yourself, too, Maggie. It's really a new day for us. But from the way you and Mama still live you'd never know it."

She put on some sunglasses that hid everything above the tip of her nose 82 and her chin.

Maggie smiled; maybe at the sunglasses. But a real smile, not scared. After 83 we watched the car dust settle I asked Maggie to bring me a dip of snuff. And then the two of us sat there just enjoying, until it was time to go in the house and go to bed.

QUESTIONS FOR READING

1. How does the narrator in this story identify herself? With whom does she compare herself? On what aspects of contemporary American culture does she draw to distinguish between the realilty of her circumstances and how she thinks Dee would like her to look and behave?

2. How does Alice Walker characterize Maggie in this story? With what does the narrator compare Maggie? What sort of future does the narrator imagine for her? How is Dee presented in the story? How do Dee and Maggie's different responses to the fire reveal their different approaches to experience? What is Dee's relationship to the simple objects in the house and how does this relationship characterize her connection to her heritage? Comment on Dee's response to the churn top and the dasher. In what ways is the narrator dependent on Dee? How does the narrator maintain her independence from Dee?

3. Comment on the importance of setting in this story. How does Walker's attention to setting prepare her readers for Dee's return? Why does Dee include the house in the Polaroid photographs she takes? How would you characterize Wangero's sensibility and values as she returns home? What, in terms of her identity, is at stake in returning home? What is she looking for?

4. Reread the section in which the narrator first describes Dee's return (paragraph 17 and following). What does the narrator notice about her as she approaches the house? How does the narrator characterize Dee's companion? Consider the exchange between the narrator and Dee over the issue of her name. How does the narrator's *diction* and syntax change at this moment? What importance does Walker attach to Dee's having taken a Muslim name and to her refusal to eat pork?

5. Discuss the dramatic function of the quilts in the story. How does Walker prepare her readers to respond when Dee says, "You just don't understand. . . . Your heritage"? How, finally, is Dee's relation to her heritage different from her mother's and Maggie's?

6. Explain the significance of the story's title. How does it serve as a commentary on Wangero's new interests? To what else in this story might the title, "Everyday Use," be applied? With what significance? How does "everyday use" characterize each person's relationship with the others as well as with art?

QUESTIONS ON CONNECTIONS

1. One of the distinctive features of Earnestine Johnson's essay, "Thank You Miss Alice Walker," (p. 128) is her honest, intense voice in responding to Walker's *The Color Purple*. Reread Johnson's essay and *compare and contrast* the narrative voice in it with the narrator's voice in "Everyday Use." What changes, if any, do you notice in each voice as the essay and story proceed? with what effect? What role does reading play in the growth of each narrator's consciousness? Comment on the relationship of Walker and Johnson to their *audiences*. How does each writer elicit the reader's sympathy and understanding?

2. *Compare and contrast* what motivates Dee to return home with the motivation described in Brenda Jacobs's essay, "Handing Down Grace" (p. 106), Ravenel Boykin Curry's essay, "A Small Town" (p. 63), and John E. Mason, Jr.'s essay, "Shared Birthdays" (p. 167). In a similar vein, in what specific ways is Dee's motivation to return home similar to and different from William Humphrey's in "The Salmon Instinct"? How is *home* defined in each? with what effect? In this respect, does Walker's depiction of home remind you in any specific ways of Ann Louise Field's essay, "The Sound of Angels" (p. 76) and Julie Reardon's essay, "The Unmarked Road" (p. 202)? Explain.

3. "Everyday Use" also examines the complexity of a daughter's relationship with a parent. How is Walker's depiction of this relationship similar to and different from Barbara Seidel's treatment of this subject in "A Tribute to My Father" (p. 212)?

SUGGESTIONS FOR WRITING

1. Reread "Everyday Use" and focus on the definitions of black identity that are explicit and implicit in it. Write an essay in which you *compare and contrast* Dee's sense of identity with her mother's. How are their responses to their black heritage different? alike? In what specific ways does Walker's use of a first-person narrator lead her readers to favor one view of black identity?

2. Review the importance of the phrase *everyday use* in this story. Identify aspects of your own daily life to which this phrase might be applied to express something significant about your own identity and your relation to your racial or ethnic heritage. Write a *narrative* essay in which you use this phrase to clarify — and exemplify — your identity and your sense of your connection to that heritage.

EMILY DICKINSON

The information about Emily Dickinson's life is startlingly simple. She died in Amherst, Massachusetts, in 1886—in the same house in which she was born fifty-six years earlier. Her father was at various times a local legislator, U.S. congressman, and treasurer of Amherst College, which her grandfather had helped found. Her mother was a semi-invalid who struggled to raise Emily, her older brother, and younger sister. Emily Dickinson attended Amherst Academy and studied for one year at Mount Holyoke Female Seminary, until her father decided that her precarious health made continuing her formal education unwise.

A shy, sensitive young woman, Dickinson devoted herself to reading, corresponding with a few friends, and writing poetry. An 1862 letter describes her experience: "I went to school, but in your manner of the phrase had no education. When a little girl, I had a friend who taught me Immortality; but venturing too near, himself, he never returned. Soon after, my tutor died, and for several years my lexicon was my only companion."

With the exception of occasional brief visits to neighboring towns and one extended trip to Washington with her father, Dickinson rarely left her Amherst home. More often than not she dressed exclusively in white. Although she wrote nearly 1,800 untitled and undated poems (gathered in handsewn packets of five and six sheets), only seven of her poems were published in her lifetime. The Poems of Emily Dickinson was published four years after her death—to mostly negative reviews. Her complete poems were not published in a reliable edition until 1958, when Thomas H. Johnson edited a three-volume collection.

A lyric poet of enormous power, Emily Dickinson addressed such traditional subjects as love, death, nature, and God with the rarest skill. Her poems on death—what she called the "mighty" reality—were written with, as one critic put it, "chilling comprehension."

I Heard a Fly Buzz—
When I Died

I heard a Fly buzz—when I died—
The Stillness in the Room
Was like the Stillness in the Air—
Between the Heaves of Storm—

The Eyes around—had wrung them dry—   5
And Breaths were gathering firm
For that last Onset—when the King
Be witnessed—in the Room—

I willed my Keepsakes—Signed away
What portion of me be   10
Assignable—and then it was
There interposed a Fly—

With Blue—uncertain stumbling Buzz—
Between the light—and me—
And then the Windows failed—and then 15
I could not see to see—

QUESTIONS FOR READING

1. How would you characterize the speaker's attitude toward death in this poem? What specific words and phrases does the poet use to convey this attitude? Does that attitude change as the poem progresses? If so, where and to what?

2. Comment on the nature of Dickinson's use of figurative language in the poem. What is the significance of "Keepsakes" in line 9? Comment on the effectiveness of Dickinson's use of "interposed" in line 12. Which "King" is referred to in lines 7–8?

3. Earlier, inaccurate printings of this poem substituted "round my form" for "in the Room" in line 2; "The eyes beside" for "The Eyes around" in line 5; "sure" for "firm" in line 5; "in his power" for "in the Room" in line 8; and "What portion of me I / Could make assignable—and then" for "What portion of me be / Assignable—and then it was" in lines 10–11. Comment on the significance of these editorial changes. What argument can you make in light of the entire poem to show that the correct version is superior in each case?

QUESTIONS ON CONNECTIONS

1. Compare the speaker's attitude toward death in this poem with that of the main character in Katherine Anne Porter's story, "The Jilting of Granny Weatherall." In what specific ways are these two characters' attitudes similar? different?

2. Compare the dramatic intensity of this speaker's behavior in facing death with that of Mrs. Trane in Beverly Dipo's essay, "No Rainbows, No Roses" (p. 70). Identify the *point of view* in each. How does each writer use details in similar ways? With similar effects?

3. *Compare and contrast* the speaker's attitude toward death in Dickinson's poem with that of Barbara Huttman in "A Crime of Compassion," James Rachels in "Active and Passive Euthanasia," and Beverly Dipo in "A Time to Die" (p. 321). In what specific ways do their responses to death coincide? differ?

SUGGESTIONS FOR WRITING

1. Reread the poem carefully, several times, and write an essay in which you discuss the effectiveness of juxtaposing a person's death with something as apparently insignificant as a fly.

2. The speaker in Emily Dickinson's poem undercuts the emotion expected of someone discussing her or his own death by refusing to grant it the significance it is usually accorded. In a similar manner, many contemporary American humorists often respond to society's traditional seriousness about death with a deadpan expression and an understated one-liner. Here are two vintage Woody Allen lines on the subject: "It is impossible to experience one's death objectively and still carry a tune." "I'm not afraid to die. I just don't want to be there when it happens." Explore some deadly serious aspect of contemporary life (terrorism, nuclear destruction, the spread of AIDS, etc.) and America's apparent fascination with making jokes about these serious matters. Write an essay in which you analyze America's fascination with juxtaposing tragic and comic sensibilities on contemporary issues of such national significance.

THOMAS HARDY

The son of a stonemason, Thomas Hardy was born in Dorsetshire, England, in 1840 and trained as an ecclesiastical architect. He also studied modern languages at King's College, Cambridge. In 1863, he earned prizes for both his architectural designs and his art criticism. At thirty, he settled into a career as a novelist and poet. Among his most celebrated novels are Far From the Madding Crowd *(1874),* The Return of the Native *(1878),* The Mayor of Casterbridge *(1886), and* Tess of the D'Urbervilles *(1891). The publication of* Jude the Obscure *in 1896 was met with such negative reviews that Hardy turned almost exclusively to writing poetry in his later years. His verse has been collected in* Wessex Poems *(1898),* Poems of the Past and Present *(1901),* Moments of Vision *(1917),* Later Lyrics and Earlier *(1922), and* Winter Words *(1928).*

Despite what was widely perceived to be Hardy's pessimistic view — that the individual is an alien in an impersonal universe subject to capriciousness and chance — he never yielded his life-long insistence that he was a meliorist and that his writing expressed his belief in the advent of a better world. When he died in 1928, he was one of England's most acclaimed writers.

Channel Firing

That night your great guns, unawares,
Shook all our coffins as we lay,
And broke the chancel window-squares,[1]
We thought it was the Judgment-day

And sat upright. While drearisome   5
Arose the howl of wakened hounds:
The mouse let fall the altar-crumb,
The worms drew back into the mounds,

The glebe cow[2] drooled. Till God called, "No;
It's gunnery practice out at sea   10
Just as before you went below;
The world is as it used to be:

[1]Window panes near the altar.
[2]The parish cow kept near the church.

"All nations striving strong to make
Red war yet redder. Mad as hatters
They do no more for Christés sake 15
Than you who are helpless in such matters.

"That this is not the judgment-hour
For some of them's a blessed thing,
For if it were they'd have to scour
Hell's floor for so much threatening. . . . 20

"Ha, ha. It will be warmer when
I blow the trumpet (if indeed
I ever do; for you are men,
And rest eternal sorely need)."

So down we lay again. "I wonder, 25
Will the world ever saner be,"
Said one, "than when He sent us under
In our indifferent century!"

And many a skeleton shook his head.
"Instead of preaching forty year," 30
My neighbor Parson Thirdly said,
"I wish I had stuck to pipes and beer."

Again the guns disturbed the hour,
Roaring their readiness to avenge,
As far inland as Stourton Tower, 35
And Camelot, and starlit Stonehenge.[3]

QUESTIONS FOR READING

1. Identify the speaker at the beginning of the poem. From what perspective does he or she speak? Who is the *you* referred to in line 1? Who else speaks in the poem? With what effect? In what specific ways does *irony* contribute to the dramatic effectiveness of what each speaker says?

[3]Stourton Tower: an eighteenth-century tower in Wiltshire, England; Camelot: the mythical center of King Arthur's court; Stonehenge: prehistoric ceremonial ruin on the Salisbury Plain in Wiltshire, England.

2. What view of modern life does Hardy present in this poem? Explain how Hardy relies on *irony* to underscore this view. Which lines best demonstrate Hardy's mastery of irony as a poetic device? Why?

3. What is the effect of Hardy's decision to carry the thought expressed in the first stanza over into the second? What does the second stanza contribute to the poem's overall effect? Characterize the sound of God's voice in this poem. What is unusual about it? What does Hardy achieve by presenting God in such a voice?

4. Reread the final stanza aloud, how has the speaker changed the sound of his or her voice? Comment on the *purpose*—and the effectiveness—of the *allusions* in the last stanza. What do they contribute to the overall impact of the poem?

QUESTIONS ON CONNECTIONS

1. Reread Nelsy Massoud's essay, "War in Paradise" (p. 175). *Compare and contrast* her attitude toward war with that expressed in "Channel Firing." In what respects are the voices that address us in that essay and in Hardy's poem alike? different? Comment on the similarities and differences in their perspectives on war. What is the nature of the *irony* evident in Massoud's essay and how is it similar to or different from Hardy's?

2. Contrast the narrative voice in "Channel Firing" with Max Ramsey's in "For Myself" (p. 197). How does each writer organize his thoughts about war? For example, does each lead his *audience* from the specific to the abstract? something else? Explain how the overall impact of "Channel Firing" is similar to or different from what is achieved in Max Ramsey's "For Myself."

3. Given Hardy's response to war in "Channel Firing," how do you think he would have reacted to Roger Rosenblatt's report on the war in Lebanon (see "Lebanon: A Legacy of Dreams and Guns")? In which specific parts of Rosenblatt's essay could Hardy find confirmation of God's judgment in the poem that "the world is as it used to be"?

SUGGESTIONS FOR WRITING

1. Reread the poem carefully several times. Write an essay in which you analyze Hardy's use of *irony* in the poem.

2. The world-renowned Indian pacifist, Mohandas Gandhi once offered the following ironic observation on war: "What difference does it make to the dead . . . whether the mad destruction is wrought under the name of totalitarianism

or the holy name of liberty or democracy?" Choose one of the world's current battlegrounds — the Middle East, Central America, Africa, etc. — and write an *expository* essay in which you illustrate the ironies evident in that conflict. To what conclusion or what general statement about war do these ironies lead you?

3. President John F. Kennedy observed that "war will exist until that distant day when the conscientious objector enjoys the same reputation and prestige that the warrior does today." Consider Kennedy's statement and write an argumentative essay in which you defend — or challenge — this proposition.

EDWIN ARLINGTON ROBINSON

A descendant of the Puritan poet Anne Bradstreet, Edwin Arlington Robinson was born in 1869 and grew up in Gardiner, Maine, the setting for many of his poems. Able to afford only two years at Harvard University, Robinson struggled at earning a living while writing poetry. His first volume of poems, The Torrent and the Night Before *(1896), was influenced by reading Thomas Hardy. A revised version,* The Children of the Night *(1897), earned increasing public attention, including the admiration of President Theodore Roosevelt, who in 1905 arranged a position for Robinson in the New York Customs House.*

Robinson's deft psychological portraits won him three Pulitzer Prizes before his death in 1935. One reviewer of his early verse observed that "the world is not beautiful to him, but a prison house," to which Robinson replied several years later: "The world is not a 'prisonhouse,' but a kind of spiritual kindergarten where bewildered infants are trying to spell God with the wrong blocks."

Richard Cory

Whenever Richard Cory went down town,
We people on the pavement looked at him:
He was a gentleman from sole to crown,
Clean favored, and imperially slim.

And he was always quietly arrayed,   5
And he was always human when he talked;
But still he fluttered pulses when he said,
"Good-morning," and he glittered when he walked.

And he was rich — yes, richer than a king —
And admirably schooled in every grace: 10
In fine, we thought that he was everything
To make us wish that we were in his place.

So on we worked, and waited for the light,
And went without the meat, and cursed the bread;
And Richard Cory, one calm summer night,   15
Went home and put a bullet through his head.

QUESTIONS FOR READING

1. In which lines does the speaker most clearly characterize him/herself? What is the effect of such phrases as "richer than a king," "glittered when he walked," and "admirably schooled"? What does "waited for the light" mean in this context? What other words and phrases help to characterize the person speaking?

2. In what specific ways is the speaker interested in Richard Cory? What does the speaker notice about him? Comment on Robinson's use of such words as *and, but,* and *so* in the poem. How do they add to the dramatic intensity of the poem's concluding lines? Comment on Robinson's use of *irony* in those lines.

3. Which lines imply that the speaker's attitude toward Cory changed at the time of his death? How would you respond to the contention that in the closing lines of the poem, the speaker is filled with grief? How does the speaker's present attitude toward Richard Cory — revealed in his *description* of Cory — cause readers to reevaluate the admiration he claims to have felt for Cory when he was alive?

4. The contemporary songwriter Paul Simon has recorded a musical retelling of "Richard Cory" (*Sounds of Silence,* Columbia Records CS9269). Listen to Simon's recording. What specific changes has he introduced? With what effect? In what ways does Simon reduce the dramatic impact of Robinson's poem? How might he improve the lyrics of his version?

QUESTION ON CONNECTIONS

1. *Compare and contrast* the speaker's point of view in "Richard Cory" to Frances Taylor's in "Carol" (p. 227). In what ways is Taylor's view of Carol similar to or different from the speaker's view of Richard Cory? Note the changes, if any, in each speaker's *point of view* as the poem and essay proceed. Comment on the use of *irony* in both. On what common notes do the poem and essay end?

SUGGESTIONS FOR WRITING

1. This poem establishes a contrast in attitudes — between the speaker and Richard Cory and between the speaker and the townspeople — which were altered by Cory's death. Reread the poem carefully, several times, and write an essay in which you (1) show how these attitdes are expressed in the language of the poem, and (2) define the speaker's final attitude toward him/herself and the townspeople.

2. In its presentation of the notion of circumscribed hope, Robinson's poem seems strikingly modern. More specifically, Robinson's rendition of Richard Cory's suicide is a compelling reminder of the hollowness of conventional American standards of success. Write an *expository* essay in which you use an incident in your own life—or in the life of someone you know—to illustrate the shallowness of traditional measures of success in the United States.

THEODORE ROETHKE

Theodore Roethke created an imposing presence — both literally and figuratively — among the poets of his generation. Although he weighed nearly 250 pounds and adopted, according to his contemporaries, "a tough, bearlike image," Roethke spent much of his life as a writer and teacher plagued by personal insecurities and nervous exhaustion. Born in Saginaw, Michigan, in 1908, he graduated from Michigan State College (now Michigan State University), studied at Harvard, and then began a life-long career as a teacher (and occasionally a tennis coach) at Lafayette College, Michigan State, Pennsylvania State, and Bennington College before moving on to the University of Washington in 1947. Roethke taught with immense energy and popularity and repeatedly urged his students, as one recalls, to "let me see evidence of an active mind. Don't be so guarded — let your mind buzz around." "A bright student," Roethke once observed, "can learn — and this is most important — much about himself and his own time."

As a poet, Roethke was deeply introspective, and he devoted much of his creative energy, as the title of his first volume, Open House *(1941), suggests, to exploring the complexities of his own life in his verse. Such later volumes as* The Lost Son *(1948) and* Praise to the End! *(1951) reveal his increasing poetic maturation.* The Waking *(1953) won him a Pulitzer Prize and* Words for the Wind *(1957) the National Book Award and a Bollingen Prize. In structure and subject, Roethke's poetry ranges from strict to free forms and from rational to surrealistic evocations of childhood and old age.*

At his death in 1963, Roethke left 277 notebooks, in one of which he noted: "I am overwhelmed by the beautiful disorder of poetry, the eternal virginity of words." For Roethke poetry served to quiet the insecure self, to allay the anxieties and fears, to cope with painful personal experiences. As poet David Wagoner, one of Roethke's renowned students, remarked, "he loved incompleteness, perhaps because it represented a promise that he would never exhaust himself."

My Papa's Waltz

The whiskey on your breath
Could make a small boy dizzy;
But I hung on like death;
Such waltzing was not easy.

We romped until the pans   5
Slid from the kitchen shelf;
My mother's countenance
Could not unfrown itself.

The hand that held my wrist
Was battered on one knuckle;   10
At every step you missed
My right ear scraped a buckle.

You beat time on my head
With a palm caked hard by dirt,
Then waltzed me off to bed   15
Still clinging to your shirt.

QUESTIONS FOR READING

1. Read this poem aloud. Comment on its rhythm. How does the rhythm reinforce
   —or run counter to—the dance described? How does the rhythm of the poem
   change in lines 2, 4, 10, and 12? with what effect? Reread lines 6 and 13. How
   does the rhythm change yet again in these lines? With what effect? How does
   the poem's rhythm reflect the father's relationship with the child?

2. Identify the speaker in this poem. From what perspective does the speaker
   describe the events of the poem? To whom is the poem addressed? For what
   purpose?

3. What is the child's reaction to the waltz? Is he terrified? delighted? some
   combination of these two extremes? Point to *specific words* and phrases to
   support your response. How is the child's response to the father dramatized in
   the last two lines of the poem?

4. How does Roethke characterize the father in this poem? What are his most
   notable traits? What do these characteristics suggest about the father? What is
   the mother's relationship to the events described? What does her response
   suggest about her relationship with the father? What does her presence in the
   poem contribute to it?

5. Comment on Roethke's use of such words as *whiskey* (line 1), *romped* (line 5),
   unfrown (line 8), *battered* (line 10), *scraped* (line 12), and *caked* (line 14).
   What are the *denotative* and *connotative* meanings of each word? Explain how
   both meanings contribute to the success of the poem. What is the effect of the
   phrase "beat time" in Line 13?

QUESTIONS ON CONNECTIONS

1. Locate a copy of Sylvia Plath's poem, "Daddy," and compare and contrast the
   nature of the father/child relationship in "My Papa's Waltz" to that depicted
   in the poem. What features of the relationship strike you as similar? In what

respects are these two poems very different? Based on your reading of Monika Jerabek's essay on Sylvia Plath's poetry (p. 118), how might you expect Jerabek to respond to "My Papa's Waltz"?

2. Contrast the father/child relationship in "My Papa's Waltz" and "Daddy" to that presented in Amber Kennish's essay, "Three Rounds with Dad" (p. 133). To what extent do fear and affection determine the relationship in each? Apply the same questions to Barbara Seidel's essay, "A Tribute to My Father" (p. 212), Tom Wicker's essay, "A Steadfast Life," and Alice Walker's short story, "Everyday Use." Which form — poetry, essay, or fiction — do you think is most suited to expressing such relationships? Why?

SUGGESTIONS FOR WRITING

1. Reread Kelly Mays's essay analyzing the structure and imagery in Andrew Marvell's "On a Drop of Dew" (p. 180). Then choose some aspect of Theodore Roethke's "My Papa's Waltz" (for example, its structure, *imagery*, rhythm, *diction*, or *point of view*) and write an essay analyzing this aspect of the poem, modeling your paper on what you regard to be the most successful features of Mays's essay.

2. In his classic essay, "Of the Affections of Fathers for Their Children," the celebrated French essayist Michel de Montaigne observed: "A father is very miserable who has no other hold on his children in affection than the need they have of assistance, if that can be called affection." Drawing on your own experience, write an essay which demonstrates — or challenges — the validity of Montaigne's observation.

WILLIAM STAFFORD

In "A Way of Writing" (1970), the poet William Stafford observes: "A writer is not so much someone who has something to say as he is someone who has found a process that will bring about new things he would not have thought of if he had not started to say them. That is, he does not draw on a resevoir; instead, he engages in an activity that brings to him a whole succession of unforeseen stories, poems, essays, plays, laws, philosophies, religions." And one of the enduring pleasures of reading William Stafford's lyric poetry results from his ability to surprise us with fresh perspectives on ordinary experience.

Born in Hutchinson, Kansas, in 1914, William Stafford declared himself a conscientious objector in the years preceding and during World War II and served with the Brethren Service, other peace organizations, the U.S. Forest Service, and the World Church Service. Having earned a Ph.D. at the University of Iowa, Stafford joined the English faculty of Lewis and Clark College in Portland, Oregon, where he still lives, in 1948. His poems have been published in such volumes as Down in My Heart (1947), West of Your City (1960), and Traveling Through the Dark (1962), which earned him the National Book Award. More recent volumes include The Rescued Year (1966), Allegiances (1970), Someday, Maybe (1973), and Stories That Could Be True (1977), from which "One Home" is drawn. Stafford's nonfiction has been collected in Friends to This Ground (1968) and Writing the Australian Crawl (1978).

One Home

Mine was a Midwest home—you can keep your world.
Plain black hats rode the thoughts that made our code.
We sang hymns in the house; the roof was near God.

The light bulb that hung in the pantry made a wan light,
but we could read by it the names of preserves—
outside, the buffalo grass, and the wind in the night.

A wildcat sprang at Grandpa on the Fourth of July
when he was cutting plum bushes for fuel,
before Indians pulled the West over the edge of the sky.

To anyone who looked at us we said, "My friend";
liking the cut of a thought, we could say, "Hello."
(But plain black hats rode the thoughts that made our
    code.)

The sun was over our town; it was like a blade.
Kicking cottonwood leaves we ran toward storms.
Wherever we looked the land would hold us up.   15

QUESTIONS ON READING

1. What overall impression of this "Midwest home" does the speaker create in the first two stanzas? What words does Stafford emphasize to convey the speaker's attitude toward "home"? What are the implications of these words and where do they reappear in the poem? With what effect?

2. Comment on Stafford's use of "plain black hats" in line 2. What is the effect of repeating line 2 in parentheses in line 12? What is the function of *but* in line 12? Comment on Stafford's use of *thoughts* in lines 2 and 12. What does the word refer to in each instance? How does he encourage us to respond to it? How does he use the word *thought* in line 11? With what effect?

3. Summarize the contrast Stafford creates in his *descriptions* of life inside and outside the house. What is the overall effect of stanza three? In what specific respects does Stafford link the "wildcat," "the Fourth of July," and "Indians"? What is the meaning of line 9 and what does it contribute to the poem?

4. What is the effect of the final stanza? What word choices there connect it to previous stanzas? Given the context of the poem, explain how the sun is "like a blade." How does the land "hold us up"?

5. Comment on the speaker's relation to the scenes described. From what perspective is the scene presented? What is the speaker's relation to the world away from "home"? In what *tone* of voice do you think "you can keep your world" (line 1) should be read? What is the effect of this line? Comment on the significance of the poem's title.

QUESTIONS ON CONNECTIONS

1. With Stafford's "One Home" in mind, reread Ravenel Boykin Curry's essay, "A Small Town" (p. 63). From what perspective does each writer view his "home"? Which aspects of rural life does each emphasize? With what effect? To what extent does each acknowledge an *audience* in his writing?

2. *Compare and contrast* the view of one's earlier years presented in "One Home" and John E. Mason, Jr.'s "Shared Birthdays" (p. 167). Which writer seems to treat this subject with greater sentimentality? Which presents his emotional reaction more directly? Point to specific words and phrases to support your response.

3. Stafford assigns great significance to the natural world in "One Home." Identify the importance of nature in the poem and then *compare and contrast* this aspect of the poem to Ann Louise Field's view of nature in "The Sound of Angels" (p. 76). What significance does each writer attach to the individual's relationship to nature? With what effects?

4. Reread William Humphrey's "The Salmon Instinct." In what ways are Humphrey's and Stafford's attitudes toward "home" similar? different? How does each writer use figurative language to convey attitude? Reread Robert Nisbet's essay, "Nostalgia." Given Nisbet's definition, identify the extent to which Humphrey's and Stafford's views of "home" are nostalgic.

SUGGESTIONS FOR WRITING

1. Find an object in your current everyday life on campus that you associate with "home." What is there about this object that you associate with home? Write a *descriptive* essay in which you use details to explain that association and to evoke the emotional connection between the object and your sense of home.

2. Stafford's poem is written in the past tense. Readers can readily imagine Stafford's desire to return to his Midwest home to experience again "the buffalo grass," "the wind in the night," "the cottonwood," and the literal and figurative strength of "the land." Recall some place from your earlier years you would like to see again. If feasible, return there and take notes on what you observe. (If not, then recall some once-familiar place on or near campus that you have not visited in some time.) Write an essay in which you *describe* how it feels to return to a familiar place after a considerable absence. How has the place changed? What once-familiar aspects of the place now appear different — and perhaps even strange? Was this a place where you felt you "belonged"? Do you still think so? Why or why not?

RICHARD WILBUR

"If a poem arises from a dynamic relation with reality, it will be fresh whatever formal difficulties the poet chooses to overcome in the writing of it. If not, it will be like a group of anthropologists demonstrating a rain dance." The quiet, inward authority with which Richard Wilbur speaks of poetry has helped earn him a secure place among the most accomplished contemporary American poets and translators. Born into a family of artists in New York City in 1921, Richard Wilbur studied at Amherst and served in World War II before taking an M.A. at Harvard University in 1947. He has taught at Harvard, Wellesley, Wesleyan, and most recently at Smith College. He has published numerous collections of poetry, including Ceremony *(1950),* A Bestiary *(1955),* Things of This World *(1956), and* Poems *(1957), which won a Pulitzer Prize. More recent volumes include* Walking to Sleep *(1969),* The Mind-Reader *(1976), and* Seven Poems *(1981). In addition to poetry, Wilbur has written a good deal of literary criticism (published as* Responses, *1976), prepared several verse translations of plays by Molière and Racine, and collaborated with Lillian Hellman and Leonard Bernstein on a comic opera based on Voltaire's* Candide.

The Writer

In her room at the <u>prow</u> of the house
Where light breaks, and the windows are tossed with linden,
My daughter is writing a story.

I pause in the stairwell, hearing
From her shut door a commotion of typewriter-keys   5
Like a chain hauled over a <u>gunwale.</u>

Young as she is, the stuff
Of her life is a <u>great cargo</u>, and some of it heavy:
I wish her a lucky passage.

But now it is she who pauses,   10
As if to reject my thought and its easy figure.
A stillness greatens, in which

The whole house seems to be thinking,
And then she is at it again with a bunched clamor
Of strokes, and again is silent.   15

700   RICHARD WILBUR

I remember the dazed starling
Which was trapped in that very room, two years ago;
How we stole in, lifted a sash

And retreated, not to affright it;
And how for a helpless hour, through the crack of the door,   20
We watched the sleek, wild, dark

And iridescent creature
Batter against the brilliance, drop like a glove
To the hard floor, or the desk-top,

And wait then, humped and bloody,   25
For the wits to try it again; and how our spirits
Rose when, suddenly sure,

It lifted off from a chair-back,
Beating a smooth course for the right window
And clearing the sill of the world.   30

It is always a matter, my darling,
Of life or death, as I had forgotten. I wish
What I wished you before, but harder.

QUESTIONS FOR READING

1. Identify the speaker in this poem. From what physical and emotional perspectives does the speaker observe the writer? What does the speaker mean by "the
   stuff / of her life is a great cargo, and some of it heavy"? Comment on the
   word *passage* in line 9.

2. Identify the *image* introduced in the first stanza. How is that image extended
   and developed in subsequent stanzas? Point to specific words and phrases to
   support your response. Comment on the significance of the phrase *easy figure*
   in line 11. To what does this refer? To what new image does it yield? Where?
   With what effect?

3. In what specific ways does Wilbur make the writer's situation analogous to the
   bird's? What is the nature of the freedom each seeks? To what extent does
   each succeed in achieving that freedom?

4. Comment on the structure of this poem. In what specific ways has Wilbur made

his poem "fresh"? What "formal difficulties," if any, has he "overcome in the writing of it"? With what effect?

5. What point does the speaker make in the last stanza about him/herself? the writer? the nature of their relationship? Comment on the significance of the poem's final line.

QUESTIONS ON CONNECTIONS

1. Reread Richard Wilbur's "The Writer." What does the poem reveal — either explicitly or implicitly — about the relationship between writer and writing? Compare and contrast the relationship between a writer and his or her own words in Wilbur's poem to Donald Murray's view of the writer and writing in his essay, "The Maker's Eye." How are Murray's views similar to or different from those expressed in Wilbur's poem?

2. "In a very real sense, the writer writes in order to teach himself, to understand himself, to satisfy himself; the publishing of his ideas, though it brings gratifications, is a curious anticlimax." With this statement by the literary critic Alfred Kazin in mind, apply it to the characters in Wilbur's "The Writer." How compatible do you think Kazin's statement is with the one explicitly and implicitly presented in Wilbur's poem? Reread Earnestine Johnson's essay, "Thank You Miss Alice Walker" (p. 128). How compatible is Kazin's statement with Johnson's view of language in general and writing in particular? Test Kazin's observation against Johnna Lynn Benson's view of writing in her essay, "Rotten at the Core" (p. 31). What other essays — both student and professional — in this collection demonstrate that their authors view writing as a means to teach the self, to understand the self, to satisfy the self? Explain.

SUGGESTIONS FOR WRITING

1. Consider your own experiences as a writer — the frustrations and the satisfactions you felt as you were at work shaping words into meaning. What *analogy* can you create to help other writers understand what it is like for your mind to be at work writing? Write an expository essay in which you explain that analogy. In describing your mind at work, make your *diction* as vivid and detailed as Wilbur's.

2. The novelist William Styron is reported to have said in a 1958 interview that "the good writing of any age has always been the product of *someone's* neurosis, and we'd have a mighty dull literature if all the writers that came along were a bunch of happy chuckleheads." With this statement in mind, review the table of contents in this book. Select one writer — either a student or a professional — and write an *expository* essay in which you use that writer's essay to illustrate the accuracy — or the inaccuracy — of Styron's observation.

GLOSSARY

abstract and concrete words An abstract word refers to an idea, quality, attitude, or state imperceptible to our senses: *equality, freedom, love, fearful, naive, courageous.* A concrete word, in contrast, refers to an object, person, place, or state that we can perceive with our senses: *magazine, bus driver, Hudson River, blushing, clear-eyed, howling.* Though abstract words are useful in conveying general concepts or impressions, they are too vague to create distinct sensory impressions in readers' minds. To make meaning precise and vivid, writers support abstractions with concrete words appealing directly to the senses of sight, hearing, touch, taste, and smell. See also **general and specific words.**

allusion A brief reference to a real or fictitious person, place, object, or event. An allusion can convey considerable meaning with few words: he was a Scrooge about money; her business tactics smacked of the robber barons. But to be effective, the allusion must refer to something readers know well.

analogy A comparison of two different things that uses some similarities between them as the basis for implying other similarities. An analogy differs from a **simile** or **metaphor** in that it involves a point-by-point rather than an overall comparison. It differs from **comparison and contrast** in that its aim is to find resemblances in two unlike things rather than to explore two related things through their common and contrasting qualities.

Like an **illustration,** an analogy adds specificity and vividness to expository writing. Brief analogies are useful for this purpose in many types of essay. "Smith fended off discovery in the grand manner of the Wizard of Oz: He sent his top subordinates out on lengthy, difficult field assignments, while generating such sound and fury from his corner office that secretaries trembled and middle managers feared to question even his most irrational statements." An extended analogy of a paragraph or more can help to clarify an explanation by relating the thing being discussed to something more familiar; or it can strengthen an argument by using a known phenomenon to illustrate the potential impact of one whose effects are not yet apparent.

Analogy is frequently used in explanations to make an abstract topic more concrete or to make a complex topic easier to understand. In science, where abstraction and complexity are common, explanations often lean heavily on detailed analogies known as *models*. For example, an early model of the atom compared it to a miniature solar system, with a nucleus at the center (the sun) and electrons orbiting around it (the planets). The human brain is sometimes compared to a computer, an analogy that has helped researchers both to understand the operation of the brain and to refine the operation of the computer. That is, scientists use the similarities they have observed to predict other similarities, which they then test.

In expository writing it is not possible to test predictions. The reader must evaluate the validity of the analogy on the basis of its plausibility: Are the subject and the analogy similar enough to justify the writer's conclusions? This is an especially important question in argumentative and persuasive writing, where the conclusions are intended to shape readers' attitudes toward the subject. For example, political observers often contend that a current scandal is (or is not) another Watergate, or that U.S. policy in Central America will (or will not) lead the nation into another Vietnam. The reason the same analogy can be used by both sides in these debates is that no two situations are ever identical. Some aspects of U.S. policy in Central America resemble U.S. policy twenty years ago in Vietnam, while others do not. Therein lies the vulnerable spot of analogy as an argumentative tool. It stresses similarities while overlooking dissimilarities that may in fact be equally (or even more) significant. It cannot provide proof of an assertion or even hard evidence; it only suggests likelihood.

The writer using this technique therefore should carefully evaluate both the similarities and the dissimilarities between his or her subject and the chosen analogy. The analogy should be exploited up to but not past its logical limits. Every analogy breaks down if pushed too far—that is, if the comparison is extended to qualities of the two things that are not in fact similar. The solar system model of the atom, for instance, breaks down when the electrons' orbits are compared with those of planets; planets move in predictable and mostly parallel paths, while electrons do not.

The reader too should evaluate analogies with caution. Has the writer accurately identified similarities, and taken account of important dissimilarities? Has he or she extended the analogy too far? To what degree does the analogy depend on emotional rather than logical appeal? In the case of a parallel such as U.S. policy in Central America and in Vietnam, the emotional power of the comparison is strong. The writer knows most readers want to avoid "another Vietnam," and he or she uses this prejudice to influence their attitude toward the situation in Central America. The reader should be aware of this and should scrutinize the analogy for dissimilarities the writer may have ignored.

Analogy can also be used as a strategy for presenting a position. Amber Kennish's "Three Rounds with Dad" (p. 133) casts an argument between two antagonists as a boxing match. Here the analogy has no direct relationship to the subject; it simply helps Kennish to dramatize the conflict. Nevertheless, it does affect readers' perceptions of the essay's substantive arguments by describing them as weak or powerful ("a quick jab" versus "a blow to the gut"), and by showing one opponent bloodied and defeated by the other.

anecdote   A brief narrative recounting an episode from personal experience.

argument and persuasion   Writing that attempts to secure readers' assent to and support for the writer's position on an issue. Technically, *argument* uses facts and logic to win the reader's rational agreement, whereas *persuasion* uses an **emotional appeal** to induce readers to think or act in a certain way. Thus, someone arguing for capital punishment might make his or her case by presenting statistics indicating that nations that use it have lower crime rates than those that do not. Someone persuading readers to vote for capital punishment might contend that killing murderers is the only way to keep them from endangering the lives of innocent people. Argument and persuasion are so often used together, however, that they are not always distinguishable. Therefore, the term *argument* is often applied to both argumentative and persuasive writing.

Neither argument nor persuasion is a rhetorical strategy like **comparison and contrast, definition, process analysis,** and the other techniques commonly used to structure an essay. Rather, the writer of an argument works within whichever of these frameworks suits his or her needs. No matter what its strategy, an argument typically opens with one or more introductory paragraphs that outline the conflict and introduce the writer's thesis. The body of the argument consists of claims supporting the thesis and evidence to back up those claims.

For example, the **thesis** of Pamela Garrettson's "Prayer in America's Public Schools: Let's Not Start a Religious War" (p. 96) is that organized spoken prayer in public schools should not be legalized. One of Garrettson's claims in support of her position is that such prayer would make nonparticipants feel uncomfortable, undermining America's tradition of protecting minority religions. As **evidence** she describes her own unease at a Hindu service she attended. Another claim is that students are already legally free to pray in school. To back up this claim, Garrettson cites a relevant Supreme Court decision.

Many writers try to arrange their arguments so that each claim forms the topic sentence of a paragraph, and the rest of the paragraph consists of information related to that claim. This is a hard pattern to follow consistently but a useful organizing goal.

Two types of logic are commonly used in constructing an argument: inductive and deductive reasoning. **Inductive reasoning** involves moving from a collection of facts to a conclusion—that is, from particular cases to a generalization. A writer arguing in favor of rent-control legislation in his or her town might interview tenants in eight of the town's apartment buildings. Suppose most or all of these people report rent increases within the past year. The writer assumes that what is true in these particular cases is probably true for the town in general, and makes the claim that local rents are on the rise. The jump from representative but limited evidence (eight buildings) to a conclusion about all possible cases (every rental unit in town) is called an *inductive leap.* What is true of eight buildings may not in fact be true of the ninth or tenth. However, the inductive leap is a reasonable one, given the difficulty of gathering enough data to prove the writer's claim beyond doubt.

Deductive reasoning involves moving from a known fact about a whole class to a conclusion about one member of that class—that is, from the general to the particular. If a newspaper reported that the town council had passed a 5 percent increase for all local rental units, the writer could accurately conclude that the rent on the mayor's apartment would go up. In deductive reasoning, unlike inductive reasoning, the logical conclusion *must* be true if it is based on accurate premises. The deductive sequence—from the general to the particular—is called a **syllogism.** It comprises two premises and a conclusion:

—Major premise: All rents in town will increase by 5 percent.

—Minor premise: The mayor lives in a rented apartment.

—Conclusion: The mayor's rent will increase by 5 percent.

If either the major premise or the minor premise is false, the conclusion may also be false. For instance, perhaps the 5 percent increase is permitted but not mandatory (major premise). In that case, the mayor's rent might or might not go up. Likewise, if the mayor moves out of his apartment and buys a house (minor premise), his rent will not increase.

When deductive reasoning is used in expository writing, one of the steps in the syllogism may be implied rather than stated:

—Thanks to the general rent increase, even the mayor will soon have to pay 5 percent more for his apartment. (minor premise implied)

—Because the mayor is a tenant rather than a homeowner, he faces a 5 percent rent increase. (major premise implied)

—All local rents are going up 5 percent; and as we know, the mayor lives in a rented apartment. (conclusion implied)

In both inductive and deductive reasoning, the writer's **conclusion**—his or her claim—is based on facts drawn from personal knowledge or research. **Evidence** is what makes the claims in an argument convincing. If someone advocating rent control states that rents are on the rise, readers will want to know why he or she thinks so. If the writer's only support for this claim is a recent increase in his or her own rent, the conclusion carries little weight. Any inductive conclusion based on inadequate evidence is called a *hasty generalization.*

Other common pitfalls in argumentative writing are the *logical fallacies*—gaps or missteps in reasoning. These include ad hominem arguments, bandwagon appeals, begging the question, ignoring the question, and non sequiturs. Each of these fallacies is defined under *logical fallacies* in this glossary.

audience   That group of readers for whom a writer intends a particular work. To communicate effectively, the writer should consider readers' knowledge of the subject, their interests in it, and their biases toward it in choosing what to say and how to say it.

cause and effect   A writing strategy in which certain events are established to explain why other events happened. Cause-and-effect analysis involves identifying the links in a chain of events and demonstrating the connections between them. This type of reasoning is typically used to explain something that has already happened, or to predict a future result, or both.

Cause and effect is a popular technique in argumentative or persuasive writing. Often the writer uses a cause-effect relationship as the basis of the recommendation that comprises his or her **thesis:** "Cigarette smoking should be outlawed because it can cause cancer and other serious health problems." In this case the writer favors alleviating an undesirable effect (cancer and other diseases) by eliminating its cause (cigarette smoking). For the argument to be effective, the writer must show that the alleged cause really is a cause. That is, he or she must present evidence that smoking does in fact lead to health problems. To be thorough, the writer would also cite data indicating that eliminating cigarettes would cause a significant decrease in these illnesses.

Cause-and-effect analysis can be used to explain as well as to argue. For instance, instead of proposing that cigarettes be outlawed, the writer interested in smoking and health problems might focus on the nature of the cause-effect relationship. What particular qualities of tobacco smoke produce an adverse impact on the human body? Which organs and systems are affected, and in what ways? Cause-and-effect reasoning can also be used to show that one set of causes is more plausible than another. Some cigarette advertising aims at convincing readers that other factors besides smoking are responsible for the ailments commonly associated with tobacco.

Cause and effect is not an easy technique to use well. The writer who chooses this strategy faces the challenge of ordering and weighing incidents or conditions that may have overlapped in time, and whose relative importance may not be obvious. Only rarely is it possible to distinguish a clear causal chain: A caused B, which caused C. "The hurricane blew down our town's power lines, therefore we had no electricity, therefore we couldn't watch the news on TV." Most sequences of events—especially those worth writing about—are more complex, and thus harder to analyze.

In writing about a cause-effect relationship, it may be preferable to begin with effects and work backward to causes, or to begin with causes and move forward to effects. The choice usually depends on the type of case being made. An explanatory essay—one that asks "why?"—typically starts with an effect in the present and goes back to causes in the past. A high proportion of American marriages end in divorce—why? The United States and the Soviet Union have enough nuclear weapons to wipe out every city on the globe several times over; what are the reasons behind this buildup? A predictive essay—one that asks "what will happen if . . . ?"—more often starts with a cause in the present and goes forward to its probable effects in the future. How is America's high divorce rate likely to affect the next generation's attitude toward marriage? Given the current arms race, what are the chances of avoiding nuclear war?

Several common pitfalls should be kept in mind when using—or evaluating—cause-and-effect reasoning. One is confusing causes with effects. Has the arms buildup caused international hostility or resulted from it? A related problem is the post hoc fallacy—assuming that because one thing follows another in time, the first is a cause and the second is an effect. The writer must demonstrate that the relationship really is causal and not merely coincidental.

The question of necessary versus sufficient cause also arises here. Does a given situation exist only because some other situation or event preceded it? Could other causes have had the same effect? For example, suppose someone dies of lung cancer after ten years of smoking two packs of cigarettes a day. The writer may view smoking as a *necessary* cause of this person's death—that is, if the victim had not smoked cigarettes, he or she probably would not have developed lung cancer. However, many people who smoke two packs a day for ten years do not die of cancer. Therefore smoking is not a *sufficient* cause of death; some other factor must also have been involved.

Another common error in cause-and-effect reasoning is confusing a cause with a symptom or sign. A married couple, one of whom drinks heavily, files for divorce. Is drinking a cause of the divorce or a symptom of deeper incompatibility between the two partners? Similarly, a given situation may appear to be a cause when in fact it is a purpose. The League of Nations was formed for the purpose of preventing international wars in the future; but its cause lies in the conflicts of the past.

chronological order   A method of organizing an essay in which events are arranged as they occurred over time, from earliest to latest. Narrative often follows a chronological order.

classification: A writing strategy that involves dividing a subject into two or more component categories and then assigning each of its parts to one of these categories. Classification is a useful way to break down a complex topic into manageable segments. It can also help the writer analyze a subject more precisely by identifying each element within it according to a logical system.

The first step in classification, called *analysis* or *division,* consists of separating the subject into categories. In "Rock Around the World" (p. 83), Erik Field divides his rock-and-roll record collection into six categories: British Invasion, Motown, Memphis, the Los Angeles sound, the San Francisco sound, and New York punk. The second step is to place each of the subject's parts in the appropriate category. Under "British Invasion," for instance, Field mentions the Beatles, the Rolling Stones, the Kinks, the Yardbirds, the Who, and the Animals. By classifying individual bands geographically according to their origin and sound, Field is able to consider a large topic (rock-and-roll) in an organized, coherent fashion. He is also able to point out significant features of many different bands without becoming repetitive.

The simplest form of classification is the *binary* type, in which the subject is split into just two categories: items that possess a certain characteristic and items that lack it. The Rh factor in human blood is a binary classification. People whose blood contains this factor are labeled Rh positive, and those who lack it are Rh negative. This is obviously a very limited way of dividing up a subject, since it provides only one piece of information about the members of each category. Indeed, for the negative group, all we know is that its members do not share a certain quality—they need not be alike in any other way. Human blood, which is a complicated substance, is classified according to numerous other criteria besides the presence or absence of the Rh factor. The best known of these are the four major blood types. A, B, AB, and O, which comprise a *complex* classification. A complex classification provides at least one piece of positive information about all the members in each group.

When using classification, the writer must be sure to keep his or her categories consistent. Erik Field's classificatin of rock-and-roll, for example, is based on geography (which also corresponds with certain types of sound). To add a seventh category such as "blues" or "having a horn section" would make his system inconsistent—some bands could fall into more than one group. In any classification, the same principle should serve as the basis for all categories.

Once the writer has divided up the subject, he or she can go on to consider each category individually. This might involve naming the category, listing its members, discussing their common features, and noting important differences and similarities between it and other categories. Sometimes a category is further subdivided, as when Field separates his Memphis group into white (a combination of Southern rhythm-and-blues and country) and black (soul). Examining each component part helps the writer to convey a sense of the whole. He or she may reinforce this larger concept by beginning or ending the essay with either an overview or a general discussion of the subject.

cliché   A worn-out, overused expression that deadens rather than enlivens writing. Examples: *few and far between, fate worse than death, sea of faces, shot in the arm, tired but happy, viable alternative.*

climactic order   A method of organizing an essay in which elements—words, sentences, examples, ideas—are arranged in order of increasing importance or drama.

coherence   The quality of effective writing that results from clear, logical connections among all the parts so that the reader can easily follow the writer's thought process. Coherence requires logic, so that each point develops naturally from those preceding it, and organization, which arranges material in the way that best focuses and directs the reader's attention. See **parallelism** and **transitions**. See also **unity**.

colloquial language   The language of conversation, including contractions (*don't, can't*) and informal words and expressions (*hassle* for an argument or fight, *mad* for angry, *to party* for attending a party). Most dictionaries label such words and expressions *colloquial* or *informal*. Colloquial language is inappropriate in formal writing such as a college term paper or a business report. But sometimes it can be used selectively to relax a piece of writing and create a friendly intimacy. See also **diction**.

comparison and contrast   A writing technique in which the qualities of two subjects are examined in relation to each other. Comparison involves identifying both the similarities and differences between the subjects; contrast focuses on the differences (though it may make use of the similarities to do so). The two processes are closely related and are almost always used together. The effectiveness of comparison and contrast comes from its comprehensive review of the two subjects' attributes: In looking carefully at each part, both writer and reader gain a fuller appreciation of the whole.

Comparison and contrast can be used to structure an entire essay whose purpose is to evaluate two phenomena. Karen Kramer's "The Little Drummer Boys," for example, is a comparison of drummers and percussionists (p. 138). Or the technique can serve as one part of a larger essay, as in David Christman's discussion of the Dionysian versus the Apollonian aspects of tattoos in "Nietzsche and the Art of Tattooing" (p. 55).

Some comparison and contrast essays are explanatory, helping the reader to understand each subject better by exploring the likenesses and discrepancies between the two. "The Little Drummer Boys" is an explanatory essay, describing how drummers and percussionists differ in attitude, equipment, and performance style. Other comparisons are evaluative, aimed at proving that one alternative is preferable to the other. Evaluative comparisons are popular in advertising: Cereal X has no added sugar whereas Cereal Y has six teaspoons; Cereal X has more fiber; Cereal X has three times the vitamin nutrition of Cereal Y. In an essay, unlike an advertisement, the writer of an evaluative comparison must be careful to consider enough characteristics of the two subjects so that the weight of the **evidence** clearly favors one over the other.

The writer setting up either type of comparison and contrast begins by jotting down aspects of the two subjects that he or she plans to compare. In Kramer's essay about drummers versus percussionists, these include (1) equipment, (2) image and attitude, (3) style of playing, (4) personal appearance and behavior, (5) relationship to the band, and (6) love of equipment. Then, for each of these aspects, the writer notes the similarities and differences between the two subjects. For example, Kramer's "equipment" category would list the instruments played by drummers and by percussionists—some of them the same (drums and cymbals) and some not (triangles, sleigh bells, woodblocks, xylophones).

Once the elements of the comparison have been identified, the writer can choose between a subject-by-subject and a point-by-point structure. The subject-by-subject comparison describes the first subject completely and then the second. The writer's outline might look like this:

1. Drummers
   a. Equipment
   b. Image and attitude
   c. Style of playing (and so on)
2. Percussionists
   a. Equipment
   b. Image and attitude
   c. Style of playing (and so on)

A subject-by-subject comparison is most appropriate for a short essay whose purpose is to give an overall impression of each subject. In a longer paper, there is some risk with this format that each description will turn into a separate essay, losing the force of the comparison. For a thorough examination of the two subjects in relation to each other, the point-by-point format is usually preferable. Here, each paragraph or section of the essay covers one element of the comparison, with plenty of room for supporting details. The writer's outline might look like this:

1. Equipment
   a. Drummers
   b. Percussionists
2. Image and attitude
   a. Drummers
   b. Percussionists (and so on)

It is often possible and desirable to combine the two formats. Kramer's essay, for instance, opens with a brief subject-by-subject comparison of drummers and percussionists and then moves into a more detailed point-by-point comparison.

Kramer's **thesis** statement appears at the end of her second paragraph, between her subject-by-subject and her point-by-point comparisons. Her very first paragraph sets the stage for her thesis by creating expectations that the thesis then overthrows. The writer of an explanatory comparison (unlike an evaluative comparison) often need such a noncomparative introduction to show why the subjects' similarities and differences are of interest.

conclusions   The sentences that bring a written work to a close and provide readers with a sense of completion, with a sense that the writer has finished. Sometimes the final point in the body of an essay may accomplish this purpose, especially if it is very important or dramatic, but usually a separate conclusion is needed. It may be a single sentence or several paragraphs, depending on the length and complexity of the piece of writing, and it may include any of the following, or a combination, depending on the writer's subject and purpose.

1. A summary of the essay's main points.
2. A statement of the essay's main idea, if it has not been previously stated; or a restatement of the main idea incorporating information from the body of the essay.
3. A comment on the significance or implications of the subject.
4. A suggestion about how readers can use the information in the essay.
5. A recommendation that readers support a proposal or action, or that they take some action themselves.
6. A prediction for the future.
7. An example, anecdote, question, or quotation that reinforces the point of the essay.

Excluded from this list are several endings that are best avoided because they tend to weaken the overall effect of an essay: (1) an example, fact, or quotation that pertains to only part of the essay; (2) an apology for the writer's ideas, for the quality of the writing, or for omissions; (3) an attempt to enlarge the significance of the essay by overgeneralizing from its ideas and evidence; (4) a new idea that requires the support of an entirely different essay.

concrete words   See **abstract and concrete words**.

connotation and denotation   A word's denotation is its literal meaning: *Factory* denotes a building where goods are manufactured; *famous* denotes the quality of being well known. A word's connotations are the associations or suggestions that go beyond its literal meaning. Some connotations are personal and vary according to an individual's experiences. *Factory*, for instance, may connote a particular place, but it may further connote a judgment on the methods of production used within that place. Other connotations are more general, calling up similar associations for all who use or hear the word. Many groups of words with essentially the same denotation vary in their connotations. *Famous, eminent,* and *notorious* all denote the quality of being well known; but *famous* connotes celebrity and popularity among contemporaries *(famous actor)*, *eminent* connotes recognition for outstanding qualities or contributions *(eminent physician)*, and *notorious* connotes sensational, even unfavorable, recognition *(notorious thief)*. Each of these words can help shape a reader's responses to the person being described. But connotative words will backfire if they set off inappropriate associations—for instance, describing a respected figure as "a notorious teacher and scholar." Frequent reference to a dictionary will safeguard against such mistakes.

contrast See **comparison and contrast**.

deductive reasoning The method of reasoning that moves from the general to the specific.

definition An explanation of the meaning of a word. Three main types of definition commonly appear in expository writing: lexical definitions, which summarize a term's meaning briefly, as in a dictionary; stipulative definitions, which specify a more limited meaning for a term in a particular context; and extended definitions, which explore a term's meaning in depth. A lexical definition is typically used to clarify a word that readers must understand in order to follow the writer's presentation. A stipulative definition enables the writer to use a word in a specialized sense that suits the purposes of his or her essay. An extended definition can fulfill either of these functions in more detail, or it can serve as the basis of a whole essay.

Lexical definitions usually characterize an object, phenomenon, or idea by classifying it in relation to other things. Such a definition normally gives the general category in which the term belongs and specific features that distinguish it from similar terms. A lexical definition of *anger* might be *a strong emotion* (general category) *of displeasure and belligerence* (distinguishing features). The term's roots might also be mentioned. One antecedent of *anger* is the Latin *angere*, "to strangle." In addition, lexical definitions sometimes include synonyms, other words that have approximately the same meaning: *wrath, rage, fury, ire*. The writer using a lexical definition in an essay chooses which of these elements to include on the basis of what readers need to know about the term in order to understand the sense in which the writer plans to apply it. If the writer's purpose is simply to clarify the meaning of a technical term, he or she may need only a phrase or two to define it. If the word may be unfamiliar and is important to the essay, a fuller definition will ensure that readers grasp it.

If the word being defined is central to the writer's goals, or controversial, or susceptible to different interpretations, a stipulative definition is appropriate. That is, the writer stipulates the special and limited sense in which the word will be used in the essay. Thu Hong Nguyen's "A Good Woman" (p. 188) opens with a stipulative definition: "A good woman means an industrious daughter, a devoted wife, and a loving mother." This definition represents traditional Vietnamese beliefs about the role of women, which is Nguyen's subject. Her essay as a whole comprises an extended definition, since she goes on to examine each phrase of her stipulative definition in more detail.

A lexical definition always reflects ordinary usage. While a stipulative definition narrows a word's meaning to suit a specialized purpose, it should not conflict with ordinary usage to a point that stretches readers' credulity. The lexical definition of anger, for example, is broad enough to fit the term in most common contexts. A stipulative definition for an essay on facial expressions might limit anger to mean "a frown or scowl accompanied by pursed lips, bared teeth, and/or flared nostrils." This definition is unusual, but consistent with readers' concept of anger. Someone could also define anger stipulatively as "a deep sadness and sense of loss," but to do so would be pointless, since readers are unlikely to accept such a definition.

An extended definition too should accord with ordinary usage. Often, however, the reason for writing an extended definition is that the term either has no clear meaning or is susceptible to different interpretations. Brenda Jacobs's "Handing Down Grace" (p. 106) tells of her realization that this phrase, like others she heard in the South, "struck a discordant note. . . . reason dictated that if grace were to be 'handed' anywhere, surely it would be sent in an upward direction." The purpose of an extended definition is usually to mirror a larger contradiction or an insight revealed by the writer's analysis of how the term is used. Jacobs's theme is not merely odd Southern expressions, but her own reconciliation with her Southern roots. Nguyen does more than describe the Vietnamese definition of a good woman; she subtly and then overtly deplores the subjugation of Vietnamese women.

denotation See **connotation and denotation.**

description The translation of a sensory image into words. By telling readers how something looks, feels, sounds, smells, or tastes, the writer enables them to share his or her experience. The thing being described may be a person, a place, an object, or even a state of mind.

Description appears in all kinds of writing. It can be used within any expository essay to convey a setting, introduce a character, or make other physical aspects of the piece more vivid. Or it can serve as the main strategy for an essay whose object is to recreate a segment of reality.

There are two general types of description: objective and subjective. An objective description emphasizes facts that could be observed by anyone: "It was a dark and stormy night, full of clouds, wind, and rain." This type of description functions mainly to paint a factual picture in the reader's mind. A subjective description, on the other hand, includes the writer's reaction or interpretation: "The sky was as dark as Helen's mood when we parted and as stormy as our good-byes." This type of description uses the picture it paints to transmit a mood. In doing so, it suggests why the writer thinks this picture is worth the reader's attention and may reveal something about the writer's attitude or values. Most descriptions combine objective and subjective elements: "Dark clouds hid the moon; gusts of wind and rain rattled the windows. It was the kind of night that makes you long for a cozy armchair in front of a fireplace." Such a description conveys both facts about the scene and clues to the writer's ideas about it.

Whether it is the essay's central focus or just one component part, a description always serves a purpose. Like every other aspect of the piece, it helps the writer to express his or her thesis. In a descriptive essay, the thesis typically takes the form of a **dominant impression.** That is, the writer tells readers about some person, place, object, or experience in a way that invests it with significance beyond its physical attributes. By sharing the writer's perceptions and viewpoint, the reader comes to understand and appreciate his or her interpretation as well.

Barbara Carter's "Momma's Cupboard" (p. 43), for example, is a descriptive essay about a pantry. Carter spends only a few sentences telling how the pantry looks. Most of her essay focuses on the exotic foods stored there and the childhood hopes and illusions represented by the pantry's contents. The essay's dominant impression is of "denials and broken dreams, the promise that never came." Carter selects and arranges the details of her description to convey this dominant impression.

The writer of a description can help to ensure success by following a series of steps. The first step is to identify the essay's topic and the dominant impression the description is meant to create. Next, he or she carefully observes the thing to be described. What are its most striking visual features? Does it have any special sound, feel, smell, or taste? Is it stationary, or do its motions help to characterize it?

The writer then chooses the most evocative and relevant details. A good description is not a catalog of facts, but an integrated picture which highlights significant qualities and omits those that do not contribute to the dominant impression. In a description of climbing a mountain, significant qualities might include the glare of sun on snow, the bite of cold wind on exposed skin, the crunch of boots on ice, the smell of wet wool, and the ache of tired muscles. Less significant would be the color of each climber's clothing, the number of rocks and trees along the path, or the brand of sunscreen used by the climbing party. Selectivity is essential in shaping an effective description.

Before putting words on paper, the writer should pick a **point of view.** This is something like the camera angle of a movie scene. For the description to feel authentic, the reader needs a sense of where the writer stands, literally and figuratively. Is this the viewpoint of someone indoors looking out? at the foot of a mountain looking up? on a high peak looking down? The point of view may be stationary or moving—for example, from the bottom of the mountain to the top, or in a panorama from side to side, or zooming in from a distance to a close-up. No matter how many elements the writer examines in the scene, his or her point of view should remain consistent. The description's dominant impression is the writer's impression, and it is established through the writer's eyes.

By the same token, elements in the description are arranged in a sequence that imitates the order in which a viewer might notice them. Frances Taylor's essay, "Carol" (p. 227) opens with Carol's most striking visual features—her mustache, her gold fillings—and then moves to the sound of her laugh, the tension of her body, her red tank top, and the sparkle in her eyes. With this picture vividly established, Taylor backs off to give us information about herself and the situation in which she met Carol. If Taylor had simply listed Carol's hair color, eye color, facial shape, and clothing, starting at the top of her head and moving to her feet, the description would be much less vivid and alive, for it would not reflect the way one person actually sees another.

Essential to an effective description is lively, specific language. Typical elements include concrete nouns and active verbs, adjectives and adverbs, and **figures of speech,** particularly similes and metaphors. Although adjectives and adverbs are often the most obvious way to make a description colorful, experienced writers recognize that the backbone of a verbal picture is its nouns and verbs. A writer telling about a climbing expedition, for example, might say, "After a long, difficult ascent we finally reached our goal." This sentence gives the reader only a vague sense of what the writer saw and felt. A more successful description would be, "After four days and nights of struggling up the mountain, we reached its snow-shrouded peak."

Similes and metaphors broaden readers' perception of the thing being described by comparing it with something else, usually something with well-known characteristics. A simile uses "like" or "as"; a metaphor does not. In using these figures of speech, the writer needs to consider not only obvious physical resemblances, but also how he or she wants the reader to react to the description. That is, similes and metaphors should contribute to the essay's dominant impression. To say, "Clouds drifted around the mountain peak like sheep in a meadow" creates a pleasant, pastoral mood. If this is not the writer's intention, he or she should choose a different comparison: "Clouds loomed over the mountain peak like portents of doom."

diction A writer's choice of words to achieve a purpose and make meaning clear. Effective diction conveys the writer's meaning exactly, emphatically, and concisely, and it is appropriate to the writer's intentions and audience. **Standard English,** the written language of educated native speakers, is expected in all writing for college, business and the professions, and publication. The vocabulary of standard English is large and varied, encompassing, for instance, both *comestibles* and *food* for edible things, both *paroxysm* and *fit* for a sudden seizure. In some writing standard English may also include words and expressions typical of conversation (see **colloquial language**). But it excludes other levels of diction that only certain groups understand or find acceptable. Most dictionaries label these levels as follows:

Nonstandard: words spoken among particular social groups, such as *ain't, yous, hisself,* and *nowheres.*

Slang: words that become dated quickly and that may not be understood by all readers, such as *uptight,* for tense or inhibited, *bread* for money, and *honcho* for one in charge.

Regional or *dialect:* words spoken in a particular region but not in the country as a whole, such as *poke* for a sack or bag, *holler* for hollow or small valley.

Obsolete: words that have passed out of use, such as *fain* to mean happy or desirous (I *fain* would go.)

See also **connotation and denotation.**

division Also called *analysis.* The method of development in which a subject is separated into its elements or parts.

dominant impression The central idea or feeling conveyed by a description of a person, place, object, or state of mind.

effect See **cause and effect.**

emotional appeal In argumentative and persuasive writing, the appeal to readers' values, beliefs, or feelings in order to win agreement or inspire action.

essay A prose composition on a single nonfiction idea or topic. An essay usually reflects the writer's personal experiences and opinions.

ethical appeal In argumentative and persuasive writing, the sense of the writer's expertise and character implied by the reasonableness of the argument, the use and quality of evidence, and the tone.

evidence The details, examples, facts, statistics, or expert opinions supporting any general statement or claim.

example An instance or representative of a general group or of an abstract concept or quality. One or more examples may provide the basic structure for developing an essay.

exposition The form of writing that explains or informs. Some essays whose primary purpose is self-expression or persuasion employ exposition to clarify ideas.

figures of speech Expressions that imply meaning beyond or different from their literal definition used to achieve vividness or force. Among the more common are simile, metaphor, personification, and hyperbole. A *simile* compares two unlike things and makes the comparison explicit with *like* or *as*: "He buttered the bread like a bricklayer"; "The child cowered in the room like a frightened bird." A *metaphor* also compares two unlike things, but more subtly, by equating them without *like* or *as*: "Mud blanketed the town"; "Cars snaked down the turnpike." *Personification* is a kind of simile or metaphor that attributes human qualities or powers to things or abstractions: "The river surged angrily over the banks"; "The city turned a cold shoulder to me." *Hyperbole* is deliberate overstatement or exaggeration: "He had a mustache as big as a dust mop"; "I paced for hours." (The opposite of hyperbole is understatement, discussed under **irony**.)

formal style See **style**.

freewriting Also called *nonstop writing*. When students freewrite, they put pen to paper and continue to write without pausing to consider elements of composition such as grammar, sentence structure, word choice, or spelling. A useful way of getting started, freewriting quickly results in putting many ideas down on paper, ideas that can be developed into successful essays. For a detailed explanation by students of the benefits of freewriting, see "Students on Writing."

general and specific words A general word refers to a group or class: *food, hobbies, clothing*. A specific word refers to a particular member of a group or class: *bread, coin collecting, socks*. General and specific are not exclusive categories but relative terms, as illustrated by the following chain from the most general to the most specific: *clothing, foot warmers, socks, wool socks, Fred's thermal wool socks*. General words are essential for referring to entire groups or classes, but they contribute little to vividness and often leave meaning unclear. Usually, the more specific a word is, the more interesting it will be for readers. See also **abstract and concrete words.**

generalization A statement about a group or a class derived from knowledge of some or all of its members: "Holiday rituals create family memories" or

"Skyscrapers deprive cities of their human scale." The more instances the generalization is based on, the more accurate it is likely to be. A generalization is the result of inductive reasoning.

hyperbole   See **figures of speech.**

illustration   The use of examples to show how an abstract or general idea applies in real situations. As the term implies, illustration is a way of adding verbal pictures to exposition. This technique can be used in any piece of writing to clarify the meaning of a concept, support an assertion, or add specificity and vitality to a discussion that might otherwise be vague. Indeed, it is a rare composition that does not benefit from examples. Illustration also can serve as the main organizing strategy of an essay aimed at demonstrating the validity of an abstraction or generalization.

Not surprisingly for such a widely used technique, illustration is an umbrella term that covers a variety of applications. Some illustrations are highly specific and require scrupulous documentation, as when an anthropologist draws a conclusion about some ancient culture based on examples from a recently opened tomb. At the other end of the spectrum are semifictional examples intended to make an idea more vivid. Matthew Holicek's essay, "Look Out Behind You!" (p. 101) describes "slasher films" by using generalized examples that represent scenes in a number of movies: "The girls all love to take late-night strolls alone through the woods. . . . The boys, eager to impress the girls, prove their manhood by descending alone into musty cellars. . . ." A writer's choice of what type of illustration to use normally depends on the topic, **purpose,** and intended **audience** of his or her essay.

In an argumentative or explanatory paper, illustrations from primary sources are often essential for substantiating the writer's statements. If the goal is to analyze or refute another writer's position, all examples may be drawn from the subject's work. Monika Jerabek quotes lines and phrases from Sylvia Plath's poems throughout "Sylvia Plath: Electra Inspired" (p. 118) to document her observations about the relationship between Plath's poetry and her adoration of her dead father.

If the writer's goal is to present an original **thesis,** examples might come from primary and secondary sources, or from his or her own experience. In "Nietzsche and the Art of Tattooing" (p. 55), David Christman supports his statement, "Tattooing is an ancient art," with the example of an Egyptian mummy from 2000 B.C. Other illustrations in Christman's essay show tattooing practices in New Zealand, Japan, Central and South America, Borneo, Europe, and the United States, as reported in sources that Christman cites in his bibliography. In contrast, Ravenel Boykin Curry's "A Small

Town" (p. 63) draws on no outside sources. Curry's opening sentence is "Junior Boy is thirty-nine and he has made it." To illustrate Junior Boy's concept of "making it," Curry quotes him as promising himself "a telephone to talk to people." Though Junior Boy's life is far from luxurious, Curry establishes his success by describing in detail the installation of his first telephone.

Just as different essay topics require the writer to choose examples from different types of sources, the paper's subject and goals affect whether its examples are few or many, brief or extended. Some of theses are best supported with a large number of short examples. A writer defending an arguable generalization such as "There is too much violence in today's popular music" would do well to cite several different songs by different groups to confirm this observation. A more limited thesis, such as "Some current music videos show great imagination and creativity," might be substantiated with two or three detailed illustrations. Or the writer could choose a combination of examples, mentioning some videos briefly and describing one or two in depth. Usually the fewer the examples, the more detailed each one should be.

The writer should select both examples and the details within examples for their relevance to his or her thesis. In some cases it may also be appropriate to include illustrations that appear to contradict the thesis and then show why the thesis is nevertheless valid.

The placement of illustrations is important. It is best not to mix examples, but to treat one at a time, as thoroughly as necessary. Each one should appear close to the statement it supports—normally right before or right after it. If the bulk of the essay consists of one or more extended illustrations, the writer should be sure to present his or her thesis clearly at the outset, reinforce it by interpreting each example, and reiterate it in a closing summary.

image   A verbal representation of sensory experience—something seen, heard, felt, tasted, or smelled. Images may be literal: "The woman sat on the park bench"; "The street lights suddenly came on." Or they may be figurative: "The women perched on the park bench like old crows in their dark coats"; "Small eyes of light illuminated the street." (See **figures of speech.**) Through images, a writer touches the reader's experiences, thus sharpening meaning and adding immediacy. See also **abstract and concrete words.**

inductive reasoning   The method of reasoning that moves from the particular to the general.

informal style   See **style.**

introductions   The sentences that open written works and set the stage for what follows. An introduction to an essay identifies and restricts the subject while establishing the writer's attitude toward it. It may require a single sentence or several paragraphs, depending on how much readers need to know before they can begin to grasp the ideas in the essay. The introduction often includes a thesis sentence which states the main idea of the essay (see **thesis**). To set up the thesis sentence, or as a substitute for it, any of the following openings alone or in combination may be effective.

1. Background on the subject establishing a time or place or providing essential information.
2. An anecdote or other reference to the writer's experience illustrating the main idea or explaining what prompted the essay.
3. An explanation of the significance of the subject.
4. An outline of the problem the essay will address, perhaps using interesting facts or statistics.
5. A statement or quotation of an opinion that the writer disagrees with.
6. A quotation or question reinforcing the main idea.

A good introduction does not mislead readers by exaggerating the significance of the subject or the essay, nor does it bore them by saying more than is neccessary. A good introduction avoids two openings that are always clumsy: (1) beginning with "The purpose of this essay is . . ." or something similar; and (2) referring to the title of the essay in the first sentence, as in "This is not as hard as it looks" or "This is a serious problem."

irony   In writing, irony is the use of words to suggest a meaning different from their literal meaning. Some irony derives from *understatement*, from saying less than is meant. But irony can also suggest a meaning exactly opposite the literal meaning. Irony can be witty, teasing, biting, or cruel. At its most humorless and heavily contemptuous, it becomes *sarcasm:* "You have a real talent for failure."

logical fallacies   Flaws in reasoning that weaken or invalidate an argument. Some of the most common fallacies are listed below.

1. *Oversimplification,* overlooking or ignoring inconsistencies or complexities in evidence: "The problems in Nicaragua would be solved if the *contras* could drive the Sandinistas from power."
2. *Hasty generalization,* leaping to a conclusion on the basis of inadequate or unrepresentative evidence: "Every one of the twenty-five students polled supports the change in course requirements, so the administration should implement it."
3. *Begging the question,* assuming the truth of a conclusion that has not

been proved: "Deforestation in Brazil is necessary for economic development, so it should continue."

4. *Ignoring the question,* shifting the argument away from the real issue: "As a wife and mother, Geraldine Ferraro would be a sensitive vice-president."

5. *Ad hominem* ("to the man") *argument,* attacking an opponent instead of the opponent's argument: "She is just a student, so we need not listen to her criticisms of economic policy."

6. *Either-or,* presenting only two alternatives when there are more choices: "To do well in a competitive industry, you have to cheat a little."

7. *Non sequitur* ("it does not follow"), deriving a wrong or illogical conclusion from stated premises: "Since students pay high rents to live off campus, they should be able to have parties any time they want."

8. *Post hoc ergo propter hoc* ("after this, therefore because of this"), assuming that one thing caused another simply because it preceded the other: "After Gerald had his wisdom teeth out, he won the lottery."

metaphor   See **figures of speech.**

narration   A technique in which the writer tells what happened by relating a succession of events in a meaningful sequence. Narration is storytelling: the writer's purpose is not to present isolated facts but to describe one or more incidents in a way that shows both the chronological and thematic connections between them.

The simplest type of narration starts at the beginning and proceeds through the middle to the end. More complex forms involve shifts in time: the writer might start *in medias res*—at some significant point part way through the action—flash back to an earlier event and then forward again toward a conclusion. Whatever the sequence, it is important for the writer to identify a beginning, middle, and end before commencing. Having done that, he or she can decide how to structure the narrative so that its opening creates the right mood and its climax comes in the most effective place.

To use narration successfully, the writer must convey not only the order in which events occurred but the relationship implied by that order. Chronology alone—A happened, then B happened, then C happened—is boring and unimpressive. Indeed, readers faced with such an unadorned factual sequence are likely to add their own interpretation, which may or may not accord with the writer's intentions. It is the writer's job to give the story meaning by selecting, arranging, and presenting its elements in a way that guides the reader's interpretation. He or she does this by paying close attention to details, duration, direction, and development.

Details are the aspects of what happened that the writer chooses to include, to leave out, and to emphasize. Having chosen a subject and a thesis, the writer knows what his or her general sequence will be and what conclusion the reader is meant to draw from it. In "The Blanket Party" (p. 39), Terry Burns decided to start with a detail that suggests an ordinary summer night: "Crickets chirped in the grass. . . ." Burns then shatters the tranquility: ". . . as four men, dressed only in white government-issue underwear, made their way through the dark barracks." A good principle is to use every detail deliberately, including only those that contribute to the essay's purpose.

Duration refers to time—the schedule by which the subject is presented. In writing, unlike life, we can stretch out a moment or skip over a year. Whatever the writer describes at length, the reader will examine and consider closely. Whatever the writer skims through, the reader will assume is not very important. The decision of how much time to devote to an incident therefore depends on its significance, not on how long it took when it happened. Most narratives depict some events in full, omit others, and mention others only briefly. Such variety maintains the pace of the story and allows the writer to emphasize those scenes that add the most impact. Patrick Kinder Lewis's "Five Minutes North of Redding" (p. 150) opens with a short paragraph about the three hours before a train arrives, then spends a long paragraph on the few seconds when the train passes through. In this way he conveys the sense of a tedious wait before a crucial instant.

Direction is a sense of forward movement or flow. The reader should have an idea of where the essay is going from the beginning, and this idea should be reinforced as the narrative progresses. Careful attention to details and duration, plus effective **transitions** between sections, contribute to direction. Particularly important is leaving out any unnecessary scenes, sentences, or words that would slow the essay's momentum. A writer describing real events must be a ruthless editor, including only what is essential to his or her goals.

Development is the writer's arrangements of the elements in a narrative so that they not only keep the story moving but build toward a climax. The climax is the point near the end of the piece when its purpose becomes dramatically clear. To achieve this sense of revelation on the reader's part, the writer organizes events in a sequence in which each one seems to add new information and meaning to what has gone before. The result is a feeling of crescendo and a conclusion that is emotionally as well as intellectually satisfying.

Three other elements are important in narration. The first is **point of view**—the writer's indication of who is telling the story. This may be a first-person "I" representing the writer or some other main character. Or it may be a third-person "they," "she," or "he." The choice of point of view is based less on who has the most important role in the story than on whose perception of events the writer wants to convey.

Voice is the tone of the story—formal or informal, serious or humorous, ironic or earnest, dispassionate or sympathetic. Word choice, sentence length, and other aspects of style help the writer to create an appropriate voice for his or her narrative. In most essays, the voice should have enough personality to represent the writer (or other narrator) authentically, without being so idiosyncratic as to lose credibility.

Some narratives include *dialogue* to communicate significant events and ideas in the voices of the people involved. Dialogue may be direct ("Yes," she said) or indirect (She said yes). In a factual essay, the speakers' words should only take the form of direct diaglogue when they are quoted exactly. While there are advantages to reporting characters' actual speeches, it is rare for people to talk concisely and to the point for more than one or two sentences. Dialogue therefore should be used judiciously. Like all the elements of a narrative, it is valuable only when it advances the writer's **purpose.**

nonstandard English   See **diction.**

paragraph   A group of related sentences, set off by an initial indention, that develops an idea. By dividing continuous text into units, paragraphs help the writer manage ideas and the reader follow those ideas. Each paragraph makes a distinct contribution to the main idea governing the entire piece of writing. The main idea of each paragraph is often stated explicitly in a topic sentence, and it is supported with sentences containing specific details, examples, and reasons. Like the larger piece of writing of which it is a part, the paragraph should be easy to follow and clearly focused (see **coherence** and **unity**).

parallelism   The use of similar grammatical form for ideas of equal importance. Within a sentence, two or more elements of equal function and importance should always be parallel to avoid confusion: "The doctor recommends swimming, bicycling, or walking" is clearer and easier to read than "The doctor recommends swimming, bicycling, or that patients walk." But parallelism can also be an emphatic stylistic device either within or among sentences. When used among sentences, parallelism also clarifies the relations among ideas (see **coherence**).

personification   See **figures of speech.**

persuasion   See **argument.**

point of view   The position of the writer in relation to the subject. In description, point of view depends on the writer's physical relation to the subject; in narration, on the writer's place in the story and on his or her relation to it in time. More broadly, point of view can also mean the writer's particular mental stance or attitude. For instance, a smoker and a nonsmoker might have different points of view toward smoking policies in a student lounge.

premise   The generalization or assumption on which an argument is based. See **syllogism.**

process analysis   An explanation of how something works, or how to do something. Just as **narration** tells *what* happened and **cause and effect** tells *why*, process analysis tells *how*. This is the strategy found in cookbooks, in instructions for playing a game or assembling a bicycle, and in descriptions of how the human heart operates or how a prince can secure political power. When used in an essay, process analysis begins with an overview of the subject and proceeds with a step-by-step discussion of each of its parts.

There are two types of process analysis: specified and informative. *Specified* process analysis tells the reader how to do something. John Siegrist's essay, "Rattlesnake: A Palatable Experience" (p. 217), is of this type, giving instructions on how to catch and cook a rattlesnake for dinner. *Informative* process analysis tells how something works. Sandra Casillas's "Cha-No-Yu, the Japanese Tea Ceremony" (p. 47) uses this technique to explain a Japanese ritual to American readers.

To understand how a process operates, we must know its **purpose** and the steps that comprise it. The thesis of a process-analysis essay tends to be simple: "how to prepare a rattlesnake meal" or "how a tea ceremony is conducted." The writer also should indicate why the process he or she has chosen to describe is of interest. Siegrist opens his essay with two paragraphs about food prejudices that often prevent people from trying new dishes and explains how he came to eat rattlesnake. Casillas conveys her reasons for writing about the Japanese tea ceremony with phrases like "the transition from chaotic modern life to the tiny tranquil chamber . . ." and a comparison of this slow traditional ritual with present-day high-speed technology.

Next, the writer identifies the steps in the process and describes each one in turn—the *analysis* part of the essay. Both Siegrist and Casillas use the second-person "you" in their analyses, suggesting that the reader is a participant. Siegrist also uses the first-person "I" when mentioning his own tactics and preferences. Other writers use the third-person "he," "she," "one," "they," or "it." The choice need not depend on whether the reader is actually likely to take part in the process being analyzed. Rather, the writer selects a mode of address that suits the subject and readers' probable reasons for being interested in it. A specified process analysis usually assumes the reader wants to learn to perform the steps described and phrases them either in the second person or in imperative commands: "Insert tab A into slot B." "Add a cup of water and stir." An informative process analysis may be about something the reader wants to understand, but in which he or she is not directly involved, such as how a hologram is made. In this case, the third person is often more practical: "The laser beam is split into two parts. One hits the object, while the other serves as a reference beam."

The steps in the process should be analyzed in a logical order. Any crucial ingredients should be specified, and unfamiliar terms identified, early enough to avoid confusion. A recipe that instructs, "Next add the egg yolks, beaten till lemon-colored" is harder to follow than one that says, "Beat the egg yolks till lemon-colored and add them to the mixture." Similarly, an explanation of holography should include definitions of "laser" and "reference beam." To be sure the analysis is clear, the writer should keep his or her **audience** in mind, covering each step in enough detail to be informative without becoming boring.

Organizing the essay in a logical order is more complicated when two or more steps take place at once. In a specified process analysis it is essential for the reader to be able to perform all the necessary actions in sequence, so the overlaps are usually small ones: "Turn cap clockwise while holding down tab with thumb." In an informative process analysis the writer may have to establish a sequence arbitrarily. Each step is described separately, but transitional phrases such as "at the same time" or "meanwhile" show when two or more steps are actually simultaneous.

If the process being analyzed is circular—photosyntehsis in leaves, for example, or the heart's pumping of blood—then the writer must also choose a starting point. Often the best place to begin is with a particularly visible step (sunlight hitting the leaf) or one that is somewhat familiar to readers (the initial thump of the heartbeat). For an especially complicated process, the writer might open with one relatively easy to explain aspect on which subsequent steps in the description can be based.

Process analysis is a technique applicable to a wide variety of subjects. Besides its more straightforward functions, it can be used humorously or ironically to explore a serious topic: "how to manage parents" or "how to take over a small country." Almost any "how" question offers material for process analysis, which is one of the most methodical ways to organize an essay.

purpose   The reason for writing, the goal the writer aims to achieve. The purpose may be to explain the subject so that readers understand it or see it in a new light; to convince readers to accept or reject an opinion or to act in a certain way; to entertain readers with a humorous or exciting story; or to express the thoughts and emotions inspired by a revealing or instructive experience. The writer's purpose overlaps the main idea—the particular point being made about the subject. In effective writing, the two together direct and control every choice the writer makes. See also **thesis** and **unity.**

rational appeal   In argumentative and persuasive writing, the appeal to readers' rational faculties—to their ability to reason logically—in order to win agreement or compel action.

rhetoric   The art of using words effectively to communicate with an audience.

satire   The combination of wit and criticism to mock or condemn human foolishness or evil. The intent of satire is to arouse readers to contempt or action, and thus it differs from comedy, which seeks simply to amuse. Much satire relies on irony—saying one thing but meaning another (see **irony**).

simile   See **figures of speech.**

slang   See **diction.**

specific words   See **general and specific words.**

standard English   See **diction.**

style   The *way* something is said, as opposed to *what* is said. Style results primarily from a writer's characteristic word choices and sentence structure. A person's writing style, like his or her speaking style, is distinctive. Viewed more broadly, style can range from formal to informal. A very formal style adheres strictly to the conventions of standard English (see **diction**), tends toward long, sophisticated sentences, and relies on learned words such as *malodorous* and *psychopathic*. A very informal style, in contrast, is more conversational (see **colloquial language**), tends toward short, uncomplicated sentences, and relies on words typical of casual speech such as *smelly* or *crazy*. The formality of style may often be modified to suit a particular audience or occasion: A college term paper demands a more formal style than an essay narrating a personal experience. See also **tone.**

syllogism   The basic form of **deductive reasoning,** in which a conclusion derives necessarily from proven or accepted premises. For example: The car never starts when it rains (the major premise). It is raining (the minor premise). Therefore, the car will not start (the conclusion).

symbol   A person, place, or thing that represents an abstract quality or concept. A red heart symbolizes love; the Statue of Liberty symbolizes the United States welcoming European immigrants; a cross symbolizes Christianity.

thesis   The main idea of a piece of writing, to which all other ideas and details relate. The main idea is often stated in a *thesis sentence* near the beginning of the essay, which asserts something about the subject and conveys the writer's purpose. Even when the writer does not state the main idea and purpose, the thesis governs all the ideas and details in the essay.

tone   The attitude toward the subject, and sometimes toward the audience and the writer's own self, expressed in choice of words and sentence structure as well as in what is said. Tone in writing is similar to tone of voice in speaking, from warm to serious, amused to angry, joyful to sorrowful, sympathetic to contemptuous.

transitions   Links between sentences and paragraphs that connect ideas and thus contribute to smoothness and clarity (see **coherence**). Some transitions are echoes of previous material that tie parts together and subtly indicate relationships: repetition and restatement can stress important words or phrases; pronouns such as *he, she, it,* and *they* can substitute for and refer back to earlier nouns; and parallelism can highlight ideas of similar importance (see **parallelism**). Other transitions are more obvious, stating the connections explicitly: transitional sentences beginning paragraphs or brief transitional paragraphs can help shift the focus or introduce new ideas; and transitional expressions can signal and specify relationships. Some common transitional expressions—by no means all—are listed below.

Space: above, below, beyond, farther away, here, nearby, opposite, there, to the right.

Time: afterward, at last, earlier, later, meanwhile, simultaneously, soon, then.

Illustration: for example, for instance, specifically, that is

Comparison: also, likewise, similarly.

Contrast: but, even so, however, in contrast, on the contrary, still, yet.

Addition or repetition: again, also, finally, furthermore, in addition, moreover, next, that is.

Cause or effect: as a result, consequently, equally important, hence, then, therefore, thus.

Summary or conclusion: all in all, in brief, in conclusion, in short, in summary, therefore, thus.

Intensification: indeed, in fact, of course, truly.

understatement   See **irony**.

unity   The quality of effective writing that results when all the parts relate to the main idea and contribute to the writer's purpose. A piece of writing must have a point, that point must be clear to readers, and they must see how every sentence relates to it. See **purpose** and **thesis**. See also **coherence**.

RHETORICAL
ARRANGEMENT

ARGUMENT AND PERSUASION

OTHER FORMS OF WRITING

Research Writing

Acknowledgments (*Continued from page iv*)

William Humphrey. "The Salmon Instinct" excerpted from the book *Farther from Heaven* by William Humphrey. Copyright © 1976, 1977 by William Humphrey. Reprinted by permission of Delacorte Press/Seymour Lawrence.

Barbara Huttman. "A Crime of Compassion" by Barbara Huttman (*Newsweek* August 8, 1983). Copyright © 1983 by Newsweek, Inc. All Rights Reserved. Reprinted by permission.

Garrison Keillor. "My Stepmother, Myself" from *Happy to be Here* by Garrison Keillor. Copyright © 1970, 1971, 1972, 1973, 1974, 1975, 1976, 1977, 1979, 1980, 1981, 1982, 1983. Reprinted by permission of Viking Penguin, Inc.

Stephen King. "On the Horror of Horror Movies" from *Danse Macabre* by Stephen King. Copyright © 1981 by Stephen King. Reprinted by permission of Dodd, Mead & Company, Inc.

Jeane J. Kirkpatrick. "The U.N. and Grenada: A Speech Never Delivered" by Jeane J. Kirkpatrick. *Strategic Review* 12, Winter 1984. Reprinted by permission.

Elisabeth Kübler-Ross. "On the Fear of Death" from *On Death and Dying* by Elisabeth Kübler-Ross. Copyright © 1969 by Elisabeth Kübler-Ross. Reprinted by permission of Macmillan Publishing Company. "Fruit Gathering," LXXIX from *Collected Poems and Plays* by Rabindranath Tagore. Copyright 1916 by Macmillan Publishing Company; renewed 1944 by Rabindranath Tagore. Reprinted by permission of Macmillan Publishing Company, New York and Macmillan, London and Basingstoke.

Doris Lessing. "The Old Chief Mshlanga" from *African Stories* by Doris Lessing. Copyright © 1951, 1953, 1954, 1957, 1958, 1963, 1964, 1965 by Doris Lessing. Reprinted by permission of Simon & Schuster, Inc. and Curtis Brown, Ltd. London.

Yukio Mishima. "Patriotism" from *Death in Midsummer* by Yukio Mishima. Copyright © 1966 by New Directions Publishing Corp. Reprinted by permission of New Directions.

Donald M. Murray. "The Maker's Eye: Revising Your Own Manuscripts" by Donald M. Murray. Copyright © 1973 by Donald M. Murray. First appeared in *The Writer*, October 1973. Reprinted by permission of Roberta Pryor, Inc.

Robert Nisbet. "Nostalgia" from *Prejudices: A Philosophical Dictionary* by Robert Nisbet. Copyright © 1982 by Robert Nisbet. Reprinted by permission of Harvard University Press.

Frank O'Connor. "Guests of the Nation" from *Collected Stories* by Frank O'Connor. Copyright © 1981 by Harriet O'Donovan Sheehy. Executrix of the Estate of Frank O'Connor. Reprinted by permission of Alfred A. Knopf, Inc. and Joan Daves.

Jo Goodwin Parker. "What is Poverty?" by Jo Goodwin Parker from *America's Other Children: Public Schools Outside Suburbia* by George Henderson. Copyright © 1971 by the University of Oklahoma Press. Reprinted by permission of Dr. George Henderson.

Sylvia Plath. Lines from "Daddy" from *The Collected Poems of Sylvia Plath* edited by Ted Hughes. Copyright © 1963 by Ted Hughes. Published by Harper & Row, Publishers, and Faber and Faber, London. Reprinted by permission of Harper & Row, Publishers, Inc., and Olwyn Hughes, representing the estate of Sylvia Plath.

Katharine Anne Porter. "The Jilting of Granny Weatherall" from *Flowering Judas and Other Stories* by Katherine Anne Porter. Copyright 1930, 1958 by Katherine Anne Porter. Reprinted by permission of Harcourt Brace Jovanovich, Inc.

James Rachels. "Active and Passive Euthanasia" by James Rachels, reprinted by permission of *The New England Journal of Medicine*. Vol. 292, pages 78–80, 1975.

Theodore Roethke. "My Papa's Waltz" by Theodore Roethke, copyright 1942 by Hearst Magazine, Inc. From *The Collected Poems of Theodore Roethke* by Theodore Roethke. Reprinted by permission of Doubleday and Company, Inc.

Roger Rosenblatt. "Lebanon: A Legacy of Dreams and Guns" by Roger Rosenblatt (*Time*, January 11, 1982). Copyright 1982 Time Inc. All rights reserved. Reprinted by permission from TIME.

Richard Selzer. "The Discus Thrower" from *Confessions of a Knife* by Richard Selzer. Copyright © 1979 by David Goodman and Janet Selzer, trustees. Reprinted by permission of Simon & Schuster, Inc.

William Stafford. "One Home" from *Stories That Could Be True* by William Stafford. Copyright © 1960 by William Stafford. Reprinted by permission of Harper & Row, Publishers, Inc.

Lewis Thomas. "The Iks" from *The Lives of a Cell: Notes of a Biology Watcher* by Lewis Thomas. Copyright © 1973 by The Massachusetts Medical Society. Originally published in *The New England Journal of Medicine*. Reprinted by permission of Viking Penguin, Inc.

Calvin Trillin. "Ordering in Japanese" from *Third Helpings* by Calvin Trillin. Copyright © 1983 by Calvin Trillin. Published by Ticknor & Fields.

Alice Walker. "Everyday Use" from *In Love & Trouble* by Alice Walker. Copyright © 1973 by Alice Walker. Reprinted from her volume *In Love & Trouble* by permission of Harcourt Brace Jovanovich, Inc.

Eudora Welty. "The Little Store" reprinted from *The Eye of the Story: Selected Essays and Reviews* by Eudora Welty. Copyright © 1975 by Eudora Welty. Reprinted by permission of Random House, Inc.

Tom Wicker. "A Steadfast Life" by Tom Wicker (*The New York Times*, October 17, 1983). Copyright © 1983 by The New York Times Company. Reprinted by permission.

Richard Wilbur. "The Writer" by Richard Wilbur from *The Mind-Reader* by Richard Wilbur. Copyright © 1971 by Richard Wilbur. Reprinted by permission of Harcourt Brace Jovanovich, Inc.

George F. Will. "Opposing Prefab Prayer" by George F. Will (*Newsweek*, June 7, 1982). Copyright © 1982 by Newsweek, Inc. All Rights Reserved. Reprinted by permission.

Richard Wright. Excerpt from *Black Boy* (pages 214–222) by Richard Wright. Copyright 1937, 1942, 1944, 1945 by Richard Wright. Reprinted by permission of Harper & Row, Publishers, Inc.

CONTEST RULES
FOR THE BEDFORD PRIZES
IN STUDENT WRITING

Bedford Books of St. Martin's Press is pleased to sponsor The Bedford Prizes in Student Writing, an annual contest designed to recognize outstanding essays written for freshman composition courses in the United States and Canada.

PRIZES

1. Each winner will receive a cash award of $175.00, to be sent by mail to the winner's home address.
2. Each instructor who sponsors a winning entry will receive a cash award of $75.00, to be sent by mail to the instructor's college address.
3. Formal certificates will be sent to the winning essayists, their instructors, and their departments.

CONTEST RULES

Eligibility and Deadline

1. The contest is open to any student enrolled in a freshman composition course at an accredited college or university in the United States and Canada.
2. Entries should be nonfiction prose essays—exposition and argument as well as narration and description—of at least 500 words. Research papers are also eligible. Fiction and poetry are not eligible. All entries must be written for and submitted for credit in a freshman composition course.
3. Although only final drafts will be judged, each entry must be accompanied by the writer's preliminary notes and drafts. Instructors may make such corrections and suggestions on prior drafts as they normally append to student papers, and the submitted version may be revised especially for entry in this contest along lines suggested by the instructor or by fellow students.
4. The contest runs on the academic year with deadlines for each semester. One set of winners will be chosen for both semesters and announced in the late fall. Entries for the fall semester must be postmarked no later than January 31, and entries for the spring semester must be postmarked no

later than May 31. *However, instructors are encouraged to submit entries at any time before these dates.* Entries should be submitted by mail to:

The Bedford Prizes in Student Writing
Bedford Books of St. Martin's Press
P.O. Box 869
Boston, MA 02117

5. There is no limit on the number of entries instructors may submit. Instructors are urged, however, to be selective in their submissions, sponsoring only those essays that in their judgment are of distinctively high quality. All entries will be judged for originality, clarity, organization, coherence, control of language and grammar, and, where applicable, reasoning and use of evidence.

Required Format and Accompanying Materials

6. Each entry must be typed, double-spaced, on one side of 8½″ × 11″ paper. The student's name should appear only on the first page of the entry in the upper right-hand corner, and the pages of the essay should be numbered. The entry should not bear the correction marks or comments of the instructor or other readers. The writer's preliminary notes and drafts should be stapled separately from the entry itself and labeled with the entrant's name.

7. Each entry must be accompanied by an official entry blank or a cover sheet containing the following information:
   Student's information: name, campus address, campus telephone number, home address, home telephone number.
   The student must also include a signed statement affirming that the essay is an original creation and that he or she has read, understood, and agreed to the rules and conditions of the contest.
   Instructor's information: name, department, college or university, address, office telephone number, home address, home telephone number, the specific assignment for the student's entry, instructor's signature.

Conditions

8. Entries must be original and may not infringe upon the rights of any third party.

9. All rights to an entry, including the copyright and other rights of reproduction and publication, are vested, upon its submission, in Bedford Books of St. Martin's Press. An entry is deemed submitted only upon its receipt by Bedford Books, which assumes no responsibility for the receipt or return

of any entry. *Students or instructors who want copies of the entries should make them before submission.*

10. Bedford Books of St. Martin's Press will publish a selection of the winning essays together in an anthology.

11. The decisions of the judges are final.

12. This contest is void where prohibited or restricted by law.

A complete list of winners, their college or university affiliations, and their sponsoring instructors will also be announced every year in *College Composition and Communication* and *College English.*